The Investor's Illustrated Guide to American Convertible and Special-Interest Automobiles, 1946–1976

1964

1967

1967

The Investor's Illustrated Guide to American Convertible and Special-Interest Automobiles, 1946-1976

Charles Webb

South Brunswick and New York: A. S. Barnes and Company
London: Thomas Yoseloff Ltd

A. S. Barnes and Co., Inc.
Cranbury, New Jersey 08512

Thomas Yoseloff Ltd
Magdalen House
136-148 Tooley Street
London SE1 2TT, England

Library of Congress Cataloging in Publication Data

Webb, Charles, 1950–
The investor's illustrated guide to American convertible and special-interest automobiles, 1946–1976.

1. Automobiles—United States—Collectors and collecting. I. Title.
TL7.W43 629.22′22′0973 77–84592
ISBN 0-498-02183-1

PRINTED IN THE UNITED STATES OF AMERICA

dedicated
to David, Robert, Merry,
and my mother Marion

Contents

Acknowledgments

I would like to thank the following people and organizations for the help they provided:

Judy Siff, Public Relations, Pontiac Motor Division, Pontiac, Michigan.

Jerry T. Robbins, Administrator, Public Relations, Oldsmobile Division, Lansing, Michigan.

Gary Josyfowycz and William O'Neill, Public Relations, Cadillac Motor Car Division, Detroit, Michigan.

Jerry Rideout and Charles H. Overy, Public Relations, Buick Motor Division, Flint, Michigan.

Carol George, Librarian, and C. R. Gawne and C. Berry, Photomedia Department, Ford Motor Company, Dearborn, Michigan.

Martin L. Whitmyer, News Relations Office, Chrysler Corporation, Detroit, Michigan.

Terry and Teresa Michaelis, T. Michaelis Corvette Supplies, Napoleon, Ohio.

Robert Webb, Los Angeles, California.

Jean Dawson, Public Relations, Chevrolet Motor Division, Detroit, Michigan.

Jim Bollman, Crosley Automobile Club International, Williamson, New York.

Don Loper, American Motors Owners Association, Janesville, Wisconsin.

Richard Quinn, Studebaker Drivers Club, Mokena, Illinois.

Richard J. McGarty, Metropolitan Owners Club, Wisconsin Chapter, Milwaukee, Wisconsin.

Larry G. Mitchell, The Classic AMX Club International, Loves Park, Illinois.

Bill Hossfield, King Midget-Eshelman Registry, Ringwood, New Jersey.

Cornelius Donovan, The Eastern Packard Club, Fairfield, Connecticut.

Will O'Neil, President, National Woodie Club, Hawthorne, California.

Marion Michaels, Black River Falls, Wisconsin.

Linda de Avila, Correspondent, *Corvette News*, Detroit, Michigan.

Wally Solberg, Whitehall, Wisconsin.

C. W. Strickler III, President, Brougham Owners Association, Atlanta, Georgia.

J. Francis Werneth, DeSoto Owners Club of Maryland, Inc., Hernando DeSoto Chapter, Baltimore, Maryland.

C. R. Maize, Metropolitan Owners Club, Somerset, Pennsylvania.

David R. Crippen, Ford Archives, Dearborn, Michigan.

Edsel Owners Club, Arvonia, Virginia.

David Webb, Black River Falls, Wisconsin.

Doug Schellinger, Assistant Editor, Daytona & Superbird Auto Club, New Berlin, Wisconsin.

Richard E. Jones, Secretary, Tucker Automobile Club of America, Orange Park, Florida.

Bill Tryon, Director, Mid-Atlantic Nomad Association, West Chester, Pennsylvania.

Elvie Nandory, Black River Falls, Wisconsin.

James Nandory, Menomonie, Wisconsin.

Ray Doern, Chrysler 300 Club, Portland, Oregon.

Joe Umphenour, President, National Nomad Club, Arvada, Colorado.

Jenny F. Waller, Editor, *Journey with Olds*, publication of the Oldsmobile Club of America, Chagrin Falls, Ohio.

Merry Michaels, Black River Falls, Wisconsin.

George Taylor, Town and Country Owners Registry, Pasadena, Texas.

Reed Mitchener, Hudsonite Family Club, Wichita, Kansas.

Mrs. Robert Dworschack, Co-editor, *Nash Times,* Clinton, Iowa.

Leonard Doud, Black River Falls, Wisconsin.

Bob Wingate, San Dimas, California.

George L. Hamlin, The Packard Club, Packard Autombile Classics, Inc., Oakland, California.

Doris Erhardt, Black River Falls, Wisconsin.

Jimmy Valentine, The Metropolitan Historical Collection, North Hollywood, California.

Richard H. Leonard, Chicago, Illinois.

Bill Tilden, Atlanta, Georgia.

Peter Booz, Hudson-Essex-Terraplane Club, Woodland Hills, California.

Evelyn Tester, Public Library, Black River Falls, Wisconsin.

Richard M. Langworth, Hopewell, New Jersey (the production figures for Kaiser-Frazers were taken from his book *Last Onslaught on Detroit*).

William D. McIntyre Library, University of Wisconsin-Eau Claire.

Pierce Library, University of Wisconsin-Stout, Menomonie, Wisconsin.

Engineering Library, University of Wisconsin-Madison.

Historical Library, University of Wisconsin-Madison.

Regenstein Library, University of Chicago.

Motor Vehicle Manufacturers Association of the United States, Inc., Detroit, Michigan.

Thomas L. Bernardin, Account Executive, McCann-Erickson, Inc., Troy, Michigan.

I'd also like to thank all the owners of ragtops and other special-interest cars I "interrogated" at car shows and swap meets.

Photo Credits

The following provided most of the photographs used in this book:

Public Relations Department, Pontiac Motor Division.
Public Relations Department, Oldsmobile Division.
Public Relations Department, Cadillac Motor Car Division.
Photomedia Department, Ford Motor Company.
Public Relations Department, Chevrolet Motor Division.
News Relations Office, Chrysler Corporation.
Public Relations Department, Buick Motor Division.
Historical Collection, Chrysler Corporation.
T. Michaelis Corvette Supplies.
Richard Quinn Collection, Studebaker Drivers Club.
Larry G. Mitchell, Loves Park, Illinois.
Richard J. McGarty, Metropolitan Owners Club.
Jim Bollman, Crosley Automobile Club.
Roger Doud, Black River Falls, Wisconsin.
GM Photographic.
The Veteran Car Museum, Denver, Colorado.
Howard and Shelby Applegate, Westchester, Pennsylvania.
Bob Wingate, San Dimas, California.
Davis and Williams, Inc., Beverly Hills, California.
John A. Conde Collection, Bloomfield Hills, Michigan.
William L. Bailey Collection, Royal Oak, Michigan.
Roaring 20 Autos, Inc., Wall, New Jersey.
Chevroland Nues, Sandy Springs, Georgia.
McCann-Erickson, Inc., Troy, Michigan.

Introduction

Many reasons have been given for the demise of the American convertible—their vulnerability to theft, the introduction of the two-door hardtop, air pollution, wind noise, leaky tops, increased use of air conditioning, above-average maintenance costs, and even the popularity of longer hair styles (no one wants to be whipped to death by his or her hairdo). While these are all possible factors, they don't tell the whole story. After all, people never bought convertibles for practical considerations anyway.

Perhaps the main reason has to do with society itself. The convertible is a friendly, extroverted, let-the-good-times-roll type of car. People today tend to be pessimistic and self-centered. It's no wonder that one sees so many vans, with tinted windows, rolling down the highways like little isolation chambers on wheels.

Still, ragtops are a symbol of the American dream to many people; they represent success, wealth, and romance.

In 1959, the rock and roll star Eddie Cochran recorded a song called "Something Else." In it he sang of the common fantasy of nearly every teenage boy: getting a girl, having lots of money, and riding around in a convertible "with the white top down." Times may have changed, but the dream about the three Rs—romance, riches, and a ragtop—is as common as ever. And not only with teens or males.

Fame, fortune, and even love may elude a person, but it is still possible to make part of that dream come true. At least once in his or her life, everyone should own a convertible. Because you haven't really lived until you've experienced the prince-of-the-world feeling of cruising "with the white top down."

The Investor's Illustrated Guide to American Convertible and Special-Interest Automobiles, 1946–1976

1
Who Wants to Buy an Old Car?

Various surveys have established the following facts about special-interest-car collectors:

1. The vast majority (over 95 percent) are men. Of these, 70 percent are between the ages of 25 and 45.
2. About 75 percent are married.
3. They are slightly above average in income. More than 50 percent earn between $15,000 to $20,000 a year, and 20 to 25 percent make $20,001 to $30,000 annually.
4. The majority have graduated from high school, and approximately 47 percent have baccalaureate degrees.

The most popular cars among collectors, according to a 1976 readers' poll by *Old Cars,* are, in order of popularity: Ford, Chevrolet, Buick, Cadillac, Studebaker, Packard, Lincoln, Chrysler, Plymouth, Dodge, Hudson, Oldsmobile, Thunderbird, Corvette, and Mercury.

There is widespread agreement that Ford and Chevrolet (in that order) are the most popular makes. This is mainly because cars that are popular when new are usually also popular when they are old. This makes an easy, and fairly accurate, method of predicting which cars will be most sought after in the future. A more precise method is to see how popular a car is on the used-car lots a couple of years after its introduction. For example, in 1957, Ford sold more cars than Chevrolet. However, the 1957 Chevy soon became the most popular used car in America. Now a 1957 Chevy will almost always bring more than a 1957 Ford of the same body type and condition.

Although Fords and Chevrolets are the most sought after, other makes are growing in popularity. A survey of the "cars wanted" sections of *Hemmings Motor News* and *Old Cars* newspaper (January 1975 through March 1977) revealed that this trend is taking place at a rapid rate.

In 1975, the cars most frequently sought (i.e., at least two different people advertised for them) were, in order of most sought after: *Fords:* 1955–57 Thunderbirds, 1956 Crown Victorias, 1962–66 Thunderbirds, 1965–66 Mustangs (hardtops and convertibles); *Chevrolets:* 1950 convertibles, 1955–57 convertibles, 1962–64 Impala two-door hardtops, 1967 Corvettes; *Cadillacs:* 1951 convertibles, 1964 two-door hardtops; *Pontiacs; Buicks:* 1953–54 Skylark convertibles; *Mercurys:* 1950 coupes and convertibles; *Studebakers:* 1950–51 convertibles, 1963–64 Avantis; *Chryslers:* 1959 Imperial convertibles; *Lincolns:* 1966 convertibles; *Oldsmobiles; Plymouths; Dodges; Ramblers; Packards.*

From January 1976 to March 1977, the cars most wanted were: *Fords:* 1950–52 convertibles, 1955–56 convertibles, Crown Victorias, 1955–57 Thunderbirds, 1959 Retractables, 1960–64 Thunderbird convertibles, 1962–66 Falcon convertibles, 1963–64 Galaxie two-door hardtops, 1965–66 Mustang convertibles and fastbacks; *Chevrolets:* 1953–67 Corvettes, 1955 two-door hardtops, 1956 Nomads and convertibles, 1957 convertibles, 1958 Impalas, 1960 convertibles, 1962 two-door hardtops, 1965 convertibles, 1967 Chevelle convertibles, 1968 Camaro convertibles; *Cadillacs:* 1950–53 convertibles, 1955 convertibles, 1957–59 Eldorado Biarritz convertibles, 1957 Sevilles, 1958 Broughams, 1964 Eldorado convertibles, 1970 De Ville convertibles; *Lincolns:* 1956–57 Mark IIs, 1956 Premiere two-door hardtops, 1961–67 convertibles; *Pontiacs:* 1959 convertibles, 1961 convertibles, 1970 GTOs; *Buicks:* 1953 Skylark convertibles, 1954 Roadmaster convertibles, 1965 Rivieras; *Chryslers:* 1957–59 300s, 1961 Imperial convertibles; *Oldsmobiles:* 1950 88 convertibles, 1953 convertibles, 1966 Toronados; *Plymouths:* 1959 Fury convertibles, 1961 convertibles; *Studebakers:* 1957–58 Golden Hawks, 1963–64 Avantis; *Mercurys:* 1950 convertibles and coupes; *Dodges:* 1969–70 Super Bees; *Packards:* 1953–56 Caribbeans; *DeSotos; Edsels.*

From January 1975 to March 1977, the number of people placing "car wanted" ads in *Hemmings Motor News* and *Old Cars* newspaper increased over 100 percent. Many of the cars people wanted were not popular ones; they were of the hard-to-find, but not particularly valuable, variety. For example, one person offered $500 just for information leading to the purchase of a 1954 Ford Country Squire station wagon in good condition.

This shows an increased interest not only in the most popular makes but also in a wide variety of old cars. It definitely shows that the hobby is expanding. Many currently unpopular makes of cars are sure to undergo some remarkable increases in value over the next five years (specific examples of these "sleepers" will be discussed in chapter four).

Old cars were not always as popular as they are today. A decade ago, about the only people who drove cars ten or more years old were the poor. Sure, there were car collectors around, but few were interested in postwar automobiles. Those who were had little trouble finding the cars they wanted at low prices. Good postwar special-interest cars selling for under $300 were a common sight then. Since they were both plentiful and cheap, only the most farsighted were investing in them.

One of my favorite pastimes in the mid-1960s was visiting used-car lots. The lots were crammed with cars from the 1950s and, to a lesser extent, the late 1940s. Some of these vehicles were clunkers, but many were very attractive. Several of the cars I fell in love with in used-car lots in 1966 were a 1958 Ford convertible ($100), a 1949 Chevy two-door fastback ($30), a 1954 Mercury convertible ($100), a 1949 Ford two-door station wagon ($15), a 1955 Chevy convertible ($50), and a 1959 Ford convertible ($200). None of the cars was in mint condition (except for the 1959 Ford—that's why it was so expensive). But all were good, solid automobiles with strong engines and little, if any, rust. In most cases, the only "restoration" needed was a wax job, seat covers, a tune-up, and, if the car was a convertible, a new top.

It wasn't until around 1970 that interest in, and demand for, postwar cars started to increase noticeably. One indication of this was the increase in the number of subscribers to *Hemmings Motor News.* Subscriptions to this publication, the bible of car collecting, more than doubled from 26,200 in June 1966 to 52,800 in May 1970 (by December 1978, there were over 166,000 subscribers). In response to the growing interest in old cars, *Hemmings Motor News* started a bi-monthly magazine, *Special Interest Autos.* As the name implies, this magazine is devoted to in-depth articles on special-interest cars, particularly postwar vehicles.

By 1971, a monthly newspaper, *Old Cars,* was established. It reported on events and people affecting the old-car hobby, and ran informative articles on postwar, and other, cars. Like those of *Hemmings Motor News* and *Special Interest Autos,* its circulation has been rising rapidly. *Old Cars* now comes out on a weekly basis.

As interest in old automobiles rose, so did prices. More and more people wanted a limited number of cars, and postwar special-interest cars were rapidly changing from a buyer's to a seller's market. Despite this high level of interest in 1970, bargains could still be readily found among cars of the 1950s and 1960s.

One that sticks in my mind was a 1950 Mercury coupe I saw in a used-car lot that year. It had just over 40,000 miles on it, but looked as if it had less than 10,000; it was beautiful. It sat on the lot for over six months. Finally, the dealer (a collector) decided to keep the car himself. Apparently, everybody thought the asking price of $350 was too much.

Actually, it *was* a little high for 1970. In December of that year I was able to pick up a virtually rust-free 1956 Pontiac four-door hardtop, with only 63,000 miles on it, for $75. The used-car dealer seemed eager to get rid of it even at that low price. I drove the Pontiac regularly, about 25,000 miles a year. In 1974, I was offered $250 for it. I refused the offer. Later, in a moment of weakness, I sold it to a friend for $150. Had I kept it, I'm sure I could easily have sold it in 1979 for $500, as is.

Even as late as 1972, one could still find nice ten- to twenty-five-year-old cars selling cheap. I bought a 1956 Chevrolet 210 station wagon that year from a used-car lot. It had a little rust, but the body was straight and sound. The original paint was very good, and the 265 V8 engine had the hot factory "power pack" (dual exhaust, four-barrel carburetor) setup. Except for a small tear on the driver's seat, and a couple of stains on the headliner, the interior was excellent; the original owner had never even bothered to remove the paper protecting the sun visors. In addition, the car came with four new tires and two-year-old snow tires. I paid a "high" $250 for the Chevy.

When I got the wagon home, I changed the oil, gave it a tune-up, polished the chrome, waxed it until its green finish gleamed, and had wide whitewall toppers put on the tires. Within a month, I received six unsolicited offers for it, ranging from $275 to $600.

That was a lot of money for a "common" sixteen-year-old four-door station wagon (hardly a hot body type). Even more interesting was the fact that only one of the people who wanted to buy my car was an old-car nut. (He offered to trade a six-year-old Chevrolet station wagon in excellent condition for it. However, back then, nice 1966 Chevy wagons were as common as "Spiro's My Hero" bumper stickers.) The other would-be purchasers were not car collectors; they were just "ordinary" people captivated by an attractive old car. And they were willing to pay more than the local going price had been for such a vehicle. Although I'd owned nice old cars all my driving life, I found this to be a novel experience.

There are several reasons for this sudden interest in old cars by "ordinary" people. Automobiles are no longer the status symbols they used to be. Sociologist Paul Blumberg believes that this decline in status began in the early 1960s. In a 1977 interview in *U.S. News and World Report,* he stated, "When almost any family could have almost any American car, when someone driving an Oldsmobile or even a Cadillac was nobody special—at that point, cars lost much of their ability to confer status." So owning a new car no longer carries the same prestige it once did.

Ford dramatically demonstrated this phenomenon when it ran ads comparing its Granada with the Cadillac Seville. The ads pointed out very convincingly how much alike the two cars looked. The premise of the ads was, "Why buy a Cadillac when you can buy a Ford for much less—and most people won't even know the difference." One Ford TV commercial reenacted a true story about a woman who got a parking ticket on her new car. On the ticket the police officer had described the car as a Cadillac, when in fact her car was a Ford.

Try to imagine anyone confusing a 1959 Cadillac with a Ford of the same year. Even someone who had spent three-fourths of his or her life in a cave in Siberia could quickly have identified the rich person's car. A mechanic recently told me, "When I was a kid, I could sit on my porch and tell every car from a block away. Now I practically have to go up and read the taillight lenses to tell them apart."

It's no wonder that people can get more admiring glances driving a shiny ten-year-old or older car than a new car of the same make. Old cars have character—a quality new cars lack.

Many people feel they are being forced by the auto makers, and rising gasoline prices, into buying the new small cars. Any time you force people to do something, even if they know it's for their own good, they are going to resent it. I've noticed that fewer and fewer people who buy new cars (especially the small ones) are actually excited about them. How many miles per gallon a car can go may be important, especially now, but it's also very boring. Buying a new car today is about as much fun as buying a new washing machine. The thrill is gone for many people.

Old cars bring back some of the fun of driving. They represent the "happy days" of the recent past. Getting behind the steering wheel of an old car is like stepping into a time machine. There isn't an old-car owner who hasn't fantasized at least once about the time when his or her car was new. This nostalgic quality old cars possess may be one of the most important factors in determining their value. (Because so many people buy Fords and Chevys, these makes have high "nostalgic value" to a large number of people.)

It may also be why "instant" collectibles, such as the 1976 Cadillac Eldorado convertible, may prove to be not as good an investment as expected. Such vehicles have little "nostalgic value." Few individuals will have had any experiences driving or riding in them, or even seeing them being driven.

This is not to say that the only reason for buying an old car is the emotional one of nostalgia (although it is the primary reason for most people—I never buy a car unless I fall in love with it). It actually makes a lot of practical sense to purchase an older car. According to the U.S. Department of Transportation, "Depreciation is the greatest single cost of owning and operating an automobile." A new car will depreciate up to 30 percent the first year, 18 percent the second, and 14 percent the third; it will continue to lose value for at least another four years.

A new car depreciates at a rapid rate, regardless of its use. A study by the Federal Highway Commission found, "In the great majority of cases, the age of a car is more important than its mileage in determining its resale or trade in value." In other words, the older it is, the less it's worth. Special-interest cars are judged differently. The age of a vehicle is less important than the quality and popularity or desirability of the car.

A person who pays $6,000 for a typical new car will lose over $3,000 in just three years. A good special-interest car can be had for around $3,000. In three years, if kept in good condition, it should be worth at least $3,000—more likely, $3,500 to $5,000, or even more.

In the booklet *Cost of Owning and Operating an Automobile 1976,* researchers for the U.S. Department of Transportation claim, "As time passes it becomes increasingly difficult and expensive to keep a car in satisfactory operating condition." Yes and no. As cars age, things are going to break down and need to be replaced. After a person owns an old car for a while she or he will come to think of replacing mufflers, tailpipes, shock absorbers, batteries, and the like as just part of routine maintenance. Since most such items can (and should) be purchased with a "lifetime" guarantee (i.e., for as long as you own the car), the cost of such repairs is minimal if you plan on keeping the car for several years.

Aside from the aforementioned items that commonly wear out, I've found the cost of keeping an old car in good working order to be reasonable. For example, in 1968, I bought a 1953 Ford for $150. It had only 43,000 original miles on its whisper-quiet, flathead V8 engine. I drove the Ford over 50,000 miles in two years, and the only major repair needed was a new fuel pump. This was a better-than-average repair rate. Still, the most expensive (repairwise) of the many old cars I've owned cost me an average of $110 a year in repairs (over a five-year period). Much of that went for an overhauled engine and a rebuilt transmission. Since those major repairs, the actual (as opposed to average) annual repair bill has dropped considerably.

This is not to say that old cars can't be expensive to repair. They can—which is why it is important to get a good one to begin with. Any old car that is used much will develop problems, but these problems don't necessarily have to bankrupt you. And if you compare the cost of repairing an old car with the money lost on depreciation of a new auto, the chances are good that you will still come out way ahead financially, even if the old car is a troublesome one.

Investing in anything is risky, and old cars are no exception. Still, it's hard to lose money if you buy the right convertible or other special-interest car, and at a reasonable price—if for no other reason than the fact that used-car prices are constantly rising. Today, one has a hard time finding any decent car for under $500. The vast majority of autos priced under that look like refugees from a junkyard. The $50-to-$100 cars of the 1960s have become the $300-to-$700 cars of the 1970s.

Just about any low-mileage, well-maintained car with a popular body type can bring close to $1,000 with no trouble. When one compares the current selling prices of most special-interest cars to what they sold for when new (or as back-row specials a few years ago), they seem high. However, when compared with those of new cars and even ordinary late-model used cars, prices for old cars are really quite reasonable. So there is plenty of room for growth in prices.

In late 1976, *Motor Trend*'s "Classic Comments" columnist, Robert J. Gottlieb, stated, "In relation to the coin, stamp, stock, or art markets, old car prices will reflect relatively few up-and-down cycles. The long-range prediction is certainly optimistic for those who have cars. . . . It's only a question of time until we see a $20,000 Nomad."

I agree, and go just a bit further. I can foresee a Nomad (probably a 1955 or 1957) selling for $25,000 within fifteen years. The combination of inflation, scarcity, and demand makes it a foregone conclusion. Of course it will be a very exceptional car, and most Nomads will sell for considerably less (but far more than what they can bring now). What's more, by then many other special-interest cars from the 50s, 60s, and 70s (especially convertibles) will be selling for over $15,000. Included among these will be cars that are currently being ignored by collectors.

The question posed by this chapter was, "Who wants to buy an old car?" The answer is, "Anyone who likes to drive a distinctive automobile, wants to save thousands of dollars on depreciation, and doesn't mind making a profit when he or she sells the car."

2
The Most Valuable Postwar American Automobiles

This chapter contains detailed information on American convertibles made from 1946 to 1976 and selected special-interest cars of other body types made from 1946 to 1970. A brief report on each car is given. It includes original selling price, number produced, estimated number existing in 1979, miles-per-gallon rating, common trouble spots, availability of parts, investment potential, and background information.

Definition of Terms

Original Price: This is what the car sold for when new. In most cases it is the base price, not including options.

Number Produced: This is the number of cars of each model that were manufactured. When the exact number is not known, an estimate is given. The letters N.A. appear when a reasonably accurate estimate cannot be made.

Estimated Number Existing in 1979: This number is based on registration figures. It is a "ball-park" figure and should not be considered the absolute number remaining. The purpose of this category is simply to give a *general* idea of the rarity of a particular automobile.

Of course, not all these cars are in good condition. For example, Larry Mitchell of the Classic AMX Club International estimates that of the 19,134 AMX's built from 1968 to 1970, about 10,000 are still registered. But, he adds, "Those 10,000 are dwindling fast, as the majority of these cars were sold in the 'Rust Belt' and are getting beyond economical restoration."

After eight to ten years all cars tend to take a sharp dive in survival, some at a greater rate than others. It is not uncommon for cars past their fourteenth birthday to disappear at the rate of 30 percent (or more) of those remaining per year. So don't be misled by a seemingly high survival rate. Plentiful cars have a way of becoming scarce in a very short period of time.

Some people argue that, since convertibles tend to deteriorate at a faster rate than closed cars, they are less likely to survive. Others believe ragtops have a higher survival rate because they are a more desirable body type. I take the middle position, and assume that ragtops will survive in the same proportion as their percentage of the original number of their make produced. That is, if a convertible was one percent of the total production of a make when new, that convertible will be one percent of the total number remaining in 1979.

For cars made from 1946 to 1961, the number surviving was usually arrived at by finding the rate of decline between the fourteenth and fifteenth years of a car's life and assuming that the car would keep vanishing at the same rate until 1979. For 1962 and newer cars, the number remaining was estimated to be the same percentage of original production as the average of several previous model years of the same make at the same stage in their life. For instance a 1969 car's survival rate in 1979 was based on that of past models of the same make at ten years of age.

In addition to registration figures, the opinions of many clubs and authorities on various makes as to the number of a particular type of car surviving were taken into account.

The figures for certain popular cars may have been slightly underestimated, because such cars are frequently rescued from junkyards and brought back to life. However, all in all, this should be a fairly accurate guide to the *approximate* number of each car existing in 1979.

Miles per Gallon: In most instances this is based on road tests made when the car was new. Personal experience and reports of present and previous owners were also taken into account.

The number of miles per gallon a driver gets from a car varies. Driving habits and the condition of the engine can affect fuel economy. The type of engine can also make a big difference. Obviously a car with a small six-cylinder engine, with single carburetor, will deliver better mileage than the same car equipped with a 400 h.p. V8, with two four-barrel carbs.

Overdrive is a good thing to look for in cars with manual transmissions. Not only does it increase the number of miles an auto can go on a gallon of gas, it also extends the life of the car's engine.

Common Trouble Spots: These are problems peculiar to the car. They are based on reports of owners, past and present, and articles in consumer and car publications. The problems listed aren't necessarily found on all cars of a certain make, but they have been reported frequently by owners of the vehicle. Often the problems have been corrected. Still, it is a good idea to be aware of possible trouble spots.

Availability of Parts: This is a guide to the *general* availability of parts (as of 1979). One can expect parts sources to deteriorate as time passes. Three basic classifications are used:

Good: Most or all parts are available, either through conventional auto-parts stores or from dealers in old-car parts.

Fair: Most parts are available, but it may take some searching to find them.

Poor: Most parts are hard to find; where available, they are extremely expensive.

Investment Potential: This refers primarily to the desirability of the car. It also is a good indicator of the car's popularity. Usually, popular cars are also desirable. However, desirable autos are not necessarily all that popular. For example, the limited-production, fuel-injected 1957 Pontiac Bonneville is not currently on the top of most collectors' car want lists. Still, it is a very desirable car.

Each car is rated on a scale from "A" to "AAA+."

A: The car is desirable, but not particularly popular or sought after.

A+: This means the car is (or should become) slightly above average in desirability and/or popularity.

AA: This rating indicates the vehicle is (or should become) above average in desirability and/or popularity.

AA+: This means the car is (or should become) slightly better than above average in desirability and/or popularity.

AAA: Autos receiving this rating are (or should become) very desirable and/or popular.

AAA+: A car with this rating is (or should become) one of the most desirable and/or popular of all postwar cars.

The condition of the specific car and the initial purchase price have a great deal to do with its profit-making potential. An auto that needs a lot of expensive repairs, or one priced well above the current market value, can be a bad buy no matter how high it is rated. However, as a rule, the higher the car's rating, the more demand there is for it, and the greater the chance of finding a buyer willing to pay your price.

It is possible to make more money per dollar invested by buying and selling "A" and "A+" rated cars than "AAA" and "AAA+" ones. The reason is that most lower-rated cars are lower-priced as well. And the less you have to pay for a car to begin with, the less you have to sell it for to make a profit. However, finding a buyer for a less popular car is usually harder to do.

For example, I know of a 1969 Pontiac Catalina convertible that has been sitting on a local used-car lot for two years. It is in good condition and reasonably priced, yet it still hasn't found a home. If it were a 1969 GTO (or other more popular car) in the same condition and at the same price, it would have been sold long ago. This isn't to say that nobody likes 1969 Catalinas, but the number of people who do like them are fewer than those who like other model years and/or series of Pontiacs.

Personally, I believe that virtually any car can be made more desirable by detailing it (i.e., shining up body and chrome, and putting on whitewall tires, etc.). Driving it is also important—people can't want what they don't know exists.

In addition to studying the old-car market, many individual collectors and car clubs were contacted in an effort to come up with a basis for judging the desirability of the cars. For example, among the members of a large Oldsmobile club, the 1950 88, 1957 98, and 1953 Fiesta convertibles rank tops. King Midget fans tend to prefer 1966 to 1969 models. Edsel lovers like the 1958 best of all although the 1960 model gets more attention from media because it is the rarest. Among Nomads, the 1955 and 1957 versions rank the highest (younger people tend to like the 1957 slightly better). The 1957 Ford Skyliner seems to be the most popular retractable, but it is easier to find a nice 1959 flip-top. Depending on what club you ask, Metropolitan owners like the 1954, 1959, and 1960 Met ragtops best. Among Chrysler 300 loyalists, the 1957 model appears to be most popular, closely followed by the 1960 and 1961. And the 1957–1958 Eldorado Broughams rate much higher than the 1959–1960 versions. (Notice that 1957 seems to be a good year for a lot of cars? Maybe the safest investment is just to buy cars built in that year. Maybe.)

Cars with the same rating will not necessarily bring the same selling price. A 1947 car rated "A" will probably sell for more than a 1970 auto with the same rating; a Cadillac will sell for more than a Dodge. What the rating does mean is that they will probably both return about the same amount of money per dollar invested.

The rating of a vehicle does not necessarily reflect the quality of the car. Many unpopular autos are very dependable and well-made, while some "hot" cars have reputations for being troublesome.

Regardless of rating, it is generally best not to buy a car until it is at least eight to ten years old. Let someone else pay for the initial maintenance, fix any inherent "bugs," and suffer the inevitable loss from depreciation during an automobile's early years. The fact that American convertibles are no longer made doesn't necessarily make them all immediately desirable; it simply adds to their nostalgic value, but the only way for a car to gain nostalgic appeal is through time.

In addition to general nostalgic appeal, personal nostalgia affects the desirability of an auto to different people. I received my initiation into the joys of cruising in a friend's '49 Chevy in the winter of 1964–1965. Since we were only 14, we had to limit our traveling to after dark, to lessen the chances of getting stopped.

With the car packed with younger siblings, the heater on high, and the lively sounds of "The Boy from New York City," "Thou Shalt Not Steal," and "Little GTO" escaping loudly from the dash, we went on our search for action." The chances of finding any "action" while driving down those rural county highways on below-zero Wisconsin nights were about as great as those of being asked by Ann-Margret to do the "Freddie" at the junior-high noon sock-hop. Still, each ride was an exciting adventure (made more so by the fact that my friend was just learning to drive).

So when I look at a 1949 Chevrolet, it brings back a carload of pleasant memories. Cruising has never been quite the same for me as it was when I was riding shotgun in "Betsy." Of course, someone else might look at a '49 Chev and recall that it was a similar car that ran over his pet frog Wilbert in 1958.

It is a personal nostalgia (as opposed to general nostalgia) that is responsible for the surprisingly high prices which some low-rated, not particularly popular cars occasionally bring at auctions and elsewhere. Some of my favorite cars have low ratings; I sometimes get the feeling that they are loved only by me and the mothers of the people who designed them.

Even the color of a car can have an effect on how desirable it is. Currently, the most popular colors for convertibles are black and red (in that order). The least popular color is green, especially army green. Also, an automobile with popular options, such as a 4-speed manual transmission, a big V8, air conditioning, fuel injection, a power package, a continental spare tire kit, and dual exhaust, can be worth substantially more than a stripped-down (six-cylinder, automatic transmission) version of the same car. Fuel injection is so popular that having it can increase a car's value by as much as $2,000 or more. However, this applies only to cars on which it was originally optional. Adding fuel injection to a car it was not offered on will *not* make that car worth more.

In the final analysis: if a car really excites you and the price is right, buy it. Chances are, if it affects you that way it will do the same to someone else. However, keep in mind that the desirability and/or popularity of the car you like among the old-car-buying public will affect the return you can expect on your investment.

Some currently low-rated cars may increase in desirability in the future, but high-rated cars are not likely to become less desirable.

Background: This consists of information on the car. In virtually all cases, the standard engine and transmission, and any optional engines and/or transmissions, are listed. Whenever possible, the percentages of this particular make and/or model sold with various optional equipment are given.

1946

1946 Buick Roadmaster Convertible

Original Price: $2,347
Number Produced: 2,587
Estimated Number Existing in 1979: 2
Miles per Gallon :11–16
Common Trouble Spots: clutch, top mechanism
Availability of Parts: poor
Investment Potential: A+

Background: The attractive Roadmaster ragtop was powered by a 144 h.p. 320.2 cu. in. eight-cylinder engine. According to Buick sales literature, this engine was "made to closer tolerances than an aircraft engine." A three-speed manual transmission was standard.

The '46 Roadmaster came with 7.00 × 15 four-ply blackwall tires. Whitewall tires were optional at extra cost, but they were not available until later in the model year.

1946 Buick Super Convertible

Original Price: $1,719
Number Produced: 5,987
Estimated Number Existing in 1979: 3
Miles per Gallon: 12–19
Common Trouble Spots: clutch, top mechanism
Availability of Parts: poor
Investment Potential: A+

Background: "Super is the name . . . and superfine is the quality," proclaimed Buick sales literature in 1946. The prestigious Super convertible was powered by a 110 h.p. 248 cu. in. eight-cylinder engine. A three-speed manual transmission and 6.50 × 16 four-ply blackwall tires were standard.

1946 Buick Super Estate Station Wagon

Original Price: $2,594
Number Produced: 798
Estimated Number Existing in 1979: 1
Miles per Gallon: 12–17
Common Trouble Spots: clutch
Availability of Parts: poor
Investment Potential: AA+

Background: The attractive Super woodie wagon was powered by a 110 h.p. 248 cu. in. eight-cylinder engine. A three-speed manual transmission was standard.

1946 Buick Super Convertible

PHOTO: BUICK MOTOR DIVISION

1946 Cadillac Series 62 Convertible

Original Price: est. $2,600
Number Produced: 1,342
Estimated Number Existing in 1979: 2
Miles per Gallon: 13–18
Common Trouble Spots: none
Availabilty of Parts: poor–fair
Investment Potential: AA

Background: Cadillac's first postwar convertible was powered by a 150 h.p. 346 cu. in. eight-cylinder engine. A three-speed manual transmission was standard. Hydra-Matic Drive automatic transmission was optional at extra cost.

1946 Cadillac Series 62 Convertible

PHOTO: CADILLAC MOTOR CAR DIVISION

1946 Chevrolet Fleetmaster Convertible

Original Price: $1,381
Number Produced: 4,508
Estimated Number Existing in 1979: 6
Miles per Gallon: 14–20
Common Trouble Spots: carburetor, piston rings
Availability of Parts: poor–fair
Investment Potential: A+

Background: The new '46 Fleetmaster ragtop was powered by a 90 h.p. 216.5 cu. in. six-cylinder engine. A three-speed manual transmission was standard.

1946 Chevrolet Fleetmaster Station Wagon

Original Price: $1,604
Number Produced: 804
Estimated Number Existing in 1979: 3
Miles per Gallon: 14–18
Common Trouble Spots: carburetor, piston rings
Availability of Parts: poor–fair
Investment Potential: AA+

Background: The attractive 1946 Fleetmaster woodie wagon was powered by a 90 h.p. 216.5 cu. in. six-cylinder engine. A three-speed manual transmission was standard.

1946 Chrysler New Yorker Convertible

Original Price: $2,193
Number Produced: est. 1,000
Estimated Number Existing in 1979: 2
Miles per Gallon: 12–17
Common Trouble Spots: brakes
Availability of Parts: poor
Investment Potential: A+

Background: The '46 New Yorker convertible was powered by a 114 h.p. 250.6 cu. in. eight-cylinder engine. A three-speed manual transmission was standard. Fluid Drive automatic transmission was optional.

Many people who have never actually seen a 1946–1948 Chrysler remember them from the cartoons of that period, for which Chryslers were often used as models.

1946 Chrysler Town and Country Convertible

Original Price: $2,743
Number Produced: est. 2,789
Estimated Number Existing in 1979: 8
Miles per Gallon: 10–15
Common Trouble Spots: brakes
Availability of Parts: poor
Investment Potential: AAA+

Background: One of the most distinctive ragtops Chrysler ever built was the '46 Town and Country. This attractive woodie convertible was powered by a 135 h.p. 323.5 cu. in. eight-cylinder engine. A three-speed manual transmission was standard. Fluid Drive automatic transmission was optional.

1946 Chrysler Town and Country Convertible

PHOTO: CHRYSLER HISTORICAL COLLECTION

1946 Chrysler Town and Country Sedan

Original Price: $2,366
Number Produced: est. 1,331
Estimated Number Existing in 1979: 4
Miles per Gallon: 10–16
Common Trouble Spots: brakes
Availability of Parts: poor
Investment Potential: AA+

Background: The swankiest four-door sedan in 1946 had to be the Town and Country. This luxurious car came with a 114 h.p. 250.6 cu. in. six-cylinder engine. Available at extra cost was a 135 h.p. 323.5 cu. in. eight-cylinder engine. The eight was not very popular; only 100 Town and Country sedans were equipped with them. A three-speed manual transmission was standard. Fluid Drive automatic transmission was optional.

1946 Chrysler Town and Country Two-Door Hardtop

Original Price: est. $2,743
Number Produced: 7
Estimated Number Existing in 1979: 1
Miles per Gallon: 10–15
Common Trouble Spots: brakes
Availability of Parts: poor
Investment Potential: AAA+

Background: This was the first two-door hardtop. Actually, it was just a prototype—a special three-passenger-coupe roof was bolted on to a convertible body.

The '46 Town and Country hardtop was powered by a 135 h.p. 323.5 cu. in. eight-cylinder engine. A three-speed manual transmission was standard. Fluid Drive automatic transmission was optional.

1946 Chrysler Town and Country Two-Door Hardtop

PHOTO: CHRYSLER CORPORATION

1946 Chrysler Windsor Convertible

PHOTO: CHRYSLER HISTORICAL COLLECTION

1946 Chrysler Windsor Convertible

Original Price: $1,861
Number Produced: est. 3,733
Estimated Number Existing in 1979: 2
Miles per Gallon: 12–18
Common Trouble Spots: brakes
Availability of Parts: poor
Investment Potential: A+

Background: The new Windsor convertible came with a 114 h.p. 250.6 cu. in. six-cylinder engine. A three-speed manual transmission was standard. Fluid Drive automatic transmission was optional.

1946 Crosley Convertible

Original Price: est. $900
Number Produced: 12
Estimated Number Existing in 1979: 1
Miles per Gallon: 25–32
Common Trouble Spots: none
Availability of Parts: poor
Investment Potential: A

Background: This was the first postwar Crosley convertible. Despite the fact that it was longer and wider than the prewar model, nobody mistook it for a Buick. It was powered by a 26 h.p. 44 cu. in. four-cylinder engine. A three-speed manual transmission was standard.

1946 Crosley Convertible

PHOTO: CROSLEY AUTOMOBILE CLUB, INC.

1946 DeSoto Custom Convertible

1946 DeSoto Custom Convertible

Original Price: est. $1,800
Number Produced: est. 2,700
Estimated Number Existing in 1979: 2
Miles per Gallon: 13–18
Common Trouble Spots: none
Availability of Parts: poor
Investment Potential: A

Background: The '46 Custom convertible was basically a warmed-over 1942 (minus the nifty hidden headlights). It was powered by a 109 h.p. 236.6 cu. in. six-cylinder engine. A three-speed manual transmission was standard. A semi-automatic transmission was optional.

1946 Dodge Custom Convertible

Original Price: $1,649
Number Produced: est. 3,166
Estimated Number Existing in 1979: 2
Miles per Gallon: 13–18
Common Trouble Spots: none
Availability of Parts: poor
Investment Potential: A

Background: Dodge's first postwar ragtop was the Custom. It was powered by a 102 h.p. 230.2 cu. in. six-cylinder engine. A three-speed manual transmission was standard.

1946 Dodge Custom Convertible

PHOTO: CHRYSLER HISTORICAL COLLECTION

1946 Ford Super Deluxe Convertible

Original Price: est. $1,500
Number Produced: 16,359
Estimated Number Existing in 1979: 16
Miles per Gallon: 15–21
Common Trouble Spots: clutch
Availability of Parts: poor–fair
Investment Potential: AA

Background: "There's a Ford in your future," predicted Ford ads in 1945, before the introduction of the first postwar models. The Ford most people dreamed of was the Super Deluxe ragtop. It was powered by a 100 h.p. 239.4 cu. in. eight-cylinder engine. A three-speed manual transmission was standard.

1946 Ford Super Deluxe Convertible

1946 Ford Super Deluxe Sportsman Convertible

Original Price: $2,041
Number Produced: 723
Estimated Number Existing in 1979: 20
Miles per Gallon: 15–21
Common Trouble Spots: clutch
Availability of Parts: poor
Investment Potential: AAA+

Background: The most beautiful car Ford had to offer in 1946 was the Sportsman convertible. This woodie softtop was a joy to behold. However, "joy" was not the word used by owners to describe the chore of keeping the car (particularly the wood portion) looking decent; a great deal of tender loving care was not just desirable but a real necessity.

The Sportsman was powered by a 100 h.p. 239.4 cu. in. eight-cylinder engine. A three-speed manual transmission was standard.

The first Ford Sportsman was sold to movie actress Ella Raines on December 25, 1945.

1946 Ford Super Deluxe Sportsman Convertible

PHOTO: FORD MOTOR COMPANY

1946 Hudson Commodore Eight Convertible Brougham

Original Price: est. $2,000
Number Produced: N.A.
Estimated Number Existing in 1979: N.A.
Miles per Gallon: 13–18
Common Trouble Spots: cooling system
Availability of Parts: poor
Investment Potential: A

Background: The new Commodore Eight looked virtually the same as the 1942 model. It was powered by a 128 h.p. 254 cu. in. eight-cylinder engine. A three-speed manual transmission was standard. Overdrive and Electromatic Drive automatic transmission were optional at extra cost.

1946 Ford Super Deluxe Station Wagon

Original Price: est. $1,500
Number Produced: 16,960
Estimated Number Existing in 1979: 17
Miles per Gallon: 14–19
Common Trouble Spots: clutch
Availability of Parts: poor
Investment Potential: AAA

Background: The attractive Super Deluxe woodie was powered by a 90 h.p. 226 cu. in. six-cylinder engine. Most buyers ordered the extra-cost 100 h.p. 239.4 cu. in. eight-cylinder engine. A three-speed manual transmission and leather upholstery were standard.

1946 Hudson Super Six Convertible Brougham

PHOTO: JOHN A. CONDE COLLECTION

1946 Ford Super Deluxe Station Wagon

PHOTO: FORD MOTOR COMPANY

1946 Hudson Super Six Convertible Brougham

Original Price: est. $1,800
Number Produced: N.A.
Estimated Number Existing in 1979: N.A.
Miles per Gallon: 13–19
Common Trouble Spots: cooling system
Availability of Parts: poor
Investment Potential: A

Background: The '46 Hudson Super Six was powered by a 102 h.p. 212 cu. in. six-cylinder engine. A three-speed manual transmission was standard. Overdrive and Electromatic Drive automatic transmission were available at extra cost.

1946 Lincoln Continental Cabriolet

Original Price: $4,476
Number Produced: 201
Estimated Number Existing in 1979: 20
Miles per Gallon: 10–15
Common Trouble Spots: none
Availability of Parts: poor
Investment Potential: AAA+

Background: The luxurious 1946 Continental convertible was powered by a 130 h.p. 305 cu. in. V12 engine. A three-speed manual transmission was standard. Overdrive was optional.

The '46 Continental was the pace car at the Indy 500. A special "pace car yellow" exterior color was offered in honor of the occasion.

1946 Lincoln Continental Coupe

PHOTO: FORD MOTOR COMPANY

1946 Lincoln Continental Cabriolet

PHOTO: FORD MOTOR COMPANY

1946 Lincoln Continental Coupe

Original Price: $4,392
Number Produced: 265
Estimated Number Existing in 1979: 26
Miles per Gallon: 10–15
Common Trouble Spots: none
Availability of Parts: poor
Investment Potential: AAA+

Background: The limited-production 1946 Continental coupe came with a 130 h.p. 305 cu. in. V12 engine. A three-speed manual transmission was standard. Overdrive was available.

The 1946 to 1948 Lincoln Continentals are probably the only postwar cars that could be considered "grand."

1946 Lincoln Convertible Coupe

Original Price: $2,883
Number Produced: N.A.
Estimated Number Existing in 1979: N.A.
Miles per Gallon: 10–15
Common Trouble Spots: none
Availability of Parts: poor
Investment Potential: AAA

Background: "On boulevards and byways, you will travel with a new distinction in the 1946 Lincoln." That statement from a Lincoln advertisement is as true today as when it was written.

The '46 Lincoln convertible was powered by a 130 h.p. 305 cu. in. V12 engine. A three-speed manual transmission was standard. Overdrive was optional.

1946 Lincoln Convertible Coupe

PHOTO: FORD MOTOR COMPANY

1946 Mercury Convertible Coupe

PHOTO: FORD MOTOR COMPANY

1946 Mercury Convertible Coupe

Original Price: est. $1,700
Number Produced: 6,044
Estimated Number Existing in 1979: 2
Miles per Gallon: 13–19
Common Trouble Spots: none
Availability of Parts: poor
Investment Potential: A+

Background: The '46 Mercury ragtop was powered by a 100 h.p. 239.4 cu. in. eight-cylinder engine. A three-speed manual transmission was standard.

1946 Mercury Sportsman Convertible Coupe

Original Price: $2,263
Number Produced: 205
Estimated Number Existing in 1979: 3
Miles per Gallon: 13–18
Common Trouble Spots: none
Availability of Parts: poor
Investment Potential: AAA+

Background: Mercury's most attractive offering in 1946 was the Sportsman woodie ragtop. It was powered by a 100 h.p. 239.4 cu. in. eight-cylinder engine. A three-speed manual transmission was standard.

1946 Mercury Sportsman Convertible Coupe

PHOTO: FORD MOTOR COMPANY

1946 Mercury Station Wagon

Original Price: est. $1,700
Number Produced: 2,797
Estimated Number Existing in 1979: 2
Miles per Gallon: 13–18
Common Trouble Spots: none
Availability of Parts: poor
Investment Potential: AA+

Background: The new 1946 Mercury wagon came equipped with a 100 h.p. 239.4 cu. in. eight-cylinder engine. A three-speed manual transmission was standard. The body featured maple framing with either birch or mahogany panels. The leather interior was available in gray, red, or tan.

1946 Nash Ambassador Suburban

Original Price: est. $2,000
Number Produced: 275
Estimated Number Existing in 1979: 2
Miles per Gallon: 13–19
Common Trouble Spots: cooling system, piston rings
Availability of Parts: poor
Investment Potential: AA

Background: Nash's answer to other makes' woodie station wagons was the attractive wood-over-metal Suburban sedan. It was powered by a 112 h.p. 234.8 cu. in. six-cylinder engine. A three-speed manual transmission was standard. Overdrive was optional.

1946 Nash Ambassador Suburban

PHOTO: JOHN A. CONDE COLLECTION

1946 Oldsmobile Custom Cruiser Series 98 Convertible

Original Price: est. $2,100
Number Produced: 874
Estimated Number Existing in 1979: 1
Miles per Gallon: 13–19
Common Trouble Spots: none
Availability of Parts: poor
Investment Potential: A+

Background: Oldsmobile's classiest car in '46 was the 98 convertible. It was powered by a 110 h.p. 257.1 cu. in. eight-cylinder engine. A three-speed manual transmission was standard. Hydra-Matic Drive automatic transmission was optional at extra cost.

1946 Oldsmobile Custom Cruiser Series 98 Convertible

PHOTO: OLDSMOBILE DIVISION

1946 Oldsmobile Special Series 66 Convertible

Original Price: est. $1,700
Number Produced: 1,409
Estimated Number Existing in 1979: 1
Miles per Gallon: 13–19
Common Trouble Spots: none
Availability of Parts: poor
Investment Potential: A+

Background: The 1946 Series 66 convertible was powered by a 100 h.p. 238.1 cu. in. six-cylinder engine. A three-speed manual transmission was standard. Hydra-Matic Drive automatic transmission was optional.

1946 Oldsmobile Special Series 66 Convertible

PHOTO: OLDSMOBILE DIVISION

1946 Oldsmobile Special Series 66 Station Wagon

PHOTO: OLDSMOBILE DIVISION

1946 Oldsmobile Special Series 66 Station Wagon

Original Price: est. $2,300
Number Produced: 140
Estimated Number Existing in 1979: 1
Miles per Gallon: 13–18
Common Trouble Spots: none
Availability of Parts: poor
Investment Potential: AA+

Background: The attractive Series 66 woodie wagon was powered by a 100 h.p. 238.1 cu. in. six-cylinder engine. A three-speed manual transmission was standard. Hydra-Matic Drive automatic transmission was optional at extra cost.

1946 Plymouth Special Deluxe Convertible

Original Price: est. $1,400
Number Produced: est. 5,098
Estimated Number Existing in 1979: 3
Miles per Gallon: 13–20
Common Trouble Spots: none
Availability of Parts: poor
Investment Potential: A

Background: The new 1946 Special Deluxe ragtop was basically just a warmed-over 1942 model. But buyers didn't mind.

It was powered by a 95 h.p. 217.8 cu. in. six-cylinder engine. A three-speed manual transmission was standard.

1946 Plymouth Special Deluxe Convertible

PHOTO: CHRYSLER HISTORICAL COLLECTION

1946 Plymouth Special Deluxe Station Wagon

PHOTO: CHRYLSER HISTORICAL COLLECTION

1946 Plymouth Special Deluxe Station Wagon

Original Price: est. $1,500
Number Produced: est. 4,304
Estimated Number Existing in 1979: 2
Miles per Gallon: 13–20
Common Trouble Spots: none
Availability of Parts: poor
Investment Potential: AA+

Background: The '46 Special Deluxe station wagon was powered by a 95 h.p. 217.8 cu. in. six-cylinder engine. A three-speed manual transmission was standard.

1946 Pontiac Streamliner Deluxe Station Wagon

PHOTO: PONTIAC MOTOR DIVISION

1946 Pontiac Streamliner Deluxe Station Wagon

Original Price: est. $2,200
Number Produced: N.A.
Estimated Number Existing in 1979: N.A.
Miles per Gallon: 13–19
Common Trouble Spots: carburetor
Availability of Parts: poor
Investment Potential: AA+

Background: The new Streamliner Deluxe was a good-looking woodie. It came with a 93.5 h.p. 239.2 cu. in. six-cylinder. But most '46 Streamliners, 53.1%, were sold with the optional 107.5 h.p. 248.9 cu. in. eight-cylinder engine. The standard transmission was a three-speed manual.

1946 Pontiac Torpedo Convertible

Original Price: est. $1,700
Number Produced: N.A.
Estimated Number Existing in 1979: N.A.
Miles per Gallon: 14–20
Common Trouble Spots: carburetor
Availability of Parts: poor
Investment Potential: A

Background: Pontiac's first postwar convertible came with a 93.5 h.p. 239.2 cu. in. six-cylinder engine. A 107.5 h.p. 248.9 cu. in. eight-cylinder engine was available at extra cost. Just 40.6% of '46 Torpedos were so equipped. The standard transmission was a three-speed manual.

According to advertisements, the '46 Pontiac featured ". . . new beautiful exterior appearance . . . new instrument panel . . . heavier chrome finish . . . improved rust resistant bodies . . . new interior trim . . . improved clutch . . . new, wider wheel rims . . . longer life muffler and tailpipe . . . improved cooling."

1946 Pontiac Torpedo Convertible

PHOTO: PONTIAC MOTOR DIVISION

1947

1947 Buick Roadmaster Convertible

Original Price: $2,455
Number Produced: 12,074
Estimated Number Existing in 1979: 2
Miles per Gallon: 11–16
Common Trouble Spots: clutch, top mechanism
Availability of Parts: poor
Investment Potential: A+

Background: Buick's luxurious Roadmaster convertible was powered by a 144 h.p. 320.2 cu. in. eight-cylinder engine. A three-speed manual transmission was standard.

1947 Buick Roadmaster Convertible

PHOTO: PUBLIC RELATIONS—BUICK MOTOR DIVISION

1947 Buick Roadmaster Estate Station Wagon

Original Price: est. $2,800
Number Produced: 300
Estimated Number Existing in 1979: 1
Miles per Gallon: 11–16
Common Trouble Spots: clutch
Availability of Parts: poor
Investment Potential: AA+

Background: The 1947 Roadmaster Estate wagon was powered by a 144 h.p. 320.2 cu. in. eight-cylinder engine. A three-speed manual transmission was standard.

1947 Buick Super Convertible

Original Price: $2,169
Number Produced: 26,297
Estimated Number Existing in 1979: 11
Miles per Gallon: 12–18
Common Trouble Spots: clutch, top mechanism
Availability of Parts: poor
Investment Potential: A+

Background: The new Super ragtop was powered by a 110 h.p. 248 cu. in. eight-cylinder engine. A three-speed manual transmission was standard.

1947 Buick Super Estate Station Wagon

Original Price: $2,559
Number Produced: 2,036
Estimated Number Existing in 1979: 2
Miles per Gallon: 12–17
Common Trouble Spots: clutch
Availability of Parts: poor
Investment Potential: AA+

Background: This was a big year for the Super wagon. Sales were up substantially from the previous year. It was powered by a 110 h.p. 248 cu. in. eight-cylinder engine. A three-speed manual transmission was standard.

1947 Cadillac Series 62 Convertible

Original Price: $2,741
Number Produced: 6,755
Estimated Number Existing in 1979: 8
Miles per Gallon: 13–18
Common Trouble Spots: none
Availability of Parts: poor–fair
Investment Potential: AA

Background: Styling changes were kept to a minimum for 1947. The "new" Series 62 convertible looked a great deal like last year's model (which was similar in appearance to the 1942 version).

It was powered by a 150 h.p. 346 cu. in. eight-cylinder engine. A three-speed manual transmission was standard. Hydra-Matic automatic transmission was optional at extra cost.

1947 Cadillac Series 62 Convertible

PHOTO: CADILLAC MOTOR CAR DIVISION

1947 Chevrolet Fleetmaster Convertible

Original Price: $1,476
Number Produced: 28,443
Estimated Number Existing in 1979: 38
Miles per Gallon: 14–20
Common Trouble Spots: none
Availability of Parts: poor–fair
Investment Potential: A+

Background: The 1947 Chevy ragtop was powered by a 90 h.p. 216.5 cu. in. six-cylinder engine. A three-speed manual transmission was standard.

1947 Chevrolet Fleetmaster Station Wagon

1947 Chevrolet Fleetmaster Station Wagon

Original Price: $1,712
Number Produced: 4,912
Estimated Number Existing in 1979: 6
Miles per Gallon: 14–18
Common Trouble Spots: none
Availability of Parts: poor–fair
Investment Potential: AA+

Background: The 1947 Chevy Fleetmaster station wagon was powered by a 90 h.p. 216.5 cu. in. six-cylinder engine. A three-speed manual transmission was standard.

Although an attractive and mechanically strong car, the '47 Chevy wagon, like most woodies, depreciated at a rather rapid rate. The main reason for this was that the wood needed a great deal of tender loving care—something it did not often receive.

1947 Chrysler New Yorker Convertible

Original Price: $2,312
Number Produced: est. 1,000
Estimated Number Existing in 1979: 2
Miles per Gallon: 12–17
Common Trouble Spots: none
Availability of Parts: poor
Investment Potential: A+

Background: The '47 New Yorker ragtop was powered by a 135 h.p. 323.5 cu. in. eight-cylinder engine. A three-speed manual transmission was standard. Fluid Drive automatic transmission was optional.

1947 Chrysler Town and Country Convertible

Original Price: $2,889
Number Produced: est. 2,789
Estimated Number Existing in 1979: 10
Miles per Gallon: 10–15
Common Trouble Spots: none
Availability of Parts: poor
Investment Potential: AAA+

Background: Few cars could match the elegance of the 1947 Town and Country convertible. It was powered by a 135 h.p. 323.5 cu. in. eight-cylinder engine. A three-speed manual transmission was standard. Fluid Drive automatic transmission was optional.

1947 Chrysler Town and Country Sedan

Original Price: $2,494
Number Produced: est. 1,331
Estimated Number Existing in 1979: 6
Miles per Gallon: 10–16
Common Trouble Spots: none
Availability of Parts: poor
Investment Potential: AA+

Background: Outside of a few minor changes, the new 1947 Town and Country four-door sedan looked the same as the previous year's model. It was powered by a 114 h.p. 250.6 cu. in. six-cylinder engine. A three-speed manual transmission was standard. Fluid Drive automatic transmission was optional.

1947 Chrysler Windsor Convertible

Original Price: $1,962
Number Produced: est. 3,733
Estimated Number Existing in 1979: 4
Miles per Gallon: 12–18
Common Trouble Spots: none
Availability of Parts: poor
Investment Potential: A+

Background: The 1947 Windsor ragtop was powered by a 114 h.p. 250.6 cu. in. six-cylinder engine. A three-speed manual transmission was standard. Fluid Drive automatic transmission was optional.

1947 Crosley Convertible

Original Price: $1,011
Number Produced: 4,005
Estimated Number Existing in 1979: 10
Miles per Gallon: 25–32
Common Trouble Spots: none
Availability of Parts: poor
Investment Potential : A

Background: The first thing many people did when seeing a Crosley was to peek in the window and look for the pedals. It was powered by a 26 h.p. 44 cu. in. four-cylinder engine. A three-speed manual transmission was standard.

The '47 Crosley ragtop is a unique little car that can squeeze a lot of miles out of a gallon of gas.

1947 DeSoto Custom Convertible

Original Price: $1,857
Number Produced: est. 2,700
Estimated Number Existing in 1979: 2
Miles per Gallon: 13–18
Common Trouble Spots: none
Availability of Parts: poor
Investment Potential : A

Background: The '47 Custom ragtop was powered by a 109 h.p. 236.6 cu. in. six-cylinder engine. A three-speed manual transmission was standard. A semi-automatic transmission was optional.

1947 DeSoto Custom Convertible

1947 Dodge Custom Convertible

Original Price: $1,739
Number Produced: est. 3,167
Estimated Number Existing in 1979: 4
Miles per Gallon: 13–18
Common Trouble Spots: none
Availability of Parts: poor
Investment Potential : A

Background: The '47 Custom ragtop was powered by a 102 h.p. 230.2 cu. in. six-cylinder engine. A three-speed manual transmission was standard.

1947 Ford Super Deluxe Convertible

Original Price: $1,531
Number Produced: 22,159
Estimated Number Existing in 1979: 29
Miles per Gallon: 15–21
Common Trouble Spots: carburetor, clutch
Availability of Parts: poor–fair
Investment Potential : AA

Background: The Ford ragtop was even more popular this year than last. It was powered by a 100 h.p. 239.4 cu. in. eight-cylinder engine. A three-speed manual transmission was standard.

1947 Ford Super Deluxe Convertible

PHOTO: FORD MOTOR COMPANY

1947 Ford Super Deluxe Sportsman Convertible

Original Price: $2,041
Number Produced: 2,774
Estimated Number Existing in 1979: 78
Miles per Gallon: 15–21
Common Trouble Spots: carburetor, clutch
Availability of Parts: poor
Investment Potential : AAA+

Background: The beautiful Sportsman woodie convertible was powered by a 100 h.p. 239.4 cu. in. eight-cylinder engine. A three-speed manual transmission was standard. It looked virtually the same as the '46. However, many (about 66%) had wood patterns that were different from the previous year's.

Among the options offered were a radio, windshield washer, heater, and fog lights.

1947 Ford Super Deluxe Sportsman Convertible

PHOTO: FORD MOTOR COMPANY

1947 Ford Super Deluxe Station Wagon

Original Price: $1,617
Number Produced: 16,104
Estimated Number Existing in 1979: 20
Miles per Gallon: 14–19
Common Trouble Spots: carburetor, clutch
Availability of Parts: poor
Investment Potential : AAA

Background: The Super Deluxe was a good-looking woodie. It came with a 90 h.p. 226 cu. in. six-cylinder engine. Available at extra cost was a 100 h.p. 239.4 cu. in. eight-cylinder engine. A three-speed manual transmission was standard.

1947 Ford Super Deluxe Station Wagon

PHOTO: FORD MOTOR COMPANY

1947 Hudson Commodore Eight Convertible Brougham

Original Price: $2,072
Number Produced: N.A.
Estimated Number Existing in 1979: N.A.
Miles per Gallon: 13–18
Common Trouble Spots: none
Availability of Parts: poor
Investment Potential : A

Background: The new Commodore Eight ragtop was powered by a 128 h.p. 254 cu. in. eight-cylinder engine. A three-speed manual transmission was standard. Overdrive and Electromatic Drive automatic transmission were optional at extra cost.

1947 Hudson Super Six Convertible Brougham

Original Price: $1,898
Number Produced: N.A.
Estimated Number Existing in 1979: N.A.
Miles per Gallon: 13–19
Common Trouble Spots: none
Availability of Parts: poor
Investment Potential : A

Background: The 1947 Super Six ragtop was powered by a 102 h.p. 212 cu. in. six-cylinder engine. A three-speed manual transmission was standard. Overdrive and Electromatic Drive automatic transmission were optional at extra cost.

1947 Lincoln Continental Cabriolet

Original Price: $4,476
Number Produced: 738
Estimated Number Existing in 1979: 73
Miles per Gallon: 10–15
Common Trouble Spots: none
Availability of Parts: poor
Investment Potential: AAA+

Background: New hubcaps and a couple of minor mechanical improvements were the main differences between the 1947 and the 1946 Continental convertibles. The only engine offered was a 130 h.p. 305 cu. in. V12. A three-speed manual transmission was standard. Overdrive was optional.

1947 Lincoln Continental Cabriolet

PHOTO: FORD MOTOR COMPANY

1947 Lincoln Continental Coupe

PHOTO: FORD MOTOR COMPANY

1947 Lincoln Continental Coupe

Original Price: $4,392
Number Produced: 831
Estimated Number Existing in 1979: 80
Miles per Gallon: 10–15
Common Trouble Spots: none
Availability of Parts: poor
Investment Potential: AAA+

Background: The plush Continental coupe was little changed for 1947. Late in the model year, the hood ornament was redesigned. It was powered by a 130 h.p. 305 cu. in. V12 engine. A three-speed manual transmission was standard. Overdrive was optional.

1947 Lincoln Convertible Coupe

Original Price: $2,883
Number Produced: N.A.
Estimated Number Existing in 1979: N.A.
Miles per Gallon: 10–15
Common Trouble Spots: none
Availability of Parts: poor
Investment Potential: AAA

Background: The '47 Lincoln ragtop was powered by a 130 h.p. 305 cu. in. V12 engine. A three-speed manual transmission was standard. Overdrive was optional.

1947 Lincoln Convertible Coupe

PHOTO: FORD MOTOR COMPANY

1947 Mercury Convertible Coupe

Original Price: $1,764
Number Produced: 10,221
Estimated Number Existing in 1979: 6
Miles per Gallon: 13–19
Common Trouble Spots: carburetor, clutch
Availability of Parts: poor
Investment Potential: A+

Background: Mercury's sportiest offering in 1947 was its convertible coupe. It came equipped with a 100 h.p. 239.4 cu. in. eight-cylinder engine. A three-speed manual transmission was standard.

1947 Mercury Convertible

PHOTO: FORD MOTOR COMPANY

1947 Mercury Station Wagon

Original Price: $1,788
Number Produced: 3,558
Estimated Number Existing in 1979: 2
Miles per Gallon: 13–18
Common Trouble Spots: carburetor, clutch
Availability of Parts: poor
Investment Potential: AA+

Background: The attractive '47 Mercury woodie wagon was powered by a 100 h.p. 239.4 cu. in. eight-cylinder engine. A three-speed manual transmission was standard.

1947 Mercury Station Wagon

PHOTO: FORD MOTOR COMPANY

1947 Nash Ambassador Suburban

Original Price: $2,049
Number Produced: 595
Estimated Number Existing in 1979: 4
Miles per Gallon: 13–19
Common Trouble Spots: cooling system, piston rings
Availability of Parts: poor
Investment Potential: AA

Background: The most expensive and distinctive Nash in 1947 was the Suburban sedan. As before, it featured wood-over-metal styling. The '47 was the most popular of the woodie Suburbans. However, it wasn't exactly a hot seller.

It was powered by a 112 h.p. 234.8 cu. in. six-cylinder engine. A three-speed manual transmission was standard. Overdrive was optional.

1947 Oldsmobile Custom Cruiser Series 98 Convertible

PHOTO: OLDSMOBILE DIVISION

1947 Oldsmobile Custom Cruiser Series 98 Convertible

Original Price: $2,181
Number Produced: 3,940
Estimated Number Existing in 1979: 1
Miles per Gallon: 13–19
Common Trouble Spots: none
Availability of Parts: poor
Investment Potential: A+

Background: The top-of-the-line 98 convertible was powered by a 110 h.p. 257.1 cu. in. eight-cylinder engine. A three-speed manual transmission was standard. Hydra-Matic Drive automatic transmission was optional at extra cost.

1947 Oldsmobile Series 60 Convertible

Original Price: $1,742
Number Produced: 6,528
Estimated Number Existing in 1979: 2
Miles per Gallon: 13–19
Common Trouble Spots: none
Availability of Parts: poor
Investment Potential: A+

Background: The Olds Series 60 convertible was powered by a 100 h.p. 238.1 cu. in. six-cylinder engine. A 110 h.p. 257.1 cu. in. eight-cylinder engine was optional; 35.5% of Series 60 ragtops were so equipped. A three-speed manual transmission was standard. Hydra-Matic Drive automatic transmission was available at extra cost.

1947 Oldsmobile Series 60 Convertible

PHOTO: OLDSMOBILE DIVISION

1947 Oldsmobile Special Series 60 Station Wagon

Original Price: $2,319
Number Produced: 1,460
Estimated Number Existing in 1979: 1
Miles per Gallon: 13–18
Common Trouble Spots: none
Availability of Parts: poor
Investment Potential: AA+

Background: The attractive Series 60 woodie wagon came with a 100 h.p. 238.1 cu. in. six-cylinder engine. A 110 h.p. 257.1 cu. in. eight-cylinder engine was optional. Most, 66.3%, had the six. A three-speed manual transmission was standard. Hydra-Matic Drive automatic transmission was available at extra cost.

1947 Oldsmobile Special Series 60 Station Wagon

PHOTO: OLDSMOBILE DIVISION

1947 Plymouth Special Deluxe Convertible

Original Price: $1,520
Number Produced: est. 5,098
Estimated Number Existing in 1979: 6
Miles per Gallon: 13–20
Common Trouble Spots: none
Availability of Parts: poor
Investment Potential: A

Background: The "new" 1947 Special Deluxe ragtop was powered by a 95 h.p. 217.8 cu. in. six-cylinder engine. A three-speed manual transmission was standard.

1947 Plymouth Special Deluxe Station Wagon

Original Price: $1,626
Number Produced: est. 4,304
Estimated Number Existing in 1979: 5
Miles per Gallon: 13–20
Common Trouble Spots: none
Availability of Parts: poor
Investment Potential: AA+

Background: The '47 Special Deluxe was a good-looking wagon. It was powered by a 95 h.p. 217.8 cu. in. six-cylinder engine. A three-speed manual transmission was standard.

1947 Pontiac Streamliner Deluxe Station Wagon

Original Price: $2,207
Number Produced: N.A.
Estimated Number Existing in 1979: N.A.
Miles per Gallon: 13–19
Common Trouble Spots: none
Availability of Parts: poor
Investment Potential: AA+

Background: The '47 Streamliner station wagon was available with either a 93.5 h.p. 239.2 cu. in. six or a 107.5 h.p. 248.9 cu. in. eight-cylinder engine. Most Streamliners, 67%, came with the eight. A three-speed manual transmission was standard.

1947 Pontiac Streamliner Deluxe Station Wagon

PHOTO: PONTIAC MOTOR DIVISION

1947 Pontiac Torpedo Convertible

Original Price: $1,711
Number Produced: N.A.
Estimated Number Existing in 1979: N.A.
Miles per Gallon: 14–20
Common Trouble Spots: none
Availability of Parts: poor
Investment Potential: A

Background: The '47 Torpedo ragtop came with a 93.5 h.p. 239.2 cu. in. six-cylinder engine. But 34.2% of Torpedo buyers ordered the extra cost 107 h.p. 248.9 cu. in. eight-cylinder engine. The transmission was a three-speed manual.

1947 Studebaker Champion Convertible

Original Price: $1,902
Number Produced: 1,988
Estimated Number Existing in 1979: 1
Miles per Gallon: 17–28
Common Trouble Spots: piston rings
Availability of Parts: poor
Investment Potential: A+

Background: The '47 Champion was the first really new postwar convertible. Its styling was considered radical in its day; next to the Champion, other 1947 cars looked ancient.

A 80 h.p. 169.6 cu. in. six-cylinder engine powered the Champion. The standard transmission was a three-speed manual with overdrive.

1947 Studebaker Champion Convertible

1947 Studebaker Commander Convertible

Original Price: est. $2,200
Number Produced: 1,318
Estimated Number Existing in 1979: 1
Miles per Gallon: 16–25
Common Trouble Spots: piston rings
Availability of Parts: poor
Investment Potential: A+

Background: The new Commander convertible created quite a sensation when it was introduced. It looked like nothing else on the road at the time.

The Commander was powered by a 94 h.p. 226.2 cu. in. six-cylinder engine. A three-speed manual transmission with overdrive was standard.

1947 Studebaker Commander Convertible

PHOTO: RICHARD QUINN COLLECTION—STUDEBAKER DRIVERS CLUB

1948

1948 Buick Roadmaster Convertible

Original Price: $2,837
Number Produced: 11,503
Estimated Number Existing in 1979: 10
Miles per Gallon: 11–17
Common Trouble Spots: top mechanism
Availability of Parts: poor
Investment Potential: A+

Background: The new Roadmaster convertible was powered by a 144 h.p. 320.2 cu. in. eight-cylinder engine. A three-speed manual transmission was standard. Dynaflow automatic transmission was optional.

1948 Buick Roadmaster Estate Station Wagon

PHOTO: WILLIAM L. BAILEY COLLECTION

1948 Buick Roadmaster Convertible

PHOTO: DAVIS-WILLIAMS, INC.

1948 Buick Roadmaster Estate Station Wagon

Original Price: $3,433
Number Produced: 350
Estimated Number Existing in 1979: 1
Miles per Gallon: 11–16
Common Trouble Spots: none
Availability of Parts: poor
Investment Potential: AA+

Background: The top-of-the-line Roadmaster woodie came equipped with a 144 h.p. 320.2 cu. in. eight-cylinder engine. A three-speed manual transmission was standard. Dynaflow automatic transmission was optional.

1948 Buick Super Convertible

1948 Buick Super Convertible

Original Price: $2,518
Number Produced: 19,017
Estimated Number Existing in 1979: 18
Miles per Gallon: 12–18
Common Trouble Spots: top mechanism
Availability of Parts: poor
Investment Potential: A+

Background: The '48 Super ragtop was powered by a 110 h.p. 248 cu. in. eight-cylinder engine. A three-speed manual transmission was standard.

1948 Buick Super Estate Station Wagon

Original Price: $3,124
Number Produced: 2,018
Estimated Number Existing in 1979: 2
Miles per Gallon: 12–17
Common Trouble Spots: none
Availability of Parts: poor
Investment Potential: AA+

Background: The new '48 Super wagon was powered by a 110 h.p. 248 cu. in. eight-cylinder engine. A three-speed manual transmission was standard.

1948 Cadillac Series 62 Convertible

Original Price: est. $3,100
Number Produced: 5,450
Estimated Number Existing in 1979: 10
Miles per Gallon: 13–18
Common Trouble Spots: none
Availability of Parts: poor–fair
Investment Potential: AA

Background: This was the car that introduced the tailfin. It was the first significantly changed Cadillac since the war. Despite the sleek new styling, it was powered by last year's 150 h.p. 346 cu. in. eight-cylinder engine. A three-speed manual transmission was standard; so were power windows. Hydra-Matic automatic transmission was optional for $186. Ninety-eight percent of all 1948 Cadillacs came with the automatic.

Buyers had their choice of a black or a tan top.

1948 Chevrolet Fleetmaster Convertible

Original Price: $1,750
Number Produced: 20,471
Estimated Number Existing in 1979: 40
Miles per Gallon: 14–20
Common Trouble Spots: none
Availability of Parts: poor–fair
Investment Potential: A+

Background: Chevrolet sales literature bragged of the "big-car quality at lowest cost" of their 1948 models. The sportiest Chevy in '48 was the Fleetmaster convertible. It was powered by a 90 h.p. 216.5 cu. in. six-cylinder engine. A three-speed manual transmission was standard.

1948 Chevrolet Fleetmaster Convertible

PHOTO: HOWARD AND SHELBY APPLEGATE

1948 Cadillac Series 62 Convertible

PHOTO: CADILLAC MOTOR CAR DIVISION

1948 Chevrolet Fleetmaster Station Wagon

Original Price: $2,013
Number Produced: 10,171
Estimated Number Existing in 1979: 19
Miles per Gallon: 14–18
Common Trouble Spots: none
Availability of Parts: poor–fair
Investment Potential: AA+

Background: The 1948 Chevy Fleetmaster wagon was powered by a 90 h.p. 216.5 cu. in. six-cylinder engine. A three-speed manual transmission was standard.

1948 Chevrolet Fleetmaster Station Wagon

1948 Chrysler New Yorker Convertible

Original Price: $2,840
Number Produced: est. 1,000
Estimated Number Existing in 1979: 2
Miles per Gallon: 12–17
Common Trouble Spots: none
Availability of Parts: poor
Investment Potential: A+

Background: The 1948 New Yorker convertible was powered by a 135 h.p. 323.5 cu. in. eight-cylinder engine. A three-speed manual transmission was standard. Fluid Drive automatic transmission was optional.

1948 Chrysler Town and Country Convertible

Original Price: $3,420
Number Produced: est. 2,789
Estimated Number Existing in 1979: 27
Miles per Gallon: 10–15
Common Trouble Spots: none
Availability of Parts: poor
Investment Potential: AAA+

Background: The luxurious Town and Country was the most distinctive convertible offered in 1948. It was powered by a 135 h.p. 323.5 cu. in. eight-cylinder engine. A three-speed manual transmission was standard. Fluid Drive automatic transmission was optional.

1948 Chrysler Town and Country Sedan

Original Price: $2,808
Number Produced: est. 1,331
Estimated Number Existing in 1979: 16
Miles per Gallon: 10–15
Common Trouble Spots: none
Availability of Parts: poor
Investment Potential: AA+

Background: The attractive 1948 Town and Country woodie sedan was powered by a 114 h.p. 250.6 cu. in. six-cylinder engine. A three-speed manual transmission was standard. Fluid Drive automatic transmission was optional.

Two desirable options were a wooden roof rack (a steel rack was standard) and spotlights.

1948 Chrysler Windsor Convertible

Original Price: $2,434
Number Produced: est. 3,733
Estimated Number Existing in 1979: 5
Miles per Gallon: 12–18
Common Trouble Spots: none
Availability of Parts: poor
Investment Potential: A+

Background: The '48 Windsor ragtop came with a 114 h.p. 250.6 cu. in. six-cylinder engine. A three-speed manual transmission was standard. Fluid Drive automatic transmission was optional.

1948 Crosley Convertible

Original Price: est. $1,000
Number Produced: 2,485
Estimated Number Existing in 1979: 11
Miles per Gallon: 25–32
Common Trouble Spots: none
Availability of Parts: poor
Investment Potential: A

Background: The early 1948 Crosleys looked almost identical to the '47 models. However, in midyear, they received a new grille. It came with a 26 h.p. 44 cu. in. four-cylinder engine. A three-speed manual transmission was standard.

1948½ Crosley Convertible

PHOTO: CROSLEY AUTOMOBILE CLUB, INC.

1948 DeSoto Custom Convertible

Original Price: est. $1,900
Number Produced: est. 2,700
Estimated Number Existing in 1979: 3
Miles per Gallon: 13–18
Common Trouble Spots: none
Availability of Parts: poor
Investment Potential: A

Background: The Custom ragtop was the sportiest car DeSoto offered in 1948. It was powered by a 109 h.p. 236.6 cu. in. six-cylinder engine. A three-speed manual transmission was standard. A semi-automatic transmission was optional.

1948 DeSoto Custom Convertible

1948 Dodge Custom Convertible

Original Price: $2,207
Number Produced: est. 3,167
Estimated Number Existing in 1979: 5
Miles per Gallon: 13–18
Common Trouble Spots: none
Availability of Parts: poor
Investment Potential: A

Background: The 1948 Dodge Custom ragtop came with a 102 h.p. 230.2 cu. in. six-cylinder engine. A three-speed manual transmission was standard.

1948 Ford Super Deluxe Convertible

Original Price: $1,700
Number Produced: 12,033
Estimated Number Existing in 1979: 27
Miles per Gallon: 15–21
Common Trouble Spots: carburetor, clutch, electrical system
Availability of Parts: poor–fair
Investment Potential: AA

Background: The new Super Deluxe convertible was powered by a 100 h.p. 239.4 cu. in. eight-cylinder engine. A three-speed manual transmission was standard.

1948 Ford Super Deluxe Sportsman Convertible

Original Price: $2,282
Number Produced: 28
Estimated Number Existing in 1979: 1
Miles per Gallon: 15–21
Common Trouble Spots: carburetor, clutch
Availability of Parts: poor
Investment Potential: AAA+

Background: The 1948 Sportsman woodie ragtops were basically just unsold 1947 models. A 100 h.p. 239.4 cu. in. eight-cylinder engine and a three-speed manual transmission were standard.

1948 Ford Super Deluxe Station Wagon

Original Price: $1,700
Number Produced: 8,912
Estimated Number Existing in 1979: 20
Miles per Gallon: 14–19
Common Trouble Spots: carburetor, clutch, electrical system
Availability of Parts: poor
Investment Potential: AAA

Background: This was the last four-door woodie wagon made by Ford. It was powered by a 90 h.p. 226 cu. in. six-cylinder engine. Available at extra cost was a 100 h.p. 239.4 cu. in. eight-cylinder engine. A three-speed manual transmission was standard.

Ford would make station wagons after 1948, but somehow they wouldn't seem quite the same.

1948 Ford Super Deluxe Station Wagon

PHOTO: FORD MOTOR COMPANY

1948 Ford Super Deluxe Convertible

PHOTO: FORD MOTOR COMPANY

1948 Hudson Commodore Eight Convertible Brougham

Original Price: est. $2,600
Number Produced: N.A.
Estimated Number Existing in 1979: N.A.
Miles per Gallon: 13–18
Common Trouble Spots: none
Availability of Parts: poor
Investment Potential: AA

Background: It's little wonder that 1948 was one of the best sales years Hudson ever had—the Hudson was one of the most attractive cars offered that year.

The '48 Commodore Eight convertible was powered by a 128 h.p. 254 cu. in. eight-cylinder engine. A three-speed manual transmission was standard. Overdrive and Drive Master automatic transmission were optional at extra cost.

1948 Hudson Commodore Eight Convertible Brougham

PHOTO: JOHN A. CONDE COLLECTION

1948 Hudson Commodore Six Convertible Brougham

Original Price: est. $2,600
Number Produced: N.A.
Estimated Number Existing in 1979: N.A.
Miles per Gallon: 13–18
Common Trouble Spots: none
Availability of Parts: poor
Investment Potential: AA

Background: The '48 Commodore Six convertible was an attractive car. It was powered by a 121 h.p. 262.2 cu. in. six-cylinder engine. A three-speed manual transmission was standard. Overdrive and Drive Master automatic transmission were optional at extra cost.

1948 Hudson Super Six Convertible Brougham

Original Price: est. $2,400
Number Produced: N.A.
Estimated Number Existing in 1979: N.A.
Miles per Gallon: 13–18
Common Trouble Spots: none
Availability of Parts: poor
Investment Potential: AA

Background: This was the first of the "step down" Hudsons. The long, low Super Six convertible was a very sleek-looking machine in its day. It was powered by a 121 h.p. 262.2 cu. in. six-cylinder engine. A three-speed manual transmission was standard. Overdrive and Drive Master automatic transmission were optional at extra cost.

1948 Lincoln Continental Cabriolet

Original Price: $4,746
Number Produced: 452
Estimated Number Existing in 1979: 45
Miles per Gallon: 10–15
Common Trouble Spots: none
Availability of Parts: poor
Investment Potential: AAA+

Background: This was the last year for the elegant Continental convertible. It came with a 130 h.p. 305 cu. in. V12 engine, which was capable of moving the 4,135 pound car from 0 to 60 in less than 16 seconds. A three-speed manual transmission was standard. Overdrive was optional.

1948 Lincoln Continental Cabriolet

PHOTO: FORD MOTOR COMPANY

1948 Hudson Commodore Six Convertible Brougham

PHOTO: WILLIAM L. BAILEY COLLECTION

1948 Lincoln Continental Coupe

Original Price: $4,662
Number Produced: 847
Estimated Number Existing in 1979: 84
Miles per Gallon: 10–15
Common Trouble Spots: none
Availability of Parts: poor
Investment Potential: AAA+

Background: The new Continental coupe was powered by a 130 h.p. 305 cu. in. V12 engine. A three-speed manual transmission was standard. Overdrive was optional.

1948 Lincoln Continental Coupe

PHOTO: FORD MOTOR COMPANY

1948 Lincoln Convertible Coupe

Original Price: est. $2,900
Number Produced: N.A.
Estimated Number Existing in 1979: N.A.
Miles per Gallon: 10–15
Common Trouble Spots: none
Availability of Parts: poor
Investment Potential: AAA

Background: The 1948 Lincoln ragtop was a big, luxurious car. It came with a 130 h.p. 305 cu. in. V12 engine. A three-speed manual transmission was standard. Overdrive was optional.

1948 Mercury Convertible Coupe

Original Price: est. $1,800
Number Produced: 7,586
Estimated Number Existing in 1979: 17
Miles per Gallon: 13–19
Common Trouble Spots: none
Availability of Parts: poor
Investment Potential: A+

Background: The new 1948 Mercury ragtop was powered by a 100 h.p. 239.4 cu. in. eight-cylinder engine. A three-speed manual transmission was standard.

1948 Mercury Station Wagon

Original Price: est. $1,800
Number Produced: 1,889
Estimated Number Existing in 1979: 4
Miles per Gallon: 13–18
Common Trouble Spots: none
Availability of Parts: poor
Investment Potential: AA+

Background: The attractive 1948 Mercury woodie wagon was powered by a 100 h.p. 239.4 cu. in. eight-cylinder engine. A three-speed manual transmission was standard.

1948 Mercury Station Wagon

PHOTO: FORD MOTOR COMPANY

1948 Mercury Convertible

PHOTO: FORD MOTOR COMPANY

1948 Nash Ambassador Convertible

Original Price: $2,345
Number Produced: 1,000
Estimated Number Existing in 1979: 4
Miles per Gallon: 13–20
Common Trouble Spots: none
Availability of Parts: poor
Investment Potential: A+

Background: This was the first postwar Nash convertible. It was also the only Ambassador convertible built until 1965. The Ambassador was powered by a 112 h.p. 234.8 cu. in. six-cylinder engine. A three-speed manual transmission was standard. Overdrive was optional.

1948 Nash Ambassador Convertible

PHOTO: JOHN A. CONDE COLLECTION

1948 Nash Ambassador Suburban

Original Price: est. $2,100
Number Produced: 130
Estimated Number Existing in 1979: 1
Miles per Gallon: 13–19
Common Trouble Spots: none
Availability of Parts: poor
Investment Potential: AA

Background: This was the last year for the attractive Suburban. Despite the fact that it was probably one of the best-looking four-door sedans on the market in 1948, sales were miserable.

The Suburban was powered by a 112 h.p. 234.8 cu. in. six-cylinder engine. A three-speed manual transmission was standard. Overdrive was optional.

1948 Oldsmobile Futuramic 98 Convertible

Original Price: est. $2,200
Number Produced: 12,914
Estimated Number Existing in 1979: 14
Miles per Gallon: 13–19
Common Trouble Spots: brakes
Availability of Parts: poor
Investment Potential: AA

Background: The 1948 Oldsmobile Futuramic 98 was one of the first cars to come out with "modern" styling. It looked very sleek compared to most of its contemporaries. It was introduced late in the model year and was well received by the car-hungry public.

Oldsmobile ran full-page ads proclaiming its arrival. One such ad stated, " 'Futuramic' is a brand new word that fills a gap in our vocabulary. It means 'the dramatic design of the future.' "

Although the 98 looked completely new, under the hood was the same 110 h.p. 257.1 cu. in. flathead eight that had been powering Oldsmobiles for years. A three-speed manual transmission was standard. Hydra-Matic Drive automatic transmission was a popular option offered for $150.

1948 Oldsmobile 60 Series Convertible

Original Price: est. $1,800
Number Produced: 3,892
Estimated Number Existing in 1979: 4
Miles per Gallon: 13–19
Common Trouble Spots: brakes
Availability of Parts: poor
Investment Potential: A+

Background: The 1948 60 Series ragtop was available with either a 100 h.p. 238.1 cu. in. six-cylinder or a 110 h.p. 257.1 cu. in. eight-cylinder engine. Most, 53.7%, had the eight. A three-speed manual transmission was standard. Hydra-Matic Drive automatic transmission was optional.

1948 Oldsmobile 60 Series Convertible

PHOTO: OLDSMOBILE DIVISION

1948 Oldsmobile 60 Series Station Wagon

Original Price: est. $2,400
Number Produced: 2,707
Estimated Number Existing in 1979: 2
Miles per Gallon: 13–18
Common Trouble Spots: brakes
Availability of Parts: poor
Investment Potential: AA+

Background: The 1948 Olds station wagon was available in both deluxe and standard versions. Buyers also had their choice of a 100 h.p. 238.1 cu. in. six-cylinder engine, or a 110 h.p. 257.1 cu. in. flathead eight. A three-speed manual transmission was standard. Hydra-Matic Drive automatic transmission was optional.

Most wagons, 51.4%, came with the six-cylinder engine. Of these, 39.6% were deluxe models. Forty-two percent of the eights were deluxe.

1948 Oldsmobile 60 Series Station Wagon

PHOTO: OLDSMOBILE DIVISION

1948 Packard Custom Eight Convertible Victoria

Original Price: est. $4,400
Number Produced: 1,103
Estimated Number Existing in 1979: 2
Miles per Gallon: 11–17
Common Trouble Spots: Electromatic clutch
Availability of Parts: poor
Investment Potential: A+

Background: The Custom Eight convertible was a popular car among the well-to-do in 1948. It was a way for bankers, lawyers, and other professional people to let the world (or at least their neighbors) know how successful they were.

The Custom Eight was powered by a 160 h.p. 356 cu. in. eight-cylinder engine. A three-speed manual transmission was standard. Overdrive and Electromatic clutch were optional.

The '48 Packard Custom Eight convertible was available in six colors: black, Cavalier maroon, French blue, golden green, Packard ivory, and Sardonyx brown.

1948 Packard Station Sedan

Original Price: $3,425
Number Produced: 1,786
Estimated Number Existing in 1979: 2
Miles per Gallon: 12–18
Common Trouble Spots: Electromatic clutch
Availability of Parts: poor
Investment Potential: AA+

Background: This was Packard's first postwar woodie. Actually, "wood-trimmed" would be a more accurate description; the body was all metal, with wood ribs and fake wood panels. The interior featured tan plastic upholstery.

The station sedan was powered by a 130 h.p. 288.6 cu. in. eight-cylinder engine. A three-speed manual transmission was standard. Overdrive and Electromatic clutch were optional.

1948 Packard Station Sedan

PHOTO: WILLIAM L. BAILEY COLLECTION

1948 Packard Super Eight Convertible Victoria

Original Price: est. $3,300
Number Produced: 4,750
Estimated Number Existing in 1979: 6
Miles per Gallon: 11–17
Common Trouble Spots: Electromatic clutch
Availability of Parts: poor
Investment Potential: A+

Background: One look at the new Super Eight and it was easy to see how it got the nickname "pregnant Packard." It was powered by a 145 h.p. 327 cu. in. eight-cylinder engine. A three-speed manual transmission was standard. Overdrive and Electromatic clutch were optional.

1948 Packard Super Eight Convertible Victoria

PHOTO: RICHARD QUINN COLLECTION

1948 Playboy Convertible

Original Price: $985
Number Produced: 97
Estimated Number Existing in 1979: 18
Miles per Gallon: 23–30
Common Trouble Spots: none
Availability of Parts: poor
Investment Potential: AA+

Background: The Playboy was designed to fill postwar America's need for low-cost, economical transportation. Although it was intended to be a mass-produced car selling thousands each year, it never got beyond the prototype stage. All Playboys were hand-built.

Three different four-cylinder engines were used in the Playboy: a 40 h.p. 91 cu. in. Continental, a 48 h.p. 133 cu. in. Hercules, and a 63 h.p. 134.2 cu. in. Willys. The Willys was the best of the three. A three-speed manual transmission was standard.

A unique feature of the Playboy was its manually operated retractable steel top. A more advanced version of this type of top was used by Ford in 1957 to 1959.

1948 Plymouth Special Deluxe Convertible

Original Price: est. $1,700
Number Produced: est. 5,098
Estimated Number Existing in 1979: 6
Miles per Gallon: 13–20
Common Trouble Spots: none
Availability of Parts: poor
Investment Potential: A

Background: The '48 Special Deluxe ragtop was powered by a 95 h.p. 217.8 cu. in. six-cylinder engine. A three-speed manual transmission was standard.

1948 Plymouth Special Deluxe Station Wagon

Original Price: est. $1,700
Number Produced: est. 4,304
Estimated Number Existing in 1979: 5
Miles per Gallon: 13–20
Common Trouble Spots: none
Availability of Parts: poor
Investment Potential: AA+

Background: The attractive Special Deluxe woodie wagon came with a 95 h.p. 217.8 cu. in. six-cylinder engine. A three-speed manual transmission was standard.

1948 Pontiac Streamliner Deluxe Station Wagon

Original Price: est. $2,200
Number Produced: N.A.
Estimated Number Existing in 1979: N.A.
Miles per Gallon: 13–19
Common Trouble Spots: none
Availability of Parts: poor
Investment Potential: AA+

Background: The attractive Streamliner woodie wagon was available with either a 93.5 h.p. 239.2 cu. in. six or a 101.5 h.p. 248.9 cu. in. eight-cylinder engine. A three-speed manual transmission was standard. Hydra-Matic automatic transmission was optional.

The vast majority of '48 Streamliner buyers, 76.5%, ordered the eight-cylinder engine, and nearly as many, 76%, bought the automatic.

1948 Pontiac Streamliner Deluxe Station Wagon

PHOTO: PONTIAC MOTOR DIVISION

1948 Pontiac Torpedo Convertible

Original Price: est. $1,800
Number Produced: N.A.
Estimated Number Existing in 1979: N.A.
Miles per Gallon: 14–20
Common Trouble Spots: none
Availability of Parts: poor
Investment Potential: A

Background: The Torpedo ragtop came with a 93.5 h.p. 239.2 cu. in. six-cylinder engine. A 101.5 h.p. 248.9 cu. in. eight-cylinder engine was available at extra cost. Only 34.2% of '48 Torpedos were so equipped. A three-speed manual transmission was standard, but not very popular—most Torpedo buyers, 66.5%, ordered the optional Hydra-Matic automatic transmission.

I can't look at a '48 Pontiac without thinking of a neighbor who owned one in the mid-1960s. The brakes were constantly failing, but that didn't keep him from using it. Whenever he would come back from a trip downtown, I'd go outside and watch him drive his car around in circles until it stopped.

1948 Pontiac Torpedo Convertible

PHOTO: PONTIAC MOTOR DIVISION

1948 Studebaker Champion Convertible

Original Price: est. $1,900
Number Produced: 9,156
Estimated Number Existing in 1979: 13
Miles per Gallon: 17–28
Common Trouble Spots: none
Availability of Parts: poor
Investment Potential: A

Background: The Champion ragtop was one of the sleekest cars available in 1948. No wonder it was the best-selling postwar convertible Studebaker made.

It was powered by an 80 h.p. 169.6 cu. in. six-cylinder engine. A three-speed manual transmission with overdrive was standard.

1948 Studebaker Commander Convertible

Original Price: est. $2,300
Number Produced: 7,560
Estimated Number Existing in 1979: 10
Miles per Gallon: 16–25
Common Trouble Spots: none
Availability of Parts: poor
Investment Potential: A

Background: Although not as popular as the Champion, the Commander ragtop sold very well in 1948. Buyers were attracted to its sleek, "modern" styling.

It was powered by a 94 h.p. 226.2 cu. in. six-cylinder engine. A three-speed manual transmission with overdrive was standard.

1948 Studebaker Commander Convertible

PHOTO: RICHARD QUINN COLLECTION, STUDEBAKER DRIVERS CLUB

1948 Tucker

Original Price: $2,495 to $5,000 (the price fluctuated greatly)
Number Produced: 51 (including one 1947 prototype)
Estimated Number Existing in 1979: 48
Miles per Gallon: 17–24
Common Trouble Spots: manual transmission, suspension
Availability of Parts: poor
Investment Potential: AAA+

Background: The 1948 Tucker was like no other postwar car. Probably the most distinctive feature of this innovative, safety-oriented vehicle was its third headlight, located midway between the other headlights. This "Cyclops eye" turned with the front wheels.

The Tucker was powered by a 150 h.p. 335 cu. in. six-cylinder Franklin helicopter engine mounted in the rear. The 1947 prototype had a 589 cu. in. engine (actually, all Tuckers were really just prototypes). Approximately 50% of Tuckers came with a Cord manual transmission; one had a Borg-Warner four-speed manual, at least one had Tuckermatic automatic, and the remainder had a Y-1 manual transmission. The Y-1 was a redesigned and improved version of the Cord transmission. Parts for it are especially hard to obtain.

As a sales brochure said, the Tucker was "the first completely new car in fifty years."

1948 Tucker

1948 Willys Jeepster Phaeton

Original Price: $1,886
Number Produced: 10,326
Estimated Number Existing in 1979: 8
Miles per Gallon: 18–30
Common Trouble Spots: none
Availability of Parts: poor
Investment Potential: A+

Background: The sporty '48 Jeepster was a handsome vehicle. In spite of its name, it was not a Jeep.

The Jeepster was introduced late in the model year. It came with a 63 h.p. 134.2 cu. in. four-cylinder engine. A three-speed manual transmission was standard.

1948 Willys Jeepster Phaeton

PHOTO: JOHN A. CONDE COLLECTION

1949

1949 Buick Roadmaster Convertible

Original Price: $3,150
Number Produced: 8,244
Estimated Number Existing in 1979: 8
Miles per Gallon: 12–17
Common Trouble Spots: automatic transmission, brakes, top mechanism
Availability of Parts: poor–fair
Investment Potential: AA+

Background: Many people consider the '49 Roadmaster convertible the best-looking Buick of the decade. It sported a handsome taillight treatment that was later imitated on other GM cars of the 1950s and 1970s. In this year the now-famous Buick portholes were introduced. As the top of the line, the Roadmaster had four portholes on each front fender; Supers had only three.

The Roadmaster ragtop came with a 150 h.p. 320.2 cu. in. eight-cylinder engine. Dynaflow automatic transmission and a power-operated top were standard.

In an article in *Special Interest Autos,* automotive writer and editor Ken Gross said the 1949 Roadmaster had "some of the most comfortable smooth-road manners of any car built in the late forties. And it's totally silent, dignified and even . . . rather majestic. It has real personality."

1949 Buick Roadmaster Convertible

PHOTO: PUBLIC RELATIONS DEPARTMENT, BUICK MOTOR DIVISION

1949 Buick Roadmaster Estate Station Wagon

Original Price: $3,734
Number Produced: 653
Estimated Number Existing in 1979: 2
Miles per Gallon: 11–16
Common Trouble Spots: automatic transmission, brakes
Availability of Parts: poor–fair
Investment Potential: AAA

Background: The 1949 Roadmaster woodie was probably the most attractive station wagon Buick made in the 1940s. It was powered by a 150 h.p. 320.2 cu. in. eight-cylinder engine. Dynaflow automatic transmission was standard.

1949 Buick Roadmaster Riviera

Original Price: $3,203
Number Produced: 4,343
Estimated Number Existing in 1979: 8
Miles per Gallon: 12–17
Common Trouble Spots: automatic transmission, brakes
Availability of Parts: poor–fair
Investment Potential: AA+

Background: Although it was the first hardtop offered in 1949, the Riviera didn't reach dealer showrooms until July of that year. It marked the beginning of the hardtop craze.

Many consider the Riviera the first real production hardtop, since Chrysler only built seven Town and Country hardtops in 1946. And they were really just prototypes—convertibles with a hardtop roof bolted on.

This was also the first year for the famous Buick portholes. Originally, the portholes were to contain lights that flashed on and off in sequence when the engine was running. However, the idea was later vetoed.

1949 Buick Roadmaster Riviera

PHOTO: WILLIAM L. BAILEY COLLECTION

Buyers could choose between leather and leather-and-cloth interiors. Strips of stainless steel were placed on the headliner to make passengers feel as though they were riding in a convertible.

The Riviera was powered by a 150 h.p. 320.2 cu. in. straight eight engine. Dynaflow automatic transmission was standard.

Attractive lines, rarity, and its historical significance as the first of the "high-production" hardtops help make the 1949 Roadmaster Riviera a desirable car.

1949 Buick Super Convertible

Original Price: $2,583
Number Produced: 22,110
Estimated Number Existing in 1979: 24
Miles per Gallon: 12–18
Common Trouble Spots: automatic transmission, brakes, top mechanism
Availability of Parts: poor–fair
Investment Potential: AA+

Background: The 1949 Super was one of the best-looking ragtops available that year. It was powered by a 115 h.p. 248.1 cu. in. eight-cylinder engine. A three-speed manual transmission was standard. Dynaflow automatic transmission was optional at extra cost.

The Super, like all '49 Buicks, had a reputation for being an oil burner. Still, it is a very desirable car.

1949 Buick Super Convertible

PHOTO: PUBLIC RELATIONS DEPARTMENT, BUICK MOTOR DIVISION

1949 Buick Super Estate Station Wagon

Original Price: $3,178
Number Produced: 1,847
Estimated Number Existing in 1979: 3
Miles per Gallon: 11–17
Common Trouble Spots: automatic transmission, brakes
Availability of Parts: poor–fair
Investment Potential: AAA

Background: The beautiful Super wagon looked virtually the same as the equally attractive Roadmaster wagon. The most noticeable difference between the two was the number of portholes on each fender; the Super had three, the Roadmaster four.

The Super was powered by a 115 h.p. 248.1 cu. in. eight-cylinder engine. A three-speed manual transmission was standard. Dynaflow automatic transmission was optional at extra cost.

1949 Cadillac Series 62 Convertible

Original Price: est. $3,600
Number Produced: 8,000
Estimated Number Existing in 1979: 21
Miles per Gallon: 12–20
Common Trouble Spots: none
Availability of Parts: poor–fair
Investment Potential: AA+

Background: The big news for Cadillac in 1949 was its new 160 h.p. 331 cu. in. V8 engine. Hydra-Matic automatic transmission and power windows were standard.

The 1949 Series 62 convertible is one of the most desirable of postwar Cadillacs.

1949 Cadillac Series 62 Convertible

PHOTO: CADILLAC MOTOR CAR DIVISION

1949 Cadillac Series 62 Coupe De Ville

Original Price: est. $3,500
Number Produced: 2,150
Estimated Number Existing in 1979: 8
Miles per Gallon: 12–20
Common Trouble Spots: none
Availability of Parts: poor–fair
Investment Potential: AA+

Background: This attractive two-door hardtop was introduced in mid-summer of 1949. It was powered by Cadillac's new 160 h.p. 331 cu. in. V8 engine, making it one of the fastest cars of its day. A three-speed manual transmission was standard. Hydra-Matic automatic transmission was optional at extra cost.

The 1949 Coupe De Ville is a beautiful and luxurious automobile. That alone is a good reason to buy one. But the presence of Cadillac's famous new engine and the fact that it was among the first production two-door hardtops make owning one all the more desirable.

1949 Chevrolet Styleline Deluxe Convertible

Original Price: $1,875
Number Produced: 32,392
Estimated Number Existing in 1979: 65
Miles per Gallon: 14–20
Common Trouble Spots: none
Availability of Parts: poor–fair
Investment Potential: AA

Background: This was Chevrolet's first new postwar convertible. Only the outside was totally new, however; the engine was little changed from that of the previous year's model. The car was powered by a 90 h.p. 216.5 cu. in. six-cylinder engine. A three-speed manual transmission was standard.

1949 Chevrolet Styleline Deluxe Station Wagon

Original Price: $2,267
Number Produced: 3,400
Estimated Number Existing in 1979: 6
Miles per Gallon: 13–18
Common Trouble Spots: none
Availability of Parts: poor–fair
Investment Potential: AA+

Background: This was the last woodie station wagon made by Chevrolet. It was also the sleekest-looking. Unfortunately, it was only available for part of the model year. During the latter part it was replaced by an all-steel wagon.

The Deluxe wagon was powered by a 90 h.p. 216.5 cu. in. six. A three-speed manual transmission was standard.

1949 Chrysler New Yorker Convertible

1949 Chrysler New Yorker Convertible

Original Price: $3,231
Number Produced: 1,137
Estimated Number Existing in 1979: 3
Miles per Gallon: 12–17
Common Trouble Spots: none
Availability of Parts: poor
Investment Potential: A+

Background: The New Yorker convertible was completely redesigned for 1949. It looked almost identical to the 1949 Windsor but had a wheelbase of 131.5, compared to the Windsor's 125.5 inch wheelbase.

The New Yorker came with a 135 h.p. 323.5 cu. in. eight-cylinder engine. A three-speed manual transmission was standard. Presto-matic automatic transmission was optional at extra cost.

A 1949 New Yorker convertible is rare. Even rarer is one equipped with the optional Highlander trim package, which included a special name plaque and leather-and-plaid upholstery.

1949 Chrysler Royal Station Wagon

Original Price: $3,151
Number Produced: 850
Estimated Number Existing in 1979: 3
Miles per Gallon: 11–16
Common Trouble Spots: none
Availability of Parts: poor
Investment Potential: AA+

Background: This was Chrysler's first station wagon since the beginning of World War II. Although somewhat boxy, it had very clean lines and was quite an attractive wagon. All-steel wagons were also made by Chrysler in 1949; but they have nowhere near the appeal of the Royal woodie.

It came with a 116 h.p. 250.6 cu. in. six-cylinder engine. A three-speed manual transmission was standard. Presto-matic automatic transmission was optional.

Because of its low production run and the rarity of well-maintained woodies, a 1949 Royal station wagon in good condition has much potential.

1949 Chrysler Royal Station Wagon

PHOTO: CHRYSLER CORPORATION

1949 Chrysler Town and Country Convertible

Original Price: $3,995
Number Produced: 1,000
Estimated Number Existing in 1979: 20
Miles per Gallon: 10–15
Common Trouble Spots: none
Availability of Parts: poor
Investment Potential: AAA+

Background: The 1949 Town and Country convertible made its debut in July of that year. It was one of the most beautiful postwar convertibles built by any manufacturer.

The Town and Country featured an all-steel body with White Ash framing. Early models had mahogany Di-Noc (metal with a wood-like pattern on it) inserts. Later models had body color panels. It was powered by a 135 h.p. 323.5 cu. in. eight-cylinder engine. A three-speed manual transmission was standard. Presto-Matic automatic transmission was optional.

1949 Chrysler Town and Country Convertible

PHOTO: CHRYSLER HISTORICAL COLLECTION

1949 Chrysler Windsor Convertible

Original Price: $2,761
Number Produced: 3,234
Estimated Number Existing in 1979: 10
Miles per Gallon: 13–18
Common Trouble Spots: none
Availability of Parts: poor
Investment Potential: A+

Background: This was the first of the really new postwar Chryslers. Some 1948 models were sold as 1949s until early 1949.

The Windsor came with a 116 h.p. 250.6 cu. in. six-cylinder engine. A three-speed manual transmission was standard. Presto-matic automatic transmission was optional at extra cost. There was a world of difference between the 1948 and the new 1949 models. The 1949 was a lot more streamlined and, although somewhat boxy in appearance, was less bulky-looking.

A special Highlander trim package was available on Windsor convertibles. It included a special identification plaque and leather-and-plaid upholstery.

1949 Crosley Convertible

Original Price: est. $1,000
Number Produced: 645
Estimated Number Existing in 1979: 5
Miles per Gallon: 25–32
Common Trouble Spots: none
Availability of Parts: poor
Investment Potential: A

Background: Sales of Crosley convertibles dropped considerably in 1949. Part of this decline was due to the new Hotshot roadster.

The '49 Crosley was powered by a 26.5 h.p. 44 cu. in. four-cylinder engine. A three-speed manual transmission was standard.

1949 Crosley Convertible

PHOTO: CROSLEY AUTOMOBILE CLUB, INC.

1949 Chrysler Windsor Convertible

PHOTO: CHRYSLER HISTORICAL COLLECTION

1949 Crosley Hotshot Roadster

PHOTO: CROSLEY AUTOMOBILE CLUB, INC.

1949 Crosley Hotshot Roadster

Original Price: $998
Number Produced: 752
Estimated Number Existing in 1979: 6
Miles per Gallon: 25–32
Common Trouble Spots: none
Availability of Parts: poor
Investment Potential: AA

Background: Many consider the Hotshot America's first postwar sports car. It was powered by a 26.5 h.p. 44 cu. in. four-cylinder engine. A three-speed manual transmission was standard.

The sporty Hotshot is easily the most desirable Crosley made in the 1940s.

1949 DeSoto Custom Convertible

Original Price: $2,500
Number Produced: 3,385
Estimated Number Existing in 1979: 10
Miles per Gallon: 13–18
Common Trouble Spots: none
Availability of Parts: poor
Investment Potential: A

Background: The '49 Custom convertible had a much sleeker look than the previous year's model. It was powered by a 112 h.p. 236.7 cu. in. six-cylinder engine. A three-speed manual transmission was standard. Tip-Toe Shift automatic transmission was optional at extra cost.

1949 DeSoto Deluxe Station Wagon

Original Price: est. $3,000
Number Produced: 850
Estimated Number Existing in 1979: 2
Miles per Gallon: 12–18
Common Trouble Spots: none
Availability of Parts: poor
Investment Potential: AA+

Background: The 1949 Deluxe wagon was a very attractive woodie. It was powered by a 112 h.p. 236.7 cu. in. six-cylinder engine. A three-speed manual transmission was standard. Tip-Toe Shift automatic transmission was optional at extra cost.

1949 Dodge Coronet Convertible

Original Price: $2,347
Number Produced: 2,411
Estimated Number Existing in 1979: 8
Miles per Gallon: 13–20
Common Trouble Spots: none
Availability of Parts: poor
Investment Potential: A

Background: The 1949 Coronet was Dodge's first real postwar convertible; the 1946–48 models were just rehashed 1942s. The Coronet convertible came with a 103 h.p. 230.2 cu. in. six-cylinder engine. A manual transmission was standard. Gyromatic automatic transmission was optional.

1949 Dodge Coronet Station Wagon

Original Price: $2,883
Number Produced: 800
Estimated Number Existing in 1979: 2
Miles per Gallon: 13–18
Common Trouble Spots: none
Availability of Parts: poor
Investment Potential: AA+

Background: The 1949 Coronet station wagon was one of the best-looking woodies on the market that year. Purists may not consider this a true woodie because the wood was really just a trim.

It was powered by a 103 h.p. 230.2 cu. in. six-cylinder engine. A three-speed manual transmission was standard. Gyromatic automatic transmission was optional.

Buyers had their choice of three exterior colors: beige, green, or maroon.

1949 Dodge Wayfarer Roadster

Original Price: $1,745
Number Produced: 5,420
Estimated Number Existing in 1979: 17
Miles per Gallon: 14–20
Common Trouble Spots: none
Availability of Parts: poor
Investment Potential: A+

Background: This sporty three-passenger car was offered for the first time in 1949. It had a back seat (if you wanted to call it that—it was apparently intended for those times when one was cruising with a couple of friends, and happened to come across a few hitchhiking Munchkins).

The Wayfarer roadster was powered by a 103 h.p. 230.2 cu. in. six-cylinder engine. A three-speed manual transmission was standard. Early models came with detachable windows. Roll-up windows were available for $35 later in the model year.

1949 Dodge Wayfarer Roadster

PHOTO: CHRYSLER CORPORATION

1949 Ford Custom Convertible

Original Price: est. $1,900
Number Produced: 51,133
Estimated Number Existing in 1979: 74
Miles per Gallon: 14–20
Common Trouble Spots: brakes
Availability of Parts: fair–poor
Investment Potential: AA

Background: This was the first of the really new postwar Fords. Originally, the '49 Ford was to have had the body that became the '49 Mercury.

The '49 Ford was credited by many as having saved the Ford Motor Company. In addition to a new body, it had a new suspension system and improved brakes.

Buyers had a choice of a 95 h.p. 225.8 cu. in. six-cylinder or a 100 h.p. 239.4 cu. in. eight-cylinder engine. A three-speed manual was standard. Overdrive was optional.

Although a significant car in many respects, the 1949 Ford has the reputation of a troublesome automobile. This should be kept in mind when considering the purchase of a '49 Custom ragtop—especially if it happens to be one of those used by the Joie Chitwood Auto Daredevils in their auto-thrill shows.

1949 Ford Custom Convertible

PHOTO: FORD MOTOR COMPANY

1949 Ford Custom Deluxe Station Wagon

Original Price: est. $2,100
Number Produced: 31,412
Estimated Number Existing in 1979: 45
Miles per Gallon: 14–19
Common Trouble Spots: brakes
Availability of Parts: poor–fair
Investment Potential: AA+

Background: The attractive Custom Deluxe wagon was available with two doors only. That gave it a very sporty look. It was powered by a 95 h.p. 225.8 cu. in. six-cylinder engine. Available at extra cost was a 100 h.p. 239.4 cu. in. eight-cylinder engine. A three-speed manual transmission was standard. Overdrive was optional at extra cost.

Buyers had their choice of seven exterior colors. The driver's seat was upholstered in leather. Passenger seats were upholstered in vinyl. Exclusive to the station wagon was a wood-grain dash.

1949 Ford Custom Station Wagon

PHOTO: FORD MOTOR COMPANY

1949 Frazer Manhattan Convertible

Original Price: est. $2,500
Number Produced: est. 33
Estimated Number Existing in 1979: 5
Miles per Gallon: 15–20
Common Trouble Spots: carburetor, cooling system, piston rings
Availability of Parts: poor
Investment Potential: AA+

Background: The new Frazer ragtop was introduced early in 1949, just after the Kaiser convertible made its debut. With the exception of minor trim and grille differences, the Frazer looked the same as the Kaiser.

The four-door Frazer convertible was powered by a 112 h.p. 226.2 cu. in. six-cylinder engine. A three-speed manual transmission, a power top, and power windows were standard.

Buyers had a choice of cloth-and-leather or all leather upholstery. The convertible top was offered in two colors, black and tan.

1949 Frazer Manhattan Convertible

PHOTO: JOHN A. CONDE COLLECTION

1949 Hudson Commodore Eight Convertible Brougham

Original Price: est. $3,000
Number Produced: N.A.
Estimated Number Existing in 1979: N.A.
Miles per Gallon: 13–18
Common Trouble Spots: none
Availability of Parts: poor
Investment Potential: AA

Background: The Commodore Eight ragtop was one of the most attractive cars available in 1949. It was powered by a 128 h.p. 254 cu. in. eight-cylinder engine. A three-speed manual transmission was standard. Overdrive and Drive Master automatic transmission were optional at extra cost.

1949 Hudson Commodore Six Convertible Brougham

Original Price: est. $2,800
Number Produced: N.A.
Estimated Number Existing in 1979: N.A.
Miles per Gallon: 13–18
Common Trouble Spots: none
Availability of Parts: poor
Investment Potential: AA

Background: The sleek 1949 Commodore Six convertible came with a 121 h.p. 262 cu. in. six-cylinder engine. A three-speed manual transmission was standard. Overdrive and Drive Master automatic transmission were optional.

1949 Hudson Super Six Convertible Brougham

Original Price: est. $2,600
Number Produced: N.A.
Estimated Number Existing in 1979: N.A.
Miles per Gallon: 13–18
Common Trouble Spots: none
Availability of Parts: poor
Investment Potential: AA

Background: The '48 Super Six ragtop was powered by a 121 h.p. 262 cu. in. six-cylinder engine. A three-speed manual transmission was standard. Overdrive and Drive Master automatic transmission were optional at extra cost.

1949 Hudson Commodore Eight Convertible Brougham

PHOTO: JOHN A. CONDE COLLECTION

1949 Kaiser Deluxe Convertible

Original Price: est. $2,200
Number Produced: est. 11
Estimated Number Existing in 1979: 5
Miles per Gallon: 15–20
Common Trouble Spots: carburetor, cooling system, piston rings
Availability of Parts: poor
Investment Potential: AA+

Background: The new Kaiser four-door convertible was an attractive car. Because so few were produced, some of the parts used in the Kaiser ragtop could be made by hand.

It was powered by a 100 h.p. 226.2 cu. in. six-cylinder engine. A three-speed manual transmission, a power top and power windows were standard.

Buyers had a choice of a cloth-and-leather or an all-leather interior. The convertible top was available in two colors, black and tan.

According to the June 17, 1949, issue of the *Kaiser-Frazer Dealers News,* the monthly payments for a Kaiser Deluxe were lowered $8.71 to $67.07.

A Kaiser convertible was chosen as the official car of the San Francisco Gold Rush Centennial. It was, naturally, painted gold.

1949 Kaiser Deluxe Convertible

1949 Kaiser Deluxe Virginian

Original Price: $2,995
Number Produced: est. 468
Estimated Number Existing in 1979: 34
Miles per Gallon: 15–20
Common Trouble Spots: carburetor, cooling system, piston rings
Availability of Parts: poor
Investment Potential: AA+

Background: "Just as a desire for a richer life actuated the founding of Virginia, land of gracious living, so the longing for a more luxurious car inspired the creation of the Kaiser 'Virginian.' " At least that's what the ads claimed.

The '49 Virginian was an attractive car, available in a wide assortment of striking color combinations. It came with a 100 h.p. 226.2 cu. in. six-cylinder engine. A three-speed manual transmission was standard.

A Custom Virginian option was offered during the early part of the model year. It featured special upholstery, interior trim, and fender insignia. Other options included a hood ornament, power windows, and leather upholstery.

1949 Kaiser Deluxe Virginian

PHOTO: JOHN A. CONDE COLLECTION

1949 Lincoln Convertible

Original Price: est. $3,100
Number Produced: N.A.
Estimated Number Existing in 1979: N.A.
Miles per Gallon: 13–18
Common Trouble Spots: automatic transmission
Availability of Parts: poor
Investment Potential: A+

Background: The new Lincoln convertible was introduced in April 1948. It was powered by a 152 h.p. 336.7 cu. in. eight-cylinder engine. A three-speed manual transmission was standard. Overdrive and (late in the model year) GM's Hydra-Matic automatic transmission were optional.

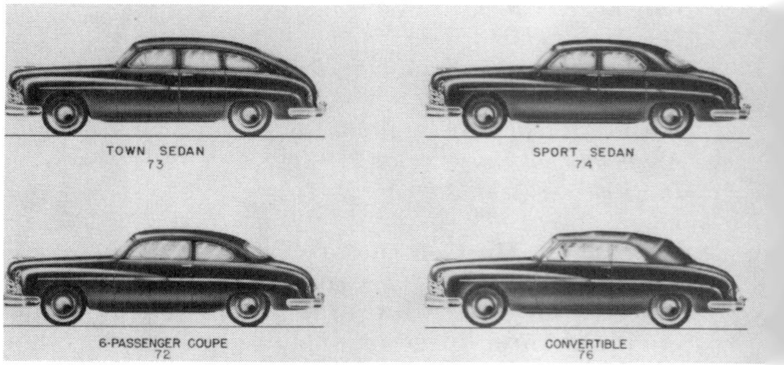

1949 Lincoln Model 76 Convertible

PHOTO: FORD MOTOR COMPANY

1949 Lincoln Cosmopolitan Convertible

Original Price: est. $3,900
Number Produced: 1,230
Estimated Number Existing in 1979: 1
Miles per Gallon: 13–17
Common Trouble Spots: automatic transmission
Availability of Parts: poor
Investment Potential: A+

Background: The '49 Cosmopolitan convertible featured sleek "modern" styling. Originally it was to have had hidden headlights (that is why the headlights are somewhat recessed). It was powered by a 152 h.p. 336.7 cu. in. eight-cylinder engine. A three-speed manual transmission was standard. Overdrive and (late in the model year) GM's Hydra-Matic automatic transmission were optional.

1949 Lincoln Cosmopolitan Convertible

PHOTO: FORD MOTOR COMPANY

1949 Mercury Convertible

Original Price: est. $2,400
Number Produced: 16,765
Estimated Number Existing in 1979: 12
Miles per Gallon: 14–19
Common Trouble Spots: none
Availability of Parts: poor–fair
Investment Potential: AAA

Background: The first really new postwar Mercury made its debut on April 29, 1948. The big Mercury convertible was one of the most attractive cars on the road in 1949. It was powered by a 110 h.p. 255.4 cu. in. eight-cylinder engine. A three-speed manual transmission was standard. Overdrive was optional at extra cost.

1949 Mercury Coupe

Original Price: est. $1,900
Number Produced: 120,616
Estimated Number Existing in 1979: 91
Miles per Gallon: 14–19
Common Trouble Spots: none
Availability of Parts: fair–poor
Investment Potential: AA+

Background: The attractive '49 Mercury coupe was powered by a 110 h.p. 255.4 cu. in. eight-cylinder engine. A three-speed manual transmission was standard. Overdrive was optional.

The 1949-51 Mercury coupes were the "in" cars to own in the 1950s. They were very popular with customizers. Magazines like *Custom Craft, Car Speed and Style, Custom Cars, Rodding and Restyling,* and others were frequently full of ways to "individualize" these cars.

1949 Mercury Coupe

PHOTO: THE VETERAN CAR MUSEUM

1949 Mercury Convertible

1949 Mercury Station Wagon

Original Price: est. $2,500
Number Produced: 8,044
Estimated Number Existing in 1979: 6
Miles per Gallon: 14–18
Common Trouble Spots: none
Availability of Parts: poor–fair
Investment Potential: AA+

Background: The new Mercury station wagon was an attractive car, sportier-looking than the previous year's model. It was powered by a 110 h.p. 255.4 cu. in. eight-cylinder engine. A three-speed manual transmission was standard.

Before buying a 1949 Mercury wagon, or any woodie, make sure the wood is in good condition. According to Will O'Neil, president of the National Woodie Club, "The main problem connected with owning a woodie is the wood. Terrible job to repair or replace it. We don't even think about sheet metal or engine repair when buying a woodie, just the wood. Doing it yourself is tough, farming it out to the experts is very expensive, and there are a lot of shoddy woodworkers around."

1949 Muntz Jet Convertible

Original Price: est. $5,000
Number Produced: 28
Estimated Number Existing in 1979: 1
Miles per Gallon: 12–17
Common Trouble Spots: engine bearings
Availability of Parts: poor–fair
Investment Potential: AA+

Background: The Muntz Jet convertible was based on the Kurtis sports car. Early ones had an aluminum body which dented very easily. Later, steel body parts were used.

It was powered by a 160 h.p. 331 cu. in. Cadillac V8. Hydra-Matic automatic transmission, seat belts, padded dash, and a luxurious vinyl interior were standard.

The Muntz had a removable steel roof that was padded inside and out.

1949 Muntz Jet Convertible

1949 Oldsmobile Futuramic 88 Convertible

Original Price: est. $2,200
Number Produced: 5,434
Estimated Number Existing in 1979: 5
Miles per Gallon: 14–18
Common Trouble Spots: carburetor, piston rings
Availability of Parts: poor
Investment Potential: AA+

Background: The Olds 88 quickly made a name for itself as one of the fastest cars on the road. Fittingly, it was chosen to be the Indianapolis 500 pace car in 1949.

The reason for its remarkable performance was the new 135 h.p. 303.7 cu. in. Rocket V8 engine. Since the 88 was slightly smaller and lighter, it could outperform the top-of-the-line 98.

Hydra-Matic automatic transmission was standard.

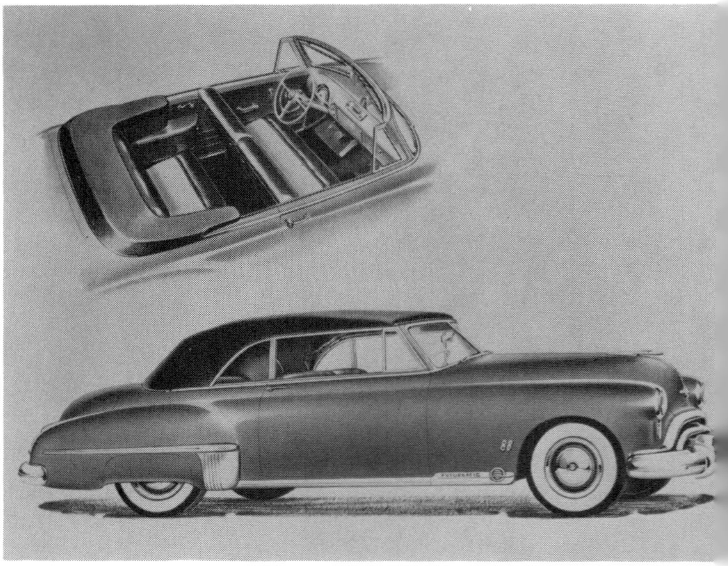

1949 Oldsmobile Futuramic 88 Convertible

PHOTO: OLDSMOBILE DIVISION

1949 Oldsmobile Futuramic 88 Deluxe Station Wagon

Original Price: est. $2,600
Number Produced: 1,355
Estimated Number Existing in 1979: 1
Miles per Gallon: 13–17
Common Trouble Spots: carburetor, piston rings
Availability of Parts: poor
Investment Potential: AA+

Background: The attractive '49 Futuramic 88 wagon came with a 135 h.p. 303.7 cu. in. V8 engine. Hydra-Matic automatic transmission was standard.

1949 Oldsmobile Futuramic 76 Convertible

PHOTO: OLDSMOBILE DIVISION

1949 Oldsmobile Futuramic 76 Convertible

Original Price: est. $2,000
Number Produced: 5,338
Estimated Number Existing in 1979: 5
Miles per Gallon: 13–19
Common Trouble Spots: none
Availability of Parts: poor
Investment Potential: A+

Background: The Futuramic 76 convertible was powered by a 105 h.p. 257.1 cu. in. six-cylinder engine. A three-speed manual transmission was standard. Hydra-Matic automatic transmission was optional at extra cost.

1949 Oldsmobile Futuramic 76 Estate Station Wagon

Original Price: est. $2,400
Number Produced: 1,545
Estimated Number Existing in 1979: 1
Miles per Gallon: 13–18
Common Trouble Spots: none
Availability of Parts: poor
Investment Potential: AA+

Background: The amount of wood used in the new 76 wagon was greatly reduced from the previous year. The trend toward all-steel station wagons was definitely at hand.

The Estate wagon was powered by a 105 h.p. 257.1 cu. in. six-cylinder engine. A three-speed manual transmission was standard. Hydra-Matic automatic transmission was optional at extra cost.

1949 Oldsmobile Futuramic 98 Convertible

PHOTO: OLDSMOBILE DIVISION

1949 Oldsmobile Futuramic 98 Convertible

Original Price: est. $2,700
Number Produced: 12,602
Estimated Number Existing in 1979: 12
Miles per Gallon: 14–17
Common Trouble Spots: piston rings
Availability of Parts: poor–fair
Investment Potential: AA

Background: Unlike the other Oldsmobile series, the 98 received only a minor facelift for 1949. The big news was the standard 135 h.p. 303.7 cu. in. Rocket V8 engine. Hydra-Matic automatic transmission was standard.

1949 Oldsmobile Futuramic 98 Deluxe Holiday Coupe

Original Price: est. $2,400
Number Produced: 3,006
Estimated Number Existing in 1979: 3
Miles per Gallon: 14–17
Common Trouble Spots: piston rings
Availability of Parts: poor–fair
Investment Potential: AA+

Background: The trend-setting Holiday two-door hardtop was introduced very late in the model year. Like GM's Buick and Cadillac "hardtop convertibles," it created quite a sensation.

The Holiday was powered by the hot new 135 h.p. 303.7 cu. in. Rocket V8. Hydramatic automatic transmission was standard.

This car is both significant (for its engine and body style) and desirable.

1949 Oldsmobile 98 Deluxe Holiday Coupe

PHOTO: OLDSMOBILE DIVISION

1949 Packard Custom Eight Convertible Victoria

Original Price: est. $4,500
Number Produced: 275 (60 of these were 1949½ models)
Estimated Number Existing in 1979: 2
Miles per Gallon: 11–17
Common Trouble Spots: Electromatic clutch
Availability of Parts: poor
Investment Potential: AA (1949½ models); A+ (regular 1949 models)

Background: The 1949 Custom Eight softtop was powered by a 160 h.p. 356 cu. in. eight-cylinder engine. A three-speed manual transmission was standard. Electromatic clutch, overdrive, and Ultramatic automatic transmission were optional at extra cost. The automatic wasn't available until May of 1949, so most Custom Eights were sold without it.

In midyear special Golden Anniversary models were produced; they featured a chrome strip that ran the length of the car. Two thousand 1949½ Packards of various models were painted gold, in honor of the occasion.

1949 Packard Custom Eight Convertible Victoria

1949 Packard Station Sedan

Original Price: est. $3,400
Number Produced: est. 1,340
Estimated Number Existing in 1979: 2
Miles per Gallon: 11–18
Common Trouble Spots: Electromatic clutch
Availability of Parts: poor
Investment Potential: AA+

Background: The "new" Station Sedan was virtually the same as the 1948 model. Some minor changes were made in mid-1949 as part of Packard's 50th anniversary celebration. It was still basically a metal station wagon with wood trim.

A 130 h.p. 288.6 cu. in. eight-cylinder engine and a three-speed manual transmission were standard. Electromatic clutch, overdrive and, in midyear, Ultramatic automatic transmission were optional at extra cost.

1949 Packard Super Eight Convertible Victoria

Original Price: est. $3,300
Number Produced: 4,921 (671 of these were 1949½ models)
Estimated Number Existing in 1979: 6
Miles per Gallon: 11–17
Common Trouble Spots: Electromatic clutch
Availability of Parts: poor
Investment Potential: AA(1949½ models); A+ (regular '49 models)

Background: The new Super Eight convertible was powered by a 145 h.p. 327 cu. in. eight-cylinder engine. A three-speed manual transmission was standard. Electromatic clutch, overdrive and Ultramatic automatic transmission were optional at extra cost. The automatic wasn't available until May of 1949.

In midyear, special Golden Anniversary models were made. These featured a full-length chrome strip on the sides of the car.

1949 Packard Station Sedan

PHOTO: THE VETERAN CAR MUSEUM

1949 Packard Super Eight Convertible Victoria

PHOTO: RICHARD QUINN COLLECTION

1949 Plymouth Special Deluxe Convertible

Original Price: est. $1,900
Number Produced: 15,240
Estimated Number Existing in 1979: 21
Miles per Gallon: 13–20
Common Trouble Spots: none
Availability of Parts: poor
Investment Potential: A

Background: This was the first really new postwar Plymouth convertible. It featured "cute" boxy styling. The Special Deluxe was powered by a 97 h.p. 217.8 cu. in. six-cylinder engine. A three-speed manual transmission was standard.

1949 Plymouth Special Deluxe Convertible

1949 Plymouth Special Deluxe Station Wagon

Original Price: est. $2,300
Number Produced: 3,443
Estimated Number Existing in 1979: 5
Miles per Gallon: 13–20
Common Trouble Spots: none
Availability of Parts: poor
Investment Potential: AA+

Background: The new Special Deluxe station wagon had a very streamlined, modern look about it compared to the previous year's model. It was powered by a 97 h.p. 217.8 cu. in. six-cylinder engine. A three-speed manual transmission was standard.

The 1949 Special Deluxe wagon is a rare and desirable woodie.

1949 Plymouth Special Deluxe Station Wagon

1949 Pontiac Chieftain Deluxe Convertible

PHOTO: PONTIAC MOTOR DIVISION

1949 Pontiac Chieftain Deluxe Convertible

Original Price: est. $2,100
Number Produced: N.A.
Estimated Number Existing in 1979: N.A.
Miles per Gallon: 14–20
Common Trouble Spots: none
Availability of Parts: poor–fair
Investment Potential: A

Background: Like most 1949 cars, the Pontiac Chieftain featured fresh, new styling, which gave it sleeker lines than the previous year's model. Buyers could order either a 93 h.p. 239.2 cu. in. six-cylinder or a 106 h.p. 248.9 cu. in. eight-cylinder engine. A three-speed manual transmission was standard. Hydra-Matic automatic transmission was available for $185.

Pontiac did its share to encourage (or at least take advantage of) the postwar marriage boom. One ad, featuring the '49 Chieftain ragtop, offered advice on what to do "when you make a sweetheart your own." The copy read, "What happier day is anyone likely to know than a wedding day—always an occasion of complete joy, a time to be long remembered. And what finer companion for every happy couple—than a beautiful new 1949 Pontiac?"

1949 Pontiac Streamliner Station Wagon

Original Price: est. $2,300
Number Produced: N.A.
Estimated Number Existing in 1979: N.A.
Miles per Gallon: 13–19
Common Trouble Spots: none
Availability of Parts: poor
Investment Potential: AA+

Background: The new Pontiac wagon was a very sleek car when compared to previous years' models. The use of wood in the body was greatly reduced.

It was powered by a 93 h.p. 239.2 cu. in. six-cylinder engine. A 106 h.p. 248.9 cu. in. eight-cylinder engine was available at extra cost. A three-speed manual transmission was standard. Hydra-Matic automatic transmission was optional.

Most 1949 Pontiacs, 77.1%, came with the eight-cylinder engine, and 66.9% had the automatic.

1949 Studebaker Champion Convertible

Original Price: est. $1,900
Number Produced: 6,780
Estimated Number Existing in 1979: 14
Miles per Gallon: 17–28
Common Trouble Spots: none
Availability of Parts: poor
Investment Potential: A

Background: The Champion convertible was an attractive car. However, since most other makes now had restyled, modern-looking cars too, it was no longer as distinctive.

It was powered by an 80 h.p. 169.6 cu. in. six-cylinder engine. A three-speed manual transmission was standard. Overdrive was optional.

1949 Studebaker Champion Convertible

1949 Studebaker Commander Convertible

Original Price: est. $2,300
Number Produced: 1,624
Estimated Number Existing in 1979: 3
Miles per Gallon: 16–25
Common Trouble Spots: none
Availability of Parts: poor
Investment Potential: A

Background: The 1949 Commander convertible was an attractive car. Studebaker's top-of-the-line ragtop was powered by a 94 h.p. 226.2 cu. in. six-cylinder engine. A three-speed manual transmission was standard. Overdrive was optional at extra cost.

1949 Studebaker Commander Convertible

1949 Willys Jeepster Phaeton

Original Price: $1,495
Number Produced: 2,960
Estimated Number Existing in 1979: 13
Miles per Gallon: 18–30
Common Trouble Spots: none
Availability of Parts: poor
Investment Potential: A+

Background: The sporty '49 Jeepster came with a 63 h.p. 134.2 cu. in. four-cylinder engine. Available at extra cost was a 72 h.p. 148.4 cu. in. six-cylinder engine. Only 22% of 1949 Jeepsters were equipped with the six. A three-speed manual transmission with overdrive was standard.

1949 Willys Jeepster Phaeton

PHOTO: JOHN A. CONDE COLLECTION

1950

1950 Buick Roadmaster Convertible

Original Price: $2.989
Number Produced: 2,964
Estimated Number Existing in 1979: 8
Miles per Gallon: 12–17
Common Trouble Spots: none
Availability of Parts: poor–fair
Investment Potential: A+

Background: The new "buck-toothed" Roadmaster was powered by a 152 h.p. 320.2 cu. in. eight-cylinder engine. Dynaflow automatic transmission was standard.

Once again, the top-of-the-line Roadmaster ragtop could be instantly differentiated from "lesser" Buicks by the four (rectangular) portholes on each side of the hood.

1950 Buick Roadmaster Estate Station Wagon

Original Price: $3,407
Number Produced: 420
Estimated Number Existing in 1979: 1
Miles per Gallon: 11–16
Common Trouble Spots: none
Availability of Parts: poor–fair
Investment Potential: AA+

Background: The Roadmaster Estate station wagon was powered by a 152 h.p. 320.2 cu. in. straight eight engine. Dynaflow automatic transmission was standard.

1950 Buick Roadmaster Convertible

PHOTO: HOWARD AND SHELBY APPLEGATE

1950 Buick Super Convertible

Original Price: $2,476
Number Produced: 12,259
Estimated Number Existing in 1979: 36
Miles per Gallon: 13–17
Common Trouble Spots: none
Availability of Parts: poor–fair
Investment Potential: A+

Background: The new Super was by far Buick's most popular convertible in 1950. It looked a great deal like the more expensive Roadmaster, at least from the front and from the rear. However, a restrained use of chrome and only three (rectangular) portholes on each side of the hood made it noticeably different from the side.

The Super ragtop was powered by a 124 h.p. 263.3 cu. in. eight-cylinder engine. Buyers could choose either a manual or Dynaflow automatic transmission. The convertible top was power operated.

1950 Buick Super Convertible

PHOTO: PUBLIC RELATIONS DEPARTMENT, BUICK MOTOR DIVISION

1950 Chevrolet Styleline Deluxe Convertible

Original Price: $1,845
Number Produced: 32,810
Estimated Number Existing in 1979: 111
Miles per Gallon: 14–20
Common Trouble Spots: none
Availability of Parts: poor–fair
Investment Potential: AA

Background: The '50 Deluxe ragtop was powered by a 92 h.p. 216.5 cu. in. six-cylinder engine when equipped with the standard three-speed manual transmission. Cars with the optional Powerglide automatic came with a 105 h.p. 235.5 cu. in. six.

1950 Buick Super Estate Station Wagon

Original Price: $2,844
Number Produced: 2,480
Estimated Number Existing in 1979: 7
Miles per Gallon: 11–17
Common Trouble Spots: none
Availability of Parts: poor–fair
Investment Potential: AA+

Background: Buick's most popular wagon in 1950 was the Super Estate. It was powered by a 124 h.p. 263.3 cu. in. straight eight engine. A three-speed manual transmission was standard. Dynaflow automatic transmission was optional at extra cost.

1950 Chevrolet Styleline Deluxe Convertible

1950 Cadillac Series 62 Convertible

Original Price: $3,654
Number Produced: 6,986
Estimated Number Existing in 1979: 36
Miles per Gallon: 12–20
Common Trouble Spots: none
Availability of Parts: poor–fair
Investment Potential: A+

Background: The new Cadillac Series 62 looked a great deal like the 1949, but wasn't quite as sleek. It featured all-leather upholstery. Buyers had a choice of either of two colors for the power convertible top—black and tan.

The Series 62 was powered by a 160 h.p. 331 cu. in. V8 engine. Hydra-Matic automatic transmission was standard.

The most famous convertible of the early 1950s was a one-of-a-kind show car called the Debutante. It was the legendary "solid gold Cadillac." This "tawny yellow" convertible featured Somaliland-leopard-and-silver-satin upholstery. Many parts were gold-plated. The car reportedly cost $35,000.

1950 Cadillac Series 62 Convertible

1950 Chrysler New Yorker Convertible

1950 Chrysler New Yorker Convertible

Original Price: $3,238
Number Produced: 899
Estimated Number Existing in 1979: 3
Miles per Gallon: 12–17
Common Trouble Spots: none
Availability of Parts: poor
Investment Potential: A+

Background: The round front signal lights and a longer wheelbase were two things that helped distinguish the New Yorker from the Windsor. Two other differences were the 323.5 cu. in. eight-cylinder engine and the optional power windows, available for the first time.

The 135 h.p. engine had a hard time pulling all that weight from a dead stop. But outside of poor acceleration (it took nearly 20 seconds to go from 0 to 60) it had little trouble once it got going. Presto-matic automatic transmission was standard.

Riding in a New Yorker was a pleasant experience. There was plenty of head and leg room. And it was available with a padded, leather-covered dash, in case the hydraulic brakes weren't able to stop the car quickly enough. Another handy feature was a warning light that would flash on and off if the emergency brake was engaged while the engine was running.

1950 Chrysler Royal Station Wagon

Original Price: $3,163
Number Produced: 599
Estimated Number Existing in 1979: 2
Miles per Gallon: 11–16
Common Trouble Spots: none
Availability of Parts: poor
Investment Potential: AA+

Background: The biggest difference between a 1949 Royal woodie and a 1950 is that the 1950 did not have a spare tire on the tailgate. Many do not consider this a real woodie because the wood was bolted onto a metal body. It was even less popular with buyers than the previous model.

It was powered by a 116 h.p. 250.6 cu. in. six-cylinder engine. A three-speed manual transmission was standard. Presto-matic automatic transmission was optional.

1950 Chrysler Town and Country Newport

Original Price: $4,003
Number Produced: 700
Estimated Number Existing in 1979: 20
Miles per Gallon: 10–15
Common Trouble Spots: none
Availability of Parts: poor
Investment Potential: AAA+

Background: This was the last year for the Town and Country woodie passenger car. It was also one of the best-looking of the series. Like the Royal wagons, it was not a true woodie—wood trim was bolted onto a metal body. However, that does little to detract from the beauty and significance of this car.

Even with a 135 h.p. 323.5 cu. in. eight-cylinder engine, the Newport gave only mediocre performance. This was primarily due to the tremendous weight of the automobile. Presto-matic automatic transmission was standard.

Low production, distinctive (and becoming) styling, and the luxurious aura of the automobile help make the 1950 Town and Country Newport one of the most desirable postwar cars made.

1950 Chrysler Town and Country Newport Hardtop

PHOTO: CHRYSLER HISTORICAL COLLECTION

1950 Chrysler Windsor Convertible

Original Price: $2,741
Number Produced: 2,201
Estimated Number Existing in 1979: 8
Miles per Gallon: 13–18
Common Trouble Spots: none
Availability of Parts: poor
Investment Potential: A+

Background: A minor facelift was all that distinguished the 1950 from the 1949 Windsor.

It came with a 116 h.p. 250.6 cu. in. six-cylinder engine and Presto-Matic automatic transmission.

The Windsor ragtop was a comfortable car to ride in, but had poor acceleration.

1950 Crosley Convertible

Original Price: $866
Number Produced: 478
Estimated Number Existing in 1979: 5
Miles per Gallon: 25–32
Common Trouble Spots: none
Availability of Parts: poor
Investment Potential: A

Background: The 1950 Crosley ragtop was the type of car the one-passenger King Midget buyer would move up to when he or she found a friend. It was powered by a 26.5 h.p. 44 cu. in. four-cylinder engine. A three-speed manual transmission was standard. A "Super" trim package was optional at extra cost.

1950 Crosley Convertible

PHOTO: CROSLEY AUTOMOBILE CLUB, INC.

1950 Crosley Hotshot Roadster

Original Price: $861
Number Produced: 742 (includes Super Sports)
Estimated Number Existing in 1979: 6 (includes Super Sports)
Miles per Gallon: 25–32
Common Trouble Spots: none
Availability of Parts: poor
Investment Potential: AA

Background: In stock form, the Hotshot wasn't exactly the terror of the stoplights. Nor was it in the habit of shutting down "Rocket 88" Oldsmobiles. However, its standard 26.5 h.p. 44 cu. in. four-cylinder engine was easily modified by owners who wanted more go. A souped-up Hotshot could go up to 90 miles per hour or more. A three-speed manual transmission was standard.

1950 Crosley Super Sports Convertible

Original Price: est. $1,000
Number Produced: 742 (includes Hotshots)
Estimated Number Existing in 1979: 6 (includes Hotshots)
Miles per Gallon: 25–32
Common Trouble Spots: none
Availability of Parts: poor
Investment Potential: AA

Background: The 1950 Super Sports ragtop was one of the most desirable Crosleys ever made. This attractive little car was basically just a fancy version of the Hotshot. It featured such luxuries as a folding top and doors that would open and shut.

The Super Sports was powered by a 26.5 h.p. 44 cu. in. four-cylinder engine. A three-speed manual transmission was standard.

1950 Crosley Super Sports Convertible

PHOTO: CROSLEY AUTOMOBILE CLUB, INC.

1950 Crosley Hotshot Roadster

PHOTO: CROSLEY AUTOMOBILE CLUB, INC.

1950 DeSoto Custom Convertible

1950 DeSoto Custom Convertible

Original Price: $2,578
Number Produced: 2,900
Estimated Number Existing in 1979: 7
Miles per Gallon: 13–18
Common Trouble Spots: none
Availability of Parts: poor
Investment Potential: A+

Background: The new Custom convertible was little changed from the previous year's model. It was powered by a 112 h.p. 236.6 cu. in. six-cylinder engine. Tip-Toe Shift automatic transmission was standard.

1950 DeSoto Custom Station Wagon

Original Price: $3,093
Number Produced: 600
Estimated Number Existing in 1979: 2
Miles per Gallon: 12–18
Common Trouble Spots: none
Availability of Parts: poor
Investment Potential: AA+

Background: The attractive '50 Custom station wagon was little changed from the previous year's model. It was powered by a 112 h.p. 236.6 cu. in. six-cylinder engine. Tip-Toe Shift automatic transmission was standard.

1950 Dodge Coronet Convertible

Original Price: $2,329
Number Produced: 1,800
Estimated Number Existing in 1979: 6
Miles per Gallon: 13–20
Common Trouble Spots: none
Availability of Parts: poor
Investment Potential: A

Background: The '50 Coronet convertible had a 123½ inch wheelbase. It was powered by a 103 h.p. 230.2 cu. in. six-cylinder engine. A three-speed manual transmission was standard. Gyromatic automatic transmission was available at extra cost.

Hundreds of 1950 Dodges spent the early parts of their lives in Chicago's Wrigley Field. Dodge dealers in that city needed a place to store their new cars, so they made a deal to have them kept in the famous ball park. The cars were parked under the stands and in the playing field. Naturally, they were only there during the off season—at least there is no record of a player hitting a ball into the stands, then driving to home plate in a Coronet convertible.

1950 Dodge Coronet Convertible

PHOTO: CHRYSLER HISTORICAL COLLECTION

1950 Dodge Coronet Station Wagon

Original Price: $2,347
Number Produced: 600
Estimated Number Existing in 1979: 3
Miles per Gallon: 13–18
Common Trouble Spots: none
Availability of Parts: poor
Investment Potential: AA+

Background: The 1950 Coronet station wagon looked virtually the same as the 1949—and that wasn't bad. As before, it was technically a wood-trimmed car—not a genuine woodie.

It was powered by a 103 h.p. 230.2 cu. in. six-cylinder engine. A three-speed manual transmission was standard. Gyromatic automatic transmission was available at extra cost.

1950 Dodge Wayfarer Roadster

Original Price: $1,745
Number Produced: 2,903
Estimated Number Existing in 1979: 10
Miles per Gallon: 14–20
Common Trouble Spots: none
Availability of Parts: poor
Investment Potential: A+

Background: Although it looked basically the same as the '49, the 1950 Wayfarer did not attract as many buyers—in fact, sales were down almost 50%.

The Wayfarer roadster was powered by a 103 h.p. 230. cu. in. six-cylinder engine. A three-speed manual transmission was standard.

1950 Ford Custom Convertible

Original Price: $1,949
Number Produced: 50,299
Estimated Number Existing in 1979: 169
Miles per Gallon: 14–20
Common Trouble Spots: brakes
Availability of Parts: fair–poor
Investment Potential: AA

Background: The 1950 Ford ragtop received a minor face-lift. Probably the easiest way to tell it from the previous year's model was to look for the Ford crest above the grille (the 1949 had the letters F-O-R-D in that location). Also, the new model had a concealed gas tank filler, while the old had one that stuck out from the car slightly.

The Custom convertible came with a 100 h.p. 239.4 cu. in. V8. A three-speed manual transmission was standard. Overdrive and Ford-O-Matic automatic transmission were optional.

It was available in eleven colors, including four shades of green. Leather and a combination of leather and Bedford cord were the upholstery materials offered. The convertible top came in black, green, and tan.

The New York Fashion Academy named the 1950 Ford "Fashion Car of the Year."

1950 Ford Custom Convertible

PHOTO: FORD MOTOR COMPANY

1950 Ford Custom Crestliner

Original Price: est. $1,590
Number Produced: 17,601
Estimated Number Existing in 1979: 59
Miles per Gallon: 14–20
Common Trouble Spots: brakes
Availability of Parts: fair–poor
Investment Potential: A+

Background: Two-door "hardtop convertibles" were hot in 1950. Unfortunately, Ford could not offer one, due to structural problems in the Ford body shell. Therefore, the Crestliner was introduced as competition to the popular hardtops. It was really just a two-door sedan with fancy trim, a vinyl roof, fender skirts, a distinctive steering wheel (black was standard, brown optional), and special chromed wheel covers.

All Crestliners were two-tone. Even the dash was painted to match the outside of the car. The seats were specially upholstered and the headliner was black imitation leather.

The Crestliner was powered by a 100 h.p. 239.4 cu. in. V8. A three-speed manual transmission was standard. Overdrive and Ford-O-Matic automatic transmission were optional.

1950 Ford Custom Crestliner

PHOTO: FORD MOTOR COMPANY

1950 Ford Custom Station Wagon

Original Price: $2,264
Number Produced: 22,929
Estimated Number Existing in 1979: 76
Miles per Gallon: 14–20
Common Trouble Spots: brakes
Availability of Parts: poor–fair
Investment Potential: AA+

Background: The new Custom station wagon looked much the same as the previous year's model. This sporty two-door woodie came with a 95 h.p. 225.9 cu. in. six. Over 90% of Custom Wagon buyers ordered the optional 100 h.p. 239.4 cu. in. V8. A three-speed manual transmission was standard. Overdrive and Ford-O-Matic automatic transmission were available at extra cost.

Buyers had their choice of any of nine exterior colors.

In mid-model year, the Custom became an all-steel wagon with wood panels placed on it.

1950 Ford Custom Station Wagon

PHOTO: FORD MOTOR COMPANY

1950 Frazer Manhattan Convertible

Original Price: $2,595
Number Produced: est. 32
Estimated Number Existing in 1979: 6
Miles per Gallon: 15–20
Common Trouble Spots: cooling system, piston rings
Availability of Parts: poor
Investment Potential: AA+

Background: All unsold 1949 Frazers (and Kaisers) at dealers, whether they were new or used, were given new serial plates and proclaimed 1950 models.

The Frazer ragtop was powered by a 112 h.p. 226.2 cu. in. six-cylinder engine. A three-speed manual transmission, a power top, and power windows were standard.

The few buyers there were had a choice of cloth-and-leather or all-leather upholstery. The convertible top came in two colors, black and tan.

1950 Frazer Manhattan Convertible

PHOTO: JOHN A. CONDE COLLECTION

1950 Hudson Commodore Eight Convertible Brougham

Original Price: $2,893
Number Produced: N.A.
Estimated Number Existing in 1979: N.A.
Miles per Gallon: 13–18
Common Trouble Spots: none
Availability of Parts: poor
Investment Potential: AA

Background: The attractive new Commodore Eight convertible was powered by a 128 h.p. 254 cu. in. eight-cylinder engine. A three-speed manual transmission was standard. Overdrive and Super Matic automatic transmission were optional.

1950 Hudson Commodore Eight Convertible Brougham

PHOTO: JOHN A. CONDE COLLECTION

1950 Hudson Commodore Six Convertible Brougham

Original Price: $2,809
Number Produced: N.A.
Estimated Number Existing in 1979: N.A.
Miles per Gallon: 13–18
Common Trouble Spots: none
Availability of Parts: poor–fair
Investment Potential: AA

Background: The 1950 Commodore Six ragtop had a sleek, low, custom-car look about it. It was powered by a 123 h.p. 262 cu. in. six-cylinder engine. A three-speed manual transmission was standard. Overdrive and Super Matic automatic transmission were optional at extra cost.

1950 Hudson Super Six Convertible Brougham

Original Price: $2,628
Number Produced: N.A.
Estimated Number Existing in 1979: N.A.
Miles per Gallon: 13–18
Common Trouble Spots: none
Availability of Parts: poor–fair
Investment Potential: AA

Background: The handsome Super Six convertible was little changed for 1950. It came with a 112 h.p. 232 cu. in. six-cylinder engine. A three-speed manual transmission was standard. Overdrive and Super Matic automatic transmission were optional at extra cost.

1950 Kaiser Deluxe Convertible

Original Price: $2,195
Number Produced: est. 11
Estimated Number Existing in 1979: 5
Miles per Gallon: 15–20
Common Trouble Spots: cooling system, piston rings
Availability of Parts: poor
Investment Potential: AA+

Background: The '50 Kaiser ragtop came with a 100 h.p. 226.2 cu. in. six-cylinder engine. A three-speed manual transmission, power top, and power windows were standard.

Buyers had a choice of cloth-and-leather or all-leather upholstery. The convertible top was offered in two colors, black and tan.

1950 Kaiser Deluxe Virginian

Original Price: $2,995
Number Produced: est. 467
Estimated Number Existing in 1979: 34
Miles per Gallon: 15–20
Common Trouble Spots: cooling system, piston rings
Availability of Parts: poor
Investment Potential: AA+

Background: The 1950 Virginian was one of the best-looking fourdoors on the road that year. Since the side window frames did not come down, it was not a real hardtop, although it looked like one.

As before, the Virginian was available in a wide range of fashionable color combinations. It was powered by a 100 h.p. 226.2 cu. in. six-cylinder engine. A three-speed manual transmission and a padded steel top were standard. Power windows and leather upholstery were among the options.

1950 Lincoln Convertible

Original Price: $3,116
Number Produced: N.A.
Estimated Number Existing in 1979: N.A.
Miles per Gallon: 13–18
Common Trouble Spots: automatic transmission
Availability of Parts: poor
Investment Potential: A+

Background: The standard 1950 Lincoln convertible was powered by a 152 h.p. 336.7 cu. in. eight-cylinder engine. A three-speed manual transmission was standard. Overdrive and Hydra-Matic automatic transmission were optional at extra cost.

1950 Lincoln Cosmopolitan Convertible

Original Price: $3,948
Number Produced: 536
Estimated Number Existing in 1979: 1
Miles per Gallon: 13–17
Common Trouble Spots: automatic transmission
Availability of Parts: poor
Investment Potential: A+

Background: The Cosmopolitan's dash was attractively redesigned for 1950. Outside of that, it looked pretty much the same as the previous year's model. It was powered by a 152 h.p. 336.7 cu. in. eight cylinder engine. A three-speed manual transmission was standard. Overdrive and Hydra-Matic automatic transmission were optional.

1950 Mercury Convertible

PHOTO: FORD MOTOR COMPANY

1950 Mercury Convertible

Original Price: $2,410
Number Produced: 8,341
Estimated Number Existing in 1979: 17
Miles per Gallon: 14–19
Common Trouble Spots: none
Availability of Parts: poor–fair
Investment Potential: AAA

Background: Despite the fact that very little was done to alter the previous year's good looks, Mercury convertible sales dropped considerably in 1950. Many people now prefer the appearance of the '50 Mercury to that of the '49.

It came with a 110 h.p. 255.4 cu. in. eight-cylinder engine. This "flathead" engine would propel the big car to a top speed of over 83.7 mph. According to *Motor Trend,* "With better tuning and a longer approach distance, it is certain that the Mercury could turn a higher top speed." A three-speed manual transmission was standard. Overdrive and Merc-O-Matic automatic transmission were available at extra cost.

The 1950 Mercury is one of the sharpest and most desirable convertibles made in the 1950s. As the ads said that year, "Go for a ride and you'll go for Mercury."

1950 Mercury Coupe

Original Price: $1,979
Number Produced: 151,489
Estimated Number Existing in 1979: 323
Miles per Gallon: 14–19
Common Trouble Spots: none
Availability of Parts: fair–*poor*
Investment Potential: AA+

Background: The 1949–50 Mercury coupes probably signify the 1950s to more people than any other car. Good looks and performance made them popular; when James Dean drove one in *Rebel Without a Cause,* he made them immortal.

The '50 Mercury coupe was powered by a 110 h.p. 255.4 cu. in. V8. A three-speed manual transmission was standard. Merc-O-Matic automatic transmission and overdrive were optional.

1950 Mercury Station Wagon

Original Price: $2,561
Number Produced: 1,746
Estimated Number Existing in 1979: 4
Miles per Gallon: 14–18
Common Trouble Spots: none
Availability of Parts: poor–fair
Investment Potential: AA+

Background: The Mercury station wagon received a minor but pleasing face-lift for 1950. It was powered by a 110 h.p. 255.4 cu. in. V8. A three-speed manual transmission was standard. Merc-O-Matic automatic and a manual with overdrive were optional at extra cost.

1950 Mercury Station Wagon

PHOTO: FORD MOTOR COMPANY

1950 Mercury Coupe

PHOTO: FORD MOTOR COMPANY

1950 Muntz Jet Convertible

Original Price: est. $5,000
Number Produced: est. 81
Estimated Number Existing in 1979: 5
Miles per Gallon: 12–17
Common Trouble Spots: none
Availability of Parts: poor–fair
Investment Potential: AA+

Background: The 1950 Muntz convertible was powered by a 154 h.p. 336.7 cu. in. Lincoln V8 engine. Hydra-Matic automatic transmission, padded dash, seat belts, radio, and a vinyl interior were standard. It had a removable padded steel roof.

The new Muntz ragtop looked virtually the same as the '49 model, but it had a 116-inch wheelbase instead of last year's 113.

1950 Nash Rambler Custom Convertible

Original Price: $1,808
Number Produced: 9,708
Estimated Number Existing in 1979: 21
Miles per Gallon: 16–25
Common Trouble Spots: none
Availability of Parts: poor
Investment Potential: A

Background: The new, unitized-body Rambler ragtop was introduced in April of 1950. It was intended to be a luxurious small car. The power-operated top was raised or lowered by steel cables sliding in tracks located in the top of the window frame. Like the Crosley ragtop's, the window frames were fixed and could not be lowered.

The Rambler was rather roomy for its size. The front seat was five inches wider than the rear. It was designed to carry five people (three in the front, two in the back).

An 82 h.p. 172.6 cu. in. six-cylinder engine and a three-speed manual transmission were standard. So were the radio and heater. Overdrive was optional at extra cost.

Special Interest Autos called the 1950 Nash Rambler "America's first successful postwar compact."

1950 Nash Rambler Custom Convertible

1950 Oldsmobile 88 Convertible

PHOTO: OLDSMOBILE DIVISION

1950 Oldsmobile 88 Convertible

Original Price: $2,294
Number Produced: 9,127
Estimated Number Existing in 1979: 20
Miles per Gallon: 14–18
Common Trouble Spots: none
Availability of Parts: poor–fair
Investment Potential: AAA

Background: A one-piece windshield was the most noticeable styling change made for 1950. It was powered by the famous 135 h.p. 303.7 cu. in. Rocket V8 engine. A three-speed manual transmission was standard. Hydra-Matic automatic transmission was optional at extra cost.

A 1950 Olds 88 was the first stock car ever tested by *Motor Trend* that went faster than 90 miles per hour. (Another 88 broke a 15-year-old record at Daytona Beach by averaging over 100 miles per hour.)

This is one of the most desirable and popular postwar Oldsmobiles.

1950 Oldsmobile 88 Holiday Coupe

Original Price: $2,294
Number Produced: 12,682
Estimated Number Existing in 1979: 28
Miles per Gallon: 14–18
Common Trouble Spots: none
Availability of Parts: poor–fair
Investment Potential: AA+

Background: "A car of power." That's how *Motor Trend* described the new Olds 88. And 88 owners proved it time and time again on racetracks and at stoplights. The Olds 88, with its 135 h.p. 303.7 cu. in. Rocket V8 engine, was one of the hottest cars of its day.

A three-speed manual transmission was standard. Hydra-Matic automatic transmission was available at extra cost.

Next to the convertibles, the 88 Holiday coupe, in either the standard or the Deluxe version (over 90% were Deluxe), is one of the most sought-after Oldsmobiles made in the 1950s. Some people like it even better than the ragtops.

One reason the 1950 88 is so popular is its suspension system, which was offered that year only. It gave the car better roadability than the suspension used before, or on preceding year's models.

1950 Oldsmobile 88 Holiday Coupe

PHOTO: OLDSMOBILE DIVISION

1950 Oldsmobile 98 Convertible

Original Price: $2,772
Number Produced: 3,925
Estimated Number Existing in 1979: 8
Miles per Gallon: 14–17
Common Trouble Spots: none
Availability of Parts: poor–fair
Investment Potential: AA

Background: The '50 Olds 98 looked much the same as the previous year's model. It was powered by a 135 h.p. 303.7 cu. in. V8 engine. A three-speed manual transmission was standard. Hydra-Matic automatic transmission was optional at extra cost.

1950 Oldsmobile 98 Convertible

PHOTO: OLDSMOBILE DIVISION

1950 Oldsmobile Series 76 Convertible

Original Price: $2,135
Number Produced: 973
Estimated Number Existing in 1979: 2
Miles per Gallon: 13–19
Common Trouble Spots: none
Availability of Parts: poor
Investment Potential: A+

Background: Once again, the 76 looked virtually the same as the 88 and 98, but it was powered by a less potent engine. It came with a 105 h.p. 257.1 cu. in. six-cylinder engine. A three-speed manual transmission was standard. Hydra-Matic automatic transmission was optional at extra cost.

1950 Packard Custom Eight Convertible Victoria

Original Price: $4,520
Number Produced: 85
Estimated Number Existing in 1979: 1
Miles per Gallon: 11–17
Common Trouble Spots: cooling system
Availability of Parts: poor
Investment Potential: A+

Background: Packard's top-of-the-line Custom Eight convertible was powered by a 160 h.p. 356 cu. in. eight-cylinder engine. Ultramatic automatic transmission was standard.

1950 Packard Station Sedan

Original Price: $3,449
Number Produced: N.A.
Estimated Number Existing in 1979: N.A.
Miles per Gallon: 11–18
Common Trouble Spots: none
Availability of Parts: poor
Investment Potential: AA+

Background: This was the last year for the attractive Station Sedan. It was the last wagon made by Packard before the merger with Studebaker.

The wood-trimmed, metal-bodied Station Sedan was powered by a 130 h.p. 288.6 cu. in. eight-cylinder engine. A three-speed manual transmission was standard. Overdrive and Ultramatic automatic transmission were optional at extra cost.

1950 Packard Super Eight Convertible Victoria Coupe

Original Price: $3,350
Number Produced: 614
Estimated Number Existing in 1979: 1
Miles per Gallon: 11–17
Common Trouble Spots: cooling system
Availability of Parts: poor
Investment Potential: A+

Background: The new Super Eight convertible was powered by a 150 h.p. 327 cu. in. eight-cylinder engine. A three-speed manual transmission was standard. Overdrive and Ultramatic automatic transmission were optional at extra cost.

1950 Packard Super Eight Convertible Victoria Coupe

PHOTO: JOHN A. CONDE COLLECTION

1950 Plymouth Special Deluxe Convertible

Original Price: $1,982
Number Produced: 12,697
Estimated Number Existing in 1979: 20
Miles per Gallon: 14–20
Common Trouble Spots: none
Availability of Parts: poor
Investment Potential: A

Background: The Special Deluxe ragtop was little changed from the previous year's model. It was powered by a 97 h.p. 217.8 cu. in. six-cylinder engine. A three-speed manual transmission was standard.

Motor Trend praised the 1950 Plymouth as "a car with riding comfort, handling ease, and good visibility." However, they did note the acceleration left something to be desired.

1950 Plymouth Special Deluxe Convertible

PHOTO: CHRYSLER CORPORATION

1950 Plymouth Special Deluxe Station Wagon

Original Price: $2,372
Number Produced: 2,057
Estimated Number Existing in 1979: 3
Miles per Gallon: 13–20
Common Trouble Spots: none
Availability of Parts: poor
Investment Potential: AA+

Background: The 1950 Special Deluxe station wagon was little changed from the previous year's model. It was powered by a 97 h.p. 217.8 cu. in. six-cylinder engine. A three-speed manual transmission was standard.

The Special Deluxe was one of the best-looking woodies made in 1950. It is both rare and desirable.

1950 Pontiac Chieftain Deluxe Convertible

Original Price: $2,122
Number Produced: N.A.
Estimated Number Existing in 1979: N.A.
Miles per Gallon: 14–19
Common Trouble Spots: none
Availability of Parts: poor–fair
Investment Potential: A

Background: Pontiac buyers could order their Chieftain with either a 90 h.p. 239.2 cu. in. six or a 108 h.p. 268.2 cu. in. eight-cylinder engine. A three-speed manual transmission was standard. Hydra-Matic automatic transmission was available at extra cost.

Most 1950 Pontiacs, 74.1%, came with the eight-cylinder engine, and 64.5% had the automatic.

1950 Pontiac Chieftain Deluxe Convertible

PHOTO: PONTIAC MOTOR DIVISION

1950 Studebaker Champion Regal Deluxe Convertible

Original Price: $1,981
Number Produced: 8,874
Estimated Number Existing in 1979: 14
Miles per Gallon: 17–28
Common Trouble Spots: choke, clutch
Availability of Parts: poor–fair
Investment Potential: AA

Background: The Champion received a new front suspension and a dramatically restyled front end. It certainly was one of the most individualistic-looking cars on the market.

It was powered by an 85 h.p. 169.6 cu. in. six-cylinder engine. A three-speed manual transmission was standard. Overdrive was optional at extra cost.

1950 Studebaker Champion Regal Deluxe Convertible

PHOTO: RICHARD QUINN COLLECTION, STUDEBAKER DRIVERS CLUB

1950 Willys Jeepster Phaeton

PHOTO: JOHN A. CONDE COLLECTION

1950 Studebaker Commander Regal Deluxe Convertible

PHOTO: RICHARD QUINN COLLECTION, STUDEBAKER DRIVERS CLUB

1950 Studebaker Commander Regal Deluxe Convertible

Original Price: $2,329
Number Produced: 2,753
Estimated Number Existing in 1979: 4
Miles per Gallon: 15–25
Common Trouble Spots: choke, clutch
Availability of Parts: poor–fair
Investment Potential: AA

Background: Wow! The bullet-nosed Commander convertible was the wildest-looking production car available in 1950. People loved it. People hated it. But they couldn't ignore it.

The Commander was powered by a 102 h.p. 245.6 cu. in. six-cylinder engine. A three-speed manual transmission was standard. Overdrive and Automatic-Drive automatic transmission were optional at extra cost.

1950 Willys Jeepster Phaeton

Original Price: $1,603
Number Produced: 5,845
Estimated Number Existing in 1979: 15
Miles per Gallon: 18–30
Common Trouble Spots: none
Availability of Parts: poor
Investment Potential: A+

Background: The Jeepster received a new grille and trim for 1950. Early models came with a 63 h.p. 134.2 cu. in. four-cylinder engine. A 72 h.p. 148.4 cu. in. six was optional. In mid-model year, these engines were replaced by a 72 h.p. 134.2 cu. in. four-cylinder and a 75 h.p. 161 cu. in. six-cylinder engine. A three-speed manual transmission was standard. Overdrive was optional at extra cost.

Most 1950 Jeepsters, over 69%, came equipped with a four-cylinder engine.

1951

1951 Buick Roadmaster Convertible

Original Price: $2,981
Number Produced: 2,911
Estimated Number Existing in 1979: 6
Miles per Gallon: 12–17
Common Trouble Spots: none
Availability of Parts: poor–fair
Investment Potential: A+

Background: The Roadmaster convertible received an attractive facelift for 1951. The most noticeable change was a return to a more conservative grille treatment, which enhanced the car's looks considerably.

It was powered by a 152 h.p. 320.2 cu. in. eight-cylinder engine. Dynaflow automatic transmission and a power-operated top were standard.

1951 Buick Roadmaster Convertible

PHOTO: PUBLIC RELATIONS DEPARTMENT, BUICK MOTOR DIVISION

1951 Buick Roadmaster Estate Station Wagon

Original Price: $3,433
Number Produced: 679
Estimated Number Existing in 1979: 2
Miles per Gallon: 11–16
Common Trouble Spots: none
Availability of Parts: poor–fair
Investment Potential: AA+

Background: The new Roadmaster wagon remained pretty much the same as the previous year's model. However, two changes were very noticeable: the flamboyant grille of the 1950 Roadmaster was replaced with a more conservative one, and the portholes (four on each side) moved from the hood back to the front fenders.

It was powered by a 152 h.p. 320.2 cu. in. eight-cylinder engine. Dynaflow automatic transmission was standard.

1951 Buick Special Deluxe Convertible

Original Price: $2,325
Number Produced: 2,099
Estimated Number Existing in 1979: 4
Miles per Gallon: 13–18
Common Trouble Spots: none
Availability of Parts: poor–fair
Investment Potential: A+

Background: Apparently Buick was in a convertible-building mood in 1951. In addition to the Roadmaster and the Super, buyers could also select the new Special Deluxe ragtop. Only a minor chrome variation distinguished it from the slightly more expensive Super; it even had three portholes on each front fender.

1951 Buick Special Deluxe Convertible

PHOTO: PUBLIC RELATIONS DEPARTMENT, BUICK MOTOR DIVISION

It was equipped with a 120 h.p. 263.3 cu. in. eight-cylinder engine. A three-speed manual transmission was standard. Dynaflow automatic transmission was optional at extra cost. Power windows and power top were standard.

1951 Buick Super Convertible

Original Price: $2,476
Number Produced: 8,116
Estimated Number Existing in 1979: 17
Miles per Gallon: 12–18
Common Trouble Spots: none
Availability of Parts: poor–fair
Investment Potential: A+

Background: The '51 Super ragtop was powered by a 124 h.p. 263.3 cu. in. eight-cylinder engine. A three-speed manual transmission was standard. Dynaflow automatic transmission was available at extra cost. The top and windows were power-operated.

Like all Buicks, the Super provided passengers with above-average riding comfort. What *Motor Trend* said in 1951 is true of all the early postwar Buicks: "All in all, the Buick ride is an adventure in luxurious moving about."

1951 Buick Super Convertible

PHOTO: HOWARD AND SHELBY APPLEGATE

1951 Buick Super Estate Station Wagon

Original Price: $2,844
Number Produced: 2,212
Estimated Number Existing in 1979: 4
Miles per Gallon: 12–17
Common Trouble Spots: none
Availability of Parts: poor–fair
Investment Potential: AA+

Background: Once again, the Super Estate wagon outsold the top-of-the-line Roadmaster. It was powered by a 124 h.p. 263.3 cu. in. eight-cylinder engine. A three-speed manual transmission was standard. Dynaflow automatic transmission was optional at extra cost.

Although this good-looking and comfortable car is popular now, there was much less demand for it when it was new or even semi-new; as late as 1961 my mother was able to buy a nice '51 Super wagon from a used-car lot for $69.50.

1951 Cadillac Series 62 Convertible

Original Price: $3,654
Number Produced: 6,117
Estimated Number Existing in 1979: 20
Miles per Gallon: 12–20
Common Trouble Spots: none
Availability of Parts: poor–fair
Investment Potential: A+

Background: The 1951 Series 62 closely resembles the 1950 version; in fact, most people have a hard time telling the two model years apart.

The only engine offered was the 160 h.p. 331 cu. in. V8. An improved Hydra-Matic automatic transmission was standard. Once again, gas mileage was quite good, and so was performance, although some owners complained of rear-end wander at speeds over 70.

1951 Cadillac Series 62 Convertible

PHOTO: CADILLAC MOTOR CAR DIVISION

1951 Chevrolet Styleline Deluxe Convertible

Original Price: $2,030
Number Produced: 20,172
Estimated Number Existing in 1979: 82
Miles per Gallon: 14–20
Common Trouble Spots: none
Availability of Parts: fair–poor
Investment Potential: AA

Background: The 1951 Chevy convertible received only a minor face-lift. Perhaps because of that, and the popularity of "hardtop convertibles," sales were down considerably from the previous year.

It was powered by a 92 h.p. 216.5 cu. in. six-cylinder engine, when equipped with the standard three-speed manual transmission. Over 36% of all '51 Chevrolets came with the optional Powerglide automatic and a 105 h.p. 235.5 cu. in. six.

1951 Chrysler New Yorker Convertible

PHOTO: CHRYSLER HISTORICAL COLLECTION

1951 Chrysler New Yorker Convertible

Original Price: $3,238
Number Produced: est. 1,100
Estimated Number Existing in 1979: 2
Miles per Gallon: 12–17
Common Trouble Spots: automatic transmission
Availability of Parts: poor
Investment Potential: AA

Background: The New Yorker featured a re-styled front end and other minor changes from the 1950 model. It was powered by a new, more powerful Fire Power V8 engine. This 331.1 cu. in. engine could develop 180 h.p. which greatly improved the New Yorker's acceleration and overall performance and helped Chrysler win *Motor Trend's* "Engineering Achievement Award." Fittingly, a New Yorker convertible was chosen as the 1951 Indianapolis 500 pace car. Presto-Matic automatic was standard.

1951 Chrysler Imperial Convertible

Original Price: $4,427
Number Produced: 650
Estimated Number Existing in 1979: 1
Miles per Gallon: 11–15
Common Trouble Spots: automatic transmission
Availability of Parts: poor
Investment Potential: AA

Background: The 1951 Imperial convertible looked a lot like a New Yorker with some of the chrome exorcised from the side.

It came with a 180 h.p. 331.1 cu. in. V8 engine. Prestomatic automatic transmission was standard.

1951 Chrysler Imperial Convertible

PHOTO: CHRYSLER HISTORICAL COLLECTION

1951 Chrysler Windsor Deluxe Convertible

Original Price: $2,741
Number Produced: est. 2,100
Estimated Number Existing in 1979: 5
Miles per Gallon: 13–18
Common Trouble Spots: automatic transmission
Availability of Parts: poor
Investment Potential: A+

Background: The Windsor convertible received a bit more of a face-lift for 1951 than it had for 1950. It still came with a 116 h.p. 250.6 cu. in. six-cylinder engine and Presto-Matic automatic transmission.

It was an attractive car, but a bit on the heavy side (almost 4,000 pounds) to be powered by a six-cylinder engine.

1951 Crosley Convertible

Original Price: $882
Number Produced: 391
Estimated Number Existing in 1979: 3
Miles per Gallon: 25–32
Common Trouble Spots: none
Availability of Parts: poor
Investment Potential: A

Background: The 1951 Crosley convertible was available in either standard or deluxe form (the deluxe models had different trim). It was powered by a 26.5 h.p. 44 cu. in. four-cylinder engine. A three-speed manual transmission was standard. The disc brakes of previous years were replaced with hydraulic ones.

1951 Crosley Super Convertible

PHOTO: CROSLEY AUTOMOBILE CLUB, INC.

1951 Crosley Hotshot Roadster

Original Price: $872
Number Produced: 646 (includes Super Sports)
Estimated Number Existing in 1979: 6 (includes Super Sports)
Miles per Gallon: 25–32
Common Trouble Spots: none
Availability of Parts: poor
Investment Potential: AA

Background: The Crosley Hotshot may not have been the biggest car on the road in 1951, but it certainly was one of the most distinctive. It was powered by a 26.5 h.p. 44 cu. in. four-cylinder engine. A three-speed manual transmission was standard.

1951 Crosley Super Sports Convertible

PHOTO: CROSLEY AUTOMOBILE CLUB, INC.

1951 Crosley Super Sports Convertible

Original Price: $925
Number Produced: 646 (includes Hotshots)
Estimated Number Existing in 1979: 6 (includes Hotshots)
Miles per Gallon: 25–32
Common Trouble Spots: none
Availability of Parts: poor
Investment Potential: AA

Background: Once again, the Super Sports was basically a fancier version of the Hotshot roadster. It was powered by a 26.5 h.p. 44 cu. in. four-cylinder engine. A three-speed manual transmission was standard.

1951 DeSoto Custom Convertible

Original Price: $2,578
Number Produced: est. 1,975
Estimated Number Existing in 1979: 5
Miles per Gallon: 13–18
Common Trouble Spots: none
Availability of Parts: poor
Investment Potential: A

Background: "There's no smoother riding car in America." That's what viewers of the popular TV show "You Bet Your Life" heard during commercials for the '51 DeSoto. The Custom convertible was powered by a 116 h.p. 250.6 cu. in. six-cylinder engine. Tip-Toe Shift automatic transmission was standard.

1951 DeSoto Custom Convertible

1951 Dodge Coronet Convertible

Original Price: $2,329
Number Produced: est. 2,775
Estimated Number Existing in 1979: 7
Miles per Gallon: 13–20
Common Trouble Spots: none
Availability of Parts: poor
Investment Potential: A

Background: The new 1951 Coronet ragtop was powered by a 103 h.p. 230.2 cu. in. six-cylinder engine. A three-speed manual transmission was standard. Gyromatic automatic transmission was optional.

1951 Dodge Coronet Convertible

1951 Dodge Wayfarer Roadster

Original Price: $1,727
Number Produced: 1,002
Estimated Number Existing in 1979: 4
Miles per Gallon: 14–20
Common Trouble Spots: none
Availability of Parts: poor
Investment Potential: A+

Background: This was the last year the Wayfarer roadster was made—unsold ones were sold as 1952 models. Although many people now consider the 1951 the best-looking model, fewer Wayfarers were sold in 1951 than in any previous year.

The Wayfarer came with hydraulic brakes and a 103 h.p. 230.2 cu. in. six-cylinder engine. A three-speed manual transmission was standard. The convertible top was also manually operated.

1951 Dodge Wayfarer Roadster

1951 Ford Custom Convertible

Original Price: $1,948
Number Produced: 40,934
Estimated Number Existing in 1979: 116
Miles per Gallon: 14–20
Common Trouble Spots: none
Availability of Parts: fair–poor
Investment Potential: AA

Background: The most noticeable styling change for the 1951 Ford Custom was the new grille, which made the car look wider. Other changes included a redesigned dash, a new hood ornament, and a different taillight lens.

The Custom convertible came with a 100 h.p. 239.4 cu. in. V8 engine. A three-speed manual transmission was standard. Overdrive and Ford-O-Matic automatic were optional.

1951 Ford Custom Convertible

PHOTO: FORD MOTOR COMPANY

1951 Ford Custom Crestliner

Original Price: $1,595
Number Produced: 8,703
Estimated Number Existing in 1979: 24
Miles per Gallon: 14–20
Common Trouble Spots: none
Availability of Parts: fair–poor
Investment Potential: A+

Background: The styling of the Crestliner coupe was little changed from the previous year's. However, many people believe that the few changes that were made altered the car for the worse.

All Crestliners were equipped with a 100 h.p. 239.4 cu. in. "flathead" V8. A three-speed manual transmission was standard. Overdrive and Ford-O-Matic automatic transmission were optional. Like the 1950 model, it had a special interior and wheel covers.

Buyers had their choice of five exterior color combinations. Most had black vinyl tops, but tops in other colors were also available.

Production of the Crestliner coupe was stopped early in the model year. With the introduction of the Victoria two-door hardtop, Ford no longer needed the Crestliner to compete with other companies' hardtops.

1951 Ford Custom Station Wagon

Original Price: $2,107
Number Produced: 29,017
Estimated Number Existing in 1979: 12
Miles per Gallon: 14–20
Common Trouble Spots: none
Availability of Parts: poor–fair
Investment Potential: AAA

Background: This was the last woodie made by Ford (some purists do not consider it a true woodie because the wood panels were placed over a metal body). The car's compact size and two-doors styling give it a sporty look.

The Custom wagon (often referred to as a "Country Squire") was powered by a 95 h.p. 225.8 cu. in. six-cylinder engine. Over 90% of all '51 Custom wagons came with the optional 100 h.p. 239.4 cu. in. V8. A three-speed manual transmission was standard. Overdrive and Ford-O-Matic automatic transmission were available at extra cost.

Of the 1949 to 1951 Ford wagons, the 1951 is the best. An article that appeared in *Consumer Reports* when the car was new stated: "The 1951 Ford is more solid in construction, quieter running, better riding and better in workmanship than its 1949 and 1950 predecessors."

1951 Frazer Manhattan Convertible

Original Price: $3,075
Number Produced: 131
Estimated Number Existing in 1979: 27
Miles per Gallon: 15–20
Common Trouble Spots: none
Availability of Parts: poor
Investment Potential: AA+

Background: The 1951 Frazer Manhattan ragtop was an attractive but very unpopular car. It was now the only four-door American convertible being produced.

The Manhattan was powered by a 115-hp 226.2 cu. in. six cylinder engine. A three-speed manual transmission and vinyl-and-leather upholstery were standard. Hydra-Matic automatic transmission was a $115 option.

1951 Hudson Commodore Eight Convertible Brougham

Original Price: $3,019
Number Produced: N.A.
Estimated Number Existing in 1979: N.A.
Miles per Gallon: 13–18
Common Trouble Spots: none
Availability of Parts: poor
Investment Potential: AA

Background: The 1951 Commodore Eight convertible came with a 128 h.p. 254 cu. in. eight-cylinder engine. A three-speed manual transmission was standard. Overdrive and Hydra-Matic automatic transmission were optional.

1951 Ford Custom (Country Squire) Station Wagon

PHOTO: FORD MOTOR COMPANY

1951 Hudson Commodore Six Custom Convertible Brougham

Original Price: $2,933
Number Produced: N.A.
Estimated Number Existing in 1979: N.A.
Miles per Gallon: 13–18
Common Trouble Spots: none
Availability of Parts: poor
Investment Potential: AA

Background: The 1951 Commodore Six convertible was powered by a 123 h.p. 262 cu. in. six-cylinder engine. A three-speed manual transmission was standard. Overdrive and Hydra-Matic automatic transmission were optional at extra cost.

1951 Hudson Hornet Six Convertible Brougham

Original Price: $3,019
Number Produced: 43,666 (includes Hornet coupes, sedans, and Hollywoods)
Estimated Number Existing in 1979: 129 (includes Hornet coupes, sedans, and Hollywoods)
Miles per Gallon: 10–17
Common Trouble Spots: none
Availability of Parts: poor
Investment Potential: AAA

Background: The Hornet Six was the hottest six-cylinder car in the country in 1951. It was powered by a 145 h.p. 308 cu. in. high-compression "H-Power" six-cylinder engine. A three-speed manual transmission and power windows were standard. Overdrive and Hydra-Matic automatic transmission were optional at extra cost.

Buyers had their choice of a black, maroon, or tan top. Upholstery was offered in red or blue leather, with harmonizing leather-grain trim. The hood ornament was plated with chrome and gold.

The Hornet was a legend at stock-car races in the early 1950s for its exceptional performance and handling. This racing reputation and its good looks make the 1951 Hornet convertible one of the most desirable of all postwar Hudsons.

1951 Hudson Hornet Six Convertible Brougham

PHOTO: JOHN A. CONDE COLLECTION

1951 Hudson Pacemaker Six Convertible Brougham

Original Price: $2,573
Number Produced: N.A.
Estimated Number Existing in 1979: N.A.
Miles per Gallon: 13–18
Common Trouble Spots: none
Availability of Parts: poor–fair
Investment Potential: AA

Background: The new Pacemaker Six convertible was powered by a 112 h.p. 232 cu. in. six-cylinder engine. A three-speed manual transmission was standard. Overdrive and Drive Master and Super Matic automatic transmissions were optional at extra cost.

1951 Hudson Super Six Convertible Brougham

Original Price: $2,753
Number Produced: N.A.
Estimated Number Existing in 1979: N.A.
Miles per Gallon: 13–18
Common Trouble Spots: none
Availability of Parts: poor
Investment Potential: AA

Background: The '51 Super Six convertible was powered by a 123 h.p. 262 cu. in. six-cylinder engine. A three-speed manual transmission was standard. Overdrive and Drive Master and Super Matic automatic transmissions were optional at extra cost.

1951 King Midget Convertible

Original Price: est. $550
Number Produced: 40
Estimated Number Existing in 1979: 2
Miles per Gallon: 50–90
Common Trouble Spots: transmission, "V" belts
Availability of Parts: good
Investment Potential: A

Background: This was the first of the two-passenger King Midget ragtops (prior to this, the King Midget was a one-passenger car). The "second series" 1951 King Midget was powered by a nine-horsepower 29 cu. in. Kohler one-cylinder engine. Automatic transmission was standard.

1951 Lincoln Cosmopolitan Convertible

Original Price: $3,950
Number Produced: 877
Estimated Number Existing in 1979: 2
Miles per Gallon: 13–17
Common Trouble Spots: automatic transmission
Availability of Parts: poor
Investment Potential: A+

Background: The new Cosmopolitan convertible looked pretty much the same as the previous year's model. It was powered by a 154 h.p. 336.7 cu. in. eight-cylinder engine. A three-speed manual transmission was standard. Overdrive and Hydra-Matic automatic transmission were optional.

1951 Lincoln Cosmopolitan Convertible

PHOTO: FORD MOTOR COMPANY

1951 Mercury Convertible

Original Price: $2,412
Number Produced: 6,759
Estimated Number Existing in 1979: 14
Miles per Gallon: 14–18
Common Trouble Spots: none
Availability of Parts: poor–fair
Investment Potential: AAA

Background: The Mercury ragtop received a minor but pleasing face-lift for 1951. It was powered by a 112 h.p. 255.4 cu. in. eight-cylinder engine. A three-speed manual transmission was standard. Overdrive and Merc-O-matic automatic transmission were optional.

1951 Mercury Convertible

PHOTO: FORD MOTOR COMPANY

1951 Mercury Coupe

Original Price: $1,875
Number Produced: 142,168
Estimated Number Existing in 1979: 304
Miles per Gallon: 14–18
Common Trouble Spots: none
Availability of Parts: fair–poor
Investment Potential: AA

Background: The popular Mercury coupe was changed just enough to make it slightly less popular with cultists than the 1949–50 models. However, it retained much of the flavor of the previous two years and so is in demand. It is an attractive car in its own right.

The Mercury coupe was powered by a 112 h.p. 255.4 cu. in. eight-cylinder engine. A three-speed manual transmission was standard. Overdrive and Merc-O-Matic automatic transmission were optional.

1951 Mercury Station Wagon

Original Price: $2,561
Number Produced: 3,812
Estimated Number Existing in 1979: 8
Miles per Gallon: 14–17
Common Trouble Spots: none
Availability of Parts: poor–fair
Investment Potential: AA+

Background: The attractive '51 Mercury wagon was powered by a 112 h.p. 255.4 cu. in. eight-cylinder engine. A three-speed manual transmission was standard. Merc-O-Matic automatic and a manual with overdrive were optional at extra cost.

1951 Muntz Jet Convertible

Original Price: est. $5,000
Number Produced: 42
Estimated Number Existing in 1979: 3
Miles per Gallon: 12–17
Common Trouble Spots: none
Availability of Parts: poor–fair
Investment Potential: AA+

Background: The 1951 Muntz Jet was powered by a 154 h.p. 336.7 cu. in. V8 engine. Hydra-Matic automatic transmission, padded dash, seat belts, radio, insulated bins in the rear armrests, and a vinyl interior were standard. It had a removable padded steel top.

1951 Nash Rambler Custom Convertible

Original Price: $1,837
Number Produced: 14,881
Estimated Number Existing in 1979: 34
Miles per Gallon: 16–25
Common Trouble Spots: none
Availability of Parts: poor
Investment Potential: A

Background: The new Rambler convertible looked virtually the same as last year's model. It was powered by a 82 h.p. 172.6 cu. in. six-cylinder engine. A three-speed manual transmission was standard. Overdrive was optional at extra cost.

1951 Nash Healey Convertible

Original Price: $4,063
Number Produced: 104
Estimated Number Existing in 1979: 10
Miles per Gallon: 16–28
Common Trouble Spots: none
Availability of Parts: poor
Investment Potential: AAA

Background: The Nash Healey sports car was introduced in early 1951. This attractive two-passenger car featured an adjustable steering wheel, leather upholstery, and an aluminum body.

It was powered by a 125 h.p. 234.8 cu. in. six-cylinder engine. A three-speed manual transmission with overdrive was standard.

1951 Oldsmobile 98 Convertible

Original Price: $2,772
Number Produced: 4,468
Estimated Number Existing in 1979: 5
Miles per Gallon: 14–18
Common Trouble Spots: none
Availability of Parts: poor–fair
Investment Potential: A+

Background: Styling changes were kept to a minimum on the new Olds 98. It was powered by a 135 h.p. 303.7 cu. in. V8 engine. A three-speed manual transmission was standard. Hydra-Matic automatic transmission was optional at extra cost.

1951 Nash Healey Convertible

PHOTO: JOHN A. CONDE COLLECTION

1951 Oldsmobile 98 Convertible

PHOTO: OLDSMOBILE DIVISION

1951 Oldsmobile Super 88 Convertible

Original Price: $2,290
Number Produced: 3,854
Estimated Number Existing in 1979: 4
Miles per Gallon: 14–18
Common Trouble Spots: none
Availability of Parts: poor–fair
Investment Potential: A+

Background: The Super 88 was powered by a 135 h.p. 303.7 cu. in. V8 engine. A three-speed manual transmission was standard. Hydra-Matic automatic transmission was optional at extra cost.

1951 Oldsmobile Super 88 Convertible

PHOTO: OLDSMOBILE DIVISION

1951 Packard 250 Convertible

Original Price: $3,400
Number Produced: N.A.
Estimated Number Existing in 1979: N.A.
Miles per Gallon: 11–17
Common Trouble Spots: none
Availability of Parts: poor–fair
Investment Potential: A+

Background: The entire Packard line was restyled for 1951. The most attractive model was the new 250 convertible. It was powered by a 150 h.p. 327 cu. in. eight-cylinder engine. A three-speed manual transmission was standard, but not very popular. Overdrive and (for $185) Ultramatic automatic transmission were optional.

1951 Packard 250 Convertible

PHOTO: RICHARD QUINN COLLECTION

1951 Plymouth Cranbrook Convertible

Original Price: $1,982
Number Produced: 7,825 (est.)
Estimated Number Existing in 1979: 13
Miles per Gallon: 14–20
Common Trouble Spots: brakes, valves
Availability of Parts: poor
Investment Potential: A

Background: The new Cranbrook convertible looked much the same as the 1950 Special Deluxe. It was powered by a 97 h.p. 217.8 cu. in. six-cylinder engine. A three-speed manual transmission was standard.

1951 Pontiac Chieftain Deluxe Convertible

Original Price: $2,122
Number Produced: N.A.
Estimated Number Existing in 1979: N.A.
Miles per Gallon: 14–19
Common Trouble Spots: none
Availability of Parts: poor–fair
Investment Potential: A+

Background: Failing to take advantage of their Silver Anniversary, Pontiac designed a Chieftain convertible for 1951 that was much the same as the 1950 model. Buyers could order either a 96 h.p. 239.2 cu. in. six-cylinder or a 116 h.p. 268.4 cu. in. eight-cylinder engine. A three-speed manual transmission was standard. Hydra-Matic automatic transmission was optional at extra cost.

Most 1951 Pontiacs, 85.5%, came with the eight-cylinder engine, and 88.2% had the automatic.

1951 Pontiac Chieftain Deluxe Convertible

PHOTO: PONTIAC MOTOR DIVISION

1951 Studebaker Champion Regal Convertible

Original Price: $2,037
Number Produced: 4,437
Estimated Number Existing in 1979: 8
Miles per Gallon: 17–28
Common Trouble Spots: none
Availability of Parts: poor–fair
Investment Potential: AA

Background: The 1951 Champion looked like the kind of car Flash Gordon would drive. It was powered by an 85 h.p. 169.6 cu. in. six-cylinder engine. A three-speed manual transmission was standard. Overdrive and Automatic-Drive automatic transmission were optional at extra cost.

1951 Studebaker Commander Convertible

Original Price: $2,244
Number Produced: 3,590
Estimated Number Existing in 1979: 6
Miles per Gallon: 14–25
Common Trouble Spots: none
Availability of Parts: poor–fair
Investment Potential: AA

Background: The unique, bullet-nose styling of the 1951 Commander ragtop made it quite a head-turner in its day. It was powered by a 120 h.p. 232.6 cu. in. V8 engine. In addition to delivering good gas mileage, it had a top speed of over 93 miles per hour. A three-speed manual transmission was standard. Overdrive and Automatic-Drive automatic transmission were optional at extra cost.

A nylon-with-vinyl-leatherette interior was standard. Leather upholstery was optional. Each door had a "weather-tight" storage pocket.

1951 Studebaker Commander Convertible

1951 Willys Jeepster Phaeton

Original Price: $1,597
Number Produced: see 1950 Jeepster
Estimated Number Existing in 1979: see 1950 Jeepster
Miles per Gallon: 18–30
Common Trouble Spots: none
Availability of Parts: poor
Investment Potential: A+

Background: The "new" Jeepsters were really just unsold 1950 models. A 72 h.p. 134.2 cu. in. OHV four-cylinder engine and a three-speed manual transmission were standard. Available at extra cost was a 75 h.p. 161 cu. in. overhead valve six and overdrive.

1952

1952 Buick Roadmaster Convertible

Original Price: $3,428
Number Produced: 2,402
Estimated Number Existing in 1979: 6
Miles per Gallon: 12–17
Common Trouble Spots: brakes
Availability of Parts: poor–fair
Investment Potential: A+

Background: The top-of-the-line Roadmaster convertible was powered by a 170 h.p. 320.2 cu. in. eight-cylinder engine (with four-barrel carburetor). Sales literature claimed that this engine was "silent as a moonbeam." Dynaflow automatic transmission, power windows, and power front seat were standard. As in previous years, passenger comfort was excellent.

1952 Buick Roadmaster Convertible

PHOTO: PUBLIC RELATIONS DEPARTMENT, BUICK MOTOR DIVISION

1952 Buick Roadmaster Estate Station Wagon

Original Price: $3,949
Number Produced: 359
Estimated Number Existing in 1979: 1
Miles per Gallon: 11–16
Common Trouble Spots: brakes
Availability of Parts: poor–fair
Investment Potential: AA+

Background: With the exception of some relatively minor trim changes, the new Roadmaster wagon looked virtually the same as the 1951. It was powered by a 170 h.p. 320.2 cu. in. eight-cylinder engine with four-barrel carburetor. Dynaflow automatic transmission was standard.

1952 Buick Special Deluxe Convertible

Original Price: $2,615
Number Produced: 600
Estimated Number Existing in 1979: 1
Miles per Gallon: 13–18
Common Trouble Spots: brakes
Availability of Parts: poor–fair
Investment Potential: A+

Background: The Special Deluxe looked very similar to the slightly higher-priced Super. Despite the similarity in appearance, it was significantly less popular with buyers.

The standard engine was a 120 h.p. 263.3 cu. in. straight eight-cylinder engine. Buyers had their choice of a three-speed manual transmission or, at extra cost, Dynaflow automatic.

1952 Buick Super Convertible

Original Price: $2,848
Number Produced: 6,904
Estimated Number Existing in 1979: 18
Miles per Gallon: 13–18
Common Trouble Sport: brakes
Availability of Parts: poor–fair
Investment Potential: A+

Background: Three portholes on the front fenders and a shorter wheelbase were the most noticeable differences between the new Super and the more expensive Roadmaster convertible.

The Super ragtop came with a 124 h.p. 263.3 cu. in. eight-cylinder engine. A three-speed manual transmission was standard. Dynaflow automatic transmission was a popular extra-cost option.

1952 Buick Super Convertible

PHOTO: PUBLIC RELATIONS DEPARTMENT, BUICK MOTOR DIVISION

1952 Buick Super Estate Station Wagon

Original Price: $3,272
Number Produced: 1,641
Estimated Number Existing in 1979: 4
Miles per Gallon: 12–17
Common Trouble Spots: brakes
Availability of Parts: poor–fair
Investment Potential: AA+

Background: The new Super wagon was little changed from the previous year's model. It was powered by a 124 h.p. 263.3 cu. in. eight-cylinder engine. A three-speed manual transmission was standard. Dynaflow automatic transmission was available at extra cost.

1952 Cadillac Series 62 Convertible

Original Price: $4,163
Number Produced: 6,400
Estimated Number Existing in 1979: 22
Miles per Gallon: 12–18
Common Trouble Spots: carburetor
Availability of Parts: poor–fair
Investment Potential: A+

Background: This was Cadillac's Golden Anniversary year. Most of the changes to the styling were minor; however, enough improvements were made in the car's handling and performance to make it *Motor Trend*'s "Car of the Year".

The Series 62 was powered by a 190 h.p. 331 cu. in. V8 engine. The only transmission offered was Hydra-Matic Dual Range automatic. Power steering was available for the first time on Cadillacs.

1952 Cadillac Series 62 Convertible

PHOTO: CADILLAC MOTOR CAR DIVISION

1952 Chevrolet Styleline Deluxe Convertible

Original Price: $1,939
Number Produced: 11,975
Estimated Number Existing in 1979: 56
Miles per Gallon: 14–20
Common Trouble Spots: piston rings, valves
Availability of Parts: fair–poor
Investment Potential: AA

Background: The '52 Deluxe ragtop was powered by a 92 h.p. 216.5 cu. in. six when equipped with the standard three-speed manual transmission. About 35% of all 1952 Chevrolets came with the optional Powerglide automatic and a 105 h.p. 235.5 cu. in. six.

New engine mountings were added this year to help reduce road noise and vibration. An automatic choke was available on the 235.5 cu. in. engine.

Buyers had their choice of fifteen exterior color combinations; leather upholstery was available. A special ornamental steering wheel was offered for $19.10.

1952 Chevrolet Styleline Deluxe Convertible

1952 Chrysler New Yorker Convertible

Original Price: $4,064
Number Produced: est. 1,100
Estimated Number Existing in 1979: 2
Miles per Gallon: 12–17
Common Trouble Spots: automatic transmission
Availability of Parts: poor
Investment Potential: AA

Background: You had to look awfully close to tell the New Yorker from last year's model—little about the car was changed. It still had the 180 h.p. 331.1 cu. in. Fire Power Hemi eight-cylinder engine. Fluid-matic Drive automatic transmission was standard. Fluid Torque Drive automatic was optional.

1952 Chrysler Windsor Deluxe Convertible

Original Price: $3,187
Production Number: est. 2,100
Estimated Numbneer in 1979: 4
Miles per Gallon: 12–18
Common Trouble Spots: automatic transmission
Availability of Parts: poor
Investment Potential: A+

Background: If you'd liked the 1951 Windsor, you liked the 1952. The new Windsor was virtually unchanged from the previous year. However, it did receive a new 264.5 cu. in. 119 h.p. six-cylinder engine. This engine improved the Windsor's acceleration and overall performance.

Fluid-Matic Drive automatic transmission was standard. Fluid Torque Drive automatic was optional.

1952 Crosley Convertible

Original Price: $1,036
Production Number: 146
Estimated Number Existing in 1979: 2
Miles per Gallon: 25–32
Common Trouble Spots: none
Availability of Parts: poor
Investment Potential: A

Background: This was the last year for the Crosley convertible. It was also the worst sales year for the little ragtop since 1946.

The Crosley was powered by a 26.5 h.p. 44 cu. in. four-cylinder engine. A three-speed manual transmission was standard.

1952 Crosley Hotshot Roadster

Original Price: $948
Production Number: 358 (includes Super Sports)
Estimated Number Existing in 1979: 6 (includes Super Sports)
Miles per Gallon: 25–32
Common Trouble Spots: none
Availability of Parts: poor
Investment Potential: AA

Background: This was the last year for the sporty Hotshot. It came with a 26.5 h.p. 44 cu. in. four-cylinder engine. A three-speed manual transmission was standard.

1952 Crosley Super Sports Convertible

Original Price: $1,029
Production Number: 358 (includes Hotshots)
Estimated Number Existing in 1979: 6 (includes Hotshots)
Miles per Gallon: 25–32
Common Trouble Spots: none
Availability of Parts: poor
Investment Potential: AA

Background: For only $81 more than the Hotshot, buyers could order the Super Sports. It came with a 26.5 h.p. 44 cu. in. four-cylinder engine. A three-speed manual transmission was standard.

1952 DeSoto Custom Convertible

Original Price: $2,976
Production Number: est. 1,975
Estimated Number Existing in 1979: 4
Miles per Gallon: 13–18
Common Trouble Spots: none
Availability of Parts: poor
Investment Potential: A+

Background: About the only way to tell the '52 Custom ragtop from the previous year's model was to look at the word DeSoto above the grille. The 1951 used script lettering; the 1952 used block lettering.

The Custom was powered by a 116 h.p. 250.6 cu. in. six-cylinder engine. Tip-Toe Shift automatic transmission (with fluid drive) was standard.

1952 DeSoto Firedome Eight Convertible

Original Price: $3,161
Production Number: 850
Estimated Number Existing in 1979: 2
Miles per Gallon: 12–18
Common Trouble Spots: valves
Availability of Parts: poor
Investment Potential: A+

Background: The '52 Firedome ragtop came with DeSoto's new "Firedome" 160 h.p. 276.1 cu. in V8 engine. A three-speed manual transmission was standard. Overdrive and two Tip-Toe Shift automatic transmissions, one with fluid drive and one with fluid torque converter, were optional. Other options included power brakes, electric windows, and (for $10.34) a "Jiffy Jet" windshield washer.

Despite the big new V8, and even functional air scoops on the hood, the '52 Firedome convertible did not have a great deal of appeal. *Motor Trend* was right when they described the '52 DeSoto as having "an engine ten years ahead of the rest of the car."

1952 Dodge Coronet Convertible

Original Price: $2,679
Production Number: est. 2,775
Estimated Number Existing in 1979: 9
Miles per Gallon: 13–20
Common Trouble Spots: none
Availability of Parts: poor
Investment Potential: A

Background: Dodge sales literature proclaimed "more new beauty in fifty-two." Yet, except for a few very minor changes, the 1952 Coronet ragtop looked identical to the 1951 model. It came with a 103 h.p. 230.2 cu. in. six-cylinder engine. A three-speed manual transmission and two-speed electric windshield wipers were standard. Gyromatic automatic transmission was optional at extra cost.

1952 Dodge Coronet Convertible

1952 Dodge Wayfarer Roadster

Original Price: $1,942
Production Number: (see 1951 Wayfarer)
Estimated Number Existing in 1979: (see 1951 Wayfarer)
Miles per Gallon: 14–20
Common Trouble Spots: none
Availability of Parts: poor
Investment Potential: A+

Background: This was just an unsold 1951 model. It was powered by a 103 h.p. 230.2 cu. in. six-cylinder engine. A three-speed manual transmission was standard.

1952 Ford Crestline Sunliner Convertible

Original Price: $2,027
Production Number: 22,534
Estimated Number Existing in 1979: 64
Miles per Gallon: 14–19
Common Trouble Spots: carburetor, cooling system, engine bearings
Availability of Parts: fair
Investment Potential: A+

Background: Ford came out with new styling in 1952 as part of its strategy to outsell Chevrolet. *Business Week* reported that Ford's "idea was to make Ford 'the most wanted car.' It hopes to generate enough desire for Fords on the part of car buyers so that when the freeze [by the National Production Authority] is off, they will switch their brand loyalty."

It was powered by a 110 h.p. 239.4 cu. in. V8. A three-speed manual was standard. Overdrive and Ford-O-Matic automatic transmission were optional.

Other new features included a hidden fuel filler behind the rear license plate and a one-piece windshield.

The 1952 Ford was available in twenty-two colors.

1952 Ford Crestline Sunliner Convertible

1952 Hudson Commodore Eight Convertible Brougham

Original Price: $3,318
Number Produced: N.A.
Estimated Number Existing in 1979: N.A.
Miles per Gallon: 13–18
Common Trouble Spots: none
Availability of Parts: poor
Investment Potential: AA

Background: Hudson's only eight-cylinder in 1952 was the Commodore. It came with a 128 h.p. 254 cu. in. engine. A three-speed manual transmission was standard. Overdrive and Hydra-Matic automatic transmission were optional.

1952 Hudson Commodore Six Convertible Brougham

Original Price: $3,224
Number Produced: N.A.
Estimated Number Existing in 1979: N.A.
Miles per Gallon: 13–18
Common Trouble Spots: none
Availability of Parts: poor
Investment Potential: AA

Background: The 1952 Commodore Six convertible was powered by a 127 h.p. 262 cu. in. six-cylinder engine. A three-speed manual transmission was standard. Overdrive and Hydra-Matic automatic transmission were optional at extra cost.

1952 Hudson Hornet Six Convertible Brougham

Original Price: $3,318
Number Produced: 35,921 (includes Hornet Coupes, Sedans, and Hollywoods)
Estimated Number Existing in 1979: 45 (includes Hornet Coupes, Sedans, and Hollywoods)
Miles per Gallon: 10–17
Common Trouble Spots: none
Availability of Parts: poor
Investment Potential: AAA

Background: The "hot" Hudson in 1952 was the Hornet. It made a winning name for itself in stock-car race after stock-car race.

The Hornet came with a 145 h.p. 308 cu. in. six-cylinder engine. A three-speed manual transmission was standard. Overdrive and Hydra-Matic automatic transmission were optional at extra cost. Other options included an electric clock, an underseat heater, a hydraulic jack, and fog lights.

1952 Hudson Pacemaker Six Convertible Brougham

Original Price: $2,790
Number Produced: N.A.
Estimated Number Existing in 1979: N.A.
Miles per Gallon: 13–18
Common Trouble Spots: none
Availability of Parts: poor
Investment Potential: AA

Background: The 1952 Pacemaker ragtop came with a 112 h.p. 232 cu. in. six-cylinder engine. A three-speed manual transmission was standard. Overdrive and Hydra-Matic automatic transmission were optional at extra cost.

1952 Hudson Wasp Convertible Brougham

Original Price: $3,026
Number Produced: N.A.
Estimated Number Existing in 1979: N.A.
Miles per Gallon: 13–18
Common Trouble Spots: none
Availability of Parts: poor
Investment Potential: AA

Background: The new Wasp convertible was powered by a 127 h.p. 262 cu. in. six-cylinder engine. A three-speed manual transmission was standard. Overdrive and Hydra-Matic automatic transmission were optional at extra cost.

1952 Hudson Wasp Convertible

PHOTO: JOHN A. CONDE COLLECTION

1952 King Midget Convertible

Original Price: est. $550
Number Produced: N.A.
Estimated Number Existing in 1979: N.A.
Miles per Gallon: 50–90
Common Trouble Spots: transmission, "V" belts
Availability of Parts: good
Investment Potential: A

Background: The little 52 King Midget ragtop was powered by a 9 h.p. 29 cu. in. one-cylinder engine. Automatic transmission was standard.

This car was very popular with college students and others seeking extremely economical transportation.

1952 Lincoln Capri Convertible

Original Price: $3,665
Number Produced: 1,191
Estimated Number Existing in 1979: 2
Miles per Gallon: 12–19
Common Trouble Spots: automatic transmission
Availability of Parts: poor
Investment Potential: A+

Background: This was the first year for the Capri convertible. It was powered by a 154 h.p. 336.7 cu. in. eight-cylinder engine. A three-speed manual transmission was standard. Overdrive and Hydra-Matic automatic transmission were optional at extra cost.

The 1952 Capri convertible was a good-looking car and handled well (although tires tended to squeal even at low speeds). Fiberglass insulation was used under the hood for a quieter ride.

Among the optional accessories were power windows, nylon or plastic seat covers, a grille guard, windshield washer, an outside rearview mirror, and a spotlight.

1952 Lincoln Capri Convertible

PHOTO: FORD MOTOR COMPANY

1952 Mercury Monterey Convertible

Original Price: $2,370
Number Produced: 5,261
Estimated Number Existing in 1979: 6
Miles per Gallon: 14–18
Common Trouble Spots: none
Availability of Parts: poor–fair
Investment Potential: A+

Background: This was the first year for the Monterey convertible. Mercury now shared its basic body with Ford rather than with Lincoln as it had for the previous three years.

It was powered by a 125 h.p. 255.4 cu. in. eight-cylinder engine. A three-speed manual transmission was standard. Overdrive and Merc-O-Matic automatic transmission were optional.

1952 Muntz Jet Convertible

Original Price: est. $5,000
Number Produced: est. 81
Estimated Number Existing in 1979: 5
Miles per Gallon: 12–17
Common Trouble Spots: none
Availability of Parts: poor–fair
Investment Potential: AA+

Background: The '52 Muntz Jet convertible was powered by a 154 h.p. 336.7 cu. in. V8 engine. Hydra-Matic automatic transmission, padded dash, seat belts, radio and a vinyl interior were standard. It had a removable padded steel top. The gas filler was located in the trunk. No options were offered.

1952 Nash Healey Convertible

Original Price: est. $5,000
Number Produced: 150
Estimated Number Existing in 1979: 15
Miles per Gallon: 16–28
Common Trouble Spots: none
Availability of Parts: poor
Investment Potential: AAA

Background: The attractive Nash Healey was restyled for 1952 by the famous designer Pinin Farina. It had an aluminum body.

Early 1952 Nash Healeys were powered by a 125 h.p. 234.8 cu. in. six-cylinder. Later models had a 135 h.p. 252.6 cu. in. six-cylinder engine. A three-speed manual transmission was standard.

1952 Nash Healey Convertible

PHOTO: JOHN A. CONDE COLLECTION

1952 Mercury Monterey Convertible

PHOTO: FORD MOTOR COMPANY

1952 Nash Rambler Custom Convertible

Original Price: $1,833
Number Produced: 3,108
Estimated Number Existing in 1979: 9
Miles per Gallon: 16–25
Common Trouble Spots: none
Availability of Parts: poor
Investment Potential: A

Background: The '52 Rambler ragtop was powered by a 82 h.p. 172.6 cu. in. six-cylinder engine. A three-speed manual was standard. Overdrive was optional at extra cost.

1952 Oldsmobile 98 Convertible

Original Price: $3,229
Number Produced: 3,544
Estimated Number Existing in 1979: 4
Miles per Gallon: 14–17
Common Trouble Spots: automatic transmission
Availability of Parts: poor–fair
Investment Potential: A+

Background: Oldsmobile's top-of-the-line 98 convertible was little changed from the previous year's model. It came with a 160 h.p. 303.7 V8 engine. A three-speed manual transmission was standard. Hydra-Matic transmission was optional at extra cost.

Available for the first time was Autronic Eye. This device automatically dimmed the car's headlights when another auto approached from the other direction.

1952 Oldsmobile 98 Convertible

PHOTO: OLDSMOBILE DIVISION

1952 Oldsmobile Super 88 Convertible

Original Price: $2,833
Number Produced: 5,162
Estimated Number Existing in 1979: 5
Miles per Gallon: 14–18
Common Trouble Spots: automatic transmission
Availability of Parts: poor–fair
Investment Potential: A+

Background: The Super 88 was powered by a 160 h.p. 303.7 cu. in. V8 engine. A three-speed manual transmission was standard. An improved Hydra-Matic automatic transmission was available at extra cost. A new option was the Autronic Eye automatic headlight dimmer.

Motor Trend clocked a Super 88 at over 105 mph. They called it "one of the fastest cars on the road today."

1952 Oldsmobile Super 88 Convertible

PHOTO: OLDSMOBILE DIVISION

1952 Packard 250 Convertible

Original Price: $3,450
Number Produced: N.A.
Estimated Number Existing in 1979: N.A.
Miles per Gallon: 11–17
Common Trouble Spots: none
Availability of Parts: poor–fair
Investment Potential: A+

Background: The biggest change in the Packard's styling from the previous year's model was the hood ornament. The '52 250 softtop was powered by a 150 h.p. 327 cu. in. eight-cylinder engine. A three-speed manual transmission was standard. Overdrive and Ultramatic automatic transmission were optional at extra cost.

1952 Packard 250 Convertible

PHOTO: RICHARD QUINN COLLECTION

1952 Plymouth Cranbrook Convertible

Original Price: $2,143
Number Produced: 7,825
Estimated Number Existing in 1979: 19
Miles per Gallon: 14–20
Common Trouble Spots: brakes, valves
Availability of Parts: poor
Investment Potential: A

Background: For all practical purposes, the "new" '52 Cranbrook was the same as the "old" 1951 model. It was powered by a 97 h.p. 217.8 cu. in. six-cylinder engine. A three-speed manual transmission was standard. Overdrive was available later in the model year.

As before, the '52 Plymouth had a superior ride and roomy interior (for its size). Electric windshield wipers were standard. Tinted glass was one of the options.

With a 0-to-60 time of over 22 seconds, it was certainly not one of the hottest cars on the road. But it was kind of cute.

1952 Pontiac Chieftain Deluxe Convertible

Original Price: $2,500
Number Produced: N.A.
Estimated Number Existing in 1979: N.A.
Miles per Gallon: 14–20
Common Trouble Spots: none
Availability of Parts: poor–fair
Investment Potential: A

Background: For the third straight year, the Chieftain received little change in styling. It was available with either a 100 h.p. 239.2 cu. in. six or a 118 h.p. 268.4 cu. in. eight-cylinder engine. A three-speed manual transmission was standard. An improved dual-range Hydra-Matic automatic transmission was optional. Most 1952 Pontiac buyers, 92.7%, ordered the eight-cylinder engine, and 88.5% bought the automatic.

The Chieftain Deluxe convertible was available in matching exterior and interior color combinations. One of the options offered was a power-operated radio antenna.

1952 Pontiac Chieftain Deluxe Convertible

PHOTO: PONTIAC MOTOR DIVISION

1952 Studebaker Champion Regal Convertible

Original Price: $2,257
Number Produced: 1,379
Estimated Number Existing in 1979: 2
Miles per Gallon: 17–28
Common Trouble Spots: none
Availability of Parts: poor–fair
Investment Potential: A+

Background: This was the last year for the Champion convertible. It was a much more conventional-looking car than the previous year's model. The Champion was powered by an 85 h.p. 169.6 cu. in. six-cylinder engine. A three-speed manual transmission was standard. Overdrive and an automatic transmission were optional at extra cost.

1952 Studebaker Commander Regal Convertible

Original Price: $2,531
Number Produced: 1,632
Estimated Number Existing in 1979: 3
Miles per Gallon: 15–23
Common Trouble Spots: piston rings
Availability of Parts: poor–fair
Investment Potential: A+

Background: Studebaker's top-of-the-line Commander convertible looked a lot tamer than last year's model. It was powered by a 120 h.p. 232.6 cu. in. V8 engine. In terms of acceleration, it was the fifth fastest car in 1952—it had a top speed of nearly 98 miles per hour. A three-speed manual transmission was standard. Overdrive and an automatic transmission were optional at extra cost.

Styling and economy were the two features of the '52 Commander ragtop emphasized by Studebaker's advertising; an ad of the period stated: "Every clean-lined inch of this trim, sleek Studebaker convertible is designed to cut your driving costs."

1952 Studebaker Commander Regal Convertible

PHOTO: RICHARD QUINN COLLECTION, STUDEBAKER DRIVERS CLUB

1953

1953 Buick Roadmaster Convertible

Original Price: $3,506
Number Produced: 3,318
Estimated Number Existing in 1979: 11
Miles per Gallon: 12–18
Common Trouble Spots: automatic transmission, brakes
Availability of Parts: poor–fair
Investment Potential: A+

Background: The '53 Roadmaster convertible was overshadowed by the beautiful Skylark. Although similar in the front, it lacked the "dream car's" charisma.

It was powered by a 188 h.p. 322 cu. in. V8 engine. Dynaflow automatic transmission was standard. Skylark chromed wire wheels were an expensive option.

The 1953 Roadmaster handled better than the previous year's model, but riding comfort wasn't as good.

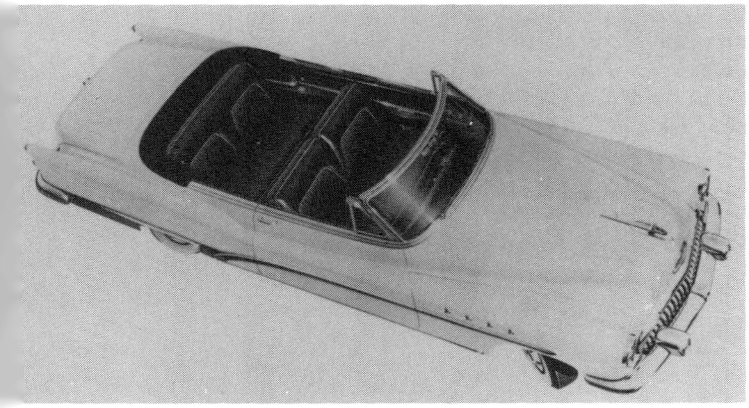

1953 Buick Roadmaster Convertible

PHOTO: PUBLIC RELATIONS, BUICK MOTOR DIVISION

1953 Buick Roadmaster Estate Station Wagon

Original Price: $4,031
Number Produced: 670
Estimated Number Existing in 1979: 3
Miles per Gallon: 10–17
Common Trouble Spots: automatic transmission, brakes
Availability of Parts: poor–fair
Investment Potential: AA+

Background: The 1953 Roadmaster Estate just might be one of the best-looking woodies of the decade—especially when equipped with the optional chromed wire wheels. Unfortunately, it was not very popular when new.

It was powered by a 188 h.p. 322 cu. in. V8 engine. Dynaflow automatic transmission was standard.

1953 Buick Skylark Convertible

Original Price: $5,500
Number Produced: 1,690
Estimated Number Existing in 1979: 40
Miles per Gallon: 12–18
Common Trouble Spots: automatic transmission, brakes
Availability of Parts: poor–fair
Investment Potential: AAA+

Background: The 1953 Skylark was a beautiful and distinctive "dream car." It was powered by a 188 h.p. 322 cu. in. V8. Dynaflow automatic transmission, tinted glass, chromed wire wheels, power brakes, power steering, and even a power antenna were standard.

A high price tag added to the car's "class appeal." It

also helped to keep production down—not a whole lot of people were willing to pay over five grand just to see their name in a medallion in the center of the Skylark steering wheel.

Still, the '53 Skylark was, and remains, a beautiful sight to behold. From its low windshield (chopped three inches to give it a customized look) and its attractive headlights (patterned after the XP-300 experimental car) to its bold taillights (similar to those used on the famous LeSabre dream car), the 1953 Skylark was a car Buick could be proud of.

1953 Buick Skylark Convertible

PHOTO: PUBLIC RELATIONS DEPARTMENT, BUICK MOTOR DIVISION

1953 Buick Special Convertible

Original Price: $2,553
Number Produced: 4,282
Estimated Number Existing in 1979: 14
Miles per Gallon: 13–18
Common Trouble Spots: automatic transmission, brakes
Availability of Parts: poor–fair
Investment Potential: A+

Background: Once again, Buick's lowest-priced convertible was the Special. It was powered by a 130 h.p. 263 cu. in. eight-cylinder engine (this was the last year for Buick's straight eight engine). A three-speed manual transmission was standard. Dynaflow automatic transmission was a popular option.

1953 Buick Special Convertible

1953 Buick Super Convertible

Original Price: $3,002
Number Produced: 6,701
Estimated Number Existing in 1979: 23
Miles per Gallon: 12–18
Common Trouble Spots: automatic transmission, brakes
Availability of Parts: poor–fair
Investment Potential: A+

Background: The mid-priced Super convertible was Buick's most popular ragtop in 1953. It was powered by a 164–h.p. 322 cu. in. V8 engine. A three-speed manual transmission was standard. Dynaflow automatic transmission was optional at extra cost.

1953 Buick Super Convertible

PHOTO: PUBLIC RELATIONS, BUICK MOTOR DIVISION

1953 Buick Super Estate Station Wagon

Original Price: $3,430
Number Produced: 1,830
Estimated Number Existing in 1979: 6
Miles per Gallon: 12–17
Common Trouble Spots: automatic transmission, brakes
Availability of Parts: poor–fair
Investment Potential: AA+

Background: The Super Estate wagon was a real eyecatcher—especially when equipped with wide whitewall tires and optional wire wheels. It was powered by a 164 h.p. 322 cu. in. V8. A three-speed manual transmission was standard. Dynaflow automatic transmission was available at extra cost.

The 1953 Super Estate station wagon is a beautiful and significant automobile. It was the last year for the Buick woodie, and the first year for the Buick V8.

1953 Buick Super Station Wagon

PHOTO: DAVIS-WILLIAMS, INC.

1953 Cadillac Eldorado Convertible

1953 Cadillac Eldorado Convertible

Original Price: $7,750
Number Produced: 532
Estimated Number Existing in 1979: 33
Miles per Gallon: 12–18
Common Trouble Spots: automatic transmission, carburetor
Availability of Parts: poor–fair
Investment Potential: AAA+

Background: The new Eldorado convertible was the star of the Cadillac line in 1953. This limited-production dream car bore a strong family resemblance to the Series 62 convertible. However, its wraparound windshield, special doors, wire wheels, and exclusive luxury interior helped set it apart.

The Eldorado was powered by a 210 h.p. 331 cu. in. V8. Dual Range Hydra-Matic automatic transmission and power steering were standard. Some 1953 Cadillacs were equipped with Buick Dyna-Flow automatic transmissions.

Only a small number of people can have the privilege of owning a 1953 Eldorado—membership in this elite group will never come cheap.

1953 Cadillac Series 62 Convertible

Original Price: $4,144
Number Produced: 8,367
Estimated Number Existing in 1979: 41
Miles per Gallon: 13–18
Common Trouble Spots: automatic transmission, carburetor
Availability of Parts: poor–fair
Investment Potential: A+

Background: Cadillac continued with the same basic styling it had used since 1950. The important changes were made under the hood.

The Series 62 was powered by a 210 h.p. 331 cu. in. V8 engine. Dual Range Hydra-Matic automatic transmission was standard. Because of a fire in the Hydra-Matic factory, some 1953 Cadillacs were equipped with Buick Dyna-Flow automatics. Power steering and air conditioning were among the extra-cost options.

1953 Chevrolet Bel Air Convertible

Original Price: $2,175
Number Produced: 24,047
Estimated Number Existing in 1979: 97
Miles per Gallon: 13–20
Common Trouble Spots: piston rings, valves
Availability of Parts: fair
Investment Potential: AA

Background: This was the first year for the Bel Air convertible. It was powered by a 108 h.p. 235.5 cu. in. six when equipped with the standard three-speed manual transmission. Those with the $187.85 optional Powerglide automatic transmission came with a 115 h.p. version of that engine. Just over 34% of all '53 Chevrolets were equipped with the automatic.

Among the accessories available at extra cost were tinted glass, radio, power steering, windshield washer, and Autronic eye.

1953 Chevrolet Bel Air Convertible

1953 Cadillac Series 62 Convertible

PHOTO: CADILLAC MOTOR CAR DIVISION

1953 Chevrolet Corvette Convertible

PHOTO: T. MICHAELIS CORVETTE SUPPLIES

1953 Chevrolet Corvette Convertible

Original Price: $3,513
Number Produced: 300
Estimated Number Existing in 1979: 15
Miles per Gallon: 14–20
Common Trouble Spots: valves
Availability of Parts: fair–good
Investment Potential: AAA+

Background: This was the first year for the fiberglass-bodied Corvette. It was originally intended to be a low-cost sports car for college kids. After the prototype received an enthusiastic reception at the GM Motorama, it went into production.

It was powered by a 150 h.p. 235.5 cu. in. six-cylinder engine. Powerglide automatic transmission was standard.

The new Corvette was available in any color the buyer wanted—as long as it was white. It had a black convertible top. A removable hard top was available.

The 1953 Corvette is one of the rarest of all 1950s dream cars. It is also one of the most valuable.

1953 Chevrolet 210 Deluxe Convertible

Original Price: $2,093
Number Produced: 5,617
Estimated Number Existing in 1979: 22
Miles per Gallon: 13–20
Common Trouble Spots: piston rings, valves
Availability of Parts: fair–poor
Investment Potential: AA

Background: A 210 ragtop was offered for the first and only time in 1953. Outside of some trim differences, it looked about the same as the top-of-the-line Bel Air. It was powered by a 108 h.p. 235.5 cu. in. six when equipped with the standard three-speed manual. Cars with optional Powerglide automatic transmission came with a 115 h.p. version of the same engine.

1953 Chrysler New Yorker Deluxe Convertible

Original Price: $4,025
Number Produced: 950
Estimated Number Existing in 1979: 3
Miles per Gallon: 12–18
Common Trouble Spots: automatic transmission
Availability of Parts: poor
Investment Potential: AA

Background: The 1953 New Yorker convertible did not attract many buyers. It looked about the same as the last couple years' models and was still powered by a 180 h.p. 331.1 cu. in. V8 engine. Fluid-Matic Drive automatic transmission was standard; Fluid Torque Drive automatic was optional. Most buyers ordered the optional power steering.

Chrysler built a special show car from a New Yorker convertible. The car, called "Thunderbolt," looked almost identical to a stock New Yorker, with some trim and upholstery changes and wire wheels.

Speaking of upholstery, some 1953 Chrysler Corporation cars featured interior and exterior color combinations based on psychological research. According to *The Iron Age,* this was quite effective. In fact, 48.3% of New Yorker hardtop buyers ordered the normally unpopular color brown (cinnamon) in 1953, presumably because it was the only color which was color-coordinated.

1953 Chrysler New Yorker Convertible

PHOTO: CHRYSLER HISTORICAL COLLECTION

1953 Chrysler Windsor Deluxe Convertible

Original Price: $3,290
Number Produced: 1,250
Estimated Number Existing in 1979: 4
Miles per Gallon: 13–18
Common Trouble Spots: automatic transmission
Availability of Parts: poor
Investment Potential: A+

Background: After two years Chrysler restyled its cars, but not dramatically; again, the Windsor bore a strong resemblance to Chryslers of the past. As in the year before, Windsors were powered by a 119 h.p. 264.5 cu. in. six-cylinder engine. Fluid-Matic Drive automatic transmission was standard. Fluid Torque Drive automatic transmission was optional.

For the first time, Windsors had a one-piece windshield. Power steering was becoming increasingly popular—the demand for it had more than doubled from 1952.

Continental spare-tire kits were a new option that helped enhance the Windsor's look. Currently, cars with dealer-installed continental kits are worth more (all other things being equal) than those without.

1953 Chrysler Windsor Deluxe Convertible

1953 DeSoto Firedome Eight Convertible

Original Price: $3,172
Number Produced: 1,700
Estimated Number Existing in 1979: 4
Miles per Gallon: 13–19
Common Trouble Spots: automatic transmission, valves
Availability of Parts: poor–fair
Investment Potential: A

Background: The Firedome ragtop was little changed from the previous year's model. Yet sales literature called it "the most superbly styled DeSoto ever built." It came with a 160 h.p. 276.1 cu. in. Firedome V8 that "lets you take off like a shot, cross intersections in split seconds." A three-speed manual transmission was standard. Overdrive and two Tip-Toe Shift automatic transmissions (one with fluid drive and one fluid torque) were optional. Other options included power steering and power brakes.

1953 DeSoto Firedome Eight Convertible

1953 Dodge Coronet Convertible

Original Price: $2,693
Number Produced: 4,100
Estimated Number Existing in 1979: 15
Miles per Gallon: 13–19
Common Trouble Spots: none
Availability of Parts: poor–fair
Investment Potential: A

Background: The most noticeable change in the Coronet was a curved-glass, one-piece windshield. It was powered by a new 140 h.p. 241.3 cu. in. V8 engine. A three-speed manual transmission was standard. Overdrive and Gyro-Torque automatic transmission were optional.

Two accessories that add to the Coronet convertible's appeal were a continental spare-tire kit and wire wheel covers.

1953 Dodge Coronet Convertible

1953 Ford Crestline Sunliner Convertible

Original Price: $2,215
Number Produced: 40,861
Estimated Number Existing in 1979: 163
Miles per Gallon: 14–19
Common Trouble Spots: carburetor, cooling system
Availability of Parts: fair
Investment Potential: AA+

Background: Although 1953 was the fiftieth anniversary of the Ford Motor Company, the Sunliner received only a minor face-lift. It came with a 101 h.p. 225.9 cu. in. six-cylinder engine. A 110 h.p. 239.4 cu. in. eight-cylinder engine was available at extra cost. A three-speed manual transmission was standard. Ford-O-Matic automatic transmission was optional for $184. Overdrive could be had for $109. Starting in June 1953, power steering was offered (for $125).

The Sunliner was available in a dozen solid and fourteen two-tone exterior colors. A small number of gold anniversary model convertibles were made. These featured a black-and-gold interior.

This was the last year for the super silent flathead eight-cylinder engine. This engine (along with the fiberglass lining under the hood) made the 1953 Ford one of the quietest cars ever produced.

1953 Ford Crestline Sunliner Convertible

PHOTO: FORD MOTOR COMPANY

1953 Hudson Hornet Convertible Brougham

Original Price: $3,342
Number Produced: 24,833 (includes Hornet coupes, sedans, and Hollywoods)
Estimated Number Existing in 1979: 26 (includes Hornet coupes, sedans, and Hollywoods)
Miles per Gallon: 10–17
Common Trouble Spots: none
Availability of Parts: poor
Investment Potential: AAA

Background: The Hornet was Hudson's top-of-the-line convertible in 1953. It was powered by a 145 h.p. 308 cu. in. six-cylinder engine. A three-speed manual transmission was standard. Overdrive and Hydra-Matic automatic transmission were optional at extra cost.

1953 Hudson Super Wasp Convertible Brougham

Original Price: $3,048
Number Produced: N.A.
Estimated Number Existing in 1979: N.A.
Miles per Gallon: 13–18
Common Trouble Spots: none
Availability of Parts: poor
Investment Potential: AA

Background: The '53 Super Wasp convertible was powered by a 127 h.p. 262 cu. in. six-cylinder engine. A three-speed manual transmission was standard. Overdrive and Hydra-Matic automatic transmission were optional at extra cost.

1953 King Midget Convertible

Original Price: est. $550
Number Produced: N.A.
Estimated Number Existing in 1979: N.A.
Miles per Gallon: 50–90
Common Trouble Spots: transmission, "V" belts
Availability of Parts: good
Investment Potential: A

Background: The '53 King Midget ragtop was powered by a 9 h.p. 29 cu. in. one-cylinder engine. Automatic transmission was standard.

Unlike many manufacturers, King Midget did not offer a limited-production "dream car" in 1953.

1953 Lincoln Capri Convertible

Original Price: $4,186
Number Produced: 2,372
Estimated Number Existing in 1979: 5
Miles per Gallon: 11–17
Common Trouble Spots: automatic transmission, brakes
Availability of Parts: poor–fair
Investment Potential: A+

Background: Good looks and its reputation as one of the legendary "Road Race" Lincolns make the 1953 Capri convertible a desirable car. It came with a 205 h.p. 317.5 cu. in. V8. Hydra-Matic automatic transmission was standard. Most '53 Lincolns, 85%, had power brakes. Buyers could also order power steering, electric windows, and a four-way power seat.

1953 Lincoln Capri Convertible

PHOTO: FORD MOTOR COMPANY

1953 Mercury Monterey Convertible

Original Price: $2,390
Number Produced: 8,463
Estimated Number Existing in 1979: 19
Miles per Gallon: 13–18
Common Trouble Spots: carburetor, cooling system
Availability of Parts: poor–fair
Investment Potential: A+

Background: The Monterey's styling was little different from last year's model. However, Monterey convertible sales were up in 1953. The new Monterey was powered by a 125 h.p. 255.4 cu. in. eight-cylinder engine. A three-speed manual transmission was standard. Overdrive and Merc-O-Matic automatic transmission were available at extra cost.

Other options offered included power steering, power brakes, tinted glass, windshield washer, four-way power seats, and electric windows.

1953 Mercury Monterey Convertible

PHOTO: FORD MOTOR COMPANY

1953 Muntz Jet Convertible

Original Price: est. $5,000
Number Produced: est. 81
Estimated Number Existing in 1979: 5
Miles per Gallon: 12–17
Common Trouble Spots: none
Availability of Parts: poor–fair
Investment Potential: AA+

Background: The '53 Muntz Jet convertible was powered by a 154 h.p. 336.7 cu. in. Lincoln V8 engine. Hydra-Matic automatic transmission, padded dash, seat belts, and a vinyl interior were standard. The car had a removable padded steel top.

1953 Nash Healey Convertible

Original Price: est. $5,000
Number Produced: 162 (includes hardtops)
Estimated Number Existing in 1979: 16 (includes hardtops)
Miles per Gallon: 16–28
Common Trouble Spots: none
Availability of Parts: poor
Investment Potential: AAA

Background: The 1953 Nash Healey sports car was a rare sight even in 1953. It was powered by a 135 h.p. 252.6 cu. in. six-cylinder engine. A three-speed manual transmission was standard.

1953 Nash Healey Convertible

PHOTO: JOHN A. CONDE COLLECTION

1953 Nash Healey Le Mans Hardtop

Original Price: est. $5,000
Number Produced: 162 (includes convertibles)
Estimated Number Existing in 1979: 16 (includes convertibles)
Miles per Gallon: 16–28
Common Trouble Spots: none
Availability of Parts: poor
Investment Potential: AAA

Background: This was the first year the Nash Healey was offered in a hardtop body style. Sleek and chic, it was one of the best-looking hardtops on the road in 1953.

The Nash Healey was powered by a 140 h.p. 252.6 cu. in. six-cylinder engine. A three-speed manual transmission was standard.

1953 Nash Rambler Custom Convertible

PHOTO: LARRY G. MITCHELL

1953 Nash Rambler Custom Convertible

Original Price: est. $1,900
Number Produced: 3,284
Estimated Number Existing in 1979: 15
Miles per Gallon: 16–25
Common Trouble Spots: cooling system
Availability of Parts: poor
Investment Potential: A

Background: The '53 Rambler convertible came with a continental spare tire. It was powered by a 85 h.p. 184 cu. in. six-cylinder engine. A 90 h.p. 195.6 cu. in. six-cylinder engine was optional. A three-speed manual transmission was standard. Overdrive and Hydra Matic automatic transmission were available at extra cost.

1953 Oldsmobile 98 Convertible

Original Price: $3,229
Number Produced: 7,521
Estimated Number Existing in 1979: 16
Miles per Gallon: 13–17
Common Trouble Spots: automatic transmission
Availability of Parts: poor–fair
Investment Potential: A+

Background: The "new" 98 looked a lot like the old one. The basic conservative styling begun in 1948 was still being used. It was powered by a 165 h.p. 303.7 cu. in. V8. A three-speed manual transmission was standard. Hydra-Matic automatic transmission was optional at extra cost. Some 98 convertibles came with Buick's Dynaflow automatic transmission.

1953 Oldsmobile 98 Convertible

PHOTO: OLDSMOBILE DIVISION

1953½ Oldsmobile 98 Fiesta Convertible

Original Price: $5,715
Number Produced: 458
Estimated Number Existing in 1979: 29
Miles per Gallon: 13–17
Common Trouble Spots: none
Availability of Parts: poor–fair
Investment Potential: AAA+

Background: This was the year of the limited-production "dream cars." Oldsmobile's offering was the beautiful Fiesta. Actually, except for the doors and wraparound windshield, it looked pretty much like a regular 98 ragtop.

It was powered by a 170 h.p. 303.7 cu. in. V8. Hydra-Matic automatic transmission, power steering, power brakes, Autronic Eye, electric windows, power seats, signal-seeking radio, padded dash, and leather upholstery (in any of five two-tone combinations) were among the many standard items. The only options were a continental spare tire and air conditioning.

Buyers had their choice of six exterior color combinations: black, surf blue and teak blue, nile green and noel green, white, red and white, or turquoise and white. The last two color combinations were the most popular. The orlon top was available in black or tan.

1953½ Oldsmobile 98 Fiesta Convertible

PHOTO: OLDSMOBILE DIVISION

1953 Oldsmobile Super 88 Convertible

Original Price: $2,853
Number Produced: 8,310
Estimated Number Existing in 1979: 10
Miles per Gallon: 14–18
Common Trouble Spots: automatic transmission
Availability of Parts: poor–fair
Investment Potential: A+

Background: Oldsmobile stylists must have taken the year off—the new Super 88 looked almost the same as last year's model.

It was powered by a 165 h.p. 303.7 cu. in. V8. A three-speed manual transmission was standard. Hydra-Matic automatic transmission was available for $178.35. Some Super 88 convertibles came with

Buick's Dynaflow automatic transmission.

Other options included power steering, power brakes, Autronic Eye, windshield washer, tinted glass, and, for a "mere" $594, an air conditioner.

The Olds Super 88 had a top speed of over 110 mph in stock form, which made it one of the hottest cars on the road in '53.

1953 Oldsmobile Super 88 Convertible

PHOTO: OLDSMOBILE DIVISION

1953 Packard Caribbean Convertible

Original Price: $5,210
Number Produced: 750
Estimated Number Existing in 1979: 50
Miles per Gallon: 11–16
Common Trouble Spots: automatic transmission, cooling system, piston rings, valves
Availability of Parts: poor–fair
Investment Potential: AAA+

Background: Like the 1953 Buick Skylark and the Cadillac Eldorado, the Caribbean was a "dream car." It was inspired by the 1952 Packard Pan America show car. Although it retained much of the show car's flavor, it was closer in appearance to the stock 1953 Packard softtop. However, the standard-equipment wire wheels, continental kit, hood scoop, and full wheel cutouts (accentuated with chrome) distinguish it.

The Caribbean was powered by a 180 h.p. 327 cu. in. straight eight engine. A three-speed manual transmission was standard. Overdrive and Ultramatic automatic transmission were optional. All power accessories were optional, but most buyers ordered them.

The understated elegance of this limited-edition dream car and the fact that it is a Packard, a name long synonymous with quality, contribute to its desirability. In addition, Caribbeans are the most valuable postwar Packards. And the 1953 is the most valuable Caribbean.

If a person couldn't afford the rather steep price, there was another way to get a Caribbean in 1953. Armour Star ran a contest with one as first prize. All the contestants had to do was dream up a screen name for movie actress Joan Weldon. In addition to the beautiful convertible, the winner would receive a two-week expense paid trip to Hollywood to meet Ms. Weldon (or whatever she would be calling herself by then).

1953 Packard Caribbean Convertible

PHOTO: HOWARD AND SHELBY APPLEGATE

1953 Packard Convertible

Original Price: $3,476
Number Produced: 1,518
Estimated Number Existing in 1979: 4
Miles per Gallon: 11–16
Common Trouble Spots: automatic transmission, cooling system, piston rings, valves
Availability of Parts: fair–poor
Investment Potential: AA

Background: The attractive new Packard convertible was powered by a 180 h.p. 327 cu. in. eight-cylinder engine. A three-speed manual transmission was standard. Overdrive and (for $199) Ultramatic automatic transmission were optional.

Other options included a radio with electric antenna, tinted glass, power steering, power windows, rear speaker, and power front seat.

1953 Packard Convertible

PHOTO: HOWARD AND SHELBY APPLEGATE

1953 Plymouth Cranbrook Convertible

Original Price: $2,288
Number Produced: 6,301
Estimated Number Existing in 1979: 23
Miles per Gallon: 14–19
Common Trouble Spots: cooling system
Availability of Parts: poor
Investment Potential: A

Background: In addition to receiving a face-lift, the new Cranbrook was lower than last year's model. It was powered by a 100 h.p. 217.8 cu. in. six-cylinder engine. A three-speed manual transmission was standard. However, this year buyers were able to order a manual with overdrive or the new Hy-Drive automatic transmission at extra cost.

Because of the location of the gas filler neck, gasoline overflow had a tendency to spill into the trunk. In addition to having to worry about a safety hazard, riders often had to put up with the fragrance of gas fumes.

The ride and handling of the '53 Cranbrook were good.

1953 Plymouth Cranbrook Convertible

1953 Pontiac Chieftain Deluxe Convertible

Original Price: $2,518
Number Produced: N.A.
Estimated Number Existing in 1979: N.A.
Miles per Gallon: 14–19
Common Trouble Spots: automatic transmission, valves
Availability of Parts: fair–poor
Investment Potential: A

Background: Chieftain buyers could order either a 115 h.p. (118 h.p. with the automatic) 239.2 cu. in. six-cylinder or a 118 h.p. (122 h.p. with automatic) 268.4 cu. in. eight-cylinder engine. A three-speed manual transmission was standard. Hydra-Matic automatic transmission was optional for $178.35. Some Chieftains were equipped with Chevrolet's Powerglide automatic.

1953 Studebaker Commander Starliner Hardtop

PHOTO: RICHARD QUINN COLLECTION, STUDEBAKER DRIVERS CLUB

Most 1953 Pontiacs, 90.7%, were sold with the eight-cylinder engine. 69.7% had the Hydra-Matic, and 5.8% had Powerglide automatic transmissions.

Other options included power steering, Autronic Eye, tinted glass, under-seat heater, lighted hood ornament, dual fog lamps, windshield washer, foldaway umbrella, and a radio.

1953 Pontiac Chieftain Deluxe Convertible

PHOTO: PONTIAC MOTOR DIVISION

1953 Studebaker Starliner Hardtop

Original Price: $2,213 (Commander); $1,955 (Champion)
Number Produced: 32,294 (total Champion and Commander Starliners)
Estimated Number Existing in 1979: 61 (total Champion and Commander Starliners)
Miles per Gallon: 17–25
Common Trouble Spots: none
Availability of Parts: fair
Investment Potential: AA

Background: "The new American car with the European look!" That's how Studebaker announced the Starliner two-door hardtop, the most acclaimed of all postwar Studebakers (with the possible exception of the Avanti). Once again, Studebaker led the industry in innovative styling.

The Commander was powered by a 120 h.p. 232.6 cu. in. V8. The Champion had a 85 h.p. 169.6 cu. in. six. A three-speed manual transmission was standard. Overdrive and Automatic-Drive automatic transmission were optional at extra cost. Both the Commander and Champion Starliner hardtops came with a Regal, deluxe-upholstery option.

1954

1954 Buick Century Convertible

Original Price: $2,962
Number Produced: 2,790
Estimated Number Existing in 1979: 8
Miles per Gallon: 12–18
Common Trouble Spots: automatic transmission, brakes
Availability of Parts: poor–fair
Investment Potential: AA

Background: This year Buick reintroduced the Century, which had been discontinued in 1942. It looked a great deal like the Super. However, it weighed less, which helped its performance.

The Century was powered by a 195 h.p. 322 cu. in. V8. A three-speed manual transmission was standard. Dynaflow automatic transmission was optional. Other standard features included an interior trimmed in leather, power front seat, and power windows.

1954 Buick Century Convertible

1954 Buick Roadmaster Convertible

Original Price: $3,506
Number Produced: 3,305
Estimated Number Existing in 1979: 9
Miles per Gallon: 12–17
Common Trouble Spots: automatic transmission, brakes
Availability of Parts: poor–fair
Investment Potential: AA

Background: Like all '54 Buicks, the new Roadmaster convertible had a wraparound windshield. It was powered by a 200 h.p. 322 cu. in. V8 engine. Dynaflow automatic transmission and power steering were standard.

1954 Buick Roadmaster Convertible

PHOTO: PUBLIC RELATIONS, BUICK MOTOR DIVISION

1954 Buick Skylark Convertible

1954 Buick Skylark Convertible

Original Price: $4,483
Number Produced: 836
Estimated Number Existing in 1979: 20
Miles per Gallon: 12–17
Common Trouble Spots: automatic transmission, brakes
Availability of Parts: poor–fair
Investment Potential: AAA

Background: The 1954 Skylark didn't have quite the pizzazz of the '53. It was powered by a 200 h.p. 322 cu. in. V8. Dynaflow automatic transmission, heater, radio, and power steering were among the standard features on this very luxurious automobile.

The 1954 Skylark may not have been a "sports car," as Buick advertising claimed, but it is a rare and desirable ragtop.

1954 Buick Special Convertible

Original Price: $2,563
Number Produced: 6,135
Estimated Number Existing in 1979: 17
Miles per Gallon: 13–18
Common Trouble Spots: automatic transmission, brakes
Availability of Parts: poor–fair
Investment Potential: AA

Background: The new Special was the lightest and lowest-priced ragtop Buick offered in 1954. It came equipped with a 143 h.p. 264 cu. in. V8. A three-speed manual transmission was standard. Dynaflow automatic transmission was a popular $193 option. Power steering was offered for $134, but the Special handled well without it.

1954 Buick Special Convertible

PHOTO: PUBLIC RELATIONS DEPARTMENT, BUICK MOTOR DIVISION

1954 Buick Super Convertible

Original Price: $2,964
Number Produced: 3,343
Estimated Number Existing in 1979: 9
Miles per Gallon: 12–18
Common Trouble Spots: automatic transmission, brakes
Availability of Parts: poor–fair
Investment Potential: AA

Background: The Super convertible continued to have three portholes on its front fenders, as opposed to the Roadmaster's four. Outside of that, the two looked much the same.

It came equipped with a 177 h.p. 322 cu. in. V8. A three-speed manual transmission was standard. Dynaflow automatic transmission was optional.

1954 Buick Super Convertible

PHOTO: PUBLIC RELATIONS DEPARTMENT, BUICK MOTOR DIVISION

1954 Cadillac Eldorado Convertible

Original Price: $5,738
Number Produced: 2,150
Estimated Number Existing in 1979: 11
Miles per Gallon: 13–17
Common Trouble Spots: none
Availability of Parts: poor–fair
Investment Potential: AA

Background: Beautiful. That's the best word to describe the new Eldorado. Clean, fresh lines and a hot but economical engine. What more could a person want?

It was powered by a 230 h.p. 331 cu. in. V8. Hydra-Matic automatic transmission and power steering were standard. At $620, air conditioning was the most expensive option.

Although the '54 Eldorado isn't as significant as the 1953, many might argue that it is better-looking, and that helps make it desirable.

1954 Cadillac Eldorado Convertible

PHOTO: CADILLAC MOTOR CAR DIVISION

1954 Cadillac Series 62 Convertible

Original Price: $4,404
Number Produced: 6,310
Estimated Number Existing in 1979: 34
Miles per Gallon: 13–17
Common Trouble Spots: none
Availability of Parts: fair–poor
Investment Potential: A+

Background: The 1954 Cadillac was attractively restyled. Gone was the bulky, "lead sled" look of previous years. The redesigned frame and liberal use of soundproofing added up to improved passenger comfort, although wind noise at speeds over 50 was rather high.

Some owners of early 1954 Cadillacs complained of gas fumes when the driver's window was down. This was caused by a defective gas filler neck and was soon corrected.

The only engine offered was a 230 h.p. 331 cu. in. V8. Hydra-Matic automatic transmission and power steering were standard. Air conditioning, power seat, chrome wire wheels, power windows, and power brakes were among the options available at extra cost.

The 1954 Series 62 convertible was one of the best-looking postwar Cadillacs. In addition, *Motor Trend* called it "the hottest performing car" of 1954.

1954 Cadillac Series 62 Convertible

PHOTO: CADILLAC MOTOR CAR DIVISION

1954 Chevrolet Bel Air Convertible

1954 Chevrolet Bel Air Convertible

Original Price: $2,185
Number Produced: 19,383
Estimated Number Existing in 1979: 105
Miles per Gallon: 13–19
Common Trouble Spots: brakes, piston rings
Availability of Parts: fair
Investment Potential: AA+

Background: According to Chevrolet sales literature, the 1954 Bel Air ragtop was "styled with a youthful, carefree spirit and luxuriously appointed." It was powered by a 115 h.p. 235.5 cu. in. six when equipped with the standard three-speed manual transmission. Cars with the $178 optional Powerglide automatic came with a 125 h.p. version of the same engine. Over 40% of all 1954 Chevrolets had the automatic.

Among the options available at extra cost were power front seat and windows, radio, heater, power steering, and power brakes.

1954 Chevrolet Corvette Convertible

Original Price: $3,523
Number Produced: 3,640
Estimated Number Existing in 1979: 90
Miles per Gallon: 14–20
Common Trouble Spots: valves
Availability of Parts: fair–good
Investment Potential: AAA+

Background: The 1954 Vette looked much the same as the previous year's model. It was powered by a 150 h.p. 235.5 cu. in. six-cylinder engine. Powerglide automatic transmission and dual exhaust were standard.

In addition to white, buyers could now choose from three other body colors—black, blue, and red. The convertible top came in tan only.

1954 Chevrolet Corvette Convertible

PHOTO: CHEVROLET MOTOR DIVISION

1954 Chrysler New Yorker Deluxe Convertible

Original Price: $3,903
Number Produced: 724
Estimated Number Existing in 1979: 5
Miles per Gallon: 12–17
Common Trouble Spots: automatic transmission
Availability of Parts: poor
Investment Potential: AA

Background: The New Yorker received a minor face-lift for 1954. Unfortunately, that didn't help sales any—they were even lower than in 1953.

It came with a hot four-barrel-carburetor, 235-h.p. version of the 331.1 cu. in. Hemi eight-cylinder engine. That shortened its 0-to-60 time to just over 12 seconds. Not bad for a luxury car.

Power Flite automatic transmission, padded dash, and power brakes were standard. Some popular options included power steering, radio, electric windows, chrome wire wheels, and even a $675 air-conditioning unit.

The upholstery was nice, but not particularly durable. Like that of all 1954 Chrysler Corporation cars, it was psychologically color-coordinated with the exterior body color. Ironically, one of the first things most new car buyers did in the 1950s was to buy seatcovers. In fact, in April 1952, *Fortune* reported that the majority of new car owners "spend up to $80 to cover the expensive fabric the auto makers spend over $100 on." However, this can be a very good thing for later owners, as covers help preserve the original interior.

1954 Chrysler New Yorker Deluxe Convertible

1954 Chrysler Windsor Deluxe Convertible

Original Price: $3,016
Number Produced: 500
Estimated Number Existing in 1979: 4
Miles per Gallon: 13–18
Common Trouble Spots: automatic transmission
Availability of Parts: poor
Investment Potential: A+

Background: This was one of the most unpopular Windsors ever, perhaps because it didn't look much different from any other Windsor made since 1950. Also, it had the same 119 h.p. 264. 5 cu. in. six-cylinder engine. A three-speed manual transmission was standard. Power Flite automatic transmission was optional.

However, the unpopularity of a Windsor Deluxe convertible when it was new makes it all the more desirable now; it is one of the rarest Chrysler convertibles made in the 1950s.

1954 DeSoto Firedome Eight Convertible

Original Price: $3,144
Number Produced: 1,025
Estimated Number Existing in 1979: 3
Miles per Gallon: 13–18
Common Trouble Spots: valves
Availability of Parts: poor–fair
Investment Potential: A

Background: Probably the best-looking feature of the new Firedome was its dash, designed by Chrysler's famous stylist Virgil Exner. On the outside, the Firedome looked pretty much the same as last year's model.

It was powered by a 170 h.p. 276.1 cu. in. V8 engine that could move the car from 0 to 60 in just under 18 seconds. The top speed was over 101 mph. A three-speed manual transmission was standard. Overdrive and Power Flite automatic transmission were optional.

Power steering, power brakes, and even a $643 air conditioner were available at extra cost.

1954 Dodge Coronet Convertible

Original Price: $2,489
Number Produced: 50
Estimated Number Existing in 1979: 1
Miles per Gallon: 12–19
Common Trouble Spots: none
Availability of Parts: poor–fair
Investment Potential: A

Background: The new Coronet convertible was powered by a 150 h.p. 241.3 cu. in. Red Ram V8. Dodge sales literature modestly called this "the most efficient engine in any American car." A three-speed manual transmission was standard. Available at extra cost were overdrive ($98) and Power Flite automatic transmission ($189). Power steering could be had for $151. Buyers had their choice of eleven exterior colors.

1954 Dodge Royal Convertible

Original Price: $2,607
Number Produced: 2,000
Estimated Number Existing in 1979: 10
Miles per Gallon: 12–19
Common Trouble Spots: none
Availability of Parts: poor–fair
Investment Potential: A+ (pace car replica); A (regular models)

Background: "A superb achievement in fine car luxury and performance." That's what Dodge sales catalogs said about the 1954 Royal ragtop. It came with a 150 h.p. 241.3 cu. in. Red Ram V8. A three-speed manual transmission was standard. Overdrive and Power Flite automatic transmission were optional. Other options included power steering and air conditioning.

The Royal convertible was the pace car at the 1954 Indianapolis 500. Approximately 700 replica pace cars, with special trim, continental kit, and wire wheels, were produced.

1954 Dodge Royal Convertible

1954 Ford Crestline Skyliner

Original Price: $2,241
Number Produced: 13,344
Estimated Number Existing in 1979: 64
Miles per Gallon: 14–18
Common Trouble Spots: carburetor, piston rings
Availability of Parts: fair
Investment Potential: AA+

Background: The Skyliner was basically just a '54 Victoria with a transparent Plexiglas insert over the front half of the car's roof. It also had special upholstery and trim. The car was popularly referred to as a "half glass" (although people who didn't like the green-tinted insert called it something else).

The problem with this roof treatment was that the interior of the car tended to get extremely hot, even with the snap-in lining in place. In addition, owners complained that the insert scratched easily.

Less than 3% of Skyliners came with the standard 115 h.p. 223 cu. in. six-cylinder engine. Most had the optional 130 h.p. 239 cu. in. V8. A three-speed manual transmission was standard. Overdrive and Ford-O-Matic automatic transmission were available at extra cost.

Unfortunately, some people have made fake Skyliners out of Victorias. So be careful when buying one—authenticity is very important.

1954 Ford Crestline Sunliner Convertible

Original Price: $2,241
Number Produced: 36,685
Estimated Number Existing in 1979: 178
Miles per Gallon: 14–18
Common Trouble Spots: carburetor, piston rings
Availability of Parts: fair
Investment Potential: AA+ (with optional transparent top), AA (without)

Background: Externally, the '54 Sunliner ragtop looked much the same as last year's model. The biggest change was a new overhead-valve 130 h.p. 239 cu. in. V8 engine. The standard engine was a 115 h.p. 223 cu. in. six cylinder. A three-speed manual transmission was standard. Overdrive and Ford-O-Matic automatic transmission were optional. Over 96% of Sunliner convertibles had the V8.

Also new was ball-joint front suspension, power windows (optional), improved brakes, a restyled hood ornament and dash, and "idiot lights" to replace the water and oil pressure gauges.

Motor Trend called the 1954 Ford "the best handling and most roadable car" of the year.

A rare option was a transparent plastic section in the convertible top. This allowed front-seat passengers a view of the sky even with the top up. It was not very popular.

1954 Ford Crestline Sunliner Convertible

PHOTO: FORD MOTOR COMPANY

1954 Hudson Hornet Convertible Brougham

Original Price: $3,400
Number Produced: 24,833 (includes Hornet coupes, sedans, and Hollywoods)
Estimated Number Existing in 1979: 48 (includes Hornet coupes, sedans, and Hollywoods)
Miles per Gallon: 10–16
Common Trouble Spots: none
Availability of Parts: poor
Investment Potential: AA+

Background: This was the last Hornet convertible and the last "real" Hudson. Hornets made in later years were basically just Nashes in special trim. It was powered by a 160 h.p. 308 cu. in. six-cylinder engine, which was rated at 170 h.p. when equipped with the optional twin carburetors. A three-speed manual transmission was standard. Overdrive and Hydra-Matic automatic transmission were available at extra cost; power steering could be had for $177.

1954 Hudson Hornet Convertible

PHOTO: JOHN A. CONDE COLLECTION

1954 Hudson Super Wasp Convertible Brougham

Original Price: est. $3,100
Number Produced: N.A.
Estimated jnumber Existing in 1979: N.A.
Miles per Gallon: 10–17
Common Trouble Spots: none
Availability of Parts: poor
Investment Potential: A+

Background: The attractive '54 Super Wasp convertible came with a 140 h.p. 262 cu. in. six-cylinder engine. This engine was rated at 149 h.p. when equipped with twin carburetors. A three-speed manual transmission was standard. Overdrive could be had for $111. Hydra-Matic automatic transmission was a $178 option.

1954 Kaiser Darrin Roadster

Original Price: $3,668
Number Produced: 435
Estimated Number Existing in 1979: 230
Miles per Gallon: 16–22
Common Trouble Spots: none
Availadility of Parts: poor
Investment Potential: AAA+

Background: Like the Corvette, the '54 Darrin was made of fiberglass. A unique feature of the Darrin was its sliding doors. It was put into production after the prototype received an enthusiastic reception at the Los Angeles Motorama in November 1952.

The Darrin came with a very Spartan padded dash. Seat belts, a heater, and wire wheels were optional. Buyers could choose from four body colors. These were, in order of popularity, white, yellow, "pine tint," and red.

It was powered by a 90 h.p. 161 cu. in. six-cylinder engine, which was rated at 135 h.p. when equipped with the optional McCulloch supercharger. However, some Darrins sold after production stopped contained a Cadillac V8 engine. A three-speed manual transmission was standard. All but one percent had overdrive.

1954 Kaiser Darrin Roadster

PHOTO: JOHN A. CONDE COLLECTION

1954 King Midget Convertible

Original Price: est. $550
Number Produced: N.A.
Estimated Number Existing in 1979: N.A.
Miles per Gallon: 50–90
Common Trouble Spots: transmission, "V" belts
Availability of Parts: good
Investment Potential: A

Background: The "new" '54 King Midget convertible was powered by a 9 h.p. 29 cu. in. one-cylinder engine. Automatic transmission was standard.

1954 Lincoln Capri Convertible

Original Price: $3,699
Number Produced: 1,951
Estimated Number Existing in 1979: 8
Miles per Gallon: 11–18
Common Trouble Spots: none
Availability of Parts: poor–fair
Investment Potential: A+

Background: This was the last year for the famous "Road Race" Lincolns. Lincolns won both first and second places in the highly publicized *Carrera Panamerica* (Pan American Road Race) held in Mexico.

The new Capri convertible was powered by a 205 h.p. 317 cu. in. V8 with a four-barrel carburetor. Hydra-Matic automatic transmission was standard. Power steering, power brakes, electric windows, and power four-way seat were among the options.

1954 Lincoln Capri Convertible

PHOTO: FORD MOTOR COMPANY

1954 Mercury Monterey Convertible

Original Price: $2,610
Number Produced: 7,293
Estimated Number Existing in 1979: 18
Miles per Gallon: 13–18
Common Trouble Spots: carburetor, engine bearings
Availability of Parts: poor–fair
Investment Potential: AA

Background: The Monterey ragtop received a minor face-lift for 1954. The most noticeable styling change was the addition of some attractive new taillights.

The Monterey was powered by a 161 h.p. 256 cu. in. V8. A three-speed manual transmission was standard. For $110, buyers could order a manual with overdrive. For $190, they could get Merc-O-Matic automatic transmission.

Other options included power steering, power brakes, a radio, and a power package with either a four-way or a two-way power front seat and power windows. *Motor Trend* called Mercury's power steering "the best power setup we've yet driven."

1954 Mercury Monterey Convertible

PHOTO: FORD MOTOR COMPANY

1954 Mercury Monterey Sun Valley

Original Price: $2,582
Number Produced: 9,761
Estimated Number Existing in 1979: 22
Miles per Gallon: 13–18
Common Trouble Spots: carburetor, engine bearing
Availability of Parts: poor–fair
Investment Potential: AA+

Background: The '54 Monterey Sun Valley was an attractive and unusual car. It featured a green tinted plastic insert over the front half of the roof.

It was powered by a 161 h.p. 256 cu. in OHV V8. A three-speed manual transmission was standard. Overdrive and Merc-O-Matic automatic transmission were optional.

1954 Mercury Monterey Sun Valley

1954 Metropolitan Series 1200 Convertible

Original Price: $1,469
Number Produced: est. 2,920
Estimated Number Existing in 1979: 19
Miles per Gallon: 27–39
Common Trouble Spots: brakes, gearshift
Availability of Parts: fair–good
Investment Potential: A

Background: The new Metropolitan was a direct descendant of the NXI (Nash Experimental International) show car of 1950. It was later called the NKI (Nash-Kelvinator International) before finally being named the Metropolitan.

The Met went into production after an extensive marketing research poll in which over a quarter of a million people participated showed there would be a demand for it.

Except for the headlights and windshield-wiper blades, the Metropolitan was made entirely in Great Britain. It was powered by a 42 h.p. 73.2 cu. in. four-cylinder Austin A-40 engine. A three-speed manual transmission was standard.

According to Nash brass, the Met was supposed to be good for "100,000 miles of normal driving."

1954 Metropolitan Series 1200 Convertible

PHOTO: LARRY G. MITCHELL

1954 Muntz Jet Convertible

Original Price: est. $5,000
Number Produced: est. 81
Estimated Number Existing in 1979: 6
Miles per Gallon: 12–17
Common Trouble Spots: none
Availability of Parts: poor–fair
Investment Potential: AA+

Background: This was the last year for the Muntz convertible. Some came with a 154 h.p. 336.7 cu. in. Lincoln V8; others had a 205 h.p. 317 cu. in. Lincoln V8. Hydra-Matic automatic transmission, padded dash, seat belts, and a radio were standard. The car had a removable padded steel top.

About eighteen '54 Muntz Jets had fiberglass fenders.

1954 Nash Healey Convertible

Original Price: est. $5,000
Number Produced: 90 (includes hardtop)
Estimated Number Existing in 1979: 9 (includes hardtops)
Miles per Gallon: 16–28
Common Trouble Spots: none
Availability of Parts: poor
Investment Potential: AAA

Background: This was the last year for the Nash Healey convertible. It was powered by a 140 h.p. 252.6 cu. in. six-cylinder engine. A three-speed manual transmission was standard.

1954 Nash Healey Le Mans Hardtop

Original Price: $5,128
Number Produced: 90 (includes convertibles)
Estimated Number Existing in 1979: 9 (includes convertibles)
Miles per Gallon: 16–28
Common Trouble Spots: none
Availability of Parts: poor
Investment Potential: AAA

Background: This was the final year for the attractive Nash Healey Le Mans. It was powered by a 140 h.p. 252.6 cu. in. six-cylinder engine. A three-speed manual transmission and upholstery made from Italian leather that was tanned in England were standard.

1954 Nash Rambler Custom Convertible

Original Price: $2,125
Number Produced: 221
Estimated Number Existing in 1979: 1
Miles per Gallon: 15–25
Common Trouble Spots: brakes, cooling system
Availability of Parts: poor
Investment Potential: A

Background: The new Rambler Custom ragtop looked virtually the same as the 1953 model, right down to the "rattle-free" continental spare tire. It was powered by a 85 h.p. 184 cu. in. six-cylinder engine with a standard

1954 Nash Rambler Custom Convertible

PHOTO: JOHN A. CONDE COLLECTION

three-speed manual transmission; a 90 h.p. 195.6 cu. in. six was standard when the car was equipped with Hydra-Matic automatic transmission. Available at extra cost were overdrive ($104) and Hydra-Matic automatic ($179).

Motor Trend called Rambler's automatic "one of the smoothest Hydra-Matics *Motor Trend* Research has had the pleasure of driving."

1954 Oldsmobile Starfire 98 Convertible

Original Price: $3,249
Number Produced: 6,800
Estimated Number Existing in 1979: 21
Miles per Gallon: 13–18
Common Trouble Spots: none
Availability of Parts: fair–poor
Investment Potential: A+

Background: The 98 convertible received a wraparound windshield and attractive styling for 1954. It was powered by a 185 h.p. 324.3 cu. in. V8 engine. A three-speed manual transmission was standard, but not very popular—most buyers paid the extra $178 for Hydra-Matic automatic transmission.

1954 Oldsmobile Starfire 98 Convertible

PHOTO: OLDSMOBILE DIVISION

1954 Oldsmobile Super 88 Convertible

PHOTO: OLDSMOBILE DIVISION

1954 Oldsmobile Super 88 Convertible

Original Price: $2,868
Number Produced: 6,452
Estimated Number Existing in 1979: 20
Miles per Gallon: 14–18
Common Trouble Spots: none
Availability of Parts: fair–poor
Investment Potential: A+

Background: "There's never been a car like this sensational new Super 88 for 1954!" So proclaimed an Oldsmobile advertisement. Despite the rather overenthusiastic ad copy, and the genuine good looks of the Super 88, sales of the convertible were down from the previous year.

The Super 88 was powered by a 185 h.p. 324.3 cu. in. V8. A three-speed manual transmission was standard. Hydra-Matic automatic transmission was a popular option.

1954 Packard Caribbean Convertible

Original Price: $6,100
Number Produced: 400
Estimated Number Existing in 1979: 40
Miles per Gallon: 11–15
Common Trouble Spots: automatic transmission, cooling system, engine bearings, valves
Availability of Parts: poor–fair
Investment Potential: AAA

Background: Sales literature stated, "There is no more glamorous car than the Packard Caribbean." Yet the Caribbean softtop looked more like the standard Packard convertible this year than last.

It was powered by a 212 h.p. 359 cu. in. eight-cylinder engine. Ultramatic automatic transmission, power steering, power brakes, windshield washer, power windows, four-way power front seat, dual (under front seat and under dash) heater and defroster, three-way radio (push-button, manual tuning, and signal-seeking), and power antenna.

Although not quite as distinctive as the 1953, the 1954 Caribbean convertible is a very desirable car.

1954 Packard Caribbean Convertible

1954 Packard Convertible

Original Price: $3,935
Number Produced: 863
Estimated Number Existing in 1979: 5
Miles per Gallon: 11–15
Common Trouble Spots: automatic transmission, cooling system, engine bearings, valves
Availability of Parts: poor–fair
Investment Potential: AA

Background: The new Packard ragtop was powered by a 212 h.p. 359 cu. in. eight-cylinder engine. Ultramatic automatic transmission was standard. Among the options were power steering, power brakes, and air conditioning. Buyers had their choice of six color combinations of leather interiors.

1954 Packard Convertible

1954 Plymouth Belvedere Convertible

Original Price: $2,281
Number Produced: 6,114
Estimated Number Existing in 1979: 17
Miles per Gallon: 14–19
Common Trouble Spots: cooling system
Availability of Parts: poor–fair
Investment Potential: A

Background: Early models of the new Belvedere came with the same 100 h.p. 217.8 cu. in. six-cylinder engine that was used in the 1953 Plymouths. Later models were powered by a 110 h.p. 230.2 cu. in. six-cylinder engine.

A three-speed manual transmission was standard. A manual with overdrive, Hy-drive automatic (in the early models), and Power Flite automatic (in the later models) were available at extra cost. Power steering was offered for $140.

Plymouth attempted to get a bigger share of the low-priced-car market in 1954 by offering "color tuned" interiors. In such cars, the upholstery, carpet, door panels, headliner, and dash matched the exterior color of the car.

1954 Plymouth Belvedere Convertible

PHOTO: CHRYSLER HISTORICAL COLLECTION

1954 Pontiac Star Chief Convertible

Original Price: $2,630
Number Produced: N.A.
Estimated Number Existing in 1979: N.A.
Miles per Gallon: 13–18
Common Trouble Spots: cooling system, engine bearings, valves
Availability of Parts: fair–poor
Investment Potential: A+

Background: This was the first year for the Star Chief convertible. It was powered by a 122 h.p. (127 h.p. with the automatic) 268.4 cu. in. eight-cylinder engine. A three-speed manual transmission was standard, but 99.5% of 1954 Star Chief buyers ordered the optional Hydra-Matic automatic transmission for $178. *Motor Trend* called the Hydra-Matic "one of the smoothest, quietest units we've tested."

Other options included a four-way power front seat, air conditioning, power steering, and power brakes.

1955

1955 Buick Century Convertible

Original Price: $2,991
Number Produced: 5,588
Estimated Number Existing in 1979: 36
Miles per Gallon: 12–17
Common Trouble Spots: automatic transmission
Availability of Parts: fair–poor
Investment Potential: A+

Background: The 1955 Century ragtop was powered by a 236 h.p. 322 cu. in. V8 with four-barrel carburetor. A three-speed manual transmission, leather upholstery, power windows, and power front seat were standard. An "improved" Dynaflow automatic transmission was available. Wire wheels were a rarely ordered option.

1955 Buick Century Convertible

PHOTO: PUBLIC RELATIONS DEPARTMENT, BUICK MOTOR DIVISION

1955 Buick Roadmaster Convertible

Original Price: $3,552
Number Produced: 4,739
Estimated Number Existing in 1979: 30
Miles per Gallon: 12–17
Common Trouble Spots: automatic transmission, brakes
Availability of Parts: fair–poor
Investment Potential: A+

Background: The top-of-the-line Roadmaster convertible was powered by a 236 h.p. 322 cu. in. V8 with four-barrel carburetor. Dynaflow automatic transmission, power steering, windshield washers, special wheel covers, and four portholes on each front fender were among the standard equipment.

1955 Buick Roadmaster Convertible

PHOTO: BUICK MOTOR DIVISION

1955 Buick Special Convertible

Original Price: $2,590
Number Produced: 10,009
Estimated Number Existing in 1979: 65
Miles per Gallon: 12–18
Common Trouble Spots: automatic transmission, brakes
Availability of Parts: fair–poor
Investment Potential: A+

Background: The Special was the only three-porthole Buick left. Now, instead of being able to tell the most expensive Buick at a glance, people could tell who was driving the cheapest one. Apparently, few buyers were concerned porthole watchers—the Special was Buick's most popular convertible by far.

It came with a 188 h.p. 264 cu. in. V8 engine. A three-speed manual transmission was standard. Dynaflow automatic transmission was optional. Power steering was also optional and was highly praised at the time for its good "feel of the road" characteristics.

1955 Buick Special Convertible

PHOTO: PUBLIC RELATIONS DEPARTMENT, BUICK MOTOR DIVISION

1955 Buick Super Convertible

Original Price: $3,225
Number Produced: 3,527
Estimated Number Existing in 1979: 23
Miles per Gallon: 12–17
Common Trouble Spots: automatic transmission, brakes
Availability of Parts: fair–poor
Investment Potential: A+

Background: Like the Roadmaster, the Super now had four portholes on each of its fenders. This made it a bit harder to tell the two apart. The Super came with a 236 h.p. 322 cu. in. V8 engine. A three-speed manual transmission was standard. Dynaflow automatic transmission was optional.

1955 Buick Super Convertible

PHOTO: PUBLIC RELATIONS DEPARTMENT, BUICK MOTOR DIVISION

1955 Cadillac Eldorado Convertible

Original Price: $6,286
Number Produced: 3,950
Estimated Number Existing in 1979: 36
Miles per Gallon: 12–17
Common Trouble Spots: automatic transmission
Availability of Parts: fair–poor
Investment Potential: AA

Background: The 1955 Eldorado looked pretty much the same from the front as last year's model. However, it now had sprouted its own unique tailfins.

The only engine offered was a 270 h.p. 331 cu. in. V8 with two four-barrel carburetors. Hydramatic automatic transmission, power steering, power brakes, and power front seat were standard.

1955 Cadillac Eldorado Convertible

PHOTO: CADILLAC MOTOR CAR DIVISION

1955 Cadillac Series 62 Convertible

PHOTO: CADILLAC MOTOR CAR DIVISION

1955 Cadillac Series 62 Convertible

Original Price: $4,448
Number Produced: 8,150
Estimated Number Existing in 1979: 74
Miles per Gallon: 12–17
Common Trouble Spots: automatic transmission
Availability of Parts: fair–poor
Investment Potential: A+

Background: The minor face-lift on the new Series 62 did nothing to detract from the attractive styling of the previous year's model. It was powered by a 250 h.p. 331 cu. in. V8 engine. Hydramatic automatic transmission and power steering were standard. A "power package" which upped the horsepower rating to 270 was available for $167.

1955 Chevrolet Bel Air Convertible

Original Price: $2,305
Number Produced: 41,292
Estimated Number Existing in 1979: 814
Miles per Gallon: 13–20
Common Trouble Spots: brakes, piston rings, electrical system
Availability of Parts: good
Investment Potential: AAA+ (with V8 and overdrive); AAA (without)

Background: "New Look! New Life (V8 or 6)! New Everything!" That is how sale literature announced the 1955 Chevy. The sportiest new Chevy was the Bel Air ragtop. It came with a 123 h.p. (136-h.p. with the automatic) 235.5 cu. in. six. But no longer did Chevrolet owners have to listen to the chant, "Six in a row won't go!"—A 162 h.p. 265 cu. in. V8 was available at extra cost. With optional power pack (dual exhaust and four-barrel carburetor), this engine was rated at 180 h.p. Late in the model year, a 195 h.p. version was available on special order. A three-speed manual transmission was standard, but overdrive and Powerglide automatic were available at extra cost.

Motor Trend called the 1955 Chevy the "best handling and most roadable car" of the year.

1955 Chevrolet Bel Air Convertible

PHOTO: GM PHOTOGRAPHIC

1955 Chevrolet Bel Air Nomad Station Wagon

Original Price: $2,571
Number Produced: 8,386
Estimated Number Existing in 1979: 1,250
Miles per Gallon: 13–19
Common Trouble Spots: brakes, piston rings, electrical system
Availability of Parts: good
Investment Potential: AAA+ (with V8 and overdrive); AAA (without)

Background: The 1955 Nomad is one of the most beautiful postwar cars made by any manufacturer. Like the Corvette, it began as a "dream car." In fact, the basic 1953 Corvette design was used for its prototype. Reception of the Nomad was so enthusiastic that GM began a crash program to produce it.

The Nomad reached dealer showrooms in early 1955, barely a year after the Waldorf Nomad was displayed at the Waldorf Astoria Motorama. The production model retained the prototype's fluted roof and European-style full rear-wheel cutouts, but it was essentially just a '55 Chevy station wagon.

It was powered by a standard 123 h.p. (136 h.p. with the automatic) 235.5 cu. in. six, but most were equipped with the new 162 h.p. 265 cu. in. V8. This engine was rated at 180 h.p. when sold with the optional power pack (four-barrel carburetor and dual exhaust). Late in the model year a 195 h.p. Special Power Kit was offered. A three-speed manual transmission was standard. Overdrive and Powerglide automatic were available at extra cost.

Chevrolet offered a great many options for the '55 Nomad. According to Bill Tryon, director of the Mid-Atlantic Nomad Association, the most popular were (and are) accessory bumper guards, gas-tank door guard, fender splash guard, bug screen, sun visor, tinted glass, Autotronic Eye, Wonder Bar radio, air conditioning (offered by Chevrolet for the first time), electric seat, electric windows, power steering, and power brakes.

1955 Chevrolet Bel Air Nomad Station Wagon

PHOTO: CHEVROLET MOTOR DIVISION

1955 Chevrolet Bel Air Sport Coupe

Original Price: $2,166
Number Produced: 185,562
Estimated Number Existing in 1979: 3,525
Miles per Gallon: 13–20
Common Trouble Spots: brakes, piston rings, electrical system
Availability of Parts: good
Investment Potential: AAA

Background: This is the third most popular '55 Chevy (the most popular are the convertible and the Nomad).

The Bel Air two-door hardtop came with a 123 h.p. (136 h.p. with the automatic) 235.5 cu. in. six. The new 162 h.p. 265 cu. in. V8 was available at extra cost. With the optional power pack (dual exhaust and four-barrel carburetor), this engine was rated at 180 h.p. Late in the model year a 195 h.p. power kit was offered. A three-speed manual transmission was standard. Overdrive and Powerglide automatic transmission were optional.

1955 Chevrolet Bel Air Sport Coupe

PHOTO: GM PHOTOGRAPHIC

1955 Chevrolet Corvette Convertible

Original Price: $2,934
Number Produced: 700
Estimated Number Existing in 1979: 25
Miles per Gallon: 14–22
Common Trouble Spots: valves, piston rings (V8)
Availability of Parts: fair-good
Investment Potential: AAA

Background: The big news for Corvette in 1955 was the availability, at extra cost, of a 195 h.p. 265 cu. in. V8 engine. The 150 h.p. (155 h.p. later in the year) 235.5 cu. in. six was standard. So was Powerglide automatic transmission.

The few buyers there were for the 1955 Vette could choose from nine body colors: black, blue, gold, green, white, two shades of copper, and two shades of red. A variety of interior colors was also available.

Next to the 1953, this is the rarest of all Corvettes.

1955 Chevrolet Corvette Convertible

PHOTO: T. MICHAELIS CORVETTE SUPPLIES

1955 Chevrolet 210 Sport Coupe

Original Price: est. $2,000
Number Produced: 11,675
Estimated Number Existing in 1979: 221
Miles per Gallon: 13–20
Common Trouble Spots: brakes, piston rings, electrical system
Availability of Parts: good
Investment Potential: AAA

Background: The attractive '55 Chevy 210 two-door hardtop was powered by a 123 h.p. (136 h.p. with the automatic) 235.5 cu. in six. A 162 h.p. 265 cu. in. V8 was available at extra cost. With the optional power pack (dual exhaust and four-barrel carburetor), this engine was rated at 180 h.p. Late in the model year, a 195 h.p. version was available on special order. A three-speed manual transmission was standard. Overdrive and Powerglide automatic transmission were offered at extra cost.

1955 Chrysler New Yorker Deluxe Convertible

Original Price: $3,869
Number Produced: 946
Estimated Number Existing in 1979: 7
Miles per Gallon: 12–17
Common Trouble Spots: none
Availability of Parts: poor
Investment Potential: AA

Background: Although completely redesigned for 1955, the New Yorker Deluxe convertible found few buyers.

It came with a 250 h.p. 331 cu. in. V8 engine, with four-barrel carburetor. Dual exhaust, padded dash, power brakes, and Power Flite automatic transmission were standard. Many options were also available, including (late in the model year) seat belts.

1955 Chrysler New Yorker Deluxe Convertible

PHOTO: CHRYSLER HISTORICAL COLLECTION

1955 Chrysler 300 Coupe

Original Price: $4,055
Number Produced: 1,725
Estimated Number Existing in 1979: 25
Miles per Gallon: 9–15
Common Trouble Spots: none
Availability of Parts: poor
Investment Potential: AAA

Background: This was the first of the famous Chrysler 300 Letter Series. It was one of the most admired (and "hot") cars of its day. *Motor Trend* called the 300 "1955's most esthetically styled car." It came equipped with a 300 h.p. 331 cu. in. Hemi engine. Power Flite automatic transmission was standard.

Among the many options were power steering, power brakes, electric windows, power seats, radio, clock, outside rear-view mirror, and wire wheels.

Buyers had their choice of three exterior colors: black, Tango red, and platinum. The interior was leather.

1955 Chrysler 300 Coupe

PHOTO: CHRYSLER HISTORICAL COLLECTION

1955 Chrysler Windsor Deluxe Convertible

Original Price: $3,035
Number Produced: 1,395
Estimated Number Existing in 1979: 10
Miles per Gallon: 12–17
Common Trouble Spots: none
Availability of Parts: poor
Investment Potential: A

Background: The Windsor was completely restyled for 1955. It was now equipped with a 188 h.p. 301 cu. in. "Spitfire" eight-cylinder engine. No six-cylinder engine was available.

A three-speed manual transmission was standard. Power Flite automatic was optional. Buyers had their choice of seventeen solid and twenty-six two-tone exterior color combinations.

1955 Chrysler Windsor Deluxe Convertible

1955 DeSoto Firedome S22 Convertible

Original Price: $2,779
Number Produced: 625
Estimated Number Existing in 1979: 3
Miles per Gallon: 12–18
Common Trouble Spots: brakes, piston rings, valves
Availability of Parts: fair–poor
Investment Potential: A+

Background: The '55 Firedome was the first really flashy DeSoto convertible—it was much sportier-looking than the boxy styles of the previous years. The Firedome was powered by a 185 h.p. 291 cu. in. V8. A three-speed manual transmission was standard. Power Flite automatic transmission was optional.

1955 DeSoto Fireflite S21 Convertible

Original Price: $3,106
Number Produced: 775
Estimated Number Existing in 1979: 4
Miles per Gallon: 12–18
Common Trouble Spots: brakes, piston rings, valves
Availability of Parts: fair–poor
Investment Potential: A+

Background: The attractive new Fireflite ragtop was powered by a 200 h.p. 291 cu. in. V8. A three-speed manual transmission was standard. Overdrive and Power Flite automatic transmission were optional at extra cost.

1955 Dodge Custom Royal Lancer Convertible

Original Price: $2,723
Number Produced: 3,302
Estimated Number Existing in 1979: 17
Miles per Gallon: 12–18
Common Trouble Spots: none
Availability of Parts: poor–fair
Investment Potential: A+

Background: Styling on the new Custom Royal seemed to have been influenced by Dodge's Granada "dream car" of 1954. The most noticeable changes for '55 were tailfins and a wraparound windshield. For the first time, Dodges could honestly be described as flashy—especially those with the new three-tone paint jobs.

The Custom Royal ragtop was powered by a 183 h.p. 270 cu. in. V8. A 193 h.p. version of this engine, with four-barrel carburetor and dual exhaust, was available. A three-speed manual transmission was standard. Power Flite automatic transmission (with shifting lever on the dash) and overdrive were optional.

1955 Ford Fairlane Crown Victoria

Original Price: $2,202
Number Produced: 33,165
Estimated Number Existing in 1979: 189
Miles per Gallon: 13–18
Common Trouble Spots: none
Availability of Parts: fair
Investment Potential: AA+

Background: New for 1955 was the beautiful Crown Victoria. It was basically just a fancy two-door sedan with special trim and upholstery.

It was available with either a 120 h.p. 223 cu. in. six-cylinder engine, a 162 h.p. 272 cu. in. V8 or a 182 h.p. "power pack" 272 cu. in. V8. Late in the model year a 193 h.p. 292 cu. in. V8 was offered. A three-speed manual transmission was standard. Overdrive and Ford-O-Matic automatic transmission were optional.

1955 Ford Fairlane Crown Victoria Skyliner

Original Price: $2,272
Number Produced: 1,999
Estimated Number Existing in 1979: 17
Miles per Gallon: 13–18
Common Trouble Spots: none
Availability of Parts: fair
Investment Potential: AAA

Background: The "half glass" Skyliner roof was now available in the new Fairlane series. Like the previous year's model, it consisted of a blue-green tinted Plexiglas insert over the front half of the car's roof. This year the lining zipped in, instead of snapping on.

Unlike the traditional rectangular radios, the Fairlane's two optional radios were circular (for 1955 only). This adds a bit of distinction to the car's interior.

The Crown Victoria looked like a two-door sedan with a wide chrome band running across the roof and inside on the headliner. It had a special interior that included a fold-down armrest in the rear seat. That, and the upholstery design, helped create a bucket-seat effect.

It was powered by a 120 h.p. 223 cu. in. six-cylinder engine. Also available were a 162 h.p. 272 cu. in. V8 (rated at 182 h.p. when equipped with a four-barrel carburetor and dual exhaust) and, late in the model year, a 193 h.p. Thunderbird 292 cu. in. V8. A three-speed manual transmission was standard. Overdrive and Ford-O-Matic automatic transmission were optional.

Special Interest Autos called the '55 Skyliner "a fine car in every way—a worthy big brother of the Thunderbird."

1955 Ford Fairlane Crown Victoria

PHOTO: FORD MOTOR COMPANY

1955 Ford Fairlane Sunliner Convertible

Original Price: $2,204
Number Produced: 49,966
Estimated Number Existing in 1979: 284
Miles per Gallon: 13–18
Common Trouble Spots: none
Availability of Parts: fair
Investment Potential: AAA

Background: The Sunliner convertible was restyled for 1955. It came with a 120 h.p. 223 cu. in. six-cylinder engine. A 162 h.p. 272 cu. in. V8, and a 182 h.p. four-barrel carburetor version of this V8 engine, were optional. Late in the model year a 193 h.p. 292 cu. in. V8 was offered. A three-speed manual transmission was standard. Overdrive and Ford-O-Matic automatic transmission were available at extra cost.

Some new features on the Sunliner this year were an automatic choke, 120-mile-per-hour speedometer, an automatic transmission gear indicator on the instrument panel, and a more rigid frame.

According to *Iron Age,* nearly half of all 1955 Fords had a two-tone paint job.

1955 Ford Fairlane Sunliner Convertible

1955 Ford Thunderbird Convertible

Original Price: $2,695
Number Produced: 16,155
Estimated Number Existing in 1979: 1,600
Miles per Gallon: 13–18
Common Trouble Spots: automatic transmission
Availability of Parts: fair
Investment Potential: AAA+

Background: "Enchantment unlimited" is how Ford described the first of the "classic" Thunderbirds. It bore a strong family resemblance to the full-size Ford Fairlane (a few '55 T-Birds even had the Fairlane's distinctive full-length side chrome piece).

It came with a 193 h.p. 292 cu. in. V8. This engine was rated at 198 h.p. when equipped with the automatic. A three-speed manual transmission was standard. Overdrive and Fordomatic automatic were optional at extra cost. All transmissions were floor mounted.

Buyers had a choice of five exterior colors: black, blue, red, white, or yellow. A hard top was standard. A soft top was available for $75. Power windows, engine dress-up kit, power seat, power steering, and simulated wire wheels were among the many options offered.

1955 Ford Thunderbird Convertible

1955 King Midget Convertible

Original Price: est. $550
Number Produced: N.A.
Estimated Number Existing in 1979: N.A.
Miles per Gallon: 50–90
Common Trouble Spots: transmission, "V" belts
Availability of Parts: good
Investment Potential: A

Background: The '55 King Midget ragtop was powered by a 9 h.p. 29 cu. in. one-cylinder engine. Automatic transmission was standard.

1955 Kurtis 500 M Sports Car

Original Price: est. $5,000
Number Produced: est. 24
Estimated Number Existing in 1979: 12
Miles per Gallon: 13–22
Common Trouble Spots: none
Availability of Parts: poor
Investment Potential: AAA

Background: The limited-production, fiberglass-bodied 1955 Kurtis 500 M was an attractive and potent car. It had a top speed of 135 mph when equipped with the standard 250 h.p. 331 cu. in. Cadillac V8 engine. A hotter version of this engine was optional.

1955 Lincoln Capri Convertible

PHOTO: FORD MOTOR COMPANY

1955 Lincoln Capri Convertible

Original Price: \$4,071
Number Produced: 1,487
Estimated Number Existing in 1979: 6
Miles per Gallon: 11–17
Common Trouble Spots: carburetor
Availability of Parts: poor–fair
Investment Potential: AA

Background: This was the last Capri convertible. It was powered by a 225 h.p. 341 cu. in. V8. Turbo-Drive automatic transmission and dual exhaust were standard.

Two novel items were among the options available on Lincoln in 1955. One was a power lubrication system which would give the car a grease job when a button on the dash was pushed. The system was good for up to 225 such operations before it had to be refilled with lubricant. The other unusual option was a unit that would automatically start the car's engine if it stalled. It was called, appropriately enough, "Startmaster."

1955 Mercury Montclair Convertible

Original Price: \$2,712
Number Produced: 10,668
Estimated Number Existing in 1979: 29
Miles per Gallon: 12–18
Common Trouble Spots: carburetor
Availability of Parts: fair–poor
Investment Potential: A+

Background: This was the first year for the Montclair convertible. It was powered by a 198 h.p. 292 cu. in. V8. A three-speed manual transmission was standard. Overdrive and Turbo-Drive automatic transmission were optional. All Montclairs came with dual exhaust.

The upholstery was available in leather, vinyl, tapestry-weave nylon, plain nylon, and woven plastics. Buyers had their choice of thirty two-tone or fifteen solid exterior colors.

A novel feature offered on the new Montclair was an automatic chassis lubrication device. All a Montclair owner had to do to lubricate his or her car was push a button on the dash.

The 1955 Mercury tied with Chevy as *Motor Trend*'s "best handling and most roadable" car of the year.

1955 Mercury Montclair Sun Valley

Original Price: \$2,711
Number Produced: 1,787
Estimated Number Existing in 1979: 6
Miles per Gallon: 12–18
Common Trouble Spots: carburetor
Availability of Parts: poor–fair
Investment Potential: AA

Background: The Sun Valley was restyled for 1955. It appeared a bit bulkier and flashier than the previous year's model. The outstanding feature of the Sun Valley was its "half glass" roof. Actually, the transparent (green-tinted) panel over the front half of the roof was made of plastic. It tended to discolor and was easily damaged.

The Sun Valley was powered by a 198 h.p. 292 cu. in. V8. A three-speed manual transmission was standard. Overdrive and Merc-O-Matic automatic transmission were optional.

1955 Mercury Montclair Sun Valley

1955 Mercury Montclair Convertible

PHOTO: FORD MOTOR COMPANY

1955 Metropolitan Series 1200 Convertible

Original Price: $1,469
Number Produced: est. 1,280
Estimated Number Existing in 1979: 8
Miles per Gallon: 27–39
Common Trouble Spots: brakes, gearshift
Availability of Parts: fair–good
Investment Potential: A

Background: The '55 Metropolitan was powered by a 42 h.p. 73.2 cu. in. four-cylinder engine. A three-speed manual transmission was standard. A radio ($60) and a heater ($69) were optional.

Many Metropolitan owners had brake troubles, but it was discovered that most of them were using the wrong kind of brake fluid. Mets also had a habit of sticking between first and second gears.

Mets sold at Nash dealerships had a Nash medallion and hubcaps. Those sold by Hudson dealers had a Hudson grille badge and hubcaps.

1955 Metropolitan Series 1200 Convertible

PHOTO: RICHARD J. MCGARTY, METROPOLITAN OWNERS CLUB

1955 Oldsmobile Starfire 98 Convertible

Original Price: $3,276
Number Produced: 9,149
Estimated Number Existing in 1979: 54
Miles per Gallon: 13–18
Common Trouble Spots: none
Availability of Parts: fair
Investment Potential: A+

Background: The attractive new 98 was powered by a 202 h.p. 324.3 cu. in. V8 engine. A three-speed manual transmission was standard. Hydra-Matic automatic transmission was optional at extra cost. All 98 convertibles had power windows and power front seats.

A novel option available on the '55 Starfire 98 ragtop was a plastic top boot cover.

1955 Oldsmobile Super 88 Convertible

Original Price: $2,894
Number Produced: 9,007
Estimated Number Existing in 1979: 53
Miles per Gallon: 14–18
Common Trouble Spots: none
Availability of Parts: fair
Investment Potential: A+

Background: The Super 88 ragtop was powered by a 202 h.p. 324.3 cu. in. V8 engine. A three-speed manual transmission was standard. Hydramatic automatic transmission was optional.

Buyers had their choice of five colors of convertible tops: black, blue, green, tan, or white. A special white orlon top and a plastic top boot were available at extra cost.

The 1955 Olds Super 88 had a top speed of over 110 mph. It could shoot from 0 to 60 in 10.6 seconds.

1955 Oldsmobile Super 88 Convertible

PHOTO: OLDSMOBILE DIVISION

1955 Oldsmobile Starfire 98 Convertible

PHOTO: OLDSMOBILE DIVISION

1955 Packard Caribbean Convertible

PHOTO: RICHARD QUINN COLLECTION

1955 Packard Caribbean Convertible

Original Price: $5,932
Number Produced: 500
Estimated Number Existing in 1979: 50
Miles per Gallon: 10–16
Common Trouble Spots: automatic transmission, cooling system
Availability of Parts: poor–fair
Investment Potential: AAA

Background: The Caribbean was restyled for 1955. A new feature was torsion-bar suspension, which made riding in a Caribbean a real delight. Another innovation was a load levelizer, which kept the car at the same level above the road regardless of how much weight it was carrying. A 275 h.p. 352 cu. in. V8, Ultramatic automatic transmission, and power steering were standard.

In June 1955, *Printers Ink* reported that Packard was experiencing "one of the biggest backlogs of new car orders in Packard history." Employees had to work overtime just to keep up with the demand. Unfortunately, the '55 Packard got the reputation of being a troublesome car, and that sealed Packard's fate.

1955 Plymouth Belvedere Convertible

Original Price: $2,351
Number Produced: 8,473
Estimated Number Existing in 1979: 39
Miles per Gallon: 13–17
Common Trouble Spots: cooling system, valves
Availability of Parts: poor–fair
Investment Potential: A+

Background: The Belvedere was attractively restyled for 1955, and Plymouth styling went from "cute" to "pretty."

It came with a 167 h.p. 260 cu. in. V8. With the optional power package, the 260 was rated at 177 h.p. A three-speed manual transmission was standard. Overdrive and Power Flite automatic transmission were offered at extra cost.

About 9% of all 1955 Plymouths were equipped with power brakes, approximately 8% had power steering, and 45.7% had the automatic transmission.

Motor Trend called the 1955 Plymouth the "softest riding in its field by far" and "the easiest car to drive" when equipped with power steering.

1955 Pontiac Star Chief Custom Safari Station Wagon

PHOTO: PONTIAC MOTOR DIVISION

1955 Pontiac Star Chief Custom Safari Station Wagon

Original Price: $2,714
Number Produced: 3,760
Estimated Number Existing in 1979: 32
Miles per Gallon: 13–18
Common Trouble Spots: automatic transmission, engine bearings, valves
Availability of Parts: fair
Investment Potential: AAA

Background: The Safari was the flashiest and sportiest station wagon Pontiac had ever offered. It was powered by a 180 h.p. 287.2 cu. in. V8. This engine was rated at 173 h.p. when equipped with the standard three-speed manual transmission. For $35, buyers could order a 200 h.p. four-barrel carburetor version of the same engine. Hydra-Matic automatic transmission was also optional.

The 1955 Safari is one of the most desirable of all postwar automobiles.

1955 Pontiac Star Chief Convertible

Original Price: $2,691
Number Produced: 19,762
Estimated Number Existing in 1979: 78
Miles per Gallon: 13–18
Common Trouble Spots: automatic transmission, engine bearings, valves
Availability of Parts: fair
Investment Potential: A+

Background: The Star Chief convertible was pleasingly restyled for 1955. It was powered by a new 180 h.p. 287.2 cu. in. V8. This engine was rated at 173 h.p. when equipped with manual transmission. For $35, one could have a 200-h.p., four-barrel carburetor, version of this engine. A three-speed manual transmission was standard. Hydra-Matic automatic transmission was optional.

Other options included power steering, power brakes, underseat heater (it worked great!), electric windows, and an air conditioner.

Although not currently one of the hot collector cars,

the 1955 Star Chief convertible has a lot of potential. In a 1977 article in *Old Cars* newspaper, columnist Tim Howley stated: "With all the emphasis on 1955-57 Chevrolets these days, a lot of collectors are passing over the far better bargain, Pontiacs of the same years, especially the '55s."

1955 Pontiac Star Chief Convertible

PHOTO: PONTIAC MOTOR DIVISION

1956

1956 Buick Century Convertible

Original Price: $3,261
Number Produced: 4,721
Estimated Number Existing in 1979: 46
Miles per Gallon: 11–17
Common Trouble Spots: automatic transmission, brakes, cooling system
Availability of Parts: fair–poor
Investment Potential: A+

Background: "Drive the Century and you command thrills that set the pulse of even a sports-car enthusiast to pounding." So claimed a '56 Buick sales catalog.

The new Century ragtop was powered by a 255 h.p. 322 cu. in. V8 with four-barrel carburetor. Dynaflow automatic transmission, power front seats, power windows, and electric clock were standard. Nearly 46% of all 1956 Buicks were equipped with power brakes, almost 52% had power steering, 87.6% had radios, 3.7% had air conditioning, 62.8% had tinted glass, and 71.7% had windshield washers. Buyers had their choice of four leather interiors.

1956 Buick Century Convertible

PHOTO: PUBLIC RELATIONS DEPARTMENT, BUICK MOTOR DIVISION

1956 Buick Roadmaster Convertible

Original Price: $3,659
Number Produced: 4,354
Estimated Number Existing in 1979: 42
Miles per Gallon: 11–17
Common Trouble Spots: automatic transmission, brakes, cooling system
Availability of Parts: fair–poor
Investment Potential: A+

Background: The luxurious Roadmaster convertible was powered by a 255 h.p. 322 cu. in. V8 with four-barrel carburetor. Dynaflow automatic transmission, power windows, power front seat, padded dash, and dual exhaust were standard. Buyers could choose from four leather interiors.

1956 Buick Roadmaster Convertible

PHOTO: PUBLIC RELATIONS DEPARTMENT, BUICK MOTOR DIVISION

1956 Buick Special Convertible

Original Price: $2,696
Number Produced: 9,712
Estimated Number Existing in 1979: 95
Miles per Gallon: 12–17
Common Trouble Spots: automatic transmission, brakes, cooling system
Availability of Parts: fair–poor
Investment Potential: A+

Background: Once again, the Special was the only Buick convertible with three portholes on each fender. It came with a 220 h.p. 322 cu. in. V8. A three-speed manual transmission was standard, but not very popular. Most '56 Buicks, 96.5%, came equipped with Dynaflow automatic transmission. Only 12.1% had power windows. A padded dash was one of the many options available.

Four "all-cordaveen" interiors, in black and ivory, two-tone blue, two-tone green, or red, were offered.

1956 Buick Special Convertible

PHOTO: PUBLIC RELATIONS DEPARTMENT, BUICK MOTOR DIVISION

1956 Buick Super Convertible

Original Price: $3,499
Number Produced: 2,489
Estimated Number Existing in 1979: 24
Miles per Gallon: 11–17
Common Trouble Spots: automatic transmission, brakes, cooling system
Availability of Parts: fair–poor
Investment Potential: A+

Background: The Super convertible continued to have four portholes on each fender, thus making it hard to distinguish from the Roadmaster. It came with a 255 h.p. 322 cu. in. V8 with four-barrel carburetor. Dynaflow automatic transmission, electric clock, power seats, and power windows were standard. Dual exhaust was among the options.

1956 Buick Super Convertible

PHOTO: PUBLIC RELATIONS DEPARTMENT, BUICK MOTOR DIVISION

1956 Cadillac Eldorado Biarritz Convertible

Original Price: $6,286
Number Produced: 2,150
Estimated Number Existing in 1979: 34
Miles per Gallon: 12–18
Common Trouble Spots: automatic transmission, brakes
Availability of Parts: fair–poor
Investment Potential: AA

Background: A new grille was the most noticeable difference between the 1956 and the 1955 Eldorado. Aside from that, both models looked much the same.

It came equipped with a 305 h.p. 365 cu. in. V8 engine. Hydramatic automatic transmission was standard. All Eldorados had power steering, power brakes, and windshield washers.

1956 Cadillac Eldorado Biarritz Convertible

PHOTO: CADILLAC MOTOR CAR DIVISION

1956 Cadillac Series 62 Convertible

PHOTO: CADILLAC MOTOR CAR DIVISION

1956 Cadillac Series 62 Convertible

Original Price: $4,448
Number Produced: 8,300
Estimated Number Existing in 1979: 105
Miles per Gallon: 12–18
Common Trouble Spots: automatic transmission, brakes
Availability of Parts: fair–poor
Investment Potential: A+

Background: The Series 62 convertible was little changed for 1956. It was powered by a 285 h.p. 365 cu. in. V8. A 305-hp version of this engine was optional. Hydramatic automatic transmission was standard.

All Cadillacs had power steering, power brakes, and windshield washers. Sixty-five percent came with power seats, 76% had power windows, and 26% were equipped with air conditioning.

A Series 62 convertible had the honor of being the one-millionth Cadillac produced.

1956 Chevrolet Bel Air Convertible

Original Price: $2,409
Number Produced: 41,268
Estimated Number Existing in 1979: 850
Miles per Gallon: 13–20
Common Trouble Spots: none
Availability of Parts: good
Investment Potential: AAA

Background: The 1956 Bel Air ragtop was, and probably always will be, a very popular car. It was powered by a 140 h.p. 235.5 cu. in. six. A 162 h.p. 265 cu. in. V8 was optional. This engine was rated at 170 h.p. when equipped with automatic, 205 h.p. with a four-barrel carburetor and dual exhaust, and 225 h.p. with two four-barrel carburetors and dual exhaust. A three-speed manual transmission was standard. Overdrive and Powerglide automatic transmission were offered at extra cost.

Most 1956 Chevrolets, 57.6%, came equipped with a V8, 60.5% had an automatic, 36% had a three-speed manual, 3.5% had overdrive, 6.3% had power brakes, 7.3% had power steering, .5% had power windows, almost 1% had an air conditioner, 16.2% had tinted glass, 24% had windshield washers, and 66.5% were sold with a radio.

1956 Chevrolet Bel Air Nomad Station Wagon

Original Price: $2,673
Number Produced: 7,886
Estimated Number Existing in 1979: 1,100
Miles per Gallon: 13–19
Common Trouble Spots: none
Availability of Parts: good
Investment Potential: AAA+ (with overdrive and a V8); AAA (without)

Background: The 1956 Nomad is a beautiful car, but, for some reason, it is the least popular Nomad. It came with a 235.5 cu. in. six. Most buyers ordered the optional 162 h.p. 265 cu. in. V8. This engine was rated at 170 h.p. when equipped with the automatic. It was rated at 205 h.p. when equipped with a four-barrel carburetor and dual exhaust, and at 225 h.p. when sold with two four-barrel carbs. Overdrive and Powerglide automatic transmission were optional. A three-speed manual was standard.

1956 Chevrolet Bel Air Nomad Station Wagon

PHOTO: GM PHOTOGRAPHIC

1956 Chevrolet Bel Air Convertible

PHOTO: GM PHOTOGRAPHIC

1956 Chevrolet Bel Air Sport Coupe

Original Price: $2,142
Number Produced: 128,382
Estimated Number Existing in 1979: 2,560
Miles per Gallon: 13–20
Common Trouble Spots: none
Availability of Parts: good
Investment Potential: AAA

Background: Anyone who has ever driven a '56 Chevy will know why *Motor Trend* named it the "best handling car of the year;" it was (and is) a pleasure to drive, even without power steering.

The Bel Air two-door hardtop came with a 140 h.p. 235.5 cu. in. six. Most buyers ordered the optional 162 h.p. 265 cu. in. V8. This engine was rated at 170 h.p. with the automatic, 205 h.p. with a four-barrel carburetor and dual exhaust, and 225 h.p. with two four-barrel carburetors and dual exhaust. A three-speed manual was standard, but not very popular. Most buyers ordered the Powerglide automatic. A small number ordered a manual with overdrive.

The 1956 Bel Air Sport Coupe is a very desirable car from both a styling and a driving standpoint. Too bad everyone knows this!

1956 Chevrolet Corvette Convertible

Original Price: $3,120
Number Produced: 3,467
Estimated Number Existing in 1979: 110
Miles per Gallon: 13–20
Common Trouble Spots: none
Availability of Parts: fair–good
Investment Potential: AAA

Background: The 1956 Corvette had classic good looks. It also had roll-up windows, and the doors could be locked. The standard engine was a 210 h.p. 265 cu. in. V8. Two other versions of this engine were available—a 225 h.p. and a 240 h.p. (equipped with the $188.30 optional high lift camshaft). A three-speed manual transmission was standard. A three-speed manual with overdrive and Powerglide automatic transmission were optional at extra cost.

Other options included power steering, power windows, radio and heater, windshield washer, and, for $215.20, a removable hard top. The hard top was offered at no cost if ordered in place of the soft top.

1956 Chevrolet Corvette Convertible

PHOTO: T. MICHAELIS CORVETTE SUPPLIES

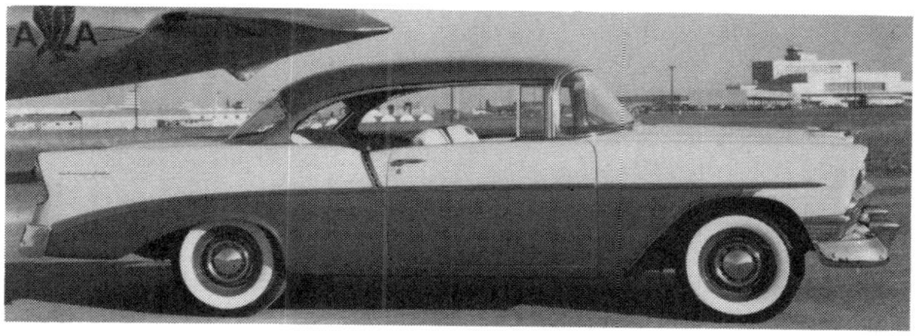

1956 Chevrolet 210 Sport Coupe

PHOTO: GM PHOTOGRAPHIC

1956 Chevrolet 210 Sport Coupe

Original Price: $2,029
Number Produced: 18,616
Estimated Number Existing in 1979: 370
Miles per Gallon: 13–20
Common Trouble Spots: none
Availability of Parts: good
Investment Potential: AAA

Background: Less flashy side trim was about all that distinguished the '56 210 two-door hardtop from the Bel Air. But apparently that was important enough to discourage a lot of buyers.

The 210 Sport Coupe came with a 140 h.p. 235.5 cu. in. six. A 162 h.p. 265 cu. in. V8 was optional. This engine was rated at 170 h.p. with the automatic, 205 h.p. when equipped with a four-barrel carburetor and dual exhaust, and 225 h.p. with two four-barrel carburetors and dual exhaust. A three-speed manual transmission was standard. Overdrive and Powerglide automatic transmission were available at extra cost.

1956 Chrysler New Yorker Convertible

Original Price: $4,136
Number Produced: 921
Estimated Number Existing in 1979: 10
Miles per Gallon: 12–17
Common Trouble Spots: none
Availability of Parts: poor
Investment Potential: AA

Background: The 1956 New Yorker ragtop was powered by a 280 h.p. 354 cu. in. V8. Power Flite automatic transmission and power brakes were standard. Later in the model year, Torque Flite automatic transmission was available.

A unique option was the "Highway Hi-Fi" record player, which could be mounted under the dash. It played through the car's radio speaker and had a tone arm that wouldn't skip when the car went over bumps. It used special seven-inch discs, made by Columbia Records, which had a playing time of forty-five minutes to an hour.

Among the other options available were air conditioning, two radios (Electro Touch Tuner Radio with foot control, and Music Master), power windows, a four-way power front seat, wire wheels, a self-winding clock set in the steering wheel, and 8.00 × 15 four-ply whitewall tires.

An interesting feature of 1956 Chryslers was that the automatic transmission shifter was placed on the dash.

1956 Chrysler New Yorker Convertible

1956 Chrysler 300-B Coupe

Original Price: $4,312
Number Produced: 1,102
Estimated Number Existing in 1979: 17
Miles per Gallon: 8–15
Common Trouble Spots: none
Availability of Parts: poor–fair
Investment Potential: AAA

Background: Styling was little changed from the 1955 model. But those changes greatly enhanced the beauty of this hot-performance car.

It came equipped with a 340 h.p. 354 cu. in. eight-cylinder engine. A 355 h.p. version of this engine was available at extra cost. Power Flite automatic transmission was standard. A three-speed manual was optional for $70. Some other accessories offered on the 300-B were power steering, power brakes, electric windows, power seats, and a clock on the steering wheel. Buyers could choose from three exterior colors: black, red, and white. The interior was leather.

1956 Chrysler 300-B Coupe

PHOTO: CHRYSLER CORPORATION

1956 Chrysler Windsor Convertible

Original Price: $3,235
Number Produced: 1,011
Estimated Number Existing in 1979: 10
Miles per Gallon: 12–17
Common Trouble Spots: none
Availability of Parts: poor
Investment Potential: AA

Background: Despite a face-lift, sales of the 1956 Windsor were down from the year before; in fact, sales were so disappointing that Chrysler dropped the Windsor convertible during the model year. That was a shame, since this was probably one of the most attractive post-war Chrysler convertibles made. In fact, it was one of the best-looking convertibles of any make.

The Windsor was powered by a 225 h.p. 331 cu. in. V8 engine. This engine was rated at 250 h.p. when equipped with the power package. A three-speed manual transmission was standard. Power Flite automatic transmission was optional. Almost all Windsor buyers chose automatic transmission. Ninety percent of all Chryslers came with power steering, although some owners complained that the power steering lacked road feel. Tinted glass was also popular; most buyers requested it.

The 1956 Windsor convertible is a beautiful and rare automobile. It has more potential than current selling prices might indicate.

1956 Continental Mark II Hardtop

Original Price: $9,538
Number Produced: 2,550
Estimated Number Existing in 1979: 1,200
Miles per Gallon: 9–16
Common Trouble Spots: brakes, carburetor, cooling system
Availability of Parts: fair
Investment Potential: AAA+

Background: The Continental Mark II was designed to be a classic in the tradition of the Continental Mark I of the 1940s.

In a 1955 interview in *Business Week,* the manager of the Continental division, William Ford, said, "The Continental is for an exclusive market—the prestige market—consisting of people of good taste who want an automobile embodying distinction, luxury, dignity and quality."

A rumor was started that the social standing of potential Mark II buyers would be checked. One Continental salesperson was quoted as saying, "I won't sell this car to a man who doesn't belong in it, even if he has the money."

Although the Mark II didn't reach showrooms until

October 21, 1955, the pre-introduction publicity was so effective that, as *Business Week* reported, dealers had 1,200 tentative orders by June of 1955. Nearly 500 of these orders carried deposits of from $500 to as much as $10,000.

The beautiful Mark II came with a 300 h.p. 368 cu. in. V8. Turbo-Drive automatic transmission was standard, as was nearly everything else. The only option was an air conditioner.

1956 Continental Mark II Hardtop

PHOTO: FORD MOTOR COMPANY

1956 DeSoto Adventurer Sport Coupe

Original Price: $3,638
Number Produced: N.A.
Estimated Number Existing in 1979: N.A.
Miles per Gallon: 10–16
Common Trouble Spots: none
Availability of Parts: fair–poor
Investment Potential: AA+

Background: The 1956 Adventurer Sport Coupe is one of the most highly prized DeSotos ever built. It was a high-performance car with a lot of flair. The Adventurer came with a 320 h.p. 341 cu. in. V8. Powerflite automatic transmission was standard.

1956 DeSoto Firedome Convertible

Original Price: $2,991
Number Produced: N.A.
Estimated Number Existing in 1979: N.A.
Miles per Gallon: 12–17
Common Trouble Spots: none
Availability of Parts: fair–poor
Investment Potential: A+

Background: The snazzy '56 Firedome ragtop was powered by a 230 h.p. 330 cu. in. V8 engine. A three-speed manual transmission was standard. Overdrive and Power Flite automatic transmission were optional. Later in the model year, Torque Flite automatic was offered.

Most 1956 DeSotos, 98.6%, came with an automatic, 1.1% had the three-speed manual, less than one-third of one percent had overdrive, 74.6% had power steering, 67.4% had power brakes, 7.4% had electric windows, 11% had power front seats, 67.3% had a radio, 50.7% had tinted glass, 49.5% had windshield washers, and 2.5% were sold with an air conditioner.

1956 DeSoto Fireflite Convertible

Original Price: $3,454
Number Produced: N.A.
Estimated Number Existing in 1979: N.A.
Miles per Gallon: 12–17
Common Trouble Spots: none
Availability of Parts: fair–poor
Investment Potential: A+

Background: The attractive '56 Fireflite convertible was available in 14 solid colors and 84 two-tone combinations. It was powered by a 255 h.p. 330 cu. in. V8 with four-barrel carburetor. Power Flite automatic transmission was standard.

Two unique options available on the Fireflite were a "Highway Hi-Fi" record player and (for $39) a fifteen-jewel watch mounted in the hub of the steering wheel.

1956 DeSoto Fireflite Pacesetter Convertible

Original Price: $3,525
Number Produced: N.A.
Estimated Number Existing in 1979: N.A.
Miles per Gallon: 12–17
Common Trouble Spots: none
Availability of Parts: fair–poor
Investment Potential: AA

Background: The Pacesetter got its name from the 1956 DeSoto Indy 500 pace car. All Pacesetters came with two-tone gold-and-white exteriors. Power brakes, electric windows, and power front seats were standard, but could be deleted if the buyer didn't want them. It was powered by a 255 h.p. 330.4 cu. in. V8 with four-barrel carburetor. The transmission was Power Flite push-button automatic.

1956 DeSoto Fireflite Pacesetter Convertible

PHOTO: CHRYSLER CORPORATION

1956 Dodge Coronet Convertible

Original Price: $2,604
Number Produced: 1,913
Estimated Number Existing in 1979: 17
Miles per Gallon: 12–18
Common Trouble Spots: none
Availability of Parts: poor–fair
Investment Potential: A+

Background: The '56 Coronet ragtop was powered by a 189 h.p. 270 cu. in. V8. A 218 h.p. 315 cu. in. V8 was available at extra cost. A three-speed manual transmission was standard. Overdrive and push-button Power Flite automatic transmission were optional. Later in the model year, Torque Flite automatic was offered.

Ninety percent of all Dodges sold in 1956 were equipped with an automatic, 1.4% had overdrive, 17.6% had power brakes, 22.5% had power steering, 21.4% had windshield washers, 23.7% had tinted glass, 47.2% had radios, 2.4% had power front seats, 2.3% had electric windows, and .7% were sold with air conditioning.

1956 Dodge Coronet Convertible

1956 Dodge Custom Royal Convertible

Original Price: $2,838
Number Produced: 1,378
Estimated Number Existing in 1979: 12
Miles per Gallon: 11–17
Common Trouble Spots: none
Availability of Parts: poor–fair
Investment Potential: A+

Background: The Custom Royal was Dodge's most expensive convertible in 1956. It came with a 230 h.p. 315 cu. in. V8. A 260 h.p. version of this engine was available at extra cost. A three-speed manual transmission was standard. Overdrive and push-button Power Flite automatic transmission were optional. Later in the model year, Torque Flite automatic was offered.

1956 Ford Fairlane Crown Victoria

Original Price: $2,099
Number Produced: 9,209
Estimated Number Existing in 1979: 78
Miles per Gallon: 13–18
Common Trouble Spots: carburetor
Availability of Parts: fair
Investment Potential: AA+

Background: The attractive Crown Victoria was little changed from the previous year's model—at least on the outside. Inside, it had a redesigned dash and a deep-dish steering wheel.

It was powered by a 137 h.p. 223 cu. in. six. Two V8s, a 173 h.p. 272 and a 200 h.p. 292, were available at extra cost. A three-speed manual transmission was standard. Overdrive and Ford-O-Matic automatic transmission were optional.

1956 Ford Fairlane Crown Victoria

PHOTO: FORD MOTOR COMPANY

1956 Dodge Custom Royal Convertible

PHOTO: CHRYSLER CORPORATION

1956 Ford Fairlane Crown Victoria Skyliner

Original Price: $2,164
Number Produced: 603
Estimated Number Existing in 1979: 8
Miles per Gallon: 13–18
Common Trouble Spots: carburetor
Availability of Parts: fair
Investment Potential: AAA

Background: This was the last year for the "half glass" Skyliner. As in previous years, the blue-green tinted Plexiglas insert had its problems: riders tended to get overly warm very fast on hot days, regardless of whether the lining was zipped in or not, and the roof insert was still very susceptible to scratches.

It was powered by a 137 h.p. 223 cu. in. six-cylinder engine. Two V8s, a 173-h.p. 272 and a 200-h.p. 292, were available at extra cost. A three-speed manual transmission was standard. Overdrive and Ford-O-Matic automatic transmission were optional.

Most 1956 Fords, 89%, were equipped with a V8, 62% had the automatic, 30% had the manual, 8% had the manual with overdrive, 19% had power steering, 2.7% had power brakes, 43% had windshield washers, 22% had tinted glass, 65% had radios, 1% had electric windows, 1% had power front seats, and 1.4% were sold with air conditioning.

1956 Ford Fairlane Sunliner Convertible

Original Price: $2,212
Number Produced: 58,147
Estimated Number Existing in 1979: 497
Miles per Gallon: 13–18
Common Trouble Spots: carburetor
Availability of Parts: fair
Investment Potential: AAA

Background: Outwardly the 1956 Sunliner resembled the '55. However, several innovations were made. A twelve-volt ignition system replaced the six-volt system of previous years. As part of its "Lifeguard Safety Program," Ford offered a new "deep center" steering wheel, better door locks, seat belts, and a padded dash. Even a new "Town and Country" signal-seeking radio and air conditioning were available.

Buyers had their choice of a 137 h.p. 223 cu. in. six-cylinder engine, or, at extra cost, a 200 h.p. 292 cu. in. V8. Most chose the V8. A three-speed manual transmission was standard. Overdrive and Ford-O-Matic automatic transmission were optional.

1956 Ford Fairlane Sunliner Convertible

PHOTO: FORD MOTOR COMPANY

1956 Ford Thunderbird Convertible

Original Price: $2,842
Number Produced: 15,631
Estimated Number Existing in 1979: 1,500
Miles per Gallon: 13–17
Common Trouble Spots: none
Availability of Parts: fair
Investment Potential: AAA+

Background: The 1956 T-Bird was virtually the same as the 1955—at least on the outside. Probably the most noticeable exterior change was the availability of a porthole hard top and a continental spare tire. Although the porthole hard top was carried over to 1957, the continental kit was not. Some say this was because the heavy rear tire affected the car's handling.

It was powered by a 202 h.p. 292 cu. in. V8. Available at extra cost was a 215 h.p. 312 cu. in. V8 (rated at 225 h.p. with an automatic) and a 260 h.p. version of this engine. (Over 90% of '56 T-Birds had a 312.) A three-speed manual transmission was standard. Overdrive and Fordomatic automatic transmission were optional at extra cost.

Buyers could choose from nine solid body colors: black, blue, coral gray, green, red, tan, white, and yellow. Five two-tone upholstery combinations were available.

1956 Ford Thunderbird Convertible

PHOTO: FORD MOTOR COMPANY

1956 King Midget Convertible

Original Price: est. $570
Number Produced: N.A.
Estimated Number Existing in 1979: N.A.
Miles per Gallon: 50–90
Common Trouble Spots: transmission, "V" belts
Availability of Parts: good
Investment Potential: A

Background: The '56 King Midget ragtop was powered by a 9 h.p. 29 cu. in. one-cylinder engine. Automatic transmission was standard.

1956 Lincoln Premier Convertible

Original Price: $4,318
Number Produced: 2,447
Estimated Number Existing in 1979: 35
Miles per Gallon: 10–16
Common Trouble Spots: brakes, carburetor, cooling system
Availability of Parts: fair–poor
Investment Potential: AAA

Background: Styling of the '56 Premier convertible was in large part taken from the 1954 XM800 Mercury "dream car." The elegant Premier convertible was powered by a 285 h.p. 368 cu. in. V8. Turbo-Drive automatic transmission and power steering were standard.

Most 1956 Lincolns, 98.4%, were equipped with power brakes, 94% had tinted glass, 86.7% had power windows, 85.1% had power seats, and 16.2% were sold with an air conditioner.

The 1956 Premier was one of the best-looking convertibles made in the 1950s.

1956 Lincoln Premier Convertible

PHOTO: FORD MOTOR COMPANY

1956 Mercury Custom Convertible

Original Price: $2,400
Number Produced: 2,311
Estimated Number Existing in 1979: 12
Miles per Gallon: 12–18
Common Trouble Spots: carburetor
Availability of Parts: fair–poor
Investment Potential: A+

Background: This was the first and only year the Custom convertible was offered as a separate series. It was powered by a 210 h.p. 312 cu. in. V8. This engine was rated at 215 h.p. when equipped with an automatic. A three-speed manual transmission was standard, but not very popular. Overdrive and Merc-O-Matic automatic transmission were optional.

1956 Mercury Montclair Convertible

Original Price: $2,612
Number Produced: 7,762
Estimated Number Existing in 1979: 40
Miles per Gallon: 12–18
Common Trouble Spots: carburetor
Availability of Parts: fair–poor
Investment Potential: A+

Background: Styling of the new Montclair was little changed from that of the previous year's model. The big news for Mercury in 1956 was the 210 h.p. 312 cu. in. V8 that was standard in the Montclair convertible. This engine was rated at 215 h.p. when equipped with an automatic. A three-speed manual transmission was standard. Overdrive and Merc-O-Matic automatic transmission were optional.

Most 1956 Mercurys, 88.9%, came with the automatic, but 8.1% had the three-speed manual, and three percent had the manual with overdrive; 27.9% had power steering, 32% had power brakes, 49.3% had windshield washers, 51% had tinted glass, 3.8% had power windows, 6.1% had power front seats, 84.6% had radios, and 1.1% were sold with an air conditioner.

1956 Mercury Montclair Convertible

PHOTO: FORD MOTOR COMPANY

1956 Mercury Custom Convertible

PHOTO: FORD MOTOR COMPANY

1956 Metropolitan Convertible

Original Price: $1,469
Number Produced: est. 1,908
Estimated Number Existing in 1979: 19
Miles per Gallon: 27–39
Common Trouble Spots: brakes, gearshift
Availability of Parts: good–fair
Investment Potential: A

Background: The early 1956 Metropolitan convertibles were of the 1200 series. They were powered by a 42 h.p. 73.2 cu. in. four-cylinder engine. In April of that year, the 1500 series Met was introduced. The facelifted 1500 was powered by a 52 h.p. 90.9 cu. in. four-cylinder engine. It had a top speed of 78 miles per hour. A three-speed manual transmission, a continental spare tire, and a radio were standard.

The 1500 series is the most popular with Metropolitan enthusiasts.

1956 Oldsmobile Starfire 98 Convertible

Original Price: $3,380
Number Produced: 8,581
Estimated Number Existing in 1979: 49
Miles per Gallon: 13–18
Common Trouble Spots: automatic transmission, piston rings
Availability of Parts: fair
Investment Potential: A+

Background: Outside of having a new grille, the Olds 98 convertible was little changed from the previous year's model. It was powered by a 240 h.p. 324.3 cu. in. V8 engine. Hydra-Matic automatic transmission was standard.

1956 Oldsmobile Starfire 98 Convertible

PHOTO: OLDSMOBILE DIVISION

1956 Oldsmobile Super 88 Convertible

PHOTO: OLDSMOBILE DIVISION

1956 Oldsmobile Super 88 Convertible

Original Price: $2,726
Number Produced: 9,561
Estimated Number Existing in 1979: 55
Miles per Gallon: 14–18
Common Trouble Spots: automatic transmission, piston rings
Availability of Parts: fair
Investment Potential: A+

Background: The Super 88 featured a grille that was inspired by the 1953 Starfire dream car. It was powered by a 240 h.p. 324.3 cu. in. V8 engine. A three-speed manual transmission was standard. Hydra-Matic automatic transmission was optional at extra cost.

Almost 99% of all 1956 Oldsmobiles came with the automatic, 70.1% had power brakes, 59.7% had power steering, 18.8% had power seats, 17.5% had power windows, 44.1% had tinted glass, 78% had windshield washers, and 4.7% came with an air conditioner.

1956 Packard Caribbean Convertible

Original Price: $5,992
Number Produced: 276
Estimated Number Existing in 1979: 30
Miles per Gallon: 10–15
Common Trouble Spots: automatic transmission, cooling system
Availability of Parts: poor–fair
Investment Potential: AAA

Background: "The greatest Packard of them all" was the 1956 model, according to that year's ads. Most postwar Packard enthusiasts consider this the last "real" Packard.

The plush and innovative Caribbean was the most expensive American convertible offered in 1956. And it was one of the most beautiful. It was powered by a 310 h.p. 374 cu. in. V8. Ultramatic automatic transmission was standard.

A unique feature of the Caribbean was its reversible seat cushions.

1956 Packard Caribbean Hardtop

Original Price: $5,495
Number Produced: 263
Estimated Number Existing in 1979: 25
Miles per Gallon: 10–15
Common Trouble Spots: automatic transmission, cooling system
Availability of Parts: poor–fair
Investment Potential: AAA

Background: This was the first and only year the luxurious Caribbean was offered in a hardtop body style. It was powered by a 310 h.p. 374 cu. in. V8 engine. Ultramatic automatic transmission and power steering were standard.

1956 Packard Caribbean Hardtop

PHOTO: WILLIAM L. BAILEY COLLECTION

1956 Plymouth Belvedere Convertible

Original Price: $2,444
Number Produced: 6,415
Estimated Number Existing in 1979: 25
Miles per Gallon: 13–17
Common Trouble Spots: valves
Availability of Parts: poor–fair
Investment Potential: A+

Background: The larger tailfins gave the new Belvedere convertible a sportier look than last year's model. It came out with a 187 h.p. 277 cu. in. V8. A 200 h.p. version of this engine was optional.

A three-speed manual transmission was standard. A manual with overdrive and push-button Power Flite automatic transmission were optional. Later in the model year, Torque Flite automatic was offered.

Most 1956 Plymouths, 61.7 percent, were equipped with the automatic, 35% had a three-speed manual, 3.3% had overdrive, 6.1% had power steering, 6% had power brakes, slightly more than .5% had electric windows, the same number had power front seats, 34.3% had radios, 28.9% had back-up lights, 19.2% had tinted glass, 19.7% had windshield washers, and .2% were sold with an air conditioner.

Also among the options offered was the "Highway Hi-Fi" phonograph, with its special long-playing discs and non-skip tone arm.

1956 Plymouth Belvedere Convertible

PHOTO: CHRYSLER HISTORICAL COLLECTION

1956 Pontiac Star Chief Convertible

Original Price: $2,818
Number Produced: 13,510
Estimated Number Existing in 1979: 87
Miles per Gallon: 13–18
Common Trouble Spots: automatic transmission, cooling system, suspension
Availability of Parts: fair
Investment Potential: A+

Background: The new Star Chief softtop was powered by a 227 h.p. 316.6 cu. in. V8. When equipped with an automatic, a 285 h.p. dual-four-barrel carburetor version of this engine was optional. A three-speed manual transmission was standard. Hydra-Matic four-speed automatic transmission was available.

Most 1956 Pontiacs, 93.1%, were equipped with either the three- or the four-speed automatic, 33% had power brakes, 27.5% had power steering, 2.4% had power front seats, 2.4% had electric windows, 2.4% had an air conditioner, 25.4% had tinted glass, and 25.2% were sold with windshield washers.

While the 1956 Pontiac may be one of the gaudier cars of the 1950s, it also was one of the better-made autos of the period. The four-speed Hydra-Matic is a pleasure to use, although it is no stranger to torque-converter problems.

1956 Pontiac Star Chief Convertible

PHOTO: PONTIAC MOTOR DIVISION

1956 Pontiac Star Chief Custom Safari Station Wagon

Original Price: $2,831
Number Produced: 4,042
Estimated Number Existing in 1979: 30
Miles per Gallon: 13–18
Common Trouble Spots: automatic transmission, cooling system, suspension
Availability of Parts: fair
Investment Potential: AAA

Background: The Safari received a minor face-lift for 1956, but it still was the flashiest station wagon offered by any manufacturer.

It came with a 227 h.p. 316.6 cu. in. V8. A 285 h.p. dual-four-barrel carburetor version of this engine was optional. A three-speed manual transmission was standard. A four-speed Hydra-Matic automatic transmission was optional. All but ten Safaris came with the automatic.

1956 Pontiac Star Chief Custom Safari Station Wagon

PHOTO: PONTIAC MOTOR DIVISION

1957

1957 Buick Century Convertible

Original Price: $3,598
Number Produced: 4,085
Estimated Number Existing in 1979: 24
Miles per Gallon: 11–17
Common Trouble Spots: automatic transmission, brakes, cooling system
Availability of Parts: fair
Investment Potential: A+

Background: The Century convertible was powered by a 300 h.p. 364 cu. in. V8 engine. Dynaflow automatic transmission was standard. Air conditioning was an unpopular option; only 6.3% of all '57 Buicks came with it. Most, 57.3%, had power brakes, 63% had power steering, 18% had power front seats, 89.7% had radios, 76% had windshield washers, and 16.8% had power windows.

1957 Buick Century Convertible

PHOTO: PUBLIC RELATIONS DEPARTMENT, BUICK MOTOR DIVISION

1957 Buick Roadmaster Convertible

Original Price: $4,066
Number Produced: 4,363
Estimated Number Existing in 1979: 26
Miles per Gallon: 11–17
Common Trouble Spots: automatic transmission, brakes, cooling system
Availability of Parts: fair
Investment Potential: A+

Background: The Roadmaster convertible was restyled inside and out for 1957. It was lower and sleeker looking than the previous year's model.

A 300 h.p. 364 cu. in. V8, Dynaflow automatic transmission and dual exhaust were standard.

1957 Buick Roadmaster Convertible

PHOTO: BUICK MOTOR DIVISION

1957 Buick Special Convertible

PHOTO: PUBLIC RELATIONS DEPARTMENT, BUICK MOTOR DIVISION

1957 Buick Special Convertible

Original Price: $2,987
Number Produced: 8,505
Estimated Number Existing in 1979: 51
Miles per Gallon: 12–17
Common Trouble Spots: automatic transmission, brakes, cooling system
Availability of Parts: fair
Investment Potential: A+

Background: Buick buyers who felt they could live with the stigma of having only three portholes ("slashes" might be a more appropriate description) on their front fenders bought the Special.

This good-looking ragtop was powered by a 250 h.p. 364 cu. in. V8. A three-speed manual transmission was standard, but not very popular. Ninety-eight percent of all '57 Buicks came with Dynaflow automatic transmission.

1957 Buick Super Convertible

PHOTO: PUBLIC RELATIONS DEPARTMENT, BUICK MOTOR DIVISION

1957 Buick Super Convertible

Original Price: $3,981
Number Produced: 2,056
Estimated Number Existing in 1979: 12
Miles per Gallon: 11–17
Common Trouble Spots: automatic transmission, brakes, cooling system
Availability of Parts: fair
Investment Potential: A+

Background: The new Super bore a strong resemblance to the top-of-the-line Roadmaster and to Buick's Centurion "dream car" of 1956. It was powered by a 300 h.p. 364 cu. in. V8 engine. Dynaflow automatic transmission and power windows were standard. Most had power brakes and power steering. Almost 18% of all '57 Buicks had power front seats.

1957 Cadillac Eldorado Biarritz Convertible

Original Price: $6,711
Number Produced: 1,800
Estimated Number Existing in 1979: 30
Miles per Gallon: 12–17
Common Trouble Spots: automatic transmission, brakes, carburetor
Availability of Parts: fair–poor
Investment Potential: AA+

Background: Although it looked much the same as the Series 62 from the front, a unique tailfin and rear-bumper treatment gave the Eldorado a very "futuristic" and sleek appearance.

It was powered by a 325 h.p. 365 cu. in. V8 engine. Hydramatic automatic transmission was standard. All Eldorados had power steering, power brakes, windshield washers and backup lights. People who wanted to flaunt their wealth could order grille, fender name script, and Sabre spoke wheels, all special and gold-plated.

In a 1975 article in *Special Interest Autos,* editor Rich Taylor stated that for high-speed cruising, the 1957 Eldorado "was one of the quietest, smoothest convertibles in my experience."

1957 Cadillac Eldorado Biarritz Convertible

PHOTO: CADILLAC MOTOR CAR DIVISION

1957 Cadillac Eldorado Brougham

Original Price: $13,074
Number Produced: 400
Estimated Number Existing in 1979: 240
Miles per Gallon: 7–15
Common Trouble Spots: automatic transmission, air suspension, carburetor, electrical system
Availability of Parts: poor–fair
Investment Potential: AAA

Background: The Eldorado Brougham was Cadillac's answer to the Continental Mark II. It was based primarily on two Cadillac "dream cars." The first of these was the Orleans, which was introduced at the 1953 Motorama. It was a four-door hardtop with a wraparound windshield. Aside from that, the Orleans looked pretty much like the standard Cadillac of the day. The second "dream car," the Park Avenue, more closely resembled the production model.

Like the Mark II, the Eldorado Brougham was designed to be a snob-mobile. Its high price was as much of a selling point as its numerous luxury features. Unlike the Mark II, however, which was totally different in appearance from anything else Ford sold, the new Brougham bore a strong resemblance to the standard Cadillac.

It was powered by a 335 h.p. 365 cu. in. V8 engine. Hydramatic automatic transmission and everything from air conditioning to the industry's first air suspension system were standard.

1957 Cadillac Eldorado Brougham

PHOTO: CADILLAC MOTOR CAR DIVISION

1957 Cadillac Series 62 Convertible

Original Price: $4,850
Number Produced: 9,000
Estimated Number Existing in 1979: 120
Miles per Gallon: 13–17
Common Trouble Spots: automatic transmission, brakes
Availability of Parts: fair
Investment Potential: A+

Background: The new Series 62 looked sleeker and flashier than last year's model. It was powered by a 300 h.p. 365 cu. in. V8. Hydramatic automatic transmission was standard. All 1957 Cadillacs came with power steering, power brakes, windshield washers, and back-up lights. Seventy-six percent had power seats, 98% had power windows, and 32% were equipped with air conditioning.

1957 Cadillac Series 62 Convertible

PHOTO: CADILLAC MOTOR CAR DIVISION

1957 Chevrolet Bel Air Convertible

Original Price: $2,611
Number Produced: 47,562
Estimated Number Existing in 1979: 1,400
Miles per Gallon: 13–19
Common Trouble Spots: Turboglide automatic, fuel injection
Availability of Parts: good
Investment Potential: AAA+ (with fuel injection); AAA (without)

Background: "Beautiful" is the word millions have used to describe the 1957 Chevy. It was (and remains) the most popular postwar car built by any manufacturer.

The Bel Air ragtop came with a 140 h.p. 235.5 cu. in. six. Available at extra cost were these V8 engines: a 162 h.p. 265, a 185 h.p. 283, a 220 h.p. 283, a 250 h.p. 283, a 270 h.p. 283 and a 283 h.p. 283. A three-speed manual transmission was standard. Overdrive and Powerglide and Turboglide automatic transmissions were optional. (Turboglide was offered only with the 283.)

The big news for 1957 was the availability of a fuel-injection unit. Chevys so equipped are highly prized, even though the early fuel-injection units had some problems.

Sixty-six percent of all '57 Chevrolets had an automatic, 31.6% had a three-speed manual, 2.4% had overdrive, 10.5% had power brakes, 15.6% had power steering, .5% had power windows, 15% had tinted glass, and 1.1% were sold with air conditioners.

The convertible top was available in beige, black, light blue, ivory, and green. Buyers had their choice of sixteen exterior colors.

1957 Chevrolet Bel Air Convertible

PHOTO: PUBLIC RELATIONS DEPARTMENT, CHEVROLET MOTOR DIVISION

1957 Chevrolet Bel Air Nomad Station Wagon

Original Price: $2,857
Number Produced: 6,103
Estimated Number Existing in 1979: 1,250
Miles per Gallon: 13–19
Common Trouble Spots: Turboglide automatic, fuel injection
Availability of Parts: good
Investment Potential: AAA+ (with fuel injection); AAA (without)

Background: The 1957 Chevy is the most popular postwar car. And the Nomad station wagon is the most popular body type—even more popular than the convertible. However, the ragtop may become the more popular of the two in the near future.

It came with a 140 h.p. 235.5 cu. in. six. Available at extra cost were several V8 engines. These included a 162 h.p. 265, a 185 h.p. 283, a 220 h.p. 283, a 250 h.p. 283, a 270 h.p. 283, and a 283 h.p. 283. A three-speed manual transmission was standard. Overdrive and Powerglide and Turboglide automatic transmissions were optional.

The 1957 Nomad is a very desirable wagon—especially when equipped with the optional fuel injection.

1957 Chevrolet Bel Air Nomad Station Wagon

PHOTO: CHEVROLET MOTOR DIVISION

1957 Chevrolet Bel Air Sport Coupe

Original Price: $2,399
Number Produced: 166,426
Estimated Number Existing in 1979: 5,000
Miles per Gallon: 13–19
Common Trouble Spots: Turboglide automatic, fuel injection
Availability of Parts: good
Investment Potential: AAA+ (with fuel injection); AAA (without)

Background: In the early 1960s, Chevrolet dealers in Los Angeles set up hundreds of billboards with a picture of a '57 Chevy, and the words, "The '57—Still *Choice* in '63." Chevy dealers could probably do the same thing in 1983 and few motorists would disagree.

The Bel Air two-door hardtop came with a 140 h.p. 235.5 cu. in. six. Available at extra cost were these V8 engines; a 162 h.p. 265, a 185 h.p. 283, a 220 h.p. 283, a 250 h.p. 283, a 270 h.p. 283, and a 283 h.p. 283. A three-speed manual transmission was standard. Overdrive and Powerglide and Turboglide automatic transmissions were optional.

The 1957 Chevrolet Bel Air Sport Coupe is one of the most popular cars ever made.

1957 Chevrolet Bel Air Sport Coupe

PHOTO: CHEVROLET MOTOR DIVISION

1957 Chevrolet Corvette Convertible

Original Price: $3,465
Number Produced: 6,339
Estimated Number Existing in 1979: 300
Miles per Gallon: 11–20
Common Trouble Spots: Fuel injection
Availability of Parts: fair–good
Investment Potential: AAA+ (with fuel injection); AAA (without)

Background: The 1957 Corvette was a beautiful car. Its classic styling, like that of the '56, was influenced by the Mercedes 300 SL and, judging by the taillights, the 1949 Buick.

It came with a 220 h.p. 283 cu. in. V8. Hotter versions of this engine were also available. These were a 245 h.p. (with two four-barrel carburetors), a 250 h.p. (with fuel injection), a 270 h.p. (with four-barrel carburetor and competition camshaft), and a 283 h.p. (with fuel injection and competition camshaft). A three-speed manual transmission was standard. Powerglide automatic and a four-speed manual transmission were optional.

Chevrolet gave the 283 h.p. fuel-injected 283 cu. in. V8 a big play in its advertising and sales literature. A brochure featuring the fuel-injected Corvette proudly proclaimed: "For the first time in automobile history—one H.P. for every cubic inch!" This theme was carried on throughout the brochure. It stated the '57 Vette was "Every inch a champion! Every inch a prized possession!"

Road & Track stated in 1957, "The fuel-injected (Corvette) engine is an absolute jewel, quiet and remarkably docile when driven gently around town, yet instantly transformable into a roaring brute when pushed hard."

The 1957 Corvette, especially those with fuel injection (only 240 were so equipped), is one of the most desirable of all postwar automobiles.

1957 Chevrolet Corvette Convertible

PHOTO: T. MICHAELIS CORVETTE SUPPLIES

1957 Chevrolet 210 Sport Coupe

Original Price: $2,304
Number Produced: 22,631
Estimated Number Existing in 1979: 700
Miles per Gallon: 13–19
Common Trouble Spots: Turboglide automatic, fuel injection
Availability of Parts: good
Investment Potential: AAA

Background: The '57 210 two-door hardtop looked just about the same as the higher-priced Bel Air. It came with a 140 h.p. 235.5 cu. in. six. A 162 h.p. 265 cu. in. V8 and a 185 h.p. 283 cu. in. V8 were offered at extra cost. Four hotter versions of the 283 were available. These were rated at 220 h.p., 250 h.p., 270 h.p. and 283 h.p. A three-speed manual transmission was standard. Overdrive and Powerglide and Turboglide automatic transmissions were optional.

1957 Chrysler New Yorker Convertible

Original Price: $4,573
Number Produced: 1,049
Estimated Number Existing in 1979: 8
Miles per Gallon: 10–16
Common Trouble Spots: automatic transmission
Availability of Parts: poor–fair
Investment Potential: AA

Background: The New Yorker not only got a face-lift, it got bigger as well.

It came with a 325 h.p. 392 cu. in. V8 engine. Torque Flite automatic transmission was standard. In 1975 *Car Classics* said that this transmission "ranks among the finest ever applied to a motor car."

Quad headlights were offered for the first time. Safety features included a padded dash and optional seat belts.

A little over 14% of all Chryslers were equipped with air conditioning. More than a third had power windows.

1957 Chrysler New Yorker Convertible

1957 Chrysler 300-C Convertible

PHOTO: CHRYSLER HISTORICAL COLLECTION

1957 Chrysler 300-C Convertible

Original Price: $5,294
Number Produced: 484
Estimated Number Existing in 1979: 6
Miles per Gallon: 8–14
Common Trouble Spots: automatic transmission
Availability of Parts: poor–fair
Investment Potential: AAA+

Background: For the first time, the 300 Series offered a convertible. A distinctive grille and trim made it easily distinguishable from the New Yorker. Like most other Chryslers, it now had four headlights.

It came with a 392 cu. in. 375 h.p. V8 engine. A 390 h.p. version of this engine was optional. Torque Flite automatic transmission was standard. A three-speed manual transmission was available.

Its position as the first of the famous 300 Series convertibles and its low production figure help make this a significant and desirable automobile. It seems to be the most popular of the 300 Letter Series convertibles.

1957 Chrysler 300-C Coupe

Original Price: $4,864
Number Produced: 1,918
Estimated Number Existing in 1979: 25
Miles per Gallon: 8–14
Common Trouble Spots: automatic transmission
Availability of Parts: poor–fair
Investment Potential: AA+

Background: The 300 was completely restyled for 1957. Despite its now rather large size, it was still a high-performance car, capable of great speed.

It came equipped with a 375 h.p. 392 cu. in. V8 engine. A 390 h.p. version of this engine was optional. Torque Flite automatic transmission was standard. A three-speed manual transmission was optional.

Like all early Chrysler 300 Letter cars, the 1957 300-C is a very desirable automobile.

1957 Chrysler 300-C Coupe

PHOTO: CHRYSLER CORPORATION

1957 Continental Mark II Convertible

PHOTO: FORD MOTOR COMPANY

1957 Continental Mark II Convertible

Original Price: est. $10,000
Number Produced: 2
Estimated Number Existing in 1979: 2
Miles per Gallon: 9–16
Common Trouble Spots: none
Availability of Parts: fair
Investment Potential: AAA+

Background: Beautiful. That is the only way to describe the 1957 Mark II convertible. It was powered by a 300 h.p. 368 cu. in. V8. Turbo-Drive automatic transmission, power steering, power brakes, and a windshield washer were among the many standard features.

The white top of this virtually one-of-a-kind car was made of orlon.

1957 Continental Mark II Hardtop

Original Price: $9,620
Number Produced: 454
Estimated Number Existing in 1979: 260
Miles per Gallon: 9–16
Common Trouble Spots: none
Availability of Parts: fair
Investment Potential: AAA+

Background: The '57 Mark II was virtually the same as the previous year's model, although the frame was lighter because only six crossmembers were used instead of seven.

It was powered by a 300 h.p. 368 cu. in. V8. Turbo-Drive automatic transmission, power steering, power brakes, electric windows, power front seat, a radio, tinted glass, carpeted trunk, and dual exhaust were among the many standard features.

People who wanted to buy a Mark II now had a harder time finding one. The number of dealers handling the car dropped from 652 to 500 by September 1956, and continued to decline until the Mark II was phased out.

1957 Continental Mark II Hardtop

PHOTO: FORD MOTOR COMPANY

1957 DeSoto Adventurer Convertible

Original Price: $4,217
Number Produced: N.A.
Estimated Number Existing in 1979: N.A.
Miles per Gallon: 8–15
Common Trouble Spots: brakes
Availability of Parts: fair–poor
Investment Potential: AA

Background: The most desirable '57 DeSoto is the top-of-the-line Adventurer convertible. It was powered by a 345 h.p. 345 cu. in. V8 engine with dual four-barrel carburetors. This car could go from 0 to 60 in less than eight seconds. Torque Flite automatic transmission, power brakes, and a 150-mile-per-hour speedometer were standard.

The Adventurer had special trim and quad headlights. It was upholstered in leather.

1957 DeSoto Firedome Convertible

Original Price: $3,311
Number Produced: N.A.
Estimated Number Existing in 1979: N.A.
Miles per Gallon: 11–16
Common Trouble Spots: brakes
Availability of Parts: fair–poor
Investment Potential: A+

Background: The flashy new Firedome ragtop was powered by a 270 h.p. 341 cu. in. V8 engine with two-barrel carburetor. A three-speed manual transmission was standard. Torque Flite automatic transmission and dual exhaust were optional.

Most 1957 DeSotos, 99.3%, came with an automatic; 81.5% had power steering, 69% had power brakes, 8% had electric windows, 8% had power front seats, 71% had radios, 31% had tinted glass, 53% had windshield washers, and 5% were sold with an air conditioner.

1957 DeSoto Fireflite Convertible

Original Price: $3,835
Number Produced: N.A.
Estimated Number Existing in 1979: N.A.
Miles per Gallon: 11–16
Common Trouble Spots: brakes
Availability of Parts: fair–poor
Investment Potential: A+

Background: The '57 Fireflite ragtop was powered by a 295 h.p. 341 cu. in. V8 engine. Torque Flite automatic transmission was standard. It had a top speed of approximately 106 mph.

1957 Dodge Coronet Convertible

PHOTO: CHRYSLER HISTORICAL COLLECTION

1957 Dodge Coronet Convertible

Original Price: $2,807
Number Produced: N.A.
Estimated Number Existing in 1979: N.A.
Miles per Gallon: 11–16
Common Trouble Spots: brakes
Availability of Parts: poor–fair
Investment Potential: A+

Background: Like all Dodges, the '57 Coronet ragtop was wider, longer, and lower than the '56. It came equipped with a 245 h.p. 325 cu. in. V8. A D-500 325 cu. in. high-performance engine, with either 285 h.p. or 310 h.p., was available at extra cost. A three-speed manual transmission was standard. Power Flite and Torque Flite automatic transmissions were optional.

One of the most distinguishing styling features of '57 Dodges, and other Chrysler products, were their large tailfins. Tailfins were the subject of a great deal of criticism that year. In a 1957 article in *Iron Age,* Virgil Exner, Chrysler's Director of Styling, defended them. He said that tailfins exerted "a stabilizing effect much as do tailfins on airplanes." He went on to say that, in cars with tailfins, "road holding stability improved, reducing steering correction by as much as 20 percent in strong crosswinds."

1957 DeSoto Fireflite Convertible

1957 Dodge Custom Royal Convertible

Original Price: $3,111
Number Produced: N.A.
Estimated Number Existing in 1979: N.A.
Miles per Gallon: 10–16
Common Trouble Spots: brakes
Availability of Parts: poor–fair
Investment Potential: A+

Background: The '57 Custom Royal softtop was flashier than last year's model. It helped to usher in the era of "full size" cars (or battleships, as some prefer to call them). In addition to a new appearance, Dodge offered torsion-bar front suspension.

The Custom Royal came with a 260 h.p. 325 cu. in. "Red Ram" V8. The optional 325 cu. in. D-500 engine, with either 285 h.p. or 310 h.p., featured dual exhaust and heavy duty suspension. A Custom Royal so equipped, and with the standard three-speed manual, could go from 0 to 60 in 8.8 seconds. Torque Flite pushbutton automatic transmission was available at extra cost.

1957 Dodge Custom Royal Convertible

1957 Dodge Royal Lancer Convertible

Original Price: est. $3,000
Number Produced: 1,957
Estimated Number Existing in 1979: 9
Miles per Gallon: 11–16
Common Trouble Spots: brakes
Availability of Parts: poor–fair
Investment Potential: A+

Background: The Royal Lancer was a slightly lower-priced version of the Custom Royal Lancer. Buyers got the same basic styling for less money.

It was powered by a 245 h.p. 325 cu. in. Red Ram V8. Also available was a 325 cu. in. D-500 engine with either 285 h.p. or 310 h.p. The D-500 featured dual exhaust, dual four-barrel carburetors and heavy duty suspension.

A three-speed manual transmission was standard but few ordered it. Ninety-seven percent of all '57 Dodges came with an automatic (Royal Lancers had Torque Flite), 50% had power steering, and 2.8% were sold with air conditioning.

1957 Ford Fairlane 500 Skyliner Retractable Hardtop

Original Price: $2,945
Number Produced: 20,766
Estimated Number Existing in 1979: 250
Miles per Gallon: 10–16
Common Trouble Spots: cooling system, engine bearings
Availability of Parts: fair
Investment Potential: AAA

Background: The 1957 Ford was introduced in the U.S.S.R. two days before its American debut—the first '57 Ford made was sent to Russia for propaganda purposes. Seven more Fords were later sold to the State Department for use in the U.S.S.R. at the bargain price of one dollar each. None were retractables. The Skyliner retractable hardtop wasn't introduced until late in the model year.

The retractable hard top was originally intended for use on the Continental Mark II. Ford reportedly spent over two million dollars to develop it. However, by the time the top was perfected in 1955, Continental had decided that, because of the anticipated low production of the Mark II, it wouldn't be economically feasible to use it.

The top mechanism is complex. It consists of over 600 feet of wire, five motors, ten solenoids, nine circuit breakers, and thirteen switches. Yet it has a reputation for being very reliable. In factory tests, the top completed 10,000 up-and-down operations without a failure.

One of the reasons Ford bothered to produce the retractable hardtop was to improve its image. This is evident in a sales brochure for the 1957 model line which stated, "The Skyliner is the prototype of a whole future generation of cars. And the fact that Ford alone has created this miracle car is important to anyone about to buy a new car. . . . For this newest new kind of Ford is dramatic proof of the engineering skill, exhaustive testing and deep-down value you get in every Ford model."

It came with a 212 h.p. 292 cu. in. V8. Available optionally were a 245 h.p. "Thunderbird" 312 cu. in. V8 and a 300 h.p. 312 cu. in. V8 with a McCulloch supercharger. A three-speed manual transmission was standard. Overdrive and Ford-O-Matic automatic transmission were optional.

The Fairlane 500 Skyliner Retractable Hardtop is the ultimate in convertibles.

1957 Ford Fairlane 500 Skyliner Retractable Hardtop

PHOTO: FORD MOTOR COMPANY

1957 Ford Fairlane 500 Sunliner Convertible

Original Price: $2,389
Number Produced: 77,728
Estimated Number Existing in 1979: 592
Miles per Gallon: 10–16
Common Trouble Spots: cooling system
Availability of Parts: fair–good
Investment Potential: AAA

Background: Beautiful. Just beautiful. Many consider the 1957 the best-looking Ford of the 1950s. It was lower, wider, and longer than previous models. Its striking good looks may help explain why Ford outsold Chevy in '57.

The Sunliner came with a 144 h.p. 223 cu. in. six-cylinder. Available at extra cost were the following V8 engines: a 206 h.p. 292 (rated at 212 h.p. with the automatic), a 245 h.p. 312, a 270 h.p. 312 (with dual four-barrel carburetors), a 285 h.p. 312 (a racing kit engine with dual four-barrel carburetors) and a 300 h.p. 312 (supercharged). The 300 h.p. replaced the 285 h.p. 312 fairly early in the model year.

A three-speed manual transmission was standard. Overdrive and Ford-O-Matic automatic transmission were optional.

Most 1957 Fords, 86.9%, were equipped with a V8, 71.4% had the automatic, 23.2% had the three-speed, 5.4% had the manual with overdrive, 27% had power steering, 9.6% had power brakes, 37.5% had windshield washers, 16.6% had tinted glass, 1.8% had electric windows, 1.9% had power front seats, 68.6% had radios, and .5% were sold with air conditioning.

1957 Ford Fairlane 500 Sunliner Convertible

PHOTO: FORD MOTOR COMPANY

1957 Ford Thunderbird Convertible

PHOTO: FORD MOTOR COMPANY

1957 Ford Thunderbird Convertible

Original Price: $3,088
Number Produced: 21,380
Estimated Number Existing in 1979: 2,100
Miles per Gallon: 13–17
Common Trouble Spots: cooling system
Availability of Parts: fair
Investment Potential: AAA+

Background: This was the last of the "classic" two-passenger T-Birds. Many consider the face-lifted 1957 model the most beautiful Thunderbird ever built. Although it had the same dimensions as the '56, it was lower. And the new styling made it look wider and more graceful.

It was powered by a 212 h.p. 292 cu. in. V8. Most were sold with one of the optional 312 cu. in. V8s with either 245 h.p., 270 h.p., 285 h.p. or 300 h.p. (supercharged). A three-speed manual transmission was standard. Overdrive and Fordomatic automatic transmission were optional.

The '57 T-Bird was offered in fifteen exterior colors and six upholstery color combinations. A removable hard-top with portholes was standard. A hard-top without portholes was available. The soft top came in four colors: black, blue, tan, and white. Among the options were seat belts, wire wheel covers, auto-home electric shaver, tonneau cover, fender skirts, signal-seeking radio, and Dial-O-Matic four-way power seats.

The supercharged models are by far the most valuable '57 T-Birds.

1957 Imperial Crown Convertible

PHOTO: CHRYSLER HISTORICAL COLLECTION

1957 Imperial Crown Convertible

Original Price: $5,523
Number Produced: 1,167
Estimated Number Existing in 1979: 10
Miles per Gallon: 9–14
Common Trouble Spots: automatic transmission, brakes
Availability of Parts: poor–fair
Investment Potential: AA

Background: The Imperial convertible was redesigned for 1957. It was a rather flamboyant automobile, especially with the optional simulated spare tire placed on the trunk lid. Priced at well over $5,000, it was definitely a car for people with a lot of money or a friend in the loan department of a bank.

It was powered by a 325 h.p. 392 cu. in. V8 engine. Torque Flite automatic transmission was standard.

1957 King Midget Convertible

Original Price: est. $600
Number Produced: N.A.
Estimated Number Existing in 1979: N.A.
Miles per Gallon: 50–90
Common Trouble Spots: transmission, "V" belts
Availability of Parts: good
Investment Potential: A

Background: Even King Midget couldn't ignore the horsepower race of 1957. New King Midget ragtops were now powered by a 10 h.p. 29 cu. in. one-cylinder engine. Automatic transmission was standard.

1957 Lincoln Premier Convertible

Original Price: est. $4,500
Number Produced: 3,676
Estimated Number Existing in 1979: 38
Miles per Gallon: 10–14
Common Trouble Spots: none
Availability of Parts: fair–good
Investment Potential: AA+

Background: The new Premier convertible was one of the flashiest cars on the road in 1957. It was powered by a 300 h.p. 368 cu. in. V8 engine. Turbo-Drive automatic transmission, power brakes, power steering, and windshield washers were standard.

Most 1957 Lincolns, 92%, came with tinted glass, 86% had power windows, 88% had power seats and 22% were sold with an air conditioner.

It had a top speed of over 124 mph.

1957 Mercury Montclair Convertible

Original Price: $3,147
Number Produced: 4,248
Estimated Number Existing in 1979: 14
Miles per Gallon: 12–17
Common Trouble Spots: automatic transmission, cooling system
Availability of Parts: fair–poor
Investment Potential: A+

Background: The attractive '57 Montclair ragtop was powered by a 255 h.p. 312 cu. in. V8. which took the Montclair from 0 to 60 in 13 seconds. A 290 h.p. 368 cu. in. V8 was available at extra cost to buyers even more impatient to get to their destination—Montclairs equipped with this engine could shoot from 0 to 60 in just 9.8 seconds. Merc-O-Matic automatic transmission was standard.

1957 Mercury Montclair Convertible

PHOTO: FORD MOTOR COMPANY

1957 Lincoln Premier Convertible

PHOTO: FORD MOTOR COMPANY

1957 Mercury Monterey Convertible

Original Price: $2,752
Number Produced: 5,033
Estimated Number Existing in 1979: 16
Miles per Gallon: 12–17
Common Trouble Spots: automatic transmission, cooling system
Availability of Parts: fair–poor
Investment Potential: A+

Background: This was the first time since 1954 that a Monterey convertible was offered. It was powered by a 255 h.p. 312 cu. in. V8. A 290 h.p. 368 cu. in. V8 was available at extra cost. A three-speed manual transmission was standard. Overdrive and Merc-O-Matic automatic transmission were optional.

Most 1957 Mercurys, 94.7%, came equipped with the automatic, 3.9% had the three-speed manual, 1.4% had the manual with overdrive, 50.9% had power steering, 48.8% had power brakes, 65.2% had windshield washers, 56.5% had tinted glass, 7.3% had power windows, 12.3% had power front seats, 88.5% had radios, and 5.3% were sold with an air conditioner.

An M-335 powerpack was offered. It featured a 368 cu. in. V8, two four-barrel carburetors, dual exhaust, and a three-speed manual. A Monterey so equipped could move from 0 to 60 in just over nine seconds.

1957 Mercury Turnpike Cruiser Convertible

Original Price: est. $4,000
Number Produced: 1,265
Estimated Number Existing in 1979: 4
Miles per Gallon: 12–16
Common Trouble Spots: automatic transmission, cooling system
Availability of Parts: fair–poor
Investment Potential: AA

Background: This was the first postwar Mercury to have its own body shell; in previous years, Mercury had shared basic bodies with Ford and Lincoln. This was also the first, and last, year for the Turnpike Cruiser convertible.

It came with a 290 h.p. 368 cu. in. V8. Merc-O-Matic automatic transmission, padded dash, power steering, power brakes, electric windows, and power "memory seat" were standard. The power front seat was rather nifty: when the driver turned the car off, the seat would move all the way back, supposedly to make it easier to get out; when the ignition was turned on, the seat moved back to a preset position.

In a 1973 interview, one of the designers of the '57 Turnpike Cruiser was asked what he thought of the car's styling now. He replied, "I call [that] period the Dark Ages of auto design."

1957 Metropolitan Series 1500 Convertible

PHOTO: RICHARD J. MCGARTY, METROPOLITAN OWNERS CLUB

1957 Metropolitan Series 1500 Convertible

Original Price: $1,551
Number Produced: est. 3,220
Estimated Number Existing in 1979: 32
Miles per Gallon: 25–35
Common Trouble Spots: brakes, gearshift
Availability of Parts: good–fair
Investment Potential: A

Background: The 1957 Metropolitan convertible was powered by a 52 h.p. 90.9 cu. in. four-cylinder engine. A three-speed manual transmission and white-vinyl-trimmed, grayish-black upholstery were standard.

1957 Oldsmobile Golden Rocket 88 Convertible

Original Price: $2,895
Number Produced: 6,423
Estimated Number Existing in 1979: 36
Miles per Gallon: 12–18
Common Trouble Spots: automatic transmission, carburetor
Availability of Parts: fair
Investment Potential: AA+ (with the J-2 powerpack); AA (without)

Background: The new Golden Rocket 88 convertible was an attractive and potent automobile. It was powered by a 277 h.p. 370.7 cu. in. V8. In early 1957, the J-2 Rocket powerpack was available. It featured three two-barrel carburetors and dual exhaust and upped the horse-power rating to 300. A three-speed manual transmission was standard. Hydra-Matic automatic transmission was optional (but it was standard with the J-2 package).

Most 1957 Oldsmobiles, 82.4%, were equipped with power brakes, 77.3% had power steering, 12.3% had power seats, 2.7% had power windows, 41.4 percent had tinted glass, 79.5% had windshield washers, and 9.9% were sold with an air conditioner.

1957 Oldsmobile Golden Rocket 88 Convertible

PHOTO: OLDSMOBILE DIVISION

1957 Oldsmobile Starfire 98 Convertible

Original Price: $3,838
Number Produced: 8,278
Estimated Number Existing in 1979: 46
Miles per Gallon: 12–17
Common Trouble Spots: automatic transmission, brakes, carburetor
Availability of Parts: fair
Investment Potential: AA+ (with the J-2 powerpack); AA (without)

Background: The 1957 Starfire 98 convertible was one of the most attractive cars of the decade. It had just the right amount of flash, without appearing gaudy.

The 98 came with a 277 h.p. 370.7 cu. in. V8. This engine was rated at 300 h.p. when equipped with the optional J-2 Rocket powerpack. It featured three two-barrel carburetors and dual exhaust. Hydra-Matic automatic transmission was standard.

1957 Oldsmobile Starfire 98 Convertible

PHOTO: OLDSMOBILE DIVISION

1957 Oldsmobile Super 88 Convertible

Original Price: $3,132
Number Produced: 7,128
Estimated Number Existing in 1979: 39
Miles per Gallon: 12–18
Common Trouble Spots: automatic transmission, carburetor
Availability of Parts: fair
Investment Potential: AA+ (with the J-2 powerpack); AA (without)

Background: The attractive new Super 88 could go from 0 to 60 in 9.5 seconds, when equipped with the standard 277 h.p. 370.7 cu. in. V8. A J-2 Rocket powerpack, producing 300 h.p., was optional. It consisted of triple two-barrel carburetors, dual exhaust, and Hydra-Matic automatic transmission.

A three-speed manual transmission was standard, but not very popular—only 1.1% of all 1957 Oldsmobiles came with it. Most buyers ordered the Hydra-Matic.

A lighted ashtray and a hidden gas filler were a couple of the minor features found on the Super 88.

1957 Plymouth Belvedere Convertible

Original Price: $2,613
Number Produced: 9,566
Estimated Number Existing in 1979: 30
Miles per Gallon: 11–16
Common Trouble Spots: automatic transmission, brakes, engine bearings, piston rings, valves
Availability of Parts: fair–poor
Investment Potential: A+

Background: The big new Belvedere convertible was the flashiest car Plymouth had ever made up to that time. It was powered by a 215 h.p. 301 cu. in. V8. A 235-h.p. power-pack version of this engine and a 290 h.p. 318 cu. in. V8 were available at extra cost.

A three-speed manual transmission was standard. A manual with overdrive and Power Flite and Torque Flite automatic transmissions were optional.

Most 1957 Plymouths, 78.6 percent, were equipped with one of the automatics, 20.2% had a three-speed manual, 1.2% had overdrive, 17.7% had power steering, 12.2% had power brakes, slightly more than .5% had electric windows, about the same number had power front seats, 31.9% had windshield washers, 17.9% had tinted glass, 47.9% had radios, and 1.5% were sold with an air conditioner.

Later-model 1957 Belvederes had extra chrome bars below the front bumpers. These chrome bars were fitted into the open slots found on the early models.

The 1957 Belvedere convertible was one of the most stylish and desirable ragtops Plymouth made in the 1950s.

1957 Plymouth Belvedere Convertible

PHOTO: CHRYSLER CORPORATION

1957 Oldsmobile Super 88 Convertible

PHOTO: OLDSMOBILE DIVISION

1957 Pontiac Bonneville Convertible

Original Price: $5,782
Number Produced: 630
Estimated Number Existing in 1979: 20
Miles per Gallon: 12–17
Common Trouble Spots: fuel injection
Availability of Parts: fair–poor
Investment Potential: AAA

Background: The new Bonneville ragtop was Pontiac's most expensive car in 1957. It was powered by a 300 h.p. 347 cu. in. V8 with fuel injection. Strato-Flight Hydra-Matic automatic transmission, power steering, power brakes, dual exhaust, eight-way power Front seat, padded dash, and power windows were standard.

The fuel-injected Bonneville could go from 0 to 60 in 8.1 seconds. It had a top speed in excess of 130 m.p.h. The most popular exterior color combination was white with blue trim.

1957 Pontiac Star Chief Convertible

Original Price: $3,105
Number Produced: 12,789
Estimated Number Existing in 1979: 104
Miles per Gallon: 12–17
Common Trouble Spots: carburetor
Availability of Parts: fair
Investment Potential: A+

Background: The new Star Chief convertible was powered by a 270 h.p. 347 cu. in. V8. Three other versions of this engine were available: a 252 h.p., a 290 h.p., and a 317 h.p. A three-speed manual transmission was standard. Hydra-Matic automatic transmission was optional for $215.

Most new Pontiacs, 96%, were equipped with an automatic, 45.1% had power brakes, 41% had power steering, 1.4% had an eight-way power front seat, 2.3% had electric windows, 23.7% had tinted glass, 24.5% had windshield washers, and 3.9% were sold with an air conditioner. A "Tri-Power" performance package, featuring three two-barrel carburetors, was also offered.

Buyers had a choice of leather-and-nylon and all-leather interiors.

1957 Pontiac Star Chief Custom Safari Station Wagon

Original Price: est. $2,900
Number Produced: 1,292 (two-door models)
Estimated Number Existing in 1979: 20
Miles per Gallon: 12–17
Common Trouble Spots: carburetor
Availability of Parts: fair–poor
Investment Potential: AAA

Background: The two-door Safari wagon had a trimmer, sleeker look in 1957. It was powered by a 227 h.p. 347 cu. in. V8. This engine was rated at 252 h.p. when equipped with automatic transmission. Also available were a 270 h.p., a 290 h.p. and a 317 h.p. version of this engine. A three-speed manual transmission was standard. Hydra-Matic automatic transmission was optional.

A four-door Safari was offered in '57; 1,894 were made. However it is not as desirable as the two-door model.

1957 Pontiac Star Chief Convertible

PHOTO: PONTIAC MOTOR DIVISION

1958

1958 Buick Century Convertible

Original Price: $3,346
Number Produced: 2,588
Estimated Number Existing in 1979: 25
Miles per Gallon: 11–17
Common Trouble Spots: none
Availability of Parts: fair
Investment Potential: A+

Background: Like all '58 Buicks, for better or for worse, the Century lost its portholes. It was powered by a 300 h.p. 364 cu. in. V8. Dynaflow automatic transmission, electric clock, trip mileage indicator, power windows, and power seats were standard. Air suspension and air conditioning were two unpopular options.

1958 Buick Century Convertible

PHOTO: PUBLIC RELATIONS DEPARTMENT, BUICK MOTOR DIVISION

1958 Buick Limited Convertible

Original Price: $4,663
Number Produced: 839
Estimated Number Existing in 1979: 8
Miles per Gallon: 11–17
Common Trouble Spots: none
Availability of Parts: fair
Investment Potential: AA

Background: Buick's highest-priced and most chrome-laden car in 1958 was the luxurious Limited convertible. The flashy Limited was powered by a 300 h.p. 364 cu. in. V8. Dynaflow automatic transmission, six-way power front seats, dual exhaust, windshield washer, electric clock, carpeting, padded dash, trip mileage indicator, electric windows, power steering, and power brakes were standard.

The 1958 Limited convertible was one of the most eye-popping cars Buick ever made.

1958 Buick Limited Convertible

PHOTO: PUBLIC RELATIONS DEPARTMENT, BUICK MOTOR DIVISION

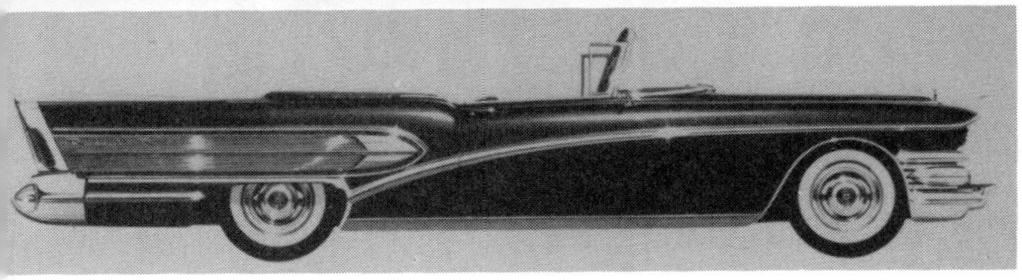

1958 Buick Roadmaster Convertible

PHOTO: PUBLIC RELATIONS DEPARTMENT, BUICK MOTOR DIVISION

1958 Buick Roadmaster Convertible

Original Price: $4,263
Number Produced: 1,181
Estimated Number Existing in 1979: 11
Miles per Gallon: 11–17
Common Trouble Spots: none
Availability of Parts: fair
Investment Potential: A+

Background: The Roadmaster appeared for the first time in years without its traditional "portholes." Stylists probably thought the side view of the "shark-finned" '58 Roadmaster distracting enough without the addition of more gimmicks.

It was powered by a 300 h.p. 364 cu. in. V8. Dynaflow automatic transmission, power windows, six-way power front seats, windshield washer, safety buzzer, trip mileage indicator, outside rearview mirror, power steering, and power brakes were standard. "Air Poise" air suspension was optional for $183.

1958 Buick Special Convertible

Original Price: $2,766
Number Produced: 5,502
Estimated Number Existing in 1979: 54
Miles per Gallon: 12–17
Common Trouble Spots: none
Availability of Parts: fair
Investment Potential: A+

Background: The '58 Special convertible came with a 250 h.p. 364 cu. in. V8. A three-speed manual transmission was standard, but not very popular. Only 1.5% of all 1958 Buicks were so equipped. Most buyers ordered the Dynaflow automatic transmission.

The majority of new Buicks, 69.2%, were sold with power steering, 60.3% had power brakes, 71.8% had windshield washers, 13.4% had power windows, 7.5% had air conditioning, and 10.7% had "Air-Poise" air suspension.

1958 Buick Special Convertible

PHOTO: PUBLIC RELATIONS DEPARTMENT, BUICK MOTOR DIVISION

1958 Cadillac Eldorado Biarritz Convertible

PHOTO: CADILLAC MOTOR CAR DIVISION

1958 Cadillac Eldorado Biarritz Convertible

Original Price: $7,500
Number Produced: 815
Estimated Number Existing in 1979: 20
Miles per Gallon: 12–17
Common Trouble Spots: air suspension
Availability of Parts: fair–poor
Investment Potential: AA+

Background: "Motordom's masterpiece"—that's how Cadillac ads described their 1958 models. The sportiest Cadillac of the year was the Eldorado Biarritz convertible. It was powered by a 335 h.p. 365 cu. in. V8 engine with three two-barrel carburetors. Hydramatic automatic transmission was standard. All Eldorados were equipped with power steering, power brakes, dual exhaust, windshield washers, and backup lights. Air suspension was optional.

1958 Cadillac Eldorado Brougham

Original Price: $13,074
Number Produced: 304
Estimated Number Existing in 1979: 182
Miles per Gallon: 7–15
Common Trouble Spots: air suspension, electrical system
Availability of Parts: poor–fair
Investment Potential: AAA

Background: The 1958 Eldorado Brougham was a flashy, luxurious automobile. It was one of the last "dream cars." The Brougham was powered by a 335 h.p. 365 cu. in. V8 engine. Hydramatic automatic transmission was standard. Other standard features included air conditioning, power steering, power brakes, electric windows, automatic headlight dimmer, tinted glass, electric clock, two cigarette lighters in the front and two in the back, power seats, and air suspension.

Despite the high selling price, buyers were getting a lot of car for their money. It reportedly cost Cadillac $23,000 to make each Brougham.

1958 Cadillac Eldorado Brougham

PHOTO: CADILLAC MOTOR CAR DIVISION

1958 Cadillac Series 62 Convertible

PHOTO: CADILLAC MOTOR CAR DIVISION

1958 Cadillac Series 62 Convertible

Original Price: $5,454
Number Produced: 7,825
Estimated Number Existing in 1979: 137
Miles per Gallon: 12–17
Common Trouble Spots: none
Availability of Parts: fair
Investment Potential: A+

Background: This was the first year for quad headlights on the Series 62. Its styling was influenced by various GM "dream cars:" 1953 Le Sabre, the 1954 El Camino and the 1955 Eldorado Brougham.

A 310 h.p. 365 cu. in. V8 powered the Series 62 convertible. Hydramatic automatic transmission was standard. All 1958 Cadillacs came with power steering, power brakes, windshield washers, dual exhaust, and backup lights. About three out of four had power front seats, 77.9% had power windows, 35% had air conditioning, and 14.2% were sold with the $215 air suspension.

1958 Chevrolet Bel Air Impala Convertible

Original Price: $2,841
Number Produced: 55,989
Estimated Number Existing in 1979: 690
Miles per Gallon: 13–17
Common Trouble Spots: Turboglide automatic
Availability of Parts: good–fair
Investment Potential: AAA (with fuel injection); AA+ (without)

Background: "Excitement on wheels" is how Chevrolet literature described the new Impala, with its "Sculpturamic styling." It came with a 145 h.p. 235.5 cu. in. six. Available at extra cost were the following V8 engines: a 185 h.p. 283 (two-barrel carburetor), a 230 h.p. 283 (four-barrel carburetor), a 250 h.p. 283 (fuel injection), a 250 h.p. 348 (four-barrel carburetor), and a 280 h.p. 348 (three two-barrel carburetors). A three-speed manual transmission was standard. Overdrive and Powerglide and Turboglide automatic transmissions were optional.

Most 1958 Chevrolets, 68.7%, came equipped with an automatic, 29.1% had a three-speed manual, 2.2% had overdrive, 24.1% had power steering, 13% had power brakes, 1% had power windows, .5% had a power front seat, 2% had air suspension, 13.4% had tinted glass, 37.6% had a six, and 1.8% were sold with an air conditioner.

During the first half of the model year, 20% of all Impala ragtops were black and 19% were painted white. The next two most popular colors were silver-blue and red.

In any color, the 1958 Impala ragtop is a beautiful car.

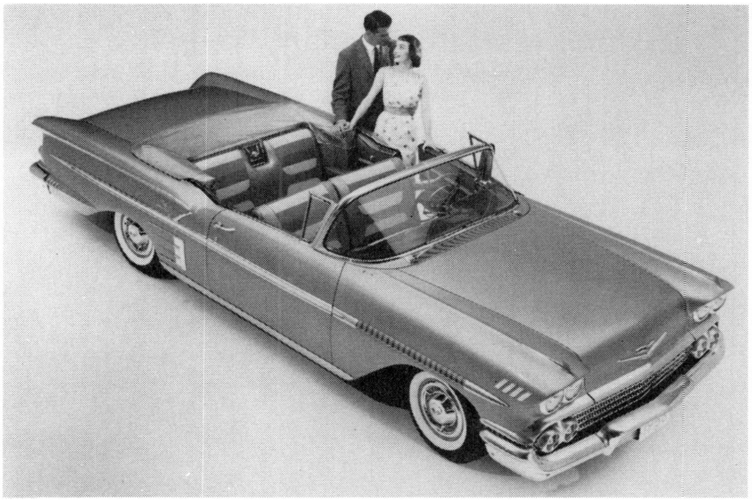

1958 Chevrolet Bel Air Impala Convertible

PHOTO: CHEVROLET MOTOR DIVISION

1958 Chevrolet Bel Air Impala Sport Coupe

Original Price: $2,693
Number Produced: est. 125,480
Estimated Number Existing in 1979: 1,549
Miles per Gallon: 13–17
Common Trouble Spots: Turboglide automatic
Availability of Parts: good–fair
Investment Potential: AAA (with fuel injection); AA+ (without)

Background: The beautiful '58 Impala Sport Coupe was an immediate hit. Even after it had been on the market for over six months, the demand for it exceeded the supply. One California Chevy dealer found a way to cash in on the Impala's popularity. For $75, he offered an Impala kit, which he sold primarily to buyers of four-door '58 Chevrolets. This kit consisted of a roof-top grille, a couple of metal body-sill moldings, a fiberglass scoop, Impala insignias (one read "Impala Special"), a couple of crossed flag-emblems, and two paint-divider emblems.

1958 Chevrolet Bel Air Impala Sport Coupe

PHOTO: GM PHOTOGRAPHIC

The Impala came with a 145 h.p. 235.5 cu. in. six. Available at extra cost were these V8 engines: a 185 h.p. 283, a 230 h.p. 283, a 250 h.p. 283, a 250 h.p. 348, and a 280 h.p. 348. A three-speed manual transmission was standard. Overdrive and Powerglide and Turboglide automatic transmissions were optional.

Among the other options available were fuel injection, air suspension, continental wheel carrier, wheel spinners, exhaust ports, wonder bar radio, air conditioning, tissue dispenser, power steering, power brakes, dual rear antennas, seat belts, and shoulder harnesses.

1958 Chevrolet Corvette Convertible

Original Price: $3,631
Number Produced: 9,168
Estimated Number Existing in 1979: 160
Miles per Gallon: 11–19
Common Trouble Spots: none
Availability of Parts: fair–good
Investment Potential: AAA

Background: The 1958 Corvette seems to be the least popular Vette of the 1950s. The reason for this is that many people believe its styling was a bit too gimmicky.

It came with a 230 h.p. 283 cu. in. V8 engine. Hotter versions of this engine were also available, including a 245 h.p., a 250 h.p. and a 290 h.p. A three-speed manual transmission was standard. Powerglide automatic and a four-speed manual transmission were optional.

Most convertible tops were manually operated. However, a power top was offered.

The most desirable '58 Vettes are those with fuel injection.

1958 Chevrolet Corvette Convertible

PHOTO: T. MICHAELIS CORVETTE SUPPLIES

1958 Chrysler New Yorker Convertible

Original Price: $4,696
Number Produced: 666
Estimated Number Existing in 1979: 6
Miles per Gallon: 10–15
Common Trouble Spots: brakes
Availability of Parts: poor–fair
Investment Potential: AA

Background: The 1958 New Yorker convertible was little changed from the previous year's model. It was powered by a 345 h.p. 392 cu. in. V8 engine with four-barrel carburetor and dual exhaust. Torque Flite automatic transmission and power steering were standard.

1958 Chrysler New Yorker Convertible

PHOTO: CHRYSLER HISTORICAL COLLECTION

1958 Chrysler 300-D Convertible

Original Price: $5,538
Number Produced: 191
Estimated Number Existing in 1979: 4
Miles per Gallon: 8–14
Common Trouble Spots: brakes
Availability of Parts: poor
Investment Potential: AAA+ (with fuel injection); AAA (without)

Background: The 1958 300-D looked about the same as the 1957. But it was even less popular.

It came with a 380 h.p. 392 cu. in. V8. A more powerful version of this engine featured a fuel-injection unit that boosted the horsepower rating to 390. A 300-D convertible so equipped was, and is, a rarity. Torque Flite automatic transmission was standard. A three-speed manual transmission was optional. Padded dash was standard.

1958 Chrysler 300-D Coupe

PHOTO: CHRYSLER CORPORATION

1958 Chrysler 300-D Coupe

Original Price: $5,108
Number Produced: 618
Estimated Number Existing in 1979: 10
Miles per Gallon: 8–14
Common Trouble Spots: brakes
Availability of Parts: poor
Investment Potential: AAA (with fuel injection); AA+ (without)

Background: Anyone who liked the 300-C would like the 300-D. Styling was virtually the same as the 1957. Even the interior hadn't changed much. The standard engine was a 380 h.p. 392 cu. in. V8. A 390 h.p. version of this engine was available at extra cost. Torque Flite automatic transmission was standard. A three-speed manual was optional.

The 300-D is a very rare and desirable automobile. *Special Interest Autos* considers the fuel-injected 300-D the most desirable car of the 300 letter series.

1958 DeSoto Adventurer Convertible

Original Price: $4,314
Number Produced: N.A.
Estimated Number Existing in 1979: N.A.
Miles per Gallon: 9–14
Common Trouble Spots: none
Availability of Parts: fair–poor
Investment Potential: AAA (with fuel injection); AA (without)

Background: Styling of the '58 Adventurer ragtop was little changed from the previous year's model. It was powered by a 345 h.p. 361 cu. in. V8. A 355 h.p. version with fuel injection was available at extra cost. Torque Flite automatic transmission was standard.

1958 DeSoto Firedome Convertible

Original Price: $3,439
Number Produced: N.A.
Estimated Number Existing in 1979: N.A.
Miles per Gallon: 10–15
Common Trouble Spots: none
Availability of Parts: fair–poor
Investment Potential: A+

Background: The addition of quad headlights was the main styling difference between the '58 Firedome ragtop and the previous year's model. It came with a 295 h.p. 361 cu. in. V8. A three-speed manual transmission was standard, but not very popular. Most buyers ordered the optional Torque Flite automatic transmission.

1958 DeSoto Fireflite Convertible

Original Price: $3,917
Number Produced: N.A.
Estimated Number Existing in 1979: N.A.
Miles per Gallon: 10–15
Common Trouble Spots: none
Availability of Parts: fair–poor
Investment Potential: A+

Background: Despite rather pleasing lines, the '58 Fireflite ragtop was not very popular with buyers. In fact, this was the worst sales year for DeSoto since 1935.

The Fireflite was powered by a 305 h.p. 361 cu. in. V8. Torque Flite automatic transmission was standard.

1958 DeSoto Fireflite Convertible

1958 DeSoto Adventurer Convertible

PHOTO: CHRYSLER HISTORICAL COLLECTION

1958 DeSoto Firesweep Convertible

Original Price: $3,174
Number Produced: N.A.
Estimated Number Existing in 1979: N.A.
Miles per Gallon: 10–15
Common Trouble Spots: none
Availability of Parts: fair–poor
Investment Potential: A+

Background: The '58 Firesweep was powered by a 280 h.p. 350 cu. in. V8. Available at extra cost was a 295 h.p. version of this engine, with four-barrel carburetor and dual exhaust. Powerflite and Torque Flite automatic transmissions were optional.

Most 1958 DeSotos, 99.5%, came with one of the automatics, 90.3% had power steering, 69.6% had power brakes, 9.3% had electric windows, 11.1% had power front seats, 67.9% had radios, 48.4% had windshield washers, 36.3% had tinted glass, and 6.2% were sold with an air conditioner.

1958 Dodge Coronet Convertible

Original Price: $2,907
Number Produced: N.A.
Estimated Number Existing in 1979: N.A.
Miles per Gallon: 10–15
Common Trouble Spots: brakes
Availability of Parts: poor–fair
Investment Potential: AA (with fuel injection); A+ (without)

Background: The '58 Coronet ragtop looked much the same as the '57 model—even the dash layout remained unchanged. It came with a 252 h.p. 325 cu. in. "Red Ram" V8. Buyers had their choice of several V8 optional engines, including a 265 h.p. 325, a 295 h.p. 350, a 305 h.p. 361, a 320 h.p. 361, and a 333 h.p. fuel-injected 361. A three-speed manual transmission was standard. Power Flite and Torque Flite automatic transmissions were optional.

Most 1958 Dodges, 96.8%, were equipped with an automatic, 65.3% had power steering, 35.3% had power brakes, 3.2% had power seats, 2.7% had electric windows, 40.9% had windshield washers, 26.4% had tinted glass, 53.2% had radios, and 3.6% were sold with the $381 air conditioner.

1958 Dodge Custom Royal Lancer Convertible

Original Price: $3,253
Number Produced: N.A.
Estimated Number Existing in 1979: N.A.
Miles per Gallon: 10–15
Common Trouble Spots: brakes
Availability of Parts: poor–fair
Investment Potential: AA (with fuel injection); A+ (without)

1958 Dodge Custom Royal Lancer Convertible

Background: The big news for Dodge this year was the availability of fuel injection. It was optional on all Dodges except station wagons.

The Custom Royal Lancer ragtop was powered by a 295 h.p. 350 cu. in. "Ram Fire" V8. In addition to the 333 h.p. fuel-injected 361 cu. in. D-500 V8, a D-500 engine with 320 h.p. (two four-barrel carburetors) and one with 305 h.p. (four-barrel carburetor) were also available. A three-speed manual transmission was standard, but most buyers ordered the optional $220 Torque Flite automatic.

1958 Edsel Citation Convertible

Original Price: $3,676
Number Produced: 930
Estimated Number Existing in 1979: 15
Miles per Gallon: 13–16
Common Trouble Spots: none
Availability of Parts: poor–fair
Investment Potential: AA+

Background: The '58 Citation ragtop is the most attractive and desirable of all Edsels. It was powered by a 345 h.p. 410 cu. in. V8. (with four-barrel carburetor and dual exhaust). Teletouch automatic transmission was standard. Air conditioning was available for $460.

Edsel's famous "horse collar" grille might not have been as distinctive if Packard had put into production its Predictor prototype, which featured an almost identical grille, intended to give the car a "classic" look.

1958 Edsel Citation Convertible

PHOTO: FORD MOTOR COMPANY

1958 Edsel Pacer Convertible

PHOTO: FORD MOTOR COMPANY

1958 Edsel Pacer Convertible

Original Price: $2,995
Number Produced: 1,876
Estimated Number Existing in 1979: 20
Miles per Gallon: 13–16
Common Trouble Spots: none
Availability of Parts: fair–poor
Investment Potential: AA

Background: The Pacer ragtop was one of the best-looking cars on the road in 1958. It was powered by a 303 h.p. 361 cu. in. V8. A three-speed manual transmission was standard. Overdrive and an automatic transmission were optional at extra cost.

Most 1958 Edsels, 91.9%, came with an automatic, 6.1% had the three-speed manual, two percent had the manual with overdrive, 48.7% had power steering, 43.3% had power brakes, 61.4% had windshield washers, 5.6% had power windows, 7.6% had power front seats, 32.9% had tinted glass, 80.3% had radios, and 1.6% were sold with air conditioning.

1958 Ford Fairlane 500 Skyliner Retractable Hardtop

Original Price: $3,138
Number Produced: 14,713
Estimated Number Existing in 1979: 166
Miles per Gallon: 10–16
Common Trouble Spots: cooling system
Availability of Parts: fair–good
Investment Potential: AAA

Background: This was the second year for the controversial retractable hardtop. Like the '57s, '58 Fords had a bad rust problem. This helped contribute to their low survival rate.

The Skyliner came with a 265 h.p. 332 cu. in. V8. Also available was a 300 h.p. 352 cu. in. V8 with four-barrel carburetor and dual exhaust. A three-speed manual transmission was standard. Overdrive and Cruise-O-Matic automatic transmission were optional.

The 1958 Skyliner is a rare and desirable car.

1958 Ford Fairlane 500 Sunliner Convertible

1958 Ford Fairlane 500 Sunliner Convertible

Original Price: $2,749
Number Produced: 35,029
Estimated Number Existing in 1979: 268
Miles per Gallon: 10–18
Common Trouble Spots: cooling system
Availability of Parts: fair–good
Investment Potential: A+

Background: Ford got in on the quad headlight fad in 1958, and that wasn't all that was new—Cruise-O-Matic automatic transmission, which featured two Drive ranges as opposed to the Ford-O-Matic's one, was introduced. Also making its debut was an optional air suspension system (less than one-half of one percent of 1958 Fords were so equipped).

Buyers had their choice of the standard 145 h.p. 223 cu. in. six-cylinder engine or two V8 engines—a 265 h.p. 332 and a 300 h.p. 352. A three-speed manual transmission was standard. Overdrive and Ford-O-Matic and Cruise-O-Matic automatics were optional.

Most 1958 Fords, 76.1%, were equipped with a V8, 69.1% had an automatic, 25.8% had a three-speed manual, 5.1% had a manual with overdrive, 27.5% had power steering, 8.4% had power brakes, 31.3% had windshield washers, 1.2% had electric windows, 1.4% had power front seats, 12.3% had tinted glass, 61.5% had radios, and 1.4% were sold with an air conditioner.

In the spring of 1958, *Motor* reported a rumor that Ford management was considering changing the rear styling of its '58 models. However this was not done because they feared they would make the earlier '58s "orphans."

1958 Ford Fairlane 500 Skyliner Retractable Hardtop

1958 Ford Thunderbird Convertible

PHOTO: FORD MOTOR COMPANY

1958 Ford Thunderbird Convertible

Original Price: est. $3,800
Number Produced: 2,134
Estimated Number Existing in 1979: 45
Miles per Gallon: 10–16
Common Trouble Spots: automatic transmission
Availability of Parts: fair
Investment Potential: AA

Background: The Thunderbird was all new for 1958. It had been enlarged to accommodate four passengers. Thus, it lost much of the sports-car flavor it originally had possessed.

The '58 T-Bird ragtop was powered by a 300 h.p. 352 cu. in. V8 that could whisk the car from 0 to 60 in 10.1 seconds. A three-speed manual transmission was standard. Overdrive and Fordomatic automatic transmission were optional.

Even though *Motor Trend* named the 1958 Thunderbird "Car of the Year" for its performance and comfort, it is not currently very popular among T-Bird collectors. However it is gaining more admirers every year.

1958 Imperial Crown Convertible

PHOTO: CHRYSLER HISTORICAL COLLECTION

1958 Imperial Crown Convertible

Original Price: $5,684
Number Produced: 675
Estimated Number Existing in 1979: 10
Miles per Gallon: 8–14
Common Trouble Spots: brakes
Availability of Parts: poor–fair
Investment Potential: AA

Background: This car dropped significantly in popularity from the previous model.

It was powered by a 392 cu. in. V8 engine that delivered 345 h.p. It came with Torque Flite automatic transmission. The seats were so designed as to give almost a "bucket-seat" effect.

Standard equipment on Imperials included power brakes, power steering, windshield washers, six-way power seats, and electric clock. About one-third came with air conditioning.

1958 King Midget Convertible

Original Price: est. $600
Number Produced: N.A.
Estimated Number Existing in 1979: N.A.
Miles per Gallon: 50–90
Common Trouble Spots: transmission, "V" belts
Availability of Parts: good
Investment Potential: A

Background: Unlike most cars in 1958, the new King Midget ragtop did not have four headlights. It was powered by a 10 h.p. 29 cu. in. one-cylinder engine. Automatic transmission was standard.

1958 King Midget Convertible

PHOTO: JOHN A. CONDE COLLECTION

1958 Lincoln Continental Mark II Convertible

1958 Lincoln Continental Mark III Convertible

Original Price: $5,792
Number Produced: 3,048
Estimated Number Existing in 1979: 38
Miles per Gallon: 8–14
Common Trouble Spots: cooling system, transmission
Availability of Parts: poor–fair
Investment Potential: A+

Background: The Continental convertible was radically restyled for 1958. It was powered by a 375 h.p. 430 cu. in. V8 engine. Turbo-Drive automatic transmission, power steering, power brakes, and a windshield washer were standard.

Most 1958 Lincolns, 85%, came with tinted glass, 85% had power windows, 62% had power seats, and 34% were sold with the $610 air conditioner.

1958 Mercury Montclair Convertible

Original Price: $3,244
Number Produced: 844
Estimated Number Existing in 1979: 8
Miles per Gallon: 9–15
Common Trouble Spots: automatic transmission, carburetor, valves
Availability of Parts: fair–poor
Investment Potential: A

Background: The '58 Montclair was the least popular convertible Mercury made in the 1950s. It came with a 330 h.p. 383 cu. in. V8. A 400 h.p. 430 cu. in. V8 was optional. Merc-O-Matic automatic transmission was standard.

1958 Mercury Monterey Convertible

Original Price: $2,822
Number Produced: 2,292
Estimated Number Existing in 1979: 24
Miles per Gallon: 9–15
Common Trouble Spots: automatic transmission, carburetor, valves
Availability of Parts: fair–poor
Investment Potential: A

Background: The Monterey was Mercury's most popular convertible in 1958, despite the fact that sales were less than half of the previous year's. The Monterey came with a 312 h.p. 383 cu. in. V8. A 400 h.p. 430 cu. in. V8 was optional. A three-speed manual transmission was standard. Overdrive and Merc-O-Matic automatic transmission were available at extra cost.

Most 1958 Mercurys, 94.2%, were equipped with an automatic, 4.8% had the three-speed manual, 1% had the manual with overdrive, 50.5% had power steering, 39.2% had power brakes, 41% had windshield washers, 35.9% had tinted glass, 6.6% had power windows, 7.9% had power front seats, 80.8% had radios, and 3.7% were sold with an air conditioner.

1958 Mercury Park Lane Convertible

Original Price: $3,788
Number Produced: 853
Estimated Number Existing in 1979: 8
Miles per Gallon: 9–14
Common Trouble Spots: automatic transmission, carburetor, cooling system
Availability of Parts: fair–poor
Investment Potential: A

Background: This was the first year for Mercury's top-of-the-line Park Lane convertible. The '58 model was also the least popular (saleswise) Park Lane ragtop ever built.

It came with a 360 h.p. 430 cu. in. V8 engine (with dual exhaust). A 400 h.p. version of this engine was optional. Multi-Drive automatic transmission was standard.

The gear selector pattern on this transmission was a bit unusual—it read: HP (high performance), CH (cruising, hill control), NS (neutral, starting), R (reverse), and BR (brake release).

1958 Metropolitan Series 1500 Convertible

Original Price: est. $1,600
Number Produced: est. 2,764
Estimated Number Existing in 1979: 27
Miles per Gallon: 25–35
Common Trouble Spots: brakes, door locks, transmission
Availability of Parts: good–fair
Investment Potential: A

Background: The 1958 Metropolitan convertible was powered by a 52 h.p. 90.9 cu. in. four-cylinder engine. A three-speed manual transmission was standard.

It is somewhat ironic that the Metropolitan, a low-cost, economical car, was most popular among well-to-do people.

1958 Oldsmobile Dynamic 88 Convertible

PHOTO: OLDSMOBILE DIVISION

1958 Oldsmobile Dynamic 88 Convertible

Original Price: $2,931
Number Produced: 4,456
Estimated Number Existing in 1979: 27
Miles per Gallon: 12–16
Common Trouble Spots: none
Availability of Parts: fair
Investment Potential: A

Background: The 1958 Dynamic 88 ragtop looked like the kind of car the "Little Blue Man" would use to pick up a hot date. It was powered by a 265 h.p. 371 cu. in. V8 engine. A 277 h.p., a 305 h.p., and a 312 h.p. version of this engine were also available. A three-speed manual transmission was standard, but not very popular—most buyers ordered the optional Hydra-Matic automatic transmission. "New-Matic Ride" air suspension was offered for the first time. However, it was an offer that most buyers decided to refuse.

1958 Oldsmobile 98 Convertible

Original Price: $3,915
Number Produced: 5,605
Estimated Number Existing in 1979: 35
Miles per Gallon: 10–14
Common Trouble Spots: none
Availability of Parts: fair
Investment Potential: A+

Background: The 1958 Olds 98 looked as if it had been designed by a chrome salesperson. It came with a 305 h.p. 371 cu. in. V8. A 312 h.p. version of this engine was available. Hydra-Matic automatic transmission was standard.

Among the many options were "New-Matic Ride" air suspension, a "Trans-Portable" radio that could be used in or out of the car, a "Safety Sentinel" speedometer that flashed and buzzed when the driver exceeded a preset speed, and an improved, transistorized Autronic Eye (headlight dimmer).

The 1958 Olds 98 ragtop is a brassy, head-turning car (some claim it does the same thing to one's stomach). It takes a gutsy, highly individualistic person to own one—and admit to it.

1958 Oldsmobile 98 Convertible

PHOTO: OLDSMOBILE DIVISION

1958 Oldsmobile Super 88 Convertible

Original Price: $3,208
Number Produced: 3,799
Estimated Number Existing in 1979: 23
Miles per Gallon: 10–15
Common Trouble Spots: carburetor
Availability of Parts: fair
Investment Potential: A

Background: Subtle it ain't; the 1958 Olds Super 88 ragtop is an ideal example of conspicuous consumption. It was powered by a 305 h.p. 371 cu. in. V8. A 312 h.p. version of this engine was also available. A three-speed manual transmission was standard. Most 1958 Olds, 98.9%, came with Hydra-Matic automatic transmission.

"New-Matic Ride" air suspension was one of the least popular options on new Oldsmobiles—only 6.1% were so equipped. Most, 86.6%, had power brakes, 85.9% had power steering, 19.4% had power front seats, 17.6% had power windows, 80.1% had tinted glass, and 12.5% were sold with an air conditioner.

1958 Oldsmobile Super 88 Convertible

PHOTO: OLDSMOBILE DIVISION

1958 Plymouth Belvedere Convertible

Original Price: $2,727
Number Produced: N.A.
Estimated Number Existing in 1979: N.A.
Miles per Gallon: 11–16
Common Trouble Spots: engine bearings, piston rings, valves
Availability of Parts: fair–poor
Investment Potential: AA+ (with fuel injection); A+ (without)

Background: With the exception of the quad headlights, styling changes for 1958 were very mild. The new Belvedere was powered by a 225 h.p. 318 cu. in. V8. A 250 h.p. version of this engine (with four-barrel carburetor) and two 350 cu. in. V8s, a 305 h.p. (with either two four-barrel carburetors or fuel injection) and a 315 h.p. (with fuel injection) were optional at extra cost.

A three-speed manual transmission was standard. Overdrive and Power Flite or Torque Flite automatic transmissions were optional.

Most 1958 Plymouths, 78.6 percent, were equipped with one of the automatics, 19.7% had a three-speed manual, 1.7% had overdrive, 33.9% had power steering, 15.9% had power brakes, 1% had electric windows, less than 1% had power front seats, 31.9% had windshield washers, 19% had tinted glass, 44.9% had radios, and 2.2% were sold with an air conditioner.

The 1958 Belvedere convertible is a smooth-riding, sporty-looking car. The ones equipped with fuel injection are especially desirable.

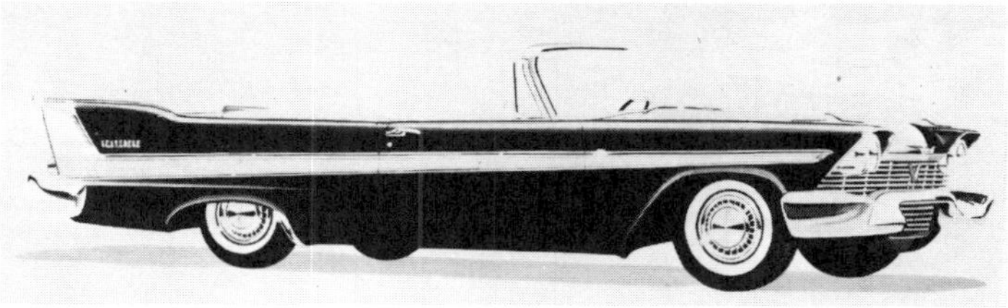

1958 Plymouth Belvedere Convertible

PHOTO: CHRYSLER HISTORICAL COLLECTION

1958 Pontiac Bonneville Convertible

Original Price: $3,277
Number Produced: 3,076
Estimated Number Existing in 1979: 21
Miles per Gallon: 10–17
Common Trouble Spots: carburetor
Availability of Parts: fair
Investment Potential: AA+ (with fuel injection); AA (without)

Background: On October 4, 1957 the Russians blasted Sputnik into orbit, and the space race began. America was quick to respond. On November 9, 1957, the new Pontiacs were introduced.

The flashy Bonneville convertible looked as if it had a rocket on each side. It was powered by a 255 h.p. 370 cu. in. V8 engine. Three other versions of this engine were available at extra cost: a 285 h.p. (with a four-barrel carburetor), a 300 h.p. (with three two-barrel carburetors), and a 310 h.p. (with fuel injection). (About 400 1958 Pontiacs had fuel injection.) A three-speed manual transmission was standard, but not very popular. Hydra-Matic automatic transmission was optional for $237.

Other "world-of-tomorrow" options included "Air-Ride" air suspension, an improved fuel-injection unit, and even a $196 "Sportable" transistor radio that could be removed from the dash and used outside the car (for up to fifty hours per set of batteries).

The '58 Bonneville was the last of the really wild, "Gee-Whiz"-styled Pontiacs.

1958 Pontiac Bonneville Convertible

PHOTO: PONTIAC MOTOR DIVISION

1958 Pontiac Chieftain Convertible

Original Price: $2,750
Number Produced: 7,359
Estimated Number Existing in 1979: 51
Miles per Gallon: 10–17
Common Trouble Spots: carburetor
Availability of Parts: fair
Investment Potential: AA (with fuel injection); A+ (without)

Background: In the fall of 1957, Americans were invited to "Meet the bold new Pontiac." And new it was. The Chieftain ragtop was radically restyled for 1958. Although basically a very attractive automobile, it was a bit gimmicky in design.

The Chieftain was powered by a 255 h.p. 370 cu. in. V8. Other versions of this engine were also available: a 270 h.p. (two-barrel carb), a 285 h.p. (four-barrel carb), a 300 h.p. (three two-barrel carbs), and a 310 h.p. (fuel injected). A three-speed manual transmission was standard. Hydra-Matic automatic transmission was optional.

Most 1958 Pontiacs, 97%, came with the automatic, 54% had power steering, 54% had power brakes, 2.4% had power front seats, 3% had electric windows, 19.7% had tinted glass, 31% had windshield washers, 3.5% had air suspension, and 5% were sold with air conditioning.

1958 Pontiac Chieftain Convertible

PHOTO: PONTIAC MOTOR DIVISION

1959

1959 Buick Electra 225 Convertible

Original Price: $4,192
Number Produced: 5,493
Estimated Number Existing in 1979: 55
Miles per Gallon: 10–16
Common Trouble Spots: automatic transmission
Availability of Parts: fair–good
Investment Potential: A+

Background: The 1959 Electra ragtop looked like the kind of car one would expect to see Batman and Robin riding in when they were off duty. It came with a 325 h.p. 401 cu. in. V8. Twin Turbine automatic transmission, power brakes, and power steering were standard. Triple Turbine automatic was optional with the economy package (four-barrel carburetor, 2.78 axle and dual exhaust). Just over 10% of all '59 Buicks had the $430 air conditioning unit.

1959 Buick Electra 225 Convertible

PHOTO: PUBLIC RELATIONS DEPARTMENT, BUICK MOTOR DIVISION

1959 Buick Invicta Convertible

Original Price: $3,620
Number Produced: 5,447
Estimated Number Existing in 1979: 55
Miles per Gallon: 11–17
Common Trouble Spots: automatic transmission
Availability of Parts: fair–good
Investment Potential: A+

Background: The '59 Invicta convertible looked nothing like the cars Buick offered in '58. It had clean, sweeping lines and a more restrained use of chrome.

The Invicta was powered by a 325 h.p. 401 cu. in. V8. Twin Turbine automatic transmission was standard. Triple Turbine automatic was available for $296.

Other options included an economy package. This consisted of Triple Turbine automatic, 2.78 axle, four-barrel carburetor, and dual exhaust. If buyers wanted a little more "go," they could order a performance package. This contained Triple Turbine automatic, 3.23 axle, and dual exhaust. Another option was a rear-seat speaker. While this did nothing for the car's performance, it did make it easier for back-seat passengers to hear Buddy Holly sing "Peggy Sue"—especially when the top was down and the car was going 75 miles per hour.

1959 Buick Invicta Convertible

PHOTO: PUBLIC RELATIONS DEPARTMENT, BUICK MOTOR DIVISION

1959 Buick LeSabre Convertible

PHOTO: PUBLIC RELATIONS DEPARTMENT, BUICK MOTOR DIVISION

1959 Buick LeSabre Convertible

Original Price: $3,129
Number Produced: 10,489
Estimated Number Existing in 1979: 106
Miles per Gallon: 11–17
Common Trouble Spots: automatic transmission
Availability of Parts: fair–good
Investment Potential: A+

Background: The LeSabre came with a 250 h.p. 364 cu. in. V8. A three-speed manual transmission was standard. If they wanted, buyers could order an economy package consisting of Triple Turbine automatic transmission, 2.78 axle, four-barrel carburetor, and dual exhaust. Also available optionally was a performance package which included Twin Turbine automatic, 3.23 axle, four-barrel carburetor, and dual exhaust.

Most 1960 Buicks, 98.8%, were equipped with an automatic, 68.7% had power brakes, 78.5% had power steering, 14.5% had power front seats, and 44.1% were sold with tinted glass.

1959 Cadillac Eldorado Biarritz Convertible

Original Price: $7,401
Number Produced: 1,320
Estimated Number Existing in 1979: 32
Miles per Gallon: 9–14
Common Trouble Spots: none
Availability of Parts: fair
Investment Potential: AA+

Background: Filthy rich. That's the first impression people had of anyone driving a new Eldorado Biarritz. There was nothing subtle about its wild, "I've got it made" styling.

The Eldorado was powered by a 345 h.p. 390 cu. in. V8 engine. Hydramatic automatic transmission, power steering, power brakes, and air suspension were standard.

The 1959 Eldorado Biarritz convertible is symbolic of the American dream of wealth and success. It is a bold, arrogant car. A meek person would be too intimidated to drive one. Even a hundred years from now, people will look at this car in a museum and instantly know it was made for the elite.

1959 Cadillac Series 62 Convertible

PHOTO: CADILLAC MOTOR CAR DIVISION

1959 Cadillac Series 62 Convertible

Original Price: $5,455
Number Produced: 11,130
Estimated Number Existing in 1979: 280
Miles per Gallon: 10–14
Common Trouble Spots: none
Availability of Parts: fair
Investment Potential: A+

Background: The Series 62 convertible was completely restyled for 1959. For people who liked big fins this was the car.

It was powered by a 325 h.p. 390 cu. in. V8 engine with a four-barrel carburetor. Hydramatic automatic transmission was standard. All 1959 Cadillacs came with power steering and power brakes. Eighty-one percent had power front seats, 83% had power windows, and 39.2 percent were equipped with air conditioning.

The 1959 Series 62 convertible is a flamboyant and luxurious automobile. It practically screams "Hey, look at me!" It was, and remains, the perfect car for people who believe in the motto, "If you got it, flaunt it."

1959 Cadillac Eldorado Biarritz Convertible

PHOTO: CADILLAC MOTOR CAR DIVISION

1959 Chevrolet Corvette Convertible

Original Price: $3,875
Number Produced: 9,670
Estimated Number Existing in 1979: 200
Miles per Gallon: 11–19
Common Trouble Spots: none
Availability of Parts: fair–good
Investment Potential: AAA

Background: The 1959 Corvette looked basically the same as the 1958. However, some of the excessive chrome found on the previous year's model was eliminated.

It was powered by a 230 h.p. 283 cu. in. V8 engine. Hotter versions of this engine were available, including a 245 h.p., a 250 h.p., and a 290 h.p. A three-speed manual transmission was standard. Powerglide automatic transmission and a four-speed manual were optional.

Buyers had their choice of seven exterior colors in solids or attractive two-tone combinations.

Road and Track said the '59 Corvette was "A pretty package with all the speed you need, and then some."

1959 Chevrolet Corvette Convertible

PHOTO: T. MICHAELIS CORVETTE SUPPLIES

1959 Chevrolet Impala Convertible

Original Price: $2,967
Number Produced: est. 69,282
Estimated Number Existing in 1979: 1,011
Miles per Gallon: 10–18
Common Trouble Spots: none
Availability of Parts: fair–good
Investment Potential: AA (with fuel injection); A+ (without)

Background: This may very well have been the most radically designed car Chevrolet ever built. It was powered by a 135 h.p. 235.5 cu. in. six. Available at extra cost were the following V8 engines: a 185 h.p. 283 (with two-barrel carburetor), a 230 h.p. 283 (with four-barrel carburetor), a 250 h.p. 283 (with fuel injection), a 290 h.p. 283 (with fuel injection), a 250 h.p. 348 (with four-barrel carburetor), a 300 h.p. 348 (with four-barrel carburetor), a 280 h.p. 348 (with three two-barrel carburetors), and a 315 h.p. 348 (with three two-barrel carburetors). A three-speed manual was standard. Overdrive, a four-speed manual, and Powerglide and Turboglide automatic transmissions were optional.

Most 1959 Chevrolets, 56%, came equipped with a V8, 65.7% had an automatic, 2.2% had overdrive, 24.1% had power steering, 11.4% had power brakes, 1.1% had power windows, almost 1% had power front seats, 18.7% had tinted glass, and 2.3% were sold with air conditioners.

1959 Chevrolet Impala Convertible

PHOTO: GM PHOTOGRAPHIC

1959 Chrysler New Yorker Convertible

Original Price: $4,800
Number Produced: 286
Estimated Number Existing in 1979: 3
Miles per Gallon: 9–14
Common Trouble Spots: brakes
Availability of Parts: poor–fair
Investment Potential: A+

Background: The face-lifted 1959 New Yorker convertible was not a very popular car. It was powered by a 350 h.p. 413 cu. in. V8 engine. Push-button Torque Flite automatic transmission and power steering were standard. One of the most interesting options offered was a swivel front seat. When the door was open, the seat could turn toward it to make exiting or entering easier. Although it sounded good in theory, some owners found it to be a nuisance.

1959 Chrysler New Yorker Convertible

1959 Chrysler 300-E Convertible

1959 Chrysler 300-E Convertible

Original Price: $5,659
Number Produced: 140
Estimated Number Existing in 1979: 5
Miles per Gallon: 8–14
Common Trouble Spots: brakes
Availability of Parts: poor–fair
Investment Potential: AAA

Background: The 300-E was similar in styling to previous 300 Series convertibles. Like them, it had a low production number.

It was powered by a 380 h.p. 413 cu. in. V8 engine. Torque Flite automatic transmission was standard. A popular option was swivel front seats.

The 300-E convertible is highly sought after by 300 Letter Series enthusiasts. It is an attractive and valuable automobile.

1959 Chrysler 300-E Coupe

Original Price: $4,852
Number Produced: 550
Estimated Number Existing in 1979: 15
Miles per Gallon: 8–14
Common Trouble Spots: brakes
Availability of Parts: poor–fair
Investment Potential: AA+

Background: The styling of the 300-E was little changed from the previous model. This may have been a factor in the decline in sales of this luxury performance car. It came equipped with a 380 h.p. 413 cu. in. V8 engine. Torque Flite automatic transmission was standard.

1959 Chrysler Windsor Convertible

Original Price: $3,555
Number Produced: 961
Estimated Number Existing in 1979: 12
Miles per Gallon: 10–16
Common Trouble Spots: brakes
Availability of Parts: poor–fair
Investment Potential: A+

Background: For the first time since 1956, a Windsor convertible was offered. It was powered by a 305 h.p. 383 cu. in. V8. A three-speed manual transmission was standard. Torque Flite automatic transmission was optional.

1959 Chrysler Windsor Convertible

1959 DeSoto Adventurer Convertible

Original Price: $4,674
Number Produced: N.A.
Estimated Number Existing in 1979: N.A.
Miles per Gallon: 9–15
Common Trouble Spots: none
Availability of Parts: fair–poor
Investment Potential: AA

Background: "What a thrill DeSoto's great luxury car is . . . styled to be stunningly beautiful . . . engineered to handle like a thoroughbred . . . built to ride as softly as passing summer clouds." That's how sales catalogs described the eye-catching 1959 Adventurer.

It came with a 350 h.p. 383 cu. in. V8 with two four-barrel carburetors. Push-button Torque Flite automatic transmission, swivel front seats, power steering, and power brakes were among the standard features.

1959 DeSoto Firedome Convertible

Original Price: $3,588
Number Produced: N.A.
Estimated Number Existing in 1979: N.A.
Miles per Gallon: 10–16
Common Trouble Spots: none
Availability of Parts: fair–poor
Investment Potential: A+

Background: The '59 Firedome ragtop was powered by a 305 h.p. 383 cu. in. V8. A 350 h.p. version of this engine, with two four-barrel carburetors and "hilift" cam, was optional. A three-speed manual transmission was standard. Torque Flite automatic transmission was available at extra cost.

Some of the accessories offered included Auto-Temp push-button heater, vanity mirror, trunk light, dual exhaust, power steering, power brakes, electric clock, Touch-Tuner radio, and ashtray light.

1959 DeSoto Fireflite Convertible

Original Price: $4,077
Number Produced: N.A.
Estimated Number Existing in 1979: N.A.
Miles per Gallon: 10–16
Common Trouble Spots: none
Availability of Parts: fair–poor
Investment Potential: A+

Background: The 1959 Fireflite convertible was a big, roomy car. It was perfect for someone with a large family, or who liked to pick up a lot of hitchhikers. It came with a 325 h.p. 383 cu. in. V8. A 350 h.p. Adventurer 383 cu. in. V8 was optional. Torque Flite automatic transmission was standard.

Among the optional accessories available at extra cost were dual exhaust, stone deflectors, three-way Prismatic mirror, Touch-Tuner radio, Station-Seeker radio, six-way power front seat, Auto-Temp push button heater, air conditioning, trunk deck lid accent stripes, automatic headlight beam changer, and dual radio antennas.

1959 DeSoto Firesweep Convertible

Original Price: $3,260
Number Produced: N.A.
Estimated Number Existing in 1979: N.A.
Miles per Gallon: 10–16
Common Trouble Spots: none
Availability of Parts: fair–poor
Investment Potential: A+

Background: This was the last year for the Firesweep convertible. It came with a 290 h.p. 361 cu. in. V8. Available at extra cost was a 350 h.p. 383 cu. in. V8. A three-speed manual transmission was standard. Powerflite and Torque Flite automatic transmissions were optional.

Most 1959 DeSotos, 99.4%, came with one of the automatics, 97% had power steering, 88.2% had power brakes, 7% had electric windows, 9.8% had power front seats, 29.1% had tinted glass, 64.8% had a radio, and 7.7% were sold with an air conditioner.

1959 Dodge Coronet Convertible

Original Price: $3,039
Number Produced: N.A.
Estimated Number Existing in 1979: N.A.
Miles per Gallon: 11–16
Common Trouble Spots: brakes
Availability of Parts: poor–fair
Investment Potential: A+

Background: Anyone who looked into his or her rear-view mirror in 1959 might feel a bit uneasy seeing a '59 Coronet approaching. It looked very aggressive—in fact, downright mean—from the front.

The Coronet was powered by a 255 h.p. 326 cu. in. V8. Optional engines included the following V8s: a 295 h.p. 361, a 305 h.p. 361, a 320 h.p. 383, and a 345 h.p. 383 (with dual four-barrel carburetors). A three-speed manual transmission was standard, but most people ordered either the Power Flite or the Torque Flite automatic transmission.

Two novel options offered were swivel seats, and self-tilting rear-view mirror. A neat gadget on the '59 Coronet ragtop was a colored bar on the speedometer. It showed green for speeds 30 mph or under, amber for 30 to 50 mph, and red for speeds over 50.

1959 Dodge Custom Royal Convertible

Original Price: $3,372
Number Produced: N.A.
Estimated Number Existing in 1979: N.A.
Miles per Gallon: 11–15
Common Trouble Spots: brakes
Availability of Parts: poor–fair
Investment Potential: A+

Background: The Custom Royal was Dodge's most expensive convertible in 1959. The Royal's highly sculptured front end was particularly striking. It had a most intimidating look about it. And with good reason—the standard engine was a "Super Ram Fire" 305 h.p. 361 cu. in. V8.

If that wasn't enough power, buyers could order a 320 h.p. or 345 h.p. 383 cu. in. V8. A three-speed manual transmission was standard. Torque Flite automatic transmission was available at extra cost.

The majority of '59 Dodges, 93.7%, were equipped with an automatic, 68.9% had power steering, 27.4% had power brakes, 20.3% had tinted glass, 1.8% had power windows, 2.5% had power seats, 46.4% had radios, and 4.5% were sold with the $379 air conditioner.

1959 Edsel Corsair Convertible

Original Price: $3,072
Number Produced: 1,343
Estimated Number Existing in 1979: 20
Miles per Gallon: 12–17
Common Trouble Spots: none
Availability of Parts: poor–fair
Investment Potential: A+

Background: Although unmistakably an Edsel, the new Corsair convertible was not as distinctive as the 1958 models. It was powered by a 225 h.p. 332 cu. in. V8. Available at extra cost was a 300 h.p. 361 cu. in. V8. A three-speed manual transmission was standard. Two Mile-O-Matic automatic transmissions, a two-speed and a dual-range three-speed, were optional.

Most 1959 Edsels, 80.5%, came with an automatic, 30.5% had power steering, 18.9% had power brakes, 8.2% had tinted glass, 1.5% had power windows, 2.3% had power front seats, 75.5% had radios, and 2.2% were sold with air conditioning.

1959 Edsel Corsair Convertible

PHOTO: FORD MOTOR COMPANY

1959 Ford Galaxie Skyliner Retractable Hardtop

Original Price: $3,346
Number Produced: 12,915
Estimated Number Existing in 1979: 310
Miles per Gallon: 10–16
Common Trouble Spots: automatic transmission, cooling system
Availability of Parts: good–fair
Investment Potential: AAA

Background: This was the last retractable hardtop made by Ford. Although production was low, it seems to have had a better survival rate than the 1957 and 1958 models.

It came with a 200 h.p. 292 cu. in. V8 (with two-barrel carb). Optional V8s were a 225 h.p. 332, a 300 h.p. 352, and a 350 h.p. 352. Buyers could choose from four transmissions: a three-speed manual, a three-speed manual with overdrive, Ford-O-Matic, and Cruise-O-Matic.

1959 Ford Galaxie Skyliner Retractable Hardtop

PHOTO: FORD MOTOR COMPANY

1959 Ford Galaxie Sunliner Convertible

Original Price: $2,957
Number Produced: 45,868
Estimated Number Existing in 1979: 614
Miles per Gallon: 10–18
Common Trouble Spots: automatic transmission, cooling system
Availability of Parts: good–fair
Investment Potential: A+

Background: Although a family resemblance remained, the 1959 Ford was noticeably restyled. In fact, the 1959 Ford won an award for "exceptional styling" at the Brussels World's Fair. While many people may feel the award was well deserved, there are many others who consider the '59 Ford downright ugly.

Buyers had their choice of four engines—a 145 h.p. 223 cu. in. six and three V8s: a 200 h.p. 292, a 225 h.p.

332, and a 300 h.p. 352. A three-speed manual transmission was standard. Overdrive and Ford-O-Matic and Cruise-O-Matic automatic transmissions were optional.

Most 1959 Fords, 70%, had an automatic, 77% had a V8, 29% had power steering, 10% had power brakes, 8% had tinted glass, 70% had radios, 1% had power windows, 1% had power front seats, and 4% had air conditioning.

1959 Ford Galaxie Sunliner Convertible

PHOTO: FORD MOTOR COMPANY

1959 Ford Thunderbird Convertible

Original Price: $3,980
Number Produced: 10,261
Estimated Number Existing in 1979: 200
Miles per Gallon: 10–14
Common Trouble Spots: cooling system
Availability of Parts: fair
Investment Potential: AA+

Background: The flashy '59 Thunderbird ragtop came with a 300 h.p. 352 cu. in. V8. Also available was a 350 h.p. 430 cu. in. V8. A three-speed manual transmission was standard. Overdrive and Cruise-O-Matic automatic transmission were optional.

Most 1959 T-Birds, 98%, were equipped with an automatic, over 95% had power steering, 56% had power windows, 47% had power front seats, 20% had air conditioning, and 40% were sold with tinted glass.

The strongly horizontal grille and rear taillight chrome treatment help make the '59 T-Bird the cleanest-looking of the 1958-1960 "Square Birds." That may be why it is now the most popular of the three years with collectors.

1959 Ford Thunderbird Convertible

PHOTO: FORD MOTOR COMPANY

1959 Imperial Crown Convertible

Original Price: $5,684
Number Produced: 555
Estimated Number Existing in 1979: 13
Miles per Gallon: 8–14
Common Trouble Spots: brakes
Availability of Parts: poor–fair
Investment Potential: AA

Background: The new Imperial softtop featured a restyled grille and other trim modifications, although a resemblance to last year's model was clearly evident.

A 350 h.p. 413 cu. in. V8 engine powered the Imperial. Torque Flite automatic transmission was standard.

Among the many options available were swivel seats, "Auto-Pilot" (a cruise control unit), "Mirror Matic" (an electronic rear-view mirror that adjusted automatically to the "night" position in response to headlights from behind), and an electronically controlled headlight dimmer.

Most 1959 Imperials, 91.5%, came with power windows, 93% had power front seats, 81.1% had tinted glass, 97.1% had radios, and 37.5% were sold with air conditioning.

1959 Imperial Crown Convertible

PHOTO: CHRYSLER HISTORICAL COLLECTION

1959 King Midget Convertible

Original Price: est. $600
Number Produced: N.A.
Estimated Number Existing in 1979: N.A.
Miles per Gallon: 50–90
Common Trouble Spots: transmission, "V" belts
Availability of Parts: good
Investment Potential: A

Background: The new '59 King Midget convertible was powered by a 10 h.p. 29 cu. in. one-cylinder engine. Automatic transmission was standard.

1959 Lincoln Continental Mark IV Convertible

PHOTO: FORD MOTOR COMPANY

1959 Lincoln Continental Mark IV Convertible

Original Price: $7,056
Number Produced: 2,195
Estimated Number Existing in 1979: 38
Miles per Gallon: 8–14
Common Trouble Spots: brakes, transmission
Availability of Parts: poor–fair
Investment Potential: A+

Background: The new Continental convertible was little changed from the previous year's model. It was powered by a 350 h.p. 430 cu. in. V8. Turbo-Drive automatic transmission, power steering, and power brakes were standard.

Most '59 Lincolns, 88.1%, had power windows, 90.3% had power seats, 82% had tinted glass, 99.6% had a radio, and 40.8% were sold with an air conditioner.

Buyers had their choice of twenty exterior colors.

1959 Mercury Monterey Convertible

Original Price: $3,150
Number Produced: 4,426
Estimated Number Existing in 1979: 75
Miles per Gallon: 11–17
Common Trouble Spots: brakes, carburetor
Availability of Parts: fair–poor
Investment Potential: A

Background: The Monterey convertible received a pleasing face-lift for 1959. It came with a 210 h.p. 312 cu. in. V8. Other V8 engines available at extra cost were a 280 h.p. 383 (two-barrel carb), a 322 h.p. 383 (four-barrel carb), and a 345 h.p. 430 (four-barrel carb). A three-speed manual transmission was standard. Merc-O-Matic automatic transmission was optional.

Most 1959 Mercurys, 97.4%, were equipped with an automatic, 69.7% had power steering, 52.5% had power brakes, 47.2% had tinted glass, 6.4% had power windows, 9.3% had power front seats, 83.1% had radios, and 7.7% were sold with an air conditioner.

1959 Mercury Park Lane Convertible

Original Price: $4,206
Number Produced: 1,257
Estimated Number Existing in 1979: 21
Miles per Gallon: 10–15
Common Trouble Spots: brakes, carburetor
Availability of Parts: fair–poor
Investment Potential: A

Background: The new Park Lane convertible was the most expensive Mercury offered in 1959. It was powered by a 345 h.p. 430 cu. in. V8. Multi-Drive automatic transmission was standard. This year, the letters on the selector pattern were changed to conform with the traditional type of lettering.

1959 Mercury Park Lane Convertible

1959 Metropolitan Series 1500 Convertible

Original Price: $1,650
Number Produced: est. 4,676
Estimated Number Existing in 1979: 63
Miles per Gallon: 25–35
Common Trouble Spots: brakes, gearshift
Availability of Parts: good–fair
Investment Potential: A

Background: The Metropolitan ragtop now had a trunk lid that opened. It was powered by a 52 h.p. 90.9 cu. in. four-cylinder engine. A three-speed manual transmission was standard.

1959 Mercury Monterey Convertible

1959 Oldsmobile Dynamic 88 Convertible

Original Price: $3,286
Number Produced: 8,491
Estimated Number Existing in 1979: 85
Miles per Gallon: 10–16
Common Trouble Spots: none
Availability of Parts: fair
Investment Potential: A

Background: The Dynamic 88 received totally new styling for 1959. It was powered by a 270 h.p. 371 cu. in. V8 engine. A three-speed manual transmission was standard, but not very popular—most buyers ordered the optional Hydra-Matic automatic transmission. Air suspension remained one of the least popular options.

1959 Oldsmobile Dynamic 88 Convertible

PHOTO: OLDSMOBILE DIVISION

1959 Oldsmobile 98 Convertible

Original Price: $4,366
Number Produced: 7,514
Estimated Number Existing in 1979: 75
Miles per Gallon: 9–15
Common Trouble Spots: none
Availability of Parts: fair
Investment Potential: A

Background: The 1959 Olds 98 was a big,.comfortable automobile. It had one of the most unusual headlight treatments to be found on any car that year.

The 98 was powered by a 315 h.p. 394 cu. in. V8 engine. Hydra-Matic automatic transmission was standard. Air suspension was available, but it wasn't very popular.

1959 Oldsmobile 98 Convertible

PHOTO: OLDSMOBILE DIVISION

1959 Oldsmobile Super 88 Convertible

Original Price: $3,595
Number Produced: 4,895
Estimated Number Existing in 1979: 48
Miles per Gallon: 9–16
Common Trouble Spots: none
Availability of Parts: fair
Investment Potential: A

Background: The 1959 Super 88 was completely restyled. It bore no resemblance to the previous year's model. It was powered by a 315 h.p. 394 cu. in. V8. A three-speed manual transmission was standard. Hydra-Matic automatic transmission was available at extra cost.

Most 1959 Oldsmobiles, 99.1%, were equipped with the automatic, 91.1% had power steering, 88.9% had power brakes, 49.1% had tinted glass, 19.7% had power windows, 13.9% had power front seats, and 16% were sold with an air conditioner.

1959 Oldsmobile Super 88 Convertible

PHOTO: OLDSMOBILE DIVISION

1959 Plymouth Belvedere Convertible

Original Price: $3,125
Number Produced: N.A.
Estimated Number Existing in 1979: N.A.
Miles per Gallon: 11–16
Common Trouble Spots: brakes
Availability of Parts: fair–poor
Investment Potential: A+

Background: The new Belvedere convertible had graceful good looks. It was powered by a 230 h.p. 318 cu. in. V8 (with two-barrel carburetor). A 260 h.p. 318 (with four-barrel carburetor) and a 305 h.p. 361 cu. in. V8 (with four-barrel carburetor) were available at extra cost.

A three-speed manual transmission was standard. A manual with overdrive and Power Flite and Torque Flite automatic transmissions were optional.

Most 1959 Plymouths, 73.1 percent, were equipped with one of the automatics, 24.6% had the three-speed manual, 2.3% had overdrive, 40.1% had power steering, 13.8% had power brakes, almost 1% had electric windows, less than .5% had power front seats, 14.7% had tinted glass, 38.8% had radios, and 2.3% were sold with air conditioning.

1959 Plymouth Sport Fury Convertible

Original Price: $3,125
Number Produced: N.A.
Estimated Number Existing in 1979: N.A.
Miles per Gallon: 10–16
Common Trouble Spots: brakes
Availability of Parts: fair–poor
Investment Potential: A+

Background: The pride of the Plymouth line for 1959 was the Sport Fury convertible. It was powered by a 260 h.p. 318 cu. in. V8 (with a four-barrel carburetor). Offered at extra cost was a 305 h.p. 361 cu. in. V8 (with four-barrel carburetor).

A three-speed manual transmission was standard. Overdrive and Torque Flite automatic transmission were optional.

An interesting option was "Mirror-Matic". It was an electronically controlled rear-view mirror that tilted slightly when the bright lights of a car behind reached it.

One of the standard features on the snazzy Sport Fury was front seats that swiveled outward to make entering and exiting easier. This feature was available at extra cost on other two-door Plymouths.

1959 Pontiac Bonneville Convertible

Original Price: $3,478
Number Produced: 11,426
Estimated Number Existing in 1979: 120
Miles per Gallon: 10–16
Common Trouble Spots: valves
Availability of Parts: fair
Investment Potential: AA

Background: The 1959 Pontiac was *Motor Trend*'s Car of the Year because it had "the year's best combination of handling, ride and performance." And as a former owner of a '59 "wide-track" Pontiac, I can only say it deserved it.

The most desirable Pontiac that year was the Bonneville ragtop. It was powered by a 260 h.p. 389 cu. in. V8 with four-barrel carburetor. Five other versions of this engine were optional: a 280 h.p., a 300 h.p., a 315 h.p., a 330 h.p., and a 345 h.p. A three-speed manual transmission was standard. Hydra-Matic automatic transmission was optional.

Good looks and performance help make the 1959 Bonneville convertible a desirable car.

1959 Pontiac Bonneville Convertible

PHOTO: PONTIAC MOTOR DIVISION

1959 Pontiac Catalina Convertible

Original Price: $3,080
Number Produced: 14,515
Estimated Number Existing in 1979: 153
Miles per Gallon: 10–17
Common Trouble Spots: carburetor, valves
Availability of Parts: fair
Investment Potential: A+

Background: Beautiful. That is the best way to describe the new Catalina convertible. It was powered by a 245 h.p. 389 cu. in. V8 with two-barrel carburetor. Seven other versions of this engine were also available: a 215 h.p. (two-barrel carb), a 260 h.p. (four-barrel carb), a

280 h.p. (two-barrel carb), a 300 h.p. (four-barrel carb), a 315 h.p. (three two-barrel carbs), a 330 h.p. (four-barrel carb), and a 345 h.p. (three two-barrel carbs). A three-speed manual transmission was standard. Hydra-Matic automatic transmission was optional.

Most 1959 Pontiacs, 97.1%, came with the automatic, 73.6% had power steering, 67.8% had power brakes, 41.5% had tinted windows, 4.6% had electric windows, 3.5% had power front seats, and 7.9% were sold with an air conditioner.

1959 Pontiac Catalina Convertible

1960

1960 Buick Electra 225 Convertible

Original Price: $4,200
Number Produced: 6,746
Estimated Number Existing in 1979: 140
Miles per Gallon: 10–16
Common Trouble Spots: none
Availability of Parts: fair–good
Investment Potential: AA

Background: The attractive Electra 225 convertible was powered by a 325 h.p. 401 cu. in. V8 engine. Twin Turbine automatic transmission power brakes and power steering were standard.

1960 Buick Invicta Convertible

Original Price: $3,620
Number Produced: 5,236
Estimated Number Existing in 1979: 60
Miles per Gallon: 11–17
Common Trouble Spots: none
Availability of Parts: fair–good
Investment Potential: AA

Background: Raised "eyebrows" above the headlights gave the Invicta an impatient look. It seemed as if the car didn't like sitting still—it wanted to move. Fast.

The Invicta ragtop was powered by a 325 h.p. 401 cu. in. V8 engine. Twin Turbine automatic transmission was standard. Most had the optional power steering and power brakes. Almost 14% of all '60 Buicks came with air conditioning.

1960 Buick Invicta Convertible

1960 Buick LeSabre Convertible

Original Price: $3,145
Number Produced: 13,588
Estimated Number Existing in 1979: 283
Miles per Gallon: 12–17
Common Trouble Spots: none
Availability of Parts: fair–good
Investment Potential: AA

Background: Like all 1960 Buicks, the LeSabre convertible was an attractive car. Even the new portholes on the fenders didn't look half bad.

The LeSabre came with a 250 h.p. 364 cu. in. V8. A 300 h.p. version of this engine was optional. A three-speed manual transmission was standard, but not very popular—only 1.1% of all 1960 Buicks were so equipped. Twin Turbine automatic transmission was available at extra cost. Other options included power steering, power brakes, and air conditioning.

1960 Cadillac Eldorado Biarritz Convertible

Original Price: $7,401
Number Produced: 1,285
Estimated Number Existing in 1979: 53
Miles per Gallon: 10–15
Common Trouble Spots: none
Availability of Parts: fair
Investment Potential: AA

Background: The new Eldorado received a minor face-lift for 1960. However, it was a little less flamboyant than last year's model. It was powered by a 345 h.p. 390 cu. in. V8. Hydramatic automatic transmission, power steering, power brakes, and leather upholstery were standard. Air conditioning was a popular option.

1960 Cadillac Eldorado Biarritz Convertible

PHOTO: CADILLAC MOTOR CAR DIVISION

1960 Cadillac Series 62 Convertible

PHOTO: CADILLAC MOTOR CAR DIVISION

1960 Cadillac Series 62 Convertible

Original Price: $5,455
Number Produced: 14,000
Estimated Number Existing in 1979: 586
Miles per Gallon: 10–15
Common Trouble Spots: none
Availability of Parts: fair
Investment Potential: A+

Background: The wild styling of the previous year was tamed a bit. The Series 62 convertible was powered by a 325 h.p. 390 cu. in. V8. Hydramatic automatic transmission was standard. All 1960 Cadillacs had power steering and power brakes. Eighty-seven percent came with power front seats, 85% had power windows, 95% had tinted glass, and 46% were equipped with air conditioning.

1960 Chevrolet Corvette Convertible

Original Price: $3,872
Number Produced: 10,261
Estimated Number Existing in 1979: 300
Miles per Gallon: 11–19
Common Trouble Spots: none
Availability of Parts: fair–good
Investment Potential: AAA

Background: The new Corvette came with a 230 h.p. 283 cu. in. V8. Hotter versions of this engine were also available. They included a 245 h.p., a 270 h.p., a 275 h.p., and a 315 h.p. The last two engines were fuel-injected. A three-speed manual transmission was standard. Powerglide automatic and a four-speed manual transmission were optional.

About 31% of 1960 Vettes were equipped with the three-speed manual, nearly 52% had the four-speed manual, and around 5% were sold with power windows.

Buyers had their choice of eight exterior colors, either solid or in two-tone combinations.

1960 Chevrolet Corvette Convertible

PHOTO: T. MICHAELIS CORVETTE SUPPLIES

1960 Chevrolet Impala Convertible

PHOTO: GM PHOTOGRAPHIC

1960 Chevrolet Impala Convertible

Original Price: $2,954
Number Produced: 79,903
Estimated Number Existing in 1979: 2,076
Miles per Gallon: 9–18
Common Trouble Spots: none
Availability of Parts: fair–good
Investment Potential: AA (with four-speed manual transmission); A+ (without)

Background: The new Impala convertible received a pleasing face-lift for 1960. It was powered by a 135 h.p. 235.5 cu. in. six. Available at extra cost were the following V8 engines: a 170 h.p. 283, a 230 h.p. 283, a 250 h.p. 348, a 280 h.p. 348, a 305 h.p. 348, a 320 h.p. 348, and a 335 h.p. 348. A three-speed manual transmission was standard. Overdrive, a four-speed manual, and Powerglide and Turboglide automatic transmissions were optional.

Buyers could order a "Police Special" kit which included an aluminum intake manifold, three two-barrel carburetors, and a special cam.

Sixty-seven percent of all 1960 Chevrolets came equipped with an automatic, 31% had a manual, 2% had overdrive, 27% had power steering, 11% had power brakes, 23% had tinted glass, 1% had power windows, 1% had power front seats, 90% had a heater, and only 3% were sold with an air conditioner.

1960 Chrysler New Yorker Convertible

Original Price: $4,800
Number Produced: 556
Estimated Number Existing in 1979: 10
Miles per Gallon: 9–14
Common Trouble Spots: automatic transmission, brakes
Availability of Parts: fair–poor
Investment Potential: AA

Background: The 1960 New Yorker convertible came with a 350 h.p. 413 cu. in. V8. Torque Flite automatic transmission was standard. Its "sun proof" vinyl interior was offered in black, blue, red, or white.

An interesting feature on Chryslers in 1960 was an electroluminescent lighting of gauges. This made the numbers on the gauges appear to be suspended in mid-air.

Most 1960 Chryslers, 80.1%, came with power brakes, 99.2% had power steering, 50.1% had tinted glass, 32.3% had power windows, 23.9% had power front seats, and 16.8% were sold with air conditioning.

1960 Chrysler New Yorker Convertible

1960 Chrysler 300-F Convertible

Original Price: $5,766
Number Produced: 248
Estimated Number Existing in 1979: 7
Miles per Gallon: 9–13
Common Trouble Spots: automatic transmission, brakes
Availability of Parts: poor–fair
Investment Potential: AAA+ (with fuel injection); AAA (without)

Background: The restyled 1960 300-F convertible maintained a strong resemblance to past 300 Letter Series cars. It came with a 375 h.p. 413 cu. in. V8 engine. A 400 h.p. fuel-injected version of this engine was available as an option. Torque Flite automatic transmission was standard. A four-speed manual transmission was optional.

The interior featured individual semi-bucket seats, both front and back.

This is a very attractive, highly desirable automobile. According to *Motor Trend,* the 300-F "rates tops in every respect."

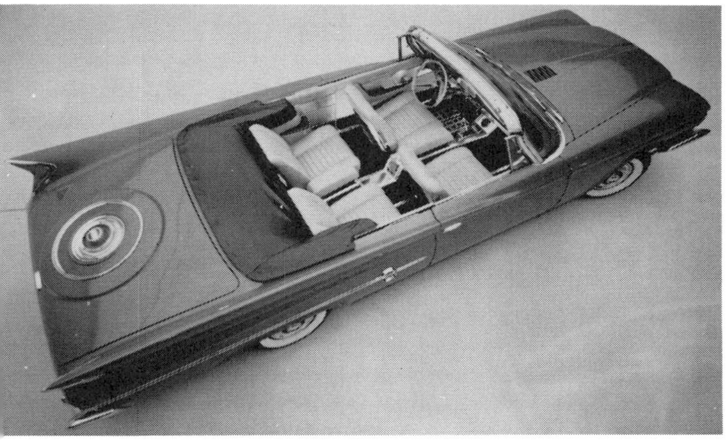

1960 Chrysler 300-F Convertible

PHOTO: CHRYSLER HISTORICAL COLLECTION

1960 Chrysler Windsor Convertible

1960 Chrysler 300-F Coupe

PHOTO: CHRYSLER CORPORATION

1960 Chrysler 300-F Coupe

Original Price: $5,336
Number Produced: 964
Estimated Number Existing in 1979: 26
Miles per Gallon: 9–13
Common Trouble Spots: automatic transmission, brakes
Availability of Parts: poor–fair
Investment Potential: AAA (with fuel injection); AA+ (without)

Background: The restyled 1960 300-F maintained its resemblance to past 300s, while at the same time offering a new look. Buyers responded favorably, and production was up by nearly 50% over the previous year.

A 375 h.p. 413 cu. in. V8 was standard equipment. A 400 h.p. fuel injected engine was also available. Torque Flite automatic transmission was standard. A four-speed manual transmission was optional.

The 300-F won the respect of performance car fans throughout the country. Its combination of style, speed, and easy-chair comfort help make it a highly sought after automobile.

1960 Chrysler Windsor Convertible

Original Price: $3,568
Number Produced: 1,467
Estimated Number Existing in 1979: 27
Miles per Gallon: 10–16
Common Trouble Spots: automatic transmission, brakes
Availability of Parts: fair–poor
Investment Potential: AA

Background: This was the last year for the Windsor convertible. It received a major face-lift from last year's model. Although tailfins were starting to go out of style, the big-finned 1960 was more popular with buyers than the 1959. The front grille treatment was obviously inspired by the 300 Letter Series cars.

A 305 h.p. 383 cu. in. engine powered the car. Torque Flite automatic transmission was standard.

1960 Dodge Dart Phoenix Convertible

Original Price: $2,868
Number Produced: N.A.
Estimated Number Existing in 1979: N.A.
Miles per Gallon: 11–17
Common Trouble Spots: brakes
Availability of Parts: fair–poor
Investment Potential: A

Background: Besides the price, the main difference between the Phoenix and the Polara convertibles was trim, interior, and engines. The Phoenix came with a 145 h.p. 225 cu. in. six-cylinder engine. A few V8 engines were available at extra cost, including a 255 h.p. 318, a 310 h.p. 361, and a 330 h.p. 383. A three-speed manual transmission was standard. Power Flite and Torque Flite automatic transmissions were optional.

1960 Dodge Polara Convertible

Original Price: $3,416
Number Produced: N.A.
Estimated Number Existing in 1979: N.A.
Miles per Gallon: 10–17
Common Trouble Spots: brakes, cooling system
Availability of Parts: fair–poor
Investment Potential: A

Background: In addition to a new body for 1960, changes were made in the Polara's interior; the seats were redesigned to give passengers more leg-, knee-, and headroom.

The Polara ragtop was powered by a 325 h.p. 383 cu. in. "Ram Fire" V8. Available at extra cost was a 330 h.p. version of this engine. A three-speed manual transmission was standard. Torque Flite automatic transmission was optional.

Most 1960 Dodges, 78.2%, were equipped with an automatic, 44.6% had power steering, 13.7% had power brakes, 34% had tinted glass, .5% had power windows, less than 1% had power front seats, 49% had radios, and 3.2% were sold with air conditioning.

1960 Dodge Polara Convertible

1960 Edsel Ranger Convertible

PHOTO: FORD MOTOR COMPANY

1960 Edsel Ranger Convertible

Original Price: est. $3,100
Number Produced: 76
Estimated Number Existing in 1979: 54
Miles per Gallon: 12–17
Common Trouble Spots: none
Availability of Parts: poor
Investment Potential: AA+

Background: What began as a very distinctive car was now little more than a Ford with fancy trim. Because it was so similar to the Ford ragtop, some people have been making "Edsels" out of Fords.

The Ranger convertible was powered by a 185 h.p. 292 cu. in. V8. Available at extra cost was a 300 h.p. 352 cu. in. V8. A three-speed manual transmission was standard. Automatic transmission was optional.

Production of all Edsels stopped in November 1959. Comedians, who had made owning an Edsel synonymous with being a "loser," no longer had the Edsel to kick around anymore.

1960 Ford Galaxie Sunliner Convertible

Original Price: $2,973
Number Produced: 44,762
Estimated Number Existing in 1979: 893
Miles per Gallon: 9–18
Common Trouble Spots: automatic transmission, cooling system
Availability of Parts: fair–good
Investment Potential: A+

Background: The Sunliner ragtop was restyled for 1960. It looked very sleek compared to the boxy style of the previous year.

Sunliner buyers had their choice of four engines—a 145 h.p. 223 cu. in. six-cylinder and the following V8s: a 185 h.p. 292, a 235 h.p. 352, and a 300 h.p. 352. A three-speed manual transmission was standard. Overdrive and Ford-O-Matic and Cruise-O-Matic automatic transmissions were optional.

Sixty-seven percent of all full-size Fords in 1960 came with an automatic, 4% had overdrive, 67.5% had a V8, 31% had power steering, 9.5% had power brakes, 1% had power windows, 1% had power front seats, 4.5% had air conditioning, and 13% had tinted glass.

1960 Ford Galaxie Sunliner Convertible

PHOTO: FORD MOTOR COMPANY

1960 Ford Thunderbird Convertible

Original Price: $4,222
Number Produced: 11,860
Estimated Number Existing in 1979: 233
Miles per Gallon: 9–15
Common Trouble Spots: none
Availability of Parts: fair
Investment Potential: AA

Background: The most noticeable change in the new T-Bird ragtop was in the taillights. Apparently Ford thought four wasn't enough, so the 1960 had six. Like the other two years of "Square Birds," the 1960 was very popular with buyers—so popular that *Motor Trend* reported some industry executives were predicting the Thunderbird would replace the Lincoln as Ford's top prestige automobile.

The '60 T-Bird convertible was powered by a 300 h.p. 352 cu. in. V8. Available at extra cost was a 350 h.p. 430 cu. in. V8. A three-speed manual transmission was standard. Overdrive and Cruise-O-Matic automatic transmission were optional.

Most 1960 Thunderbirds, 98%, came equipped with an automatic, 1% had a three-speed manual, 1% had a manual with overdrive, 97% had power steering, 89% had power brakes, 53% had tinted glass, 54% had electric windows, 44% had power front seats, 98% had radios, and 25% were sold with air conditioners.

1960 Ford Thunderbird Convertible

1960 Imperial Crown Convertible

Original Price: $5,684
Number Produced: 618
Estimated Number Existing in 1979: 17
Miles per Gallon: 8–14
Common Trouble Spots: automatic transmission, brakes
Availability of Parts: poor–fair
Investment Potential: AA

Background: The 1960 Imperial convertible received a minor face-lift. It was powered by a 350 h.p. 413 cu. in. V8 engine. A push-button Torque Flite automatic transmission, power steering, and power brakes were standard. It also featured an unusual rectangular steering wheel.

Most 1960 Imperials, 92.9%, came with power windows, 92.7% had power seats, 84.6% had tinted glass, 98% had radios, and 44.7% were sold with air conditioning.

1960 Imperial Crown Convertible

PHOTO: CHRYSLER HISTORICAL COLLECTION

3469 Investors Guide pp 598-609 js

1960 King Midget Convertible

Original Price: est. $650
Number Produced: 221
Estimated Number Existing in 1979: 14
Miles per Gallon: 50–90
Common Trouble Spots: transmission, "V" belts
Availability of Parts: good
Investment Potential: A

Background: Once again, the King Midget ragtop had the lowest sticker price and the highest miles-per-gallon rating of any car on the market. It was powered by a 10 h.p. 29 cu. in. one-cylinder engine. Automatic transmission was standard.

1960 Lincoln Continental Mark V Convertible

Original Price: $7,056
Number Produced: 2,044
Estimated Number Existing in 1979: 57
Miles per Gallon: 8–15
Common Trouble Spots: cooling system
Availability of Parts: poor–fair
Investment Potential: A+

Background: The new Continental convertible looked almost identical to the previous year's model. It did, however, have improved brakes and handling.

A 315 h.p. 430 cu. in. V8 powered the Continental. Turbo-Drive automatic transmission was standard. All 1960 Lincolns had power steering, power brakes, and a radio. Most, 92.5%, were equipped with power windows, 93% had power seats, 90% had tinted glass, and 49% were sold with an air conditioner.

1960 Mercury Monterey Convertible

Original Price: $3,077
Number Produced: 6,062
Estimated Number Existing in 1979: 127
Miles per Gallon: 13–17
Common Trouble Spots: none
Availability of Parts: fair–poor
Investment Potential: A+

Background: The new Monterey had a cleaner look than the previous year's model. It came with a 205 h.p. 312 cu. in. V8. A 280 h.p. 383 cu. in. V8 was available at extra cost. A three-speed manual transmission was standard. Merc-O-Matic automatic transmission was optional.

Most 1960 Mercurys, 92.8%, were equipped with the automatic, 66% had power steering, 48% had power brakes, 77% had tinted glass, 6.5% had power windows, 7.6% had power front seats, 74% had radios, and 15% were sold with an air conditioner.

1960 Mercury Park Lane Convertible

Original Price: $4,018
Number Produced: 1,525
Estimated Number Existing in 1979: 31
Miles per Gallon: 10–16
Common Trouble Spots: none
Availability of Parts: fair–poor
Investment Potential: A+

Background: The Park Lane convertible was restyled for 1960. It came with a 310 h.p. 430 cu. in. V8 engine. Multi-Drive automatic transmission was standard.

1960 Metropolitan Series 1500 Convertible

Original Price: est. $1,700
Number Produced: est. 2,920
Estimated Number Existing in 1979: 59
Miles per Gallon: 25–35
Common Trouble Spots: brakes, gearshift
Availability of Parts: good–fair
Investment Potential: A

Background: The 1960 Metropolitan convertible was powered by a 52 h.p. 90.9 cu. in. four-cylinder engine. A three-speed manual transmission was standard.

This was the last year Metropolitans were made. Rambler dropped it in favor of the new compact American. Unsold 1960 Mets were offered in 1961 and 1962.

1960 Metropolitan Series 1500 Convertible

PHOTO: RICHARD J. MCGARTY, METROPOLITAN OWNERS CLUB

1960 Mercury Park Lane Convertible

PHOTO: FORD MOTOR COMPANY

1960 Oldsmobile Dynamic 88 Convertible

PHOTO: OLDSMOBILE DIVISION

1960 Oldsmobile Dynamic 88 Convertible

Original Price: $3,284
Number Produced: 12,271
Estimated Number Existing in 1979: 230
Miles per Gallon: 10–16
Common Trouble Spots: none
Availability of Parts: fair
Investment Potential: A+

Background: The Olds Dynamic 88 was attractively restyled for 1960. Mercifully, the wild-looking grille and headlight treatment of the previous year was replaced.

It was powered by a 240 h.p. 371 cu. in. V8. A 260 h.p. version of this engine was available at extra cost. A three-speed manual transmission was standard. Hydra-Matic automatic transmission was optional and very popular. Most 1960 Oldsmobiles, 98.8%, were equipped with the automatic. The vast majority also had power brakes and power steering.

The 1960 Dynamic 88 convertible is one of the best-looking Oldsmobiles made in the 1960s.

1960 Oldsmobile 98 Convertible

Original Price: $4,362
Number Produced: 7,284
Estimated Number Existing in 1979: 136
Miles per Gallon: 9–15
Common Trouble Spots: none
Availability of Parts: fair
Investment Potential: A+

Background: Any way one looked at it, the 1960 Olds 98 ragtop was an attractive car. Especially when compared to many of its contemporaries. Having spent many high school nights (and days) cruising in a friend's 1960 98, I know they are as nice to ride in as they are to behold. Fiberglass material was applied around the firewall, rear tires, trunk, and trunk lid to reduce road noise.

The 98 was powered by a 315 h.p. 394 cu. in. V8 engine. Hydra-Matic automatic transmission was standard.

Big, comfortable and beautiful—that's the 1960 Olds 98 convertible.

1960 Oldsmobile Super 88 Convertible

Original Price: $3,592
Number Produced: 5,830
Estimated Number Existing in 1979: 109
Miles per Gallon: 10–15
Common Trouble Spots: none
Availability of Parts: fair
Investment Potential: A+

Background: The 1960 Super 88 ragtop was a very attractive car. It was powered by a 315 h.p. 394 cu. in. V8. A three-speed manual transmission was standard, but not very popular—only 1.2% of all 1960 Oldsmobiles were so equipped. Most buyers ordered the optional Hydra-Matic automatic transmission.

The majority of new Olds, 94.6%, came with power steering, 91.2% had power brakes, 66% had tinted glass, 10.1% had power windows, 14.2% had power front seats, and 18.8% were sold with an air conditioner.

1960 Oldsmobile Super 88 Convertible

PHOTO: OLDSMOBILE DIVISION

1960 Oldsmobile 98 Convertible

PHOTO: OLDSMOBILE DIVISION

1960 Plymouth Fury Convertible

1960 Plymouth Fury Convertible

Original Price: $2,932
Number Produced: N.A.
Estimated Number Existing in 1979: N.A.
Miles per Gallon: 11–17
Common Trouble Spots: brakes
Availability of Parts: fair–poor
Investment Potential: A+

Background: The new Fury convertible was powered by a 230 h.p. 318 cu. in. V8. Several other V8 engines were available at extra cost: a 260 h.p. 318 (four-barrel carburetor), a 305 h.p. 361 (four-barrel carburetor), a 310 h.p. 361 (two four-barrel carburetors), a 325 h.p. 383 (four-barrel carburetor), and two 330 h.p. 383s (both with two four-barrel carburetors). All the optional engines came with dual exhaust.

A three-speed manual transmission was standard. Power Flite and Torque Flite automatic transmissions were optional.

Most 1960 Plymouths, 73.7 percent, came equipped with one of the automatic transmissions, 26.3% had a three-speed manual, 45.1% had power steering, 14.7% had power brakes, 16.5% had tinted glass, almost 1% had electric windows, nearly as many had power seats, 47.9% had radios, and 2.9% were sold with an air conditioner.

1960 Pontiac Bonneville Convertible

Original Price: $3,476
Number Produced: 17,062
Estimated Number Existing in 1979: 345
Miles per Gallon: 10–16
Common Trouble Spots: none
Availability of Parts: fair
Investment Potential: A+

Background: The '60 Bonneville was powered by a 281 h.p. 389 cu. in. V8. Five other versions of this engine were available at extra cost: a 215 h.p. (two-barrel carb), a 303 h.p. (four-barrel carb), a 318 h.p. (three two-barrel carbs), a 333 h.p. (four-barrel carb), and a 348 h.p. (three two-barrel carbs). A three-speed manual transmission was standard, but not very popular—only 2.7% of all Pontiacs were so equipped. Most buyers ordered the optional Hydra-Matic automatic transmission.

1960 Pontiac Catalina Convertible

Original Price: $3,078
Number Produced: 17,172
Estimated Number Existing in 1979: 347
Miles per Gallon: 10–17
Common Trouble Spots: carburetor
Availability of Parts: fair
Investment Potential: A

Background: The Catalina received a major face-lift for 1960. It was powered by a 215 h.p. 389 cu. in. V8. Five other versions of this engine were optional at extra cost: a 283 h.p. (two-barrel carb), a 303 h.p. (four-barrel carb), a 318 h.p. (three two-barrel carbs), a 333 h.p. (four-barrel carb), and a 348 h.p. (three two-barrel carbs). A three-speed manual transmission was standard. Hydra-Matic automatic transmission was optional.

Most 1960 Pontiacs, 97.3%, came with the automatic, 83% had power steering, 79.5% had power brakes, 45% had tinted glass, 6.2% had electric windows, 6% had power front seats, and 10.2% were sold with an air conditioner.

1960 Studebaker Lark Regal Convertible

Original Price: $2,756
Number Produced: 8,306
Estimated Number Existing in 1979: 65
Miles per Gallon: 14–22
Common Trouble Spots: automatic transmission, brakes, carburetor, cooling system, engine bearings
Availability of Parts: fair–poor
Investment Potential: A

Background: This was the first year for the Lark ragtop. It was available with either a 90 h.p. 169.6 cu. in. six-cylinder engine or, for a little over $100 more, a 180 h.p. 259.2 cu. in. V8 with a two-barrel carburetor. A 195 h.p. version of the V8 engine was an extra-cost option.

A three-speed manual transmission was standard. Overdrive and Flightomatic automatic transmission were optional.

Just over 40% of 1960 Studebakers were equipped with the automatic, 39.4% had the three-speed manual, 20.4% had the manual with overdrive, 52.2% had a six-cylinder engine, 7.2% had power steering, 3.5% had power brakes, 4.9% had tinted glass, 17.2% had radios, and .6% were sold with air conditioning.

1960 Pontiac Bonneville Convertible

PHOTO: PONTIAC MOTOR DIVISION

1961

1961 Buick Electra 225 Convertible

Original Price: $4,192
Number Produced: 7,158
Estimated Number Existing in 1979: 340
Miles per Gallon: 10–16
Common Trouble Spots: none
Availability of Parts: fair
Investment Potential: A+

Background: The Electra convertible received major restyling for 1961. It was a smaller, more conservatively styled car than the previous year's model. About the only gimmicky aspect of the design was the four portholes on each front fender.

The Electra was powered by a 325 h.p. 401 cu. in. V8. Turbine Drive automatic transmission, power steering, and power brakes were standard. Air conditioning continued to grow in popularity—twenty-five percent of all full-size '61 Buicks came with it.

1961 Buick Electra 225 Convertible

1961 Buick Invicta Convertible

Original Price: $3,620
Number Produced: 3,953
Estimated Number Existing in 1979: 189
Miles per Gallon: 11–17
Common Trouble Spots: none
Availability of Parts: fair
Investment Potential: A+

Background: The fins were gone on the 1961 Invicta convertible, although the portholes remained. It was powered by a 325 h.p. 401 cu. in. V8. Turbine Drive automatic transmission was standard. The vast majority of Invicta convertibles came with power brakes and power steering.

1961 Buick LeSabre Convertible

Original Price: $3,382
Number Produced: 11,951
Estimated Number Existing in 1979: 560
Miles per Gallon: 12–17
Common Trouble Spots: none
Availability of Parts: fair
Investment Potential: A+

Background: The new LeSabre ragtop was powered by a 250 h.p. 364 cu. in. V8 engine. Turbine Drive automatic transmission was standard. Power steering and power brakes were popular options. Tinted glass was ordered by 45.8% of 1961 full-size Buick buyers. Just under 17% bought power front seats.

1961 Cadillac Eldorado Biarritz Convertible

Original Price: $6,477
Number Produced: 1,450
Estimated Number Existing in 1979: 68
Miles per Gallon: 8–12
Common Trouble Spots: none
Availability of Parts: fair–good
Investment Potential: AA

Background: As in the past, the Eldorado Biarritz was Cadillac's most expensive and luxurious convertible. It was powered by a 325 h.p. 390 cu. in. V8 engine. Hydramatic automatic transmission, power steering, power brakes, and leather upholstery were standard.

1961 Cadillac Eldorado Biarritz Convertible

PHOTO: CADILLAC MOTOR CAR DIVISION

1961 Cadillac Series 62 Convertible

Original Price: $5,455
Number Produced: 15,500
Estimated Number Existing in 1979: 733
Miles per Gallon: 8–12
Common Trouble Spots: none
Availability of Parts: fair–good
Investment Potential: A+

Background: The 1961 Series 62 convertible was a big, luxurious automobile. New this year were a redesigned front suspension and a smaller steering wheel. The car was powered by a 325 h.p. 390 cu. in. V8 engine with four-barrel carburetor. Hydramatic automatic transmission and leather upholstery were standard.

All 1961 Cadillacs had power steering and power brakes. The vast majority, 99%, came with power front seats, 91% had power windows, and 51.7% were equipped with air conditioning.

1961 Cadillac Series 62 Convertible

PHOTO: CADILLAC MOTOR CAR DIVISION

1961 Chevrolet Corvette Convertible

Original Price: $3,934
Number Produced: 10,939
Estimated Number Existing in 1979: 387
Miles per Gallon: 11–19
Common Trouble Spots: none
Availability of Parts: fair–good
Investment Potential: AAA

Background: The most noticeable change in the 1961 Corvette was its new rear end. The graceful flowing rear section of the past few years was replaced by a "duck-tail"-styled one.

The standard engine was a 230 h.p. 283 cu. in. V8 (with four-barrel carburetor). Other, higher-horsepower versions of this engine were also available: a 245 h.p. (with dual four-barrel carburetors), a 270 h.p. (with dual four-barrel carburetors), a 275 h.p. (with fuel injection), and a 315 h.p. (with fuel injection).

A three-speed manual transmission was standard. Most buyers, 64.1%, ordered the optional four-speed manual. Only 13.3% came with Powerglide automatic transmission. And 6.4% were sold with power windows.

Buyers had their choice of seven exterior colors in either solid colors or two-tone combinations.

1961 Chevrolet Corvette Convertible

PHOTO: T. MICHAELIS CORVETTE SUPPLIES

1961 Chevrolet Impala Convertible

PHOTO: GM PHOTOGRAPHIC

1961 Chevrolet Impala Convertible

Original Price: $2,954
Number Produced: 64,624
Estimated Number Existing in 1979: 2,291
Miles per Gallon: 9–18
Common Trouble Spots: carburetor
Availability of Parts: fair–good
Investment Potential: AA (with Super Sport option); A+ (without)

Background: The Impala was attractively restyled for 1961. It came with a 135 h.p. 235.5 cu. in. six. Available at extra cost were these V8 engines: a 170 h.p. 283, a 230 h.p. 283, a 250 h.p. 348, a 280 h.p. 348, a 305 h.p. 348, a 340 h.p. 348, a 350 h.p. 348, and a 360 h.p. 409. A three-speed manual transmission was standard. Overdrive, a four-speed manual, and Powerglide and Turboglide automatic transmissions were optional.

Most full-size '61 Chevrolets, 57.4%, came equipped with a V8, 70.2% had an automatic, 28.3% had a manual, 1.5% had overdrive, 32.9% had power steering, 11.3% had power brakes, 30.5% had tinted glass, 1.2% had power windows, almost 1% had power front seats, and 5.6% were sold with air conditioning.

In the summer of 1961, a Super Sport kit, featuring bucket seats and special trim, was made available.

The most popular exterior color for Chevys in '61 was white. Twenty-five percent of all Chevrolets made that year were painted that color. The second most popular color was beige—it was found on 18% of 1961 Chevrolets.

1961 Chrysler New Yorker Convertible

Original Price: $4,592
Number Produced: 576
Estimated Number Existing in 1979: 8
Miles per Gallon: 9–14
Common Trouble Spots: brakes
Availability of Parts: fair–poor
Investment Potential: A+

Background: The '61 New Yorker ragtop came with a 350 h.p. 413 cu. in. V8 with a four-barrel carburetor. Torque Flite automatic transmission was standard.

1961 Chrysler Newport Convertible

Original Price: $3,442
Number Produced: 2,135
Estimated Number Existing in 1979: 34
Miles per Gallon: 9–14
Common Trouble Spots: brakes
Availability of Parts: fair–poor
Investment Potential: A+

Background: The new slanted-headlight styling attracted a lot of buyers. Unlike other manufacturers, Chrysler kept the tailfin styling so popular in the mid-to-late 1950s.

The Newport convertible came with a 265 h.p. 361 cu. in. V8 and a two-barrel carburetor. Torque Flite automatic transmission was still available, although a floor-mounted three-speed manual transmission was standard.

Most 1961 Chryslers, 95.7%, came equipped with the automatic, 95.1% had power steering, 52% had power brakes, 46% had tinted glass, 16.7% had power windows, 19% had power seats, 70.4% had radios, and 17.8% were sold with air conditioning.

1961 Chrysler Newport Convertible

1961 Chrysler New Yorker Convertible

1961 Chrysler 300-G Convertible

Original Price: $5,841
Number Produced: 337
Estimated Number Existing in 1979: 8
Miles per Gallon: 9–13
Common Trouble Spots: brakes
Availability of Parts: poor–fair
Investment Potential: AAA

Background: The 1961 looked like a modified version of the 1960. It was powered by a 375 h.p. 413 cu. in. V8 engine. Torque Flite automatic transmission was standard. A floor-mounted manual transmission was optional. The interior featured four individual bucket seats and a center console that extended from the front to the back seat of the car. The seats were ventilated in an effort to lessen stickiness caused by perspiration.

The 1961 300-G convertible is highly sought after by 300 Letter Series enthusiasts.

1961 Chrysler 300-G Convertible

PHOTO: CHRYSLER HISTORICAL COLLECTION

1961 Chrysler 300-G Coupe

Original Price: $5,411
Number Produced: 1,280
Estimated Number Existing in 1979: 30
Miles per Gallon: 9–13
Common Trouble Spots: brakes
Availability of Parts: fair–poor
Investment Potential: AA+

Background: Styling for the new 300-G was only a slight variation of that used on the 300-F. It was still one of the few high-performance cars that could honestly be considered elegant.

It was powered by a 375 h.p. 413 cu. in. V8 engine. Torque Flite automatic transmission was standard. A four-speed manual was optional.

Most enthusiasts consider this the last "real" 300 Letter Series car. The cars that followed in this series seemed little more than trim and engine options on the new 300 Sport Series. They were, so to speak, impostors.

1961 Chrysler 300-G Coupe

PHOTO: CHRYSLER HISTORICAL COLLECTION

1961 Dodge Dart Phoenix Convertible

Original Price: $2,988
Number Produced: N.A.
Estimated Number Existing in 1979: N.A.
Miles per Gallon: 11–15
Common Trouble Spots: brakes
Availability of Parts: fair–poor
Investment Potential: A+

Background: The '61 Phoenix ragtop was powered by a 230 h.p. 318 cu. in. V8. Several other V8 engines were available at extra cost: a 305 h.p. 361, a 325 h.p. 383, two 330 h.p. 383s, a 340 h.p. 383, a 350 h.p. 413, and two 375 h.p. 413s. A three-speed manual transmission was standard. Torque Flite and Power Flite automatic transmissions were optional.

1961 Dodge Dart Phoenix Convertible

1961 Dodge Polara Convertible

Original Price: $3,252
Number Produced: N.A.
Estimated Number Existing in 1979: N.A.
Miles per Gallon: 11–15
Common Trouble Spots: brakes
Availability of Parts: fair–poor
Investment Potential: A+

Background: The 1961 Polara convertible was one of the most attractive postwar Dodges made. It came with a 265 h.p. 361 cu. in. V8. Four 383 cu. in. V8s, rated at 325 h.p. (two), 330 h.p., and 340 h.p., were available at extra cost. A three-speed manual transmission was standard. Torque Flite automatic was optional.

A D-500 performance package, featuring ram induction, two four-barrel carburetors, and a special "500" insignia, was offered.

1961 Ford Galaxie Sunliner Convertible

Original Price: $2,963
Number Produced: 44,614
Estimated Number Existing in 1979: 1,638
Miles per Gallon: 9–18
Common Trouble Spots: automatic transmission, rear axle
Availability of Parts: good–fair
Investment Potential: A+

Background: The Sunliner ragtop was restyled for 1961. Buyers had their choice of six engines—a 135 h.p. 223 cu. in. six-cylinder and the following V8s: a 220 h.p. 352, a 175 h.p. 292, a 300 h.p. 390, a 330 h.p. 390, and a 375 h.p. 390. A three-speed manual transmission was standard. Overdrive and Ford-O-Matic and Cruise-O-Matic automatic transmissions were optional.

Seventy-two percent of all 1961 Fords were equipped with an automatic, 4.1% had overdrive, 74.8% had a V8, 39.1% had power steering, 11.1% had power brakes, 1% had power windows, 1.2% had power seats, 14.3% had tinted glass, and 6.2% were sold with air conditioning.

1961 Ford Galaxie Sunliner Convertible

1961 Ford Thunderbird Convertible

Original Price: $4,222
Number Produced: 10,516
Estimated Number Existing in 1979: 385
Miles per Gallon: 8–14
Common Trouble Spots: none
Availability of Parts: fair
Investment Potential: AA+

Background: The Thunderbird convertible was tastefully restyled for 1961. Rather than resembling (well, sort of) the Ford Fairlane, it now looked more like the Lincoln Continental, at least in the front. That wasn't surprising, since the basic styling used on the '61 Continental was originally planned for the T-Bird. However, Lincoln executives liked it so much that they used it for their car.

The '61 Thunderbird was powered by a 300 h.p. 390 cu. in. V8. Cruise-O-Matic automatic transmission, power steering, and power brakes were standard.

Most new T-Birds, 76.6%, came with power windows, 62% had tinted glass, 46.6% had power front seats, 98% had radios, and 32.6% were sold with air conditioning.

The convertible top was available in three colors: black, blue, and white.

1961 Ford Thunderbird Convertible

PHOTO: FORD MOTOR COMPANY

1961 Imperial Crown Convertible

Original Price: \$5,774
Number Produced: 429
Estimated Number Existing in 1979: 17
Miles per Gallon: 8–13
Common Trouble Spots: automatic transmission
Availability of Parts: poor–fair
Investment Potential: AA+

Background: The new Imperial convertible received a face-lift for 1961. Its most notable feature was its free-standing headlights. The purpose of this style headlights was to recapture the feel of the classic cars of the 1930s. Whether or not the designers succeeded is debatable.

A 350 h.p. 413 cu. in. V8 was standard on the Imperial. So were push-button Torque Flite automatic transmission, power steering, and power brakes.

Most 1961 Imperials, 87.1%, came with power windows, 85.3% had power seats, 85.8% had tinted glass, 97.6% had radios, and 50.2% were sold with air conditioning.

1961 Imperial Crown Convertible

PHOTO: CHRYSLER HISTORICAL COLLECTION

1961 King Midget Convertible

Original Price: est. \$650
Number Produced: 148
Estimated Number Existing in 1979: 9
Miles per Gallon: 50–90
Common Trouble Spots: transmission, "V" belts
Availability of Parts: good
Investment Potential: A

Background: The '61 King Midget ragtop was powered by a 10 h.p. 29 cu. in. one-cylinder engine. Automatic transmission was standard.

According to Bill Hossfield, of the King Midget-Eshelman Registry, "There are countless problems with these cars, but the two biggest are that they are very underpowered and the clutches and V belts slip." If that wasn't bad enough, Mr. Hossfield adds, "In traffic you are so small people almost run you over."

Despite these few flaws, the King Midget is definitely one of the most unique automobiles of the postwar period.

1961 Lincoln Continental Convertible

Original Price: \$6,713
Number Produced: 2,857
Estimated Number Existing in 1979: 250
Miles per Gallon: 10–15
Common Trouble Spots: automatic transmission, brakes, top mechanism
Availability of Parts: fair
Investment Potential: AAA

Background: Not since the "classic" Mark II had a Lincoln received as much acclaim as the 1961 Continental. Its styling influenced the entire automobile industry.

Yet the new Continental had more going for it than just beauty. Late in 1961 *Motor Trend* said, "The 1961 Continental established a new standard of quality of mass-produced automobiles." Every engine and transmission were thoroughly inspected before being put in the car. After they were installed, a technician took the car for a twelve-mile road test. (Body shake was common in early models at speeds over 50. This problem was corrected later in the model year.)

The Continental was powered by a 300 h.p. 430 cu. in. V8 engine. Turbo-Drive automatic transmission, power steering, power brakes, electric windows, power front seats, and a radio were standard. Most '61 Lincolns, 65%, had air conditioning.

The 1961 Lincoln Continental is one of the most beautiful, and desirable, of all postwar convertibles.

1961 Lincoln Continental Convertible

PHOTO: FORD MOTOR COMPANY

1961 Mercury Monterey Convertible

Original Price: $3,126
Number Produced: 7,053
Estimated Number Existing in 1979: 287
Miles per Gallon: 11–18
Common Trouble Spots: carburetor, cooling system
Availability of Parts: fair–poor
Investment Potential: A

Background: The Monterey was the only convertible offered by Mercury in 1961. It was noticeably smaller than the previous year's model. The grille was similar to the 1960's, but the taillight treatment showed the influence of the 1958 Lincoln.

The Monterey came with a 175 h.p. 292 cu. in. V8 (two-barrel carb). Two other V8 engines, a 220 h.p. 352 (two-barrel carb) and a 300 h.p. 390 (four-barrel carb), were available at extra cost. A three-speed manual transmission was standard. Merc-O-Matic and Multi-Drive automatic transmissions were optional.

Most 1961 Mercurys, 89.5%, were equipped with an automatic, 66.1% had power steering, 41.6% had power brakes, 34.5% had tinted glass, 5.6% had power windows, 6.7% had power front seats, 68.9% had radios, and 10.2% were sold with an air conditioner.

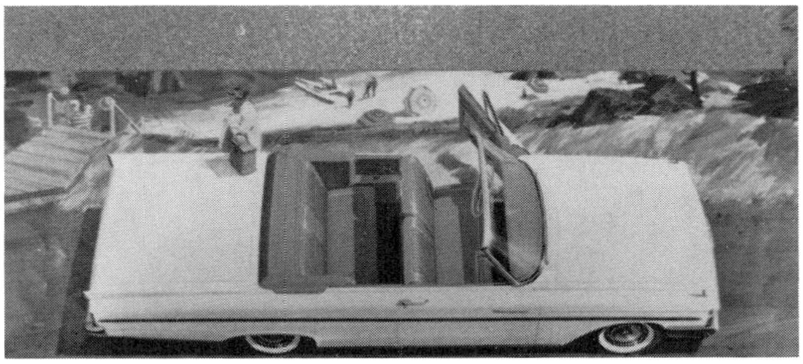

1961 Mercury Monterey Convertible

1961 Metropolitan Series 1500 Convertible

Original Price: est. $1,700
Number Produced: est. 204
Estimated Number Existing in 1979: 5
Miles per Gallon: 25–35
Common Trouble Spots: brakes, gearshift
Availability of Parts: good–fair
Investment Potential: A

Background: "Light-hearted adventure for you!" That's how American Motors described the "new" 1961 Metropolitan. It was powered by a 52 h.p. 90.9 cu. in. four-cylinder engine. A three-speed manual transmission was standard.

1961 Oldsmobile Dynamic 88 Convertible

Original Price: $3,284
Number Produced: 9,049
Estimated Number Existing in 1979: 262
Miles per Gallon: 10–16
Common Trouble Spots: none
Availability of Parts: fair
Investment Potential: A+

Background: Early Dynamic 88s came with a 250 h.p. 394 cu. in. V8. Later, a 371 cu. in. V8 was made standard and the 394 cu. in. V8 became optional. A three-speed manual transmission was standard, but not very popular. Most 1961 Oldsmobiles, 99.3%, were equipped with Hydra-Matic automatic transmission.

1961 Oldsmobile Dynamic 88 Convertible

PHOTO: OLDSMOBILE DIVISION

1961 Oldsmobile 98 Convertible

Original Price: $4,362
Number Produced: 3,804
Estimated Number Existing in 1979: 110
Miles per Gallon: 9–15
Common Trouble Spots: none
Availability of Parts: fair
Investment Potential: A+

Background: The traditionally top-of-the-line 98 convertible was overshadowed this year by the new Starfire ragtop. The 98 came with a 371 cu. in. V8. A 325 h.p. 394 cu. in. V8 was also available. An improved, lighter weight Hydra-Matic automatic transmission was standard.

1961 Oldsmobile 98 Convertible

PHOTO: OLDSMOBILE DIVISION

1961 Oldsmobile Super 88 Convertible

PHOTO: OLDSMOBILE DIVISION

1961 Oldsmobile Super 88 Convertible

Original Price: $3,592
Number Produced: 2,624
Estimated Number Existing in 1979: 76
Miles per Gallon: 10–15
Common Trouble Spots: automatic transmission
Availability of Parts: fair
Investment Potential: A+

Background: The Super 88 was restyled for 1961. The rear leaf springs of the previous year were replaced by coil springs.

It was powered by a 371 cu. in. V8. A 325 h.p. 394 cu. in. V8 was available at extra cost (this engine was standard in early models). A three-speed manual transmission was standard. Hydra-Matic automatic transmission was a popular option.

Most 1961 full-size Oldsmobiles, 96.9%, came with power steering, 94.3% had power brakes, 34.4% had tinted windows, 8.1% had power windows, 15.5% had power front seats, and 23% were sold with an air conditioner.

1961 Oldsmobile Super 88 Starfire Convertible

Original Price: $4,647
Number Produced: 7,600
Estimated Number Existing in 1979: 220
Miles per Gallon: 9–15
Common Trouble Spots: none
Availability of Parts: fair
Investment Potential: AA

Background: "Adventure in motoring excitement." That's what Oldsmobile ads promised buyers of the new Starfire convertible. The Starfire took its name from the 1953 Oldsmobile "dream car." It was introduced late in the model year.

A 330 h.p. 394 cu. in. V8 engine, with four-barrel carburetor, powered this sporty luxury car. Hydra-Matic automatic transmission, dual exhaust, leather bucket seats (in front, with a bench seat in back), and a special high-performance camshaft were standard.

1961 Plymouth Fury Convertible

Original Price: $2,967
Number Produced: N.A.
Estimated Number Existing in 1979: N.A.
Miles per Gallon: 12–17
Common Trouble Spots: brakes
Availability of Parts: fair–poor
Investment Potential: A+

Background: Although it no longer had fins, the Fury was still a rather wild-looking car. It was powered by a 230 h.p. 318 cu. in. V8. Eight other V8 engines were available at extra cost: a 305 h.p. 361 (four-barrel carburetor), two 330 h.p. 383s (both having two four-barrel carburetors), a 325 h.p. 383 (four-barrel carburetor), a 340 h.p. 383 (two four-barrel carburetors), a 350 h.p. 413 (four-barrel carburetor), and two 375 h.p. 413s (both having two four-barrel carburetors). All the optional engines came with dual exhaust.

A three-speed manual transmission was standard. Power Flite and Torque Flite automatic transmissions were optional.

Most 1961 Plymouths, 78.2%, were equipped with one of the automatics, 49.1% had power steering, 17% had power brakes, 17.5% had tinted glass, 3.9% had power windows, 2.8% had power front seats, 44.1% had radios, and 4% were sold with air conditioning.

A couple of rather unusual optional items were a square steering wheel and an in-car record player.

1961 Plymouth Fury Convertible

PHOTO: CHRYSLER CORPORATION

1961 Oldsmobile Super 88 Starfire Convertible

1955 Oldsmobile Super 88 Convertible
PHOTO: OLDSMOBILE DIVISION

1953 Oldsmobile 98 Convertible
PHOTO: OLDSMOBILE DIVISION

1964 Oldsmobile Jetstar 88 Convertible
PHOTO: OLDSMOBILE DIVISION

1967 Oldsmobile Cutlass Convertible
PHOTO: OLDSMOBILE DIVISION

1968 Buick GS 400 Convertible
PHOTO: BUICK MOTOR DIVISION

1968 Buick LeSabre Convertible
PHOTO: BUICK MOTOR DIVISION

1971 Buick Centurion Convertible
PHOTO: MC CANN-ERICKSON, INC.

1971 Buick GS Convertible
PHOTO: MC CANN-ERICKSON, INC.

1971 Buick LeSabre Custom Convertible
PHOTO: MC CANN-ERICKSON, INC.

1971 Buick Skylark Custom Convertible
PHOTO: MC CANN-ERICKSON, INC.

1972 Buick Centurion Convertible
PHOTO: MC CANN-ERICKSON, INC.

1972 Buick LeSabre Custom Convertible
PHOTO: MC CANN-ERICKSON, INC.

1972 Buick Skylark Custom Convertible
PHOTO: MC CANN-ERICKSON, INC.

1974 Buick LeSabre Luxus Convertible
PHOTO: MC CANN-ERICKSON, INC.

1960 Oldsmobile 98 Convertible
PHOTO: OLDSMOBILE DIVISION

1961 Pontiac Bonneville Convertible

PHOTO: PONTIAC MOTOR DIVISION

1961 Pontiac Bonneville Convertible

Original Price: $3,476
Number Produced: 18,264
Estimated Number Existing in 1979: 475
Miles per Gallon: 10–16
Common Trouble Spots: automatic transmission
Availability of Parts: fair
Investment Potential: A+

Background: A 1961 Bonneville softtop had the distinction of being the 75,000,000th car built by General Motors.

The standard Bonneville engine was a 235 h.p. 389 cu. in. V8. Five other versions of this engine were available at extra cost: a 303 h.p. (four-barrel carb), a 230 h.p. (two-barrel carb), a 318 h.p. (three two-barrel carbs), a 333 h.p. (four-barrel carb), and a 348 h.p. (three two-barrel carbs).

A three-speed manual transmission was standard, but not very popular. Hydra-Matic automatic and a four-speed manual were optional. Another option was front bucket seats.

1961 Pontiac Catalina Convertible

Original Price: $3,078
Number Produced: 12,379
Estimated Number Existing in 1979: 322
Miles per Gallon: 10–17
Common Trouble Spots: automatic transmission
Availability of Parts: fair
Investment Potential: A+

Background: The '61 Catalina convertible had a fresh, clean look more reminiscent of the '59 than the '60 model. It was powered by a 215 h.p. 389 cu. in. V8. Six other versions of this engine were also available at extra cost: a 235 h.p. (four-barrel carb), a 267 h.p. (two-barrel carb), a 287 h.p. (four-barrel carb), a 230 h.p. (two-barrel carb), a 318 h.p. (three two-barrel carbs), a 333 h.p. (four-barrel carb), and a 348 h.p. (three two-barrel carbs).

A three-speed manual transmission was stândard. Hydra-Matic automatic and a four-speed manual transmission were optional.

Most full-size 1961 Pontiacs, 95.9%, came with an automatic, 85.1% had power steering, 77.6% had power brakes, 49.1% had tinted glass, 8.3% had electric windows, 8.1% had power front seats, and 14% were sold with an air conditioner.

1961 Pontiac Catalina Convertible

PHOTO: PONTIAC MOTOR DIVISION

1961 Rambler American Convertible

Original Price: $2,369
Number Produced: 12,918
Estimated Number Existing in 1979: 308
Miles per Gallon: 16–25
Common Trouble Spots: carburetor
Availability of Parts: fair–poor
Investment Potential: A

Background: This was the first year for the Rambler American softtop. It was powered by a 125 h.p. 195.6 cu. in. OHV six-cylinder engine. A three-speed manual transmission was standard. Overdrive and Flash-O-Matic automatic transmission were available at extra cost.

Most 1961 Ramblers, 52.1%, were equipped with the automatic, 36.4% had a three-speed manual, 11.5% had a manual with overdrive, 15.7% had power steering, 7.9% had power brakes, 9% had tinted glass, 28.8% had a radio, 6.9% had power windows, and 4.6% were sold with an air conditioner.

1961 Rambler American Convertible

PHOTO: LARRY G. MITCHELL

1961 Studebaker Lark Regal Convertible

Original Price: $2,554
Number Produced: 1,898
Estimated Number Existing in 1979: 38
Miles per Gallon: 14–22
Common Trouble Spots: none
Availability of Parts: fair–poor
Investment Potential: A

Background: The 1961 Lark Regal came with a new 112 h.p. 169.6 OHV six-cylinder engine. A 180 h.p. 259.2 cu. in. V8 and a 195 h.p. (four-barrel carburetor) version of this engine were available at extra cost. A three-speed manual transmission was standard. Flightomatic automatic transmission and what *Motor Trend* called "one of the best overdrive units currently available on domestic cars" were optional.

Most 1961 Studebakers, 57%, were equipped with the six, 48.4% had the automatic, 37% had the three-speed manual, 14.6% had overdrive, 8.8% had power steering, 2.4% had power brakes, 8.7% had tinted glass, 18.1% had radios, and 1.1% were sold with air conditioning.

A unique feature available on Larks equipped with the manual transmission was a "hill-holder" device. When stopped on hills, the driver had only to press down on the clutch pedal; there was no need to step on the brake to keep the car from rolling back.

1961 Studebaker Lark Regal Convertible

PHOTO: RICHARD QUINN COLLECTION, STUDEBAKER DRIVERS CLUB

1962

1962 Buick Electra 225 Convertible

Original Price: $4,366
Number Produced: 7,894
Estimated Number Existing in 1979: 436
Miles per Gallon: 11–16
Common Trouble Spots: none
Availability of Parts: good–fair
Investment Potential: A+

Background: The 1962 Electra convertible was powered by a 325 h.p. 401 cu. in. V8. The standard transmission was Turbine Drive automatic. Power steering and power brakes were also standard.

Twenty-three percent of all full-size '62 Buicks had power seats and 26.8% had air conditioning.

1962 Buick Electra 225 Convertible

1962 Buick Invicta Convertible

Original Price: $3,617
Number Produced: 13,471
Estimated Number Existing in 1979: 913
Miles per Gallon: 11–17
Common Trouble Spots: none
Availability of Parts: good–fair
Investment Potential: A+

Background: The big new Invicta convertible was powered by a 325 h.p. 401 cu. in. V8. Turbine Drive automatic transmission was standard. Power brakes were a popular option, 86.8% of all full-size '62 Buicks had them. A whopping 95.6% of big Buicks had power steering.

For around $400 or so, buyers could get a detachable hardtop for their Invicta (or any GM) convertible. This top was made of fiberglass and weighed 80 pounds. It was offered in black or white. But for $100 more, a silver or gold "starburst" version was available.

1962 Buick Invicta Convertible

1962 Buick Special Convertible

1962 Buick Special Convertible

Original Price: $2,587
Number Produced: 7,918
Estimated Number Existing in 1979: 532
Miles per Gallon: 15–23
Common Trouble Spots: cooling system
Availability of Parts: good–fair
Investment Potential: A

Background: The 1962 Buick Special was named *Motor Trend*'s "Car of the Year." It came with a 135 h.p. 198 cu. in. six-cylinder engine. A 190 h.p. 215 cu. in. V8 was available at extra cost. A three-speed manual transmission was standard. Dual Path Turbine Drive automatic and a four-speed manual were optional.

Nearly 60% of all 1962 Specials were equipped with the six, 86.5% had the automatic, 12.1% had power brakes, 42.3% had power steering, 9.7% had air conditioning, and 54.7% had tinted glass.

Specials were very popular cars in 1962. Especially the six-cylinder models. *Automotive News* quoted a Cincinnati Buick dealer's remarks about the '62 Special: "They go out as fast as we get them in. I don't think there is an unsold Special in town." Buick dealers across the country were saying the same thing.

1962 Buick Special Deluxe Convertible

Original Price: $2,879
Number Produced: 8,332
Estimated Number Existing in 1979: 560
Miles per Gallon: 15–23
Common Trouble Spots: cooling system
Availability of Parts: good–fair
Investment Potential: A

Background: Outside of a few trim changes, the Special Deluxe was a dead ringer for the Special. It came with a 155 h.p. 215 cu. in. V8. A 190 h.p. version of this engine was optional. A three-speed manual transmission was standard. Dual Path Turbine Drive automatic transmission and a four-speed manual were available at extra cost.

Just over 41% of all 1962 Specials were equipped with a V8; only 13.5% had a manual transmission.

1962 Buick Special Deluxe Convertible

1962 Buick Special Skylark Convertible

Original Price: $3,012
Number Produced: 8,913
Estimated Number Existing in 1979: 599
Miles per Gallon: 15–22
Common Trouble Spots: cooling system
Availability of Parts: good–fair
Investment Potential: A+

Background: The sporty new Skylark convertible was powered by a 190 h.p. 215 cu. in. V8 engine. A three-speed manual transmission was standard. An automatic transmission and a four-speed manual (floor mounted) were optional. Power brakes were optional with the automatic.

1962 Cadillac Eldorado Biarritz Convertible

Original Price: $6,610
Number Produced: 1,450
Estimated Number Existing in 1979: 70
Miles per Gallon: 8–12
Common Trouble Spots: none
Availability of Parts: fair–good
Investment Potential: AA

Background: The new Eldorado featured lower fins and trim changes. It was powered by a 325 h.p. 390 cu. in. V8 engine. Hydramatic automatic transmission, power steering, electric windows, and power brakes were standard.

1962 Cadillac Eldorado Biarritz Convertible

PHOTO: CADILLAC MOTOR CAR DIVISION

1962 Cadillac Series 62 Convertible

Original Price: $5,588
Number Produced: 16,800
Estimated Number Existing in 1979: 818
Miles per Gallon: 8–12
Common Trouble Spots: none
Availability of Parts: fair–good
Investment Potential: A+

Background: The Series 62 convertible was powered by a 325 h.p. 390 cu. in. V8 engine with a four-barrel carburetor. Hydramatic automatic transmission, power steering, electric windows, and power brakes were standard. Over 89% of all 1962 Cadillacs came with power seats; 59.4% were equipped with air conditioning.

1962 Cadillac Series 62 Convertible

PHOTO: CADILLAC MOTOR CAR DIVISION

1962 Chevrolet Chevy II Nova Convertible

Original Price: $2,475
Number Produced: 23,741
Estimated Number Existing in 1979: 1,583
Miles per Gallon: 16–24
Common Trouble Spots: none
Availability of Parts: fair–good
Investment Potential: AA

Background: This was the first year for the cute Nova convertible. It came with a 120 h.p. 194 cu. in. six-cylinder engine. A three-speed manual transmission was standard. Powerglide automatic was optional.

Most 1962 Chevy IIs, 59.9%, came equipped with the automatic, 40.1% had a three-speed manual, 9.5% had power steering, 32.6% had tinted glass, 2% had power brakes, 4.7% had power windows, 40.5% had radios, and 2.2% were sold with air conditioners.

1962 Chevrolet Chevy II Nova Convertible

PHOTO: GM PHOTOGRAPHIC

1962 Chevrolet Corvair Monza Convertible

Original Price: $2,483
Number Produced: 16,569
Estimated Number Existing in 1979: 1,104
Miles per Gallon: 16–27
Common Trouble Spots: carburetor, heating system
Availability of Parts: good–fair
Investment Potential: AA (with Spyder package); A+ (without)

Background: This is the car that saved the Corvair (at least for a while). Chevrolet was about to discontinue the Corvair, but response to the Monza convertible at the Chicago Auto Show was so enthusiastic that the ragtop was quickly put into production.

It was powered by an 80 h.p. 145 cu. in. six. Also available were an 84 h.p. and a 102 h.p. version of this engine. A three-speed manual transmission was standard. Powerglide automatic transmission was optional.

Fifty-two percent of all 1962 Corvairs came equipped with the three-speed manual, 55.1% had radios, 41.8% had tinted glass, and 2.5% were sold with air conditioning.

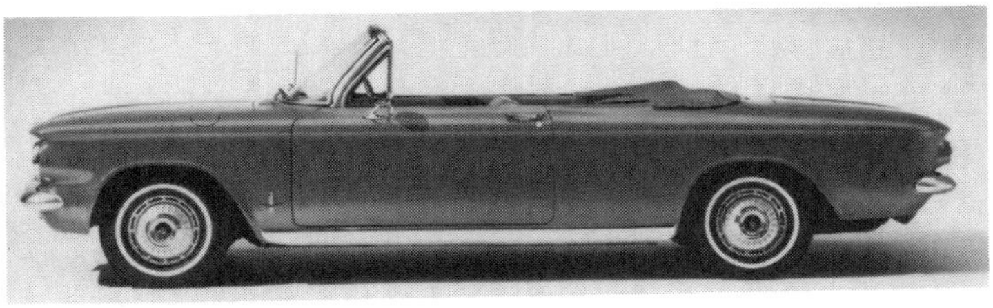

1962 Chevrolet Corvair Monza Convertible

PHOTO: GM PHOTOGRAPHIC

In mid-model year, the Monza Spyder performance package was offered for $421.95. It featured metallic brakes; four-speed manual transmission; heavy duty suspension; 150 h.p. Turbocharged 145 cu. in. six; special trim, instrument cluster, and insignia; and 3.55 to 1 axle gears.

1962 Chevrolet Corvette Convertible

Original Price: $4,038
Number Produced: 14,531
Estimated Number Existing in 1979: 968
Miles per Gallon: 11–18
Common Trouble Spots: none
Availability of Parts: fair–good
Investment Potential: AAA

Background: The '62 Corvette was little changed from the previous year's model. It was powered by a 250 h.p. 327 cu. in. V8. Three other versions of this engine were optional: a 300 h.p. (with four-barrel carburetor), a 340 h.p. (with four-barrel carburetor), and a 360 h.p. (with fuel injection). A three-speed manual transmission was standard. Almost 78% came with a four-speed manual, and a little over 10% had Powerglide automatic transmission. Only 6.8% had power windows.

Buyers had their choice of seven exterior colors.

1962 Chevrolet Corvette Convertible

PHOTO: T. MICHAELIS CORVETTE SUPPLIES

1962 Chevrolet Impala Convertible

Original Price: $3,026
Number Produced: 75,719
Estimated Number Existing in 1979: 5,040
Miles per Gallon: 8–18
Common Trouble Spots: none
Availability of Parts: good
Investment Potential: AA+ (with Super Sport option); AA (without)

Background: The attractive '62 Impala ragtop came with a 135 h.p. 235 cu. in. six. Several V8 engines were available at extra cost. These included a 170 h.p. 283, a 250 h.p. 327, a 300 h.p. 327, a 380 h.p. 409, and a 409 h.p. 409. A three-speed manual transmission was standard. Overdrive, a four-speed manual, and Powerglide automatic transmission were optional.

Also available at extra cost was the Super Sport kit, consisting of a special interior, trim, and insignia, bucket seats, dual exhaust, and a 409 cu. in. V8.

Most full-size 1962 Chevrolets, 72.6%, came with the automatic, 65.1% had a V8, 41.2% had power steering, 15.3% had power brakes, 40.1% had tinted glass, 6.6% had power windows, .9% had power front seats, 45.4% had radios, and 9.8% were sold with an air conditioner.

1962 Chevrolet Impala Convertible

PHOTO: GM PHOTOGRAPHIC

1962 Chevrolet Impala Sport Coupe

PHOTO: CHEVROLET MOTOR DIVISION

1962 Chevrolet Impala Sport Coupe

Original Price: $2,776
Number Produced: 323,427 (includes Bel Air Sport Coupe)
Estimated Number Existing in 1979: 21,566 (includes Bel Air Sport Coupe)
Miles per Gallon: 8–18
Common Trouble Spots: none
Availability of Parts: good
Investment Potential: AA+ (with Super Sport option); AA (without)

Background: The '62 Impala two-door hardtop came with a 135 h.p. 235 cu. in. six, but almost two out of three new Chevys were ordered with one of the optional V8 engines. These were a 170 h.p. 283, a 250 h.p. 327, a 300 h.p. 327, a 380 h.p. 409, and a 409 h.p. 409. A three-speed manual transmission was standard. Overdrive, a four-speed manual and Powerglide automatic transmission were available at extra cost.

The optional Super Sport kit featured a special interior, trim and insignia, bucket seats, dual exhaust, and a 409 cu. in. V8.

1962 Chrysler Newport Convertible

Original Price: $3,399
Number Produced: 2,051
Estimated Number Existing in 1979: 72
Miles per Gallon: 10–16
Common Trouble Spots: electrial system
Availability of Parts: fair–poor
Investment Potential: A+

Background: From the front, the 1962 Newport ragtop looked virtually the same as the 1961. However, the tailfins, which so long had been popular on Chrysler Corporation automobiles, were gone. In addition to styling changes, mechanical and structural improvements were made. Included among these was a smaller automatic transmission.

The Newport was powered by a 265 h.p. 361 cu. in. V8 engine. A floor-mounted three-speed manual transmission was standard. Torque Flite automatic transmission was optional.

Most 1962 Chryslers, 96.1%, came with power steering, 64.7% had power brakes, 36.7% had tinted glass, 20.8% had power windows, 15.3% had power seats, 70.9% had radios, and 21.1% were sold with air conditioning.

1962 Chrysler 300-H Convertible

Original Price: $5,461
Number Produced: 123
Estimated Number Existing in 1979: 7
Miles per Gallon: 8–13
Common Trouble Spots: electrical system
Availability of Parts: poor–fair
Investment Potential: AA

Background: Fans of the 300 Letter Series don't consider the 300-H a "real" 300 car. Externally, it was a dead ringer for the lower-priced 300 Sports Series. However, it did feature a special luxury interior package.

The standard engine in the 300-H was a 380 h.p. 413 cu. in. V8. It had a four-barrel carburetor, special cam shaft, dual exhausts, and a heavy-duty radiator. Torque Flite automatic transmission was standard. Late in the model year, a 426 cu. in. V8 was offered.

Although not as significant as previous 300 Letter Series convertibles, the 300-H is of some interest, if only for its low production quantity. An article on the 300s in *Car Classics* called the 300-H "one of Chrysler's most lavish automobiles of any era."

1962 Chrysler 300-H Convertible

PHOTO: CHRYSLER HISTORICAL COLLECTION

1962 Chrysler Newport Convertible

1962 Chrysler 300 Sport Series Convertible

1962 Chrysler 300 Sport Series Convertible

Original Price: $3,883
Number Produced: 1,848
Estimated Number Existing in 1979: 65
Miles per Gallon: 9–14
Common Trouble Spots: electrical system
Availability of Parts: fair–poor
Investment Potential: A+

Background: It was easy to confuse the 300 Sport with the 300-H; they looked almost exactly the same. However, the Sport was a much cheaper car. A 305 h.p. 383 cu. in. V8 was standard. Available at extra cost were a 340 h.p. 413 and a 380 h.p. 413. Late in the model year, a 426 cu. in. engine was available. It was also offered on the 300-H. This engine became very popular with the hot rod set.

The 426 engine wasn't the only thing on the 1962 300 worthy of praise. *Motor Trend* called the optional Torque Flite transmission "the only automatic on the market that we would unhesitantly choose over a three-speed manual" (a floor-mounted three-speed manual transmission was standard).

The 300 Sport had semi-bucket seats in the front, but a bench seat in the rear.

1962 Dodge Dart 440 Convertible

Original Price: $2,945
Number Produced: N.A.
Estimated Number Existing in 1979: N.A.
Miles per Gallon: 12–17
Common Trouble Spots: none
Availability of Parts: fair–poor
Investment Potential: A+ (with "Ramcharger 413" performance package); A (without)

Background: The Dart was dramatically restyled for 1962. It bore no resemblance whatever to the 1961 model. It was powered by a 230 h.p. 318 cu. in. V8 with two-barrel carburetor. Optional V8 engines included a 260 h.p. 318, a 310 h.p. 361, a 305 h.p. 361, a 330 h.p. 383, a 335 h.p. 383, a 385 h.p. 413, a 365 h.p. 413, and a 410 h.p. 413. A three-speed manual transmission was standard. Torque Flite automatic was optional.

Also optional was the "Ramcharger 413" performance package, which *Motor Trend* described as "probably the wildest performance package Detroit has ever offered."

1962 Dodge Custom 880 Convertible

Original Price: $3,251
Number Produced: N.A.
Estimated Number Existing in 1979: N.A.
Miles per Gallon: 12–17
Common Trouble Spots: none
Availability of Parts: fair–poor
Investment Potential: A+ (with "Ramcharger 413" performance package); A (without)

Background: Although a new series, the Custom 880 looked remarkably like the '61 Dodge, especially from the front. From the back it resembled a Chrysler.

The Custom 880 ragtop was powered by a 265 h.p. 316 cu. in. V8. Available at extra cost was the hot new "Ramcharger 413" performance package which featured a 413 cu. in. V8 engine. A three-speed manual transmission was standard. Torque Flite automatic transmission was optional.

1962 Dodge Polara Convertible

Original Price: $3,268
Number Produced: N.A.
Estimated Number Existing in 1979: N.A.
Miles per Gallon: 10–16
Common Trouble Spots: none
Availability of Parts: fair–poor
Investment Potential: A+

Background: The Polara convertible was restyled for 1962. It came with a 305 h.p. 361 cu. in. V8 with four-barrel carburetor, dual exhaust, and a special camshaft. Buyers wanting really hot performance could order the new "Ramcharger 413" Performance package. This option included heavy duty transmission and drive shaft. A Dodge so equipped was able to zip from 0 to 60 in 5.8 seconds.

Other V8 engines offered included a 310 h.p. 361, a 330 h.p. 383, a 335 h.p. 383, a 365 h.p. 413, a 385 h.p. 413, and a 410 h.p. 413. A three-speed manual transmission was standard. Torque Flite automatic transmission was optional.

Most 1962 Dodges, 82.3%, were equipped with the automatic, 57.1% had power steering, 13.5% had power brakes, 41.6% had tinted glass, 6.5% had power windows, .6% had power front seats, 97.7% had heaters, and 6.8% were sold with air conditioning.

1962 Ford Galaxie 500 Sunliner Convertible

Original Price: $3,033
Number Produced: 42,646
Estimated Number Existing in 1979: 2,829
Miles per Gallon: 9–18
Common Trouble Spots: rear axle
Availability of Parts: good–fair
Investment Potential: A+

Background: Galaxie 500 convertible buyers had their choice of nine engines—a 138 h.p. 223 cu. in. six and the following V8s: a 170 h.p. 292, a 220 h.p. 352, a 300 h.p. 390, a 330 h.p. 390, a 375 h.p. 390, a 401 h.p. 390, a 385 h.p. 406, and a 405 h.p. 406. A three-speed manual transmission was standard. Overdrive and Ford-O-Matic and Cruise-O-Matic automatic transmissions were optional (automatic transmission was not offered with the 406 V8).

Seventy-eight percent of all 1962 Galaxies came with an automatic, 3.1% had overdrive, 85.6% had a V8, 51.6% had power steering, 15% had power brakes, 4.1% had power windows, 1.8% had power front seat, 39% had tinted glass, and 9.2% were equipped with air conditioning.

A rare option, offered late in the model year, was a removable hard top called the "Starlift."

1962 Ford Galaxie 500 Sunliner Convertible

PHOTO: FORD MOTOR COMPANY

1962½ Ford Galaxie 500 XL Convertible

Original Price: $3,358
Number Produced: 13,183
Estimated Number Existing in 1979: 874
Miles per Gallon: 9–17
Common Trouble Spots: rear axle
Availability of Parts: good–fair
Investment Potential: AA+

Background: This sporty mid-model-year convertible featured bucket seats and special trim and interior. It was powered by a 170 h.p. 292 cu. in. V8. Buyers had their choice of six other V8 engines: a 220 h.p. 352, a 330 h.p. 390, a 375 h.p. 390, a 401 h.p. 390, a 385 h.p. 406, and a 405 h.p. 406. A three-speed manual was standard. Overdrive, a four-speed manual and Cruise-O-Matic automatic transmission were optional.

The 500 XL was offered in five exterior colors: black, gold, red, silver, and white.

1962 Ford Thunderbird Convertible

Original Price: $4,788
Number Produced: 7,030
Estimated Number Existing in 1979: 463
Miles per Gallon: 8–14
Common Trouble Spots: cooling system
Availability of Parts: fair
Investment Potential: AA+

Background: The '62 Thunderbird ragtop was powered by a 300 h.p. 390 cu. in. V8. A 340 h.p. version of this engine was optional. Cruise-O-Matic automatic transmission was standard.

All 1962 T-Birds had power steering and power brakes. Just over 71% came with power windows, 67% had tinted glass, 53.9% had power seats, 96.8% had radios, and 39.6% were sold with air conditioning.

Buyers had their choice of vinyl-and-cloth, all-vinyl, and all-leather interiors. The convertible top was available in three colors: black, blue, and white.

Like the 1961, the '62 Thunderbird convertible is beautiful from both the sidewalk and the driver's seat.

1962 Ford Thunderbird Convertible

PHOTO: FORD MOTOR COMPANY

1962 Ford Thunderbird Sports Roadster

Original Price: $5,439
Number Produced: 1,427
Estimated Number Existing in 1979: 140
Miles per Gallon: 8–14
Common Trouble Spots: cooling system
Availability of Parts: fair
Investment Potential: AAA

Background: The Sports Roadster was basically a '62 T-Bird with a fiberglass tonneau covering the rear seat. The idea of a tonneau covering was not new to Thunderbird; a vinyl version had been available on the classic T-Birds of the mid 1950s.

Although the tonneau cover looked as though it could be removed and placed on a standard T-Bird convertible, it couldn't. At least that's what Ford Motor

1962 Ford Thunderbird Sports Roadster

PHOTO: FORD MOTOR COMPANY

Company engineers said at the time. Since then, many fake roadsters have been made.

In addition to the tonneau, the Sports Roadster had a passenger assist bar ("sissy bar"), special insignias, and chromed wire wheels. The convertible top was available in only two colors, black and white.

It was powered by a 300 h.p. 390 cu. in. V8. A 340 h.p. (triple two-barrel carburetor) version of this engine was optional. Cruise-O-Matic automatic transmission, power steering, and power brakes were standard.

Car Life said of the 1962 Sports Roadster, "There is something special about owning/driving a Thunderbird; on the boulevard it announces to all that here's a person of sporting taste, on the highway it's quiet and smooth, in front of your house it will turn your neighbors green with envy. And the Sports Roadster even turns other 'Bird owners a nice shade of chartreuse."

1962 Imperial Crown Convertible

Original Price: $5,770
Number Produced: 554
Estimated Number Existing in 1979: 40
Miles per Gallon: 8–14
Common Trouble Spots: automatic transmission
Availability of Parts: poor–fair
Investment Potential: AA+

Background: The Imperial continued to sport free-standing headlights. New for 1962 were free-standing taillights similar to those used on Imperials in the mid-1950s. That helped to improve the overall integrity of the design—the fins of the 1961 tended to distract from the classic look the stylists were hoping to achieve.

A 340 h.p. 413 cu. in. V8 powered the Imperial. Torque Flite automatic transmission, power steering and power brakes were standard.

The all-leather interior added to the car's luxury appeal. Most 1962 Imperials, 95.1%, came with power windows, 94.4% had power seats, 91.1% had tinted glass, 97.6% had radios, and 60.3% were sold with air conditioning.

Chrysler used a rather unique method of selling Imperials: they hired sales specialists who sold Imperials only. This was intended to increase the number of contacts and demonstration rides given to prospective customers. In the 180 dealerships which made use of these specialists, 1962 Imperial sales were up by 25% compared to the previous year.

1962 King Midget Convertible

Original Price: est. $650
Number Produced: 166
Estimated Number Existing in 1979: 12
Miles per Gallon: 50–90
Common Trouble Spots: transmission, "V" belts
Availability of Parts: good
Investment Potential: A

Background: The '62 King Midget convertible was powered by a 10 h.p. 29 cu. in. one-cylinder engine. Automatic transmission was standard.

1962 King Midget Convertible

PHOTO: JOHN A. CONDE COLLECTION

1962 Imperial Crown Convertible

PHOTO: CHRYSLER HISTORICAL COLLECTION

1962 Lincoln Continental Convertible

PHOTO: FORD MOTOR COMPANY

1962 Lincoln Continental Convertible

Original Price: $6,720
Number Produced: 3,212
Estimated Number Existing in 1979: 312
Miles per Gallon: 10–15
Common Trouble Spots: brakes, top mechanism
Availability of Parts: fair
Investment Potential: AAA

Background: The most noticeable difference between the 1962 Continental convertible and the previous year's model was a new grille.

It was powered by a 300 h.p. 430 cu. in. V8 engine. Turbo-Drive automatic transmission, power brakes, power steering, radio, and power windows were standard. Most 1962 Lincoln Continentals, 96%, had power seats, 94.4% had tinted glass, and 73% were sold with air conditioning.

Some new options offered were power antenna, power trunk release, automatic headlight dimmer, and a remote-control outside rearview mirror.

As before, each Continental underwent extensive testing before leaving the factory.

1962 Mercury Monterey Custom Convertible

Original Price: $3,222
Number Produced: 6,804
Estimated Number Existing in 1979: 488
Miles per Gallon: 9–18
Common Trouble Spots: brakes, cooling system
Availability of Parts: fair–poor
Investment Potential: A+ (with S-55 package); A (without)

Background: The '62 Monterey Custom came with a 170 h.p. 292 cu. in. V8. Five other V8 engines were available at extra cost: a 220 h.p. 352, a 300 h.p. 390, a 330 h.p. 390, a 385 h.p. 406, and a 405 h.p. 406. A three-speed manual transmission was standard. Multi-Drive automatic and (with the 406 cu. in. V8) a four-speed manual were optional.

Most 1962 Montereys, 95.4%, were equipped with the automatic, 82.4% had power steering, 53.9% had power brakes, 59% had tinted glass, 22.4% had power windows, 10.3% had power brakes, 75.2% had radios, and 16.1% were sold with air conditioning.

In mid-year an S-55 package was offered, featuring special trim and bucket-seat interior. Thirty-two percent of all 1962 Montereys were ordered this way.

1962 Metropolitan Series 1500 Convertible

Original Price: est. $1,800
Number Produced: est. 88
Estimated Number Existing in 1979: 2
Miles per Gallon: 25–35
Common Trouble Spots: brakes, gearshift
Availability of Parts: good–fair
Investment Potential: A

Background: This is the last year Metropolitan convertibles were sold. Actually, it was just a leftover 1960 model; production of Metropolitans ceased in the middle of that year.

It was powered by a 52 h.p. 90.9 cu. in. four-cylinder engine. A three-speed manual transmission was standard.

1962 Oldsmobile Dynamic 88 Convertible

Original Price: $3,381
Number Produced: 12,212
Estimated Number Existing in 1979: 548
Miles per Gallon: 10–16
Common Trouble Spots: none
Availability of Parts: fair–good
Investment Potential: A+

Background: The face-lifted Dynamic 88 was powered by a 280 h.p. 394 cu. in. V8. A 260 h.p., and a 330 h.p. version of that engine were available at extra cost. A three-speed manual transmission was standard, but not very popular. Hydra-Matic automatic transmission was optional.

Most full-size 1962 Oldsmobiles, 98%, came with power steering, 95.4% had power brakes, 76.8% had tinted glass, 26.6% had power windows, 18% had power front seats, and 29.9% were sold with air conditioning.

1962 Mercury Monterey Custom Convertible

PHOTO: FORD MOTOR COMPANY

1962 Oldsmobile 98 Convertible

PHOTO: OLDSMOBILE DIVISION

1962 Oldsmobile 98 Convertible

Original Price: $4,459
Number Produced: 3,693
Estimated Number Existing in 1979: 165
Miles per Gallon: 9–15
Common Trouble Spots: none
Availability of Parts: fair–good
Investment Potential: A+

Background: The 98 was Oldsmobile's biggest ragtop in 1962; it had a wheelbase of 126 inches. A 330 h.p. 394 cu. in. V8 engine and Hydra-Matic automatic transmission were standard. A removable fiberglass hard top was available from Olds dealers.

1962 Oldsmobile F-85 Convertible

Original Price: $2,760
Number Produced: 3,660
Estimated Number Existing in 1979: 163
Miles per Gallon: 13–20
Common Trouble Spots: none
Availability of Parts: fair–good
Investment Potential: A

Background: This was the first year for the F-85 convertible. It was powered by a 155 h.p. 215 cu. in. V8. A 185 h.p. version of this engine, with four-barrel carburetor, was available at extra cost. A three-speed manual transmission was standard. Hydra-Matic automatic transmission and a four-speed manual were optional. Most buyers ordered the automatic.

Many 1962 F-85s, 50.3%, came with power steering, 2.6% had power brakes, 56.8% had tinted glass, 87.1% had radios, 7.8% had power windows, and 8.1% were sold with air conditioning. A detachable fiberglass hard top was offered (by Olds dealers).

1962 Oldsmobile F-85 Convertible

PHOTO: OLDSMOBILE DIVISION

1962 Oldsmobile F-85 Cutlass Convertible

Original Price: $2,971
Number Produced: 9,893
Estimated Number Existing in 1979: 444
Miles per Gallon: 13–20
Common Trouble Spots: none
Availability of Parts: fair–good
Investment Potential: A+

Background: The new F-85 Cutlass was basically a dressed-up regular F-85. It came with a 155 h.p. 215 cu. in. V8. A 185 h.p. version of this engine, with four-barrel carburetor, was available at extra cost. A three-speed manual transmission was standard. Hydra-Matic automatic transmission and a four-speed manual were optional.

1962 Oldsmobile Starfire Convertible

Original Price: $4,744
Number Produced: 7,149
Estimated Number Existing in 1979: 320
Miles per Gallon: 9–15
Common Trouble Spots: automatic transmission
Availability of Parts: fair–good
Investment Potential: AA

Background: The Starfire convertible was Oldsmobile's sportiest full-size car in 1962. It was powered by a 345 h.p. 394 cu. in. V8. Manual transmission was standard. Hydra-Matic automatic transmission was a popular option.

Oldsmobile, and other GM dealers, offered a detachable fiberglass hardtop for all their convertibles. The exact number of Starfire buyers who purchased one of these is not known. However, *Automotive News* estimated that five percent of all GM convertible buyers ordered a removable hardtop.

1962 Plymouth Fury Convertible

Original Price: $2,924
Number Produced: N.A.
Estimated Number Existing in 1979: N.A.
Miles per Gallon: 11–17
Common Trouble Spots: none
Availability of Parts: fair
Investment Potential: A

Background: After several years of flamboyant styles, Plymouth once again became a rather ordinary (but pleasant) looking car. In addition to a more conservative design, the new Fury was several inches shorter and narrower than last year's model.

The Fury came with a 230 h.p. 318 cu. in. V8. A 260 h.p. version of this engine and a 305 h.p. 361 cu. in. V8 and a 410 h.p. 413 cu. in. V8 were available at extra cost.

A three-speed manual transmission was standard. Torque Flite automatic transmission was optional.

Most 1962 Plymouths, 74.4 percent, were equipped with the automatic, 46.8% had power steering, 11.4% had power brakes, 26.8% had tinted glass, 8.2% had electric windows, a little more than .5% had power front seats, and 5.2% were sold with an air conditioner.

1962 Plymouth Fury Convertible

1962 Plymouth Sport Fury Convertible

Original Price: $2,822
Number Produced: N.A.
Estimated Number Existing in 1979: N.A.
Miles per Gallon: 10–16
Common Trouble Spots: none
Availability of Parts: fair
Investment Potential: A+

Background: "Nobody Passes a New Plymouth Fury Without the Owner's Permission!" At least that's what the Plymouth ads were saying in 1962. And there was a lot of truth to that statement.

The Sport Fury came with a 305 h.p. 361 cu. in. V8. A new 410 h.p. Super Stock 413 cu. in. V8 engine was available at extra cost. A three-speed manual transmission was standard, but not very popular. Most Sport Furys came with the optional push-button Torque Flite automatic transmission.

1962 Pontiac Bonneville Convertible

Original Price: $3,570
Number Produced: 21,582
Estimated Number Existing in 1979: 832
Miles per Gallon: 9–17
Common Trouble Spots: automatic transmission
Availability of Parts: fair–good
Investment Potential: A+

Background: The Bonneville was Pontiac's highest-priced and most popular convertible in 1962. It was powered by a 235 h.p. 389 cu. in. V8. Five other versions of this engine were available at extra cost: a 230 h.p. (Rochester two-barrel carb), a 303 h.p. (Carter four-barrel carb), a 318 h.p. (three Rochester two-barrel carbs and dual exhaust), a 333 h.p. (Carter four-barrel carb), and a 348 h.p. (three Rochester two-barrel carbs).

A three-speed manual transmission was standard, but not very popular. Hydra-Matic automatic and a four-speed manual were optional.

Pontiac dealers (not the factory) offered a detachable hard top for the Bonneville and other Pontiac convertibles. It came in four colors: black, white, and, for $100 extra, "Starburst" gold or silver.

1962 Pontiac Bonneville Convertible

PHOTO: PONTIAC MOTOR DIVISION

1962 Pontiac Catalina Convertible

Original Price: $3,172
Number Produced: 16,877
Estimated Number Existing in 1979: 650
Miles per Gallon: 9–17
Common Trouble Spots: automatic transmission
Availability of Parts: fair–good
Investment Potential: A

Background: The new Catalina convertible was powered by a 215 h.p. 389 cu. in. V8. Six other versions of this engine were available at extra cost: a 230 h.p. (Rochester two-barrel carb), a 235 h.p. (Carter four-barrel carb), 267 h.p. (Rochester two-barrel carb), a 303 h.p. (Carter four-barrel carb), a 318 h.p. (three Rochester two-barrel carbs), a 333 h.p. (Carter four-barrel carb), and a 348 h.p. (three Rochester two-barrel carbs).

A three-speed manual transmission was standard. Hydra-Matic automatic and a four-speed manual transmission were optional.

Most 1962 full-sized Pontiacs, 95%, came with an automatic, 87.7% had power steering, 79.1% had power brakes, 60.5% had tinted glass, 15.8% had electric windows, 5.1% had power front seats, and 19.6% were sold with an air conditioner.

1962 Pontiac Tempest Deluxe Convertible

Original Price: $2,564
Number Produced: 5,076
Estimated Number Existing in 1979: 195
Miles per Gallon: 13–23
Common Trouble Spots: brakes
Availability of Parts: fair–good

Background: This was the first year for the Tempest ragtop. It was powered by a 110 h.p. 194.5 cu. in. four-cylinder engine. Four other versions of this engine, a 115 h.p., a 120 h.p., a 140 h.p., and a 166 h.p., plus a 185 h.p. 215 cu. in. V8, were available at extra cost. A three-speed manual transmission was standard. Tempes Torque automatic and a-four speed manual transmission were optional.

Most 1962 Tempests, 79.8%, came with the automatic, 8.7% had power steering, 36.8% had tinted glass, 1.1% had the V8, 3.6% had electric windows, and 3.6% were sold with an air conditioner.

The Le Mans package was available on the Tempest convertible. It featured semi-bucket front seats, special interior, and name plates. A manually operated top was standard. The eight millionth car produced by Pontiac was a 1962 Le Mans convertible.

1962 Rambler American Convertible

Original Price: $2,344
Number Produced: 13,497
Estimated Number Existing in 1979: 550
Miles per Gallon: 15–25
Common Trouble Spots: none
Availability of Parts: fair–poor
Investment Potential: A

Background: The 1962 American looked the same as the previous year's model. However, mechanical improvements were made. It was powered by a 125 h.p. 195.6 cu. in. OHV six-cylinder engine. A three-speed manual transmission was standard. Flash-O-Matic automatic and the new "E-Stick" transmission with overdrive were optional. So were reclining bucket seats.

Most 1962 Ramblers, 53.9%, were equipped with the automatic, 34.8% had the three-speed manual, 11.3% had "E-Stick", 15% had power steering, 7.9% had power brakes, 10% had tinted glass, 28.5% had a radio, .4% had power windows, and 6.5% were sold with an air conditioner.

A Louisiana Rambler dealer had a rather unique way of selling cars: he parked a new American convertible by a billboard advertising his dealership and had an attractive model sit in it and wave at passing motorists.

1962 Studebaker Gran Turismo Hawk

1962 Studebaker Gran Turismo Hawk

Original Price: $3,095
Number Produced: 7,842
Estimated Number Existing in 1979: 229
Miles per Gallon: 14–21
Common Trouble Spots: none
Availability of Parts: fair–poor
Investment Potential: AA+

Background: Motor Trend called the elegant new Hawk "an automobile that is completely masculine in character and somehow reminiscent of some of the really great cars of the early '30s." Studebaker literature referred to it as a "family sports classic . . . designed and made in the meticulous tradition of the great European road cars and offering the comforts and conveniences preferred by the discerning American motorist."

It came with a 210 h.p. 289 cu. in. V8. A 225 h.p. version of this engine and a 180 h.p. 259.2 cu. in. V8 were available at extra cost. A three-speed manual transmission was standard. Overdrive, a four-speed manual, and Flightomatic automatic transmission were optional. So were reclining bucket seats, safety belts, and an all-vinyl interior (a vinyl-and-cloth interior was standard).

Automotive News praised the Hawk's interior saying, "It's obvious the Hawk was built for the driver. The instrument panel is covered by a dull wood-like finish and contains one of the finest collections of instruments this side of a jetliner."

Many options were offered, including air conditioning, electric clock, climatizer, tachometer, power steering, power brakes, two radios, padded sun visor, and electric windshield washer.

1962 Rambler American Convertible

1962 Studebaker Lark Daytona Convertible

1962 Studebaker Lark Daytona Convertible

Original Price: $2,814
Number Produced: (see Lark Regal)
Estimated Number Existing in 1979: (see Lark Regal)
Miles per Gallon: 14–20
Common Trouble Spots: none
Availability of Parts: fair–poor
Investment Potential: A+

Background: The new Daytona convertible featured reclining bucket seats and a padded center console. It came with a 112 h.p. 169.6 cu. in. six-cylinder engine. Several V8 engines could be had, including a 180 h.p. 259.2, a 195 h.p. 259.2, a 210 h.p. 289, and a 225 h.p. 289. A three-speed manual transmission was standard. Overdrive, a four-speed manual and Flightomatic automatic transmission were available at extra cost.

After a road test, *Automotive News* called the Daytona "a well-trimmed highly comfortable compact with enough zip to make driving an exciting adventure rather than a prosaic means of transportation."

The Lark Daytona ragtop was the Indy 500 pace car in 1962.

1962 Studebaker Lark Regal Convertible

1962 Studebaker Lark Regal Convertible

PHOTO: RICHARD QUINN COLLECTION, STUDEBAKER DRIVERS CLUB

Original Price: $2,589
Number Produced: 2,599 (includes Daytonas)
Estimated Number Existing in 1979: 76 (includes Daytonas)
Miles per Gallon: 14–20
Common Trouble Spots: none
Availability of Parts: fair–poor
Investment Potential: A

Background: "Glamorously new both inside and out." That's how Studebaker described the '62 Regal softtop. It was powered by a 112 h.p. 169.6 cu. in. six-cylinder engine. Two 259.2 cu. in. V8s (rated at 180 h.p. and 195 h.p.) and two 289 cu. in. V8s (rated at 210 h.p. and 225 h.p.) were available at extra cost. A three-speed manual transmission was standard. Overdrive and Flightomatic automatic transmission were optional.

Most 1962 Studebakers, 53.2%, were equipped with the six-cylinder engine, 52.4% had the automatic, 29.9% had manual transmission, 12.1% had the manual with overdrive, 16.1% had power steering, 4.3% had power brakes, 13.3% had tinted glass, 26.2% had radios, and 1.9% were sold with air conditioning.

1963

1963 Buick Electra 225 Convertible

Original Price: $4,365
Number Produced: 6,367
Estimated Number Existing in 1979: 267
Miles per Gallon: 9–15
Common Trouble Spots: brakes
Availability of Parts: good–fair
Investment Potential: A+

Background: The luxurious new Electra convertible came with a 325 h.p. 401 cu. in. V8 engine. Turbine Drive automatic transmission, power steering, power brakes, heater, and windshield washers were standard. A three-speed manual and a four-speed manual were optional.

Most full-size 1963 Buicks, 99%, were equipped with an automatic, and 32.7% had an air conditioner. Bucket seats and a seven-position tilting steering wheel were among the options offered.

1963 Buick Electra 225 Convertible

1963 Buick Special Convertible

1963 Buick LeSabre Convertible

Original Price: $3,339
Number Produced: 9,975
Estimated Number Existing in 1979: 420
Miles per Gallon: 10–16
Common Trouble Spots: none
Availability of Parts: good–fair
Investment Potential: A+

Background: The LeSabre convertible closely resembled the Electra. Three portholes on each front fender, as opposed to the Electra's four, was the quickest way of telling the two apart from a distance.

It was powered by a 280 h.p. 401 cu. in. V8. Two other versions of this engine, a 265 h.p. and a 325 h.p., were available at extra cost. A three-speed manual transmission was standard. Turbine Drive automatic and a four-speed manual were optional.

Eighty-eight percent of all full-size '63 Buicks came with power brakes, 96.5% had power steering, 26.8% had power front seats, and 31.8% were equipped with power windows.

1963 Buick Special Convertible

Original Price: $2,591
Number Produced: 8,082
Estimated Number Existing in 1979: 340
Miles per Gallon: 15–23
Common Trouble Spots: none
Availability of Parts: good–fair
Investment Potential: A

Background: The compact new Special ragtop bore a strong family resemblance to the full-size Buicks. It came with a 135 h.p. 198 cu. in. V6. Two 215 cu. in. V8s, a 155 h.p. and a 200 h.p., were available at extra cost. A three-speed manual transmission was standard. Turbine Drive automatic and a four-speed manual were optional.

Just over 88% of all 1963 Specials came with an automatic, 59.3% had a V8 engine, 9.5% had power brakes, 47.5% had power steering, and 11.1% were equipped with air conditioning.

1963 Buick Special Skylark Convertible

Original Price: $3,011
Number Produced: 10,212
Estimated Number Existing in 1979: 430
Miles per Gallon: 14–20
Common Trouble Spots: none
Availability of Parts: good–fair
Investment Potential: A+

Background: The sporty Skylark convertible was powered by a 200 h.p. 215 cu. in. V8. A three-speed manual transmission was standard. Turbine Drive automatic and a four-speed manual transmission were optional at $189 and $199.80 respectively. Only 11.8% of all 1963 Specials had manual transmissions. Front seat belts were an $18.83 mandatory option.

1963 Buick Riviera Sport Coupe

Original Price: $4,333
Number Produced: 40,000
Estimated Number Existing in 1979: 1,686
Miles per Gallon: 11–15
Common Trouble Spots: none
Availability of Parts: good
Investment Potential: AAA

Background: The 1963 Riviera was originally planned for the Cadillac division of GM. After Cadillac decided not to produce it, Buick took it over.

Buick management predicted they would be able to sell at least 50,000 Rivieras in 1963. However, they deliberately made 20% less in order to increase the car's appeal.

It was powered by a 325 h.p. 401 cu. in. V8. A 340 h.p. 425 cu. in. V8 was available at extra cost. Turbine Drive automatic transmission, a heater, power steering, and a windshield washer were standard. Leather upholstery and air conditioning were among the options.

This Rolls-Royce-inspired luxury personal car is easily the most attractive Buick of the 1960s.

1963 Buick Riviera Sport Coupe

1963 Buick Wildcat Convertible

1963 Buick Wildcat Convertible

Original Price: $3,961
Number Produced: 6,021
Estimated Number Existing in 1979: 253
Miles per Gallon: 9–16
Common Trouble Spots: none
Availability of Parts: good–fair
Investment Potential: A+

Background: The '63 Wildcat convertible was powered by a 325 h.p. 401 cu. in. V8. A three-speed manual transmission was standard. Turbine Drive automatic and a four-speed manual transmission were optional. All Wildcat convertibles had power steering and power brakes. Many came with bucket seats.

1963 Cadillac Eldorado Biarritz Convertible

Original Price: $6,608
Number Produced: 1,825
Estimated Number Existing in 1979: 189
Miles per Gallon: 9–16
Common Trouble Spots: none
Availability of Parts: fair–good
Investment Potential: AA+

Background: The big news for 1963 was Cadillac's new engine; it was the first major change in the make's engine since 1949. In addition to being more durable, the new 325 h.p. 390 cu. in. V8 was 52 pounds lighter than last year's. Hydramatic automatic transmission, power steering, electric windows, and power brakes were standard. Many options were also available.

1963 Cadillac Eldorado Biarritz Convertible

PHOTO: CADILLAC MOTOR CAR DIVISION

1963 Cadillac Series 62 Convertible

PHOTO: CADILLAC MOTOR CAR DIVISION

1963 Cadillac Series 62 Convertible

Original Price: $5,590
Number Produced: 17,600
Estimated Number Existing in 1979: 1,829
Miles per Gallon: 9–16
Common Trouble Spots: none
Availability of Parts: fair–good
Investment Potential: AA

Background: The attractive new Series 62 convertible was powered by a lighter 325 h.p. 390 cu. in. V8 (with a four-barrel carburetor). Hydramatic automatic transmission, power steering, electric windows, and power brakes were standard.

A record 143 interior options were available in 1963. Among these were bucket seats, AM-FM radio, and cruise control. Nearly all 1963 Cadillacs, 91.9%, had power seats, 66% had air conditioning, and 28% were equipped with a six-position tilting steering wheel.

In 1963, *Advertising Age* reported, Cadillac was trying to capture the youth market (at least the wealthier segments of it). Younger models were used in ads "in more youthful settings and situations."

1963 Chevrolet Chevy II Nova Convertible

Original Price: $2,472
Number Produced: 24,823
Estimated Number Existing in 1979: 2,363
Miles per Gallon: 16–22
Common Trouble Spots: none
Availability of Parts: good
Investment Potential: AA

Background: The '63 Nova convertible was an attractive little car, especially when equipped with the optional Super Sport package. It came with a 120 h.p. 194 cu. in. six. A three-speed manual transmission was standard. Powerglide automatic transmission was available at extra cost.

Almost 65% of all 1963 Chevy IIs came equipped with the automatic, 11.1% had power steering, 40.1% had tinted glass, 2.9% had power brakes, 5.4% had power front seats, 45.6% had radios, and 3.6% were sold with air conditioners.

1963 Chevrolet Chevy II Nova Convertible

PHOTO: GM PHOTOGRAPHIC

1963 Chevrolet Corvair Monza Convertible

Original Price: $2,808
Number Produced: 44,165
Estimated Number Existing in 1979: 4,204
Miles per Gallon: 16–27
Common Trouble Spots: piston rings
Availability of Parts: good
Investment Potential: AA (with the Spyder package); A+ (without)

Background: The Corvair "has emerged as one of the few cars ever manufactured in the United States that have attained a true personality." At least that is what *Motor Trend* had to say about the new 1963 Corvair.

The Monza ragtop came with an 80 h.p. 145 cu. in. six-cylinder engine. Three other versions of this engine, with 84 h.p., 102 h.p., or 150 h.p. were available at extra cost. A three-speed manual transmission was standard. Powerglide automatic and a four-speed manual transmission were optional.

Forty-four percent of all 1963 Corvairs came equipped with the automatic, 55.9% had radios, 48% had tinted glass, and 2.5% were sold with air conditioning.

Once again, the Spyder performance package was offered.

1963 Chevrolet Corvair Monza Convertible

PHOTO: GM PHOTOGRAPHIC

1963 Chevrolet Corvette Convertible

PHOTO: T. MICHAELIS CORVETTE SUPPLIES

1963 Chevrolet Corvette Stingray Convertible

Original Price: $4,037
Number Produced: 10,919
Estimated Number Existing in 1979: 1,020
Miles per Gallon: 11–18
Common Trouble Spots: brakes
Availability of Parts: good
Investment Potential: AAA

Background: The restyled '63 Vette had a very futuristic look about it. It was powered by a 250 h.p. 327 cu. in. V8. Three other versions of this engine, a 300 h.p. (with four-barrel carburetor), a 340 h.p. (with four-barrel carburetor), and a 360 h.p. (with fuel injection), were optional. A three-speed manual transmission was standard. Most 1963 Corvettes, 83.5%, came with the optional four-speed manual. Slightly over 12% had Powerglide automatic transmission.

A little over 1% of '63 Vettes were equipped with an air conditioner, 14.2% had power steering, 15.5% had power brakes, and 17.4% were sold with power windows. Most convertible buyers, 52.5%, ordered the optional hard top.

1963 Chevrolet Corvette Stingray Sport Coupe

Original Price: $4,252
Number Produced: 10,594
Estimated Number Existing in 1979: 1,008
Miles per Gallon: 11–18
Common Trouble Spots: brakes
Availability of Parts: good
Investment Potential: AAA+ (with fuel injection); AAA (without)

Background: The split-window 1963 Stingray coupe is one of the most beautiful and desirable of all Corvettes. The standard engine was a 250 h.p. 327 cu. in. V8. Three other versions of this engine, a 300 h.p. (with four-barrel carburetor), a 340 h.p. (with four-barrel carburetor), and a 360 h.p. (with fuel injection), were optional. A three-speed manual transmission was standard, but not very popular; only 4.3% of '63 Vettes were sold that way. Most had the optional four-speed manual transmission. Just 12.2% had Powerglide automatic transmission.

Buyers had their choice of three exterior colors—blue, red, and silver. A leather interior was optional at extra cost.

1963 Chevrolet Corvette Stingray Sport Coupe

PHOTO: CHEVROLET MOTOR DIVISION

The Stingray coupe was so popular in 1963 that Chevrolet was unable to keep up with the demand. Many buyers had to wait at least two months before they were able to take delivery of their new Vettes.

The Stingray split-window coupe hasn't lost any of its appeal over the years. It is one of the most valuable and prized postwar cars made by any manufacturer.

1963 Chevrolet Impala Convertible

Original Price: $3,024
Number Produced: 82,659
Estimated Number Existing in 1979: 7,868
Miles per Gallon: 9–18
Common Trouble Spots: automatic transmission
Availability of Parts: good
Investment Potential: AA+ (with Super Sport option); AA (without)

Background: On September 30, 1962, Chevrolet ran a 330-second commercial to show off its new models. The stars from the Chevy-sponsored TV shows "My Three Sons," "Bonanza," and "Route 66" were on hand to help sell the viewing public on the virtues of the '63 Chevys.

The top-of-the-line Chevrolet in 1963 was the Impala ragtop. It was powered by a 140 h.p. 230 cu. in. six. Also available were the following V8 engines: a 195 h.p. 283, a 250 h.p. 327, a 300 h.p. 327, a 340 h.p. 409, a 400 h.p. 409, and a 425 h.p. 409. A three-speed manual transmission was standard. Powerglide automatic transmission and a four-speed manual were optional.

Most full-size 1963 Chevrolets, 70.2%, came equipped with a V8, 73.6% had the automatic, 46.7% had power steering, 16.8% had power brakes, 46.5% had tinted glass, 7.3% had power windows, almost 1% had power front seats, and 12.5% were sold with an air conditioner.

A Super Sport trim package was optional.

1963 Chevrolet Impala Convertible

PHOTO: GM PHOTOGRAPHIC

1963 Chevrolet Impala Sport Coupe

Original Price: $2,774
Number Produced: 399,244
Estimated Number Existing in 1979: 38,005
Miles per Gallon: 9–18
Common Trouble Spots: automatic transmission
Availability of Parts: good
Investment Potential: AA+ (with Super Sport option); AA (without)

Background: The '63 Impala two-door hardtop was one of the best-looking full-size Chevrolets made in the 1960s. It was powered by a 140 h.p. 230 cu. in. six. Most buyers ordered one of the optional V8 engines, which included a 195 h.p. 283, a 250 h.p. 327, a 300 h.p. 327, a 340 h.p. 409, a 400 h.p. 409, and a 425 h.p. 409. A three-speed manual transmission was standard. Powerglide automatic and a four-speed manual transmission were optional.

A Super Sport performance and trim package was once again offered at extra cost.

1963 Chevrolet Impala Sport Coupe

PHOTO: CHEVROLET MOTOR DIVISION

1963 Chrysler 300 Sport Series Convertible

Original Price: $3,790
Number Produced: 3,396
Estimated Number Existing in 1979: 202
Miles per Gallon: 9–14
Common Trouble Spots: none
Availability of Parts: poor–fair
Investment Potential: A+

Background: Standard on the 300 Sport convertible was a 305 h.p. 383 cu. in. V8 engine. Available at extra cost was a 360 h.p. 413 cu. in. V8. A floor-mounted three-speed manual transmission was standard. Torque Flite automatic transmission was optional.

Two popular options were power seats and air conditioning. About one out of every four 1963 Chryslers came with these items.

Late in the model year, an Indianapolis 500 pace car trim package was available. It consisted of special upholstery, paint, and emblem. A total of 1,836 1963 300 Sport ragtops came with this option.

1963 Chrysler 300 Sports Series Convertible

1963 Chrysler Newport Convertible

Original Price: $3,400
Number Produced: 2,093
Estimated Number Existing in 1979: 125
Miles per Gallon: 10–16
Common Trouble Spots: none
Availability of Parts: fair–poor
Investment Potential: A+

Background: The restyled 1963 Newport convertible was a very attractive automobile. It was powered by a 265 h.p. 361 cu. in. V8 engine. It was available with the standard floor-mounted three-speed manual or with optional Torque Flite automatic transmission. The vast majority of buyers chose the automatic; less than four percent of all 1963 Chryslers had manual transmissions.

Most 1963 Chryslers, 96.4%, came with power steering, 68.1% had power brakes, 63.3% had tinted glass, 25.7% had power windows, 16.6% had power seats, 73.2% had radios, and 26% were sold with air conditioning.

1963 Chrysler Newport Convertible

1963 Dodge Custom 880 Convertible

Original Price: $3,251
Number Produced: N.A.
Estimated Number Existing in 1979: N.A.
Miles per Gallon: 11–16
Common Trouble Spots: brakes
Availability of Parts: fair
Investment Potential: A+

Background: The new 880 convertible looked like a mildly customized version of the previous year's model. Buyers had a choice of either vinyl or 100 percent nylon interior.

It was powered by a 265 h.p. 361 cu. in. V8. A 305 h.p. 383 cu. in. "power pack" V8 was available at extra cost. A three-speed manual transmission was standard. Torque Flite Eight automatic was optional.

Most 1963 880s, 99%, were equipped with the automatic, 95% had power steering, 63.3% had power brakes, 72.3% had tinted glass, 70.4% had radios, 23.6% had power windows, 6.8% had power front seats, and 20% were sold with air conditioning.

1963 Dodge Dart GT Convertible

Original Price: $2,512
Number Produced: N.A.
Estimated Number Existing in 1979: N.A.
Miles per Gallon: 15–23
Common Trouble Spots: none
Availability of Parts: fair
Investment Potential: A+

Background: The Dart GT was a fancy version of the Dart 270 that featured special trim and bucket seats. It was powered by a 101 h.p. 170 cu. in. slant six. A 145 h.p. 225 cu. in. slant six was available at extra cost. A three-speed manual transmission was standard. Torque Flite automatic transmission was a popular option.

At least one Dart dealer in '63 offered fur-lined seat belts. They could be had in chinchilla ($200), mink ($100), or ocelot ($70).

1963 Dodge Dart GT Convertible

1963 Dodge Dart 270 Convertible

1963 Dodge Dart 270 Convertible

Original Price: $2,385
Number Produced: N.A.
Estimated Number Existing in 1979: N.A.
Miles per Gallon: 15–23
Common Trouble Spots: none
Availability of Parts: fair
Investment Potential: A

Background: The compact Dart 270 ragtop was the first Dodge in years to come with a six-cylinder engine. Besides the 101 h.p. 170 cu. in. slant six, buyers could order a 145 h.p. 225 cu. in. slant six. Both engines had one-barrel carburetors. A three-speed manual transmission was standard. Push button Torque Flite automatic transmission was optional.

Most 1963 Darts, 70%, were equipped with the automatic, 16.6% had power steering, 30% had tinted glass, 42.1% had radios, 1.9% had power windows, and 1.8% were sold with an air conditioner.

1963 Dodge Polara Convertible

Original Price: $3,196
Number Produced: N.A.
Estimated Number Existing in 1979: N.A.
Miles per Gallon: 11–15
Common Trouble Spots: brakes
Availability of Parts: fair
Investment Potential: A+

Background: The '63 Polara softtop was powered by a 230 h.p. 318 cu. in. V8. Other V8 engines were available, including a 305 h.p. 383 (which was standard with the optional 500 power and trim package), a 330 h.p. 383, a 415 h.p. 426, and a 425 h.p. 426 (the 426 was considered a 1963½ engine). A three-speed manual transmission was standard. Torque Flite Eight automatic and a four-speed manual were optional.

Most 1963 Dodges, 82.8%, came equipped with an automatic, 58.8% had power steering, 63.3% had power brakes, 40.9% had tinted glass, 49.8% had radios, 9.5% had power windows, .6% had power front seats, and 9.5% were sold with air conditioning.

1963 Ford Falcon Futura Convertible

PHOTO: FORD MOTOR COMPANY

1963 Ford Falcon Futura Convertible

Original Price: $2,470
Number Produced: 31,192
Estimated Number Existing in 1979: 1,696
Miles per Gallon: 15–24
Common Trouble Spots: electrical system
Availability of Parts: good–fair
Investment Potential: A+

Background: The new Futura ragtop was available with optional bucket seats and center console. It had a power-operated top. The Futura was powered by a 85 h.p. 144 cu. in. six-cylinder engine. A 101 h.p. 170 cu. in. six was optional. A three-speed manual transmission was standard, and Ford-O-Matic automatic and a floor-mounted four-speed manual were offered at extra cost.

Just over 50% of all 1963 Falcons came with the automatic, 4.7% had power windows, 51.4% had radios, 23.3% had tinted glass, and 1.7% were equipped with an air conditioner. Most Futura convertibles, 64.6%, had bucket seats.

1963 Ford Falcon Sprint Convertible

Original Price: $2,837
Number Produced: 4,602
Estimated Number Existing in 1979: 250
Miles per Gallon: 13–20
Common Trouble Spots: electrical system
Availability of Parts: good–fair
Investment Potential: AA

Background: The most desirable Falcon in 1963 was the top-of-the-line Sprint convertible. It was powered by a 164 h.p. 260 cu. in. V8. A three-speed manual transmission was standard; Ford-O-Matic automatic and a floor-mounted four-speed manual were optional. In August of 1963, Bendix-Dunlop disc brakes were made a $198 option.

1963 Ford Falcon Sprint Convertible

PHOTO: FORD MOTOR COMPANY

1963 Ford Galaxie 500 Convertible

Original Price: $2,924
Number Produced: 36,876
Estimated Number Existing in 1979: 2,006
Miles per Gallon: 10–18
Common Trouble Spots: piston rings
Availability of Parts: good–fair
Investment Potential: A+

Background: The Galaxie 500 was powered by a 138 h.p. 223 cu. in. six-cylinder engine. A few V8 engines were available, including a 164 h.p. 260, a 220 h.p. 352, a 300 h.p. 390, a 410 h.p. 427, and a 425 h.p. 427. A three-speed manual transmission was standard. Overdrive, a four-speed manual and Cruise-O-Matic automatic transmission were optional.

Most 1963 Galaxies, 90.5%, came with a V8, 78% had the automatic, 2.5% had overdrive, 57.7% had power steering, 16% had power brakes, 11.8% had power windows, 1.7% had power front seats, 1.2% had "swing away" steering wheels, 34% had tinted glass, and 11.4% were equipped with an air conditioner.

1963 Ford Galaxie 500 Convertible

PHOTO: FORD MOTOR COMPANY

1963 Ford Galaxie 500 XL Convertible

Original Price: $3,518
Number Produced: 18,551
Estimated Number Existing in 1979: 1,009
Miles per Gallon: 9–16
Common Trouble Spots: piston rings
Availability of Parts: good–fair
Investment Potential: AA+

Background: The sporty Galaxie 500 XL received a minor face-lift for 1963. Early models came with a 220 h.p. 352 cu. in. V8. The new Challenger 195 h.p. 289 cu. in. V8 was standard on later ones. Other V8 engines available were a 300 h.p. 390, a 330 h.p. 390, a

1963 Ford Galaxie 500 XL Convertible

410 h.p. 427, and a 425 h.p. 427. Cruise-O-Matic automatic transmission was standard. A three-speed manual, a four-speed manual, and overdrive were optional.

The 1963 500 XL is the most popular Galaxie XL.

1963 Ford Thunderbird Convertible

Original Price: $4,912
Number Produced: 5,457
Estimated Number Existing in 1979: 296
Miles per Gallon: 8–14
Common Trouble Spots: none
Availability of Parts: fair
Investment Potential: AA+

Background: Outside of a few minor changes to the grille and trim (and the addition of about 140 pounds of sound-deadening materials), the 1963 T-Bird ragtop was much the same as the 1962 model. It came with a 300 h.p. 390 cu. in. V8. Optional at extra cost was a 340 h.p. version of this engine. Cruise-O-Matic automatic transmission, power steering, and power brakes were standard.

Most 1963 T-Birds, 70.9%, had power windows, 69.7% had tinted glass, 52.4% had power seats, and 43.5% had air conditioning.

1963 Ford Thunderbird Convertible

1963 Ford Thunderbird Sports Roadster

Original Price: $5,563
Number Produced: 455
Estimated Number Existing in 1979: 50
Miles per Gallon: 8–14
Common Trouble Spots: none
Availability of Parts: fair
Investment Potential: AAA

Background: This was the last year for the Sports Roadster as a separate series. As before, it came with a removable tonneau which covered the rear seat, special insignia, chrome wire wheels, and a passenger assist bar.

It was powered by a 300 h.p. 390 cu. in. V8. A 340 h.p. version of this engine was optional. Cruise-O-Matic automatic transmission, power steering, and power brakes were standard. Buyers had their choice of a black, blue, or white top.

The 1963 Sports Roadster is a rare and beautiful convertible.

1963 Ford Thunderbird Sports Roadster

PHOTO: FORD MOTOR COMPANY

1963 Imperial Crown Convertible

Original Price: $5,782
Number Produced: 531
Estimated Number Existing in 1979: 31
Miles per Gallon: 8–15
Common Trouble Spots: none
Availability of Parts: poor–fair
Investment Potential: AA+

Background: Although the free-standing headlights remained, the 1963 Imperial was obviously a more refined (or watered-down) version of the 1962.

An improved 340 h.p. 413 cu. in. engine with a four-barrel carburetor powered the Imperial. Torque Flite automatic transmission was standard.

Buyers had a choice of sixteen solid colors and twenty-one upholstery combinations. These included leather and cloth, vinyl and cloth, and all leather. For just under $100, they could buy an "Auto-Pilot" control. This allowed the driver to set the control at

1963 Imperial Crown Convertible

PHOTO: CHRYSLER HISTORICAL COLLECTION

any speed from 40 to 85. The unit would be disengaged when the driver put on the brakes.

All Imperials came equipped with power brakes, power steering, power windows, and remote control outside mirror. Almost 65% had air conditioning, and over 90% had tinted glass.

1963 King Midget Convertible

Original Price: est. $700
Number Produced: 156
Estimated Number Existing in 1979: 10
Miles per Gallon: 50–90
Common Trouble Spots: transmission, "V" belts
Availability of Parts: good
Investment Potential: A

Background: The '63 King Midget convertible was powered by a 10 h.p. 29 cu. in. one-cylinder engine. Automatic transmission was standard.

1963 Lincoln Continental Convertible

Original Price: $6,916
Number Produced: 3,138
Estimated Number Existing in 1979: 300
Miles per Gallon: 9–14
Common Trouble Spots: top mechanism
Availability of Parts: fair
Investment Potential: AAA

Background: The Continental four-door convertible was as beautiful as ever in 1963. It was available in eighteen colors. Buyers had a choice of a black, blue, or white top.

A 320 h.p. 430 cu. in. V8 engine powered the Continental. Turbo-Drive automatic transmission was standard. The engine and transmission were thoroughly tested and broken in before, and after, being installed.

All 1963 Continentals came with power steering, power brakes, electric windows, power seats, and radios. Most, 95.5%, had tinted glass, and 79.5% were sold with air conditioning.

1963 Lincoln Continental Convertible

PHOTO: FORD MOTOR COMPANY

1963 Mercury Comet Custom Convertible

Original Price: $2,557
Number Produced: 7,354
Estimated Number Existing in 1979: 379
Miles per Gallon: 15–23
Common Trouble Spots: none
Availability of Parts: fair
Investment Potential: A

Background: This was the first year for the Comet Custom convertible. Its resemblance to the '59 Edsel is not just a coincidence; the Comet was originally planned as an Edsel.

It came with an 85 h.p. 144.3 cu. in. six. A 101 h.p. 170 cu. in. six was available at extra cost. A three-speed manual transmission was standard. Merc-O-Matic automatic and a four-speed manual were optional.

Most 1963 Comets, 64.3%, were equipped with the automatic, 7.4% had power steering, 34% had tinted glass, 2.4% had power windows, 50.3% had radios, and 2% were sold with air conditioning.

1963 Mercury Comet S-22 Convertible

Original Price: $2,710
Number Produced: 5,757
Estimated Number Existing in 1979: 297
Miles per Gallon: 14–23
Common Trouble Spots: none
Availability of Parts: fair
Investment Potential: AA

Background: The sporty S-22 ragtop came with bucket seats and a center console. It was powered by an 85 h.p. 144.3 cu. in. six. A 101 h.p. 170 cu. in. six was optional. Later in the model year, a 1963½ S-22 was introduced. It was available with a 170 cu. in. six or a 260 cu. in. V8. A three-speed manual was standard. Merc-O-Matic automatic and a four-speed manual transmission were optional.

1963 Mercury Comet S-22 Convertible

PHOTO: FORD MOTOR COMPANY

1963 Mercury Monterey Custom Convertible

PHOTO: FORD MOTOR COMPANY

1963 Mercury Monterey Custom Convertible

Original Price: $3,333
Number Produced: 3,783
Estimated Number Existing in 1979: 195
Miles per Gallon: 9–16
Common Trouble Spots: none
Availability of Parts: fair
Investment Potential: A

Background: The new Monterey convertible looked more like the 1961 model than the '62. It came with a 250 h.p. 390 cu. in. V8. Four other V8 engines were available: a 300 h.p. 390, a 330 h.p. 390, a 385 h.p. 406, and a 405 h.p. 406. A three-speed manual transmission was standard. Multi-Drive automatic and a four-speed manual were optional.

Most 1963 Mercurys, 96.6%, were equipped with the automatic, 89.8% had power steering, 62% had power brakes, three percent had a tilting steering wheel, 9.7% had power windows, 17% had power front seats, 77% had radios, 64% had tinted glass, and 20% were sold with air conditioners.

1963 Mercury Monterey S-55 Convertible

Original Price: $3,900
Number Produced: 1,379
Estimated Number Existing in 1979: 70
Miles per Gallon: 9–16
Common Trouble Spots: none
Availability of Parts: fair
Investment Potential: A+

Background: The sporty '63 Monterey S-55 ragtop came with a 250 h.p. 390 cu. in. V8. Four other V8 engines were available: a 300 h.p. 390, a 330 h.p. 390, a 385 h.p. 406, and a 405 h.p. 406. A three-speed manual transmission was standard. Multi-Drive automatic and a four-speed manual were optional. The four-speed manual was the only transmission offered with either of the "Marauder" 406 V8s.

An unusual option available on Mercurys in 1963 was a Citizens Band (CB) radio.

1963 Oldsmobile Dynamic 88 Convertible

Original Price: $3,379
Number Produced: 12,551
Estimated Number Existing in 1979: 503
Miles per Gallon: 10–16
Common Trouble Spots: brakes
Availability of Parts: good–fair
Investment Potential: A+

Background: The new Dynamic 88 was Oldsmobile's lowest-priced full-size convertible in 1963. However, it looked much the same as the higher-priced Olds.

It was powered by a 280 h.p. 394 cu. in. V8. A 260 h.p. and a 330 h.p. version of this engine were available at extra cost. A three-speed manual transmission was standard, but not very popular; most 1963 Oldsmobiles, 99.5%, were equipped with Hydra-Matic automatic transmission.

1963 Oldsmobile F-85 Cutlass Convertible

Original Price: $2,971
Number Produced: 12,149
Estimated Number Existing in 1979: 486
Miles per Gallon: 12–19
Common Trouble Spots: automatic transmission, carburetor
Availability of Parts: good–fair
Investment Potential: A+

Background: The new F-85 looked a bit more like the full-size Olds than last year's model had. It was powered by a 185 h.p. 215 cu. in. V8. A 195 h.p. version of this engine, with four-barrel carburetor, was available at extra cost. A three-speed manual transmission was standard. Hydra-Matic automatic and a four-speed manual transmission were optional.

Most F-85s, 88.6%, came with the automatic, 58.1% had power steering, 21.1% had power brakes, 62.3% had tinted glass, 3% had power windows, 3.3% had power front seats, 86.5% had a radio, and 10.8% were ordered with an air conditioner.

Buyers had their choice of fifteen exterior colors.

1963 Oldsmobile F-85 Cutlass Convertible

PHOTO: OLDSMOBILE DIVISION

1963 Oldsmobile 98 Convertible

PHOTO: OLDSMOBILE DIVISION

1963 Oldsmobile 98 Convertible

Original Price: $4,457
Number Produced: 4,267
Estimated Number Existing in 1979: 170
Miles per Gallon: 9–15
Common Trouble Spots: brakes
Availability of Parts: good–fair
Investment Potential: A+

Background: The new 98 convertible was powered by a 330 h.p. 394 cu. in. V8 engine. Hydra-Matic automatic transmission was standard.

A "Tilt-Away" steering wheel was optional on Olds equipped with power steering. Although 98.5% of all 1963 Oldsmobiles came with power steering, only 15.9% had the tilting steering wheel. Twenty-six percent had power windows, 27.2% had power front seats, 79.3% had tinted glass, and 35% were sold with air conditioning.

1963 Oldsmobile Starfire Convertible

Original Price: $4,742
Number Produced: 4,401
Estimated Number Existing in 1979: 176
Miles per Gallon: 10–15
Common Trouble Spots: brakes
Availability of Parts: good–fair
Investment Potential: AA

Background: The sporty big 1963 Starfire ragtop was powered by a 345 h.p. 394 cu. in. V8. Hydra-Matic automatic transmission was standard. Although not exactly a head-turner, the Starfire convertible was Oldsmobile's flashiest car of the year.

1963 Oldsmobile Starfire Convertible

PHOTO: OLDSMOBILE DIVISION

1963 Plymouth Fury Convertible

Original Price: $2,924
Number Produced: N.A.
Estimated Number Existing in 1979: N.A.
Miles per Gallon: 10–17
Common Trouble Spots: brakes
Availability of Parts: fair
Investment Potential: A

Background: The new Fury received a pleasing face-lift for 1963. It was powered by a 230 h.p. 318 cu. in. V8. Three other V8 engines were available at extra cost: a 265 h.p. 361, a 330 h.p. 383, and a 365 h.p. 426 cu. in. Super Stock.

A three-speed manual was standard. A four-speed manual and Torque Flite automatic transmission were optional.

Most 1963 Plymouths, 76.1 percent, were equipped with the automatic transmission, 50.9% had power steering, 12.8% had power brakes, 32.2% had tinted glass, 8.7% had electric windows, .5% had power front seats, and 8.1% were sold with air conditioning.

1963 Plymouth Sport Fury Convertible

Original Price: $3,082
Number Produced: N.A.
Estimated Number Existing in 1979: N.A.
Miles per Gallon: 10–17
Common Trouble Spots: brakes
Availability of Parts: fair
Investment Potential: A+

Background: The Sport Fury convertible was Plymouth's top-of-the-line car for 1963. It came with a 230 h.p. 318 cu. in. V8. Three other V8s were available at extra cost: a 265 h.p. 361, a 330 h.p. 383, and, late in the model year, the famous 365 h.p. 426 cu. in. Super Stock.

A three-speed manual transmission was standard. A four-speed manual and Torque Flite Eight automatic transmission were optional.

1963 Plymouth Valiant Signet 200 Convertible

Original Price: $2,454
Number Produced: N.A.
Estimated Number Existing in 1979: N.A.
Miles per Gallon: 15–25
Common Trouble Spots: none
Availability of Parts: fair
Investment Potential: A+

Background: For $114 more than the price of the V 200 convertible, Valiant buyers could purchase the Signet 200. It came with a 101 h.p. 170 cu. in. six-cylinder engine. A 145 h.p. 225 cu. in. six-cylinder engine was optional. A three-speed manual transmission was standard. Torque Flite Six automatic transmission was optional.

1963 Plymouth Valiant V200 Convertible

1963 Plymouth Valiant V 200 Convertible

Original Price: $2,340
Number Produced: N.A.
Estimated Number Existing in 1979: N.A.
Miles per Gallon: 15–25
Common Trouble Spots: none
Availability of Parts: fair
Investment Potential: A+

Background: This was the first year the Valiant was offered in a convertible body style. The Valiant V 200 was powered by a 101 h.p. 170 cu. in. six-cylinder engine. A 145 h.p. 225 cu. in. six-cylinder engine was optional.

A three-speed manual transmission was standard (the early manuals differed somewhat from those installed on the later 1963 V 200s). Torque Flite Six automatic transmission was available at extra cost.

Most 1963 Valiants, 64%, were equipped with the automatic, 10.3% had power steering, 19.8% had tinted glass, 38.3% had radios, 1.9% had electric windows, and 1.6% were sold with air conditioning.

The 1963 Valiant V 200 is an attractive and economical little car.

1963 Pontiac Bonneville Convertible

Original Price: $3,568
Number Produced: 23,459
Estimated Number Existing in 1979: 1,119
Miles per Gallon: 9–16
Common Trouble Spots: automatic transmission, carburetor
Availability of Parts: fair–good
Investment Potential: A+

Background: The attractive new Bonneville convertible was powered by a 235 h.p. 389 cu. in. V8. Three other versions of this engine were available at extra cost: a 230 h.p., a 303 h.p., and a 313 h.p. Later in the model year, a Tri-Power package, featuring a 421 cu. in. V8, was offered.

A three-speed manual transmission was standard, but not very popular. Hydra-Matic automatic and a four-speed manual were optional.

1963 Pontiac Catalina Convertible

Original Price: $3,171
Number Produced: 18,249
Estimated Number Existing in 1979: 868
Miles per Gallon: 9–17
Common Trouble Spots: automatic transmission, carburetor
Availability of Parts: fair–good
Investment Potential: A+

Background: This was the first year for the vertical quad headlights that would become a Pontiac trademark for the next few years.

The Catalina was powered by a 215 h.p. 389 cu. in. V8. Five other versions of this engine were available at extra cost: a 235 h.p., a 303 h.p., a 230 h.p., a 267 h.p., and a 313 h.p. Later in the model year, a Tri-Power package, featuring a 421 cu. in. V8, was offered. A three-speed manual transmission was standard. Hydra-Matic automatic and a four-speed manual were also offered.

Most full-size '63 Pontiacs, 95%, were equipped with the automatic, 90.5% had power steering, 81.4% had power brakes, less than 1% had a tilting steering wheel, 64.7% had tinted glass, 18.7% had power windows, 7% had power front seats, and 24.5% were sold with an air conditioner.

1963 Pontiac Catalina Convertible

PHOTO: PONTIAC MOTOR DIVISION

1963 Pontiac Bonneville Convertible

PHOTO: PONTIAC MOTOR DIVISION

1963 Pontiac Le Mans Convertible

Original Price: $2,742
Number Produced: 15,957
Estimated Number Existing in 1979: 759
Miles per Gallon: 12–22
Common Trouble Spots: carburetor
Availability of Parts: fair–good
Investment Potential: A+

Background: The Le Mans came with a 115 h.p. 194.5 cu. in. four-cylinder engine. Three other versions of this engine, a 120 h.p., a 140 h.p., and a 166 h.p., plus a 260 h.p. 326 cu. in. V8, were available at extra cost. Over 40% of Le Mans convertibles were sold with the V8. A three-speed manual transmission was standard. Tempes Torque automatic and a four-speed manual transmission were optional.

1963 Pontiac Le Mans Convertible

PHOTO: PONTIAC MOTOR DIVISION

1963 Pontiac Tempest Deluxe Convertible

Original Price: $2,564
Number Produced: 5,012
Estimated Number Existing in 1979: 238
Miles per Gallon: 12–22
Common Trouble Spots: carburetor
Availability of Parts: fair–good
Investment Potential: A

Background: The Tempest Deluxe was powered by a 115 h.p. 194.5 cu. in. four-cylinder engine. Three other versions of this engine, a 120 h.p., a 140 h.p., and a 166 h.p., plus a 260 h.p. 326 cu. in V8, were available at extra cost. A three-speed manual transmission was standard. Tempes Torque automatic and a four-speed manual were optional.

Most 1963 Tempests, 73.6%, came with an automatic, 38.2% had the V8, 19.7% had power steering, 3.1% had power brakes, 40.7% had tinted glass, 2.6% had power windows, and 5% were sold with an air conditioner. "Idiot lights" were standard, but buyers could order the optional gauge kit.

1963 Rambler American Convertible

Original Price: $2,344
Number Produced: 4,750
Estimated Number Existing in 1979: 190
Miles per Gallon: 15–25
Common Trouble Spots: none
Availability of Parts: fair–poor
Investment Potential: A

Background: The 1963 American convertible was powered by a 125 h.p. 195.6 cu. in. six-cylinder engine. A 138 h.p. version of this engine was optional. A three-speed manual transmission was standard. Overdrive and Flash-O-Matic automatic transmission were available at extra cost.

Most '63 Ramblers, 57.4%, came equipped with the automatic, 30.2% had the three-speed manual, 12.4% had overdrive, 18.3% had power steering, 8.1% had power brakes, 25.2% had tinted glass, .5% had power windows, 34.2% had radios, and 8.2% were sold with air conditioning.

1963 Rambler American Convertible

PHOTO: LARRY G. MITCHELL

1963 Studebaker Avanti

PHOTO: RICHARD QUINN COLLECTION, STUDEBAKER DRIVERS CLUB

1963 Studebaker Avanti

Original Price: $4,445
Number Produced: 3,744
Estimated Number Existing in 1979: 1,500
Miles per Gallon: 12–18
Common Trouble Spots: none
Availability of Parts: fair–good
Investment Potential: AAA+

Background: This was the car that was meant to save the Studebaker-Packard Corporation (there was some consideration given to calling it "Packard"). The beautiful Avanti was conceived, designed, and put into production in record time.

The Avanti was introduced in July 1962 as a 1963 model. It came with a 225 h.p. 289 cu. in. V8. Also available was a 240 h.p. 289, and for $210 a hotter 300 h.p. Supercharged version of this engine. A three-speed floor-mounted transmission was standard. Power-Shift automatic ($210) and a four-speed manual ($182.30) were optional. Seat belts could be had for $9.75.

In July of 1962, *Car Life* said of the Avanti, "When Studebaker called the Hawk the Gran Turismo, it gave the right name to the wrong car. If ever we saw one, the Avanti is a Gran Turismo in the fullest sense of the term."

Just over two dozen people received free '63 Avantis; from October to December 1962, Studebaker held a "Drive of the Future" contest, and twenty-five Avantis were offered as prizes.

1963 Studebaker Gran Turismo Hawk

Original Price: $3,095
Number Produced: 3,649
Estimated Number Existing in 1979: 163
Miles per Gallon: 14–21
Common Trouble Spots: none
Availability of Parts: fair–poor
Investment Potential: AA+

Background: "Classic styling . . . timeless elegance" is how Studebaker literature described the new GT Hawk. It came with a 210 h.p. 289 cu. in. V8 engine. A 305 h.p. 304.5 cu. in. V8 and three hotter versions of the 289 cu. in. V8 engine were available: a 225 h.p., a 240 h.p. R-1, and a 290 h.p. R-2 Supercharged. A three-speed manual transmission was standard. Overdrive, a four-speed manual transmission and two automatics, Flightomatic and Borg-Warner AS2-10, were available (the Warner was optional on the 304.5 cu. in. V8).

1963 Studebaker Gran Turismo Hawk

In mid–model year a 160 mph speedometer replaced the 120 mph unit. For $581.70 buyers could order the "Super" package. It featured the R-2 engine, tachometer, rear anti-roll bar, power disc brakes, and a heavy-duty suspension.

1963 Studebaker Lark Daytona Convertible

Original Price: $2,679
Number Produced: 773
Estimated Number Existing in 1979: 34
Miles per Gallon: 13–20
Common Trouble Spots: none
Availability of Parts: fair
Investment Potential: AA (with "Super" option); A+ (without)

Background: September 27, 1962, was the first day 1963 Larks were made available to the public. Buyers of the new Daytona convertible had their choice of several engines—a 112 h.p. 169.6 cu. in. six-cylinder and the following V8s: a 180 h.p. 259.2, a 195 h.p. 259.2, a 210 h.p. 289, a 225 h.p. 289, a 240 h.p. Jet Thrust 289, and a 290 h.p. Jet Thrust Supercharged 289.

A three-speed manual transmission was standard. Overdrive, a four-speed manual, and Flightomatic automatic transmission were optional.

Most 1963 Studebakers, 52%, were equipped with a V8 engine, 57.4% had the automatic, 30.1% had a manual, 12.5% had a manual with overdrive, 17.7% had power steering, 14.4% had power brakes, 18.3% had tinted glass, 4% had power windows, 29.6% had radios, and 3.2% were sold with air conditioning.

In mid-year a "Super" performance option was offered. It featured heavy-duty suspension, bucket seats, disc brakes, and special emblem.

1963 Studebaker Lark Daytona Convertible

PHOTO: RICHARD QUINN COLLECTION, STUDEBAKER DRIVERS CLUB

1964

1964 Buick Electra 225 Convertible

Original Price: $4,364
Number Produced: 7,181
Estimated Number Existing in 1979: 423
Miles per Gallon: 11–15
Common Trouble Spots: none
Availability of Parts: good–fair
Investment Potential: A

Background: The Electra convertible received a pleasing face-lift for 1964. It didn't look quite as dull as the previous year's model.

The Electra came equipped with a 325 h.p. 401 cu. in. V8. Two 425 cu. in. V8s, rated at 340 h.p. and 360 h.p., were available. Super Turbine 400 automatic transmission, power steering, power brakes, and power windows were standard.

1964 Buick LeSabre Convertible

Original Price: $3,304
Number Produced: 6,685
Estimated Number Existing in 1979: 394
Miles per Gallon: 12–17
Common Trouble Spots: brakes
Availability of Parts: good–fair
Investment Potential: A+

Background: A different grille treatment and side trim made the LeSabre easily distinguishable from the Wildcat. It also was, and looked, lighter, and therefore sportier.

The LeSabre came equipped with a 210 h.p. 300 cu. in. V8. Buyers could also order a 250 h.p. version of this engine. A three-speed manual transmission was standard. Super Turbine 300 automatic transmission was optional.

Most full-size 1964 Buicks, 99.2%, came with an automatic, 97.8% had power steering, 89.9% had power brakes, 88.5% had tinted glass, 13.4% had a tilting steering wheel, 22.9% had power windows, 23.1% had power front seats, and 37.1% were sold with air conditioning.

1964 Buick LeSabre Convertible

1964 Buick Riviera Sport Coupe

Original Price: $4,374
Number Produced: 37,658
Estimated Number Existing in 1979: 2,221
Miles per Gallon: 11–15
Common Trouble Spots: none
Availability of Parts: good
Investment Potential: AA+

Background: The new Riviera was basically the same as the 1963. It was powered by a 340 h.p. 425 cu. in. V8. A 360 h.p. version of this engine was optional. Super Turbine 400 automatic transmission was standard.

1964 Buick Skylark Convertible

Original Price: $2,823
Number Produced: 10,225
Estimated Number Existing in 1979: 603
Miles per Gallon: 13–20
Common Trouble Spots: none
Availability of Parts: good–fair
Investment Potential: AA

Background: The new Skylark looked a lot like a shrunken LeSabre. It was powered by a 155 h.p. 225 cu. in. V6. Two 300 cu. in. V8s, rated at 210 h.p. and 250 h.p., were available at extra cost. A three-speed manual transmission was standard. Super Turbine 300 automatic and a four-speed manual were optional. Other options included power steering, power brakes, and bucket seats.

1964 Buick Special Convertible

Original Price: $2,594
Number Produced: 6,308
Estimated Number Existing in 1979: 372
Miles per Gallon: 15–20
Common Trouble Spots: none
Availability of Parts: good–fair
Investment Potential: A

Background: The Special ragtop received a new chassis and a pleasing face-lift for 1964. It was powered by a 155 h.p. 255 cu. in. V6 engine. Two 300 cu. in. V8s, rated at 210 h.p. and 250 h.p., were also available. A three-speed manual transmission was standard. Super Turbine 300 automatic and a four-speed manual were optional.

Most 1964 Specials, 64.4%, came with a V8, 88.6% had an automatic, 9.6% had a three-speed manual, 1.8% had a four-speed manual, 62% had power steering, 22.3% had power brakes, 63.6% had tinted glass, 1.5% had a tilting steering wheel, 3.2% had power windows, 2.7% had power front seats, 87.1% had radios, and 17.3% were sold with air conditioning.

1964 Buick Wildcat Convertible

Original Price: $3,445
Number Produced: 7,850
Estimated Number Existing in 1979: 463
Miles per Gallon: 10–15
Common Trouble Spots: none
Availability of Parts: good–fair
Investment Potential: A+

Background: The new Wildcat convertible looked a lot like last year's model. It was powered by a 325 h.p. 401 cu. in. V8. Two 425 cu. in. V8s, rated at 340 h.p. and 360 h.p., were available at extra cost. A three-speed

1964 Buick Wildcat Convertible

manual transmission was standard. Super Turbine 400 automatic and a four-speed manual were optional. Other options included power steering, power brakes, and bucket seats.

1964 Cadillac Fleetwood Eldorado Biarritz Convertible

Original Price: $6,608
Number Produced: 1,870
Estimated Number Existing in 1979: 235
Miles per Gallon: 10–16
Common Trouble Spots: none
Availability of Parts: good–fair
Investment Potential: AA+

Background: The Eldorado received an attractive but minor face-lift for 1964. It came with a 340 h.p. 429 cu. in. V8 engine. Turbo Hydramatic automatic transmission, power steering, electric windows, and power brakes were standard.

The optional air conditioner was equipped with an electric comfort control thermostat; all the driver had to do was set the temperature he or she desired. The air conditioner could supply warm air as well as cold.

1964 Cadillac Eldorado Biarritz Convertible

PHOTO: CADILLAC MOTOR CAR DIVISION

1964 Cadillac De Ville Convertible

PHOTO: CADILLAC MOTOR CAR DIVISION

1964 Cadillac De Ville Convertible

Original Price: $5,590
Number Produced: 17,900
Estimated Number Existing in 1979: 2,255
Miles per Gallon: 10–16
Common Trouble Spots: none
Availability of Parts: good–fair
Investment Potential: AA

Background: The 1964 De Ville convertible was one of the most attractive Cadillacs made in the 1960s. It was powered by a 340 h.p. 429 cu. in. V8 engine. A modified Hydramatic automatic transmission, power steering, electric windows, and power brakes were standard. One of the most interesting options offered in '64 was a device that turned the car's lights on at dusk, and shut them off at dawn.

1964 Chevrolet Chevelle Malibu Convertible

Original Price: $2,576
Number Produced: 23,158
Estimated Number Existing in 1979: 2,547
Miles per Gallon: 11–20
Common Trouble Spots: carburetor, electrical system, automatic transmission
Availability of Parts: good
Investment Potential: AA+ (with Super Sport option); AA (without)

Background: This was the first year for the Chevelle convertible. It came with a 120 h.p. 194 cu. in. six-cylinder engine. Also available was a 155 h.p. 230 cu. in. six and several V8s: a 195 h.p. 283, a 220 h.p. 283, a 250 h.p. 327, a 300 h.p. 327, and a 365 h.p. 327. A three-speed manual transmission was standard. Overdrive, a four-speed manual, and Powerglide automatic transmission were optional.

A Super Sport package, featuring special trim, bucket seats, and a console mounted shifting lever, was available at extra cost.

Most 1964 Chevelles, 59.7%, came equipped with a V8, 65.1% had an automatic, 25.3% had a three-speed manual, 8.2% had a four-speed manual, 30.1% had power steering, 10.9% had power brakes, 1% had a tilting steering wheel, 49.6% had tinted glass, 57% had radios, 5.4% had power windows, .2% had power front seats, and 8.9% had air conditioning.

1964 Chevrolet Corvair Monza Convertible

Original Price: $2,481
Number Produced: 35,806
Estimated Number Existing in 1979: 3,938
Miles per Gallon: 16–27
Common Trouble Spots: valves
Availability of Parts: good
Investment Potential: AA (with Spyder package); A+ (without)

Background: The Monza ragtop received a minor face-lift for 1964. It was powered by a 95 h.p. 164 cu. in. six. A 110 h.p. and a 150 h.p. Turbocharged 164 cu. in. six were optional. A three-speed manual transmission was standard. Powerglide automatic and a four-speed manual were available at extra cost.

The Spyder performance and trim package was optional. All Spyders came with the Turbo 150 h.p. 164 cu. in. six. A total of 4,761 Corvairs were sold with this option.

Most '64 Corvairs, 57.8%, came equipped with radios, 47% had the automatic, 13.5% had the three-speed manual, 39.5% had the four-speed manual, 47.8% had tinted glass, and 3.1% had air conditioners.

1964 Chevrolet Corvair Monza Spyder Convertible

PHOTO: GM PHOTOGRAPHIC

1964 Chevrolet Chevelle Convertible

1964 Chevrolet Corvette Stingray Convertible

Original Price: $4,037
Number Produced: 13,925
Estimated Number Existing in 1979: 1,531
Miles per Gallon: 12–16
Common Trouble Spots: none
Availability of Parts: good
Investment Potential: AAA

Background: The new Corvette was powered by a 250 h.p. 327 cu. in. V8. Other versions of this engine, a 300 h.p. (with four-barrel carburetor), a 365 h.p. (with four-barrel carburetor), and a 375 h.p. (with fuel injection), were available at extra cost. A three-speed manual transmission was standard, but not very popular; most 1964 Vettes, 85.7%, came with the optional four-speed manual. Just over 11% came with Powerglide automatic transmission.

Nearly 9% of new Vettes were equipped with an air conditioner, 14% had power steering, 10% had power brakes, and 16.6% were sold with power windows. Slightly over half of all Corvette convertible buyers purchased the detachable hard top.

Road & Track called the '64 Vette's optional power steering "one of the best we have ever encountered."

1964 Chevrolet Corvette Convertible

PHOTO: GM PHOTOGRAPHIC

1964 Chevrolet Corvette Stingray Sport Coupe

Original Price: $4,252
Number Produced: 8,304
Estimated Number Existing in 1979: 1 500
Miles per Gallon: 12–16
Common Trouble Spots: none
Availability of Parts: good
Investment Potential: AAA+ (with fuel injection); AAA (without)

Background: The new Stingray coupe looked basically the same as last year's model, except that it didn't have a split rear window.

It was powered by a 250 h.p. 327 cu. in. V8. Other versions of this engine, a 300 h.p. (with four-barrel carburetor), a 365 h.p. (with four-barrel carburetor), a 375 h.p. (with fuel injection), were available at extra cost. A three-speed manual transmission was standard, but only 3.2% of all '64 Vettes had it; the vast majority came with the optional four-speed manual. Just 11.1% were equipped with Powerglide automatic transmission.

1964 Chevrolet Corvette Stingray Sport Coupe

PHOTO: T. MICHAELIS CORVETTE SUPPLIES

1964 Chevrolet Impala Convertible

Original Price: $3,024
Number Produced: 81,897
Estimated Number Existing in 1979: 9,008
Miles per Gallon: 10–18
Common Trouble Spots: automatic transmission
Availability of Parts: good
Investment Potential: AA+ (with Super Sport option); AA (without)

Background: The '64 Impala convertible came with a

1964 Chevrolet Impala Convertible

PHOTO: CHEVROLET MOTOR DIVISION

140 h.p. 230 cu. in. six. Buyers could choose from several V8 engines at extra cost: a 195 h.p. 283, a 250 h.p. 327, a 300 h.p. 327, a 340 h.p. 409, a 400 h.p. 409, and a 425 h.p. 409. A three-speed manual transmission was standard. Overdrive, a four-speed manual transmission, and Powerglide automatic were optional.

The Super Sport package was again offered in 1964.

Most '64 full-size Chevrolets, 76%, came equipped with a V8, 76% had an automatic, 28.1% had a three-speed manual, 4.2% had a four-speed manual, .8% had overdrive, 52.8% had power steering, 17.4% had power brakes, 2.6% had a tilting steering wheel, 52.8% had tinted glass, 7.7% had power windows, 17.7% had air conditioning, .9% had power front seats, and 56.7% had radios.

1964 Chevrolet Impala Sport Coupe

Original Price: $2,936
Number Produced: 442,292
Estimated Number Existing in 1979: 48,652
Miles per Gallon: 10–18
Common Trouble Spots: automatic transmission
Availability of Parts: good
Investment Potential: AA+ (with Super Sport option); AA (without)

Background: The '64 Impala two-door hardtop is the favorite of many Chevy fans. It came with a 140 h.p. 230 cu. in. six-cylinder engine. Most buyers ordered one of the optional V8s. These included a 195 h.p. 283, a 250 h.p. 327, a 300 h.p. 327, a 340 h.p. 409, a 400 h.p. 409, and a 425 h.p. 409. A three-speed manual transmission was standard. Overdrive, a four-speed manual, and Powerglide automatic transmission were available at extra cost.

The Super Sport kit was optional. It featured special trim, insignias, and bucket seats.

1964 Chevrolet Impala Sport Coupe

1964 Chrysler Newport Convertible

Original Price: $3,334
Number Produced: 2,176
Estimated Number Existing in 1979: 156
Miles per Gallon: 10–16
Common Trouble Spots: brakes, piston rings
Availability of Parts: fair–poor
Investment Potential: A

Background: The new Newport convertible received only a minor face-lift; the big changes were in the interior. New features included a seven-position adjustable steering wheel, head rests, reclining seats, console-mounted automatic transmission, and other options. A padded dash was standard.

The Newport was powered by a 265 h.p. 361 cu. in. V8. A floor-mounted three-speed manual transmission was standard. Torque Flite Eight automatic transmission was optional.

Most 1964 Chryslers, 98.3%, came with power steering, 73.4% had power brakes, 6.1% had a tilting steering wheel, 27.4% had power windows, 17.6% had power seats, 70.2% had tinted glass, 77.7% had radios, and 33.8% were sold with air conditioning.

1964 Chrysler 300 Convertible

Original Price: $3,803
Number Produced: 1,401
Estimated Number Existing in 1979: 100
Miles per Gallon: 9–14
Common Trouble Spots: brakes
Availability of Parts: fair–poor
Investment Potential: A+

Background: The 1964 300 ragtop came with a 305 h.p. 383 cu. in. V8. A 360 h.p. 413 cu. in. V8 was available as an option. A floor-mounted three-speed manual was standard. Torque Flite Eight automatic and a four-speed manual were optional. Most buyers ordered the automatic. Also available were reclining seats, head rests, adjustable steering wheel, and a console-mounted automatic transmission.

1964 Chrylser 300 Convertible

1964 Chrysler 300-K Convertible

Original Price: $4,522
Number Produced: 625
Estimated Number Existing in 1979: 45
Miles per Gallon: 8–13
Common Trouble Spots: brakes
Availability of Parts: fair–poor
Investment Potential: A+

Background: The '64 300-K came with a 360 h.p. 413 cu. in. V8. With performance options (special manifold and dual four-barrel carburetors), this engine could be boosted to 390 h.p. Chrysler sales literature called cars so equipped "hairy chested enough to match your wildest dreams." A four-speed manual transmission, power steering, power brakes, between-seat console, electric clock, windshield washers, and dual exhaust were standard. Torque Flite Eight automatic transmission was optional.

1964 Dodge Custom 880 Convertible

Original Price: $3,251
Number Produced: N.A.
Estimated Number Existing in 1979: N.A.
Miles per Gallon: 11–17
Common Trouble Spots: brakes
Availability of Parts: fair
Investment Potential: A+

Background: The '64 Custom softtop was powered by a 265 h.p. 361 cu. in. V8 with a two-barrel carburetor. Buyers could also order a 305 h.p. 383 cu. in. V8. A three-speed manual transmission was standard. Torque Flite Eight automatic and a four-speed manual were available at extra cost.

Most 1964 Dodge 880s, 98.8%, came equipped with an automatic, 1% had a three-speed manual, .2% had a four-speed manual, 94.4% had power steering, 62.2% had power brakes, 76.4% had tinted glass, 6.2% had a tilting steering wheel, 26.2% had power windows, 8.8% had power front seats, 78.8% had radios, and 26.9% were sold with air conditioning.

1964 Dodge Custom 880 Convertible

1964 Chrysler 300-K Convertible

1964 Dodge Dart GT Convertible

1964 Dodge Dart GT Convertible

Original Price: $2,524
Number Produced: N.A.
Estimated Number Existing in 1979: N.A.
Miles per Gallon: 15–23
Common Trouble Spots: brakes
Availability of Parts: fair
Investment Potential: A+

Background: The Dart GT convertible was basically a dressed-up Dart 270. The special trim added to the car's looks, and the bucket seat interior was also nicely done.

It was powered by a 101 h.p. 170 cu. in. slant six. A 145 h.p. 225 cu. in. slant six and, late in the model year, a "1964½" 180 h.p. 273 cu. in. V8 were extra-cost options. A three-speed manual transmission was standard. Torque Flite automatic and a four-speed manual were also available.

1964 Dodge Dart 270 Convertible

Original Price: $2,377
Number Produced: N.A.
Estimated Number Existing in 1979: N.A.
Miles per Gallon: 15–23
Common Trouble Spots: brakes
Availability of Parts: fair
Investment Potential: A

Background: The Dart 270 ragtop was powered by a 101 h.p. 170 cu. in. slant six. A 145 h.p. 225 cu. in. slant six and a 180 h.p. 273 cu. in. V8, were available at extra cost. The V8 wasn't offered until late in the model year; it was known as a 1964½ engine. A three-speed manual transmission was standard. Torque Flite automatic and a four-speed manual were optional.

Most 1964 Darts, 88.4%, came equipped with a six, 70% had an automatic, 24.9% had the three-speed manual, 5.1% had the four-speed manual, 20.7% had power steering, .3% had power brakes, 32.4% had tinted glass, 2% had power windows, 51.1% had radios, and 2.7% were sold with air conditioning.

1964 Dodge Dart 270 Convertible

1964 Dodge Polara Convertible

1964 Dodge Polara Convertible

Original Price: $3,131
Number Produced: N.A.
Estimated Number Existing in 1979: N.A.
Miles per Gallon: 11–16
Common Trouble Spots: brakes
Availability of Parts: fair
Investment Potential: AA (with 500 option); A+ (without)

Background: The 1964 Polara was restyled for Dodge's 50th Anniversary. It had clean, uncluttered good looks from any angle. It was powered by a 230 h.p. 318 cu. in. V8. Other V8 engines available included a 305 h.p. 383, a 330 h.p. 383, a 365 h.p. 426, a 415 h.p. 426, and a 425 h.p. 426. A three-speed manual transmission was standard. Torque Flite Eight automatic and a four-speed manual were optional.

A 500 trim option was offered. Polaras with this option had special trim and upholstery and came with a 305 h.p. 383 cu. in. V8, but buyers could order hotter engines. The four-speed manual and Torque Flite automatic transmissions were mounted on the floor console.

Most 1964 Dodges, 84.7%, came with an automatic, 13.1% had a three-speed manual, 2.2% had a four-speed manual, 64% had power steering, 13.7% had power brakes, 46.9% had tinted glass, 8.7% had electric windows, .6% had power seats, 59.1% had radios, and 14.2% were sold with air conditioning.

1964 Ford Falcon Futura Convertible

Original Price: $2,470
Number Produced: 16,200
Estimated Number Existing in 1979: 1,296
Miles per Gallon: 14–23
Common Trouble Spots: none
Availability of Parts: good
Investment Potential: A+

Background: The new Futura was the lowest-priced Ford convertible offered in 1964. It was powered by a 101 h.p. 170 cu. in. six-cylinder engine. A 116 h.p. 200 cu. in. six and a 164 h.p. 260 cu. in. V8 were optional. A three-speed manual transmission was standard. Ford-omatic automatic and a four-speed manual were available at extra cost.

Most Futura softtops, 77.5%, had bench seats.

1964 Ford Falcon Futura Sprint Convertible

Original Price: $2,824
Number Produced: 4,278
Estimated Number Existing in 1979: 342
Miles per Gallon: 13–20
Common Trouble Spots: none
Availability of Parts: good
Investment Potential: AA

Background: The new Falcon Sprint had a look a bit more sculptured than the previous year's model. It featured a 164-h.p. 260 cu. in. V8. A three-speed manual transmission was standard. Fordomatic automatic and a four-speed manual were optional.

The Sprint had a modified heavy-duty chassis, a dash-mounted tach, and a special air cleaner and exhaust system. Most had bucket seats, but 17% were sold with bench seats.

A high performance "Cobra Kit" was available at extra cost.

1964 Ford Galaxie 500 Convertible

Original Price: $3,045
Number Produced: 37,311
Estimated Number Existing in 1979: 2,984
Miles per Gallon: 10–19
Common Trouble Spots: none
Availability of Parts: good
Investment Potential: A+

Background: The '64 Galaxie 500 was powered by a 138 h.p. 223 cu. in. six-cylinder engine. Also available were several V8 engines: a 195 h.p. 289, a 250 h.p. 352, a 300 h.p. 390, a 330 h.p. 390, a 410 h.p. 427, and a 425 h.p. 427. A three-speed manual transmission was standard. Overdrive, a four-speed manual, and Cruise-O-Matic automatic were optional.

Performance "Cobra Kits" were offered on the Galaxie and most other 1964 Fords. These kits ranged from a single four-barrel carburetor to four two-barrel carburetors.

Most 1964 Galaxies, 91.4%, came with a V8, 78.1% had an automatic, 13% had a three-speed manual, 1.8% had overdrive, 3.1% had a four-speed manual, 61.4% had power steering, 16.6% had power brakes, 35.1% had tinted glass, 3.2% had a tilting steering wheel, 16.6% had electric windows, 1.4% had power front seats, 60.7% had radios, and 13.3% were sold with air conditioning.

1964 Ford Falcon Futura Sprint Convertible

PHOTO: FORD MOTOR COMPANY

1964 Ford Galaxie 500 XL Convertible

Original Price: $3,484
Number Produced: 15,169
Estimated Number Existing in 1979: 1,213
Miles per Gallon: 10–18
Common Trouble Spots: none
Availability of Parts: good
Investment Potential: AA+

Background: The 1964 Galaxie 500 XL was powered by a 195 h.p. 289 cu. in. V8. Other V8s were also available including a 250 h.p. 352, a 300 h.p. 390, a 330 h.p. 390, a 410 h.p. 427, and a 425 h.p. 427. Cruise-O-Matic automatic transmission was standard. A three-speed manual, overdrive, and a four-speed manual were optional.

Buyers had their choice of five seat-belt colors: beige, black, blue, gold and red. A glass rear window was standard.

Many Galaxie XL enthusiasts believe the 1964 model was the best performing XL.

1964 Ford Galaxie 500 XL Convertible

PHOTO: FORD MOTOR COMPANY

1964½ Ford Mustang Convertible

PHOTO: FORD MOTOR COMPANY

1964½ Ford Mustang Convertible

Original Price: est. $2,600
Number Produced: 28,833
Estimated Number Existing in 1979: 2,306
Miles per Gallon: 13–23
Common Trouble Spots: none
Availability of Parts: good
Investment Potential: AAA

Background: "Birth of a new breed of car." That's how Ford ads announced the new Mustang. The Mustang was the biggest thing to happen to Ford, and the entire auto industry, in 1964. It was an instant success. As *Motor Trend* said in November 1964, "No other recent car has enjoyed anything like the instant popularity of Mustang. It hit first place in compact sales and fourth overall in its second month."

The Mustang used a modified Falcon chassis and standard Falcon front and rear suspension. It came with a 101 h.p. 170 cu. in. six-cylinder engine. A 164 h.p. 260 cu. in. V8 and a 210 h.p. and a 271 h.p. 289 cu. in. V8 were optional. A three-speed manual transmission was standard. Fordomatic automatic and a four-speed manual were available at extra cost.

A "Rallye Pack" option, consisting of a tach and clock mounted on the steering wheel column, was offered.

The 1964½ Mustang convertible is one of the most popular cars made in the 1960s.

1964½ Ford Mustang Two-Door Hardtop

Original Price: est. $2,300
Number Produced: 92,705
Estimated Number Existing in 1979: 7,416
Miles per Gallon: 13–23
Common Trouble Spots: none
Availability of Parts: good
Investment Potential: AAA

Background: Early Ford Mustangs are the rising stars of collector automobiles, and the 1964½ may be the most desirable of them all. It came with a 101 h.p. 170 cu. in. six-cylinder engine, but only about 27% of all Mustangs were sold that way; most came with one of the optional V8 engines: a 164 h.p. 260, a 210 h.p. 289, and a 271 h.p. 289. A three-speed manual was standard. Ford-O-Matic automatic and a four-speed manual were available at extra cost. So was a "Rallye Pack" option, consisting of a tach and clock mounted on the steering wheel column.

The 1964½ Mustang has been credited with starting the pony car craze. In 1974, *Special Interest Autos* editor Michael Lamm called the 1964½ Mustang "the milestone car of the 1960s." He went on to say, "No other automobile of that decade exerted greater influence on the industry."

1964½ Ford Mustang Two-Door Hardtop

PHOTO: FORD MOTOR COMPANY

1964 Ford Thunderbird Convertible

Original Price: $4,953
Number Produced: 9,198
Estimated Number Existing in 1979: 735
Miles per Gallon: 9–15
Common Trouble Spots: electrical system
Availability of Parts: fair–good
Investment Potential: AA

Background: The Thunderbird received major restyling inside and out for 1964. It was powered by a 300 h.p. 390 cu. in. V8. Cruise-O-Matic automatic transmission, power steering, and power brakes were standard.

Although the Sports Roadster was gone, buyers could order a tonneau cover, but few did. Other options included a four-way emergency flasher and leather upholstery. Most 1964 T-Birds, 75%, came with power windows, 52.4% had power seats, 72.6% had tinted glass, and 50.6% were sold with an air conditioner.

1964 Ford Thunderbird Convertible

PHOTO: FORD MOTOR COMPANY

1964 Imperial Crown Convertible

Original Price: $6,003
Number Produced: 922
Estimated Number Existing in 1979: 82
Miles per Gallon: 8–14
Common Trouble Spots: none
Availability of Parts: fair–poor
Investment Potential: AA

Background: The Imperial received the biggest face-lift in the Chrysler line. The "classic inspired" free-standing headlights were gone. That made the 1964 Imperial look more like its contemporaries. Whether that was good or bad is a matter of personal taste. Apparently most buyers liked the change, because sales of the convertible were up significantly.

It was powered by a 340 h.p. 413 cu. in. V8 engine. Torque Flite Eight automatic transmission was standard. So were removable head rests, power windows, remote control outside mirror, electric clock, and upholstery made of leather and nylon Bedford cord. All-leather upholstery was optional. A traditional round steering wheel replaced the square one of previous models.

Customers had a choice of seventeen solid body colors. Each car received nine coats of paint. Tops were available in tan, black, white, or blue.

Most 1964 Imperials, 97.7%, came with power seats, 28.8% had a tilting steering wheel, 98.8% had radios, 95% had tinted glass, and 77.5% were sold with air conditioning.

1964 Imperial Crown Convertible

PHOTO: CHRYSLER HISTORICAL COLLECTION

1964 Lincoln Continental Convertible

PHOTO: FORD MOTOR COMPANY

1964 King Midget Convertible

Original Price: est. $750
Number Produced: 130
Estimated Number Existing in 1979: 8
Miles per Gallon: 50–90
Common Trouble Spots: transmission, "V" belts
Availability of Parts: good
Investment Potential: A

Background: The economical '64 King Midget convertible was powered by a 10 h.p. 29 cu. in. one-cylinder engine. Automatic transmission was standard.

1964 Lincoln Continental Convertible

Original Price: $6,916
Number Produced: 3,328
Estimated Number Existing in 1979: 400
Miles per Gallon: 8–13
Common Trouble Spots: none
Availability of Parts: fair–good
Investment Potential: AAA

Background: The '64 Continental four-door convertible was three inches longer than the previous year's model. The convertible's roofline and dash were changed.

It was powered by a 320 h.p. 430 cu. in. V8. Turbo-Drive automatic transmission, a trip odometer, map lights, a fuel warning light, and an automatic parking brake release were standard. For $281, buyers could order a package featuring front seats that were individually adjustable and a center console.

All 1964 Lincolns had power steering, power brakes, electric windows, and power front seats. Most, 96%, had tinted glass, seven percent had a tilting steering wheel, and 86% had air conditioning.

1964 Mercury Comet Caliente Convertible

PHOTO: FORD MOTOR COMPANY

1964 Mercury Comet Caliente Convertible

Original Price: $2,733
Number Produced: 9,039
Estimated Number Existing in 1979: 686
Miles per Gallon: 12–20
Common Trouble Spots: none
Availability of Parts: good
Investment Potential: A+

Background: This was the first year for the sporty Caliente convertible. It came with a 101 h.p. 170 cu. in. six. A 116 h.p. 200 cu. in. six and a 164 h.p. 260 cu. in. V8 were optional. A three-speed manual transmission was standard. Two automatics, Merc-O-Matic and Multi-Drive, and a four-speed manual were available at extra cost.

Among the options offered were air conditioning, padded dash, tinted glass, and bucket seats. Just over 29% of '64 Caliente convertibles had bucket seats.

1964 Mercury Monterey Convertible

Original Price: $3,215
Number Produced: 2,592
Estimated Number Existing in 1979: 196
Miles per Gallon: 9–16
Common Trouble Spots: electrical system
Availability of Parts: fair–good
Investment Potential: A

Background: The '64 Monterey convertible came with a 250 h.p. 390 cu. in. V8. Five other V8 engines were available: a 266 h.p. 390 (two-barrel carb), a 300 h.p. 390 (four-barrel carb), a 330 h.p. 390 (four-barrel carb), a 410 h.p. 427 (four-barrel carb), and a 425 h.p. 427 (two four-barrel carbs). A three-speed manual transmission was standard. Multi-Drive automatic and a four-speed manual transmission were optional.

Buyers could choose from fourteen solid exterior colors: anniversary silver, burgundy, carnival red, fawn, glacier blue, onyx, pacific blue, palomino, platinum beige, pink frost, polar white, peacock, silver turquoise, and yellow mist. The all-vinyl interior could be ordered in beige, black, blue, or red.

1964 Mercury Park Lane Convertible

1964 Mercury Park Lane Convertible

Original Price: $3,538
Number Produced: 1,967
Estimated Number Existing in 1979: 149
Miles per Gallon: 9–15
Common Trouble Spots: electrical system
Availability of Parts: fair–good
Investment Potential: A+ (with bucket seats); A (without)

Background: "When you want more than the usual in luxury, step into Mercury's finest medium priced car—the Park Lane." So invited Mercury ads in 1964.

The Park Lane was the most luxurious convertible offered by Mercury during its twenty-fifth anniversary. It came with a 300 h.p. 390 cu. in. V8. Three other V8 engines were available at extra cost: a 330 h.p. 390 (four-barrel carb), a 410 h.p. 427 (four-barrel carb), and a 425 h.p. 427 (two four-barrel carbs). A three-speed manual transmission was standard. Multi-Drive automatic and a four-speed manual were optional.

In addition to the fourteen exterior colors available on the Monterey ragtop, two more, Aztec gold and bittersweet, were offered. The all-vinyl interior could be had in black, blue, palomino, red, or turquoise. Nearly 45% of 1964 Park Lane convertibles were equipped with bucket seats.

1964 Mercury Monterey Convertible

1964 Oldsmobile Dynamic 88 Convertible

PHOTO: OLDSMOBILE DIVISION

1964 Oldsmobile Dynamic 88 Convertible

Original Price: $3,378
Number Produced: 10,042
Estimated Number Existing in 1979: 592
Miles per Gallon: 10–17
Common Trouble Spots: brakes, carburetor
Availability of Parts: good
Investment Potential: A+

Background: The Dynamic 88 was powered by a 280 h.p. 394 cu. in. V8. Two other versions of this engine, a 260 h.p. and a 330 h.p., were available at extra cost. A three-speed manual transmission was standard. Hydra-Matic automatic transmission was optional.

1964 Oldsmobile F-85 Cutlass Convertible

Original Price: $2,973
Number Produced: 12,822
Estimated Number Existing in 1979: 756
Miles per Gallon: 11–19
Common Trouble Spots: none
Availability of Parts: good
Investment Potential: AA (with the 4-4-2 option); A+ (without)

Background: The new F-85 convertible looked a lot like a shrunken full-size Olds. It was powered by a 290 h.p. 330 cu. in. V8. A three-speed manual transmission was standard. Jetaway automatic transmission and a four-speed manual were optional. All F-85s had bucket seats.

Late in the model year, a 4-4-2 option was made available for $285.14. It consisted of a 310 h.p. 330 cu. in. Jetfire Rocket V8, four-barrel carburetor, floor-mounted four-speed manual transmission, dual exhaust, heavy duty chassis, and "red line" tires.

The 4-4-2 option was officially known as Option Number B-09 Police Apprehender Pursuit. Just how many law officers went around chasing bad guys in F-85 convertibles so equipped is not known. However, an educated guess would be none. After all, with the top down, where could they put the big flashing red light? Approximately one out of every four F-85s came with the 4-4-2 option.

1964 Oldsmobile Jetstar 88 Convertible

Original Price: $3,308
Number Produced: 3,903
Estimated Number Existing in 1979: 230
Miles per Gallon: 11–17
Common Trouble Spots: brakes, carburetor
Availability of Parts: good
Investment Potential: A+

Background: The 1964 Jetstar 88 ragtop was not especially popular in its day. It was powered by a 245 h.p. 330 cu. in. V8. A 290 h.p. version of this engine was available at extra cost. A three-speed manual transmission was standard. Jetaway automatic transmission was optional.

1964 Oldsmobile 98 Convertible

Original Price: $4,457
Number Produced: 4,004
Estimated Number Existing in 1979: 236
Miles per Gallon: 10–15
Common Trouble Spots: brakes, carburetor
Availability of Parts: good
Investment Potential: A+

Background: The 1964 98 convertible had a larger wheelbase and weighed more than the other Olds ragtops. However, it was priced slightly lower than the glamorous Starfire.

It was powered by a 330 h.p. 394 cu. in. V8. A 345 h.p. version of this engine was available at extra cost. Hydra-Matic automatic transmission, bucket seats, power steering, and power brakes were standard.

1964 Oldsmobile F-85 Cutlass Convertible

PHOTO: OLDSMOBILE DIVISION

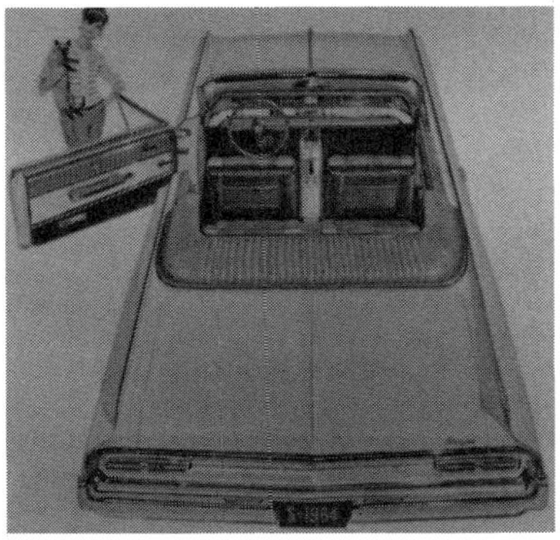

1964 Oldsmobile Starfire Convertible

1964 Oldsmobile Starfire Convertible

Original Price: $4,742
Number Produced: 2,410
Estimated Number Existing in 1979: 142
Miles per Gallon: 9–15
Common Trouble Spots: brakes, carburetor
Availability of Parts: good
Investment Potential: AA

Background: The Starfire ragtop received a pleasing, but minor, face-lift for 1964. It was powered by a 345 h.p. 394 cu. in. V8. Hydra-Matic automatic transmission, electric windows, power steering, dual exhaust, special interior, and power brakes were standard.

Among the options were a seven-way adjustable steering wheel, cruise control, and a power front seat.

1964 Plymouth Fury Convertible

Original Price: $2,937
Number Produced: N.A.
Estimated Number Existing in 1979: N.A.
Miles per Gallon: 12–18
Common Trouble Spots: brakes
Availability of Parts: fair
Investment Potential: A

Background: The styling of the 1964 Fury convertible was similar to the previous year's model. The Fury came with a 145 h.p. 225 cu. in. six-cylinder engine. Four V8 engines were available at extra cost: a 230 h.p. 318, a 265 h.p. 361, a 330 h.p. 383, and a 365 h.p. 426.

A three-speed manual transmission was standard. Torque Flite Eight automatic and a four-speed manual transmission were optional.

The Fury convertible came with an all-vinyl interior in one of six colors: black, blue, copper, red, tan, and turquoise. The exterior was available in nine colors.

Most 1964 Plymouths, 72.9%, were powered by a V8, 79.3% had an automatic, 4.1% had a four-speed manual, 16.6% had a three-speed manual, 55.7% had power steering, 16.1% had power brakes, 40.3% had tinted glass, 7.5% had electric windows, .6% had power seats, 56.8% had radios, and 12.1% were sold with air conditioning.

1964 Plymouth Sport Fury Convertible

1964 Plymouth Sport Fury Convertible

Original Price: $3,095
Number Produced: N.A.
Estimated Number Existing in 1979: N.A.
Miles per Gallon: 9–16
Common Trouble Spots: brakes
Availability of Parts: fair
Investment Potential: A+

Background: "Fastest on the block." That's how the rock and roll group the Super Stocks described Plymouth's hot 426 cu. in. V8 in their song "426 Super Stock." The 365 h.p. 426 Super Stock V8 was one of four V8s available in the Sport Fury. The others were a 230 h.p. 318 (the standard engine), a 265 h.p. 361, and a 330 h.p. 383.

A three-speed manual transmission was standard for all cars except those with the 426 engine. A four-speed floor-mounted manual was standard with the 426. The four-speed manual and Torque Flite Eight automatic transmission were optional with all engines.

Among the standard equipment on the '64 Sport Fury ragtop were all-vinyl bucket seats, deluxe wheel covers, padded dash, electric clock, deep-pile carpeting, self-adjusting brakes, and compartment console. The interior was available in black, blue, copper, red, or turquoise. Ten exterior colors were offered.

1964 Plymouth Fury Convertible

1964 Plymouth Valiant Barracuda Two-Door Hardtop

1964 Plymouth Valiant Barracuda Two-Door Hardtop

Original Price: $2,365
Number Produced: N.A.
Estimated Number Existing in 1979: N.A.
Miles per Gallon: 16–21
Common Trouble Spots: none
Availability of Parts: good
Investment Potential: A+

Background: The sporty Barracuda made its debut in May of 1964. It featured front bucket seats and a rear bench seat that could be folded forward.

The Barracuda came with a 101 h.p. 170 cu. in. six-cylinder engine. A 145 h.p. 225 cu. in. six and a 180 h.p. 273 cu. in. V8 were available at extra cost. Torque Flite automatic transmission and a four-speed manual were optional.

1964 Plymouth Valiant Signet 200 Convertible

Original Price: $2,473
Number Produced: N.A.
Estimated Number Existing in 1979: N.A.
Miles per Gallon: 16–21
Common Trouble Spots: none
Availability of Parts: fair
Investment Potential: A+

Background: The '64 Signet 200 was a good-looking little car. It came with a 101 h.p. 170 cu. in. six-cylinder engine. A 145 h.p. 225 cu. in. six and a 180 h.p. 273 cu. in. V8 were available at extra cost. A three-speed manual transmission, bucket seats, and deep-pile carpeting were standard. Torque Flite automatic and a four-speed manual transmission were optional.

Four all-vinyl interiors were offered: black, blue, red, and tan. Twelve exterior colors were available: black, light blue, medium blue metallic, dark blue metallic, light turquoise, medium turquoise metallic, medium gray metallic, red, Signet Royal red, light tan, medium tan metallic, and white.

1964 Plymouth Valiant Signet 200 Convertible

1964 Plymouth Valiant V 200 Convertible

Original Price: $2,349
Number Produced: N.A.
Estimated Number Existing in 1979: N.A.
Miles per Gallon: 16–21
Common Trouble Spots: none
Availability of Parts: fair
Investment Potential: A+

Background: The Valiant received an attractive face-lift for 1964. It was powered by a 101 h.p. 170 cu. in. six-cylinder engine. A 145 h.p. 225 cu. in. six-cylinder and a 180 h.p. 273 cu. in. V8 were available at extra cost. A four-speed manual and Torque Flite automatic transmission were optional.

A new item was a blue convertible top with blue upholstery.

Most 1964 Valiants, 82%, came with a six-cylinder engine, 65.8% had an automatic, 27.5% had a three-speed manual, 6.7% had a four-speed manual, 15% had power steering, .7% had power brakes, 1.7% had electric windows, 27.1% had tinted glass, 49.5% had radios, and 2.3% were sold with air conditioning.

1964 Plymouth Valiant V200 Convertible

1964 Pontiac Bonneville Convertible

Original Price: $3,568
Number Produced: 22,016
Estimated Number Existing in 1979: 1,541
Miles per Gallon: 9–16
Common Trouble Spots: automatic transmission, brakes
Availability of Parts: good–fair
Investment Potential: AA

Background: The attractive new Bonneville had sharp, clean lines. It was powered by a 306 h.p. 389 cu. in. V8. Six other V8s were available at extra cost: a 320 h.p. 421 (three two-barrel carbs), a 230 h.p. 389 (two-barrel carb), a 303 h.p. 389 (four-barrel carb), a 330 h.p. 389 (three two-barrel carbs), a 350 h.p. 421 (three two-barrel carbs) and a 370 h.p. 421 (three two-barrel carbs).

A three-speed manual transmission was standard, but not very popular. Hydra-Matic automatic and a four-speed manual transmission were optional.

The 1964 Bonneville was one of the better-looking big cars made in the 1960s.

1964 Pontiac Catalina Convertible

Original Price: $3,170
Number Produced: 18,673
Estimated Number Existing in 1979: 1,307
Miles per Gallon: 9–17
Common Trouble Spots: automatic transmission, brakes
Availability of Parts: good–fair
Investment Potential: AA (with 2+2 option); A+ (without)

Background: The new Catalina was powered by a 235 h.p. 389 cu. in. V8 with two-barrel carburetor. Nine other V8 engines were available at extra cost: a 320 h.p. 421 (three two-barrel carbs), a 230 h.p. 389 (two-barrel carb), a 267 h.p. 389 (two-barrel carb), a 283 h.p. 389 (two-barrel carb), a 303 h.p. 389 (four-barrel carb), a 306 h.p. 389 (four-barrel carb), a 330 h.p. 389 (three two-barrel carbs), a 350 h.p. 421 (three two-barrel carbs), and a 370 h.p. 421 (three two-barrel carbs).

A three-speed manual transmission was standard. Hydra-Matic automatic and a four-speed manual were optional. Most full-size '64 Pontiacs, 95.8%, were equipped with the automatic, 2.4% had the three-speed manual, 1.8% had the four-speed manual, 93.4% had power steering, 83.6% had power brakes, 12.2% had electric windows, 8.3% had a tilting steering wheel, 36.3% had tinted glass, 17.6% had power front seats, and 16.5% had air conditioners.

For $290.52, Catalina buyers could order the 2+2 option, which featured vinyl bucket seats, a center console, special wheel discs, and a distinctive steering wheel and trim. Over 8% of all 1964 Catalinas came with this option.

1964 Pontiac Bonneville Convertible

PHOTO: PONTIAC MOTOR DIVISION

1964 Pontiac Le Mans Convertible

Original Price: $2,785
Number Produced: 24,203 (6,644 had the GTO option)
Estimated Number Existing in 1979: 1,694
Miles per Gallon: 11–19
Common Trouble Spots: carburetor
Availability of Parts: good–fair
Investment Potential: AA+ (with the GTO option); A+ (without)

Background: This was the first year the LeMans was a separate series and not just an option. It came with a 140 h.p. 215 cu. in. six-cylinder engine. Four V8s were available at extra cost: a 250 h.p. 326, a 280 h.p. 326, a 325 h.p. 389, and a 348 h.p. 389. A three-speed manual transmission was standard. A four-speed manual and an automatic transmission were optional.

A new and popular option was the GTO package, offered for $295. The GTO featured a 325 h.p. 389 cu. in. V8 with four-barrel carburetor (a 348 h.p. 389 cu. in. V8 with three two-barrel carburetors was also available); special valve lifters, camshaft and trim; a stiffer suspension; dual exhaust; distinctive emblems; chromed valve covers; and a chromed air cleaner.

According to a Pontiac ad, the GTO was "for the man who wouldn't mind riding a tiger if someone'd put wheels on it."

A 1964 Le Mans convertible with the GTO package is a very desirable car.

1964 Pontiac Le Mans Convertible

PHOTO: PONTIAC MOTOR DIVISION

1964 Pontiac Le Mans GTO Two-Door Hardtop

Original Price: $2,545
Number Produced: 18,422
Estimated Number Existing in 1979: 1,289
Miles per Gallon: 10–17
Common Trouble Spots: carburetor
Availability of Parts: good–fair
Investment Potential: AA+

Background: Many consider the '64 Le Mans with the GTO option the first muscle car. It featured a 325 h.p. 389 cu. in. V8 with four-barrel carburetor (a 348 h.p. 389 with three two-barrel carburetors was also available); special valve lifters, camshaft, and trim; stiffer suspension; dual exhaust; distinctive emblems; chromed valve covers; and a chromed air cleaner. A three-speed manual transmission was standard. A four-speed manual and an automatic transmission were optional.

For only $295, Pontiac buyers were able to transform the ordinary Le Mans into a legend—the GTO.

1964 Pontiac Tempest Custom Convertible

Original Price: $2,630
Number Produced: 7,987
Estimated Number Existing in 1979: 559
Miles per Gallon: 12–20
Common Trouble Spots: carburetor
Availability of Parts: good–fair
Investment Potential: A

Background: The 1964 Tempest was a good-looking little ragtop. It was powered by a 140 h.p. 215 cu. in. six-cylinder engine. Four V8 engines were available at extra cost: a 250 h.p. 326, a 280 h.p. 326, a 325 h.p. 389, and a 348 h.p. 389. A three-speed manual transmission was standard. A four-speed manual and an automatic transmission were optional.

Most '64 Tempests, 70.2%, were equipped with the automatic, 16.1% had the three-speed manual, 13.7% had the four-speed manual, 41.1% had power steering, 18.3% had power brakes, 1.6% had a tilting steering wheel, 1.5% had power windows, 2% had power front seats, 15.1% had tinted glass, 90.2% had radios, and 9.9% were sold with air conditioning.

1964 Pontiac Tempest Custom Convertible

PHOTO: PONTIAC MOTOR DIVISION

1964 Rambler American Convertible

Original Price: $2,335
Number Produced: 8,907
Estimated Number Existing in 1979: 578
Miles per Gallon: 14–23
Common Trouble Spots: valves
Availability of Parts: fair–poor
Investment Potential: A+

Background: The American received attractive new styling for 1964. It also had a roomier interior and new front (and improved rear) suspension.

It was powered by a 138 h.p. 195.6 cu. in. six-cylinder engine. A three-speed manual transmission was standard. Overdrive, "Twin Stick" (a floor-mounted three-speed manual with overdrive), and Flash-O-Matic automatic transmission were optional.

Most 1964 Ramblers, 61.6%, came equipped with the automatic, 29.1% had a three-speed manual, 9.3% had overdrive, 20.7% had power steering, 9% had power brakes, 8.6% had tinted glass, 2.6% had a tilting steering wheel, 3.9% had power windows, 36.9% had radios, and 9% were sold with air conditioning.

Buyers had their choice of fourteen solid exterior colors and forty-two two-tone combinations.

1964 Rambler American Convertible

PHOTO: LARRY G. MITCHELL

1964 Studebaker Avanti

Original Price: $4,445
Number Produced: est. 795
Estimated Number Existing in 1979: 350
Miles per Gallon: 12–18
Common Trouble Spots: none
Availability of Parts: fair–good
Investment Potential: AAA+

Background: The Avanti was as beautiful as ever in 1964. Actually, changes in the Avanti were not made on a model-year basis. The most noticeable styling change (made in August 1963) was the switch from round to square headlight frames. Most Avantis, 3,871, had the round ones. Just 752 have square ones.

The Avanti came with a 225 h.p. 289 cu. in. V8. Hotter V8s were available at extra cost. These were a 240 h.p. 289, a 290 h.p. 289 (R-2 Jet Thrust Supercharged), a 335 h.p. 304.5 (R-3 Supercharged), and a 304.5 (R-4 with dual four-barrel carburetors). Only nine R-3's, and no R-4's, were sold. However, many Avanti owners later bought R-3-like performance packages.

The 1964 Avanti was, and always will be, a very attractive and desirable automobile.

1964 Studebaker Avanti

PHOTO: RICHARD QUINN COLLECTION, STUDEBAKER DRIVERS CLUB

1964 Studebaker Gran Turismo Hawk

Original Price: $2,958
Number Produced: 1,484
Estimated Number Existing in 1979: 108
Miles per Gallon: 14–21
Common Trouble Spots: none
Availability of Parts: fair–poor
Investment Potential: AA+

Background: The attractive 1964 Hawk came with a 210 h.p. 289 cu. in. V8. Available at extra cost were three hotter versions of this engine: a 225 h.p., a 240 h.p. R-1,

1964 Studebaker Gran Turismo Hawk

PHOTO: RICHARD QUINN COLLECTION, STUDEBAKER DRIVERS CLUB

and a 290 h.p. R-2. A 305 h.p. 304.5 cu. in. V8 was also offered. A three-speed manual transmission was standard. Overdrive, a four-speed manual, and two automatics, Flightomatic and Borg-Warner, were optional (the Warner was optional on the 304.5 cu. in. V8.)

A new option was a "half vinyl" roof that covered the front section of the car's roof.

1964 Studebaker Lark Daytona Convertible

Original Price: $2,797
Number Produced: 411
Estimated Number Existing in 1979: 26
Miles per Gallon: 12–19
Common Trouble Spots: none
Availability of Parts: fair–poor
Investment Potential: AA (with "Super" package); A+ (without)

Background: This was the last year for the Daytona convertible. It came with a 180 h.p. 259.2 cu. in. V8. Five other V8s were available at extra cost: a 195 h.p. 259.2, a 210 h.p. 289, a 225 h.p. 289, a 305 h.p. 304.5, a Jet Thrust 304.5, and a Jet Thrust Supercharged 289.

A three-speed manual transmission was standard. Overdrive, a four-speed manual, Flightomatic automatic, and Warner AS2-10 automatic transmission were optional (the four-speed manual was standard on the 304.5 cu. in. V8).

A "Super" performance package was offered. It featured heavy duty suspension, a 160 mph speedometer, bucket seats, disc brakes, tachometer, and special "S" emblem. *Motor Trend* called Larks so equipped "among the fastest production cars in the country."

1964 Studebaker Lark Daytona Convertible

PHOTO: RICHARD QUINN COLLECTION, STUDEBAKER DRIVERS CLUB

1965

1965 Buick Electra 225 Custom Convertible

Original Price: $4,440
Number Produced: 8,508
Estimated Number Existing in 1979: 740
Miles per Gallon: 10–15
Common Trouble Spots: none
Availability of Parts: good
Investment Potential: A+

Background: The new Electra convertible was powered by a 325 h.p. 401 cu. in. V8. Two 425 cu. in. V8s, rated at 340 h.p. and 360 h.p. were available. Super Turbine automatic transmission, power brakes, and power steering were standard. Air conditioning was a popular option; just over 46% of all full-size Buicks came with it.

1965 Buick LeSabre Custom Convertible

Original Price: $3,325
Number Produced: 6,543
Estimated Number Existing in 1979: 569
Miles per Gallon: 11–16
Common Trouble Spots: none
Availability of Parts: good
Investment Potential: A

Background: The LeSabre convertible received a new look for 1965. It had a bit more flair than last year's model. It came with a 210 h.p. 300 cu. in. V8. A 250 h.p. version of this engine was available. A three-speed manual transmission was standard. Super Turbine automatic transmission was optional.

Just over 91% of all full-size Buicks had power brakes, 98.7% had power steering, 26.4% had power windows, and 24.3% had power seats.

1965 Buick Riviera Sport Coupe

Original Price: $4,408
Number Produced: 34,586
Estimated Number Existing in 1979: 3,008
Miles per Gallon: 10–15
Common Trouble Spots: none
Availability of Parts: good
Investment Potential: AA+

Background: The Riviera received an attractive face-lift for 1965. It looked somewhat like a mildly customized version of the original design. It was powered by a 325 h.p. 401 cu. in. V8. Two 425 cu. in. V8s, rated at 340 h.p. and 360 h.p. were optional. Super Turbine automatic transmission was standard.

All 1965 Rivieras had power steering and power brakes; 74.2% had power windows, 55.5% had power seats, 69.5% had air conditioning, 94.2% had tinted glass, and 92.8% were equipped with a tilting steering wheel.

1965 Buick Riviera Sport Coupe

1965 Buick Skylark Convertible

Original Price: $2,834
Number Produced: 11,637
Estimated Number Existing in 1979: 1,012
Miles per Gallon: 13–20
Common Trouble Spots: none
Availability of Parts: good
Investment Potential: AA

Background: The new Skylark convertible was available in either standard form or, in mid–model year, with the Gran Sport package. This $252.86 option included bucket seats, heavy duty radiator, dual exhaust, heavy duty brakes, padded dash, and a 325 h.p. 400 cu. in. V8. Exactly 1,181 Skylark convertibles were so equipped.

The standard Skylark engine was a 155 h.p. 225 cu. in. V6. A 210 h.p. and a 250 h.p. 300 cu. in. V8 were available at extra cost. A three-speed manual transmission was standard. Super Turbine automatic transmission and a four-speed manual were optional.

1965 Buick Special Convertible

Original Price: $2,605
Number Produced: 6,722
Estimated Number Existing in 1979: 584
Miles per Gallon: 13–21
Common Trouble Spots: none
Availability of Parts: good
Investment Potential: A+ (with Gran Sport package); A (without)

Background: The 1965 Special convertible came with a 155 h.p. 225 cu. in. V6 engine. A 210 h.p. and a 250 h.p. 300 cu. in. V8 were also available. A three-speed manual transmission was standard. Super Turbine automatic and a four-speed manual were optional.

Only 25.1% of all '65 Specials came equipped with the V6, 91% had the automatic, 2.3% had the four-speed manual, 29.8% had power brakes, 71.7% had power steering, 18% had power windows, 2.9% had power front seats, 68.5% had tinted glass, and 20% were sold with air conditioning.

A total of 3,357 1965 Special ragtops came with the optional Gran Sport package.

1965 Buick Wildcat Custom Convertible

Original Price: $3,727
Number Produced: 4,398
Estimated Number Existing in 1979: 382
Miles per Gallon: 10–15
Common Trouble Spots: none
Availability of Parts: good
Investment Potential: A+

Background: The main difference between the Wildcat Custom and the lower-priced Wildcat Deluxe was that the Custom had bucket seats, rear radio speaker, and center console. It came with a 325 h.p. 401 cu. in. V8. Two 425 cu. in. V8s, rated at 340 h.p., and 360 h.p., were available at extra cost. A three-speed manual transmission was standard. Super Turbine automatic and a four-speed manual were optional. Power steering and power brakes were popular options.

1965 Buick Wildcat Deluxe Convertible

Original Price: $3,502
Number Produced: 4,616
Estimated Number Existing in 1979: 401
Miles per Gallon: 10–15
Common Trouble Spots: none
Availability of Parts: good
Investment Potential: A

Background: The 1965 Wildcat Deluxe convertible came with a 325 h.p. 401 cu. in. V8. A 340 h.p. or 360 h.p. 425 cu. in. V8 was optional. A three-speed manual transmission was standard. Super Turbine automatic and a four-speed manual were optional. Power steering and power brakes were available at extra cost; both were very popular.

1965 Cadillac Fleetwood Eldorado Convertible

Original Price: $6,738
Number Produced: 2,125
Estimated Number Existing in 1979: 340
Miles per Gallon: 10–14
Common Trouble Spots: piston rings
Availability of Parts: good–fair
Investment Potential: AA

Background: The Eldorado was restyled for 1965. It looked bulkier than last year's model. The only engine offered was a 340 h.p. 429 cu. in. V8 with four-barrel carburetor. A new Turbo Hydra-Matic automatic transmission, power steering, electric windows, and power brakes were standard.

An interesting option was "Automatic Level Control," a device which kept the car's body level no matter how heavy a load it was carrying (Packard enthusiasts are quick to point out who had this first). It cost $80.65.

Like the De Ville convertible, the Eldorado had a glass rear window.

1965 Cadillac De Ville Convertible

Original Price: $5,639
Number Produced: 19,200
Estimated Number Existing in 1979: 3,072
Miles per Gallon: 10–14

1965 Chevrolet Chevelle Malibu Super Sport Convertible

PHOTO: GM PHOTOGRAPHIC

1965 Cadillac De Ville Convertible

PHOTO: CADILLAC MOTOR CAR DIVISION

Common Trouble Spots: piston rings
Availability of Parts: good–fair
Investment Potential: A+

Background: The restyled De Ville was powered by a 340 h.p. 429 cu. in. V8 engine with four-barrel carburetor. Turbo Hydra-Matic automatic transmission, power steering, electric windows, and power brakes were standard. Eighty-three percent of all 1965 Cadillacs had air conditioning and 36.1% were equipped with a tilting and telescoping steering wheel. Buyers had their choice of over 170 upholstery combinations.

1965 Chevrolet Chevelle Malibu Convertible

Original Price: $2,588
Number Produced: (see 1965 Chevelle Malibu Super Sport)
Estimated Number Existing in 1979: (see 1965 Chevelle Malibu Super Sport)
Miles per Gallon: 9–20
Common Trouble Spots: none
Availability of Parts: good
Investment Potential: AA

Background: The boxy Malibu convertible was powered by a 120 h.p. 194 cu. in. six. A 140 h.p. 230 cu. in. six was available at extra cost. Most came with one of the optional V8s, which included a 195 h.p. 283, a 250 h.p. 327, a 300 h.p. 327, and a 350 h.p. 327. A three-speed manual transmission was standard. Powerglide automatic and a four-speed manual were optional.

The majority of '65 Chevelles, 62%, came equipped with a V8, 67.3% had an automatic, 10.3% had the four-speed manual, 33.2% had power steering, 7.7% had power brakes, 2.4% had a tilting steering wheel, 3.6% had power windows, 53.1% had tinted glass, and 11.1% were sold with an air conditioner.

1965 Chevrolet Chevelle Malibu Super Sport Convertible

Original Price: $2,750
Number Produced: 19,765 (includes regular Malibu ragtops)
Estimated Number Existing in 1979: 2,767 (includes regular Malibu ragtops)
Miles per Gallon: 9–20
Common Trouble Spots: none
Availability of Parts: good
Investment Potential: AAA (with RPO Z16 package); AA+ (without)

Background: The Malibu Super Sport was basically a dressed-up version of the regular Malibu. It was powered by a 120 h.p. 194 cu. in. six. A 140 h.p. 230 cu. in. six and several V8 engines, were available at extra cost. The V8s included a 195 h.p. 283, a 250 h.p. 327, a 300 h.p. 327, and a 350 h.p. 327. A three-speed manual transmission was standard. Powerglide automatic and a four-speed manual were available optionally.

An optional RPO Z16 package, featuring a 396 cu. in. V8, was offered later in the model year. *Motor Trend* called a Malibu with this option "without a doubt the hottest and finest car of its type ever made."

1965 Chevrolet Corvair Corsa Convertible

Original Price: $2,665
Number Produced: 8,353
Estimated Number Existing in 1979: 1,169
Miles per Gallon: 16–25
Common Trouble Spots: carburetor
Availability of Parts: good
Investment Potential: AA

Background: The beautiful new Corsa convertible came with a 140 h.p. Turbo-Air 164 cu. in. six. A 180 h.p. Turbocharged 164 cu. in. six was optional. A three-speed manual transmission was standard. A four-speed manual was available at extra cost.

Buyers had their choice of black, blue, and beige tops and thirteen exterior colors. Among the many options were a stereo tape system, deck lid carrier, air conditioner, electric clock, fire extinguisher, and even a tissue dispenser.

The 1965 Corsa convertible is one of the most popular and desirable Corvairs made. It really was, as sales literature put it, "a new stunner in style and spirit."

1965 Chevrolet Corvair Monza Convertible

Original Price: $2,493
Number Produced: 26,466
Estimated Number Existing in 1979: 3,705
Miles per Gallon: 16–27
Common Trouble Spots: carburetor
Availability of Parts: good
Investment Potential: A+

Background: "Open Sesame to driving adventure." That was the promise made to potential Monza buyers by Chevy sales literature. The Monza was powered by a 95 h.p. 164 cu. in. six. Also available were a 110 and a 140 h.p. version of this engine. A three-speed manual transmission was standard. Powerglide automatic and a four-speed manual were optional.

Most 1965 Corvairs, 53.1%, came equipped with an automatic, 33.6% had a four-speed manual, 3.7% had a tilting steering wheel, 49.8% had tinted glass, and 4% were sold with an air conditioner.

Buyers had their choice of all-vinyl upholstery in eight colors: black, blue, fawn, red, saddle, slate, white with aqua, and black with white.

1965 Chevrolet Corvair Monza Convertible

PHOTO: CHEVROLET MOTOR DIVISION

1965 Chevrolet Corvette Stingray Convertible

Original Price: $4,106
Number Produced: 15,376
Estimated Number Existing in 1979: 2,152
Miles per Gallon: 9–17
Common Trouble Spots: none
Availability of Parts: good
Investment Potential: AAA

Background: The new Corvette was powered by a 250 h.p. 327 cu. in. V8. Other versions of this engine included a 300 h.p. (with Holly four-barrel carburetor), a 350 h.p. (with Carter four-barrel carburetor), a 365 h.p. (with Carter four-barrel), a 375 h.p. (with fuel injection), and, late in the model year, a 425 h.p. Turbo-Jet 396.

A three-speed manual was standard (except on the 396 V8). Most 1965 Vettes, 89.7%, were equipped with the optional four-speed manual. Only 8.6% had the Powerglide automatic.

The majority of new Corvettes, 63.1%, came with power steering, 8.5% had power windows, 3.8% had a tilting steering wheel, 58.7% had tinted windows, 22.5% had power brakes, 1.1% had power seats, and 24.4% had an air conditioner. A little more than half of all Vette convertibles were sold with a detachable hard top.

1965 Chevrolet Corvette Convertible

PHOTO: GM PHOTOGRAPHIC

1965 Chevrolet Corvette Stingray Sport Coupe

Original Price: $4,321
Number Produced: 8,186
Estimated Number Existing in 1979: 1,600
Miles per Gallon: 9–17
Common Trouble Spots: brakes
Availability of Parts: good
Investment Potential: AAA

Background: The Stingray received a face-lift for 1965. It was powered by a 250 h.p. 327 cu. in. V8. Other versions of this engine, a 300 h.p. (with Holly four-barrel carburetor), a 350 h.p. (with Carter four-barrel carburetor), a 365 h.p. (with Carter four-barrel carburetor), and a 375 h.p. (with fuel injection), were available at extra cost. Late in the model year, a 425 h.p. 396 cu. in. V8 was optional.

A three-speed manual transmission was standard, but only 1.7% of 1965 Vettes came with it; most had the optional four-speed manual transmission. Only 8.6% had Powerglide automatic transmission.

Power steering was one of the most popular options. Nearly two out of three 1965 Corvettes were sold with it.

Buyers could choose from nine exterior colors: black, blue, green, maroon, red, silver, white, and two shades of yellow.

1965 Chevrolet Corvette Stingray Sport Coupe

PHOTO: T. MICHAELIS CORVETTE SUPPLIES

1965 Chrysler Newport Convertible

1965 Chevrolet Impala Convertible

Original Price: $3,051
Number Produced: 72,760 (includes Super Sport ragtops)
Estimated Number Existing in 1979: 10,186 (includes Super Sport ragtops)
Miles per Gallon: 10–18
Common Trouble Spots: brakes, electrical system, automatic transmission
Availability of Parts: good
Investment Potential: A+

Background: The Impala ragtop was powered by a 140 h.p. 230 cu. in. six. Most came with one of the optional V8 engines, a 195 h.p. 283, a 250 h.p. 327, a 300 h.p. 327, a 300 h.p. 396, a 325 h.p. 396, a 425 h.p. 396, a 340 h.p. 409, and a 400 h.p. 409. A three-speed manual transmission was standard. Powerglide automatic and a four-speed manual transmission were optional.

Most full-size 1965 Chevrolets, 81.5%, came equipped with a V8, 81.6% had an automatic, 3.8% had the four-speed manual, 63.1% had power steering, 22.5% had power brakes, 3.8% had a tilting steering wheel, 8.5% had power windows, 1.1% had a power front seat, 58.7% had tinted glass, and 24.4% were sold with an air conditioner.

1965 Chevrolet Impala Super Sport Convertible

Original Price: $3,212
Number Produced: (see 1965 Chevrolet Impala)
Estimated Number Existing in 1979: (see 1965 Chevrolet Impala)
Miles per Gallon: 10–18
Common Trouble Spots: brakes, electrical system, automatic transmission
Availability of Parts: good
Investment Potential: AA

Background: Chevy's top-of-the-line convertible for 1965 was the new Impala Super Sport. It came with a 140 h.p. 230 cu. in. six. Most Super Sport buyers, over 98%, ordered one of the optional V8s, which included a 195 h.p. 283, a 250 h.p. 327, a 300 h.p. 327, a 300 h.p. 396, a 325 h.p. 396, a 425 h.p. 396, a 340 h.p. 409, and a 400 h.p. 409. A three-speed manual transmission was standard. Powerglide automatic and a four-speed manual were optional.

1965 Chevrolet Impala Super Sport Convertible

PHOTO: GM PHOTOGRAPHIC

1965 Chrysler Newport Convertible

Original Price: $3,442
Number Produced: 3,192
Estimated Number Existing in 1979: 446
Miles per Gallon: 10–16
Common Trouble Spots: brakes, piston rings
Availability of Parts: fair–good
Investment Potential: A+

Background: Newports were given a major face-lift this year that was well received by buyers; sales of Newport convertibles were up about 50 percent.

The standard engine was a 270 h.p. 383 V8. It came with a two-barrel carburetor. A 315 h.p. four-barrel carburetor version of this engine was available. A three-speed manual transmission was standard. Torque Flite Eight automatic transmission was optional. All Newports made from April 1, 1965, on had safety belts in the rear seats (front seat belts had been standard equipment since early 1964).

Most 1965 Chryslers, 99.3%, came equipped with the automatic, 99.6% had power steering, 79.5% had power brakes, 7.4% had a tilting steering wheel, 77% had tinted glass, 22% had power seats, 28% had power windows, and 42.7% were sold with air conditioning.

1965 Chrysler 300 Convertible

Original Price: $3,911
Number Produced: 1,418
Estimated Number Existing in 1979: 198
Miles per Gallon: 8–14
Common Trouble Spots: brakes, piston rings
Availability of Parts: fair–good
Investment Potential: A+

Background: The '65 300 convertible was powered by a 315 h.p. 383 cu. in. FirePower V8 with four-barrel carburetor. A 360 h.p. 413 cu. in. V8 with four-barrel carburetor was optional. A three-speed manual transmission and front bucket seats were standard. Torque Flite Eight automatic and a four-speed manual were available. Most 300s came with the automatic. Rear seat belts became standard in the model year.

Buyers could choose a black, blue, gold, red, tan, or white vinyl interior. Black or red leather upholstery was offered at extra cost.

1965 Chrysler 300-L Convertible

Original Price: $4,618
Number Produced: 440
Estimated Number Existing in 1979: 61
Miles per Gallon: 8–13
Common Trouble Spots: brakes, piston rings
Availability of Parts: fair–good
Investment Potential: A+

Background: The '65 300-L was almost a twin in appearance to the 300 convertible. It was powered by a 360 h.p. 413 cu. in. V8 with four-barrel carburetor and dual exhaust. Buyers had their choice of a four-speed manual or Torque Flite Eight automatic transmission.

Standard features included between-seat console, power steering, power brakes, carpeted trunk, windshield washers, and clock. Some options were leather upholstery, reclining seats with headrests, and "Auto Pilot" (a cruise-control device).

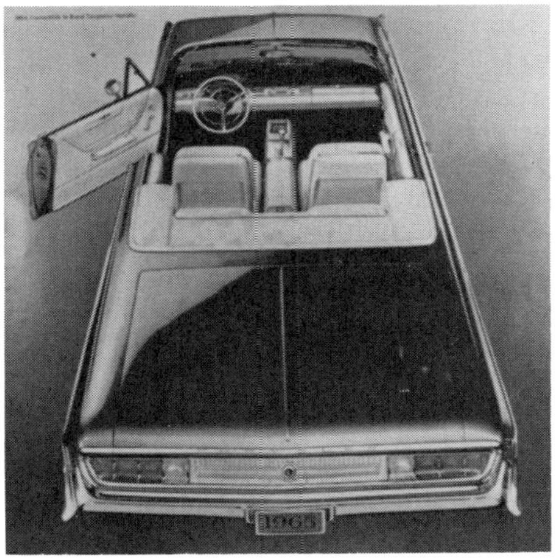

1965 Chrysler 300-L Convertible

1965 Dodge Coronet 500 Convertible

Original Price: $2,869
Number Produced: N.A.
Estimated Number Existing in 1979: N.A.
Miles per Gallon: 10–18
Common Trouble Spots: none
Availability of Parts: fair–good
Investment Potential: A+

Background: The 500 was Coronet's sportiest ragtop in 1965. It featured special wheel covers and trim and an interior that included front bucket seats, padded dash, and seat belts.

It was powered by a 180 h.p. 273 cu. in. V8. Buyers could also choose one of the optional V8 engines: a 230 h.p. 318, a 265 h.p. 361, a 330 h.p. 383, a 330 h.p. 426, a 365 h.p. 426, or a 425 h.p. 426. With the smaller engines, a three-speed manual transmission was standard, and Torque Flite automatic and a four-speed manual were optional. The four-speed manual transmission and heavy-duty brakes and suspension were standard with the 426 V8s.

Dodge advertised the Coronet as an "Animal Tamer." It challenged other manufacturers by saying, "Bring on the [Ford] Mustangs, [Buick] Wildcats, [Chevy] Impalas . . . We'll even squash a few [Corvair] Spyders while we're at it. Dodge has made it a little harder to survive in the asphalt jungle. They just uncaged the Coronet."

1965 Dodge Coronet 500 Convertible

1965 Dodge Coronet 440 Convertible

Original Price: $2,718
Number Produced: N.A.
Estimated Number Existing in 1979: N.A.
Miles per Gallon: 12–19
Common Trouble Spots: none
Availability of Parts: fair–good
Investment Potential: A

Background: The Coronet 440 ragtop came with a 145 h.p. 225 cu. in. slant six. Several V8 engines were available at extra cost: a 180 h.p. 273, a 230 h.p. 318, a 265 h.p. 361, a 330 h.p. 383, and a 365 h.p. 426. A three-speed manual transmission was standard. Torque Flite automatic and a four-speed manual were optional.

Most 1965 Coronets, 75.3%, were equipped with a V8, 84.7% had an automatic, 12.1% had a three-speed manual, 2.2% had a four-speed manual, 61.1% had power steering, 8.4% had power brakes, 46% had tinted glass, 7.1% had power windows, and 14.9% were sold with air conditioning.

1965 Dodge Custom 880 Convertible

Original Price: $3,335
Number Produced: N.A.
Estimated Number Existing in 1979: N.A.
Miles per Gallon: 10–15
Common Trouble Spots: none
Availability of Parts: fair–good
Investment Potential: A

Background: The Custom 880 convertible had clean, boxy styling. Although it wasn't exactly a headturner, it did come with some very potent engines. The standard engine was a 270 h.p. 383 cu. in. V8. A 315 h.p. version of this engine, a 340 h.p. 413 cu. in. V8, a 365 h.p. 426 cu. in. V8, and a 425 h.p. 426 cu. in. Hemi V8, were available at extra cost. A three-speed manual transmission was standard. Torque Flite automatic and a four-speed manual were optional.

1965 Dodge Dart GT Convertible

Original Price: $2,628
Number Produced: N.A.
Estimated Number Existing in 1979: N.A.
Miles per Gallon: 15–23
Common Trouble Spots: none
Availability of Parts: fair–good
Investment Potential: A+

Background: Although not quite as distinctive as the 1964, the '65 Dart GT convertible was a good-looking car. It was powered by a 101 h.p. 170 cu. in. slant six. Available at extra cost were a 145 h.p. 225 cu. in. six, a 180 h.p. 273 cu. in. V8, and a 235 h.p. 273 cu. in. V8. A three-speed manual transmission was standard. Torque Flite automatic and a four-speed manual were optional.

1965 Dodge Dart 270 Convertible

Original Price: $2,481
Number Produced: N.A.
Estimated Number Existing in 1979: N.A.
Miles per Gallon: 15–23
Common Trouble Spots: none
Availability of Parts: fair–good
Investment Potential: A

Background: People who liked the sporty styling of the Dart GT, but could not quite afford it, bought the equally attractive Dart 270. It came with a 101 h.p. 170 cu. in. slant six. Available at extra cost were a 145 h.p. 225 cu. in. six, a 180 h.p. 273 cu. in. V8, and a 235 h.p. 273 cu. in. V8. A three-speed manual transmission was standard. Torque Flite automatic and a four-speed manual were optional.

In keeping with the trend of automakers in the mid-1960s, the lower-priced 270 had more chrome than the GT. This was a complete reverse from the 1950s idea that the more chrome a car had, the more expensive it was (compared to other cars in its series).

Most 1965 Darts, 82.9%, were equipped with a six, 74.3% had an automatic, 32.5% had a three-speed manual, 3.2% had a four-speed manual, 25.6% had power steering, 1.6% had power brakes, .1% had disc brakes, 1.4% had power windows, 38.4% had tinted glass, and 7.2% were sold with an air conditioner.

1965 Dodge Polara Convertible

Original Price: $3,131
Number Produced: N.A.
Estimated Number Existing in 1979: N.A.
Miles per Gallon: 10–16
Common Trouble Spots: none
Availability of Parts: fair–good
Investment Potential: AA (with 500 option); A+ (without)

Background: The boxy new Polara came with a 270 h.p. 383 cu. in. V8 with two-barrel carburetor. A four-barrel, 315 h.p version of this engine, a 340 h.p. 413 cu. in. V8, and a 365 h.p. 426 cu. in. V8 were available at extra cost. A three-speed manual transmission was standard. Torque Flight Eight automatic and a four-speed manual were optional.

As in previous years, a 500 trim package was offered. It included special trim, front bucket seats, and console mounted shifting lever.

Most 1965 Polaras, 98.1%, were equipped with the automatic, 1.3% had the three-speed manual, .6% had the four-speed manual, 96.2% had power steering, 56.9% had power brakes, 5.3% had a tilting steering wheel, 22.5% had power windows, 74.1% had tinted glass, 7.1% had power front seats, and 29.9% were sold with air conditioning.

1965 Ford Falcon Futura Convertible

Original Price: $2,481
Number Produced: 6,315
Estimated Number Existing in 1979: 682
Miles per Gallon: 14–22
Common Trouble Spots: none
Availability of Parts: good
Investment Potential: A+

Background: This was the last Falcon convertible made. And it was a very attractive car. It was powered by a 105 h.p. 170 cu. in. six-cylinder engine. A 120 h.p. 200 cu. in. six and a 200 h.p. 289 cu. in. V8 were optional. A three-speed manual transmission was standard. Cruise-O-Matic automatic and a four-speed manual were available at extra cost.

Most 1965 Falcons, 57.3%, came with the automatic, 18.3% had a V8, 2.4% had a four-speed manual, 8.1% had power steering, 20.4% had tinted glass, and 3.3% were equipped with an air conditioner. Almost 2% of Futura convertibles had bucket seats.

1965 Ford Falcon Futura Convertible

PHOTO: FORD MOTOR COMPANY

1965 Ford Galaxie 500 Convertible

Original Price: $2,950
Number Produced: 31,930
Estimated Number Existing in 1979: 3,448
Miles per Gallon: 9–19
Common Trouble Spots: none
Availability of Parts: good
Investment Potential: A+

Background: The 1965 Galaxie 500 may have cost less than the XL, but it looked just about the same. It was powered by a 150 h.p. 240 cu. in. six-cylinder engine. Buyers had their choice of five V8 engines: a 200 h.p. 289, a 250 h.p. 352, a 300 h.p. 390, a 330 h.p. 390, and a 425 h.p. 427. A three-speed manual transmission was standard. Overdrive, a four-speed manual, and Cruise-O-Matic automatic transmission were optional.

1965 Ford Galaxie 500 XL Convertible

Original Price: $3,493
Number Produced: 9,849
Estimated Number Existing in 1979: 1,063
Miles per Gallon: 9–19
Common Trouble Spots: none
Availability of Parts: good
Investment Potential: A+

Background: The new Galaxie XL was powered by a 200 h.p. 289 cu. in. V8. Four other V8 engines were also available: a 250 h.p. 352, a 300 h.p. 390, a 330 h.p. 390, and a 425 h.p. 427. A three-speed manual transmission was standard. Overdrive, a four-speed manual, and Cruise-O-Matic automatic transmission were optional at extra cost. The vast majority of buyers chose the automatic.

1965 Ford Galaxie 500 XL Convertible

PHOTO: FORD MOTOR COMPANY

1965 Ford Mustang Convertible

Original Price: $2,614
Number Produced: 73,112
Estimated Number Existing in 1979: 7,896
Miles per Gallon: 13–23
Common Trouble Spots: automatic transmission
Availability of Parts: good
Investment Potential: AAA

Background: The new Mustang was powered by a 120 h.p. 200 cu. in. six-cylinder engine. However, most Mustang buyers, 64.4%, chose one of the optional 289 cu. in. V8s, rated at 200 h.p., 225 h.p. and 271 h.p. A high-performance engine package, with heavy-duty suspension, was available for $31.30 on any engine. A three-speed manual transmission was standard. Cruise-O-Matic Drive automatic and a four-speed manual were available at extra cost.

Most 1965 Mustangs, 53.6%, came with the automatic, 14.5% had the four-speed manual, almost 25% had power steering, 4.3% had power brakes, 6.7% had disc brakes, 33.8% had tinted glass, and 9.1% were equipped with an air conditioner.

Buyers had their choice of sixteen exterior colors and five vinyl upholsteries.

1965 Ford Mustang Convertible

PHOTO: FORD MOTOR COMPANY

1965 Ford Mustang Fastback

Original Price: $2,589
Number Produced: 77,079
Estimated Number Existing in 1979: 8,324
Miles per Gallon: 13–23
Common Trouble Spots: none
Availability of Parts: good
Investment Potential: AA+

Background: This was the first year for the Mustang fastback. It came with a 120 h.p. 200 cu. in. six-cylinder engine. Most buyers ordered one of the optional 289 cu. in. V8s, with 200 h.p., 225 h.p., or 271 h.p. A high-performance engine package was available on all engines for only $31.30.

1965 Ford Mustang Fastback

PHOTO: FORD MOTOR COMPANY

A three-speed manual transmission was standard. Most 1965 Mustangs, 53.6%, were equipped with Cruise-O-Matic automatic transmission. The least popular transmission was the optional four-speed manual.

1965 Ford Mustang Two-Door Hardtop

Original Price: $2,372
Number Produced: 409,260
Estimated Number Existing in 1979: 44,200
Miles per Gallon: 13–23
Common Trouble Spots: none
Availability of Parts: good
Investment Potential: AA+

Background: The standard engine in the '65 Mustang was a 120 h.p. 200 cu. in. six-cylinder, but just 35.6% of all Mustangs were so equipped. Most buyers chose one of the optional 289 cu. in. V8s with 200 h.p., 225 h.p., or 271 h.p. For $31.30, a high-performance package could be had.

A three-speed manual transmission was standard, yet only 31.9% came with it. Most had the Cruise-O-Matic automatic. A four-speed manual was optional.

1965 Ford Thunderbird Convertible

Original Price: $4,953
Number Produced: 6,846
Estimated Number Existing in 1979: 739
Miles per Gallon: 8–15
Common Trouble Spots: electrical system
Availability of Parts: fair–good
Investment Potential: AA

Background: The attractive '65 Thunderbird convertible was powered by a 300 h.p. 390 cu. in. V8. Cruise-O-Matic automatic transmission, power steering, power disc brakes, and a tilting steering wheel were standard.

Most '65 Thunderbirds, 77.2%, came with power windows, 73% had tinted glass, 50% had power seats, and 55.7% were sold with air conditioning. A new option was power vent windows.

An interesting feature of the new T-Bird was its sequential turn signals. Many owners were plagued by friends and neighbors who wanted them to turn on their signal lights so they could see the "show."

1965 Ford Thunderbird Convertible

PHOTO: FORD MOTOR COMPANY

1965 Imperial Crown Convertible

Original Price: $6,194
Number Produced: 633
Estimated Number Existing in 1979: 75
Miles per Gallon: 8–14
Common Trouble Spots: none
Availability of Parts: fair–good
Investment Potential: AA

Background: The Imperial softtop was pleasingly restyled for 1965. Like the 1964 model, it had a slight bulge on the trunk to simulate a budding Continental kit. It was especially classy from the front. The headlights were covered by a piece of glass.

It was powered by a 340 h.p. 413 cu. in. V8 engine. Torque Flite Eight automatic transmission, power steering, power brakes, and electric windows were standard. As in previous years, the interior was very plush and comfortable.

More than 60% of all Imperials sold in 1965 came with the optional leather interior. A whopping 93% had air conditioning, 96.7% had power seats, 96.9% had tinted glass, and 29.9% came with a tilting steering wheel.

Unlike some Imperials (and other cars), the 1965 has the sort of clean, elegant styling that remains attractive over the years. Beauty, luxury, and low production make this a car to watch.

1965 King Midget Convertible

Original Price: $800
Number Produced: 141
Estimated Number Existing in 1979: 9
Miles per Gallon: 50–90
Common Trouble Spots: transmission, "V" belts
Availability of Parts: good
Investment Potential: A

Background: The 1965 King Midget convertible was powered by a 10 h.p. 29 cu. in. one-cylinder engine. Automatic transmission was standard.

1965 Lincoln Continental Convertible

Original Price: $6,938
Number Produced: 3,356
Estimated Number Existing in 1979: 466
Miles per Gallon: 9–13
Common Trouble Spots: none
Availability of Parts: fair–good
Investment Potential: AAA

Background: The Continental received a pleasing face-lift for 1965. It was powered by a 320 h.p. 430 cu. in. V8. Turbo-Drive automatic transmission was standard.

All 1965 Lincolns were equipped with power steering, power disc brakes, electric windows, and power front seats. Most, 97.5%, had tinted glass, 26.4% had a tilting steering wheel, and 90.6% were sold with air conditioning.

Buyers had their choice of a black, blue, tan, or white top.

1965 Mercury Comet Caliente Convertible

Original Price: $2,664
Number Produced: 6,035
Estimated Number Existing in 1979: 706
Miles per Gallon: 12–20
Common Trouble Spots: none
Availability of Parts: good–fair
Investment Potential: A+

Background: The new Caliente convertible came with a 120 h.p. 200 cu. in. six. Two V8 engines, a 200 h.p. 289 and a 225 h.p. 289, were available at extra cost. A three-speed manual transmission was standard. Multi-Drive automatic and a four-speed manual were optional.

Most 1965 Comets, 51.3%, were equipped with a V8, 65.5% had the automatic, 7.5% had the four-speed manual, 25.7% had power steering, 3.8% had power brakes, 33.5% had tinted glass, 1.9% had power windows, and 5.4% had an air conditioner. Many 1965 Caliente convertibles, 26.9%, had bucket seats.

1965 Mercury Monterey Convertible

Original Price: $3,230
Number Produced: 4,762
Estimated Number Existing in 1979: 557
Miles per Gallon: 9–16
Common Trouble Spots: none
Availability of Parts: good–fair
Investment Potential: A+

Background: The expensive looking '65 Monterey convertible came with a 250 h.p. 390 cu. in. V8. Three other V8 engines, a 300 h.p. 390, a 330 h.p. 390, and a 425 h.p. 427, were available at extra cost. A three-speed manual transmission was standard. Overdrive, a four-speed manual, and Multi-Drive automatic transmission were optional.

Most 1965 Mercurys, 97.1, were equipped with an automatic, .3% had a four-speed manual, 94.2% had power steering, 59.8% had power brakes, 6.4% had a tilting steering wheel, 64.6% had tinted glass, 21.6% had power windows, 9.7% had power front seats, and 29.6% were sold with an air conditioner. Six percent of 1965 Monterey convertibles had bucket seats. These were offered in blue, palomino, or white. The standard all-vinyl interior came in black, blue, palomino, red, or white. Seventeen solid exterior colors were available.

1965 Mercury Monterey Convertible

PHOTO: FORD MOTOR COMPANY

1965 Mercury Comet Caliente Convertible

PHOTO: FORD MOTOR COMPANY

1965 Mercury Park Lane Convertible

PHOTO: FORD MOTOR COMPANY

1965 Mercury Park Lane Convertible

Original Price: $3,599
Number Produced: 3,006
Estimated Number Existing in 1979: 351
Miles per Gallon: 9–15
Common Trouble Spots: none
Availability of Parts: good–fair
Investment Potential: A+

Background: The attractive '65 Park Lane convertible came with a 300 h.p. 390 cu. in. V8. Two other V8 engines, a 330 h.p. 390 and a 425 h.p. 427, were available at extra cost. A three-speed manual was standard. Multi-Drive automatic and a four-speed manual were optional. Over 30% of 1965 Park Lane convertibles had bucket seats.

Seventeen exterior colors were offered: aquamarine, blue ice, burgundy, carnival red, fawn, ivy gold, midnight blue, olive mist, ocean turquoise, onyx, pecan frost, pearl gray, polar white, Tiffany blue, sanddrift, silver turquoise, and yellow mist.

The standard all-vinyl interior was available in black, blue, ivy, gold, palomino, red, turquoise, or white. Leather bench seats could be had in burgundy or palomino. Optional bucket seats came in black, blue, palomino, red, or white.

1965 Oldsmobile Dynamic 88 Convertible

Original Price: $3,408
Number Produced: 8,832
Estimated Number Existing in 1979: 768
Miles per Gallon: 10–16
Common Trouble Spots: carburetor
Availability of Parts: good
Investment Potential: A+

Background: The new Dynamic 88 softtop had the same 123″ wheelbase as the previous year's model, but it was slightly lighter. Like all 1965 Olds, it was attractively restyled.

A 310 h.p. 425 cu. in. V8 powered the Dynamic 88. Two other versions of this engine, a 300 h.p. and a 360 h.p., were available at extra cost. A three-speed manual transmission was standard, but not many were sold that way. Turbo Hydra-Matic automatic transmission and a four-speed manual were optional.

1965 Oldsmobile F-85 Cutlass Convertible

Original Price: $2,983
Number Produced: 12,628
Estimated Number Existing in 1979: 1,098
Miles per Gallon: 11–17
Common Trouble Spots: carburetor
Availability of Parts: good
Investment Potential: AA (with the 4-4-2 option); A+ (without)

Background: The F-85 Cutlass received attractive new styling for 1965. It was powered by a 315 h.p. 330 cu. in. V8. A three-speed manual transmission was standard, but not very popular; most F-85s, 86.4%, came with the optional Jetaway automatic transmission. Only 7.9% were equipped with a four-speed manual transmission.

Just over 79% of all F-85s had power steering, 50.6% had power brakes, 3.9% had a tilting steering wheel, 20.9% had power windows, 2.9% had power front seats, 69.1% had tinted glass, and 27.4% were sold with air conditioning.

Once again the "hot" 4-4-2 performance package was available. It featured a 345 h.p. 400 cu. in. V8 engine and special trim inside and out. Approximately one out of every four 1965 F-85 Cutlass convertibles came with the 4-4-2 option.

1965 Oldsmobile F-85 Cutlass Convertible

PHOTO: OLDSMOBILE DIVISION

1965 Oldsmobile Dynamic 88 Convertible

PHOTO: OLDSMOBILE DIVISION

1965 Oldsmobile Jetstar 88 Convertible

PHOTO: OLDSMOBILE DIVISION

1965 Oldsmobile Starfire Convertible

Original Price: $4,778
Number Produced: 2,236
Estimated Number Existing in 1979: 194
Miles per Gallon: 9–14
Common Trouble Spots: carburetor
Availability of Parts: good
Investment Potential: A+

Background: Oldsmobile's top-of-the-line Starfire convertible was attractively restyled for the new year. It was powered by a 360 h.p. 425 cu. in V8. Turbo Hydra-Matic automatic transmission was standard.

1965 Oldsmobile Jetstar 88 Convertible

Original Price: $3,337
Number Produced: 2,879
Estimated Number Existing in 1979: 250
Miles per Gallon: 12–17
Common Trouble Spots: carburetor
Availability of Parts: good
Investment Potential: A+

Background: The new Jetstar 88 convertible had attractive styling. It was powered by a 260 h.p. 330 cu. in. V8. A 315 h.p. version of this engine was available at extra cost. A three-speed manual transmission was standard, but not very popular. The vast majority came with optional Jetaway automatic transmission. Only one-fifth of one percent of all full-size 1965 Oldsmobiles had the optional four-speed manual.

1965 Oldsmobile 98 Convertible

Original Price: $4,493
Number Produced: 4,903
Estimated Number Existing in 1979: 426
Miles per Gallon: 8–14
Common Trouble Spots: carburetor
Availability of Parts: good
Investment Potential: A+

Background: The new 98 convertible had more graceful lines than last year's model. It was powered by a 360 h.p. 425 cu. in. V8. A 370 h.p. version of this engine was available at extra cost. Turbo Hydra-Matic automatic transmission was standard.

Air conditioning was a popular option on full-size Olds in 1965; nearly 49% were so equipped. Only 3.9% had a tilting steering wheel, 20.9% had power windows, and a mere 2.7% had power front seats.

1965 Plymouth Belvedere Satellite Convertible

Original Price: $2,869
Number Produced: N.A.
Estimated Number Existing in 1979: N.A.
Miles per Gallon: 10–17
Common Trouble Spots: none
Availability of Parts: fair–good
Investment Potential: A+

Background: The new Satellite came with a 180 h.p. 273 cu. in. V8. Five other V8 engines were available at extra cost: a 230 h.p. 318, a 265 h.p. 361, a 330 h.p. 383, a 365 h.p. 426, a 415 h.p. 426, and a 425 h.p. 426 Hemi. A three-speed manual transmission was standard. A four-speed manual and Torque Flite Eight automatic transmission were optional.

Most 1965 Belvederes, 75%, were equipped with an automatic transmission, 4% had the four-speed manual, 42.6% had power steering, 6.6% had power brakes, 35.6% had tinted glass, 4.8% had power windows, and 10.3% were sold with air conditioning.

1965 Plymouth Belvedere Satellite Convertible

1965 Plymouth Belvedere II Convertible

1965 Plymouth Belvedere II Convertible

Original Price: $2,693
Number Produced: 1,921
Estimated Number Existing in 1979: 249
Miles per Gallon: 10–19
Common Trouble Spots: none
Availability of Parts: fair–good
Investment Potential: A

Background: For the first time since 1959, Plymouth offered a Belvedere convertible. It came with a 145 h.p. 225 cu. in. six-cylinder engine. Six V8 engines were available at extra cost: a 180 h.p. 273, a 230 h.p. 318, a 265 h.p. 361, a 330 h.p. 383, a 365 h.p. 426, a 415 h.p. 426, and a 425 h.p. 426. Nearly 66% of all 1965 Belvederes came with a V8 engine.

A three-speed manual transmission was standard, except with the 426, which came with a standard four-speed floor-mounted manual. The four-speed manual was optional with the 361 and 383 V8s. Torque Flite automatic transmission was optional with all engines.

1965 Plymouth Fury III Convertible

Original Price: $3,048
Number Produced: N.A.
Estimated Number Existing in 1979: N.A.
Miles per Gallon: 10–18
Common Trouble Spots: none
Availability of Parts: fair–good
Investment Potential: A+

Background: The 1965 Fury III came with a 145 h.p. 225 cu. in. six-cylinder engine. Four V8 engines were available at extra cost: a 230 h.p. 318, a 270 h.p. 383, a 330 h.p. 383, and a 365 h.p. 426. A three-speed manual transmission was standard. A four-speed manual and Torque Flite automatic transmission were optional.

Most 1965 Furys, 89.3 percent, were equipped with a V8 engine, 89.3% had an automatic, 2.6% had a four-speed manual, 75.4% had power steering, 23.8% had power brakes, 1.4% had a tilting steering wheel, 54% had tinted glass, 11.8% had power windows, 1.1% had power front seats, and 20.4% were sold with air conditioning.

1965 Plymouth Sport Fury Convertible

Original Price: $3,209
Number Produced: N.A.
Estimated Number Existing in 1979: N.A.
Miles per Gallon: 10–16
Common Trouble Spots: none
Availability of Parts: fair–good
Investment Potential: A+

Background: The new Sport Fury was the flashiest Plymouth in 1965. It came with a 230 h.p. 318 cu. in. V8. Three other V8s were available at extra cost: a 270 h.p. 383, a 330 h.p. 383, and a 365 h.p. 426.

A three-speed manual transmission was standard except with the 426, which came with a standard floor-mounted four-speed manual transmission. The four-speed manual and Torque Flite Eight automatic transmission were optional with all engines. The vast majority of Sport Furys came with automatic transmission.

A new option available on the Sport Fury this year was Auto-Pilot speed control. Buyers had their choice of fifteen exterior colors.

1965 Plymouth Sport Fury Convertible

1965 Plymouth Fury III Convertible

1965 Plymouth Valiant Signet Convertible

Original Price: $2,561
Number Produced: N.A.
Estimated Number Existing in 1979: N.A.
Miles per Gallon: 15–21
Common Trouble Spots: none
Availability of Parts: fair–good
Investment Potential: A+

Background: The face-lifted Signet convertible was a good-looking little car. It came with a 101 h.p. 170 cu. in. six-cylinder engine. A 145 h.p. 225 cu. in. six and two V8s, a 180 h.p. 273 and a 235 h.p. 273, were available at extra cost. Less than 10% of all Valiants were equipped with a V8.

A three-speed manual transmission was standard. Torque Flite automatic and a four-speed manual were optional.

1965 Plymouth Valiant 200 Convertible

Original Price: $2,437
Number Produced: N.A.
Estimated Number Existing in 1979: N.A.
Miles per Gallon: 15–21
Common Trouble Spots: none
Availability of Parts: fair–good
Investment Potential: A+

Background: The new Valiant 200 was powered by a 101 h.p. 170 cu. in. six-cylinder engine. A 145 h.p. 225 cu. in. six and two V8s, a 180 h.p. 273 and a 235 h.p. 273, were available at extra cost. A three-speed manual transmission was standard. Torque Flite automatic and a four-speed manual transmission were optional.

Most 1965 Valiants, 90.3 percent, were equipped with a six-cylinder engine, 66.8% had an automatic, 1.3% had a four-speed manual, 14.6% had power steering, 1.6% had power brakes, .5% had disc brakes, 2.1% had electric windows, 27.6% had tinted glass, and 4.6% were sold with air conditioning.

1965 Pontiac Bonneville Convertible

Original Price: $3,594
Number Produced: 21,050
Estimated Number Existing in 1979: 2,526
Miles per Gallon: 8–16
Common Trouble Spots: brakes, carburetor
Availability of Parts: good–fair
Investment Potential: A+

Background: The '65 Bonneville convertible was powered by a 333 h.p. 389 cu. in. V8 with four-barrel carburetor. Four other V8 engines were available at extra cost: a 338 h.p. 389 (three two-barrel carbs), a 338 h.p. 421 (four-barrel carb), a 356 h.p. 421 (three two-barrel carbs), and a 376 h.p. 421 (three two-barrel carbs).

A Ford (that's right, Ford) three-speed manual transmission was standard. Turbo Hydra-Matic automatic transmission and a four-speed manual were optional.

Most full-size 1965 Pontiacs, 96.3%, came with the automatic, 95.7% had power steering, 86.5% had power brakes, 9% had a tilting steering wheel, 73.2% had tinted glass, 22.9% had electric windows, 7.6% had power front seats, and 39% were sold with air conditioning. A new feature available on the air conditioner was an automatic temperature control. Leather interior was also offered.

1965 Pontiac Bonneville Convertible

PHOTO: PONTIAC MOTOR DIVISION

1965 Pontiac Catalina Convertible

Original Price: $3,196
Number Produced: 18,347
Estimated Number Existing in 1979: 2,201
Miles per Gallon: 9–16
Common Trouble Spots: brakes, carburetor
Availability of Parts: good–fair
Investment Potential: AA (with 2+2 option); A+ (without)

Background: The new Catalina convertible was a bit flashier than the previous year's model. It was powered by a 256 h.p. 389 cu. in. V8. Five other V8 engines were available at extra cost: a 290 h.p. 389, a 333 h.p. 389, a 338 h.p. 389, a 338 h.p. 421, a 356 h.p. 421, and a 376 h.p. 421. A Ford three-speed manual transmission was standard. Turbo Hydra-Matic automatic and a four-speed manual were optional.

The 2+2 option was once again offered. The price this year was $397. It featured a 421 cu. in V8, 3.42 performance rear axle, floor-mounted three-speed, dual exhaust, heavy-duty shocks and springs, engine dress-up kit, and distinctive trim and interior. In mid-model year, buyers could order special striping in their choice of three colors. Approximately 10% of Catalina softtops were sold with this option.

1965 Pontiac Le Mans Convertible

Original Price: $2,797
Number Produced: 25,208 (11,311 with the GTO option)
Estimated Number Existing in 1979: 3,024
Miles per Gallon: 11–19
Common Trouble Spots: carburetor
Availability of Parts: good–fair
Investment Potential: AA+ (with GTO option); AA (without)

Background: The '65 Le Mans convertible had very sporty lines. It was powered by a 140 h.p. 215 cu. in. six-cylinder engine with a one barrel carburetor. Three V8 engines were available at extra cost: a 250 h.p. 326 (two-barrel carb), a 285 h.p. 326 (four-barrel carb), and a 335 h.p. 389 (four-barrel carb). A three-speed manual transmission was standard. A four-speed manual and an automatic transmission were optional.

Speaking of options, the Le Mans had the most famous one in the industry—the GTO. The GTO came with a 335 h.p. 389 cu. in. V8 with four-barrel carburetor. Buyers could also order a 360 h.p. version of this engine with three two-barrel carburetors. A three-speed, floor-mounted manual transmission was standard. A four-speed manual and an automatic were optional.

Among the other standard features on the GTO were bucket seats, dual exhaust, chromed air cleaner, oil filler cap, and rocker panels. In mid-model year, customers could get hand-painted special striping in one of three colors.

A special gold-painted GTO, with distinctive "tiger appointed interior," was offered as a prize in a contest sponsored by Hurst Performance Products. Contestants had to count the number of times the word "tiger" was sung in the song "GeeTo Tiger" by a group named (you guessed it) the Tigers. They also had to write, in twenty-five words or less, "Why I would like to own the original GeeTo Tiger."

1965 Pontiac Le Mans Convertible

PHOTO: PONTIAC MOTOR DIVISION

1965 Pontiac Tempest Custom Convertible

Original Price: $2,691
Number Produced: 8,346
Estimated Number Existing in 1979: 1,001
Miles per Gallon: 12–20
Common Trouble Spots: carburetor
Availability of Parts: good–fair
Investment Potential: A+

Background: The 1965 Tempest Custom convertible was a sharp-looking little car. It had a bolder, more assertive appearance than last year's model.

The Custom was powered by a 140 h.p. 215 cu. in. six-cylinder engine with a one-barrel carburetor. Three V8 engines were available at extra cost: a 250 h.p. 326 (two-barrel carb), a 285 h.p. 326 (four-barrel carb), and a 335 h.p. 389 (four-barrel carb). A three-speed manual transmission was standard. A four-speed manual and an automatic transmission were optional.

Most 1965 Tempests, 68.9%, came with the automatic, 77.1% had one of the V8 engines, 54.7% had power steering, 25.4% had power brakes, 1.6% had a tilting steering wheel, 4.3% had electric windows, just under 1% had power front seats, 53% had tinted glass, and 14.9% were sold with air conditioning.

1965 Rambler Ambassador Convertible

Original Price: $2,955
Number Produced: 3,499
Estimated Number Existing in 1979: 314
Miles per Gallon: 13–19
Common Trouble Spots: none
Availability of Parts: fair
Investment Potential: A

Background: This was the first Ambassador convertible since 1948. It featured a padded dash and all-vinyl upholstery. Tops were offered in aqua, blue, black, and white.

The Ambassador softtop came with a 155 h.p. 232 cu. in. six-cylinder engine. Two V8 engines, a 198 h.p. 287 and a 270 h.p. 327, were available at extra cost. A three-speed manual transmission was standard. Overdrive and Flash-O-Matic automatic transmission were optional.

1965 Rambler American Convertible

Original Price: $2,418
Number Produced: 3,882
Estimated Number Existing in 1979: 349
Miles per Gallon: 14–23
Common Trouble Spots: none
Availability of Parts: fair–poor
Investment Potential: A+

1965 Rambler American Convertible

Background: The American ragtop received a pleasing face-lift for 1965. It was powered by a 125 h.p. 195.6 cu. in. six-cylinder engine. A 155 h.p. 232 cu. in. six was available at extra cost. A three-speed manual transmission was standard. Overdrive and Flash-O-Matic automatic transmission were optional (the automatic was standard with the 232 cu. in. six).

1965 Rambler Classic Convertible

Original Price: $2,696
Number Produced: 4,953
Estimated Number Existing in 1979: 564
Miles per Gallon: 13–19
Common Trouble Spots: automatic transmission
Availability of Parts: fair
Investment Potential: A

Background: This was the first year for the Classic convertible. It came with a 145 h.p. 232 cu. in. six-cylinder engine. A 155 h.p. version of this engine and two V8s, a 198 h.p. 287 and a 270 h.p. 327, were available at extra cost. A three-speed manual transmission was standard. Overdrive and Flash-O-Matic automatic transmission were optional.

Most 1965 Ramblers, 70.2%, were equipped with the automatic, 72.4% had a six-cylinder engine, 32.9% had power steering, 17.9% had power brakes, 4.3% had disc brakes, 4.7% had power windows, 3.4% had a tilting steering wheel, 34.6% had tinted glass, and 12.1% were sold with air conditioning.

1965 Rambler Classic Convertible

1965 Shelby American GT 350 Fastback

Original Price: est. $4,400
Number Produced: 550
Estimated Number Existing in 1979: 59
Miles per Gallon: 9–15
Common Trouble Spots: none
Availability of Parts: fair–good
Investment Potential: AAA

Background: This was the first of the famous Shelby GT 350s. Many believe that the 1965 and 1966 models were the best. It came with a 306 h.p. 289 cu. in. V8 that could propel the car from 0 to 60 in 5.7 seconds. A four-speed manual transmission was standard.

1965 Shelby American GT 350 Fastback

PHOTO: HOWARD AND SHELBY APPLEGATE

1966

1966 Buick Electra 225 Custom Convertible

Original Price: \$4,378
Number Produced: 7,175
Estimated Number Existing in 1979: 1,004
Miles per Gallon: 9–15
Common Trouble Spots: none
Availability of Parts: good
Investment Potential: A+

Background: The Electra convertible received a minor face-lift for 1966. It was powered by a 325 h.p. 401 cu. in. V8 with four-barrel carburetor. Also available was a 340 h.p. 425 cu. in. V8. Super Turbine automatic transmission was standard. Power brakes and power steering were also standard. Bucket seats and air conditioning were among the options.

1966 Buick Electra 225 Custom Convertible

1966 Buick LeSabre Custom Convertible

Original Price: \$3,326
Number Produced: 4,994
Estimated Number Existing in 1979: 699
Miles per Gallon: 12–17
Common Trouble Spots: none
Availability of Parts: good
Investment Potential: A

Background: The new LeSabre ragtop was powered by a 220 h.p. 340 cu. in. V8 with two-barrel carburetor. Also available was a 260 h.p. four-barrel-carburetor version of this engine. A three-speed manual transmission was standard. Super Turbine automatic transmission was a very popular option.

Bench seats were standard, bucket seats optional. Almost 93% of all full-size Buicks came with power brakes, 99.1% had power steering, 28% had power windows, 25.9% had power seats, and 54.4% were ordered with air conditioning.

1966 Buick LeSabre Custom Convertible

1966 Buick Skylark Convertible

Original Price: $2,837
Number Produced: 8,784
Estimated Number Existing in 1979: 1,229
Miles per Gallon: 12–19
Common Trouble Spots: none
Availability of Parts: good
Investment Potential: AA (with Gran Sport package); A+ (without)

Background: The attractive '66 Skylark convertible was powered by a 160 h.p. 225 cu. in. V6. Also available were a 210 h.p. 300 cu. in. V8 and a 260 h.p. 340 cu. in. V8. A three-speed manual transmission was standard. Super Turbine automatic was optional. Most people ordered the automatic and a V8.

The Skylark was also available with the Gran Sport package. It featured an optional engine dress-up kit, heavy-duty suspension, all-vinyl interior, 325 h.p. 400 cu. in. V8, red-line or whitewall tires, full wheel covers, simulated airscoops on the hood, carpeting, and special insignias. A total of 2,047 Skylark convertibles were so equipped in 1966.

The 1964 to 1969 Skylarks have a reputation among used-car dealers as being of unusually high quality. Therefore, mid-to-late 1960s Skylarks tend to command higher prices than many of their contemporaries. Despite this they usually sell quickly. Especially the two-door hardtops and convertibles with Gran Sport packages.

1966 Buick Special Convertible

Original Price: $2,604
Number Produced: 3,393
Estimated Number Existing in 1979: 475
Miles per Gallon: 13–20
Common Trouble Spots: none
Availability of Parts: good
Investment Potential: A+ (with Gran Sport package); A (without)

Background: The Special continued to be Buick's lowest-priced ragtop. It came with a 160 h.p. 225 cu. in. V6 engine (only 18.3% of Special convertibles were so equipped). A 210 h.p. 300 cu. in. V8 was optional. A three-speed manual was standard, but only 5.5% of all Specials were sold with it; the vast majority of buyers ordered the optional Super Turbine automatic.

Eighty percent of '66 Specials had power steering, 35.2% had power brakes, 17.9% had power windows, 3% had power front seats, and 27.7% came with air conditioning.

A Gran Sport package was offered.

1966 Buick Wildcat Convertible

Original Price: $3,480
Number Produced: 2,690
Estimated Number Existing in 1979: 376
Miles per Gallon: 9–15
Common Trouble Spots: none
Availability of Parts: good
Investment Potential: A

Background: The new Wildcat convertible came with a 325 h.p. 401 cu. in. V8 with four-barrel carburetor. Also available was a 340 h.p. 425 cu. in. V8. A three-speed manual transmission was standard, but not very popular; a whopping 99.8% of all full-size '66 Buicks were ordered with automatic transmission.

1966 Buick Wildcat Custom Convertible

Original Price: $3,701
Number Produced: 2,790
Estimated Number Existing in 1979: 378
Miles per Gallon: 9–15
Common Trouble Spots: none
Availability of Parts: good
Investment Potential: A+

Background: The Wildcat Custom convertible was powered by a 325 h.p. 401 cu. in. V8 with four-barrel carburetor. Also available was a 340 h.p. 425 cu. in. V8. A three-speed manual transmission was standard. But most people ordered the Super Turbine automatic.

An optional Gran Sport package was offered. It featured a 340 h.p. 425 cu. in. V8, heavy-duty suspension, dual exhaust, and engine dress-up kit.

1966 Cadillac Eldorado Convertible

PHOTO: CADILLAC MOTOR CAR DIVISION

1966 Cadillac Fleetwood Eldorado Convertible

Original Price: $6,631
Number Produced: 2,250
Estimated Number Existing in 1979: 495
Miles per Gallon: 10–14

Common Trouble Spots: none
Availability of Parts: good–fair
Investment Potential: AA

Background: One might call this the first "last" Eldorado convertible. Cadillac wouldn't make another Eldorado softtop until 1971. It came with a 340 h.p. 429 cu. in. V8 engine. Turbo Hydra-Matic automatic transmission, power brakes, electric windows, and a new power steering were standard. Air conditioning was one of the most popular options (even though it cost over $500).

1966 Cadillac De Ville Convertible

Original Price: $5,555
Number Produced: 19,200
Estimated Number Existing in 1979: 4,224
Miles per Gallon: 10–14
Common Trouble Spots: none
Availability of Parts: good–fair
Investment Potential: A+

Background: The De Ville was powered by a 340 h.p. 429 cu. in. V8 engine. Turbo Hydra-Matic automatic transmission, power brakes, electric windows, and a new power steering were standard.

A rather unique option offered on 1966 Cadillacs was an electric seat warmer. It had to be turned on manually, but it would go off when the heater fan came on (or the driver turned it off). Over 88% of all 1966 Cadillacs were so equipped.

1966 Cadillac De Ville Convertible

PHOTO: CADILLAC MOTOR CAR DIVISION

1966 Chevrolet Chevelle Malibu Convertible

Original Price: $2,588
Number Produced: N.A.
Estimated Number Existing in 1979: N.A.
Miles per Gallon: 9–20
Common Trouble Spots: none
Availability of Parts: good
Investment Potential: AA

Background: The 1966 Malibu convertible was powered by a 120 h.p. 194 cu. in. six. A 140 h.p. 230 cu. in. six was available at extra cost. Several V8 engines were offered: a 195 h.p. 283, a 220 h.p. 283, and a 275 h.p. 327. A three-speed manual transmission was standard. Overdrive, a four-speed manual, and Powerglide automatic transmission were optional.

Most '66 Chevelles, 73.9%, came equipped with a V8, 65.4% had an automatic, 17.2% had a three-speed manual, 17.4% had a four-speed manual, 41.4% had power steering, 7.5% had power brakes, 1.4% had a tilting steering wheel, 3.4% had power windows, one-third of 1% had a power front seat, 59.8% had tinted glass, and 13.6% were sold with an air conditioner.

1966 Chevrolet Chevelle Super Sport Convertible

Original Price: $2,984
Number Produced: N.A.
Estimated Number Existing in 1979: N.A.
Miles per Gallon: 9–15
Common Trouble Spots: none
Availability of Parts: good
Investment Potential: AA+

Background: The new Chevelle Super Sport ragtop came with a 325 h.p. 396 cu. in. V8. Buyers also had their choice of a 360 h.p. and a 375 h.p. version of this engine. A floor-mounted three-speed manual transmission was standard. Powerglide automatic and a four-speed manual were optional.

The Chevelle Super Sport had stiffer coil springs and a heavier front stabilizer than the Malibu. It also had a special grille, hood, insignias, and chromed rocker arm covers and air cleaner. The interior was all vinyl.

1966 Chevrolet Chevelle Super Sport Convertible

PHOTO: GM PHOTOGRAPHIC

1966 Chevrolet Corvair Corsa Convertible

Original Price: $2,662
Number Produced: 3,142
Estimated Number Existing in 1979: 659
Miles per Gallon: 16–23
Common Trouble Spots: none
Availability of Parts: good
Investment Potential: AA

Background: This was the last year for the attractive Corsa convertible. It was powered by a 140 h.p. 164 cu. in. six. A 180 h.p. version of this engine was available at extra cost. A three-speed manual transmission was standard. A four-speed manual transmission was optional.

The 1966 Corsa convertible is one of the most desirable and popular of all Corvairs.

1966 Chevrolet Corvair Corsa Convertible

PHOTO: GM PHOTOGRAPHIC

1966 Chevrolet Corvair Monza Convertible

Original Price: $2,493
Number Produced: 10,345
Estimated Number Existing in 1979: 2,172
Miles per Gallon: 16–25
Common Trouble Spots: none
Availability of Parts: good
Investment Potential: A+

Background: The '66 Monza ragtop was a very attractive little car. It came with a 95 h.p. 164 cu. in. six. Buyers could order a 110 h.p. or a 140 h.p. version of this engine at extra cost. A three-speed manual transmission was standard. Powerglide automatic and a four-speed manual were optional.

Most 1966 Corvairs, 57.2%, came equipped with the automatic, 16.1% had a three-speed manual, 26.7% had the four-speed manual, 2.2% had a tilting steering wheel, 47.9% had tinted glass, and 4.6% were sold with an air conditioner.

1966 Chevrolet Corvair Monza Convertible

1966 Chevrolet Corvette Stingray Convertible

Original Price: $4,084
Number Produced: 17,762
Estimated Number Existing in 1979: 3,730
Miles per Gallon: 9–18
Common Trouble Spots: none
Availability of Parts: good
Investment Potential: AAA

Background: The '66 Vette ragtop was powered by a 300 h.p. 327 cu. in. V8. Other V8 engines included a 350 h.p. 327, a 390 h.p. 427, and a 425 h.p. 427. A three-speed manual transmission was standard (except on the 427). Most 1966 Vettes, 89.3%, had the optional four-speed manual transmission. Only 8.7% had Powerglide automatic transmission.

Slightly over 20% of new Corvettes had power steering, 19.7% had power brakes, 13.2% had a tilting steering wheel, 76.2% had tinted glass, 16.5% had power windows, and 12.7% were sold with an air conditioner. A little over half of 1966 Corvette convertible buyers purchased the detachable hard top.

1966 Chevrolet Corvette Convertible

PHOTO: T. MICHAELIS CORVETTE SUPPLIES

1966 Chevrolet Corvette Stingray Sport Coupe

Original Price: $4,295
Number Produced: 9,958
Estimated Number Existing in 1979: 2,000
Miles per Gallon: 9–18
Common Trouble Spots: none
Availability of Parts: good
Investment Potential: AAA

Background: The '66 Stingray came with a 300 h.p. 327 cu. in. V8. Other V8 engines available at extra cost included a 350 h.p. 327, a 390 h.p. 427, and a 425 h.p. 427. A three-speed manual transmission was standard (except on the 427 cu. in. V8). Nearly nine out of ten 1966 Vettes were equipped with the optional four-speed manual. Only 8.7% had Powerglide automatic transmission.

Buyers had their choice of ten exterior colors. Leather upholstery was optional.

1966 Chevrolet Impala Convertible

Original Price: $2,935
Number Produced: N.A.
Estimated Number Existing in 1979: N.A.
Miles per Gallon: 9–18
Common Trouble Spots: carburetor, electrical system
Availability of Parts: good
Investment Potential: A+

Background: The new Impala convertible came with a 155 h.p. 250 cu. in. six. Optional V8 engines included a a 195 h.p. 283, a 250 h.p. 327, a 300 h.p. 327, a 300 h.p. 396, a 390 h.p. 427, and a 425 h.p. 427. A three-speed manual transmission was standard. Overdrive, a four-speed manual, and Powerglide automatic were available at extra cost.

Most 1966 full-size Chevrolets, 86.2%, came equipped with a V8, 85.3% had an automatic, 12.5% had the three-speed manual, 2.1% had the four-speed manual, 69.3% had power steering, 24.2% had power brakes, 3.1% had a tilting steering wheel, 10.5% had power windows, 1.6% had power front seats, 65.4% had tinted glass, and 29.8% were sold with an air conditioner.

1966 Chevrolet Impala Super Sport Convertible

Original Price: $3,093
Number Produced: N.A.
Estimated Number Existing in 1979: N.A.
Miles per Gallon: 9–18
Common Trouble Spots: carburetor, electrical system
Availability of Parts: good
Investment Potential: AA

Background: The attractive new Impala Super Sport ragtop was powered by a 155 h.p. 250 cu. in. six. Most Super Sport buyers ordered one of the optional V8 engines: a 195 h.p. 283, a 220 h.p. 283, a 275 h.p. 327, a 325 h.p. 396, a 390 h.p. 427, and a 425 h.p. 427. A three-speed manual transmission was standard. Overdrive, a four-speed manual and Powerglide automatic transmission were available at extra cost.

1966 Chevrolet Impala Super Sport Convertible

PHOTO: GM PHOTOGRAPHIC

1966 Chrysler Newport Convertible

Original Price: $3,476
Number Produced: 3,085
Estimated Number Existing in 1979: 678
Miles per Gallon: 9–17
Common Trouble Spots: none
Availability of Parts: good
Investment Potential: A+

Background: The 1966 Newport softtop was powered by a 270 h.p. 383 cu. in. V8. Also available were a 325 h.p. version of this engine and a 365 h.p. 440 cu. in. V8. A three-speed manual transmission was standard. Torque Flite Eight automatic transmission was optional.

Other options included disc brakes, bucket seats, a telescoping and tilting steering wheel, full-length console, ash-receiver light, power rear antenna, rear-seat heater, electric clock, tinted windshield, six-way power seats, and reclining passenger seat.

Most 1966 Chryslers, 99.6%, came with the automatic, 99.4% had power steering, 80.5% had power brakes, 1.8% had disc brakes, 26.4% had power windows, 20.5% had power front seats, 81.8% had tinted glass, 1.6% had a tilting steering wheel, and 50.9% were sold with air conditioning.

Newport convertible buyers had their choice of twenty exterior colors and nineteen vinyl interiors.

1966 Chrysler Newport Convertible

1966 Chrysler 300 Convertible

Original Price: $3,936
Number Produced: 2,500
Estimated Number Existing in 1979: 550
Miles per Gallon: 8–14
Common Trouble Spots: none
Availability of Parts: good–fair
Investment Potential: A+

Background: "Just the sight of this Chrysler cruising down your street will impress a lot of people." That's what Chrysler sales literature modestly claimed about the 1966 300 convertible. It was powered by a 325 h.p. 383 cu. in. V8 with four-barrel carburetor. A special "TNT" performance package was available for $303.70. It included fifteen-inch wheels, disc brakes, heavy-duty suspension, a 365 h.p. 440 cu. in. V8, four-barrel carburetor, and dual exhaust. A 300 so equipped could go from 0 to 60 in just over eight seconds.

A three-speed manual transmission was standard. Torque Flite Eight automatic transmission was optional. Other options included a rear-seat heater, Auto-Pilot, disc brakes, console, power steering, electric windows, tinted glass, vanity mirror, rear power antenna, three radios (AM, AM Search-Tune Pedal Control, and AM-FM), electric door locks, outside remote-control mirror, power brakes, and fender-mounted turn-signal indicators.

The vinyl bucket seats were offered in black, blue, red, silver, tan, or white. Leather seats could be had in black or red metallic. A combination cloth and vinyl interior was also available.

1966 Chrysler 300 Convertible

PHOTO: CHRYSLER HISTORICAL COLLECTION

1966 Dodge Coronet 500 Convertible

Original Price: $2,921
Number Produced: N.A.
Estimated Number Existing in 1979: N.A.
Miles per Gallon: 10–19
Common Trouble Spots: none
Availability of Parts: good–fair
Investment Potential: A+

Background: The Coronet 500 convertible featured shell-type, all-vinyl bucket seats and a center console. It was powered by a 145 h.p. 225 cu. in. six. Five V8s were also available: a 180 h.p. 273, a 230 h.p. 318, a 265 h.p. 361, a 325 h.p. 383, and a 425 h.p. 426. A three-speed manual transmission was standard. Torque Flite Eight automatic and a four-speed manual were optional.

Slightly over 87% of all 1966 Coronets came with the automatic, 10.2% had the three-speed manual, 2.5% had the four-speed manual, 72.8% had power steering, 9.5% had power brakes, .1% had disc brakes, 7.3% had power windows, 55.6% had tinted glass, and 21% were sold with an air conditioner.

One of the most notable things about the 1966 Dodges was the popular "Dodge Rebellion" ad campaign, whose light-hearted advertisements, starring actress Pam Austin, helped Dodge to shake off its image as an automobile for the Lawrence Welk set.

1966 Dodge Coronet 500 Convertible

1966 Dodge Coronet 440 Convertible

Original Price: $2,766
Number Produced: N.A.
Estimated Number Existing in 1979: N.A.
Miles per Gallon: 12–19
Common Trouble Spots: none
Availability of Parts: fair–good
Investment Potential: A+

Background: The 440 was the low-priced version of the 500; it came with bench seats and a less luxurious interior. However, its full-length side chrome piece made it look sleeker than the more expensive Coronet.

The standard engine was a 145 h.p. 225 cu. in. slant six. Available at extra cost were the following V8 engines: a 180 h.p. 273, a 230 h.p. 318, a 265 h.p. 361, a 325 h.p. 383, and a 425 h.p. 426. A three-speed manual transmission was standard. Torque Flite automatic and a four-speed manual were optional.

1966 Dodge Dart GT Convertible

Original Price: $2,700
Number Produced: N.A.
Estimated Number Existing in 1979: N.A.
Miles per Gallon: 15–25
Common Trouble Spots: none
Availability of Parts: good–fair
Investment Potential: AA

Background: Buyers of the '66 Dart GT had their choice of seventeen exterior colors and six interior combinations. The GT ragtop was powered by a 101 h.p. 170 cu. in. six. Also available were a 145 h.p. 225 cu. in. six, a 180 h.p. 273 cu. in. V8, and a 235 h.p. 273 cu. in. V8. A three-speed manual transmission was standard. Torque Flite automatic and a four-speed manual were optional.

1966 Dodge Dart GT Convertible

1966 Dodge Dart 270 Convertible

Original Price: $2,570
Number Produced: N.A.
Estimated Number Existing in 1979: N.A.
Miles per Gallon: 15–25
Common Trouble Spots: none
Availability of Parts: good–fair
Investment Potential: A+

Background: The sporty Dart 270 ragtop was powered by a 101 h.p. 170 cu. in. slant six. Also available were a 145 h.p. 225 cu. in. six, a 180 h.p. 273 cu. in. V8, and a 235 h.p. 273 cu. in. V8. A three-speed manual transmission was standard. Torque Flite automatic transmission and a four-speed manual were optional.

Slightly over 80% of all '66 Darts came with an automatic, 1.6% had a four-speed manual, 18.1% had a three-speed manual, 14.7% had a V8, 33.5% had power steering, 1.2% had power brakes, .9% had disc brakes, 41.4% had tinted glass, 1.6% had power windows, and 10.3% were sold with an air conditioner.

1966 Dodge Dart 270 Convertible

1966 Dodge Polara Convertible

Original Price: $3,161
Number Produced: N.A.
Estimated Number Existing in 1979: N.A.
Miles per Gallon: 9–16
Common Trouble Spots: none
Availability of Parts: good–fair
Investment Potential: A+ (with 500 option); A (without)

Background: The '66 Polara softtop came with a 270 h.p. 383 cu. in. V8. A four-barrel-carburetor, 325 h.p. version of this engine and a 350 h.p. 440 cu. in. V8, were available at extra cost. A three-speed manual transmission was standard. Torque Flight Eight automatic and a four-speed manual were optional.

Most 1966 Polaras, 99.2%, came equipped with an automatic, .2% had the four-speed manual, 43% had air conditioning, 81% had tinted glass, 96.9% had power steering, 72% had power brakes, and 20% had power windows.

The Polara 500 trim option was again available. This option featured a special all-vinyl interior (with bucket seats) and a console-mounted shifting lever.

1966 Dodge Polara Convertible

1966 Ford Fairlane 500 Convertible

Original Price: $2,603
Number Produced: 9,299
Estimated Number Existing in 1979: 1,534
Miles per Gallon: 11–22
Common Trouble Spots: none
Availability of Parts: good
Investment Potential: A+

Background: This was Ford's lowest-priced convertible in 1966. Just over 17% of all Fairlanes came with the standard 120 h.p. 200 cu. in. six-cylinder engine. Most came with one of the optional V8s: a 200 h.p. 289, a 265 h.p. 390, a 275 h.p. 390, and a 315 h.p. 390. A three-speed manual transmission was standard. Overdrive, a four-speed manual and Cruise-O-Matic automatic were available at extra cost.

Over 42% of '66 Fairlanes came equipped with power steering, 5.7% had power windows, 6.1% had power brakes, 37.1% had tinted glass, and 12.4% were sold with air conditioning.

1966 Ford Fairlane 500 GT Convertible

Original Price: $3,068
Number Produced: 4,327
Estimated Number Existing in 1979: 713
Miles per Gallon: 9–16
Common Trouble Spots: none
Availability of Parts: good
Investment Potential: AA

Background: The most expensive convertible offered in the Fairlane series in '66 was the GT (GT/A if equipped with automatic transmission). It was made to compete with Pontiac's GTO. In addition to a special trim package and engine dress-up kit, the GT had heavy-duty suspension.

Both the GT and GT/A were powered by a 335 h.p. 390 cu. in. V8. Cruise-O-Matic automatic transmission was standard in the GT/A. A four-speed manual was standard in the GT.

1966 Ford Fairlane 500 GT Convertible

PHOTO: FORD MOTOR COMPANY

1966 Ford Fairlane 500 XL Convertible

Original Price: $2,768
Number Produced: 4,560
Estimated Number Existing in 1979: 752
Miles per Gallon: 11–22
Common Trouble Spots: none
Availability of Parts: good
Investment Potential: AA

Background: The intermediate-price Fairlane convertible was the 500 XL. This attractive, mid-size car came with a 120 h.p. 200 cu. in. six-cylinder engine. But over 82.9% of all 1966 Fairlanes were equipped with one of the optional V8 engines—a 200 h.p. 289, a 265 h.p. 390, a 275 h.p. 390, and a 315 h.p. 390. A three-speed manual transmission was standard. Overdrive, a four-speed manual, and Cruise-O-Matic automatic were available at extra cost.

1966 Ford Fairlane 500 XL Convertible

PHOTO: FORD MOTOR COMPANY

1966 Ford Galaxie 500 Convertible

Original Price: $3,042
Number Produced: 27,454
Estimated Number Existing in 1979: 4,529
Miles per Gallon: 8–18
Common Trouble Spots: none
Availability of Parts: good
Investment Potential: A+

Background: This was the lowest-priced of the Galaxie ragtops in 1966. But, like the others, it had a padded dash and seat belts (front and rear) as standard equipment.

It was powered by a 150 h.p. 240 cu. in. six-cylinder engine. Most buyers ordered one of the optional V8s—a 200 h.p. 289, a 250 h.p. 352, a 275 h.p. 390, a 315 h.p. 390, a 360 h.p. 427, a 410 h.p. 427, a 345 h.p. 428, and a 425 h.p. 428. A three-speed manual transmission was standard. Overdrive, a four-speed manual and Cruise-O-Matic automatic transmission were optional. The vast majority of Galaxie 500 convertibles came with the automatic.

1966 Ford Galaxie 500 XL Convertible

PHOTO: FORD MOTOR COMPANY

1966 Ford Galaxie 500 XL Convertible

Original Price: $3,480
Number Produced: 6,360
Estimated Number Existing in 1979: 1,049
Miles per Gallon: 8–18
Common Trouble Spots: none
Availability of Parts: good
Investment Potential: A+

Background: The new Galaxie 500 XL had a more luxurious look than last year's model. A padded dash and front and rear seat belts were among the standard items.

It was powered by a 200 h.p. 289 cu. in. V8 engine. Also available were the following V8s: a 250 h.p. 352, a 275 h.p. 390, a 315 h.p. 390, a 360 h.p. 427, a 410 h.p. 427, a 345 h.p. 428, and a 425 h.p. 428. A three-speed manual transmission was standard. Overdrive, a four-speed manual, and Cruise-O-Matic automatic transmission were optional.

1966 Ford Galaxie 7-Litre Convertible

Original Price: $3,872
Number Produced: 2,368
Estimated Number Existing in 1979: 390
Miles per Gallon: 8–17
Common Trouble Spots: none
Availability of Parts: good
Investment Potential: AA

Background: This was Ford's top-of-the-line softtop for 1966. Among its standard features were special wheel covers, trim, and paint stripes and power front disc brakes. An eight-track tape player was among the many options.

The 7-Litre convertible came with a 345 h.p. 428 cu. in. V8. If that wasn't hot enough for them, buyers could order a 425 h.p. version of that engine, or either a 360 h.p. or a 410 h.p. 427 cu. in. V8. A four-speed manual transmission was optional. Cruise-O-Matic automatic was standard.

1966 Ford Galaxie 7-Litre Convertible

PHOTO: FORD MOTOR COMPANY

1966 Ford Mustang Convertible

Original Price: $2,653
Number Produced: 72,119
Estimated Number Existing in 1979: 11,899
Miles per Gallon: 12–21
Common Trouble Spots: none
Availability of Parts: good
Investment Potential: AAA

Background: The new Mustang was little changed from the 1965 model. However, all Mustangs now had fourteen-inch wheels and tires (previously, six-cylinder cars had come with thirteen-inch wheels).

It was powered by a 120 h.p. 200 cu. in. six-cylinder. Three 289 cu. in. V8s, rated at 200 h.p., 225 h.p., and 271 h.p., were available. A three-speed manual transmission was standard. Cruise-O-Matic automatic and a four-speed manual were optional at extra cost.

Over 62% of 1966 Mustangs were equipped with the automatic, 7.1% had the four-speed manual, 41.7% had a six-cylinder engine, 28.9% had power steering, 3.3% had power brakes, 6.7% had disc brakes, 36.4% had tinted glass, and 9.5% were sold with air conditioning.

Among the items standard in the 1966 Mustang were windshield washers, emergency flasher, vinyl bucket seats, padded dash and sun visors, front and rear seat belts, heater-defroster (buyers could ask not to have this and receive a discount from the car's price), and carpeting. The top was offered in black or white.

Ads described the '66 Mustang as "America's favorite fun car." Many people still agree with that statement.

1966 Ford Mustang Convertible

PHOTO: FORD MOTOR COMPANY

1966 Ford Mustang Fastback 2 + 2

Original Price: $2,607
Number Produced: 35,698
Estimated Number Existing in 1979: 5,890
Miles per Gallon: 12–21
Common Trouble Spots: none
Availability of Parts: good
Investment Potential: AA+

Background: The sporty '66 Mustang Fastback came with a 120 h.p. 200 cu. in. six-cylinder engine. Three 289 cu. in. V8s were available: a 200 h.p. Challenger, a 225 h.p. Challenger Special, and a 271 h.p. Cobra. A three-speed manual was standard with all engines except the Cobra. Cruise-O-Matic automatic and a four-speed manual were optional.

Buyers had their choice of sixteen single-tone exterior colors and over seventy options, including an attractive set of wire-style wheel covers.

1966 Ford Mustang Fastback

PHOTO: FORD MOTOR COMPANY

1966 Ford Mustang Two-Door Hardtop

PHOTO: FORD MOTOR COMPANY

1966 Ford Mustang Two-Door Hardtop

Original Price: $2,416
Number Produced: 499,751
Estimated Number Existing in 1979: 82,458
Miles per Gallon: 12–21
Common Trouble Spots: none

Availability of Parts: good
Investment Potential: AA+

Background: The attractive '66 Mustang hardtop came with a 120 h.p. 200 cu. in. six-cylinder engine. Buyers wanting a little more "go" could order one of three optional V8s: a 200 h.p. (with two-barrel carburetor), a 225 h.p. (with four-barrel carburetor), and a 271 h.p. (with four-barrel carburetor and dual exhaust) 289.

A fully synchronized three-speed manual transmission was standard, but it was not available with the 271 h.p. V8. Cruise-O-Matic automatic and a four-speed manual transmission were available at extra cost.

Most 1966 Mustang hardtops, 96%, were sold with the standard bucket seats. The rest had bench seats.

1966 Ford Thunderbird Convertible

PHOTO: FORD MOTOR COMPANY

1966 Ford Thunderbird Convertible

Original Price: $4,879
Number Produced: 5,049
Estimated Number Existing in 1979: 833
Miles per Gallon: 8–15
Common Trouble Spots: electrical system
Availability of Parts: good–fair
Investment Potential: AA+

Background: This was the last year for the T-Bird convertible. It was powered by a 315 h.p. 390 cu. in. V8. Available at extra cost was a 345 h.p. 428 cu. in. V8. Cruise-O-Matic automatic transmission, power steering, power disc brakes, and a tilting steering wheel were standard.

Most '66 Thunderbirds, 79.1%, came with power windows, 51.6% had power seats, 77% had tinted glass, and 63.7% were sold with an air conditioner.

Buyers had their choice of more than a dozen upholstery combinations. The convertible top came in black, blue, or white.

1966 Imperial Crown Convertible

Original Price: $6,146
Number Produced: 514
Estimated Number Existing in 1979: 71
Miles per Gallon: 8–14
Common Trouble Spots: none
Availability of Parts: fair–good
Investment Potential: AA

Background: The Imperial convertible was available with only one engine, a 350 h.p. 440 cu. in. V8. The engine featured a special "silenced" air cleaner and dual exhaust. Torque Flite automatic transmission, power steering, power brakes, electric windows, and six-way adjustable bucket seats were standard. Bench seats were optional.

A customized version of the Imperial hardtop was used on the TV series "The Green Hornet." Three such cars were made.

Most 1966 Imperials, 96.3%, came with power seats, 30.4% had a tilting steering wheel, 97.5% had tinted glass, and 92.5% were sold with air conditioning.

1966 Imperial Crown Convertible

PHOTO: CHRYSLER HISTORICAL COLLECTION

1966 King Midget Convertible

Original Price: est. $875
Number Produced: 152
Estimated Number Existing in 1979: 20
Miles per Gallon: 50–90
Common Trouble Spots: transmission, "V" belts
Availability of Parts: good
Investment Potential: A

Background: Early '66 King Midget convertibles were powered by a 10 h.p. 29 cu. in. one-cylinder engine. In mid-model year, a 12 h.p. version of this engine was offered. Automatic transmission was standard.

According to Bill Hossfield, of the King Midget-Eshelman Registry, the 12 h.p. engine "was the best improvement ever, giving it more power and torque." King Midgets so equipped were the first to be able to go 50 mph.

1966 Lincoln Continental Convertible

Original Price: $6,383
Number Produced: 3,180
Estimated Number Existing in 1979: 588
Miles per Gallon: 9–13
Common Trouble Spots: none
Availability of Parts: good–fair
Investment Potential: AAA

Background: The attractive '66 Continental four-door convertible was powered by a 340 h.p. 462 cu. in. V8. Turbo-Drive automatic transmission was standard.

All 1966 Lincolns came with power steering, power disc brakes, electric windows, and power seats. Most, 97.7% had tinted glass, 34.9% had a tilting steering wheel, and 93.5% were sold with air conditioning.

Among the options were a stereo tape player, an automatic headlight dimmer, and a nine-inch TV set. The key-operated top had a glass window.

1966 Mercury Comet Caliente Convertible

Original Price: $2,841
Number Produced: 3,922
Estimated Number Existing in 1979: 670
Miles per Gallon: 11–20
Common Trouble Spots: none
Availability of Parts: good–fair
Investment Potential: A+

Background: The '66 Caliente ragtop came with a 120 h.p. 200 cu. in. six. Three V8 engines were available at extra cost: a 200 h.p. 289, a 265 h.p. 390, and a 275 h.p. 390. A three-speed manual transmission was standard. Merc-O-Matic automatic and a four-speed manual were optional.

Most 1966 Comets, 63.7%, were equipped with a V8, 72% had the automatic, 20.1% had the three-speed manual, 7.9% had the four-speed manual, 39.4% had power steering, 9.1% had power brakes, 37.7% had tinted glass, 4.3% had power windows, almost 1% had power front seats, and 10.1% were sold with an air conditioner. Nearly 16% of 1966 Caliente ragtops had bucket seats.

1966 Mercury Comet Caliente Convertible

PHOTO: FORD MOTOR COMPANY

1966 Mercury Comet Cyclone Convertible

Original Price: $2,961
Number Produced: 1,305
Estimated Number Existing in 1979: 223
Miles per Gallon: 11–20
Common Trouble Spots: none
Availability of Parts: good–fair
Investment Potential: A+

Background: This was the first year for the sporty Cyclone ragtop. It came with a 120 h.p. 200 cu. in. six-cylinder engine. Three V8 engines were available at extra cost: a 200 h.p. 289, a 265 h.p. 390, and a 275 h.p. 390. A three-speed manual was standard. Merc-O-Matic automatic and a four-speed manual were optional. Most buyers ordered the automatic.

One of the most novel options offered on Cyclones in 1966 was a nine-inch TV set.

1966 Mercury Comet Cyclone GT Convertible

Original Price: $3,152
Number Produced: 2,158
Estimated Number Existing in 1979: 369
Miles per Gallon: 9–15
Common Trouble Spots: none
Availability of Parts: good–fair
Investment Potential: AA

Background: This was the first year the Cyclone GT convertible was offered. It was powered by a 335 h.p. 390 cu. in. V8. A three-speed manual transmission was standard. Merc-O-Matic automatic and a four-speed manual were optional.

1966 Mercury Monterey Convertible

Original Price: $3,237
Number Produced: 3,279
Estimated Number Existing in 1979: 560
Miles per Gallon: 10–18
Common Trouble Spots: none
Availability of Parts: good–fair
Investment Potential: A

Background: The new Monterey ragtop came with a 265 h.p. 390 cu. in. V8. Three other V8 engines were available at extra cost: a 275 h.p. 390, a 330 h.p. 410, and a 345 h.p. 428. A three-speed manual transmission was standard. Multi-Drive automatic and a four-speed manual were optional.

Most 1966 Mercurys, 98.2%, were equipped with the automatic, 1.5% had a three-speed manual, .3% had a four-speed manual, 97% had power steering, 65.6% had power brakes, 2.1% had disc brakes, 25.4% had power windows, 11.6% had power front seats, and 39.5% were sold with an air conditioner.

1966 Mercury Park Lane Convertible

Original Price: $3,608
Number Produced: 2,546
Estimated Number Existing in 1979: 435
Miles per Gallon: 9–14
Common Trouble Spots: none
Availability of Parts: good–fair
Investment Potential: A+

Background: The luxurious Park Lane convertible came with a 330 h.p. 410 cu. in. V8. A 345 h.p. 428 cu. in. V8 was available at extra cost. A three-speed manual transmission was standard. Multi-Drive automatic and a four-speed manual were optional.

Among the options offered in 1966 were a stereo tape player and a small TV set that could be plugged into the padded dash. Many Park Lane ragtops, 23.6%, had bucket seats.

1966 Mercury Park Lane Convertible

PHOTO: FORD MOTOR COMPANY

1966 Mercury S-55 Convertible

Original Price: $3,614
Number Produced: 669
Estimated Number Existing in 1979: 114
Miles per Gallon: 9–14
Common Trouble Spots: none
Availability of Parts: good–fair
Investment Potential: A+

Background: The sportiest full-size Mercury convertible in 1966 was the S-55. It featured bucket seats, a center console, and special trim inside and out. The S-55 was powered by a 345 h.p. 428 "Super Marauder" V8 engine (with four-barrel carburetor and dual exhaust). A three-speed manual was standard. Multi-Drive automatic and a four-speed manual were optional.

1966 Mercury S-55 Convertible

PHOTO: FORD MOTOR COMPANY

1966 Oldsmobile Cutlass Convertible

Original Price: $2,965
Number Produced: 12,154
Estimated Number Existing in 1979: 1,701
Miles per Gallon: 10–17
Common Trouble Spots: carburetor
Availability of Parts: good
Investment Potential: AA (with the 4-4-2 option); A+ (without)

Background: The Cutlass was powered by a 310 h.p. 330 cu. in. V8. A 320 h.p. version of this engine was available at extra cost. A three-speed manual transmission was standard. Jetaway automatic and a four-speed manual transmission were optional.

A 4-4-2 performance package, featuring a 350 h.p. 400 cu. in. V8, was offered. About one out of three 1966 Cutlasses came with it. The Tri-Carb performance package (three two-barrel carburetors) was optional on the 4-4-2.

1966 Oldsmobile Cutlass Convertible

PHOTO: OLDSMOBILE DIVISION

1966 Oldsmobile Delta 88 Convertible

Original Price: $3,588
Number Produced: 4,303
Estimated Number Existing in 1979: 602
Miles per Gallon: 9–16
Common Trouble Spots: carburetor
Availability of Parts: good
Investment Potential: A

Background: The new Delta 88 was powered by a 300 h.p. 425 cu. in. V8. Three other versions of this engine were optional: a 310 h.p., a 365 h.p., and a 375 h.p. A three-speed manual transmission was standard, but very few 88s came that way. Turbo Hydra-Matic automatic and a four-speed manual transmission were optional.

1966 Oldsmobile Dynamic 88 Convertible

Original Price: $3,404
Number Produced: 5,540
Estimated Number Existing in 1979: 775
Miles per Gallon: 9–16
Common Trouble Spots: carburetor
Availability of Parts: good
Investment Potential: A

Background: The Dynamic 88 was Oldsmobile's most popular ragtop in 1966. It was powered by a 300 h.p. 425 cu. in. V8. Three other versions of this engine—a 310 h.p., a 365 h.p., and a 375 h.p.—were available at extra cost. A three-speed manual transmission was standard, but not very popular—most buyers ordered the optional Turbo Hydra-Matic automatic transmission. A very small number chose the four-speed manual (only .1% of all full-size 1966 Oldsmobiles had four-speed manual transmissions).

1966 Oldsmobile 98 Convertible

Original Price: $4,443
Number Produced: 4,568
Estimated Number Existing in 1979: 639
Miles per Gallon: 9–14
Common Trouble Spots: carburetor
Availability of Parts: good
Investment Potential: A

Background: The new Olds 98 was powered by a 365 h.p. 425 cu. in. V8. A 375 h.p. version of this engine was available at extra cost. Turbo Hydra-Matic automatic transmission was standard. Air conditioning was a popular option—over 58% of all full-size 1966 Oldsmobiles came with it.

1966 Oldsmobile Delta 88 Convertible

PHOTO: OLDSMOBILE DIVISION

1966 Oldsmobile Dynamic 88 Convertible

PHOTO: OLDSMOBILE DIVISION

1966 Oldsmobile Toronado

Original Price: $4,617
Number Produced: 40,963
Estimated Number Existing in 1979: 5,734
Miles per Gallon: 10–14
Common Trouble Spots: none
Availability of Parts: good
Investment Potential: AAA

Background: The beautiful Toronado was one of the most outstanding cars built in the 1960s. It featured radical styling that doesn't seem to age.

The front-wheel-drive Toronado was powered by a 385 h.p. 425 cu. in. V8 engine with a four-barrel carburetor. Turbo Hydra-Matic automatic transmission, power steering, and power brakes were standard.

It was offered in either a standard or deluxe model. The only difference between the two was the interior. About 85% came in the deluxe version.

Most Toronados, 64.9%, were equipped with power windows, 54% had power front seats, 51.5% had a tilting steering wheel, 90.7% had tinted glass, and 73.7% were sold with an air conditioner.

According to *Special Interest Autos* editor Michael Lamm, "If ever two cars shared attributes—though mechanical and spiritual—it's the coffin-nosed Cord and the 1966 Olds Toronado. Had Cord survived, the Toronado might reasonably have become its 1966 model." Many people agree with Mr. Lamm.

1966 Plymouth Belvedere II Convertible

Original Price: $2,738
Number Produced: N.A.
Estimated Number Existing in 1979: N.A.
Miles per Gallon: 10–18
Common Trouble Spots: none
Availability of Parts: good–fair
Investment Potential: A

Background: The new Belvedere II came with a 145 h.p. 225 cu. in. V8 engine. Four other V8 engines were optional: a 180 h.p. 273 cu. in., a 230 h.p. 318, a 265 h.p. 361, and 325 h.p. 383, and a 425 h.p. 426. Belvederes ordered with the 426 had heavy-duty brakes and suspension.

A three-speed manual transmission was standard. Torque Flite automatic transmission and a four-speed manual transmission were available at extra cost.

Most 1966 Belvederes, 80.9%, were equipped with an automatic transmission, 14.3% had a three-speed manual transmission, 4.8% had a four-speed manual transmission, 54.9% had power steering, 7.3% had power brakes, .1% had disc brakes, 5.9% had electric windows, 47.7% had tinted glass, and 15.3% were sold with an air conditioner.

1966 Plymouth Fury III Convertible

Original Price: $3,074
Number Produced: N.A.
Estimated Number Existing in 1979: N.A.
Miles per Gallon: 10–18
Common Trouble Spots: none
Availability of Parts: good–fair
Investment Potential: A+

Background: The new Fury III came with a 145 h.p. 225 cu. in. six-cylinder engine. Four V8 engines were optional: a 230 h.p. 318, a 270 h.p. 383, a 325 h.p. 383 and a 365 h.p. 440. A three-speed manual transmission was standard. Torque Flite automatic and a four-speed manual transmission were available at extra cost.

Most 1966 Furys, 93%, had a V8 engine, 91.4% had an automatic transmission, 7.9% had a three-speed manual transmission, 1.6% had a four-speed manual transmission, 83.8% had power steering, 25.9% had power brakes, less than 1% had disc brakes, 12.5% had power windows, 1.5% had a power front seat, .8% had a tilting steering wheel, 64.8% had tinted glass, and 32.1% were sold with an air conditioner.

1966 Plymouth Satellite Convertible

1966 Plymouth Satellite Convertible

Original Price: $2,910
Number Produced: N.A.
Estimated Number Existing in 1979: N.A.
Miles per Gallon: 10–18
Common Trouble Spots: none
Availability of Parts: good–fair
Investment Potential: A+

Background: The 1966 Satellite came with a 180 h.p. 273 cu. in. V8 engine. Four other V8 engines were available at extra cost: a 230 h.p. 318, a 265 h.p. 361, a 325 h.p. 383, and a 425 h.p. 426 Hemi.

A three-speed manual transmission was standard. Torque Flite Eight and a four-speed manual transmission were optional.

Satellites equipped with the 426 Hemi had two four-barrel carburetors, dual exhaust, and heavy-duty brakes and suspension. Those '66 Satellites with a 426 Hemi sold in late 1965 were available only with a floor-mounted four-speed manual transmission. After January 1, 1966, the Torque Flite Eight automatic was offered.

A unique Western-motif vinyl upholstery was available only on the Satellite.

1966 Plymouth Sport Fury Convertible

Original Price: $3,251
Number Produced: N.A.
Estimated Number Existing in 1979: N.A.
Miles per Gallon: 10–16
Common Trouble Spots: none
Availability of Parts: good–fair
Investment Potential: A+

Background: Plymouth's glamor car, the Sport Fury, came with a 230 h.p. 318 cu. in. V8 engine. Three other V8s were available at extra cost: a 270 h.p. 383, a 325 h.p. 383, and a 365 h.p. 440.

A three-speed manual transmission was standard. Torque Flite Eight automatic and a four-speed manual transmission were optional (the automatic was standard with the 440 cu. in. V8.).

1966 Plymouth Sport Fury Convertible

1966 Plymouth Valiant Signet Convertible

Original Price: $2,527
Number Produced: N.A.
Estimated Number Existing in 1979: N.A.
Miles per Gallon: 15–21
Common Trouble Spots: none
Availability of Parts: good–fair
Investment Potential: A+

Background: The top-of-the-line Valiant convertible in 1966 was the Signet convertible. It came with a 101 h.p. 170 cu. in. six-cylinder engine. A 145 h.p. 225 cu. in. six and two 273 cu. in. V8s, rated at 180 h.p. and 235 h.p., were available at extra cost. Less than nine percent of all 1966 Valiants were equipped with a V8.

A three-speed manual was standard. Torque Flite automatic and (with the 273 V8) a four-speed manual transmission were optional.

This was the last Signet convertible.

1966 Plymouth Valiant 200 Convertible

Original Price: est. $2,400
Number Produced: N.A.
Estimated Number Existing in 1979: N.A.
Miles per Gallon: 15–21
Common Trouble Spots: none
Availability of Parts: good–fair
Investment Potential: A

Background: The new Valiant 200 came with a 101 h.p. 170 cu. in. six-cylinder engine. A 145 h.p. 225 cu. in. six and two V8s, a 180 h.p. 273 and a 235 h.p. 273, were available at extra cost. A three-speed manual transmission was standard. Torque Flite automatic and a four-speed manual transmission were optional.

Most 1966 Valiants, 91.2%, were equipped with a six-cylinder engine, 73.2% had an automatic, 26.3% had a three-speed manual, .5% had a four-speed manual, 23.3% had power steering, 1.6% had power brakes, .3% had disc brakes, 30.3% had tinted glass, and 6.9% were sold with an air conditioner.

This was the last Valiant 200 convertible.

1966 Pontiac Bonneville Convertible

Original Price: $3,586
Number Produced: 16,299
Estimated Number Existing in 1979: 2,770
Miles per Gallon: 9–15
Common Trouble Spots: none
Availability of Parts: good–fair
Investment Potential: A+

Background: Of the many convertibles offered by Pontiac in 1966, none was more luxurious than the Bonneville. It came with a 333 h.p. 389 cu. in. V8. Five other V8 engines were available at extra cost: a 256 h.p. 389 (two-barrel carburetor), a 325 h.p. 389 (four-barrel carburetor), a 338 h.p. 421 (four-barrel carburetor), a 356 h.p. 421 (three two-barrel carburetors), and a 376 h.p. 421 (three two-barrel carburetors).

A three-speed manual transmission was standard, but not very popular. A four-speed manual and Turbo Hydra-Matic automatic transmission were optional.

The '66 Bonneville convertible was offered in fifteen exterior colors: starlight black, blue charcoal, cameo ivory, Fontaine blue, nightwatch blue, palmetto green, reef turquoise, marina turquoise, burgundy, barrier blue, Montero red, Martinique bronze, mission beige, platinum, and candlelite cream.

1966 Pontiac Bonneville Convertible

PHOTO: PONTIAC MOTOR DIVISION

1966 Pontiac Catalina Convertible

Original Price: $3,219
Number Produced: 14,837
Estimated Number Existing in 1979: 2,522
Miles per Gallon: 9–15

Common Trouble Spots: none
Availability of Parts: good–fair
Investment Potential: AA (with 2+2 option); A+ (without)

Background: The big new Catalina was powered by a 256 h.p. 389 cu. in. V8. Four V8 engines were available at extra cost: a 290 h.p. 389 (two-barrel carb), a 325 h.p. 389 (four-barrel carb), a 333 h.p. 389 (four-barrel carb), a 338 h.p. 421 (four-barrel carb), 356 h.p. 421 (three two-barrel carbs), and a 376 h.p. 421 (three two-barrel carbs).

A three-speed manual transmission was standard. Turbo Hydra-Matic automatic and a four-speed manual transmission were optional.

Most full-size 1966 Pontiacs, 98.1%, came with the automatic, 1.1% had a three-speed manual, .8% had a four-speed manual, 97.6% had power steering, 89.6% had power brakes, 11.6% had a tilting steering wheel, 77.5% had tinted glass, 16.8% had electric windows, 7.5% had power front seats, and 45% were sold with air conditioning.

Approximately 7% of 1966 Catalina ragtops came with the 2+2 option.

1966 Pontiac Catalina 2 + 2 Convertible

1966 Pontiac Le Mans Convertible

Original Price: $2,806
Number Produced: 13,080
Estimated Number Existing in 1979: 2,223
Miles per Gallon: 12–20
Common Trouble Spots: carburetor
Availability of Parts: good–fair
Investment Potential: AA

Background: The sporty '66 Le Mans convertible was powered by a 165 h.p. 230 cu. in. six-cylinder engine. A 207 h.p. version of this engine and two V8s, a 250 h.p. 326 and a 285 h.p. 326, were available at extra cost. A three-speed manual transmission was standard, but not very popular. A four-speed manual and an automatic transmission were optional. Most Le Mans ragtops had the automatic.

A new OHC Sports Package was offered, featuring sport striping, heavy-duty suspension, chromed air cleaner, special emblems, and a three-speed manual transmission (a four-speed manual was optional).

1966 Pontiac Le Mans Convertible

1966 Pontiac GTO Convertible

Original Price: $3,082
Number Produced: 12,798
Estimated Number Existing in 1979: 2,175
Miles per Gallon: 9–15
Common Trouble Spots: carburetor
Availability of Parts: good–fair
Investment Potential: AA+

Background: The GTO was now a separate series. It came with a 335 h.p. 389 cu. in. V8. A 360 h.p. version of this engine, with three two-barrel carburetors, was available at extra cost. Both required premium fuel. A three-speed manual transmission was standard. A four-speed manual and an automatic transmission were optional.

Buyers had their choice of fifteen exterior colors. The expanded Morrokide interior could be had in black, blue, bronze, parchment, red, or turquoise.

1966 Pontiac GTO Convertible

PHOTO: PONTIAC MOTOR DIVISION

1966 Pontiac Tempest Custom Convertible

Original Price: $2,655
Number Produced: 5,557
Estimated Number Existing in 1979: 944
Miles per Gallon: 12–21
Common Trouble Spots: carburetor
Availability of Parts: good–fair
Investment Potential: A+

Background: The new Tempest Custom ragtop came with a 165 h.p. 230 cu. in. six-cylinder engine. A 207 h.p. version of this engine and two V8s, a 250 h.p. 326 and a 285 h.p. 326, were available at extra cost. A three-speed manual transmission was standard. A four-speed manual and a two-speed automatic transmission were optional.

Most 1966 Tempests, 69.8%, had the automatic, 63.5% had power steering, 29.7% had power brakes, 1.7% had a tilting steering wheel, 1.9% had electric windows, just less than 1% had power front seats, 58.7% had tinted glass, and 19.2% were sold with an air conditioner.

The '66 Tempest Custom convertible was available in twelve exterior colors. The all Morrokide interior could be ordered in black, blue, bronze, or red.

1966 Rambler Ambassador Convertible

Original Price: $2,968
Number Produced: 1,798
Estimated Number Existing in 1979: 212
Miles per Gallon: 13–21
Common Trouble Spots: none
Availability of Parts: fair–good
Investment Potential: A

Background: Rambler's most luxurious convertible in 1966 was the Ambassador. It came with a 155 h.p. 232 cu. in. six. Three V8 engines, a 198 h.p. 287, a 250 h.p. 327, and a 270 h.p. 327, were available at extra cost. A three-speed manual transmission was standard. Overdrive, a four-speed manual, and Flash-O-Matic automatic transmission were optional.

1966 Rambler Ambassador Convertible

PHOTO: LARRY G. MITCHELL

1966 Rambler American Convertible

Original Price: $2,486
Number Produced: 2,092
Estimated Number Existing in 1979: 246
Miles per Gallon: 14–25
Common Trouble Spots: none
Availability of Parts: fair–good
Investment Potential: A

Background: The '66 American convertible came with a 128 h.p. 199 cu. in. six-cylinder engine. A 155 h.p. 232 cu. in. six and two 290 cu. in. V8s, a 200 h.p. and a 225 h.p., were available at extra cost. The 290 cu. in. V8 wasn't available until mid-model year. A three-speed manual transmission was standard, but it was not available with a V8. Overdrive, a four-speed manual, and Flash-O-Matic automatic transmission were optional.

1966 Rambler Classic Convertible

Original Price: $2,616
Number Produced: 1,806
Estimated Number Existing in 1979: 213
Miles per Gallon: 13–21
Common Trouble Spots: none
Availability of Parts: fair
Investment Potential: A

Background: The new Classic ragtop came with a 145 h.p. 232 cu. in. six-cylinder engine. Available at extra cost were a 155 h.p. version of this engine and three V8s, a 198 h.p. 287, a 250 h.p. 327, and a 270 h.p. 327. A three-speed manual transmission was standard. Overdrive, a four-speed manual, and Flash-O-Matic automatic transmission were optional. Among the other options was "Cruise-Command" automatic speed control, available with the automatic transmission.

Most 1966 Ramblers, 68.7%, were equipped with a six, 75.3% had an automatic, 23.2% had a three-speed manual, 1.5% had a four-speed manual, 40.1% had power steering, 26.4% had power brakes, 4% had disc brakes, 37.7% had tinted glass, 4% had a tilting steering wheel, 5.5% had power windows, and 14.8% were sold with air conditioning.

1966 Rambler Classic Convertible

PHOTO: LARRY G. MITCHELL

1966 Shelby American GT 350 Fastback

Original Price: $4,428
Number Produced: 2,378
Estimated Number Existing in 1979: 392
Miles per Gallon: 9–15
Common Trouble Spots: none
Availability of Parts: fair–good
Investment Potential: AAA

Background: The '66 GT 350 was a little lighter than the previous year's model. It was powered by a 306 h.p. 289 cu. in. V8. A 350 h.p. version of this engine was also available. The standard transmission was a four-speed manual. Cruise-O-Matic automatic transmission was optional. Two other options were mag wheels and a back seat.

Hertz Rent-A-Car ordered 1,000 GT 350s and had them painted black with gold stripes. Most of the GT 350s Hertz bought, 91.5%, came equipped with the automatic.

Six GT 350 convertibles were handmade in 1966, but they were not offered to the general public.

1967

1967 Buick Electra 225 Custom Convertible

Original Price: $4,421
Number Produced: 6,941
Estimated Number Existing in 1979: 1,665
Miles per Gallon: 8–14
Common Trouble Spots: none
Availability of Parts: good
Investment Potential: A+

Background: The big Electra convertible grew even larger in 1967. It was powered by a 360 h.p. 430 cu. in. V8 engine. Super Turbine automatic transmission, power steering, and power brakes were standard. Air conditioning was a popular option; over 63% of all full-size Buicks were so equipped.

1967 Buick Electra 225 Custom Convertible

PHOTO: BUICK MOTOR DIVISION

1967 Buick LeSabre Custom Convertible

Original Price: $3,388
Number Produced: 4,624
Estimated Number Existing in 1979: 1,109
Miles per Gallon: 9–18
Common Trouble Spots: none
Availability of Parts: good
Investment Potential: A

Background: The '67 LeSabre ragtop was a big car—and looked it. It was powered by a 220 h.p. 340 cu. in. V8. Also available were a 260 h.p. version of this engine and a 340 h.p. 400 cu. in. V8. A three-speed manual transmission was standard. Super Turbine automatic transmission was optional.

Most full-size 1967 Buicks, 99.9%, came with the automatic, 31.6% had power windows, 7.7% had power front seats, one-third of 1% had disc brakes, and 92.5% had tinted glass. Power steering and power brakes were ordered by most LeSabre buyers.

A 400 Package, consisting of Super Turbine automatic, a four-barrel 340 cu. in. engine, and special insignia, was optional.

1967 Buick Skylark Convertible

Original Price: $2,945
Number Produced: 6,319
Estimated Number Existing in 1979: 1,516
Miles per Gallon: 12–19
Common Trouble Spots: none
Availability of Parts: good
Investment Potential: AA

Background: The sporty '67 Skylark convertible was

1967 Buick Skylark Convertible

powered by a 160 h.p. 225 cu. in. V6. A 210 h.p. 300 cu. in. V8 and a 260 h.p. 340 cu. in. V8 were optional. A three-speed manual transmission was standard. Super Turbine automatic transmission (column or console shift) was a popular option. Many Skylarks were sold with the optional power brakes and power steering.

1967 Buick Skylark GS 400 Convertible

Original Price: $3,167
Number Produced: 2,140
Estimated Number Existing in 1979: 513
Miles per Gallon: 9–16
Common Trouble Spots: none
Availability of Parts: good
Investment Potential: AA

Background: The GS 400 was a fancy version of the regular Skylark convertible. It had heavy-duty suspension, a special grille, fake hood scoops, and dual exhaust.

The GS 400 came with a 340 h.p. 400 cu. in. V8 with four-barrel carburetor. A three-speed manual transmission was standard. Super Turbine automatic and a four-speed manual were optional. The automatic was the most popular, the four-speed the least.

Available only in California was a special yellow GS 400 called, appropriately enough, "the California."

1967 Buick Skylark GS 400 Convertible

1967 Buick Wildcat Convertible

Original Price: $3,536
Number Produced: 2,276
Estimated Number Existing in 1979: 546
Miles per Gallon: 8–14
Common Trouble Spots: none
Availability of Parts: good
Investment Potential: A

Background: With the exception of a few trim differences, the Wildcat ragtop looked virtually the same as the Wildcat Custom. It was powered by a 360 h.p. 430 cu. in. V8. Super Turbine automatic transmission and power steering were standard. A console-shift version of this automatic was available. Power brakes and air conditioning were very popular options.

An optional Gran Sport package was available at extra cost.

1967 Buick Wildcat Convertible

1967 Buick Wildcat Custom Convertible

Original Price: $3,757
Number Produced: 2,913
Estimated Number Existing in 1979: 699
Miles per Gallon: 8–14
Common Trouble Spots: none
Availability of Parts: good
Investment Potential: A+ (with Gran Sport package); A (without)

Background: The new Wildcat convertible was powered by a 360 h.p. 430 cu. in. V8. Super Turbine automatic transmission (column shift) and power steering were standard. A console-shift version of this automatic was optional. Power brakes and air conditioning were popular options.

An optional Gran Sport package was offered, featuring special chromed wheels, grille, and trim.

1967 Cadillac De Ville Convertible

PHOTO: CADILLAC MOTOR CAR DIVISION

1967 Cadillac De Ville Convertible

Original Price: $5,238
Number Produced: 18,200
Estimated Number Existing in 1979: 5,824
Miles per Gallon: 10–14
Common Trouble Spots: none
Availability of Parts: good
Investment Potential: A+

Background: Although a good year for Cadillac sales in general, 1967 saw a decline in the sale of De Ville convertibles.

The new De Ville was powered by a 340 h.p. 429 cu. in. V8 engine with four-barrel carburetor. Turbo Hydra-Matic automatic transmission, power steering, and power brakes were standard. Virtually all 1967 Cadillacs, 93.5%, were equipped with air conditioning, 45.1% had a tilting steering wheel, and 3.9% came with disc brakes.

1967 Cadillac Fleetwood Eldorado Coupe

Original Price: $6,277
Number Produced: 17,930
Estimated Number Existing in 1979: 5,737
Miles per Gallon: 10–14
Common Trouble Spots: none
Availability of Parts: good
Investment Potential: AA

Background: This was the first year for the front-wheel-drive Eldorado coupe. Cadillac had been working on it since 1959. It was meant to be a "personal car" successor to the Brougham. One prototype even had four doors like the Brougham. Another looked a great deal like the 1963 Buick Riviera. This is not surprising, since the Riviera design was originally planned for Cadillac.

The Eldorado was powered by a 340 h.p. 429 cu. in. V8 engine. Turbo Hydra-Matic automatic transmission, power brakes, power steering, and power front seats were standard.

1967 Cadillac Fleetwood Eldorado Coupe

PHOTO: CADILLAC MOTOR CAR DIVISION

1967 Chevrolet Camaro Super Sport Convertible

PHOTO: GM PHOTOGRAPHIC

1967 Chevrolet Camaro Convertible

Original Price: $2,704
Number Produced: 220,900 (includes Sport Coupes)
Estimated Number Existing in 1979: 66,270 (includes Sport Coupes)
Miles per Gallon: 10–21
Common Trouble Spots: none
Availability of Parts: good
Investment Potential: AAA

Background: This was the first year for the attractive, sporty Camaro convertible. Many people consider a Camaro the next best thing to a Corvette.

The '67 Camaro was powered by a 140 h.p. 230 cu. in. six. A 155 h.p. 250 cu. in. six was also available, as were several V8 engines: a 210 h.p. 327, a 275 h.p. 327, and a 295 h.p. 350. A three-speed manual transmission was standard. Powerglide automatic and a four-speed manual were offered at extra cost. After January 1, 1967, a dealer-installed 396 cu. in. V8 was available.

Most new Camaros, 73.4%, were equipped with a V8, 56.2% had an automatic, 22.3% had a three-speed manual, 21.5% had a four-speed manual, 41.7% had power steering, 11.1% had power brakes, 6.7% had disc brakes, 81.6% had radios, 2.2% had power windows, 3.6% had a tilting steering wheel, 52.8% had tinted glass, 97% had bucket seats, and 12.8% were sold with an air conditioner.

In addition to fifteen exterior colors, Camaro convertible buyers could order one of two extra-cost performance packages: for $210.65, the SS 350, which featured "Bumble Bee" strips, wide-oval tires, hidden headlights, special hood, and a special handling package; for $105.35, the Rally Sport, which featured a black grille, special trim, emblems, body side strips, and a unique taillight treatment.

1967 Chevrolet Camaro Sport Coupe

PHOTO: CHEVROLET MOTOR DIVISION

1967 Chevrolet Camaro Sport Coupe

Original Price: $2,465
Number Produced: (see 1967 Camaro convertible)
Estimated Number Existing in 1979: (see 1967 Camaro convertible)
Miles per Gallon: 10–21
Common Trouble Spots: none
Availability of Parts: good
Investment Potential: AAA (with Z-28 option); AA+ (without)

Background: The '67 Camaro was one of the best-looking cars Chevrolet ever made. Chevrolet reportedly used a computer to help design the car so it wouldn't be too affected by wind gusts. It came with a 140 h.p. 230 cu. in. six. A 155 h.p. 250 cu. in. six was also available. Most Camaros were powered by one of the optional V8 engines. These included a 210 h.p. 327, a 275 h.p. 327, and a 295 h.p. 350. A three-speed manual transmission was standard. Powerglide automatic and a four-speed manual were offered at extra cost. A dealer-installed 396 cu. in. V8, with up to 375 h.p., was available after January 1, 1967.

The optional performance packages included the SS 350, the Rally Sport, and, in mid-model year, the famous Z-28 package, which included a 290 h.p. 302 cu. in. V8, two wide strips on the hood and trunk, a spoiler on the rear deck, dual exhaust, heavy duty suspension, disc brakes, and a four-speed manual transmission. Only 602 1967 Camaros were so equipped.

1967 Chevrolet Chevelle Malibu Convertible

Original Price: $2,637
Number Produced: N.A.
Estimated Number Existing in 1979: N.A.
Miles per Gallon: 9–20
Common Trouble Spots: none
Availability of Parts: good
Investment Potential: AA

Background: The attractive Malibu ragtop was powered by a 140 h.p. 230 cu. in. six. A 155 h.p. 250 cu. in. six was also available, as were several V8 engines: a 195 h.p. 283, a 275 h.p. 327, and a 325 h.p. 327. A three-speed manual was standard, Powerglide automatic overdrive, and a four-speed manual were optional.

Most 1967 Chevelles, 69.5%, came equipped with the automatic, 14.8% had a three-speed manual, 15.2% had a four-speed manual, 77.8% had a V8, 50% had power steering, 9.2% had power brakes, 1.3% had disc brakes, 3.9% had power windows, 1.6% had a tilting steering wheel, 63.8% had tinted glass, 21.5% had bucket seats, and 18.6% were sold with an air conditioner.

1967 Chevrolet Chevelle Malibu Convertible

1967 Chevrolet Chevelle SS 396 Convertible

Original Price: $3,033
Number Produced: N.A.
Estimated Number Existing in 1979: N.A.
Miles per Gallon: 9–15
Common Trouble Spots: none
Availability of Parts: good
Investment Potential: AA+

Background: The Chevelle convertible looked sportier this year than last. It was powered by a 325 h.p. 396 cu. in. V8. A 350 h.p. version of that engine was available at extra cost. A three-speed manual transmission was standard. Turbo Hydra-Matic automatic and a four-speed manual transmission were optional.

1967 Chevrolet Corvair Monza Convertible

Original Price: $2,540
Number Produced: 2,109
Estimated Number Existing in 1979: 631
Miles per Gallon: 16–25
Common Trouble Spots: none
Availability of Parts: good
Investment Potential: A+

Background: The new Monza convertible was a sporty, stylish little car. It was powered by a 95 h.p. 164 cu. in. six-cylinder engine. A 110 h.p. version of this engine was optional. A three-speed manual transmission was standard. Powerglide automatic transmission and a four-speed manual were available at extra cost.

Most 1967 Corvairs, 67.9%, were equipped with an automatic, 17.3% had a three-speed manual, 14.8% had a four-speed manual, 1.1% had a tilting steering wheel, 42.2% had tinted glass, and 5.1% were sold with an air conditioner.

1967 Chevrolet Corvette Stingray Convertible

Original Price: $4,141
Number Produced: 14,436
Estimated Number Existing in 1979: 4,330
Miles per Gallon: 8–18
Common Trouble Spots: none
Availability of Parts: good
Investment Potential: AAA

Background: The new Corvette ragtop was powered by a 300 h.p. 327 cu. in. V8. Optional V8 engines included: a 350 h.p. 327, a 390 h.p. 427, a 400 h.p. 427, and a 435 h.p. 427. A three-speed manual transmission was standard. Most 1967 Vettes, 88%, were equipped with a four-speed manual. Only 10.1% had Powerglide automatic transmission.

Just over 25% of new Corvettes had power steering, 20.8% had power brakes, 10.5% had a tilting steering wheel, 17.6% had power windows, 78% had tinted glass, 96.7% had radios, and 16.5% were sold with an air conditioner. Close to 48% of Vette convertibles were purchased with a detachable hard top.

Although they found some minor faults with the quality control of '67 Corvettes, *Road & Track* stated that it "ranks with the best sports/GT cars the world has to offer, regardless of price."

1967 Chevrolet Corevette Stingray Sport Coupe

Original Price: $4,353
Number Produced: 8,504
Estimated Number Existing in 1979: 3,000
Miles per Gallon: 8–18
Common Trouble Spots: none
Availability of Parts: good
Investment Potential: AAA

Background: This was the last year for the Stingray fastback coupe. It was powered by a 300 h.p. 327 cu. in. V8. Other V8 engines included: a 350 h.p. 327, a 390 h.p. 427, a 400 h.p. 427, and a 435 h.p. 427. A three-speed manual transmission was standard, but not very popular; only 1.9% of all 1967 Vettes came with it. Most were equipped with the four-speed manual. Around one in ten had Powerglide automatic transmission.

1967 Chevrolet Corvette Stingray Sport Coupe

PHOTO: T. MICHAELIS CORVETTE SUPPLIES

1967 Chevrolet Impala Convertible

Original Price: $3,097
Number Produced: N.A.
Estimated Number Existing in 1979: N.A
Miles per Gallon: 9–19
Common Trouble Spots: none
Availability of Parts: good
Investment Potential: AA

Background: The Impala convertible received an attractive face-lift for 1967—it looked a bit flashier than the previous year's model.

It was powered by a 155 h.p. 250 cu. in. six. Most buyers ordered one of the optional V8 engines. These included a 195 h.p. 283, a 275 h.p. 327, a 325 h.p. 396, and a 385 h.p. 427. A three-speed manual transmission was standard. Overdrive, a four-speed manual, and Powerglide automatic transmission were available at extra cost.

Almost 89% of all full-size '67 Chevys came equipped with an automatic, 9.8% had a three-speed manual, 1.2% had a four-speed manual, 77.2% had power steering, 89.9% had a V8, 29% had power brakes, .5% had disc brakes, 4.2% had a tilting steering wheel, 11.6% had power windows, 1.7% had power front seats, 70.4% had tinted glass, 7.2% had bucket seats, and 39.3% were sold with an air conditioner.

1967 Chevrolet Impala Super Sport Convertible

Original Price: $3,254
Number Produced: N.A.
Estimated Number Existing in 1979: N.A.
Miles per Gallon: 9–19
Common Trouble Spots: none
Availability of Parts: good
Investment Potential: AA+

Background: The '67 Super Sport convertible looked less "sporty," from the outside, than the lower-priced standard Impala convertible. The Super Sport had no chrome on the sides of its body. This tended to make it look fat.

It was powered by a 155 h.p. 250 cu. in. six. However, not many were sold that way. Most came with one of the optional V8 engines. These included a 195 h.p. 283, a 275 h.p. 327, a 325 h.p. 396, and a 385 h.p. 427. A three-speed manual transmission was standard. Overdrive, a four-speed manual, and Powerglide automatic transmission were available at extra cost.

1967 Chrysler Newport Convertible

Original Price: $3,583
Number Produced: 2,891
Estimated Number Existing in 1979: 823
Miles per Gallon: 8–17
Common Trouble Spots: none
Availability of Parts: good
Investment Potential: A+

Background: The '67 Newport ragtop was powered by a 270 h.p. 383 cu. in. V8 with a two-barrel carburetor. Two other V8s, a 325 h.p. 383, and a 375 h.p. 440 were available. A three-speed transmission was standard, but not very popular. Most Newports were equipped with the Torque Flite automatic transmission.

Only.3% of all 1967 Chryslers came with the three-speed manual, 99.5% had power steering, 76.2% had power brakes, 6.2% had disc brakes, 27.2% had power windows, 21.9% had power seats, 4.8% had a tilting steering wheel, 86.5% had tinted glass, and 62% were sold with air conditioning.

1967 Chrysler 300 Convertible

Original Price: $4,289
Number Produced: 1,594
Estimated Number Existing in 1979: 454
Miles per Gallon: 8–14
Common Trouble Spots: brakes, electrical system
Availability of Parts: good
Investment Potential: A+

Background: A special grille and trim helped to distin-

1967 Chevrolet Impala Super Sport Convertible

PHOTO: GM PHOTOGRAPHIC

guish the 300 ragtop from the lower-cost Newport. It was also about four inches longer.

It was powered by a 350 h.p. 440 cu. in. V8. Available at extra cost was a 375 h.p. version of this engine. Torque Flite Eight automatic transmission was standard. A four-speed manual was optional. Bucket seats were one of many options available.

1967 Chrysler 300 Convertible

1967 Dodge Coronet 500 Convertible

Original Price: $3,013
Number Produced: N.A.
Estimated Number Existing in 1979: N.A.
Miles per Gallon: 11–19
Common Trouble Spots: none
Availability of Parts: good
Investment Potential: A+

Background: The '67 Coronet 500 ragtop was powered by a 145 h.p. 225 cu. in. slant six. Optional V8 engines available included a 180 h.p. 273, a 230 h.p. 318, a 270 h.p. 383, a 325 h.p. 383, and a 425 h.p. 426. A three-speed manual transmission and front bucket seats were standard. Torque Flite automatic and a four-speed manual transmission were optional.

The Coronet 500 convertible could be ordered in one of nineteen exterior colors, including a special buffed silver metallic. The all-vinyl interior was offered in black, blue, copper, gold and black, red, or white and black. The top could be had in black, blue, or white.

1967 Dodge Coronet 500 Convertible

1967 Dodge Coronet 440 Convertible

Original Price: $2,834
Number Produced: N.A.
Estimated Number Existing in 1979: N.A.
Miles per Gallon: 11–19
Common Trouble Spots: none
Availability of Parts: good
Investment Potential: A+

Background: The 440 convertible was powered by a 145 h.p. 225 cu. in. slant six. Optional V8 engines available included a 180 h.p. 273, a 230 h.p. 318, a 270 h.p. 383, a 325 h.p. 383, and a 425 h.p. 426. A three-speed manual transmission was standard. Torque Flite automatic and a four-speed manual were optional.

Most 1967 Coronets, 88.3%, were equipped with a V8, 92.3% had an automatic, 6% had a three-speed manual, 1.7% had a four-speed manual, 83.9% had power steering, 10.8% had power brakes, 1.6% had disc brakes, 4.9% had power windows, 80.9% had radios, 62% had tinted glass, 17.7% had bucket seats, and 28.4% were sold with air conditioning.

Buyers had their choice of nineteen exterior colors, including a special buffed silver metallic. The all vinyl interior was offered in black, black and white, blue, or red. The top was available in black, blue, or white.

1967 Dodge Coronet 440 Convertible

1967 Dodge Coronet R/T Convertible

Original Price: $3,438
Number Produced: N.A.
Estimated Number Existing in 1979: N.A.
Miles per Gallon: 8–15
Common Trouble Spots: none
Availability of Parts: good
Investment Potential: AA

Background: The new Coronet R/T (Road and Track) was a hot-performing car even in its standard form. It came with a 375 h.p. 440 cu. in. V8, either a four-speed manual or Torque Flite Eight automatic, heavy-duty brakes and suspension, dual exhaust, Red Streak tires, front bucket seats, body stripes, and R/T medallions. An even hotter 425 h.p. 426 V8 was available.

1967 Dodge Dart GT Convertible

Original Price: $2,732
Number Produced: N.A.
Estimated Number Existing in 1979: N.A.
Miles per Gallon: 13–23
Common Trouble Spots: none
Availability of Parts: good
Investment Potential: AA

Background: The new Dart GT convertible was powered by a 115 h.p. 170 cu. in. slant six. Also available were a 145 h.p. 225 cu. in. six, two 273 cu. in. V8s (rated at 180 h.p. and 235 h.p.), and, late in the model year, a 325 h.p. 383 (with four-barrel carburetor and front disc brakes). A three-speed manual transmission was standard. Torque Flite automatic and a four-speed manual were optional.

Most 1967 Darts, 76.2%, came equipped with a six, 81.8% had an automatic, 16.6% had a three-speed manual, 1.6% had a four-speed manual, 48.9% had power steering, 2.3% had power brakes, 1.6% had disc brakes, 49.3% had tinted glass, and 17.1% were sold with air conditioning.

Dart GT buyers could order one of nineteen exterior colors. The all-vinyl interior came in black, blue, copper, red, white and black, white and blue, or white and red. The top was either black, blue, or white. Bucket seats were optional.

1967 Dodge Dart GT Convertible

1967 Dodge Polara Convertible

Original Price: $3,241
Number Produced: N.A.
Estimated Number Existing in 1979: N.A.
Miles per Gallon: 9–16
Common Trouble Spots: none
Availability of Parts: good
Investment Potential: A+ (with 500 option); A (without)

Background: The new Polara ragtop was a bit flashier than last year's model. It came with a 270 h.p. 383 cu. in. V8. Optional V8 engines included a 325 h.p. 383, a 350 h.p. 440, and a 375 h.p. 440. A three-speed manual transmission was standard. Torque Flite Eight automatic and a four-speed manual were optional at extra cost.

Most '67 Polaras, 97.9%, were equipped with the automatic, 2% had the three-speed manual, .1% had the four-speed manual, 98.1% had power steering, 69.7% had power brakes, 3.1% had disc brakes, 2.4% had power windows, 2.7% had power front seats, almost 1% had a tilting steering wheel, 81.7% had tinted glass, 12.1% had bucket seats, and 45.9% were sold with air conditioning.

The Polara was also available with the 500 option, which included special trim, a center console, and bucket seats.

1967 Ford Fairlane 500 Convertible

Original Price: $2,664
Number Produced: 5,428
Estimated Number Existing in 1979: 1,275
Miles per Gallon: 11–22
Common Trouble Spots: none
Availability of Parts: good
Investment Potential: A+

Background: The attractive Fairlane 500 was powered by a 120 h.p. 200 cu. in. six-cylinder engine. Most were ordered with one of the optional V8s: a 200 h.p. 289, a 270 h.p. 390, and a 320 h.p. 390. A three-speed manual transmission was standard. Overdrive, a four-speed manual, and Cruise-O-Matic automatic transmission were available at extra cost.

The majority of 1967 Fairlanes, 81%, had the automatic, 4.5% had the four-speed manual, 15.4% had a six, 51.6% had power steering, 6% had power brakes, 10% had disc brakes, 8.2% had power windows, 39.4% had tinted glass, and 16.3% came with an air conditioner.

1967 Ford Fairlane 500 XL Convertible

Original Price: $2,843
Number Produced: 1,943
Estimated Number Existing in 1979: 456
Miles per Gallon: 10–22
Common Trouble Spots: none
Availability of Parts: good
Investment Potential: A+

Background: The new Fairlane 500 XL came with a 120 h.p. 200 cu. in. six-cylinder engine. Most buyers ordered one of the optional V8s: a 200 h.p. 289, a 270 h.p. 390, and a 320 h.p. 390. A three-speed manual transmission was standard, but not very popular. Overdrive, a four-speed manual, and Cruise-O-Matic automatic were available at extra cost.

1967 Ford Fairlane 500 XL Convertible

PHOTO: FORD MOTOR COMPANY

1967 Ford Fairlane 500 GT Convertible

PHOTO: FORD MOTOR COMPANY

1967 Ford Fairlane 500 XL Gran Turismo Convertible

Original Price: $3,064
Number Produced: 2,117
Estimated Number Existing in 1979: 497
Miles per Gallon: 10–22
Common Trouble Spots: none
Availability of Parts: good
Investment Potential: AA

Background: The most expensive Fairlane convertible in 1967 came with a 120 h.p. 200 cu. in. six-cylinder. Buyers had their choice of several V8s at extra cost: a 200 h.p. 289, a 270 h.p. 390, and a 320 h.p. 390. A three-speed manual transmission was standard. Cruise-O-Matic automatic, overdrive, and a four-speed manual were optional.

The Fairlane Gran Turismo came in two versions, the GT and the GT/A. The only difference between the two was that the GT had a manual transmission and the GT/A had the Cruise-O-Matic. Most 1967 Fairlanes, 81%, came with the automatic.

1967 Ford Galaxie 500 Convertible

Original Price: $3,003
Number Produced: 19,068
Estimated Number Existing in 1979: 4,480
Miles per Gallon: 9–18
Common Trouble Spots: none
Availability of Parts: good
Investment Potential: A+

Background: A 150 h.p. 240 cu. in. six-cylinder engine was standard in the 1967 Galaxie 500. However, most came with one of the optional V8s: a 200 h.p. 289, a 270 h.p. 390, a 315 h.p. 390, a 410 h.p. 427, a 425 h.p. 427, a 345 h.p. 428, and a 360 h.p. 428. A three-speed manual transmission was standard. Overdrive, a four-speed manual, and Cruise-O-Matic automatic were optional at extra cost.

Most full-size 1967 Fords, 93.9%, came with automatic transmission, 94.9% had a V8, 5.4% had a three-speed manual, about a third of 1% had a four-speed manual, 83.9% had power steering, 33.5% had power brakes, 3.7% had disc brakes, 18% had power windows, 2.6% had power front seats, 55.5% had tinted glass, and 39.7% were equipped with an air conditioner.

1967 Ford Galaxie 500 XL Convertible

Original Price: $3,493
Number Produced: 5,161
Estimated Number Existing in 1979: 1,212
Miles per Gallon: 9–18
Common Trouble Spots: none
Availability of Parts: good
Investment Potential: AA

Background: The new Galaxie 500 XL came with a 200 h.p. 289 cu. in. V8, all vinyl interior, bucket seats, command console, and Cruise-O-Matic automatic transmission. A four-speed manual and the following V8s were optional: a 270 h.p. 390, a 315 h.p. 390, a 410 h.p. 427, a 425 h.p. 427, a 345 h.p. 428, and a 360 h.p. 428.

A 7-Litre trim and performance package was opional on Galaxie 500 XLs.

1967 Ford Galaxie 500 XL Convertible

PHOTO: FORD MOTOR COMPANY

1967 Ford Mustang Convertible

Original Price: $2,698
Number Produced: 44,808
Estimated Number Existing in 1979: 10,529
Miles per Gallon: 11–20
Common Trouble Spots: none
Availability of Parts: good
Investment Potential: AA+

Background: The good, clean lines of the original 1964½ Mustang were modified only slightly for 1967. It was powered by a 120 h.p. 200 cu. in. six-cylinder engine. Several V8s were available: a 200 h.p. 289, a 225 h.p. 289, a 271 h.p. 289, and a 320 h.p. 390. A three-speed manual transmission was standard. Cruise-O-Matic automatic and a four-speed manual were optional. A competition handling package was offered for $389.

Seventy percent of all 1967 Mustangs came with a V8, almost 68% had the automatic, 7.3% had the four-speed manual, 43.9% had power steering, 13% had disc brakes, 2.7% had tilting steering wheels, 34.2% had tinted glass, and 15.8% were equipped with an air conditioner. Only 2.6% of Mustang convertibles had bench seats.

A kit that could transform a stock Mustang convertible into a station wagon, was available from an aftermarket source. The kit, called the "Hobo," cost $595.

Buyers had their choice of sixteen exterior colors and sixteen vinyl interiors.

1967 Ford Mustang Convertible

PHOTO: FORD MOTOR COMPANY

1967 Imperial Crown Convertible

Original Price: $6,244
Number Produced: 577
Estimated Number Existing in 1979: 138
Miles per Gallon: 8–14
Common Trouble Spots: none
Availability of Parts: good–fair
Investment Potential: A+

Background: The Imperial convertible was beginning to look more and more like just another Chrysler. The restyled 1967 was smaller than the previous model. Some might consider that an improvement.

It came equipped with a 350 h.p. 440 cu. in. V8 engine. Torque Flite Eight automatic transmission was standard. A new feature on Imperial convertibles was the introduction of a tempered glass rear window, instead of the plastic window formerly used.

All 1967 Imperials came with power steering, power disc brakes, and electric windows. Most, 96%, had power seats, 94.7% had tilting steering wheels, 98% had tinted glass, 21.6% had bucket seats, and 95.1% were sold with air conditioning.

1967 Imperial Crown Convertible

PHOTO: CHRYSLER HISTORICAL COLLECTION

1967 King Midget Convertible

Original Price: est. $995
Number Produced: 195
Estimated Number Existing in 1979: 30
Miles per Gallon: 50–90
Common Trouble Spots: transmission, "V" belt
Availability of Parts: good
Investment Potential: A

Background: The '67 King Midget convertible was powered by a 12 h.p. 29 cu. in. one-cylinder engine. Automatic transmission was standard.

1967 Lincoln Continental Convertible

Original Price: $6,449
Number Produced: 2,276
Estimated Number Existing in 1979: 589
Miles per Gallon: 8–14
Common Trouble Spots: none
Availability of Parts: good–fair
Investment Potential: AAA

Background: This was the last year for the luxurious four-door Continental convertible. It was powered by a 340 h.p. 462 cu. in. V8. Turbo-Drive automatic transmission was standard.

All 1967 Lincolns were equipped with power steering, power disc brakes, electric windows, and power seats. Most, 98.4%, had tinted glass, 40.9% had a tilting steering wheel, and 96.5% were sold with an air conditioner.

1967 Lincoln Continental Convertible

PHOTO: FORD MOTOR COMPANY

1967 Mercury Comet Caliente Convertible

Original Price: $2,818
Number Produced: 1,539
Estimated Number Existing in 1979: 392
Miles per Gallon: 13–22
Common Trouble Spots: none
Availability of Parts: good
Investment Potential: A+

Background: The new Caliente convertible came with a

120 h.p. 200 cu. in. six-cylinder engine. Two V8 engines were available at extra cost: a 200 h.p. 289 and a 270 h.p. 390. A three-speed manual transmission was standard. Merc-O-Matic automatic and a four-speed manual were optional.

Most '67 Comets, 67.4%, were equipped with a V8, 82.4% had the automatic, 14.2% had the three-speed manual, 3.4% had the four-speed manual, 49.6% had power steering, 8.4% had power brakes, 1.2% had disc brakes, 6.4% had power windows, less than 1% had power front seats, 39.4% had tinted glass, and 15.5% were sold with an air conditioner.

The '67 Caliente ragtop could be had in one of fifteen exterior colors. The crinkle-vinyl interior came in aqua, black, blue, parchment, red, or saddle. Three colors of tops—black, blue, and white—were offered.

1967 Mercury Comet Caliente Convertible

PHOTO: FORD MOTOR COMPANY

1967 Mercury Comet Cyclone Convertible

Original Price: $2,997
Number Produced: 431
Estimated Number Existing in 1979: 109
Miles per Gallon: 11–18
Common Trouble Spots: none
Availability of Parts: good
Investment Potential: AA (with GT option); A+ (without)

Background: The '67 Cyclone ragtop came with a 200 h.p. 289 cu. in. V8. Two 390 cu. in. V8 engines, a 270 h.p. and a 320 h.p., were available at extra cost. A three-speed manual transmission was standard. Merc-O-Matic automatic and a four-speed manual were optional.

A GT package was offered. It featured a 320 h.p. 390 cu. in. V8, four-barrel carburetor, console-mounted transmission, bucket seats, high-lift cam, wide-rim wheels, engine dress-up kit, and twin-scoop GT hood. A little less than half (about 47%) of '67 Cyclone convertibles came with this option.

Cyclone buyers could choose from fifteen exterior colors. The all-vinyl bucket seats (front only) came in black, blue, parchment, red, and saddle. The top came in black, blue, and white.

1967 Mercury Cougar Two-Door Hardtop

PHOTO: FORD MOTOR COMPANY

1967 Mercury Cougar Hardtop

Original Price: $2,851
Number Produced: 150,893
Estimated Number Existing in 1979: 38,477
Miles per Gallon: 12–18
Common Trouble Spots: none
Availability of Parts: good
Investment Potential: AA

Background: Across the country in 1966, there were billboards with a picture of a ferocious-looking cougar and the caption, "Mercury Cougar—unleased Sept. 30!"

Motor Trend named the sporty new Cougar its "Car of the Year." It came with a 200 h.p. 289 cu. in. V8. Available at extra cost were a 225 h.p. version of this engine and a 320 h.p. 390 cu. in. V8. A three-speed manual transmission was standard. Merc-O-Matic automatic and a four-speed manual were optional. All transmissions were floor shifted.

Most 1967 Cougars, 80.9%, were equipped with an automatic, 13.8% had the three-speed manual, 5.3% had the four-speed manual, 76.8% had power steering, 22.2% had power brakes, 13.9% had disc brakes, 10.1% had a tilting steering wheel, 59.7% had tinted glass, and 33% were sold with an air conditioner.

For $323.85, buyers could order a GT package. Other options included a black, blue, or parchment bench seat with folding arm rest (bucket seats were standard and offered in aqua, black, blue, ivy gold, parchment, red, or saddle) and a TV set. Sixteen exterior colors were available.

1967 Mercury Comet Cyclone Convertible

1967 Mercury Monterey Convertible

1967 Mercury Monterey Convertible

Original Price: $3,311
Number Produced: 2,818
Estimated Number Existing in 1979: 718
Miles per Gallon: 9–17
Common Trouble Spots: none
Availability of Parts: good
Investment Potential: A+ (with S-55 option); A (without)

Background: The new Monterey ragtop came with a 270 h.p. 390 cu. in. V8. Three other V8 engines were available at extra cost: a 330 h.p. 410, a 345 h.p. 428, and a 360 h.p. 428. A three-speed manual transmission was standard. Merc-O-Matic automatic transmission and a four-speed manual were optional.

Most full-size 1967 Mercurys, 99.2%, were equipped with the automatic, .7% had the three-speed manual, .1% had the four-speed manual, 98.5% had power steering, 33.7% had power brakes, 43.1% had disc brakes, 34.9% had power windows, 15.1% had power front seats, 10.6% had a tilting steering wheel, 75.7% had tinted glass, and 50% were sold with an air conditioner.

A S-55 package was optional. It featured bucket seats, center console, a 428 cu. in. V8 (with either 345 h.p. or 360 h.p.), and special trim. Only about 5% of all '67 Monterey ragtops were ordered with this option.

1967 Mercury Park Lane Convertible

Original Price: $3,984
Number Produced: 1,191
Estimated Number Existing in 1979: 303
Miles per Gallon: 9–14
Common Trouble Spots: none
Availability of Parts: good
Investment Potential: A

Background: The luxurious Park Lane came with a 330 h.p. 410 cu. in. V8. Two 428 cu. in. V8 engines, a 345 h.p. and a 360 h.p., were available at extra cost. Buyers had their choice of Merc-O-Matic automatic or a four-speed manual transmission. Most ordered the automatic.

One interesting option was a "speed-actuated power door locks" system. This automatically locked all doors when the car reached a speed exceeding eight miles per hour. Other options included dual exhaust, power transfer axle, speed control, power antenna, power windows, power steering, six-way power front seat, cornering lights, interval selector windshield wipers, remote control deck-lid release, tinted glass, wire wheel covers, two radios (AM and AM/FM), and shoulder belts.

The '67 Park Lane convertible was offered in eighteen exterior colors: burgundy, cardinal red, cinnamon frost, Cumberland beige, Caspian blue, fawn, lime frost, glacier blue, Jamaican yellow, Inverness green, onyx, polar white, sage gold, Sheffield silver, sea foam green, Trafalgar blue, Tiffany blue, and turquoise. The vinyl interior was available in aqua, black, blue, ivy gold, parchment, red, or saddle; the top in black, blue, or white.

1967 Oldsmobile Cutlass Convertible

Original Price: $2,770
Number Produced: 4,344
Estimated Number Existing in 1979: 1,042
Miles per Gallon: 11–19
Common Trouble Spots: none
Availability of Parts: good
Investment Potential: A+

Background: The new Cutlass convertible was powered by a 155 h.p. 250 cu. in. six-cylinder engine. Three 330 cu. in. V8s, a 250 h.p., a 310 h.p., and a 320 h.p., were available. A three-speed manual transmission was standard, but not very popular. Jetaway automatic and a four-speed manual transmission were optional.

Also offered at extra cost was the "Rocket Rally Pac," which featured a clock, ammeter, tach, temperature, and oil pressure gauges.

1967 Oldsmobile Cutlass Convertible

PHOTO: OLDSMOBILE DIVISION

1967 Oldsmobile Cutlass Supreme Convertible

PHOTO: OLDSMOBILE DIVISION

1967 Oldsmobile Cutlass Supreme Convertible

Original Price: $3,026
Number Produced: 10,897
Estimated Number Existing in 1979: 2,615
Miles per Gallon: 10–15
Common Trouble Spots: none
Availability of Parts: good
Investment Potential: AA (with the 4-4-2 option); A+ (without)

Background: The 1967 Cutlass Supreme was powered by a 320 h.p. 330 cu. in. V8. A 310 h.p. version of this engine and a 350 h.p. 400 cu. in. V8 were available at extra cost. A three-speed manual transmission was standard, but not very popular. Jetaway automatic and a four-speed manual transmission were optional. Turbo Hydra-Matic automatic was optional on the 400 cu. in. V8.

Over 28% of all Cutlass Supremes were ordered with the optional 4-4-2 performance package. It included heavy-duty shocks and coil springs, wide oval tires, and a special front stabilizer bar. The standard 4-4-2 engine was a 350 h.p. 400 cu. in. V8.

Also offered at extra cost was the "Rocket Rally Pac," which featured a clock, ammeter, tach, temperature, and oil gauges.

A limited number of Cutlass Supreme convertibles were made with a special yellow paint job, top, upholstery, and carpeting.

1967 Oldsmobile Delmont 88 Convertible

Original Price: $3,462
Number Produced: 3,525
Estimated Number Existing in 1979: 846
Miles per Gallon: 8–17
Common Trouble Spots: none
Availability of Parts: good
Investment Potential: A

Background: This was the first year for the Delmont 88 convertible. It was powered by a 250 h.p. 330 cu. in. V8. Buyers could choose from six optional V8 engines: a 260 h.p. 330, a 300 h.p. 425, a 320 h.p. 330, a 310 h.p. 425, a 365 h.p. 425, and a 375 h.p. 425.

A three-speed manual transmission was standard, but not very popular. Virtually all full-size 1967 Olds, 99.9%, came with the optional Turbo Hydra-Matic automatic transmission.

1967 Oldsmobile Delta 88 Convertible

Original Price: $3,646
Number Produced: 2,447
Estimated Number Existing in 1979: 587
Miles per Gallon: 8–16
Common Trouble Spots: none
Availability of Parts: good
Investment Potential: A

Background: The new Delta 88 ragtop was powered by a 300 h.p. 425 cu. in. V8. Three other versions of this engine, a 310 h.p., a 365 h.p., and a 375 h.p., were available at extra cost. A three-speed manual transmission was standard, but not very popular; only one-tenth of 1% of all full-size 1967 Oldsmobiles were so equipped. Most buyers ordered the optional Turbo Hydra-Matic automatic transmission.

1967 Oldsmobile Delta 88 Convertible

PHOTO: OLDSMOBILE DIVISION

1967 Oldsmobile Delmont 88 Convertible

PHOTO: OLDSMOBILE DIVISION

1967 Oldsmobile 98 Convertible

PHOTO: OLDSMOBILE DIVISION

1967 Oldsmobile 98 Convertible

Original Price: $4,498
Number Produced: 3,769
Estimated Number Existing in 1979: 904
Miles per Gallon: 8–14
Common Trouble Spots: none
Availability of Parts: good
Investment Potential: A

Background: Oldsmobile's top-of-the-line 98 convertible came with a 365 h.p. 425 cu. in. V8. A 375 h.p. version of this engine was available at extra cost. Turbo Hydra-Matic automatic transmission was standard.

1967 Plymouth Barracuda Convertible

Original Price: $2,779
Number Produced: N.A.
Estimated Number Existing in 1979: N.A.
Miles per Gallon: 11–21
Common Trouble Spots: none
Availability of Parts: good
Investment Potential: A+

Background: This was the first time the Barracuda was available as a convertible. It was an attractive little car.

The Barracuda came with a 145 h.p. 225 cu. in. six-cylinder engine. Three V8s were available: a 180 h.p. 273, a 235 h.p. 273, and a 280 h.p. 383. A three-speed manual transmission was standard. Torque Flite automatic and a four-speed manual transmission were optional.

Most 1967 Barracudas, 71.5%, were equipped with a V8 engine, 79.6% had an automatic transmission, 10.7% had a three-speed manual transmission, 9.7% had a four-speed manual transmission, 46% had power steering, 6.1% had power brakes, 8% had disc brakes, 54.8% had tinted glass, 61.4% had bucket seats, and 14.1% were sold with an air conditioner.

A Formula S package was offered on Barracudas. It featured dual exhaust, medallions, front disc brakes, stiffer springs, shocks, torsion bars, anti-sway bar, and wide oval tires.

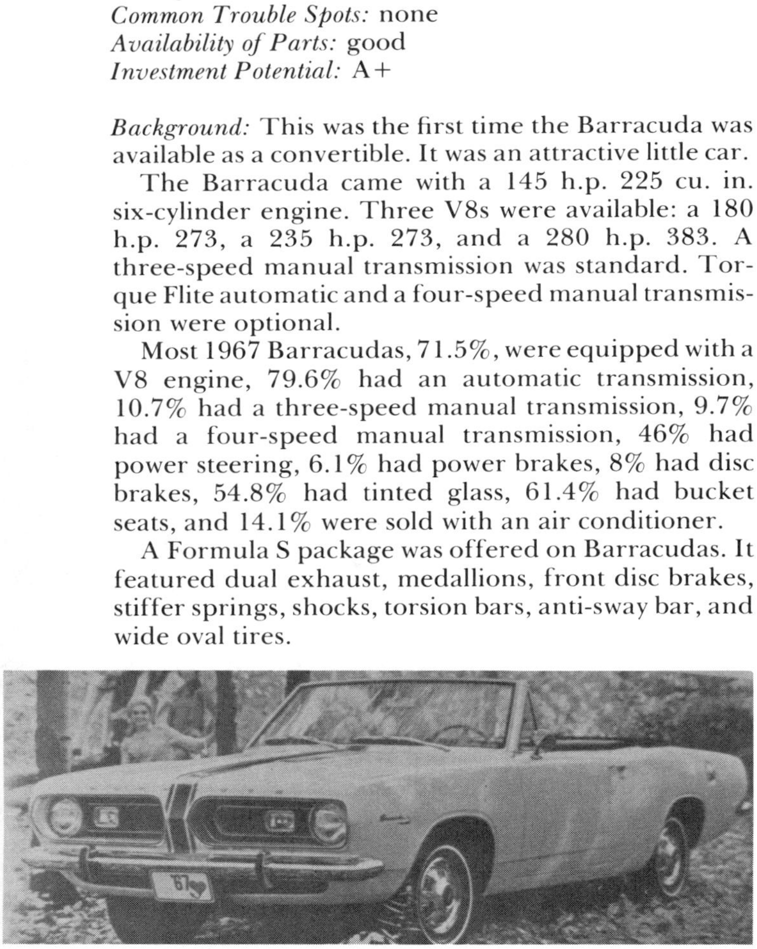

1967 Plymouth Barracuda Convertible

1967 Plymouth Belvedere II Convertible

Original Price: $2,789
Number Produced: N.A.
Estimated Number Existing in 1979: N.A.
Miles per Gallon: 10–18
Common Trouble Spots: none
Availability of Parts: good
Investment Potential: A+

Background: The new Belvedere II came with a 145 h.p. 225 cu. in. six-cylinder engine. Four V8 engines were available: a 180 h.p. 273, 230 h.p. 318, a 270 h.p. 383, and a 325 h.p. 383. A three-speed manual transmission was standard. Torque Flite automatic transmission was optional.

Most 1967 Belvederes, 71.5%, were equipped with a V8, 79.6% had an automatic transmission, 64.7% had power steering, 8.5% had power brakes, 2% had disc brakes, 75.6% had radios, 6.1% had power windows, 21.2% had bucket seats, 54.4% had tinted glass, and 24.4% were sold with an air conditioner.

This was the last year for the Belvedere II convertible.

1967 Plymouth Belvedere II Convertible

1967 Plymouth Fury III Convertible

Original Price: $3,118
Number Produced: N.A.
Estimated Number Existing in 1979: N.A.
Miles per Gallon: 10–18
Common Trouble Spots: none
Availability of Parts: good
Investment Potential: A+

Background: The new Fury III came with a 145 h.p. 225 cu. in. six-cylinder engine. Five V8 engines were available: a 230 h.p. 318, a 270 h.p. 383, a 325 h.p. 383, a 350 h.p. 440, and a 375 h.p. 440. A three-speed manual transmission was standard. Torque Flite Eight automatic and a four-speed manual transmission were optional.

Most 1967 Furys, 95.3%, had a V8 engine, 97% had an automatic transmission, 2.7% had a three-speed manual transmission, .3% had a four-speed manual transmission, 89.7% had power steering, 32.7% had power brakes, 3.4% had disc brakes, 13.5% had power windows, 2.2% had power front seats, almost 1% had a tilting steering wheel, 70.7% had tinted glass, and 45.2% were sold with an air conditioner.

1967 Plymouth Fury III Convertible

1967 Plymouth GTX Convertible

Original Price: $3,418
Number Produced: est. 12,000 (includes GTX two-door hardtops)
Estimated Number Existing in 1979: 2,796 (includes GTX two-door hardtops)
Miles per Gallon: 8–14
Common Trouble Spots: none
Availability of Parts: good
Investment Potential: AA

Background: This was the first year for the GTX convertible. It came with a 375 h.p. 440 cu. in. V8 engine. Plymouth's famous 425 h.p. 426 cu. in. "Super Stock" V8 was available at extra cost. Torque Flite Eight automatic transmission was standard. A four-speed manual transmission was optional.

Some options available on the GTX were a Sports console, a console-mounted electric tachometer, a wood-grain steering wheel, dual sport strips on the hood and trunk, and front disc brakes.

In 1967, Chrysler Corporation offered a five-year or 50,000-mile warranty on all of its cars except those equipped with the 426 cu. in. Hemi V8. Autos with that engine came with a 12-month or 12,000-mile warranty. Chrysler knew muscle cars like the GTX tended to "live fast and die young."

1967 Plymouth GTX Convertible

1967 Plymouth Satellite Convertible

1967 Plymouth Satellite Convertible

Original Price: $2,986
Number Produced: N.A.
Estimated Number Existing in 1979: N.A.
Miles per Gallon: 10–17
Common Trouble Spots: none
Availability of Parts: good
Investment Potential: A+

Background: The new Satellite came with a 180 h.p. 273 cu. in. V8 engine. Three other V8 engines were available at extra cost: a 230 h.p. 318, a 270 h.p. 383, and a 325 h.p. 383. A three-speed manual transmission was standard, but not very popular; most Satellite buyers ordered the optional Torque Flite Eight automatic transmission.

1967 Plymouth Sport Fury Convertible

Original Price: $3,279
Number Produced: N.A.
Estimated Number Existing in 1979: N.A.
Miles per Gallon: 9–17
Common Trouble Spots: none
Availability of Parts: good
Investment Potential: A+

Background: The 1967 Sport Fury convertible came with a 230 h.p. 318 cu. in. V8 engine. Three other V8s were available at extra cost: a 270 h.p. 383, a 325 h.p. 383, and a 375 h.p. 440. A three-speed manual transmission was standard. Torque Flite Eight automatic and a four-speed manual transmission were optional.

1967 Plymouth Sport Fury Convertible

1967 Pontiac Bonneville Convertible

Original Price: $3,680
Number Produced: 8,902
Estimated Number Existing in 1979: 2,047
Miles per Gallon: 8–15
Common Trouble Spots: none
Availability of Parts: good
Investment Potential: AA

Background: The 1967 Bonneville softtop had striking good looks. It came with a 333 h.p. 400 cu. in. V8. Four other V8s were available at extra cost: a 265 h.p. 400, a 325 h.p. 400, a 360 h.p. 428, and a 376 h.p. 428. The 265 h.p. 400, the only Bonneville engine equipped with a two-barrel carburetor, was made to run on regular gasoline; the others required premium.

A three-speed manual transmission was standard. Turbo Hydra-Matic automatic and a four-speed manual transmission were optional.

Among the many options offered on the '67 Bonneville convertible were tinted glass, air conditioning, bucket seats, power seats (bucket or bench), power brakes, cruise control, power steering, rear deck lid release, power windows, seven-position tilting steering wheel, Verbra-Phonic rear speaker system, electric antenna, eight-track tape player, spotlight, underhood lamp, reclining passenger seat, hood-mounted tachometer, and fender skirts.

The 1967 Bonneville is one of the best-looking ragtops made in the 1960s.

1967 Pontiac Catalina Convertible

Original Price: $3,276
Number Produced: 10,033
Estimated Number Existing in 1979: 2,307
Miles per Gallon: 9–16
Common Trouble Spots: none
Availability of Parts: good
Investment Potential: AA (with 2+2 option); A+ (without)

Background: The 1967 Catalina was an attractive car. It came with a 265 h.p. 400 cu. in. V8. Five other V8 engines were available at extra cost: a 290 h.p. 400, a 325 h.p. 400, a 333 h.p. 400, a 360 h.p. 428, and a 376 h.p. 428. A three-speed manual transmission was standard. Turbo Hydra-Matic automatic and a four-speed manual transmission were optional.

Most 1967 full-size Pontiacs, 98.8%, had the automatic, less than .5% had a four-speed manual transmission, 98.4% had power steering, 88.9% had power brakes, 1.7% had disc brakes, 23.4% had electric windows, 7.8% had a power front seat, 81.4% had tinted glass, and 55.6% were sold with an air conditioner. Approximately 2% of all 1967 Catalina convertibles (and two-door hardtops) came with the 2 + 2 option. A Ventura option was also offered.

1967 Pontiac Bonneville Convertible

PHOTO: PONTIAC MOTOR DIVISION

1967 Pontiac Firebird Convertible

Original Price: $2,903
Number Produced: 15,582
Estimated Number Existing in 1979: 3,583
Miles per Gallon: 10–20
Common Trouble Spots: none
Availability of Parts: good
Investment Potential: AAA

Background: The new Firebird convertible was the sportiest-looking ragtop Pontiac offered in 1967. It was also the most popular.

The Firebird was powered by a 165 h.p. 230 cu. in. six-cylinder engine. A 215 h.p. "Sprint" version of this engine, and four V8s were available at extra cost: a 250 h.p. 326, a 285 h.p. 326, and two 325 h.p. 400s. A three-speed manual transmission was standard. A four-speed manual transmission, a two-speed automatic, and (with the 400 cu. in V8) Turbo Hydra-Matic automatic were optional.

1967 Pontiac Firebird Convertible

PHOTO: PONTIAC MOTOR DIVISION

1967 Pontiac Firebird Two-Door Hardtop

Original Price: $2,666
Number Produced: 67,032
Estimated Number Existing in 1979: 15,417
Miles per Gallon: 10–20
Common Trouble Spots: none
Availability of Parts: good
Investment Potential: AA+

Background: The sleek new Firebird made its debut in February 1967. It came with a 165 h.p. 230 cu. in. six-cylinder engine. A 215 h.p. "Sprint" version of this engine and four V8s were available at extra cost. The V8s were a 250 h.p. 326, a 285 h.p. 326, and two 325 h.p. 400s. A three-speed manual transmission was standard. A two-speed automatic, Turbo Hydra-Matic automatic (only with the 400 cu. in. V8), and a four-speed manual were optional.

Most 1967 Firebirds, 78.6%, were equipped with one of the V8s, 66.1% had an automatic, 17.9% had the four-speed manual, 7.3% had disc brakes, 65.5% had power steering, 26.4% had power brakes, 2.7% had electric windows, 95.3% had bucket seats, and 17.9% were sold with air conditioning.

1967 Pontiac Firebird Two-Door Hardtop

PHOTO: PONTIAC MOTOR DIVISION

1967 Pontiac Grand Prix Convertible

Original Price: $3,813
Number Produced: 5,856
Estimated Number Existing in 1979: 1,346
Miles per Gallon: 8–15
Common Trouble Spots: none
Availability of Parts: good
Investment Potential: AA

Background: This was the first year for the Grand Prix convertible. Hidden headlights (and windshield wipers) were two of the design features that help make this a very sleek-looking car (considering its size).

It came with a 350 h.p. 400 cu. in. V8. Three other V8s were available at extra cost: a 265 h.p. 400, a 360 h.p. 428, and a 376 h.p. 428. A three-speed manual transmission was standard, but not very popular. Turbo Hydra-Matic automatic and a four-speed manual transmission were optional.

Among the many options available was a vinyl tonneau cover.

1967 Pontiac GTO Convertible

PHOTO: PONTIAC MOTOR DIVISION

1967 Pontiac GTO Convertible

Original Price: $3,165
Number Produced: 9,517
Estimated Number Existing in 1979: 2,188
Miles per Gallon: 9–16
Common Trouble Spots: none
Availability of Parts: good
Investment Potential: AA+

Background: "The Great One"—that's how Pontiac literature described the new GTO. It came with a 335 h.p. 400 cu. in. V8. A 255 h.p. and a 360 h.p. version of this engine were available. A three-speed manual transmission was standard. A four-speed manual and Turbo Hydra-Matic automatic transmission were optional.

Among the standard items were bucket seats, heavy-duty springs, shocks, and stabilizer bar, dual exhaust, and either whitewall or red-line tires. Many options were offered; as the Pontiac sales catalog so aptly put it, the GTO had "an option list as long as your arm and twice as hairy." Virtually everything from an eight-track tape player to a vinyl tonneau cover was included.

A "Ram Air" package was available on the 360 h.p. 400 cu. in. V8 for $263.30. It featured, among other things, functional air scoops, special camshaft, and stronger valve springs.

Good looks and the GTO charisma make the 1967 GTO convertible a very desirable automobile.

1967 Pontiac Grand Prix Convertible

PHOTO: PONTIAC MOTOR DIVISION

1967 Pontiac Le Mans Convertible

Original Price: $2,881
Number Produced: 9,820
Estimated Number Existing in 1979: 2,258
Miles per Gallon: 12–21
Common Trouble Spots: none
Availability of Parts: good
Investment Potential: AA

Background: The attractive Le Mans convertible was powered by a 165 h.p. 230 cu. in. overhead-cam six. A 215 h.p. version of this engine and two V8s, a 250 h.p. 326 and a 285 h.p. 326, were available at extra cost. A three-speed manual transmission was standard. A four-speed manual and a two-speed automatic transmission were optional.

An all Morrokide interior was standard. Buyers had their choice of either notch-back bench seats with center armrest or bucket seats.

1967 Pontiac Tempest Custom Convertible

Original Price: $2,723
Number Produced: 4,082
Estimated Number Existing in 1979: 938
Miles per Gallon: 12–21
Common Trouble Spots: none
Availability of Parts: good
Investment Potential: A+

Background: The Tempest convertible was powered by a 165 h.p. 230 cu. in. six-cylinder engine. A 215 h.p. "Sprint" version of this engine and two V8s, a 250 h.p. 326 and a 285 h.p. 326, were available at extra cost. A three-speed manual transmission was standard. A four-speed manual and an automatic transmission were optional.

Most 1967 Tempests, 76.9%, came with the automatic, 9.5% had the three-speed manual, 13.6% had the four-speed manual, 78.5% had a V8 engine, 73.8% had power steering, 31.3% had power brakes, 2.4% had disc brakes, 4.7% had electric windows, 1.9% had a tilting steering wheel, 63.4% had tinted glass, and 27.5% were sold with air conditioning.

A manually operated top was standard, but a power top was offered.

1967 Rambler Ambassador DPL Convertible

Original Price: $3,143
Number Produced: 1,260
Estimated Number Existing in 1979: 302
Miles per Gallon: 10–20
Common Trouble Spots: none
Availability of Parts: good
Investment Potential: A+

Background: The luxurious Ambassador DPL came with a 200 h.p. 290 cu. in. V8. Two 343 cu. in. V8 engines were available at extra cost. These were rated at 235 h.p. and 280 h.p. A three-speed manual transmission was standard. Overdrive, a four-speed manual, and Flash-O-Matic automatic transmission were optional.

Most 1967 Ambassadors, 96.1%, were equipped with the automatic, 2.2% had the three-speed manual, .6% had the four-speed manual, 81.4% had power steering, 56.5% had power brakes, 7% had disc brakes, 59.9% had tinted glass, 5.1% had power windows, 14.1% had a tilting steering wheel, 23.2% had bucket seats, and 33.1% were sold with air conditioning.

1967 Rambler American Rogue Convertible

Original Price: $2,611
Number Produced: 921
Estimated Number Existing in 1979: 221
Miles per Gallon: 13–23
Common Trouble Spots: none
Availability of Parts: fair–good
Investment Potential: A+

Background: The '67 Rogue convertible came with a 128 h.p. 199 cu. in. six. Available at extra cost were two 232 cu. in. six-cylinder engines, a 145 h.p. and a 155 h.p., and three V8s, a 200 h.p. 290, a 225 h.p. 290, a 280 h.p. 343. A three-speed manual transmission was standard. Overdrive, a four-speed manual and Flash-O-Matic automatic transmission were optional.

1967 Rambler Rogue Convertible

PHOTO: LARRY G. MITCHELL

1967 Rambler Rebel SST Convertible

Original Price: $2,782
Number Produced: 1,686
Estimated Number Existing in 1979: 404
Miles per Gallon: 12–20
Common Trouble Spots: none
Availability of Parts: good
Investment Potential: A

Background: This was the first Rebel SST convertible. It came with a 145 h.p. 232 cu. in. six-cylinder engine. A 155 h.p. version of this engine and three V8s, a 200 h.p. 290, a 235 h.p. 343, and a 280 h.p. 343, were available at extra cost. A three-speed manual transmission was standard. Overdrive, a four-speed manual, and Flash-O-Matic automatic transmission were optional.

Most 1967 Rebels, 85.3%, were equipped with the automatic, 10.3% had the three-speed manual, 1.2% had the four-speed manual, 54.2% had a six, 16.2% had bucket seats, 53.5% had power steering, 24% had power brakes, 1.5% had disc brakes, 62.5% had radios, 44% had tinted glass, .4% had power windows, and 18.8% were sold with air conditioning.

1967 Rambler Rebel SST Convertible

PHOTO: LARRY G. MITCHELL

1968

1968 Buick Electra 225 Custom Convertible

Original Price: $4,568
Number Produced: 7,976
Estimated Number Existing in 1979: 2,823
Miles per Gallon: 8–14
Common Trouble Spots: none
Availability of Parts: good
Investment Potential: A+

Background: The Electra received an attractive face-lift for 1968. It was powered by a 360 h.p. 430 cu. in. V8 with four-barrel carburetor. Super Turbine automatic transmission was standard. All Electras had power steering, power brakes, and power windows. Air conditioning was an extremely popular option—most Electras, 86.8%, were air conditioned. One of the least popular options was disc brakes—only 2.4% of '68 Electras had them.

1968 Buick Gran Sport 400 Convertible

Original Price: $3,294
Number Produced: 2,454
Estimated Number Existing in 1979: 868
Miles per Gallon: 9–15
Common Trouble Spots: none
Availability of Parts: good
Investment Potential: AA

Background: The Gran Sport 400 ragtop came with a 340 h.p. 400 cu. in. V8 with four-barrel carburetor. A three-speed manual transmission was standard, but not very popular. Even less popular was the optional four-speed manual. Most people ordered the Super Turbine automatic.

1968 Buick GS 400 Convertible

1968 Buick LeSabre Custom Convertible

Original Price: $3,527
Number Produced: 5,257
Estimated Number Existing in 1979: 1,860
Miles per Gallon: 9–16
Common Trouble Spots: none
Availability of Parts: good
Investment Potential: A+

Background: The attractive '68 LeSabre convertible was powered by a 230 h.p. 350 cu. in. V8. A 280 h.p. version of this engine was optional. A three-speed manual transmission was standard. Super Turbine automatic transmission was available.

Most 1968 LeSabres, 99.8%, came with the automatic, 90.6% had power brakes, .5% had disc brakes, 6.4% had power windows, 4.1% had power front seats, and 57.7% were equipped with air conditioning.

1968 Buick LeSabre Custom Convertible

PHOTO: PUBLIC RELATIONS DEPARTMENT, BUICK MOTOR DIVISION

1968 Buick Skylark Custom Convertible

Original Price: $3,121
Number Produced: 8,188
Estimated Number Existing in 1979: 2,898
Miles per Gallon: 10–19
Common Trouble Spots: none
Availability of Parts: good
Investment Potential: AA

Background: The 1968 Skylark convertible was a good-looking car. It was powered by a standard 155 h.p. 250 cu. in. V6, but most buyers ordered either the 230 h.p. or the 280 h.p. 350 cu. in. V8. A three-speed manual transmission was standard. Super Turbine automatic transmission was a popular option.

1968 Buick Wildcat Custom Convertible

Original Price: $3,896
Number Produced: 3,572
Estimated Number Existing in 1979: 1,264
Miles per Gallon: 8–14
Common Trouble Spots: none
Availability of Parts: good
Investment Potential: A

Background: The big Wildcat convertible was powered by a 360 h.p. 430 cu. in. V8 with four-barrel carburetor. A three-speed manual transmission was standard. Super Turbine automatic transmission was optional.

Virtually all Wildcats, 99.9%, were equipped with the automatic, 98.1% had power brakes, 2% had disc brakes, 99.8% had power steering, 26.7% had power windows, and 69% had air conditioning.

1968 Cadillac De Ville Convertible

Original Price: $5,767
Number Produced: 18,025
Estimated Number Existing in 1979: 7,750
Miles per Gallon: 9–14
Common Trouble Spots: none
Availability of Parts: good
Investment Potential: A+

Background: The biggest change in the Cadillac for 1968 was its new 375 h.p. 472 cu. in. V8 engine. A different grille was the major change in styling. Turbo Hydra-Matic automatic transmission, power steering, power windows, and power brakes were standard.

Nearly all 1968 Cadillacs, 97.8%, came equipped with power front seats, 95.9% had air conditioning, 55.5% had a tilting steering wheel, and 21.6% had disc brakes.

1968 Chevrolet Camaro Convertible

Original Price: $2,908
Number Produced: 235,100 (includes Sport Coupes)
Estimated Number Existing in 1979: 88,397 (includes Sport Coupes)
Miles per Gallon: 10–21
Common Trouble Spots: none
Availability of Parts: good
Investment Potential: AAA

Background: The sleek new Camaro ragtop was powered by a 140 h.p. 230 cu. in. six. A 155 h.p. 250 cu. in. six was also available. Buyers could choose from several V8 engines: a 210 h.p. 327, a 275 h.p. 327, a 210 h.p. 350, a 295 h.p. 350, and a 325 h.p. 396. A three-speed manual transmission was standard. Powerglide and Turbo Hydra-Matic automatics and a four-speed manual were optional at extra cost.

Most 1968 Camaros, 78.3%, came equipped with a V8, 57.7% had an automatic, 22.1% had a three-speed manual, 20.2% had a four-speed manual, 49% had power steering, 27.4% had power brakes, 8.6% had disc brakes, 1.4% had power windows, 2.3% had a tilting steering wheel, 53.6% had tinted glass and, 15.3% were sold with air conditioning.

A Rally Sport and a Super Sport option package were offered. Cars so equipped had distinctive grilles, trim, and insignia.

1968 Chevrolet Camaro Rally Sport Convertible

1968 Cadillac De Ville Convertible

PHOTO: CADILLAC MOTOR CAR DIVISION

1968 Chevrolet Camaro Sport Coupe

Original Price: $2,694
Number Produced: (see 1968 Camaro Convertible)
Estimated Number Existing in 1979: (see 1968 Camaro Convertible)
Miles per Gallon: 10–21
Common Trouble Spots: none
Availability of Parts: good
Investment Potential: AAA (with Z-28 option); AA+ (without)

Background: The '68 Camaro coupe looked much the same as the previous year's model (minus vent windows). Handling was improved. It came with a 140 h.p. 230 cu. in. six, and 155 h.p. 250 cu. in. six was also available, but most Camaros were sold with one of the optional V8 engines: a 210 h.p. 327, a 275 h.p. 327, a 210 h.p. 350 a 295 h.p. 350, a 325 h.p. 396, and a 290 h.p. 302. A three-speed manual transmission was standard. Powerglide and Turbo Hydra-Matic automatics and a four-speed manual were optional at extra cost.

The Rally Sport, Super Sport, and Z-28 packages were once again offered. A total of 7,199 Camaro coupes were sold with the Z-28 option in 1968.

1968 Chevrolet Chevelle Malibu Convertible

Original Price: $2,780
Number Produced: N.A.
Estimated Number Existing in 1979: N.A.
Miles per Gallon: 9–20
Common Trouble Spots: none
Availability of Parts: good
Investment Potential: AA

Background: The new Malibu convertible came with a 140 h.p. 230 cu. in. six. A 155 h.p. 250 cu. in. six was also available, as were the following V8s: a 200 h.p. 307, a 250 h.p. 327, a 275 h.p. 327, and a 325 h.p. 327. A three-speed manual transmission was standard. Overdrive, a four-speed manual, and Powerglide automatic transmission were offered at extra cost.

Most 1968 Chevelles, 82.2%, were equipped with a V8, 76.5% had an automatic, 12.2% had a three-speed manual, 11% had a four-speed manual, and 13% had a tilting steering wheel.

1968 Chevrolet Chevelle Malibu Convertible

1968 Chevrolet Chevelle SS 396 Convertible

1968 Chevrolet Chevelle SS 396 Convertible

Original Price: $3,125
Number Produced: N.A.
Estimated Number Existing in 1979: N.A.
Miles per Gallon: 9–15
Common Trouble Spots: none
Availability of Parts: good
Investment Potential: AA

Background: The Chevelle SS 396 ragtop received an attractive face-lift for 1968. It was powered by a 325 h.p. 396 cu. in. V8. A 350 h.p. version of this engine was optional. A three-speed manual transmission was standard. A four-speed manual and Powerglide and Turbo Hydra-Matic automatic transmissions were available at extra cost.

1968 Chevrolet Corvair Monza Convertible

Original Price: $2,649
Number Produced: 1,386
Estimated Number Existing in 1979: 521
Miles per Gallon: 16–25
Common Trouble Spots: none
Availability of Parts: good
Investment Potential: A+

Background: The new Monza ragtop looked virtually the same as last year's model—but that wasn't bad. It was powered by a 95 h.p. 164 cu. in. six. Buyers could order, at extra cost, a 110 h.p. or a 140 h.p. version of this engine. A three-speed manual transmission was standard. Powerglide automatic and a four-speed manual transmission were optional.

Most 1968 Corvairs, 69.8%, came equipped with the automatic, 17.2% had the three-speed manual, 13% had the four-speed manual, 1.5% had a tilting steering wheel, and 33.5% had tinted glass.

1968 Chevrolet Corvette Stingray Convertible

Original Price: $4,347
Number Produced: 18,630
Estimated Number Existing in 1979: 7,004
Miles per Gallon: 8–17
Common Trouble Spots: none
Availability of Parts: good
Investment Potential: AAA

Background: Road & Track probably provided the best description of the new Vette: "If there's such a thing as a psychedelic car, the 1968 Corvette is it. One almost expects strobe lights to come up when those monstrous flaps out front start lifting at the pull of the headlight switch." They called it "a car that can take a trip without going anywhere."

It was powered by a 300 h.p. 327 cu. in. V8. Other V8 engines were available at extra cost—a 350 h.p. 327, a 390 h.p. 427, a 400 h.p. 427, and a 435 h.p. 427. A three-speed manual transmission was standard. Most 1968 Vettes, 81.1%, came with the optional four-speed manual. Only 17.7% had the Turbo Hydra-Matic automatic transmission.

A little over 36% of all new Vettes were equipped with power steering, 33.7% had power brakes, 22.7% had a tilting steering wheel, 24.7% had power windows, 81% had tinted glass, and 19.8% had air conditioning.

1968 Chevrolet Corvette Convertible

PHOTO: GM PHOTOGRAPHIC

1968 Chevrolet Impala Super Sport Convertible

PHOTO: GM PHOTOGRAPHIC

1968 Chevrolet Impala Convertible

Original Price: $2,989
Number Produced: N.A.
Estimated Number Existing in 1979: N.A.
Miles per Gallon: 9–19
Common Trouble Spots: none
Availability of Parts: good
Investment Potential: A+

Background: The 1968 Impala ragtop was a big, roomy car. It came with a standard 155 h.p. 250 cu. in. six, but most were ordered with one of the optional V8s—a 200 h.p. 307, a 250 h.p. 327, a 275 h.p. 327, a 325 h.p. 396, and a 385 h.p. 427. A three-speed manual transmission was standard. Overdrive, a four-speed manual, and Powerglide and Turbo Hydra-Matic automatic transmissions were available at extra cost.

Over 93% of all full-size '68 Chevrolets came equipped with an automatic, 6.1% had the three-speed manual, a little more than .5% had the four-speed manual, 84.6% had power steering, 93.1% had a V8, 34.8% had power brakes, 2.4% had disc brakes, 3.6% had power windows, 1.8% had power seats, 3.8% had a tilting steering wheel, 70.2% had tinted glass, and 47.6% were sold with air conditioning.

A Super Sport option, featuring bucket seats, fender louvers, and special trim, was offered.

1968 Chrysler Newport Convertible

Original Price: $3,729
Number Produced: 2,847
Estimated Number Existing in 1979: 1,053
Miles per Gallon: 8–16
Common Trouble Spots: none
Availability of Parts: good
Investment Potential: A+

Background: The 1968 Newport had a more sculptured look than the 1967. That livened up its appearance—it made it look less conservative. Despite this, sales were down slightly.

A 290 h.p. 383 cu. in. V8 powered the Newport. Available at extra cost were a 330 h.p. version of this engine and a 375 h.p. 440 cu. in. V8. A three-speed manual transmission was standard. Torque Flite automatic transmission was optional. Late in the model year, a special fake wood-grain trim was made optional.

Most 1968 Chryslers, 99.6%, came with power steering, 84.5% had power brakes, 8.4% had disc brakes, 34.2% had electric windows, 22.7% had power seats, 7.3% had a tilting steering wheel, 88.3% had tinted glass, and 68.7% were sold with air conditioning.

1968 Chrysler 300 Convertible

Original Price: $4,362
Number Produced: 2,161
Estimated Number Existing in 1979: 799
Miles per Gallon: 8–14
Common Trouble Spots: none
Availability of Parts: good
Investment Potential: A+

Background: The 1968 300 convertible was a very sporty-looking car, considering its size. Apparently many buyers thought so as well because sales were up about 25% over last year.

The 300 came with a 350 h.p. 440 cu. in. V8 engine. A 375 h.p. version of this engine was available at extra cost. Torque Flite automatic transmission was standard. Many optional accessories were also offered.

This was one of the better-looking convertibles offered in the 300 Sport Series.

1968 Chrysler 300 Convertible

PHOTO: CHRYSLER HISTORICAL COLLECTION

1968 Dodge Dart GT Convertible

Original Price: $2,856
Number Produced: N.A.
Estimated Number Existing in 1979: N.A.
Miles per Gallon: 13–23
Common Trouble Spots: none
Availability of Parts: good
Investment Potential: A+

Background: Because of a slightly different grille treatment, the GT looked lower and wider than the higher-priced GTS. It was powered by a 115 h.p. 170 cu. in. slant six. Also available were a 145 h.p. 225 cu. in. six and two V8s, a 190 h.p. 273 and a 230 h.p. 318. Torque Flite automatic and a four-speed manual transmission were optional.

Most 1968 Darts, 71.9%, came equipped with a six, 87.3% had an automatic, 10.5% had a three-speed manual, 2.2% had a four-speed manual, 54.7% had power steering, 4.2% had power brakes, 1.2% had disc brakes, 45.7% had tinted glass, about .9% had bucket seats, and 20.3% were sold with air conditioning.

1968 Dodge Dart GT Convertible

1968 Dodge Dart GTS Convertible

Original Price: $3,408
Number Produced: N.A.
Estimated Number Existing in 1979: N.A.
Miles per Gallon: 12–19
Common Trouble Spots: none
Availability of Parts: good
Investment Potential: AA

Background: The attractive new Dart GTS ragtop came with a 275 h.p. 340 cu. in. V8 with four-barrel carburetor. A hot 300 h.p. 383 cu. in. V8 with four-barrel carburetor was available at extra cost. Buyers had their choice of Torque Flite automatic or a four-speed manual.

Special trim, hood, and heavy-duty suspension helped set the GTS apart from "ordinary" Darts. It was available in any of seventeen exterior colors: dark blue metallic, bright blue metallic, light blue metallic, medium turquoise metallic, racing green metallic, medium green metallic, light green metallic, medium gold metallic, medium tan metallic, beige, yellow, bronze metallic, burgundy metallic, red, silver metallic, white, and black.

1968 Dodge Dart GT Sport Convertible

1968 Dodge Coronet R/T Convertible

1968 Dodge Coronet 500 Convertible

Original Price: $3,061
Number Produced: N.A.
Estimated Number Existing in 1979: N.A.
Miles per Gallon: 10–17
Common Trouble Spots: none
Availability of Parts: good
Investment Potential: A+

Background: The attractive new Coronet convertible was powered by a 230 h.p. 318 cu. in. V8. Two 383 cu. in. V8s, rated at 290 h.p. and 330 h.p., were available at extra cost. A three-speed manual transmission was standard. Torque Flite automatic and a four-speed manual were optional.

Most 1968 Coronets, 87.6%, were equipped with an automatic, 9.3% had a three-speed manual, 3.1% had a four-speed manual, 81.6% had power steering, 13% had power brakes, 1.7% had disc brakes, 86% had radios, 11.9% had power windows, 61.3% had tinted glass, 1.4% had bucket seats, and 32.7% were sold with air conditioning.

1968 Dodge Coronet 500 Convertible

1968 Dodge Coronet R/T Convertible

Original Price: $3,638
Number Produced: N.A.
Estimated Number Existing in 1979: N.A.
Miles per Gallon: 8–14
Common Trouble Spots: none
Availability of Parts: good
Investment Potential: AA

Background: Special trim and performance equipment helped to distinguish the R/T (Road and Track) from the less expensive Coronet 500. It came with a 375 h.p. 440 cu. in. V8. If that wasn't hot enough, buyers could order a 425 h.p. 426 cu. in. Hemi V8. Two transmissions were offered, Torque Flite automatic and a four-speed manual.

1968 Dodge Polara Convertible

Original Price: $3,313
Number Produced: N.A.
Estimated Number Existing in 1979: N.A.
Miles per Gallon: 8–16
Common Trouble Spots: brakes; cooling, electrical and ignition systems; suspension
Availability of Parts: good
Investment Potential: A+ (with 500 package); A (without)

Background: The stylish '68 Polara convertible came with a 230 h.p. 318 cu. in. V8. Other V8s were available at extra cost—a 290 h.p. 383, a 330 h.p. 383, a 350 h.p. 440, and a 375 h.p. 440. A three-speed manual transmission was standard. Torque Flite automatic transmission was optional.

Most 1968 Polaras, 99%, were equipped with the automatic, 97.8% had power steering, 70.9% had power brakes, 5.1% had power front seats, 3.1% had a tilting steering wheel, 80.6% had tinted glass, 1.6% had bucket seats, and 58.4% were sold with air conditioning.

The Polara 500 package, featuring special trim and interior, was optional.

1968 Ford Fairlane 500 Convertible

PHOTO: FORD MOTOR COMPANY

1968 Ford Fairlane 500 Convertible

Original Price: $2,822
Number Produced: 3,761
Estimated Number Existing in 1979: 1,350
Miles per Gallon: 10–21
Common Trouble Spots: none
Availability of Parts: good
Investment Potential: A+

Background: The attractive Fairlane 500 came with a 115 h.p. 200 cu. in. six-cylinder engine. Most had one of the optional V8s. These included a 210 h.p. 302, a 265 h.p. 390, and a 335 h.p. 390. A three-speed manual transmission was standard. Cruise-O-Matic automatic, and a four-speed manual were optional at extra cost.

The majority of 1968 Fairlanes, 68.5%, had power steering, 19.9% had power disc brakes, 10.3% had the six, .5% had power windows, 38.5% had tinted glass, and 24.3% were equipped with an air conditioner. Nine percent of Fairlane 500 convertibles had bucket seats.

1968 Ford Fairlane Torino GT Convertible

Original Price: $3,001
Number Produced: 5,310
Estimated Number Existing in 1979: 1,906
Miles per Gallon: 9–18
Common Trouble Spots: none
Availability of Parts: good
Investment Potential: AA

Background: The new Torino was Fairlane's top-of-the-line convertible. It bore a strong family resemblance to the big Galaxie 500. A 210 h.p. 302 cu. in. V8 was standard on early models. Those sold after January 1, 1968, came with a 195 h.p. 289 cu. in. V8. Three other V8s were optional: a 265 h.p. 390, and a 335 h.p. 390, and a 390 h.p. 427. A three-speed manual transmission was standard, but only 10.4% of all 1968 Fairlanes were so equipped. Most came with the optional Cruise-O-Matic automatic, and 4.2% had the four-speed manual.

The Torino softtop was the pace car for the 1968 Indy 500.

1968 Ford Galaxie 500 Convertible

Original Price: $3,108
Number Produced: 11,832
Estimated Number Existing in 1979: 4,247
Miles per Gallon: 9–18
Common Trouble Spots: none
Availability of Parts: good
Investment Potential: A+

Background: The attractive Galaxie 500 ragtop came with a standard 150 h.p. 240 cu. in. six-cylinder engine, but less than 1% of all 1968 Galaxies were sold with it. Most had one of the optional V8s—a 210 h.p. 302, a 265 h.p. 390, a 315 h.p. 390, a 390 h.p. 427, and a 340 h.p. 428. A three-speed manual transmission was standard. Cruise-O-Matic automatic transmission and a four-speed manual were available at extra cost.

The majority of new Galaxies, 97.6%, came with the automatic, a mere .1% had the four-speed manual, 94.6% had power steering, 47% had tinted glass, nearly 1% had a tilting steering wheel, 31.3% had power brakes, and 44.7% were equipped with an air conditioner.

Galaxie 500 buyers had their choice of six all-vinyl interiors.

1968 Ford Galaxie 500 Convertible

PHOTO: FORD MOTOR COMPANY

1968 Ford Fairlane Torino GT Convertible

PHOTO: FORD MOTOR COMPANY

1968 Ford Galaxie 500 XL Convertible

Original Price: $3,214
Number Produced: 6,066
Estimated Number Existing in 1979: 2,177
Miles per Gallon: 9–18
Common Trouble Spots: none
Availability of Parts: good
Investment Potential: AA

Background: Hidden headlights were probably the most noticeable change made in the Galaxie XL for 1968. They made the car look "ritzy."

The Galaxie XL came with a 150 h.p. 240 cu. in. six-cylinder engine. Most Galaxie buyers, 99.1%, ordered one of the optional V8s, which included a 210 h.p. 302, a 265 h.p. 390, a 315 h.p. 390, a 390 h.p. 427, and a 340 h.p. 428. A three-speed manual transmission was standard. Cruise-O-Matic automatic and a four-speed manual were available at extra cost.

The XL's vinyl power top was offered in black, blue, and parchment. Buyers had their choice of fifteen exterior colors and seven all-vinyl upholsteries.

Bucket seats, padded dash, carpeting, electric clock, and padded full-length console were standard.

1968 Ford Mustang Convertible

Original Price: $2,814
Number Produced: 25,376
Estimated Number Existing in 1979: 9,109
Miles per Gallon: 12–22
Common Trouble Spots: none
Availability of Parts: good
Investment Potential: AA+

Background: A sales brochure described the new Mustang as "2,900 pounds of pure delight." And the most delightful of all was the convertible.

It was powered by a 115 h.p. 200 cu. in. six-cylinder engine. Several V8s were optional: a 195 h.p. 289, a 230 h.p. 302, a 280 h.p. 390, a 325 h.p. 390, and a 390 h.p. 427. A three-speed manual transmission was standard. Cruise-O-Matic automatic and a four-speed manual were available at extra cost.

Most 1968 Mustangs, 71.7%, came with the automatic, 5.7% had the four-speed manual, 70.7% had a V8, 51.8% had power steering, 13.1% had power brakes, 2.7% had a tilting steering wheel, 91% had radios, 31.7% had tinted glass, 97.3% had bucket seats, and 17.5% were equipped with air conditioning.

1968 Ford Mustang Convertible

PHOTO: FORD MOTOR COMPANY

1968 Imperial Crown Convertible

Original Price: $6,522
Number Produced: 474
Estimated Number Existing in 1979: 208
Miles per Gallon: 8–14
Common Trouble Spots: none
Availability of Parts: good
Investment Potential: A+

Background: The 1968 Imperial convertible looked like a customized 1967 Newport from the front. Although it was an expensive and luxurious automobile, it was becoming less and less distinctive. Sales were down by about 20 percent.

The Imperial was powered by a 350 h.p. 440 cu. in. V8 engine. Torque Flite automatic transmission, power steering, power disc brakes, and electric windows were standard.

Most 1968 Imperials, 90.2%, had power seats, 71.1% had a tilting steering wheel, 98.5% had tinted glass, and 97.2% were sold with air conditioning.

1968 Imperial Crown Convertible

PHOTO: CHRYSLER HISTORICAL COLLECTION

1968 King Midget Convertible

Original Price: est. $1,000
Number Produced: 95
Estimated Number Existing in 1979: 28
Miles per Gallon: 50–90
Common Trouble Spots: clutch, "V" belt
Availability of Parts: good
Investment Potential: A

Background: The 1968 King Midget convertible was powered by a 12 h.p. 29 cu. in. one-cylinder engine. Automatic transmission was standard.

1968 Mercury Monterey Convertible

Original Price: $3,436
Number Produced: 1,515
Estimated Number Existing in 1979: 474
Miles per Gallon: 9–16
Common Trouble Spots: none
Availability of Parts: good
Investment Potential: A

Background: The '68 Monterey ragtop came with a 265 h.p. 390 cu. in. V8. Three other V8 engines were available at extra cost: a 280 h.p. 390, a 315 h.p. 390, and a 340 h.p. 428. A three-speed manual transmission was standard. Merc-O-Matic automatic transmission was optional.

Most 1968 Mercurys, 99.6%, were equipped with the automatic, 99.2% had power steering, 76.5% had power brakes, 32.8% had electric windows, 14.8% had power front seats, 9.7% had a tilting steering wheel, 74.2% had tinted glass, and 59.5% were sold with air conditioning.

1968 Mercury Monterey Convertible

PHOTO: FORD MOTOR COMPANY

1968 Mercury Montego MX Convertible

Original Price: $2,935
Number Produced: 3,248
Estimated Number Existing in 1979: 1,016
Miles per Gallon: 10–19
Common Trouble Spots: none
Availability of Parts: good
Investment Potential: A+

Background: This was the first year for the Montego MX convertible. It came with a 115 h.p. 200 cu. in. six-cylinder engine, and five V8 engines were available at extra cost: a 210 h.p. 302, a 230 h.p. 302, a 265 h.p. 390, a 335 h.p. 390, and a 390 h.p. 427. A three speed manual transmission was standard. Cruise-O-Matic automatic and a four-speed manual were optional.

Many Montego MX convertibles, 29.6%, were equipped with bucket seats.

1968 Mercury Montego MX Convertible

PHOTO: FORD MOTOR COMPANY

1968 Mercury Park Lane Convertible

Original Price: $3,822
Number Produced: 1,112
Estimated Number Existing in 1979: 348
Miles per Gallon: 9–15
Common Trouble Spots: none
Availability of Parts: good
Investment Potential: A

Background: The Park Lane was Mercury's most luxurious convertible in 1968. It came with a standard 315 h.p. 390 cu. in. V8; a 340 h.p. 428 cu. in. V8 was optional. Merc-O-Matic automatic transmission was standard. A wood-grain-type exterior trim was available at extra cost.

1968 Oldsmobile Cutlass Convertible

Original Price: $2,972
Number Produced: 14,077
Estimated Number Existing in 1979: 4,406
Miles per Gallon: 12–19
Common Trouble Spots: none
Availability of Parts: good
Investment Potential: A+

Background: The 1968 Cutlass was by far the most popular Oldsmobile convertible of the year. It was powered by a 155 h.p. 250 cu. in. six-cylinder engine, but less than 5% of all Cutlass ragtops were so equipped; the vast majority of buyers ordered the optional 350 cu. in. V8, with either 250 h.p. or 310 h.p. A three-speed manual transmission was standard. Jetaway automatic and a four-speed manual transmission were optional.

Other options offered were simulated wire wheels, a stereo tape player, and an anti-spin differential, to mention a few.

1968 Oldsmobile Cutlass Convertible

PHOTO: OLDSMOBILE DIVISION

1968 Oldsmobile Delmont 88 Convertible

Original Price: $3,538
Number Produced: 2,812
Estimated Number Existing in 1979: 880
Miles per Gallon: 8–17
Common Trouble Spots: none
Availability of Parts: good
Investment Potential: A

Background: This was Oldsmobile's least popular convertible in 1968. It was powered by a 250 h.p. 350 cu. in. V8. Some other V8s, a 310 h.p. 350, a 320 h.p. 455, and a 365 h.p. 455, were available at extra cost. A three-speed manual transmission was standard. Jetaway automatic transmission was optional.

Most 1968 Delmonts, 99.7%, came with the automatic transmission, 99.5% had power steering, 95.3% had power brakes, less than 1% had disc brakes, 4.2% had power windows, 2.3% had power seats, 4.2% had tilting steering wheel, 84% had tinted glass, and 55.7% were sold with air conditioning.

1968 Oldsmobile Dynamic 88 Convertible

Original Price: est. $3,500
Number Produced: 2,843
Estimated Number Existing in 1979: 889
Miles per Gallon: 8–17
Common Trouble Spots: none
Availability of Parts: good
Investment Potential: A

Background: The 1968 Dynamic 88 is a typical big, late-1960s convertible. It came with a 250 h.p. 350 cu. in. V8. Three other V8s, a 310 h.p. 350, a 320 h.p. 455, and a 365 h.p. 455, were available at extra cost. A three-speed manual transmission was standard. Jetaway automatic transmission was optional.

1968 Oldsmobile 4-4-2 Convertible

Original Price: $3,364
Number Produced: 5,142
Estimated Number Existing in 1979: 1,609
Miles per Gallon: 9–15
Common Trouble Spots: none
Availability of Parts: good
Investment Potential: AA

Background: The 4-4-2 was now a separate series; before, it had been an option package. It came with a 350 h.p. 400 cu. in. V8. Three other versions of this engine were also available, rated at 290 h.p., 325 h.p., and 360 h.p. A three-speed manual transmission was standard. Turbo Hydra-Matic automatic and a four-speed manual were optional.

1968 Oldsmobile 4-4-2 Convertible

PHOTO: OLDSMOBILE DIVISION

1968 Oldsmobile Delmont 88 Convertible

PHOTO: OLDSMOBILE DIVISION

1968 Oldsmobile 98 Convertible

PHOTO: OLDSMOBILE DIVISION

1968 Plymouth Fury III Convertible

1968 Oldsmobile 98 Convertible

Original Price: $4,641
Number Produced: 3,942
Estimated Number Existing in 1979: 1,233
Miles per Gallon: 8–14
Common Trouble Spots: none
Availability of Parts: good
Investment Potential: A

Background: The 98 was the most popular full-size Oldsmobile ragtop in 1968. It was powered by a 365 h.p. 455 cu. in. V8. Turbo Hydra-Matic automatic transmission, power steering, and power brakes were standard.

Most 98s, 90%, came with air conditioning, 7.5% had disc brakes, 96.6% had tinted glass, and 45.7% had a tilting steering wheel.

1968 Plymouth Barracuda Convertible

Original Price: $2,932
Number Produced: N.A.
Estimated Number Existing in 1979: N.A.
Miles per Gallon: 11–21
Common Trouble Spots: none
Availability of Parts: good
Investment Potential: A+

Background: The sporty new Barracuda came with a 145 h.p. 225 cu. in. six-cylinder engine. Three V8 engines were available: a 230 h.p. 318, a 275 h.p. 340, and a 300 h.p. 383. A three-speed manual transmission was standard. Torque Flite automatic and a four-speed manual transmission were optional.

Most 1968 Barracudas, 72.5%, were equipped with a V-8 engine, 84.5% had an automatic transmission, 6.3% had a three-speed manual transmission, 9.2% had a four-speed manual transmission, 57.6% had power steering, 8.3% had power brakes, 6.1% had disc brakes, 84% had radios, 54.5% had tinted glass, 9.5% had bucket seats, and 19.1% were sold with a $334.60 air conditioner.

The Formula S package was again offered. It was available with either a 340 cu. in. (for $186.30) or a 383 cu. in. V8 engine (for $221.65). A four-speed manual transmission was standard. Torque Flite automatic transmission was optional.

1968 Plymouth Fury III Convertible

Original Price: $3,261
Number Produced: N.A.
Estimated Number Existing in 1979: N.A.
Miles per Gallon: 9–17
Common Trouble Spots: none
Availability of Parts: good
Investment Potential: A+

Background: The new Fury III ragtop came with a 145 h.p. 225 cu. in. six-cylinder engine. Four V8 engines were available at extra cost: a 230 h.p. 318 (two-barrel carburetor), a 290 h.p. 383 (two-barrel carburetor), a 330 h.p. 383 (four-barrel carburetor), and a 375 h.p. 440 (four-barrel carburetor).

A three-speed manual transmission was standard. Torque Flite automatic transmission and a four-speed manual transmission were optional.

Most 1968 Fury IIIs, over 97%, were equipped with a V8 engine, 96.9% had an automatic transmission, 2.9% had a three-speed manual transmission, .2% had a four-speed manual transmission, 93.8% had power steering, 39.2% had power brakes, 4.1% had disc brakes, 13.4% had electric windows, 1.7% had power front seats, 72.4% had tinted glass, about .2% had bucket seats, and 56.2% were sold with an air conditioner.

1968 Plymouth GTX Convertible

Original Price: $3,615
Number Produced: N.A.
Estimated Number Existing in 1979: N.A.
Miles per Gallon: 8–14
Common Trouble Spots: none
Availability of Parts: good
Investment Potential: AA

Background: Plymouth's most expensive convertible in 1968 was the GTX. It came with a 375 h.p. 440 cu. in. V8 engine (with four-barrel carburetor). A 425 h.p. 426 cu. in. V8 (with two four-barrel carburetors) was available at extra cost. Buyers had their choice of either Torque Flite automatic transmission or a four-speed manual transmission.

1968 Plymouth Satellite Convertible

Original Price: $2,943
Number Produced: N.A.
Estimated Number Existing in 1979: N.A.
Miles per Gallon: 9–18
Common Trouble Spots: none
Availability of Parts: good
Investment Potential: A

Background: The new Satellite convertible came with a 145 h.p. 225 cu. in. six-cylinder engine. Five V8 engines were available at extra cost: a 190 h.p. 273, a 230 h.p. 318, a 290 h.p. 383, a 330 h.p. 383, and a 425 h.p. 426. A three-speed manual transmission was standard. Torque Flite automatic and a four-speed manual transmission were optional.

1968 Plymouth Sport Satellite Convertible

Original Price: $3,061
Number Produced: N.A.
Estimated Number Existing in 1979: N.A.
Miles per Gallon: 9–16
Common Trouble Spots: none
Availability of Parts: good
Investment Potential: A+

Background: The fanciest Satellite convertible for 1968 was the Sport. It came with a 230 h.p. 318 cu. in. V8 engine (with two-barrel carburetor). Two other V8 engines were available at extra cost: a 330 h.p. 383 (with four-barrel carburetor) and a 425 h.p. 426 (with two four-barrel carburetors).

Buyers could choose from Torque Flite automatic or a four-speed manual transmission.

1968 Plymouth Sport Fury Convertible

Original Price: $3,450
Number Produced: N.A.
Estimated Number Existing in 1979: N.A.
Miles per Gallon: 9–16
Common Trouble Spots: none
Availability of Parts: good
Investment Potential: A+

Background: The big new Sport Fury convertible came with a 230 h.p. 318 cu. in. V8 engine (with two-barrel carburetor). Three other V8 engines were available at extra cost: a 290 h.p. 383 (two-barrel carburetor), a 330 h.p. 383 (four-barrel carburetor), and a 375 h.p. 440 (four-barrel carburetor).

A three-speed manual transmission was standard. Torque Flite automatic transmission and a four-speed manual transmission were optional.

1968 Pontiac Bonneville Convertible

Original Price: $3,823
Number Produced: 7,358
Estimated Number Existing in 1979: 2,575
Miles per Gallon: 8–15
Common Trouble Spots: none
Availability of Parts: good
Investment Potential: A

Background: "Elegant styling, precision engineering and new safety features make the 1968 Bonnevilles a new experience in driving comfort and convenience." That's how a Pontiac public relations release described the new Bonneville.

The Bonneville came with a 340 h.p. 400 cu. in. V8. Three other V8 engines were available at extra cost: a 265 h.p. 400, a 375 h.p. 428, and a 390 h.p. 428. A three-speed manual transmission was standard, but not very popular; the vast majority of buyers ordered the optional Turbo Hydra-Matic automatic transmission.

1968 Plymouth Sport Fury Convertible

1968 Pontiac Bonneville Convertible

PHOTO: PONTIAC MOTOR DIVISION

1968 Pontiac Catalina Convertible

Original Price: $3,414
Number Produced: 7,339
Estimated Number Existing in 1979: 2,568
Miles per Gallon: 8–17
Common Trouble Spots: none
Availability of Parts: good
Investment Potential: A

Background: Pontiac's lowest-priced full-size convertible suffered a significant drop in popularity in 1968. It came with a 290 h.p. 400 cu. in. V8. Four other V8 engines were available at extra cost: a 265 h.p. 400, a 340 h.p. 400, a 375 h.p. 428, and a 390 h.p. 428. A three-speed manual transmission was standard. Turbo Hydra-Matic automatic transmission was optional.

Most full-size 1968 Pontiacs, 99.3%, came with the automatic, 98.9% had power steering, 90.9% had power brakes, 2.4% had disc brakes, 21.6% had electric windows, 7.5% had power front seats, 14.4% had a tilting steering wheel, 83.1% had tinted glass, and 63.6% were sold with an air conditioner.

1968 Pontiac Catalina Convertible

1968 Pontiac Firebird Convertible

Original Price: $3,019
Number Produced: 16,960
Estimated Number Existing in 1979: 5,936
Miles per Gallon: 10–20
Common Trouble Spots: none
Availability of Parts: good
Investment Potential: AAA

Background: The Firebird ragtop was even more popular this year than last. It was powered by a 175 h.p. 250 cu. in. six-cylinder engine. A 215 h.p. version of this engine was also available. Most Firebird buyers, 82.7%, ordered one of the optional V8s: a 265 h.p. 350, a 320 h.p. 350, a 330 h.p. 400, and a 335 h.p. 400.

A three-speed manual transmission was standard. A four-speed manual and an automatic transmission were optional.

Most 1968 Firebirds, 69.3%, came with the automatic, 13.7% had the three-speed manual, 17% had the four-speed manual, 79% had power steering, 37.2% had power brakes, 6.3% had disc brakes, 95.7% had radios, 3% had power windows, 5.6% had a tilting steering wheel, 59.6% had tinted glass, 96.4% had bucket seats, and 23.2% had an air conditioner.

1968 Pontiac Firebird Convertible

1968 Pontiac GTO Convertible

Original Price: $3,350
Number Produced: 9,980
Estimated Number Existing in 1979: 3,493
Miles per Gallon: 8–16
Common Trouble Spots: none
Availability of Parts: good
Investment Potential: AA

Background: The GTO came with a 350 h.p. 400 cu. in. V8—the same engine that was standard in the big, top-of-the-line Grand Prix. Three other V8s were available at extra cost: a 265 h.p. 400, and two 360 h.p. 400s. A three-speed manual transmission was standard. Turbo Hydra-Matic automatic and a four-speed manual transmission were optional.

1968 Pontiac GTO Convertible

PHOTO: PONTIAC MOTOR DIVISION

1968 Pontiac Le Mans Convertible

Original Price: $3,038
Number Produced: 8,820
Estimated Number Existing in 1979: 3,087
Miles per Gallon: 10–20
Common Trouble Spots: none
Availability of Parts: good
Investment Potential: A+

Background: The Le Mans ragtop came with a 175 h.p. 250 cu. in. six-cylinder engine. A 215 h.p. version of this engine was available. Two 350 cu. in. V8s, with either 265 h.p. or 320 h.p. were optional. Most Le Mans buyers ordered one of the V8s.

A three-speed manual transmission was standard, but not very popular. A four-speed manual transmission and an automatic transmission were optional at extra cost. Both of these were more popular than the three-speed.

1968 Pontiac Tempest Custom Convertible

Original Price: $2,862
Number Produced: 3,518
Estimated Number Existing in 1979: 1,231
Miles per Gallon: 10–20
Common Trouble Spots: none
Availability of Parts: good
Investment Potential: A+

Background: The Tempest Custom was the only '68 Pontiac softtop with a base price under $3,000. It was also Pontiac's least popular convertible.

The Custom came with a 175 h.p. 250 cu. in. six-cylinder engine. A 215 h.p. version of this engine was also available. Most Tempest buyers ordered one of the optional V8s—the 265 h.p. 350 or the 320 h.p. 350. A three-speed manual transmission was standard. A four-speed manual and an automatic transmission were optional.

Most 1968 Tempests, 82.5%, were equipped with the automatic, 7% had the three-speed manual, 10.5% had the four-speed manual, 84.6% had a V8 engine, 84.3% had power steering, 41.5% had power brakes, 3.2% had disc brakes, 95% had radios, 5.1% had electric windows, 56.7% had bucket seats, 1.1% had power front seats, 66% had tinted glass, and 36.9% were sold with air conditioning.

1968½ Rambler AMX Sport Coupe

Original Price: $3,245
Number Produced: 6,725
Estimated Number Existing in 1979: 2,360
Miles per Gallon: 10–18
Common Trouble Spots: none
Availability of Parts: good
Investment Potential: AAA

Background: American Motors made the sporty two-passenger AMX in an effort to improve their image with the performance crowd. They succeeded. The AMX came with a 225 h.p. 290 cu. in. V8. Two other V8s, a 280 h.p. 343 and a 315 h.p. 390, were available at extra cost. A four-speed manual was standard. Shift-Command automatic transmission was optional.

Most 1968½ AMXs, 54.6%, were equipped with the automatic, 45.4% had the four-speed manual, 68.7% had power steering, 77% had power brakes, 60.9% had disc brakes, 21.9% had a tilting steering wheel, 78.3% had radios, 52.2% had tinted glass, and 13.9% were sold with air conditioning.

1968½ Rambler AMX Sport Coupe

PHOTO: LARRY G. MITCHELL, THE CLASSIC AMX CLUB INT.

1968 Rambler Rebel 550 Convertible

Original Price: $2,736
Number Produced: 377
Estimated Number Existing in 1979: 132
Miles per Gallon: 12–19
Common Trouble Spots: none
Availability of Parts: good
Investment Potential: A

Background: The 1968 Rebel 550 convertible came with a 145 h.p. 232 cu. in. six. A 155 h.p. version of this engine and four V8s, a 200 h.p. 290, a 235 h.p. 343, a 280 h.p. 343, and a 315 h.p. 390, were available at extra cost. A three-speed manual transmission was standard. Overdrive, a four-speed manual, and Shift-Command automatic transmission were optional.

Most '68 Rebels, 54.3%, were equipped with a six, 88.9% had the automatic, 8.1% had the three-speed manual, .6% had the four-speed manual, 53.7% had power steering, 22.3% had power brakes, 1.2% had disc brakes, seven percent had power windows, 36.9% had tinted glass, 2.4% had a tilting steering wheel, and 16.4% were sold with air conditioning.

1968 Rambler Rebel SST Convertible

Original Price: $2,999
Number Produced: 823
Estimated Number Existing in 1979: 288
Miles per Gallon: 10–18
Common Trouble Spots: none
Availability of Parts: good
Investment Potential: A+

Background: This was the last year for the Rebel SST convertible. It came with a 200 h.p. 290 cu. in. V8. Three other V8s; a 235 h.p. 343, a 280 h.p. 343, and a 315 h.p. 390, were available at extra cost. A three-speed manual transmission was standard. Overdrive, a four-speed manual, and Shift-Command automatic transmission were optional.

1968 Shelby American Cobra GT 500 Convertible

Original Price: est. $5,000
Number Produced: est. 574
Estimated Number Existing in 1979: 206
Miles per Gallon: 8–14
Common Trouble Spots: none
Availability of Parts: fair–good
Investment Potential: AAA

Background: The '68 Shelby American GT 500 ragtop came with a 360 hp 428 cu. in. V8 (with four-barrel Holley carburetor). If that wasn't enough power, GT 500 buyers could order a 400 h.p. 427 cu. in. V8. A four-speed manual transmission was standard. Cruise-O-Matic automatic transmission was optional.

1968 Shelby American Cobra GT 350 Convertible

Original Price: est. $4,500
Number Produced: est. 550
Estimated Number Existing in 1979: 197
Miles per Gallon: 9–15
Common Trouble Spots: none
Availability of Parts: fair–good
Investment Potential: AAA

Background: This was the first year for the hot Shelby GT 350 ragtop. It came with a 250 h.p. 302 cu. in. V8 (with high-volume intake manifold and four-barrel carburetor). This engine was rated at 335 h.p. when equipped with the optional Cobra centrifugal supercharger. A four-speed manual transmission was standard. Cruise-O-Matic automatic transmission was available.

1968 Shelby American Cobra GT 500 Convertible

PHOTO: FORD MOTOR COMPANY

1969

1969 Buick Electra Custom 225 Convertible

Original Price: $4,625
Number Produced: 8,294
Estimated Number Existing in 1979: 3,674
Miles per Gallon: 8–14
Common Trouble Spots: cooling system
Availability of Parts: good
Investment Potential: A+

Background: The '69 Electra convertible looked even more luxurious this year than last. It was powered by a 360 h.p. 430 cu. in. V8. Turbo Hydra-Matic automatic transmission was standard.

All Electras had power steering and power brakes. Nearly 80% had power windows, 74% had power seats, 6.3% had disc brakes, and 93.2% came with air conditioning.

1969 Buick GS 400 Convertible

Original Price: $3,308
Number Produced: 1,776
Estimated Number Existing in 1979: 786
Miles per Gallon: 8–15
Common Trouble Spots: cooling system
Availability of Parts: good
Investment Potential: AA

Background: The GS 400 was basically just a fancy Skylark. It was powered by a 340 h.p. 400 cu. in. V8. A three-speed manual transmission was standard. Most buyers ordered the optional Turbo Hydra-Matic automatic transmission. The least popular transmission was the four-speed manual.

The majority of GS 400s had power steering. Power brakes were less popular.

1969 Buick GS 400 Convertible

1969 Buick LeSabre Custom Convertible

Original Price: $3,562
Number Produced: 3,620
Estimated Number Existing in 1979: 1,603
Miles per Gallon: 9–17
Common Trouble Spots: cooling system
Availability of Parts: good
Investment Potential: A

Background: The LeSabre received an attractive facelift for 1969. It was powered by a 230 h.p. 350 cu. in. V8. A 280 h.p. version of this engine was optional. A three-speed manual transmission was standard, but not very popular. Most LeSabres, 99.9%, came with the optional Super Turbine automatic transmission. Power steering was on 99.4% of '69 LeSabres, power brakes on 92.3%, power windows on 6.9%, and a $421 air conditioning unit came on 70%.

1969 Buick LeSabre Custom Convertible

PHOTO: BUICK MOTOR DIVISION

1969 Buick Skylark Custom Convertible

Original Price: $3,135
Number Produced: 6,552
Estimated Number Existing in 1979: 2,902
Miles per Gallon: 10–18
Common Trouble Spots: cooling system
Availability of Parts: good
Investment Potential: AA

Background: This was Buick's lowest priced ragtop in 1969. It was powered by a 230 h.p. 350 cu. in. V8. A 280 h.p. version of this engine was available at extra cost. A three-speed manual transmission was standard. Turbo Hydra-Matic automatic transmission was a very popular option.

Most buyers ordered the $100 power steering and $42 power brakes. The $376 air conditioning unit was also very popular.

1969 Buick Skylark Custom Convertible

PHOTO: BUICK MOTOR DIVISION

1969 Buick Wildcat Custom Convertible

Original Price: $3,931
Number Produced: 2,374
Estimated Number Existing in 1979: 1,051
Miles per Gallon: 8–14
Common Trouble Spots: cooling system
Availability of Parts: good
Investment Potential: A+

Background: The Wildcat convertible was powered by a 360 h.p. 430 cu. in. V8. A three-speed manual transmission was standard, but not very popular. Most Wildcats, 99.9%, had the optional Turbo Hydra-Matic automatic transmission. Virtually all, 98.6%, had power brakes, 99.8% had power steering, 27.3% had power windows, 76.9% had air conditioning, and 4.9% were equipped with disc brakes.

1969 Cadillac De Ville Convertible

Original Price: $5,887
Number Produced: 16,445
Estimated Number Existing in 1979: 9,044
Miles per Gallon: 9–14
Common Trouble Spots: none
Availability of Parts: good
Investment Potential: A+

Background: For the first time since 1964, Cadillac headlights were horizontal. Other styling changes were made in both the body and the interior.

The De Ville was powered by a 375 h.p. 472 cu. in. V8 engine. Turbo Hydra-Matic automatic transmission, power steering, power disc brakes, and power windows were standard. Air conditioning was available optionally for $516. Nearly all 1969 Cadillacs, 97.2% came with it.

1969 Cadillac De Ville Convertible

PHOTO: CADILLAC MOTOR CAR DIVISION

1969 Chevrolet Camaro Convertible

Original Price: $2,835
Number Produced: 243,100 (includes Sport Coupes)
Estimated Number Existing in 1979: 121,550 (includes Sport Coupes)
Miles per Gallon: 10–21
Common Trouble Spots: cooling system, automatic transmission
Availability of Parts: good
Investment Potential: AAA

Background: This was the last year for the sporty Camaro convertible. It came with a 140 h.p. 230 cu. in. six. Also available were a 155 h.p. 250 cu. in. six and three V8 engines—a 210 h.p. 327, a 255 h.p. 350, a 300 h.p. 350, and a 325 h.p. 396. A three-speed manual transmission was standard. A four-speed manual and Powerglide and Turbo Hydra-Matic automatic transmissions were optional.

Over 57% of all 1969 Camaros came equipped with an automatic, 18.5% had the three-speed manual, 23.9% had the four-speed manual, 85% had a V8, 57.3% had power steering, 35.7% had power brakes, 29% had disc brakes, 1.4% had power windows, 3%

had a tilting steering wheel, 48.4% had tinted glass, and 18.1% were sold with an air conditioner.

Rally Sport and Super Sport packages were available optionally. A total of 3,675 Camaro convertible Indy 500 Pace Car replicas were produced.

1969 Chevrolet Camaro Rally Sport Convertible

PHOTO: GM PHOTOGRAPHIC

1969 Chevrolet Camaro Sport Coupe

Original Price: $2,621
Number Produced: (see 1969 Camaro convertible)
Estimated Number Existing in 1979: (see 1969 Camaro convertible)
Miles per Gallon: 10–21
Common Trouble Spots: cooling system, automatic transmission
Availability of Parts: good
Investment Potential: AAA (with Z-28 option); AA+ (without)

Background: The '69 Camaro coupe came with a 140 h.p. 230 cu. in. six. A 155 h.p. 250 cu. in. six was also available. Most buyers ordered one of the optional V8 engines—the 210 h.p. 327, the 255 h.p. 350, the 300 h.p. 350, the 290 h.p. 302, or the 325 h.p. 396. A three-speed manual transmission was standard. A four-speed manual and Powerglide and Turbo Hydra-Matic automatic transmissions were optional.

Once again, the Rally Sport, Super Sport and the Z-28 packages were offered. The Z-28 option included a 290 h.p. 302 cu. in. V8, special suspension, hood and rear-deck stripes, power disc brakes, quick-ratio steering, four-speed manual transmission, and Z-28 emblems. A total of 20,302 Camaro coupes were so equipped in 1969.

1969 Chevrolet Chevelle Malibu Convertible

Original Price: $2,763
Number Produced: N.A.
Estimated Number Existing in 1979: N.A.
Miles per Gallon: 9–20
Common Trouble Spots: clutch, cooling system
Availability of Parts: good
Investment Potential: AA

Background: The new Malibu convertible was little changed from last year's model. It came with a 140 h.p. 230 cu. in. six. Optional V8 engines included a 200 h.p. 307, a 255 h.p. 350, a 325 h.p. 396, and a 350 h.p. 396. A three-speed manual transmission was standard. A four-speed manual and Powerglide and Turbo Hydra-Matic automatic transmissions were optional at extra cost.

Over 78% of all 1969 Chevelles were equipped with an automatic, 9.7% had the three-speed manual, 11.9% had the four-speed manual, 89.1% had a V8, 72.7% had power steering, 32.7% had power brakes, 22% had disc brakes, 15.8% had bucket seats, 2.1% had a tilting steering wheels, 6% had power windows, 88.1% had radios, 61.4% had tinted glass, and 34.3% were sold with air conditioning.

1969 Chevrolet Chevelle Malibu Convertible

1969 Chevrolet Corvair Monza Convertible

Original Price: $2,625
Number Produced: 521
Estimated Number Existing in 1979: 260
Miles per Gallon: 16–25
Common Trouble Spots: none
Availability of Parts: good
Investment Potential: AA+

Background: This was the last year for the compact Corvair Monza ragtop. It was powered by a 95 h.p. 164 cu. in. six. Buyers could order, at extra cost, a 110 h.p. or a 140 h.p. version of this engine. A three-speed manual transmission was standard. Powerglide automatic and a four-speed manual were optional.

Over 72% of all 1969 Corvairs came with an automatic, 13.7% had a three-speed manual, 13.9% had a four-speed manual, 53.9% had bucket seats, 83.1% had radios, 2.6% had a tilting steering wheel, and 25.9% were sold with tinted glass.

1969 Chevrolet Corvette Stingray Convertible

Original Price: $4,420
Number Produced: 16,608
Estimated Number Existing in 1979: 8,304

Miles per Gallon: 8–16
Common Trouble Spots: clutch; cooling, electrical, and ignition systems
Availability of Parts: good
Investment Potential: AAA

Background: The '69 Corvette was powered by a 300 h.p. 350 cu. in. V8. Other V8 engines were available: a 350 h.p. 350, a 390 h.p. 427, a 400 h.p. 427, and a 435 h.p. 427. A three-speed manual transmission was standard. Most Vettes, 78.4%, came with the four-speed manual. Almost 20% were equipped with Turbo Hydra-Matic automatic transmission.

The majority of new Corvettes, 56.6%, came with power steering, 42.5% had power brakes, 27.2% had a tilting steering wheel, 26.8% had power windows, 80.5% had tinted glass, and 29.9% were sold with air conditioning.

The convertible top came in black, blue, and white. Buyers could order a special black vinyl covering for the detachable hard top.

1969 Chevrolet Impala Convertible

Original Price: $3,244
Number Produced: N.A.
Estimated Number Existing in 1979: N.A.
Miles per Gallon: 9–19
Common Trouble Spots: cooling system
Availability of Parts: good
Investment Potential: A+

Background: The big new Impala convertible came with a 155 h.p. 250 cu. in. six. V8 engines available at extra cost included a 255 h.p. 350, a 265 h.p. 396, a 335 h.p. 427, and a 390 h.p. 427. A three-speed manual transmission was standard. A four-speed manual transmission and Powerglide and Turbo Hydra-Matic automatic transmissions were optional.

Ninety-six percent of all full-size 1969 Chevrolets came with an automatic, 3.6% had a three-speed manual, slightly less than one-half of 1% had a four-speed manual, 95.7% had a V8, 91.7% had power steering, 42.5% had power brakes, 11% had disc brakes, 2.4% had bucket seats, 16% had power windows, 2% had power front seats, 6.4% had a tilting steering wheel, 74.6% had tinted glass, and 62.1% were sold with an air conditioner.

1969 Chevrolet Impala Convertible

PHOTO: GM PHOTOGRAPHIC

1969 Chrysler Newport Convertible

Original Price: $3,806
Number Produced: 2,169
Estimated Number Existing in 1979: 1,084
Miles per Gallon: 8–16
Common Trouble Spots: electrical, cooling, fuel, and ignition systems
Availability of Parts: good
Investment Potential: A+

Background: The '69 Newport ragtop was powered by a 290 h.p. 383 cu. in. V8 with a two-barrel carburetor. A 330 h.p. version of this engine and a 375 h.p. 440 cu. in. V8 were available at extra cost. A three-speed manual transmission was standard. Torque Flite automatic transmission was optional.

Most 1969 Newports, 99.8%, came with the automatic, 99.5% had power steering, 82.2% had power brakes, 5.5% had disc brakes, 4.1% had power windows, 3.9% had power seats, 1.3% had a tilting steering wheel, and 71.5% were sold with air conditioning.

1969 Chrysler Newport Convertible

1969 Chrysler 300 Convertible

Original Price: $4,433
Number Produced: 1,933
Estimated Number Existing in 1979: 966
Miles per Gallon: 8–14
Common Trouble Spots: brakes, electrical, and ignition systems
Availability of Parts: good
Investment Potential: AA

Background: The 300 continued to feature hidden headlights in a restyled body. From the front, it bore a striking resemblance to the Imperial.

The standard engine in the 300 was a 350 h.p. 440 cu. in. V8. A 375 h.p. version of this engine was available at extra cost. Torque Flite automatic transmission was standard.

Most 1969 300s, 99.9%, came with power steering, 97% had power brakes, 30% had disc brakes, 39.6%

had power windows, 34.5% had power seats, 11.8% had a tilting steering wheel, 94.4% had tinted glass, and 83.8% were sold with the $406 air conditioning unit.

1969 Chrysler 300 Convertible

1969 Dodge Charger 500 Daytona

Original Price: est. $3,900
Number Produced: 505
Estimated Number Existing in 1979: 252
Miles per Gallon: 13–16
Common Trouble Spots: brakes; cooling, electrical, fuel, and ignition systems; manual transmission
Availability of Parts: good
Investment Potential: AAA

Background: The limited-production Daytona was basically an aerodynamically designed Charger. It was capable of speeds in excess of 200 mph. The Daytona was so popular that, even before it hit the showrooms, Chrysler had to tell dealers to stop taking orders for it. Virtually every one made was sold before it left the factory.

This winged beauty came with a 440 cu. in. Magnum V8 with four-barrel carburetor. Also available was a 425 h.p. 426 cu. in. Hemi with two four-barrel carburetors. Buyers could choose a four-speed manual or Torque Flite automatic transmission.

At a Daytona-SuperBird Auto Club meet in 1977, a Chrysler chief engineer was quoted as saying "Chrysler was never able to come up with a better car than the Daytona."

1969 Dodge Coronet 500 Convertible

Original Price: $3,052
Number Produced: N.A.
Estimated Number Existing in 1979: N.A.
Miles per Gallon: 8–17
Common Trouble Spots: brakes; cooling, electrical, fuel, and ignition systems; manual transmission
Availability of Parts: good
Investment Potential: A+

Background: The sleek Coronet 500 came with a 230 h.p. 318 cu. in. V8. Optional V8 engines included a 330 h.p. 383 and a 425 h.p. 426. A three-speed manual transmission was standard. Torque Flite automatic and a four-speed manual transmission were available at extra cost.

Most 1969 Coronets, 87.7%, were equipped with the automatic, 8.3% had the four-speed manual, 4% had the three-speed manual, 83.6% had power steering, 15.7% had power brakes, 3.2% had disc brakes, .5% had power windows, 63.9% had tinted glass, and 39.5% were sold with air conditioning.

Coronet 500 buyers had their choice of eighteen exterior colors.

1969 Dodge Coronet 500 Convertible

1969 Dodge Coronet R/T Convertible

Original Price: $3,660
Number Produced: N.A.
Estimated Number Existing in 1979: N.A.
Miles per Gallon: 8–14
Common Trouble Spots: cooling, electrical, fuel, and ignition systems; clutch
Availability of Parts: good
Investment Potential: AA

Background: The Coronet R/T (Road and Track) received a minor face-lift for 1969. It was a bit more flashy than the previous year's model. Distinctive trim, interior, hood, and taillight treatment helped set it apart from the Coronet 500.

It was powered by a 375 h.p. 440 cu. in. V8 with four-barrel carburetor. A 425 h.p. 426 cu. in. Hemi V8 was available at extra cost. Both engines required premium fuel. Torque Flite automatic transmission was standard. A four-speed manual was optional.

Buyers of the 1969 Coronet R/T could choose from eighteen exterior colors. Twelve of these were metallic—medium blue, bright blue, light blue, bright turquoise, dark green, medium green, light green, gold, copper, light bronze, dark bronze, and silver. The rest—beige, black, cream, red, yellow, and white—were regular paints.

1969 Dodge Coronet R/T Convertible

1969 Dodge Polara Convertible

Original Price: $3,360
Number Produced: N.A.
Estimated Number Existing in 1979: N.A.
Miles per Gallon: 9–16
Common Trouble Spots: brakes; cooling, electrical, and ignition systems; suspension
Availability of Parts: good
Investment Potential: A+

Background: The good-looking Polara convertible came equipped with a 230 h.p. 318 cu. in. V8. Optional V8 engines included a 290 h.p. 383, a 330 h.p. 383, and a 375 h.p. 440. A three-speed manual transmission was standard. Torque Flite automatic was available at extra cost.

1969 Dodge Dart GT Convertible

Original Price: $2,945
Number Produced: N.A.
Estimated Number Existing in 1979: N.A.
Miles per Gallon: 13–23
Common Trouble Spots: brakes, clutch
Availability of Parts: good
Investment Potential: A+

Background: The Dart GT convertible came with a 115 h.p. 170 cu. in. slant six. Available at extra cost were a 145 h.p. 225 cu. in. six and two V8s: a 190 h.p. 273 and a 230 h.p. 318. A three-speed manual transmission was standard. Torque Flite automatic and a four-speed manual were optional.

Most 1969 Darts, 64.6%, were equipped with a six, 84.4% had the automatic, 8.5% had the three-speed manual, 7.1% had the four-speed manual, 57% had power steering, 3.5% had power brakes, 2.6% had disc brakes, 43.4% had tinted glass, and 23.1% were sold with air conditioning.

1969 Dodge Dart GT Sport Convertible

Original Price: $3,402
Number Produced: N.A.
Estimated Number Existing in 1979: N.A.
Miles per Gallon: 12–19
Common Trouble Spots: brakes, clutch
Availability of Parts: good
Investment Potential: AA

Background: The '69 Dart GT Sport ragtop had a lot to offer performance-car enthusiasts on a budget. It was powered by a 275 h.p. 340 cu. in. V8. A 330 h.p. 383 V8 was available at extra cost. Buyers had their choice of Torque Flite automatic or a four-speed manual transmission.

1969 Dodge Polara 500 Convertible

Original Price: $3,559
Number Produced: N.A.
Estimated Number Existing in 1979: N.A.
Miles per Gallon: 9–16
Common Trouble Spots: brakes; cooling, electrical, and ignition systems; suspension
Availability of Parts: good
Investment Potential: A+

Background: The 1969 Polara 500 was an attractive, stylish ragtop. It came with a 230 h.p. 318 cu. in. V8. Other engines available included a 290 h.p. 383, a 330 h.p. 383, a 350 h.p. 440, and a 375 h.p. 440. A three-speed manual transmission was standard. Torque Flite automatic transmission was optional.

1969 Dodge Polara 500 Convertible

1969 Ford Fairlane 500 Convertible

PHOTO: FORD MOTOR COMPANY

1969 Ford Fairlane Torino GT Convertible

PHOTO: FORD MOTOR COMPANY

1969 Ford Fairlane 500 Convertible

Original Price: $2,834
Number Produced: 2,264
Estimated Number Existing in 1979: 1,023
Miles per Gallon: 10–20
Common Trouble Spots: brakes, clutch, suspension
Availability of Parts: good
Investment Potential: A+

Background: The attractive new Fairlane 500 came with a 155 h.p. 250 cu. in. six-cylinder engine. Several V8 engines were available at extra cost: a 210 h.p. 302, a 250 h.p. 351, a 290 h.p. 351, a 315 h.p. 390, a 390 h.p. 427, and a 335 h.p. 428. A three-speed manual transmission was standard. Most buyers choose the optional Select Shift automatic. A small number selected the four-speed manual.

Most 1969 Fairlanes, 71.8%, had power steering, 86.6% had the automatic, 4.6% had the four-speed manual, 25.3% had power brakes, 38% had tinted glass, 27.3% had an air conditioner, 6.5% had power windows, and about one-third of 1% were equipped with power front seats. Just 9.6% of Fairlane 500 convertibles had bucket seats.

1969 Ford Fairlane Torino GT Convertible

Original Price: $3,022
Number Produced: 2,552
Estimated Number Existing in 1979: 1,153
Miles per Gallon: 9–17
Common Trouble Spots: brakes, clutch, suspension
Availability of Parts: good
Investment Potential: AA

Background: The new Torino GT came with a 220 h.p. 302 cu. in. V8. Other V8s available at extra cost were a 250 h.p. and a 290 h.p. 351, a 320 h.p. 390, a 390 h.p. 427, and a 335 h.p. 428. A three-speed manual transmission was standard, but not very popular. Select-Shift automatic and a four-speed manual were optional. Thirty-six percent of Torino GT convertibles had bucket seats.

1969 Ford Galaxie 500 Convertible

Original Price: $3,142
Number Produced: 6,910
Estimated Number Existing in 1979: 3,123
Miles per Gallon: 9–18
Common Trouble Spots: manual transmission
Availability of Parts: good
Investment Potential: A+

Background: The new Galaxie 500 came with a 150 h.p. 240 cu. in. six-cylinder. But the standard engine was not very popular; in fact, only 1.9% of all full-size '69 Fords were equipped with the six. Most were powered by one of the optional V8s—the 210 h.p. 302, the 280 h.p. 390, or the 320 h.p. 429.

A three-speed manual transmission was standard. Select-Shift automatic was a very popular option. Virtually all big Fords, 98%, were sold with it.

1969 Ford Mustang Convertible

Original Price: $2,832
Number Produced: 14,746
Estimated Number Existing in 1979: 6,665
Miles per Gallon: 11–22
Common Trouble Spots: automatic transmission, brakes, clutch
Availability of Parts: good
Investment Potential: AA+

Background: The Mustang received a major face-lift for 1969. It also gained about 400 pounds. A 115 h.p. 200 cu. in. six-cylinder engine was standard. A 155 h.p. 250 cu. in. six was available, but most Mustangs were powered by one of the optional V8s. These included a 210 h.p. 302, a 250 h.p. 351, a 290 h.p. 351, a 320 h.p. 390, and two 335 h.p. 428s (one with "Jet-Ram Air"). A three-speed manual transmission was standard. Select-Shift automatic and a four-speed manual were optional at extra cost.

The majority of 1969 Mustangs, 71.1%, had the automatic, 17.2% had the three-speed manual, 11.7% had the four-speed manual, 18.4% had the six, 65.9% had power steering, 30.5% had power brakes, 3.2%

had a tilting steering, 38.8% had tinted glass, 98.4% had bucket seats, and 23.2% were equipped with an air conditioner.

"Get a Mustang convertible and have something to tell your grandchildren." That's what a sales catalog urged in 1969, and it's still not a bad idea.

1969 Ford Mustang Convertible

PHOTO: FORD MOTOR COMPANY

1969 Ford XL Convertible

Original Price: $3,280
Number Produced: 7,402
Estimated Number Existing in 1979: 3,345
Miles per Gallon: 9–18
Common Trouble Spots: clutch
Availability of Parts: good
Investment Potential: A+

Background: The new XL ragtop was basically a dressed-up version of the Galaxie 500. It came with a 150 h.p. 240 cu. in. six-cylinder engine. Nearly all buyers selected one of the optional V8s, which included a 210 h.p. 302, a 280 h.p. 390, and 320 h.p. 429. A three-speed manual was standard. Select-Shift automatic transmission was optional at extra cost.

Almost 95% of all full-size Fords in 1969 had power steering, 62.9 had power brakes, 2.9% had a tilting steering wheel, 68.4% had tinted glass, 3.7% had power front seats, 20.8% had power windows, and 64.3% were equipped with an air conditioner.

1969 Ford XL Convertible

PHOTO: FORD MOTOR COMPANY

1969 King Midget Convertible

Original Price: $1,029
Number Produced: N.A.
Estimated Number Existing in 1979: N.A.
Miles per Gallon: 50–90
Common Trouble Spots: clutch, "V" belt
Availability of Parts: good
Investment Potential: A+

Background: This was the last year for the economical King Midget convertible. It was powered by a 12 h.p. 29 cu. in. one-cylinder engine. Automatic transmission was standard.

1969 Lincoln Continental Mark III

Original Price: $6,741
Number Produced: 30,858
Estimated Number Existing in 1979: 15,120
Miles per Gallon: 9–15
Common Trouble Spots: none
Availability of Parts: good
Investment Potential: AA+

Background: Work began on the Mark III in mid 1965. It was introduced in the spring of 1968 as a 1969 model.

The attractive Mark III was powered by a 365 h.p. 460 cu. in. V8. Select-Shift automatic transmission, power disc brakes, power steering, electric windows, power front seat, dual exhaust, nylon carpeting, and even a rear-lamp monitoring system were among the many standard features.

The plush interior was available, at extra cost, in either nylon fabric and vinyl or leather with vinyl. Buyers had their choice of twenty-one exterior colors.

Some of the options included a vinyl roof, AM/FM radio, AM radio/stereo tape system, six-way power seat with reclining passenger seat, air conditioning, and a tilting steering wheel.

1969 Lincoln Continental Mark III

PHOTO: FORD MOTOR COMPANY

1969 Mercury Cougar Convertible

PHOTO: FORD MOTOR COMPANY

1969 Mercury Cougar Convertible

Original Price: $3,365
Number Produced: 5,796
Estimated Number Existing in 1979: 2,492
Miles per Gallon: 10–17
Common Trouble Spots: brakes; electrical and ignition systems; manual transmission, suspension
Availability of Parts: good
Investment Potential: AA

Background: This was the first year for the sporty Cougar convertible. It came with a 250 h.p. 351 cu. in. V8. Available at extra cost were a 290 h.p. version of this engine and two other V8s; a 320 h.p. 390, and a 335 h.p. 428. A three-speed manual transmission was standard. Select Shift automatic and a four-speed manual were optional.

Most 1969 Cougars, 89.4%, were equipped with the automatic, 7.5% had the three-speed manual, 3.1% had the four-speed manual, 92.4% had power steering, 58.9% had power brakes, 9.5% had a tilting steering wheel, 6.3% had power windows, 57% had tinted glass, and 53.2% were sold with an air conditioner.

1969 Mercury Cougar XR-7 Convertible

Original Price: $3,578
Number Produced: 4,024
Estimated Number Existing in 1979: 1,730
Miles per Gallon: 10–17
Common Trouble Spots: brakes; electrical, and ignition systems; manual transmission, suspension
Availability of Parts: good
Investment Potential: AA

Background: Mercury sales literature called the '69 XR-7 "a higher breed of Cougar." Although it looked basically the same as the standard Cougar ragtop, it was a bit more luxurious.

The XR-7 came with a 250 h.p. 351 cu. in. V8. Three other V8 engines, a 290 h.p. 351, a 320 h.p. 390, and a 335 h.p. 428, were available at extra cost. A three-speed manual transmission was standard. Select Shift automatic and a four-speed manual were optional.

1969 Mercury Marquis Convertible

PHOTO: FORD MOTOR COMPANY

1969 Mercury Marquis Convertible

Original Price: $4,107
Number Produced: 2,319
Estimated Number Existing in 1979: 997
Miles per Gallon: 8–14
Common Trouble Spots: electrical system
Availability of Parts: good
Investment Potential: A+

Background: The Marquis may well have been the most beautiful ragtop in its price class for 1969. Its styling was definitely influenced by the Lincoln Continental, and Mercury sales literature was quick to point that out.

The Marquis was powered by a 320 h.p. 429 cu. in. V8 with two-barrel carburetor. A 360 h.p. version of this engine was optional. Select Shift automatic transmission was standard.

Most 1969 Marquis's, 99.9%, had power steering, 98.7% had power brakes, 26.8% had a tilting steering wheel, 44.7% had power windows, 42.7% had power seats, 92.3% had tinted glass, and 88.5% were sold with a "Whisper-Aire" air conditioner. A wood-toned steering wheel was among the many other options offered.

1969 Mercury Monterey Convertible

Original Price: $3,528
Number Produced: 1,297
Estimated Number Existing in 1979: 557
Miles per Gallon: 8–16
Common Trouble Spots: electrical system
Availability of Parts: good
Investment Potential: A

Background: The 1969 Monterey convertible came with a 265 h.p. 390 cu. in. V8. Four other V8s were available at extra cost; a 280 h.p. 390, a 320 h.p. 390, a 335 h.p. 428, and a 360 h.p. 429. A three-speed manual transmission was standard. Select Shift automatic transmission was optional.

Most '69 Montereys, 99.5%, came equipped with the automatic, 99.1% had power steering, 74.8% had power brakes, 2.6% had a tilting steering wheel, 1.5% had power windows, 2% had power front seats, 59.8% had tinted glass, and 59.2% were sold with an air conditioner.

An all-vinyl interior was standard.

1969 Mercury Montego MX Convertible

PHOTO: FORD MOTOR COMPANY

1969 Mercury Montego MX Convertible

Original Price: $2,979
Number Produced: 1,725
Estimated Number Existing in 1979: 741
Miles per Gallon: 8–18
Common Trouble Spots: brakes
Availability of Parts: good
Investment Potential: A+

Background: "Liveliness and luxury combined at a popular price." That's how Mercury sales catalogs described the 1969 Montego MX. It came with a 155 h.p. 250 cu. in. six-cylinder engine. Four V8 engines were available at extra cost: a 290 h.p. 351, a 320 h.p. 390, a 390 h.p. 427, and a 360 h.p. 429. A three-speed manual was standard. Select Shift automatic and a four-speed manual transmission were optional.

Most 1969 Montegos, 86.9%, were equipped with a V8, 92.4% had the automatic, 5.8% had the three-speed manual, 1.8% had the four-speed manual, 82.9% had power steering, 35% had power brakes, 1.5% had power windows, almost 1% had power front seats, 45.1% had tinted glass, and 40.1% were sold with an air conditioner. Many Montego MX ragtops, 21%, had bucket seats.

1969 Oldsmobile Cutlass "S" Convertible

Original Price: $2,981
Number Produced: 13,734
Estimated Number Existing in 1979: 6,084
Miles per Gallon: 11–19
Common Trouble Spots: suspension
Availability of Parts: good
Investment Potential: A+

Background: Once again, the Cutlass was Oldsmobile's most popular softtop. It was powered by a 155 h.p. 250 cu. in. six-cylinder engine. But less than 2% of new Cutlass convertibles were so equipped. Most came with either the 310 h.p. or 325 h.p. 350 cu. in. V8. A three-speed manual transmission was standard, but not very popular. Jetaway automatic transmission and a four-speed manual were optional. Air conditioning could be had for $376.

1969 Oldsmobile Delta 88 Convertible

Original Price: $3,573
Number Produced: 5,294
Estimated Number Existing in 1979: 2,345
Miles per Gallon: 8–17
Common Trouble Spots: suspension
Availability of Parts: good
Investment Potential: A

Background: The big new Delta 88 convertible came with a 250 h.p. 350 cu. in. V8. Three 455 cu. in. V8s were optional, a 310 h.p., a 365 h.p., and a 390 h.p. A three-speed manual transmission was standard, but not very popular. Most 88 buyers, 99.9%, ordered the optional Turbo Hydra-Matic automatic transmission.

1969 Oldsmobile Delta 88 Convertible

PHOTO: OLDSMOBILE DIVISION

1969 Oldsmobile Cutlass "S" Convertible

PHOTO: OLDSMOBILE DIVISION

1969 Oldsmobile 4-4-2 Convertible

PHOTO: OLDSMOBILE DIVISION

1969 Oldsmobile 4-4-2 Convertible

Original Price: $3,378
Number Produced: 4,295
Estimated Number Existing in 1979: 1,902
Miles per Gallon: 9–15
Common Trouble Spots: suspension
Availability of Parts: good
Investment Potential: AA

Background: The 1969 4-4-2 ragtop came with a 350 h.p. 400 cu. in. V8. Two other versions of this engine, a 325 h.p. and a 360 h.p., were available at extra cost. A three-speed manual transmission was standard. Turbo Hydra-Matic automatic and a four-speed manual transmission were optional.

1969 Oldsmobile 98 Convertible

Original Price: $4,702
Number Produced: 4,288
Estimated Number Existing in 1979: 1,899
Miles per Gallon: 8–14
Common Trouble Spots: suspension
Availability of Parts: good
Investment Potential: A

Background: The 1969 98 convertible was more popular than the previous year's model. It was powered by a 365 h.p. 455 cu. in. V8. Turbo Hydra-Matic automatic transmission, power steering, and power brakes were standard.

Many 98s, 22.1%, had a tilting steering wheel, 13.3% had disc brakes, and 80.2% were sold with the $421 air conditioner.

1969 Plymouth Barracuda Convertible

Original Price: $2,959
Number Produced: N.A.
Estimated Number Existing in 1979: N.A.
Miles per Gallon: 10–20
Common Trouble Spots: none
Availability of Parts: good
Investment Potential: A+

Background: The new Barracuda came with a 145 h.p. 225 cu. in. six-cylinder engine. Three V8 engines were available: a 230 h.p. 318, a 275 h.p. 340, and a 335 h.p. 383. A three-speed manual transmission was standard. Torque Flite automatic transmission and a four-speed manual transmission were optional.

Most 1969 Barracudas, 77.7%, were equipped with a V8 engine, 83.6% had an automatic transmission, 5% had a three-speed manual transmission, 11.4% had a four-speed manual transmission, 64.9% had power steering, 10.2% had power brakes, 8.3% had disc brakes, 56.2% had tinted glass, 71.5% had bucket seats, and 21.9% were sold with an air conditioner.

A Formula S performance package was offered. This option was available with either a 275 h.p. 340 cu. in. or a 335 h.p. high performance 383 cu. in. V8 engine.

1969 Oldsmobile 98 Convertible

PHOTO: OLDSMOBILE DIVISION

1969 Plymouth Fury III Convertible

Original Price: $3,307
Number Produced: N.A.
Estimated Number Existing in 1979: N.A.
Miles per Gallon: 9–16
Common Trouble Spots: none
Availability of Parts: good
Investment Potential: A+

Background: The new Fury III came with a 290 h.p. 383 cu. in. V8. A 330 h.p. version of this engine was available at extra cost. A three-speed manual transmission was standard. Torque Flite automatic transmission was optional.

Most 1969 Furys, 98.7% had an automatic transmission, 96% had power steering, 53% had power brakes; 8.8% had disc brakes, 91.4% had radios, 2.5% had power windows, 2.2% had power front seats, 1.6% had a tilting steering wheel, 79.5% had tinted glass, .2% had bucket seats, and 67.1% were sold with an air conditioner.

1969 Plymouth GTX Convertible

Original Price: $3,618
Number Produced: N.A.
Estimated Number Existing in 1979: N.A.
Miles per Gallon: 8–14
Common Trouble Spots: none
Availability of Parts: good
Investment Potential: AA

Background: This was the last year for the GTX convertible. It came with a 375 h.p. 440 cu. in. V8 engine. A 425 h.p. 426 cu. in. V8 was optional. Torque Flite automatic transmission was standard. A four-speed manual transmission was available at extra cost.

1969 Plymouth Road Runner Convertible

Original Price: $3,296
Number Produced: N.A.
Estimated Number Existing in 1979: N.A.
Miles per Gallon: 8–14
Common Trouble Spots: none
Availability of Parts: good
Investment Potential: A+

Background: The sporty Road Runner convertible came with a 335 h.p. 383 cu. in. V8 engine (with four-barrel carburetor). A 425 h.p. 426 cu. in. V8 engine (with two four-barrel carburetors) was available at extra cost. A four-speed manual transmission was standard. Torque Flite automatic transmission was optional.

1969 Plymouth Satellite Convertible

Original Price: $2,858
Number Produced: N.A.
Estimated Number Existing in 1979: N.A.
Miles per Gallon: 9–18
Common Trouble Spots: none
Availability of Parts: good
Investment Potential: A

Background: The new Satellite came with a 145 h.p. 225 cu. in. six-cylinder engine. Four V8 engines were available: a 230 h.p. 318, a 290 h.p. 383, a 330 h.p. 383, and a 425 h.p. 426. A three-speed manual transmission was standard. Torque Flite automatic and a four-speed manual transmission were optional.

1969 Plymouth Sport Fury Convertible

Original Price: $3,485
Number Produced: N.A.
Estimated Number Existing in 1979: N.A.
Miles per Gallon: 9–16
Common Trouble Spots: none
Availability of Parts: good
Investment Potential: A+

Background: The 1969 Sport Fury convertible was a big and rather luxurious automobile. It came with a 230 h.p. 318 cu. in. V8 engine. Two 383 cu. in. V8 engines, with 290 h.p., and 330 h.p., and a 375 h.p. 440 cu. in. V8, were available at extra cost. A three-speed manual transmission was standard, but not very popular; only 1.3% of all 1969 Sport Furys were so equipped. Most buyers ordered the $208, Turbo Flite automatic transmission.

Other popular options included power steering ($100), power brakes ($43), and air conditioning ($365).

This was the last year for the Sport Fury convertible.

1969 Plymouth Sport Satellite Convertible

Original Price: $3,064
Number Produced: N.A.
Estimated Number Existing in 1979: N.A.
Miles per Gallon: 9–16
Common Trouble Spots: none
Availability of Parts: good
Investment Potential: A

Background: The 1969 Sport Satellite convertible came with a 230 h.p. 318 cu. in. V8 engine. Three other V8 engines were available at extra cost: a 290 h.p. 383 (two-barrel carburetor), a 330 h.p. 383 (four-barrel carburetor), and a 425 h.p. 426 (two four-barrel carburetors). A three-speed manual transmission was standard. Torque Flite automatic transmission and a four-speed manual were optional.

1969 Pontiac Bonneville Convertible

Original Price: $3,879
Number Produced: 5,438
Estimated Number Existing in 1979: 2,501
Miles per Gallon: 8–15
Common Trouble Spots: suspension
Availability of Parts: good
Investment Potential: A

Background: Despite Pontiac's public-relations department's claim of "new styling," the 1969 Bonneville looked very similar to the previous year's model.

It came with a 360 h.p. 428 cu. in. V8. Two other V8s were available at extra cost: a 265 h.p. 400 and a 390 h.p. 428. A three-speed manual transmission was standard, but few Bonnevilles were sold that way; in fact, less than one-third of one percent of all full-size 1969 Pontiacs were so equipped. Most buyers ordered the $227 optional Turbo Hydra-Matic automatic transmission.

Power steering was $116 extra and very popular. So were power brakes at $72. Even the $421 air conditioner was sold to nearly three out of every four full-size-Pontiac buyers.

1969 Pontiac Bonneville Convertible

PHOTO: PONTIAC MOTOR DIVISION

1969 Pontiac Catalina Convertible

Original Price: $3,459
Number Produced: 5,436
Estimated Number Existing in 1979: 2,500
Miles per Gallon: 8–16
Common Trouble Spots: suspension
Availability of Parts: good
Investment Potential: A

Background: The big new Catalina came with a 290 h.p. 400 cu. in. V8. Buyers could also order a 265 h.p. 400 cu. in. V8 and a 360 h.p. or a 390 h.p. 428 cu. in. V8. A three-speed manual transmission was standard, but nearly all 1969 big Pontiacs, 99.7%, were equipped with the $227 optional Turbo Hydra-Matic automatic transmission.

Most full-size Pontiacs, 96.7%, had power steering, 94.9% had power brakes, 53.8% had disc brakes, 15.5% had power windows, 8.4% had power front seats, 13.7% had a tilting steering wheel, 87.7% had tinted glass, and 74.4% were sold with air conditioning.

1969 Pontiac Catalina Convertible

1969 Pontiac Firebird Convertible

Original Price: $3,028
Number Produced: 11,649
Estimated Number Existing in 1979: 5,358
Miles per Gallon: 10–20
Common Trouble Spots: automatic transmission, cooling system, manual transmission, suspension
Availability of Parts: good
Investment Potential: AAA

Background: The '69 Firebird ragtop was a popular car. It was powered by a 175 h.p. 250 cu. in. six-cylinder engine. A 215 h.p. "Sprint" version of this engine was available. Most Firebirds, 86.5%, came with one of the optional V8 engines, which included a 265 h.p. 350, a 325 h.p. 350, a 330 h.p. 400, a 335 h.p. 400, and a 345 h.p. 400 (Ram Air IV). A three-speed manual transmission was standard. A four-speed manual and two automatic transmissions were optional.

Most 1969 Firebirds, 75.3%, came with an automatic, 11.4% had a three-speed manual, 13.3% had a four-speed manual, 85.6% had power steering, 45.2% had power brakes, 24.8% had disc brakes, 3.5% had electric windows, 1.2% had power front seats, 6.3% had a tilting steering wheel, 65.3% had tinted glass, 98% had bucket seats, and 31.4% were sold with air conditioning.

1969 Pontiac Firebird Convertible

PHOTO: PONTIAC MOTOR DIVISION

1969 Pontiac GTO Convertible

Original Price: $3,365
Number Produced: 7,436
Estimated Number Existing in 1979: 3,420
Miles per Gallon: 9–16
Common Trouble Spots: clutch, cooling system
Availability of Parts: good
Investment Potential: AA

Background: The new GTO ragtop came with a 350 h.p. 400 cu. in V8. Buyers also had their choice of three other 400 cu. in. V8s, rated at 265 h.p., 366 h.p., and 370 h.p. A three-speed manual transmission was standard. Turbo Hydra-Matic automatic and a four-speed manual transmission were optional. Just over 60% of all 1969 GTOs were ordered with the automatic. Only 108 1969 GTO convertibles came with the "Judge" performance package.

1969 Pontiac Le Mans Convertible

Original Price: $3,047
Number Produced: 5,676
Estimated Number Existing in 1979: 2,610
Miles per Gallon: 10–20
Common Trouble Spots: automatic transmission, clutch, cooling system
Availability of Parts: good
Investment Potential: A+

Background: The Le Mans ragtop came with a 175 h.p. 250 cu. in. six-cylinder engine. Two hotter versions of this engine, a 215 h.p. and a 230 h.p., were offered at extra cost. Buyers could also order two 350 cu. in. V8s, with either 265 h.p. or 330 h.p. A three-speed manual transmission was standard, but not very popular. A four-speed manual and two automatic transmissions were optional.

1969 Pontiac Tempest Custom Convertible

Original Price: $2,871
Number Produced: 2,379
Estimated Number Existing in 1979: 1,094
Miles per Gallon: 10–20
Common Trouble Spots: automatic transmission, clutch, cooling system
Availability of Parts: good
Investment Potential: A+

Background: This was the last year for the Tempest Custom softtop. It came with a 175 h.p. 250 cu. in. six-cylinder engine. Two other versions of this engine, a 215 h.p. and a 230 h.p. and two V8s, a 265 h.p. 350 and a 330 h.p. 350, were available at extra cost. A three-speed manual transmission was standard. Two automatics and a four-speed manual transmission were optional.

Most '69 Tempests, 88.3%, were equipped with a V8, 83.9% had automatic transmissions, 10.4% had a four-speed manual, 88.9% had power steering, 49.2% had power brakes, 26.7% had disc brakes, 2.7% had electric windows, 1.1% had power front seats, 3.2% had a tilting steering wheel, 71.5% had tinted glass, and 31.4% were sold with an air conditioner.

1969 Pontiac Le Mans Convertible and Firebird Two-Door Hardtop

PHOTO: PONTIAC MOTOR DIVISION

1969 Rambler AMX Sport Coupe

Original Price: $3,297
Number Produced: 8,293
Estimated Number Existing in 1979: 3,706
Miles per Gallon: 10–17
Common Trouble Spots: none
Availability of Parts: good
Investment Potential: AAA

Background: The attractive new AMX came with a 225 h.p. 290 cu. in. V8. Two other V8s, a 280 h.p. 343 and a 315 h.p. 390, were available at extra cost. A four-speed manual transmission was standard. Shift-Command automatic transmission was optional.

Most 1969 AMXs, 61.3%, were equipped with the four-speed manual, 67.4% had power steering, 81.4% had power brakes, 75.7% had disc brakes, 21.2% had a tilting steering wheel, 61.8% had tinted glass, and 21% were sold with air conditioning.

1969 Rambler AMX Sport Coupe

1969 Shelby American GT 500 Convertible

Original Price: est. $6,300
Number Produced: 335
Estimated Number Existing in 1979: 151
Miles per Gallon: 8–14
Common Trouble Spots: none
Availability of Parts: fair–good
Investment Potential: AAA

Background: The new Shelby GT 500 convertible came with a 335 h.p. 428 cu. in. V8. A four-speed manual transmission was standard. Select Shift Cruise-O-Matic automatic transmission was optional.

1969 Shelby American GT 500 Convertible

PHOTO: HOWARD AND SHELBY APPLEGATE

1969 Shelby American GT 350 Convertible

Original Price: est. $6,000
Number Produced: 194
Estimated Number Existing in 1979: 87
Miles per Gallon: 9–15
Common Trouble Spots: none
Availability of Parts: fair–good
Investment Potential: AAA

Background: The '69 GT 350 ragtop came with a 290 h.p. 351 cu. in. V8. Buyers had their choice of either a four-speed manual or Select Shift Cruise-O-Matic automatic transmission.

1970

1970 AMX Sport Coupe

Original Price: $3,395
Number Produced: 4,116
Estimated Number Existing in 1979: 2,210
Miles per Gallon: 9–17
Common Trouble Spots: none
Availability of Parts: good
Investment Potential: AAA

Background: This was the last of the two-passenger AMXs. It came with a 245 h.p. 360 cu. in. V8. A 325 h.p. 390 cu. in. V8 was available at extra cost. A four-speed manual transmission was standard. Shift-Command automatic transmission was optional.

Most 1970 AMXs, 60%, were equipped with the four-speed manual, 69.7% had power steering, 86.5% had power brakes, 82.2% had disc brakes, 20% had a tilting steering wheel, 62.8% had tinted glass, and 25.7% were sold with air conditioning.

1970 Buick Electra Custom 225 Convertible

Original Price: $4,802
Number Produced: 6,045
Estimated Number Existing in 1979: 3,475
Miles per Gallon: 7–14
Common Trouble Spots: cooling system
Availability of Parts: good
Investment Potential: A+

Background: This was the last year for the luxurious Electra convertible. The only engine offered was a 370 h.p. 455 cu. in. V8 which required premium fuel. Turbo Hydra-Matic automatic transmission, power brakes, and power steering were standard.

Electra ragtop buyers had their choice of fifteen exterior colors: aqua mist, bamboo cream, burgundy mist, burnished saddle, coronet gold, desert gold, diplomat blue, fire red, harvest gold, glacier white, gulfstream blue, regal black, seamist green, silver mist, and sherwood green. The expanded vinyl interior came in black, burnished saddle, red, and sandalwood.

1970 AMX Sport Coupe

1970 Buick Electra Custom 225 Convertible

1970 Buick GS 455 Convertible

1970 Buick Gran Sport 455 Convertible

Original Price: $3,469
Number Produced: 1,416
Estimated Number Existing in 1979: 814
Miles per Gallon: 8–15
Common Trouble Spots: none
Availability of Parts: good
Investment Potential: AA

Background: A special grille and trim, hood scoops, chrome wheels, and a performance package were the main differences between the GS 455 and the standard Skylark. It was powered by a 350 h.p. 455 cu. in. V8. A 360 h.p. version of this engine was also available. A three-speed manual transmission was standard. Turbo Hydra-Matic automatic and a four-speed manual were optional.

1970 Buick LeSabre Custom Convertible

Original Price: $3,700
Number Produced: 2,487
Estimated Number Existing in 1979: 1,430
Miles per Gallon: 7–16
Common Trouble Spots: cooling system
Availability of Parts: good
Investment Potential: A+

Background: The 1970 LeSabre convertible came with a 260 h.p. 350 cu. in. V8. A 285 h.p. and a 310 h.p. version of this engine and a 370 h.p. 455 cu. in. V8 were available. A three-speed manual transmission was standard. Turbo Hydra-Matic automatic transmission was optional.

Almost 98% of all full-size '70 Buicks came with power brakes, 99.9% had power steering, 46.2% had power windows, 6.7% had disc brakes, and 85.6% were sold with air conditioning.

LeSabre convertible buyers had their choice of all-vinyl bench seats in black, blue, red, or saddle.

1970 Buick Skylark Custom Convertible

Original Price: $3,275
Number Produced: 4,954
Estimated Number Existing in 1979: 2,848
Miles per Gallon: 9–17
Common Trouble Spots: none
Availability of Parts: good
Investment Potential: AA

Background: The '70 Skylark convertible had somewhat more conservative styling than the previous year's model. It was powered by a 260 h.p. 350 cu. in. V8. A 285 h.p. and a 310 h.p. version of this engine were available. A three-speed manual transmission was standard. Turbo Hydra-Matic automatic transmission was optional at extra cost.

Almost 98% of all Skylarks came with the automatic, 96.1% had power steering, 54.4% had power brakes, 8.8% had power windows, 2.4% had power seats, 5.6% had disc brakes, and 63.2% came with air conditioning.

All-vinyl bench seats, in black or sandalwood, were standard. Black, burnished saddle, or pearl white all-vinyl bucket seats were optional at extra cost.

1970 Buick Skylark Custom Convertible

1970 Buick LeSabre Custom Convertible

1970 Buick Wildcat Custom Convertible

Original Price: $4,079
Number Produced: 1,244
Estimated Number Existing in 1979: 715
Miles per Gallon: 7–14
Common Trouble Spots: cooling system
Availability of Parts: good
Investment Potential: A+

Background: This was the last year for the Wildcat Custom convertible. It was powered by a 370 h.p. 455 cu. in. V8. A three-speed manual transmission was standard. Virtually all came with the Turbo Hydra-Matic automatic transmission. The vast majority had power steering and power brakes.

1970 Buick Wildcat Custom Convertible

1970 Cadillac De Ville Convertible

Original Price: $6,399
Number Produced: 15,172
Estimated Number Existing in 1979: 10,013
Miles per Gallon: 9–14
Common Trouble Spots: none
Availability of Parts: good
Investment Potential: AA

Background: This was the last year the De Ville convertible was offered. It was powered by a 375 h.p. 472 cu. in. V8 engine. Turbo Hydra-Matic automatic transmission, power disc brakes, power steering, electric windows, and power seats were standard. Ninety-nine percent of all 1970 De Villes were equipped with air conditioning, 99.3% had tinted glass, and 64.1% had a tilting steering wheel.

1970 Cadillac De Ville Convertible

PHOTO: CADILLAC MOTOR CAR DIVISION

1970 Chevrolet Chevelle Malibu Convertible

Original Price: $3,009
Number Produced: N.A.
Estimated Number Existing in 1979: N.A.
Miles per Gallon: 9–19
Common Trouble Spots: clutch, cooling system
Availability of Parts: good
Investment Potential: AA

Background: The '70 Chevelle ragtop came with a 155 h.p. 250 cu. in. six-cylinder engine. Optional V8 engines included a 200 h.p. 307, a 325 h.p. 396, a 350 h.p. 402, a 330 h.p. 402, and a 360 h.p. 454. A three-speed manual transmission was standard. Powerglide automatic and a four-speed manual were available at extra cost.

Over 85% of all '70 Chevelles were equipped with an automatic, 93.5% had a V8, 4.5% had a three-speed manual, 9.9% had a four-speed manual, 82.5% had power steering, 40.7% had power brakes, 31.6% had disc brakes, 6.8% had power windows, 3.2% had a tilting steering wheel, 70.7% had tinted glass, and 45.7% were sold with an air conditioner.

1970 Chevrolet Chevelle Malibu Convertible

1970 Chevrolet Corvette Stingray Convertible

Original Price: $4,848
Number Produced: 6,648
Estimated Number Existing in 1979: 4,188
Miles per Gallon: 8–16
Common Trouble Spots: electrical and ignition systems
Availability of Parts: good
Investment Potential: AAA

Background: The new Corvette was powered by a 300 h.p. 350 cu. in. V8. Other V8 engines were available optionally: a 350 h.p. 350, a 390 h.p. 427, a 400 h.p. 427, and a 435 h.p. 427. Most 1970 Vettes, 70.5%, came with a four-speed manual transmission. The rest had Turbo Hydra-Matic automatic transmissions.

Nearly 69% of new Corvettes were equipped with power steering, 51.9% had power brakes, 33.5% had a tilting steering wheel, 27.8% had power windows, and 38.5% were sold with air conditioning.

1970 Chevrolet Impala Convertible

Original Price: $3,377
Number Produced: N.A.
Estimated Number Existing in 1979: N.A.
Miles per Gallon: 8–16
Common Trouble Spots: none
Availability of Parts: good
Investment Potential: A+

Background: The new Impala came with a 250 h.p. 350 cu. in. V8. Optional V8 engines included a 265 h.p. 400, a 345 h.p. 454, and a 390 h.p. 454. A three-speed manual transmission was standard. Powerglide automatic transmission was available at extra cost.

Almost 98% of all full-size 1970 Chevrolets were equipped with an automatic, 2.1% had a three-speed manual, 97.5% had a V8, 95.2% had power steering, 60.5% had power brakes, 44.3% had disc brakes, 19% had power windows, 8.5% had a tilting steering wheel, 2.5% had a power front seat, 79.9% had tinted glass, and 71.8% were sold with an air conditioner.

1970 Chrysler Newport Convertible

Original Price: $3,925
Number Produced: 1,124
Estimated Number Existing in 1979: 663
Miles per Gallon: 8–15
Common Trouble Spots: electrical, fuel, and ignition systems; suspension
Availability of Parts: good
Investment Potential: A+

Background: A minor face-lift was given the 1970 Newport. It still strongly resembled the 1969 and to a lesser degree the 1967.

The Newport was powered by a 290 h.p. 383 cubic inch V8. A 330 h.p. version of this engine and a 375 h.p. 440 cu. in. V8 were also available as options. A three-speed manual transmission was standard. Torque Flite automatic transmission was optional.

Most 1970 Newports, 99.7%, were equipped with power steering, 83% had power brakes, 15% had disc brakes, 4.6% had power windows, 4.2% had power seats, 1.6% had a tilting steering wheel, 72.5% had tinted glass, and 76.8% were sold with air conditioning.

1970 Chrysler 300 Convertible

Original Price: $4,580
Number Produced: 1,077
Estimated Number Existing in 1979: 635
Miles per Gallon: 8–14
Common Trouble Spots: none
Availability of Parts: good
Investment Potential: AA+ (300 "H"); AA (the rest)

Background: Hidden headlights were again used on the restyled 1970 300. It was an especially attractive car from the front, although the entire design was well done. Apparently many buyers did not think so, as sales were down by almost 50 percent.

It came with a 350 h.p. 440 cu. in. V8. A 375 h.p. version of this engine was available optionally. Torque Flite automatic transmission was standard.

This is one of the best-looking full-size convertibles Chrysler made. That, plus the fact that it had a low production run and was the last 300 convertible made, add to the 1970 300's investment appeal.

Most 1970 300s, 99.9%, were equipped with power steering, 97.8% had power brakes, 49.6% had disc brakes, 46% had power windows, 40.1% had power seats, 15.9% had a tilting steering wheel, 88.2% had tinted glass, and 89.4% were sold with air conditioning.

Extremely rare is the 1970 300 "H" (for Hurst) ragtop; only one was built.

1970 Chevrolet Impala Convertible

PHOTO: GM PHOTOGRAPHIC

1970 Dodge Challenger Convertible

Original Price: $3,222
Number Produced: 3,173
Estimated Number Existing in 1979: 1,960
Miles per Gallon: 9–17
Common Trouble Spots: automatic transmission; cooling, electrical, fuel, and ignition systems; manual transmission
Availability of Parts: good
Investment Potential: A+

Background: The attractive new Challenger ragtop came with a 145 h.p. 225 cu. in. slant six. Several V8 engines were available at extra cost: a 230 h.p. 318, a 275 h.p. 340, a 290 h.p. 383, a 330 h.p. 383, and a 335 h.p. 383. A three-speed manual transmission was standard. Torque Flite automatic and a four-speed manual were optional.

Most 1970 Challengers, 86.1%, were equipped with a V8, 70.9% had the automatic, 16.7% had a three-speed manual, 12.4% had a four-speed manual, 74.7% had power steering 26.9% had power brakes, 18.1% had disc brakes, 3.4% had power windows, 62.5% had tinted glass, and 34.9% were sold with an air conditioner.

1970 Dodge Challenger R/T Convertible

Original Price: $3,535
Number Produced: 1,070
Estimated Number Existing in 1979: 661
Miles per Gallon: 8–14
Common Trouble Spots: automatic and manual transmission; cooling, fuel, and ignition systems; suspension
Availability of Parts: good
Investment Potential: AA

Background: The Challenger R/T (Road and Track) convertible was a very attractive addition to the 1970 Dodge line. It came with a 330 h.p. 383 cu. in. V8. Other V8s also available were a 375 h.p. 440, a 390 h.p. 440, and a 425 h.p. 426. A three-speed manual transmission was standard. Torque Flite automatic and a four-speed manual were optional.

1970 Dodge Coronet 500 Convertible

Original Price: $3,188
Number Produced: 924
Estimated Number Existing in 1979: 571
Miles per Gallon: 9–17
Common Trouble Spots: cooling, electrical, fuel, and ignition systems; suspension
Availability of Parts: good
Investment Potential: A

Background: This was the last year for the Coronet 500 ragtop. It came with a 230 h.p. 318 cu. in. V8. A 290 h.p., and a 330 h.p. 383 cu. in. V8 were available at extra cost. A three-speed manual transmission was standard. Torque Flite automatic and a four-speed manual were optional.

Most 1970 Coronets, 91.7%, were equipped with the automatic, 2.6% had the three-speed manual, 5.7% had the four-speed manual, 86.3% had power steering, 21.4% had power brakes, 9.9% had disc brakes, one half of one percent had power windows, 65.2% had tinted glass, and 46.9% were sold with air conditioning.

1970 Dodge Coronet 500 Convertible

1970 Dodge Coronet R/T Convertible

Original Price: $3,785
Number Produced: 296
Estimated Number Existing in 1979: 182
Miles per Gallon: 8–14
Common Trouble Spots: cooling, electrical, fuel, and ignition systems, manual transmission, suspension
Availability of Parts: good
Investment Potential: AA

Background: The '70 Coronet R/T (Road and Track) convertible was a rare sight even when new. It came with a 375 h.p. 440 cu. in. V8. Two hotter engines were available at extra cost—a 390 h.p. 440 cu. in. V8 and a 425 h.p. 426 cu. in. Hemi V8. Torque Flite automatic transmission was standard. A four-speed manual was optional.

Buyers had their choice of eighteen exterior colors with such names as hemi orange, sublime, banana, go-mango, and plum-crazy.

1970 Dodge Coronet R/T Convertible

1970 Dodge Polara Convertible

Original Price: $3,527
Number Produced: 842
Estimated Number Existing in 1979: 520
Miles per Gallon: 9–16
Common Trouble Spots: none
Availability of Parts: good
Investment Potential: A

Background: Styling for the 1970 Polara seemed to take a step backward. While the '69 had a fresh, sharp appearance, the new model looked bland and fat.

It came with a 230 h.p. 318 cu. in. V8. Available at extra cost was a 350 h.p. 440 cu. in. V8. A three-speed manual transmission was standard. Torque Flite automatic transmission was optional.

1970 Ford Mustang Convertible

Original Price: $3,126
Number Produced: 7,673
Estimated Number Existing in 1979: 4,649
Miles per Gallon: 10–21
Common Trouble Spots: clutch, ignition system
Availability of Parts: good
Investment Potential: AA

Background: Just over 15% of 1970 Mustangs were sold with the standard 120 h.p. 200 cu. in. six-cylinder engine or optional 155 h.p. 250 cu. in. six. Most buyers ordered one of the optional V8s, which included a 220 h.p. 302, a 290 h.p. 302, a 250 h.p. 351, a 300 h.p. 351, and two 335 h.p. 428s ("Cobra" and "Cobra Jet").

A three-speed manual transmission was standard. Select Shift automatic and a four-speed manual were optional.

The majority of 1970 Mustangs, 74.7%, were equipped with the automatic, 10.9% had the four-speed manual, 14.4% had the three-speed manual, 73.5% had power steering, 30.6% had power brakes, 2.3% had a tilting steering wheel, 42.2% had tinted glass, and 29.7% came with an air conditioner.

1970 Ford Mustang Convertible

PHOTO: FORD MOTOR COMPANY

1970 Ford Torino GT Convertible

Original Price: $3,212
Number Produced: 3,939
Estimated Number Existing in 1979: 2,387
Miles per Gallon: 8–17
Common Trouble Spots: clutch, suspension
Availability of Parts: good
Investment Potential: AA

Background: The Torino GT was restyled for 1970. It came with a 220 h.p. 302 cu. in. V8. Other V8s available at extra cost were a 210 h.p. 351, a 300 h.p. 351, a 360 h.p. 429, and two 370 h.p. 429s (Cobra and Cobra Jet). A three-speed manual transmission was standard on all engines except the 429 V8. It had a four-speed manual transmission. Select Shift automatic transmission was optional.

Most 1970 Torinos, 90.4%, came with the automatic, 6.6% had the three-speed manual, 3% had the four-speed manual, 79.1% had power steering, 28.2% had disc brakes, 42.6% had tinted glass, almost 1% had power windows, .5% had power seats, and 39.1% were equipped with an air conditioner.

1970 Ford Torino GT Convertible

PHOTO: FORD MOTOR COMPANY

1970 Ford XL Convertible

Original Price: $3,501
Number Produced: 6,348
Estimated Number Existing in 1979: 3,846
Miles per Gallon: 8–17
Common Trouble Spots: brakes
Availability of Parts: good
Investment Potential: A+

Background: The '70 XL came with a 250 h.p. 351 cu. in. V8. A 265 h.p. 390 and a 320 h.p. and a 360 h.p. 429 cu. in. V8 were optional at extra cost. A three-speed manual transmission was standard. Select Shift automatic transmission was optional.

Virtually all full-size 1970 Fords, 99%, had the automatic, 97.3% had power steering, 74.8% had power brakes, 3.2% had a tilting steering wheel, 72.7%

had tinted glass, 4.3% had power windows, 3.5% had power front seats, and 72.8% were equipped with air conditioning.

This was the last Ford XL convertible.

1970 Ford XL Convertible

PHOTO: FORD MOTOR COMPANY

1970 Mercury Cougar Convertible

Original Price: $3,264
Number Produced: 2,322
Estimated Number Existing in 1979: 1,325
Miles per Gallon: 10–17
Common Trouble Spots: clutch; cooling, electrical, and ignition systems; suspension
Availability of Parts: good
Investment Potential: AA

Background: The attractive new Cougar convertible came with a 220 h.p. 302 cu. in. V8. Three other V8s were optional: a 290 h.p. 302, a 300 h.p. 351, and a 335 h.p. 428 cu. in. V8. A three-speed manual transmission was standard. Select Shift automatic and a four-speed manual were available at extra cost.

Most 1970 Cougars, 92.2%, were equipped with the automatic, 5% had the three-speed manual, 2.8% had the four-speed manual, 95.6% had power steering, 67.6% had power disc brakes, 12.1% had a tilting steering wheel, 5.9% had power windows, 63.9% had tinted glass, and 61.7% were sold with an air conditioner.

1970 Mercury Cougar Convertible

1970 Mercury Cougar XR-7 Convertible

PHOTO: FORD MOTOR COMPANY

1970 Mercury Cougar XR-7 Convertible

Original Price: $3,465
Number Produced: 1,977
Estimated Number Existing in 1979: 1,128
Miles per Gallon: 10–17
Common Trouble Spots: clutch; cooling, electrical, and ignition systems; suspension
Availability of Parts: good
Investment Potential: AA

Background: The flashy 1970 XR-7 ragtop came with a 220 h.p. 302 cu. in. V8. Other V8s were optional: a 290 h.p. 302, a 300 h.p. 351, and a 335 h.p. 428. A three-speed manual transmission was standard. Select Shift automatic and a four-speed manual were available at extra cost.

1970 Mercury Marquis Convertible

Original Price: $4,047
Number Produced: 1,233
Estimated Number Existing in 1979: 704
Miles per Gallon: 8–15
Common Trouble Spots: none
Availability of Parts: good
Investment Potential: AA

Background: "Luxury far beyond its medium price." That is how Mercury sales literature described the attractive new Marquis convertible. It was powered by a 265 h.p. 390 cu. in. V8. Two 429 cu. in. V8 engines, a 320 h.p. and a 360 h.p. were available at extra cost. Select Shift automatic transmission was standard.

Most 1970 Marquis, 99.9% came equipped with power steering, 98.8% had power disc brakes, 21.5% had a tilting steering wheel, 30.6% had power windows, 31.2% had power seats, 92.6% had tinted glass, and 90.1% were sold with an air conditioner.

Buyers had their choice of seventeen exterior colors: black, white, medium brown metallic, light gold, medium blue metallic, dark blue, pastel blue, dark maroon, light gray metallic, red, dark ivy green metallic, medium ivy green metallic, light ivy yellow, yellow, medium gold metallic, medium bronze metallic, or dark aqua metallic. The standard vinyl bench-seat interior could be had in black, medium blue, dark red, dark brown, or white. Optional vinyl "Twin Comfort Lounge Seats" came in black or white. The top was also either black or white.

1970 Mercury Marquis Convertible

PHOTO: FORD MOTOR COMPANY

1970 Mercury Monterey Convertible

Original Price: $3,429
Number Produced: 581
Estimated Number Existing in 1979: 331
Miles per Gallon: 8–15
Common Trouble Spots: none
Availability of Parts: good
Investment Potential: A+

Background: This was the last year the Monterey convertible was offered. It came with a 265 h.p. 390 cu. in. V8. Two 429 cu. in. V8 engines, rated at 320 h.p. and 360 h.p. were available at extra cost. A three-speed manual transmission was standard. Select Shift automatic transmission was optional.

Most 1970 Montereys, 99.7%, came equipped with the automatic, 94.6% had power steering, 80.3% had power disc brakes, 3.3% had a tilting steering wheel, 70.5% had tinted glass, 1.3% had power windows, 1.8% had power seats, and 71% were sold with an air conditioner.

1970 Oldsmobile Cutlass Supreme Convertible

Original Price: est. $3,100
Number Produced: 11,354
Estimated Number Existing in 1979: 6,528
Miles per Gallon: 9–16
Common Trouble Spots: none
Availability of Parts: good
Investment Potential: AA

Background: The attractive new Cutlass Supreme ragtop was powered by a 310 h.p. 350 cu. in. V8. Available at extra cost were a 250 h.p. and a 325 h.p. version of this engine and a 320 h.p. 455 cu. in. V8. A three-speed manual transmission was standard, but not very popular. Turbo Hydra-Matic automatic and a four-speed manual transmission were optional.

An "SX" package was available. It featured a 455 V8, dual exhaust, Turbo Hydra-Matic transmission, and special trim.

1970 Oldsmobile Cutlass Supreme Convertible

PHOTO: OLDSMOBILE DIVISION

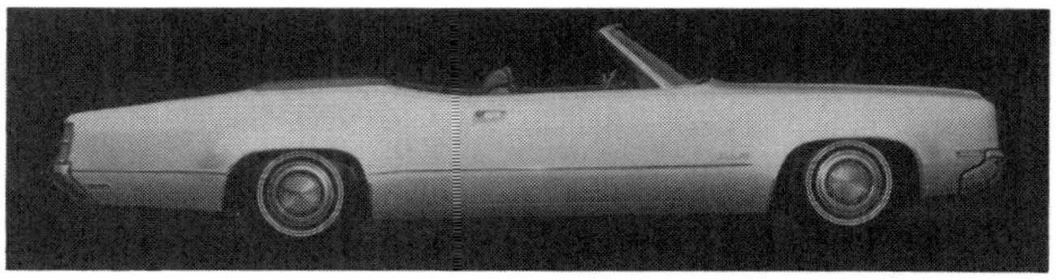

1970 Oldsmobile Delta 88 Convertible

PHOTO: OLDSMOBILE DIVISION

1970 Oldsmobile Delta 88 Convertible

Original Price: est. $3,600
Number Produced: 3,095
Estimated Number Existing in 1979: 1,779
Miles per Gallon: 8–16
Common Trouble Spots: none
Availability of Parts: good
Investment Potential: A

Background: The new Delta 88 convertible was powered by a 250 h.p. 350 cu. in. V8. Three 455 cu. in. V8s, a 310 h.p., a 365 h.p., and a 390 h.p., were available at extra cost. All 1970 Delta 88s were sold with Turbo Hydra-Matic automatic transmission.

Buyers had their choice of ten exterior colors: Porcelain white, copper, platinum, burnished gold, Azure blue, Galleon gold, Aspen green, Sherwood green, and, on special order, nugget gold and Aegean aqua.

1970 Oldsmobile 4-4-2 Convertible

Original Price: est. $3,400
Number Produced: 2,933
Estimated Number Existing in 1979: 1,686
Miles per Gallon: 8–14
Common Trouble Spots: none
Availability of Parts: good
Investment Potential: AA

Background: The 4-4-2 was powered by a 365 h.p. 455 cu. in. V8. A 370 h.p. version of this engine was available at extra cost. A three-speed manual transmission was standard. Turbo Hydra-Matic automatic and a four-speed manual transmission were optional.

A "W-30" package was offered. It featured a fiberglass hood with rally stripes, pin locks, and cold air scoops; side body stripes; 370 h.p. 455 cu. in V8; aluminum manifold; anti-spin performance axle; and special "W" emblems on the front fenders.

1970 Oldsmobile 4-4-2 Convertible

PHOTO: OLDSMOBILE DIVISION

1970 Oldsmobile 98 Convertible

PHOTO: OLDSMOBILE DIVISION

1970 Oldsmobile 98 Convertible

Original Price: est. $4,800
Number Produced: 3,161
Estimated Number Existing in 1979: 1,817
Miles per Gallon: 8–14
Common Trouble Spots: none
Availability of Parts: good
Investment Potential: A

Background: The luxurious 98 convertible was slipping in popularity. Sales were down by more than 25% from 1969.

The 98 came with a 365 h.p. 455 cu. in. V8. Turbo Hydra-Matic automatic transmission was standard.

1970 Plymouth Barracuda Convertible

Original Price: $3,135
Number Produced: N.A.
Estimated Number Existing in 1979: N.A.
Miles per Gallon: 11–20
Common Trouble Spots: none
Availability of Parts: good
Investment Potential: A+

Background: The Barracuda was one of the sportiest-looking American-made convertibles in 1970. It came with a 145 h.p. 225 cu. in. six-cylinder engine. V8 engines available at extra cost included a 230 h.p. 318, 290 h.p. 383, and a 335 h.p. 383. A three-speed manual transmisson was standard. Torque Flite automatic transmission and a four-speed manual transmission were optional.

Most 1970 Barracudas, 88.1%, were equipped with a V8 engine, 72.4% had an automatic transmission, 6.8% had a three-speed manual transmission, 20.8% had a four-speed manual transmission, 62.9% had power steering, 19.8% had power brakes, 13.2% had disc brakes, 2.1% had electric windows, 28.2% had tinted glass, and 22% were sold with an air conditioner.

1970 Plymouth Cuda Convertible

Original Price: $3,433
Number Produced: N.A.
Estimated Number Existing in 1979: N.A.
Miles per Gallon: 8–15
Common Trouble Spots: none
Availability of Parts: good
Investment Potential: AA

Background: The Cuda convertible came with a 335 h.p. 383 cu. in. V8. Other V8s available were a 275 h.p. 340, a 290 h.p. 383, a 375 h.p. 440, and a 425 h.p. 426. A three-speed manual transmission was standard. Torque Flite automatic and a four-speed manual transmission were optional.

1970 Plymouth Fury III Convertible

Original Price: $3,415
Number Produced: N.A.
Estimated Number Existing in 1979: N.A.
Miles per Gallon: 10–17
Common Trouble Spots: none
Availability of Parts: good
Investment Potential: A+

Background: The Fury III was the biggest convertible offered by Plymouth in 1970. It came with a 230 h.p. 318 cu. in. V8 engine. A 290 h.p. 383 cu. in. V8 was optional. A three-speed manual transmission was standard. Turbo Flite automatic transmission was optional.

Most 1970 Fury IIIs, 99.9%, were equipped with an automatic transmission, 99.4% had power steering, 51.4% had power brakes, 8.2% had disc brakes, 1.3% had power windows, 1.7% had power front seats, almost 1% had a tilting steering wheel, 65.8% had tinted glass, and 79.9% were sold with an air conditioner.

This was the last year for the Fury III convertible.

1970 Plymouth Road Runner Convertible

Original Price: $3,289
Number Produced: N.A.
Estimated Number Existing in 1979: N.A.
Miles per Gallon: 8–15
Common Trouble Spots: none
Availability of Parts: good
Investment Potential: A+

Background: This was the last year for the Road Runner convertible. It came with a 290 h.p. 383 cu. in. V8 engine. Two other V8 engines, a 425 h.p. 426 and a 390 h.p. 440, were available at extra cost. A three-speed manual transmission was standard. Torque Flite automatic transmission and a four-speed manual transmission were optional.

1970 Plymouth Road Runner Superbird

Original Price: $4,298
Number Produced: 1,873
Estimated Number Existing in 1979: 1,123
Miles per Gallon: 12–16
Common Trouble Spots: none
Availability of Parts: good–fair
Investment Potential: AAA

Background: "Wild" is the best word to describe the limited-edition Superbird. It was powered by a 375 h.p. 440 cu. in. V8. Available at extra cost were a 390 h.p. version of this engine ($119) and a 425 h.p. 426 Hemi ($679). Buyers had their choice of Torque Flite automatic transmission (which came with the "Performance Axle Package"), or a four-speed manual (which came with the "Track Pak").

Standard equipment included a black vinyl roof, competition-type hood, power brakes, power steering, heavy-duty suspension, black or white vinyl bench seats (bucket seats in the same colors were optional), and a "beep-beep" horn. It was available in seven exterior colors: white, orange, yellow, green, blue metallic, red, and blue.

One of the reasons Chrysler built the Superbird was to increase sales of its other cars. As a sales brochure aimed at Plymouth dealers stated, the Superbird's "wild appearance can be just what you need to draw car enthusiasts to your dealership. Once there, you'll be able to interest them in something a bit milder—a regular Road Runner, perhaps; or maybe a GTX, or a 'Cuda, or a Duster 340."

1970 Plymouth Road Runner Superbird

1970 Plymouth Satellite Convertible

Original Price: $3,096
Number Produced: N.A.
Estimated Number Existing in 1979: N.A.
Miles per Gallon: 8–18
Common Trouble Spots: none
Availability of Parts: good
Investment Potential: A

Background: This was the last year for the Satellite convertible. It was powered by a 145 h.p. 225 cu. in. six-cylinder engine. Four V8s were optional: a 230 h.p. 318, a 290 h.p. 383, a 330 h.p. 383, and a 335 h.p. 383. A three-speed manual transmission was standard. Turbo Flite automatic and a four-speed manual transmission were available at extra cost.

1970 Pontiac Bonneville Convertible

Original Price: est. $3,900
Number Produced: 7,033
Estimated Number Existing in 1979: 4,079
Miles per Gallon: 8–15
Common Trouble Spots: suspension
Availability of Parts: good
Investment Potential: AA

Background: The new Bonneville convertible had a classy look about it. It came with Pontiac's new 360 h.p. 455 cu. in. V8. Two other V8s, a 265 h.p. 400 and a 370 h.p. 455, were available at extra cost. A three-speed manual transmission was standard, but few Bonnevilles were sold that way. In fact, only .2% of all full-size 1970 Pontiacs were so equipped; the vast majority came with the Turbo Hydra-Matic automatic transmission.

The 1970 Bonneville convertible is one of the more attractive full-size Pontiacs made in the late 1960s to early 1970s. It is also the last Bonneville softtop.

1970 Pontiac Bonneville Convertible

PHOTO: PONTIAC MOTOR DIVISION

1970 Pontiac Catalina Convertible

Original Price: est. $3,500
Number Produced: 3,688
Estimated Number Existing in 1979: 2,139
Miles per Gallon: 8–16
Common Trouble Spots: suspension
Availability of Parts: good
Investment Potential: A+

Background: The Catalina received a pleasing face-lift for 1970. It was powered by a 255 h.p. 350 cu. in. V8. Three other V8s were available at extra cost—a 265 h.p. 400, a 330 h.p. 400, and a 370 h.p. 455. A three-speed manual transmission was standard. Turbo Hydra-Matic automatic transmission was optional.

Most full-size 1970 Pontiacs, 99.8%, came with the automatic, 99.4% had power steering, 92.7% had power brakes, 53.3% had disc brakes, 29.2% had electric windows, 7.4% had a power front seat, 11.7% had a tilting steering wheel, 89.4% had tinted glass, and 80.5% were sold with an air conditioner.

1970 Pontiac Le Mans Sport Convertible

Original Price: est. $3,000
Number Produced: 4,670
Estimated Number Existing in 1979: 2,708
Miles per Gallon: 11–19
Common Trouble Spots: clutch, cooling system
Availability of Parts: good
Investment Potential: A+

Background: The new Sport was now the only Le Mans ragtop offered. It came with a 155 h.p. 250 cu. in. six-cylinder engine. Two 400 cu. in. V8s, a 265 h.p. and a 330 h.p., were available at extra cost. Most buyers ordered one of the V8s.

A three-speed manual transmission was standard, but not very popular; the majority of Le Mans convertibles were equipped with one of the two optional automatic transmissions. Most also had power steering and power brakes.

1970 Pontiac GTO Convertible

Original Price: est. $3,400
Number Produced: 3,783
Estimated Number Existing in 1979: 2,194
Miles per Gallon: 8–14
Common Trouble Spots: clutch, cooling system
Availability of Parts: good
Investment Potential: AA

Background: "GTO spells Go." That's how Pontiac's public relations department described the new GTO ragtop. It came with a 350 h.p. 400 cu. in. V8. Three other V8s were offered—a 366 h.p. 400, a 370 h.p. 400, and a 370 h.p. 455.

A three-speed manual transmission was standard. Turbo Hydra-Matic automatic and a four-speed manual transmission were optional. Just over 60% of all 1970 GTOs were equipped with the automatic.

Only 168 1970 GTO convertibles were sold with the "Judge" performance option. It featured a 455 cu. in. Ram Air V8, heavy-duty transmission, a rear airfoil, an "air dam" on the hood, special body strips, and "The Judge" decals.

1970 Pontiac GTO Convertible

PHOTO: PONTIAC MOTOR DIVISION

1970 Shelby American GT 500 Convertible

Original Price: est. $6,300
Number Produced: N.A.
Estimated Number Existing in 1979: N.A.
Miles per Gallon: 8–14
Common Trouble Spots: none
Availability of Parts: fair–good
Investment Potential: AAA

Background: The sporty 1970 Shelby GT 500 ragtop was powered by a 335 h.p. 428 cu. in. V8. A four-speed manual transmission and a padded roll bar were standard. Select Shift Cruise-O-Matic automatic transmission was optional.

It was basically just an unsold 1969 GT 500. Hood strips and new serial numbers were about the only changes.

1970 Shelby American GT 350 Convertible

Original Price: est. $6,000
Number Produced: N.A.
Estimated Number Existing in 1979: N.A.
Miles per Gallon: 9–15
Common Trouble Spots: none
Availability of Parts: fair–good
Investment Potential: AAA

Background: The 1970 Shelby GT 350 ragtop was basically a "souped-up" Mustang. It came with a padded roll bar and a 290 h.p. 351 cu. in. V8. Buyers had their choice of Select Shift Cruise-O-Matic automatic and a fully synchronized four-speed manual transmission.

Some extra-cost options included "Tilt-Away" steering wheel, AM/FM radio, AM radio/stero tape system, tinted glass, air conditioning, and heavy-duty battery.

1971

1971 Buick Centurion Convertible

Original Price: $4,446
Number Produced: 2,161
Estimated Number Existing in 1979: 1,558
Miles per Gallon: 7–15
Common Trouble Spots: none
Availability of Parts: good
Investment Potential: A+

Background: The Centurion took its name from Buick's 1956 GM Motorama show car. Its styling appeared to have been influenced by the Riviera. A 315 h.p. 455 cu. in. V8 and a three-speed manual transmission were standard. Turbo Hydra-Matic automatic transmission was a popular $242 option.

All Centurion convertibles came with power steering and power disc brakes. The vast majority were equipped with the $442 air conditioning unit.

1971 Buick GS Convertible

Original Price: $3,475
Number Produced: 902
Estimated Number Existing in 1979: 650
Miles per Gallon: 9–15
Common Trouble Spots: none
Availability of Parts: good
Investment Potential: AA

Background: The 1971 GS softtop was basically a dressed-up, hotter version of the Skylark. It came with a 230 h.p. 350 cu. in. V8. Three 455 cu. in V8s, rated at 315 h.p., 330 h.p., and 345 h.p. were available. A three-speed manual transmission was standard. Turbo Hydra-Matic automatic transmission was optional. Power steering and power brakes were popular options.

1971 Buick LeSabre Custom Convertible

Original Price: $4,127
Number Produced: 1,856
Estimated Number Existing in 1979: 1,338
Miles per Gallon: 9–15
Common Trouble Spots: none
Availability of Parts: good
Investment Potential: A+

Background: The LeSabre ragtop received an attractive face-lift for 1971. It was powered by a 230 h.p. 350 cu. in. V8. A 260 h.p. version of this engine was available at extra cost. A three-speed manual transmission was standard, but not very popular; Turbo Hydra-Matic automatic transmission was the choice of the majority of buyers.

Power steering and power disc brakes were standard. Air conditioning cost $442; still, 90.3% of all full-size Buicks came with it.

1971 Buick Skylark Custom Convertible

Original Price: $3,461
Number Produced: 3,993
Estimated Number Existing in 1979: 2,878
Miles per Gallon: 10–17
Common Trouble Spots: none
Availability of Parts: good
Investment Potential: AA

Background: The '71 Skylark Custom ragtop looked a lot like last year's model. It was powered by a 230 h.p. 350 cu. in. V8. A 260 h.p. version of this engine was available. A three-speed manual transmission was standard. Turbo Hydra-Matic automatic transmission was optional for $222.

Almost 98% of all Skylarks had power steering, 61.2% had power brakes, 10.4% had power windows, 1.8% had power seats, 69.4% had air conditioning, and 17.4% came with disc brakes.

1971 Cadillac Fleetwood Eldorado Convertible

PHOTO: CADILLAC MOTOR CAR DIVISION

1971 Chevrolet Corvette Convertible

PHOTO: GM PHOTOGRAPHIC

1971 Cadillac Fleetwood Eldorado Convertible

Original Price: $7,784
Number Produced: 6,800
Estimated Number Existing in 1979: 5,535
Miles per Gallon: 9–14
Common Trouble Spots: none
Availability of Parts: good
Investment Potential: AA

Background: For the first time since 1966, Cadillac offered the Eldorado convertible. It was one of the best-looking convertibles available in 1971.

The Eldorado came with a 365 h.p. 500 cu. in. V8 engine. Turbo Hydra-Matic automatic transmission, power disc brakes, power steering, electric windows, and power seats were standard. Nearly all Eldorados, 99.6%, were equipped with the $537 air conditioning unit, 99.4% had tinted glass, and 65.5% had a tilting steering wheel.

1971 Chevrolet Chevelle Malibu Convertible

Original Price: $3,255
Number Produced: N.A.
Estimated Number Existing in 1979: N.A.
Miles per Gallon: 8–17
Common Trouble Spots: clutch
Availability of Parts: good
Investment Potential: AA

Background: The '71 Chevelle ragtop had Monte-Carlo-inspired styling. It came with a 200 h.p. 307 cu. in. V8. Several other V8 engines were available at extra cost: a 330 h.p. 350, a 300 h.p. 402, and a 365 h.p. 454. A three-speed manual transmission was standard. Powerglide automatic and a four-speed manual were optional.

Close to 94% of all '71 Chevelles were equipped with an automatic, 93.4% came with a V8, 3.1% had a three-speed manual, 3.2% had a four-speed manual, 90.5% had power steering, 55.1% had power brakes, 22.2% had disc brakes, 7.6% had power windows, 4.1% had a tilting steering wheel, 75.3% had tinted glass, and 55.3% were sold with an air conditioner.

1971 Chevrolet Corvette Stingray Convertible

Original Price: $5,299
Number Produced: 7,121
Estimated Number Existing in 1979: 5,347
Miles per Gallon: 8–16
Common Trouble Spots: electrical and cooling system
Availability of Parts: good
Investment Potential: AAA

Background: The new Corvette was powered by a 270 h.p. 350 cu. in. V8. Other V8 engines were available at extra cost—a 330 h.p. 350, a 365 h.p. 454, and a 425 h.p. 454. Almost 54% of 1971 Corvettes came with a four-speed manual transmission. The rest had Turbo Hydra-Matic automatic transmission.

Most new Vettes, 82.1%, had power steering, 62.2% had power brakes, 37.3% had a tilting steering wheel, 28.4% had power windows, and 52.7% were sold with an air conditioner. Only 36.8% of Vette convertible buyers ordered a detachable hard top.

1971 Chevrolet Impala Convertible

Original Price: est. $3,600
Number Produced: N.A.
Estimated Number Existing in 1979: N.A.
Miles per Gallon: 8–16
Common Trouble Spots: none
Availability of Parts: good
Investment Potential: A+

Background: The '71 Impala ragtop seemed to have Eldorado-inspired styling. It came with a 270 h.p. 350 cu. in. V8. Optional V8s included a 255 h.p. 400, a 300 h.p. 402, and a 365 h.p. 454. A three-speed manual transmission was standard. Powerglide and Turbo Hydra-Matic automatic transmissions were optional.

Over 99% of all full-size 1971 Chevrolets were equipped with an automatic, 98.5% had a V8, 99.8% had power steering, all had power disc brakes, 9.4% had power windows, 3.3% had a power front seat, 12.2% had a tilting steering wheel, 84.9% had tinted glass, and 81.2% were sold with an air conditioner.

1971 Dodge Challenger R/T Convertible

PHOTO: CHRYSLER CORPORATION

1971 Dodge Challenger Convertible

Original Price: $3,105
Number Produced: 2,165
Estimated Number Existing in 1979: 1,623
Miles per Gallon: 8–17
Common Trouble Spots: none
Availability of Parts: good
Investment Potential: AA+ (with R/T option); AA (without)

Background: The Challenger ragtop was the pace car for the Indianapolis 500 in 1971. It was powered by a 125 h.p. 198 cu. in. slant six. Available at extra cost were a 145 h.p. 225 cu. in. six-cylinder and several V8 engines—a 300 h.p. 383, a 290 h.p. 340, a 385 h.p. 440, and a 425 h.p. 426. A three-speed manual transmission was standard. Torque Flite automatic and a four-speed manual transmission were optional.

Most '71 Challengers, 93.1%, were equipped with a V8, 88.8% had the automatic, 5.9% had a three-speed manual, 5.3% had the four-speed, 85.2% had power steering, 24.8% had power brakes, 18.9% had disc brakes, 2.7% had power windows, 64.8% had tinted glass, and 48.1% were sold with air conditioning.

1971 Ford LTD Convertible

Original Price: $3,746
Number Produced: 5,750
Estimated Number Existing in 1979: 4,076
Miles per Gallon: 8–16
Common Trouble Spots: none
Availability of Parts: good
Investment Potential: A+

1971 Ford LTD Convertible

PHOTO: FORD MOTOR COMPANY

Background: This was the first year for the LTD convertible. It came with a 240 h.p. 351 cu. in. V8. Other V8s were offered at extra cost—a 255 h.p. 390, a 260 h.p. 400, and a 320 h.p. 429. A three-speed manual transmission was standard, but not very popular. In Ford's LTD sales catalog, copywriters advised, "Select-Shift Cruise-O-Matic transmission, which you can shift manually or automatically, is a silkily efficient option you'll likely want to include." Most buyers apparently agreed, as 99.5% of all full-size '71 Fords came with the automatic.

White all-vinyl upholstery was standard. The vinyl power top, which featured a stain-and scratch-resistant glass rear window, was available in black or white. Bucket seats were optional.

The majority of full-size 1971 Fords, 98%, had power steering, 4.3% had a five-position tilting steering wheel, 80% had tinted glass, 5.4% had power windows, 4.4% had six-way power seats, and 80.1% were equipped with an air conditioner.

1971 Ford Mustang Convertible

Original Price: $3,322
Number Produced: 6,121
Estimated Number Existing in 1979: 4,339
Miles per Gallon: 9–20
Common Trouble Spots: clutch
Availability of Parts: good
Investment Potential: AA

Background: The new Mustang convertible was an attractive, sporty personal car. The standard engine was a 145 h.p. 250 cu. in. six-cylinder. Most came with one of the five optional V8s—the 210 h.p. 302, the 240 h.p. 351, the 285 h.p. 351, the 370 h.p. 429, or the 370 h.p. 429 with Dual Ram Induction.

A three-speed manual transmission was standard. Select Shift automatic and a four-speed manual transmission were optional at extra cost.

Most '71 Mustangs, 89.9% came with the automatic, 9.8% had the six, 5.3% had a four-speed manual, 86% had power steering, 40.9% had power brakes, 3.2% had a tilting steering wheel, 47.7% had tinted glass, 1.9% had power windows, and 40.5% were sold with an air conditioner.

Buyers could choose from sixteen exterior colors, five standard vinyl interior colors, and six knitted-vinyl colors.

1971 Ford Mustang Convertible

PHOTO: FORD MOTOR COMPANY

1971 Ford Torino GT Convertible

Original Price: $3,408
Number Produced: 1,613
Estimated Number Existing in 1979: 1,143
Miles per Gallon: 8–16
Common Trouble Spots: none
Availability of Parts: good
Investment Potential: AA

Background: The '71 Torino GT ragtop came with a 240 h.p. 351 cu. in. V8. Two other V8s were available, a 285 h.p. 351 and a 370 h.p. 429. A four-speed manual transmission was standard. So was power steering. Select Shift automatic transmission was optional.

Most Torinos, 95%, were equipped with the automatic, 33.1% had power disc brakes, and 50.8% were sold with the $412 air conditioner.

1971 Mercury Cougar Convertible

Original Price: $3,681
Number Produced: 1,723
Estimated Number Existing in 1979: 1,195
Miles per Gallon: 9–17
Common Trouble Spots: electrical system, suspension
Availability of Parts: good
Investment Potential: AA

Background: The Cougar ragtop received an attractive face-lift for 1971. It came with a 240 h.p. 351 cu. in. V8. A 285 h.p. version of this engine and a 370 h.p. 429 cu. in. V8 was optional. A three-speed manual transmission was standard. Select Shift automatic and a four-speed manual were available.

Most 1971 Cougars, 96.9%, were equipped with the automatic, 1% had a four-speed manual, 98.5% had power steering, 79.7% had power disc brakes, 17% had a tilting steering wheel, 8.9% had power windows, 4.6% had power seats, 77.9% had tinted glass, and 75% were sold with the $408 air conditioner.

1971 Mercury Cougar XR-7 Convertible

PHOTO: FORD MOTOR COMPANY

1971 Mercury Cougar XR-7 Convertible

Original Price: $3,877
Number Produced: 1,717
Estimated Number Existing in 1979: 1,191
Miles per Gallon: 9–17
Common Trouble Spots: electrical system, suspension
Availability of Parts: good
Investment Potential: AA

Background: The XR-7 was basically just a fancy version of the standard '71 Cougar convertible. It came with a 240 h.p. 351 cu. in. V8. Available at extra cost were a 285 h.p. version of this engine and a 370 h.p. 429 cu. in. V8. Select Shift automatic and a four-speed manual were optional. A three-speed manual transmission was standard.

The high-back bucket seats in the XR-7 were upholstered in leather. Buyers had their choice of black, blue, ginger, green, red, or white. A console with a storage compartment was offered.

1971 Oldsmobile Cutlass Supreme Convertible

Original Price: $3,506
Number Produced: 10,255
Estimated Number Existing in 1979: 7,393
Miles per Gallon: 9–16
Common Trouble Spots: none
Availability of Parts: good
Investment Potential: A+

Background: The Cutlass Supreme remained Oldsmobile's most popular ragtop. It was powered by a 240 h.p. 350 cu. in. V8. A 260 h.p. version of this engine and a 455 cu. in. V8 were available at extra cost. A three-speed manual transmission was standard. Turbo Hydra-Matic automatic transmission was optional for $222.

Other popular options included power steering ($119), power brakes ($47), disc brakes ($70), and air conditioning ($408).

1971 Oldsmobile Delta 88 Royale Convertible

Original Price: $4,325
Number Produced: 2,883
Estimated Number Existing in 1979: 2,078
Miles per Gallon: 9–16
Common Trouble Spots: none
Availability of Parts: good
Investment Potential: A

Background: The luxurious Delta 88 Royale was Oldsmobile's top-of-the-line convertible in 1971. It was powered by a 240 h.p. 350 cu. in. V8. A 280 h.p. 455 cu. in. V8 was available at extra cost. Turbo Hydra-Matic automatic transmission, power steering, and power disc brakes, were standard.

Ninety percent of 1971 88s were equipped with the $442 air conditioner, 43.2% had power windows, 30.8% had a tilting steering wheel, and 36.5% came with power front seats.

1971 Oldsmobile Delta 88 Royale Convertible

PHOTO: OLDSMOBILE DIVISION

1971 Oldsmobile 4-4-2 Convertible

Original Price: $3,742
Number Produced: 1,304
Estimated Number Existing in 1979: 940
Miles per Gallon: 8–14
Common Trouble Spots: none
Availability of Parts: good
Investment Potential: AA

Background: The 4-4-2 was powered by a 340 h.p. 455 cu. in. V8 engine. A three-speed manual transmission was standard. Turbo Hydra-Matic automatic and a four-speed manual transmission were optional. Other popular options included power steering ($116), power disc brakes ($70), and air conditioning ($408).

1971 Plymouth Barracuda Convertible

Original Price: $3,124
Number Produced: N.A.
Estimated Number Existing in 1979: N.A.
Miles per Gallon: 9–20
Common Trouble Spots: none
Availability of Parts: good
Investment Potential: AA

Background: This was the last Barracuda convertible made. It came with a 125 h.p. 198 cu. in. six-cylinder engine. Four V8 engines were available: a 230 h.p. 318, a 275 h.p. 340, a 275 h.p. 383, and a 300 h.p. 383. A three-speed manual transmission was standard. Torque Flite automatic transmission, and a four-speed manual were optional.

Most 1971 Barracudas, 81.8%, were equipped with a V8 engine, 79.4% had an automatic; 8.5% had a three-speed manual, 12.1% had a four-speed manual, 71.8% had power steering, 31% had power brakes, 25% had disc brakes, 2.8% had power windows, 54.9% had tinted glass, and 29.5% had an air conditioner.

1971 Plymouth Cuda Convertible

Original Price: $3,412
Number Produced: N.A.
Estimated Number Existing in 1979: N.A.
Miles per Gallon: 8–11
Common Trouble Spots: none
Availability of Parts: good
Investment Potential: AA

Background: This was the last year for the sporty Cuda convertible. It came with a 300 h.p. 383 cu. in. V8. Two other V8s, a 385 h.p. 440 cu. in., and a 425 h.p. 426 cu. in., were available at extra cost. A three-speed manual transmission was standard. Torque Flite automatic and a four-speed manual transmission were optional.

1971 Oldsmobile 4-4-2 Convertible

PHOTO: OLDSMOBILE DIVISION

1971 Pontiac Catalina Convertible

Original Price: $3,807
Number Produced: 2,036
Estimated Number Existing in 1979: 1,404
Miles per Gallon: 8–16
Common Trouble Spots: suspension
Availability of Parts: good
Investment Potential: A+

Background: The new Catalina was powered by a 250 h.p. 350 cu. in. V8. Other V8s available at extra cost were a 265 h.p. 400, a 300 h.p. 400, a 280 h.p. 455, and a 325 h.p. 455. A three-speed manual transmission was standard. Turbo Hydra-Matic automatic transmission was optional for $243.

Most Catalinas, 99.9%, came with the automatic, 99.9% had power steering, all had power brakes, 5.8% had a tilting steering wheel, 3.7% had electric windows, 1.7% had power front seats, 89% had tinted glass, and 81.1% were sold with a $442 air conditioner.

1971 Pontiac Catalina Convertible

1971 Pontiac Grand Ville Convertible

Original Price: $4,464
Number Produced: 1,789
Estimated Number Existing in 1979: 1,234
Miles per Gallon: 7–13
Common Trouble Spots: suspension
Availability of Parts: good
Investment Potential: A+

Background: This was the first year for Pontiac's new top-of-the-line Grand Ville convertible. It came with a 325 h.p. 455 cu. in. V8. Turbo Hydra-Matic automatic transmission, power steering, and power disc brakes were standard.

Most Grand Villes, 70.8%, were equipped with electric windows, 43.9% had power front seats, 43.9% had a tilting steering wheel, 98.2% had tinted glass, and 96.8% were sold with an air conditioner.

1971 Pontiac GTO Convertible

Original Price: $3,676
Number Produced: 678
Estimated Number Existing in 1979: 467
Miles per Gallon: 8–14
Common Trouble Spots: clutch
Availability of Parts: good
Investment Potential: AA

Background: The '71 GTO ragtop had a very wild-looking front end. It came with a 300 h.p. 400 cu. in. V8. Buyers could also order other V8s, a 325 h.p. 455 and a 335 h.p. 455, at extra cost. A three-speed manual transmission was standard. A four-speed manual and an automatic transmission were optional.

Most GTOs, 75.4%, were equipped with the automatic, 5% had the three-speed manual, 19.6% had the four-speed manual, 93.4% had power steering, 79.9% had power brakes, 8.9% had electric windows, 3.3% had power front seats, 5.9% had a tilting steering wheel, 82.9% had tinted glass, and 60.2% were sold with an air conditioner.

Especially desirable are those equipped with the "Judge" performance package. Only seventeen 1971 GTO convertibles came with this option, which featured a 455 cu. in. Ram Air V8, heavy-duty suspension, a rear airfoil, a Ram Air hood, special body strips, and "The Judge" decals.

This was the last GTO convertible made.

1971 Pontiac GTO Convertible

PHOTO: PONTIAC MOTOR DIVISION

1971 Pontiac Grand Ville Convertible

1971 Pontiac Le Mans Sport Convertible

Original Price: $3,359
Number Produced: 3,865
Estimated Number Existing in 1979: 2,666
Miles per Gallon: 9–19
Common Trouble Spots: clutch
Availability of Parts: good
Investment Potential: A+

Background: The new Le Mans Sport was the lowest-priced convertible offered by Pontiac in 1971. It came with a 145 h.p. 250 cu. in. six-cylinder engine. But 99% of all 1971 Le Mans Sports were sold with one of the optional V8s, which included a 250 h.p. 350, a 265 h.p. 400, a 325 h.p. 455, and a 335 h.p. 455. A three-speed manual transmission was standard. An automatic transmission and a four-speed manual were optional.

Most Le Mans Sports, 96.8%, came equipped with the automatic, 1.5% had a three-speed manual, 1.7% had a four-speed manual, 98.4% had power steering, 24.7% had power brakes, 50% had disc brakes, 4.6% had electric windows, 1.6% had a power front seat, 3.7% had a tilting steering wheel, 86.6% had tinted glass, and 72% had the $408 optional air conditioner.

1971 Pontiac Le Mans Sport Convertible

1972

1972 Buick Centurion Convertible

Original Price: $4,616
Number Produced: 2,396
Estimated Number Existing in 1979: 1,849
Miles per Gallon: 8–14
Common Trouble Spots: none
Availability of Parts: good
Investment Potential: A

Background: The Centurion softtop came with a 455 cu. in. V8 engine. Turbo Hydra-Matic automatic transmission, power steering, and power disc brakes were standard. Most Centurions had the $431 optional air conditioning unit.

1972 Buick GS Convertible

Original Price: $3,406
Number Produced: 852
Estimated Number Existing in 1979: 656
Miles per Gallon: 9–15
Common Trouble Spots: none
Availability of Parts: good
Investment Potential: AA

This was the last year for the GS ragtop. It was powered by a 350 cu. in V8. A hotter version of this engine and a 455 cu. in. V8 were optional. A three-speed manual transmission was standard, but not very popular. Turbo Hydra-Matic automatic and a four-speed manual were available at extra cost. Most people ordered the automatic.

1972 Buick LeSabre Custom Convertible

Original Price: $4,291
Number Produced: 2,037
Estimated Number Existing in 1979: 1,572
Miles per Gallon: 8–15
Common Trouble Spots: none
Availability of Parts: good
Investment Potential: A+

Background: This was the last LeSabre convertible built. It had a 350 cu. in. V8 engine. Two other versions of this engine were available. Turbo Hydra-Matic automatic transmission was standard, as were power steering and power disc brakes.

Fifty-six percent of all full-size '72 Buicks came with power windows, 43.1% had power front seats, and 93.1% had the $431 air conditioner.

1972 Buick Skylark Custom Convertible

Original Price: $3,393
Number Produced: 3,608
Estimated Number Existing in 1979: 2,785
Miles per Gallon: 10–17
Common Trouble Spots: none
Availability of Parts: good
Investment Potential: AA

Background: This was the last year for the Skylark convertible. It was powered by a 350 cu. in. V8 engine. Two hotter versions of this engine were also available. A three-speed manual transmission was standard, but not very popular; most skylark buyers, 99.2%, ordered the optional Turbo Hydra-Matic automatic transmission.

Just over 69% of all '72 Skylarks had power brakes, 98.3% had power steering, 10.6% had power windows, 2.6% had power seats, 10.5% had a tilting steering wheel, and 75.2% came with air conditioning.

1972 Cadillac Fleetwood Eldorado Convertible

PHOTO: CADILLAC MOTOR CAR DIVISION

1972 Cadillac Fleetwood Eldorado Convertible

Original Price: $7,546
Number Produced: 7,975
Estimated Number Existing in 1979: 6,627
Miles per Gallon: 9–14
Common Trouble Spots: none
Availability of Parts: good
Investment Potential: AA

Background: The attractive new Eldorado convertible was powered by a 500 cu. in. V8 engine. Turbo Hydra-Matic automatic transmission, power disc brakes, power steering, electric windows, and power seats were standard.

Nearly all 1972 Eldorados, 99.8%, came with air conditioning, 99.6% had tinted glass, and 85.7% had a tilting steering wheel.

1972 Chevrolet Chevelle Malibu Convertible

Original Price: $3,187
Number Produced: N.A.
Estimated Number Existing in 1979: N.A.
Miles per Gallon: 8–17
Common Trouble Spots: clutch, fuel system
Availability of Parts: good
Investment Potential: AA

Background: The '72 Malibu came with a 307 cu. in. V8. Optional V8s included a 350, a 402, and a 454. A three-speed manual was standard. Powerglide automatic and a four-speed manual were optional.

Almost 95% of all Chevelles came equipped with an automatic, 2.7% had a three-speed manual, 2.5% had a four-speed manual, 92.9% had power steering, 72.7% had power brakes, 30.2% had disc brakes, 8.9% had power windows, 80.5% had tinted glass, 5% had a tilting steering wheel, and 62.8% were sold with an air conditioner.

1972 Chevrolet Corvette Convertible

PHOTO: GM PHOTOGRAPHIC

1972 Chevrolet Corvette Stingray Convertible

Original Price: $5,246
Number Produced: 6,508
Estimated Number Existing in 1979: 5,323
Miles per Gallon: 8–15
Common Trouble Spots: none
Availability of Parts: good
Investment Potential: AAA

Background: The new Corvette was powered by a 350 cu. in. V8. A hotter version of that engine and a 454 cu. in. V8 were available at extra cost. Most 1972 Vettes, 53.9%, were equipped with the optional Turbo Hydra-Matic automatic transmission; the rest came with the standard four-speed manual transmission.

Just over 88% of new Corvettes had power steering, 69.5% had power brakes, 48.1% had a tilting steering wheel, 35.2% had power windows, and 63.8% were sold with the $452 optional air conditioner. Close to 41% of 1972 Corvette ragtop buyers ordered the detachable hard top.

1972 Chevrolet Impala Convertible

Original Price: $3,978
Number Produced: N.A.
Estimated Number Existing in 1979: N.A.
Miles per Gallon: 8–16
Common Trouble Spots: none
Availability of Parts: good
Investment Potential: A+

Background: The new Impala received a flattering face-lift for 1972. This year's convertible looked even ritzier than last year's model.

It came with a 350 cu. in. V8. Optional V8 engines included a 400, a 402, and a 454. Turbo Hydra-Matic automatic transmission was standard.

Virtually all 1972 full-size Chevrolets, 99.6%, came equipped with a V8, 99.8% had an automatic, 13.8% had a tilting steering wheel, 89.5% had tinted glass, 16.4% had power windows, 4.3% had power front seats, and 84.5% were sold with an air conditioner. Power steering and power disc brakes were standard.

1972 Chevrolet Impala Convertible

PHOTO: GM PHOTOGRAPHIC

1972 Ford LTD Convertible

Original Price: $4,073
Number Produced: 4,234
Estimated Number Existing in 1979: 3,213
Miles per Gallon: 8–16
Common Trouble Spots: none
Availability of Parts: good
Investment Potential: AA

Background: This was the last year for the LTD convertible. It came with a 351 cu. in. V8. A 400 cu. in. V8 and a 429 cu. in. V8 were available at extra cost. Select Shift automatic transmission, power steering, power disc brakes, and vinyl interior were standard.

Almost 33% of all full-size 1972 Fords had power windows, 6.1% had power front seats, 6.6% had a tilting steering wheel, 85.1% had tinted glass, and 85.6% had an air conditioner.

1972 Ford LTD Convertible

1972 Ford Mustang Convertible

Original Price: $3,015
Number Produced: 6,401
Estimated Number Existing in 1979: 4,858
Miles per Gallon: 10–20
Common Trouble Spots: suspension
Availability of Parts: good
Investment Potential: AA

Background: The standard engine in the new Mustang was a 250 cu. in. six-cylinder. Buyers could choose from three optional V8 engines—a 302 and two 351s. A three-speed manual transmission was standard. Select Shift automatic and a four-speed manual were optional.

The vast majority of '72 Mustangs, 90.4%, came with the automatic, 6.9% had the three-speed manual, 90.2% had power steering, 54.9% had power brakes, 3.9% had a tilting steering wheel, 61.6% had tinted glass, 2% had power windows, and 48.5% were sold with an air conditioner.

1972 Ford Mustang Convertible

PHOTO: FORD MOTOR COMPANY

1972 Mercury Cougar Convertible

Original Price: $3,420
Number Produced: 1,240
Estimated Number Existing in 1979: 933
Miles per Gallon: 9–17
Common Trouble Spots: brakes, electrical system, suspension
Availability of Parts: good
Investment Potential: AA

Background: The sporty '72 Cougar ragtop came with a 351 cu. in. V8. Two hotter versions of this engine were available at extra cost. A three-speed manual was standard. Select Shift automatic and a four-speed manual were optional.

Most 1972 Cougars, 98.5%, were equipped with the automatic, 1% had the three-speed manual, .5% had the four-speed manual, 99.1% had power steering, 87.9% had power disc brakes, 83.5% had tinted glass, 10.6% had power windows, 5.7% had power seats, and 81.2% were sold with an air conditioner.

1972 Mercury Cougar XR-7 Convertible

Original Price: $3,597
Number Produced: 1,929
Estimated Number Existing in 1979: 1,452
Miles per Gallon: 9–17
Common Trouble Spots: brakes, electrical system, suspension
Availability of Parts: good
Investment Potential: AA

Background: The attractive new XR-7 came with a 351 cu. in. V8. Two hotter versions of this engine were optional at extra cost. A three-speed manual transmission was standard. Select Shift automatic and a four-speed manual were offered. Most buyers chose the automatic.

1972 Mercury Cougar XR-7 Convertible

PHOTO: FORD MOTOR COMPANY

1972 Oldsmobile Cutlass Supreme Convertible

Original Price: $3,433
Number Produced: 11,571
Estimated Number Existing in 1979: 9,719
Miles per Gallon: 9–16
Common Trouble Spots: none
Availability of Parts: good
Investment Potential: AA

Background: a 1972 Oldsmobile sales catalog referred to the Cutlass Supreme as "our little limousine." It was powered by a 350 cu. in. V8 with a four-barrel carburetor. Three other versions of this engine and two 455 cu. in. V8s were available at extra cost. A three-speed manual transmission was standard. Turbo Hydra-Matic automatic and a four-speed manual were optional.

The 4-4-2 Sport/Handling package and the W30 Performance Package were available for buyers who wanted to put a little more "go" into their Cutlass.

This was the last Cutlass convertible.

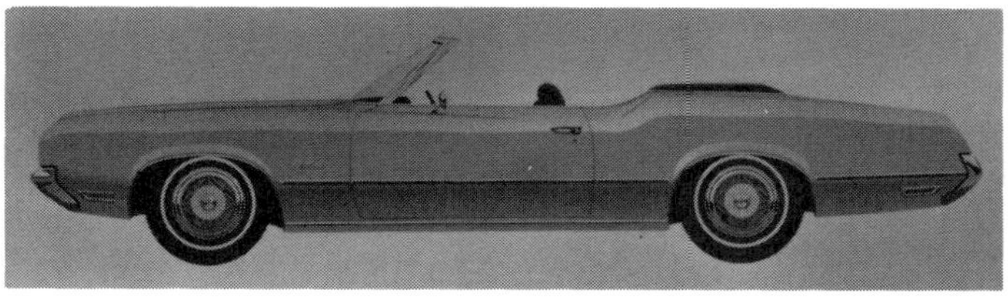

1972 Oldsmobile Cutlass Supreme Convertible

PHOTO: OLDSMOBILE DIVISION

1972 Oldsmobile Delta 88 Royale Convertible

Original Price: $4,387
Number Produced: 3,900
Estimated Number Existing in 1979: 3,276
Miles per Gallon: 9–15
Common Trouble Spots: none
Availability of Parts: good
Investment Potential: A

Background: "Not just another pretty car." That's the way a 1972 Oldsmobile sales catalog described the attractive new Delta 88 Royale.

It came with a 350 cu. in. V8 engine with a two-barrel carburetor. A hotter four-barrel-carburetor version of this engine and a 455 cu. in. V8 were available at extra cost. Turbo Hydra-Matic automatic transmission, power disc brakes, power steering, and chrome wheel discs were standard.

Most 1972 88s, 90%, were equipped with an air conditioner, 43.2% had power windows, 36.5% had six-way power front seats, and 30.8% were sold with a "Tilt-Away" steering wheel.

Buyers had their choice of twenty-one exterior colors. The Madrid-grained Moroceen (vinyl) interior was offered in black, green, white, or saddle.

1972 Oldsmobile Delta 88 Royale Convertible

PHOTO: OLDSMOBILE DIVISION

1972 Pontiac Catalina Convertible

Original Price: $4,080
Number Produced: 2,399
Estimated Number Existing in 1979: 1,950
Miles per Gallon: 8–15
Common Trouble Spots: none
Availability of Parts: good
Investment Potential: A+

Background: The new Catalina convertible was powered by a 400 cu. in. V8 with two-barrel carburetor. Three other V8s were available at extra cost: a 400 (with four-barrel carburetor), a 455 (with two-barrel carburetor), and a 455 (with four-barrel carburetor). Turbo Hydra-Matic automatic transmission, power steering, power disc brakes, and all-Morrokide interior were standard.

Most full-size 1972 Pontiacs, 90.5%, were equipped with an air conditioner, 35.5% had power windows, 12% had a power front seat, 22% had a tilting steering wheel, and 94.2% came with tinted glass.

This was the last Catalina convertible.

1972 Pontiac Catalina Convertible

1972 Pontiac Grand Ville Convertible

Original Price: $4,640
Number Produced: 2,213
Estimated Number Existing in 1979: 1,799
Miles per Gallon: 7–13
Common Trouble Spots: none
Availability of Parts: good
Investment Potential: A+

Background: Pontiac sales literature called the Grand Ville their "smoothest, quietest, most elegant full sized car for 1972." It was powered by a 455 cu. in V8 with a four-barrel carburetor. Turbo Hydra-Matic automatic transmission was standard.

Even though it cost $431, air conditioning was one of the most popular options on Grand Villes. Other options included power windows and door locks, cruise control, 8-track tape player, seven-position steering wheel, six-way power seat, deck-lid release, and even trailer towing packages.

1972 Pontiac Le Mans Sport Convertible

Original Price: $3,228
Number Produced: 3,438
Estimated Number Existing in 1979: 2,795
Miles per Gallon: 9–19
Common Trouble Spots: none
Availability of Parts: good
Investment Potential: AA

Background: The attractive Le Mans came with bucket seats and a 250 cu. in. six-cylinder engine. Five V8 engines were also offered: a 350 (with two-barrel carburetor), a 400 (with four-barrel carburetor), a 400 (with two-barrel carburetor), a 455 (with four-barrel carburetor), and a 455 H.O. (with four-barrel carburetor).

A three-speed manual transmission was standard. A four-speed manual and two automatic transmissions were optional.

Most 1972 Le Mans, 94%, were equipped with an automatic, 4.4% had a three-speed manual, 1.6% had a four-speed manual, 96.6% had one of the V8 engines, 96.4% had power steering, 68.9% had power brakes, 49% had disc brakes, 3.8% had electric windows, 1.3% had power front seats, 5% had a tilting steering wheel, 82.4% had tinted glass, and 70.7% were sold with an air conditioner.

This was the last year for the Le Mans convertible.

1972 Pontiac Le Mans Sport Convertible

1972 Pontiac Grand Ville Convertible

1973

1973 Buick Centurion Convertible

Original Price: $4,534
Number Produced: 5,739
Estimated Number Existing in 1979: 5,073
Miles per Gallon: 8–14
Common Trouble Spots: none
Availability of Parts: good
Investment Potential: A+

Background: This was the only convertible Buick offered in 1973. And it was quite handsome.

The new Centurion was powered by a 455 cu. in. V8 engine. Turbo Hydra-Matic automatic transmission, power steering, and power brakes were standard. Over 57% of all full-size Buicks had power windows, 44.2% had power front seats, and 94.3% came with air conditioning.

1973 Cadillac Fleetwood Eldorado Convertible

Original Price: $6,782
Number Produced: 9,315
Estimated Number Existing in 1979: 8,122
Miles per Gallon: 9–14
Common Trouble Spots: none
Availability of Parts: good
Investment Potential: AA

Background: The 1973 Eldorado convertible was an attractive car, inside and out. While some people complained that it was starting to look a lot like a Chevy (at least from a distance), it still retained the Cadillac flair.

It was powered by a 500 cu. in. V8 engine. Turbo Hydra-Matic automatic transmission, power disc brakes, power steering, electric windows, and power seats were standard. Virtually all Eldorados, 99.8%, had air conditioning, 99.7% had tinted glass, and 88.3% had a tilting steering wheel.

1973 Chevrolet Caprice Convertible

Original Price: $4,345
Number Produced: N.A.
Estimated Number Existing in 1979: N.A.
Miles per Gallon: 8–15
Common Trouble Spots: none
Availability of Parts: good
Investment Potential: A+

Background: This was the first year for the Caprice convertible. It was powered by a 400 cu. in. V8 engine. A 454 cu. in. V8 was optional. Automatic transmission, power steering, and power disc brakes were standard.

Over 26% of all full-size '73 Chevys had power windows, 19% had a tilting steering wheel, 5.7% had power front seats, 90.2% had tinted glass, and 84.7% were sold with an air conditioner.

Its power-operated top was available in black or white. The all-vinyl interior could be had in green, neutral, or white.

1973 Chevrolet Caprice Convertible

PHOTO: GM PHOTOGRAPHIC

1973 Cadillac Fleetwood Eldorado Convertible

PHOTO: CADILLAC MOTOR CAR DIVISION

1973 Chevrolet Corvette Stingray Convertible

Original Price: $5,399
Number Produced: N.A.
Estimated Number Existing in 1979: N.A.
Miles per Gallon: 8–15
Common Trouble Spots: air conditioning unit
Availability of Parts: good
Investment Potential: AAA

Background: This was the 20th anniversary of the Corvette. The new Vette was powered by a 350 cu. in. V8. A hotter version of that engine and a 454 cu. in. V8 were available at extra cost. Most 1973 Corvettes, 58.8%, came with the optional Turbo Hydra-Matic automatic transmission. The rest were equipped with the standard four-speed manual.

Over 91% of all new Corvettes had power steering, 79.3% had power brakes, 58.9% had a tilting steering wheel, 46% had power windows, and 70.8% were sold with an air conditioner.

Buyers could choose from ten body colors: medium blue metallic, dark blue metallic, blue/green metallic, orange metallic, yellow, yellow metallic, Mille Miglia Red, Elkhart green, and classic white.

The standard interior was all vinyl. It came in five colors: black, blue, red, dark saddle, or medium saddle. A leather-and-vinyl interior, in black, dark saddle, or medium saddle, was optional at extra cost.

1973 Chevrolet Corvette Convertible

1973 Ford Mustang Convertible

Original Price: $3,102
Number Produced: 11,853
Estimated Number Existing in 1979: 9,956
Miles per Gallon: 10–21
Common Trouble Spots: brakes, suspension
Availability of Parts: good
Investment Potential: AA+

1973 Ford Mustang Convertible

PHOTO: FORD MOTOR COMPANY

Background: This was the last year for the Mustang convertible. It came with a 250 cu. in. six-cylinder engine, but only 5.8% of Mustangs were ordered that way in 1973. Optional at extra cost were two 351 cu. in. V8s. A three-speed manual transmission was standard. An automatic transmission and a four-speed manual were optional.

Most '73 Mustangs, 90.4%, were equipped with the automatic, 6.7% had the three-speed manual, 2.9% had the four-speed manual, 92.9% had power steering, 77.9% had power brakes, 5.6% had a tilting steering wheel, 62.8% had tinted glass, 3.2% had power windows, and 56.2% were sold with an air conditioner.

A special decor group was optional. It featured a black grille with "sport lamps," a body side strip, and wheel trim rings.

Three facts about the 1973 Mustang ragtop will ensure its continued desirability: it's a convertible, it has sporty good looks, and it's a Ford.

1973 Mercury Cougar Convertible

Original Price: $3,903
Number Produced: 1,284
Estimated Number Existing in 1979: 1,069
Miles per Gallon: 9–17
Common Trouble Spots: brakes; electrical, fuel, and ignition systems; suspension
Availability of Parts: good
Investment Potential: AA

Background: This was the last year for the Mercury convertible. The Cougar ragtop came with a 351 cu. in. V8. A hotter version of this engine was available at extra cost. Select Shift automatic transmission and power disc brakes were standard. A four-speed manual transmission was optional.

Most 1973 Cougars, 99.3%, were equipped with the automatic, 99.1% had power steering, 28% had a tilting steering wheel, 14.7% had power windows, 8.4% had power seats, 86.2% had tinted glass, and 84.5% came equipped with an air conditioner.

1973 Mercury Cougar Convertible

1973 Mercury Cougar XR-7 Convertible

Original Price: est. $4,100
Number Produced: 3,165
Estimated Number Existing in 1979: 2,636
Miles per Gallon: 9–17
Common Trouble Spots: brakes; electrical, fuel, and ignition systems; suspension
Availability of Parts: good
Investment Potential: AA+

Background: The attractive '73 Cougar XR-7 ragtop came with a 351 cu. in. V8 engine. A hotter version of this engine was optional. Select Shift automatic transmission was standard; a four-speed manual was optional, but not very popular.

1973 Oldsmobile Delta 88 Royale Convertible

Original Price: $4,442
Number Produced: 7,088
Estimated Number Existing in 1979: 6,230
Miles per Gallon: 8–15
Common Trouble Spots: cooling system
Availability of Parts: good
Investment Potential: A

Background: Sales of the Delta 88 Royale ragtop were up substantially from last year. Part of the reason for this may have been because the Royale was now the only convertible Oldsmobile offered.

It was powered by a 350 cu. in. V8. A 455 cu. in. V8 was optional. Automatic transmission power steering and power disc brakes were standard.

Most full-size 1973 Oldsmobiles, 93.9%, came with an air conditioner, 46.6% had power windows, 41.1% had power front seats, 96.6% had tinted glass, and 44.2% were sold with a tilting steering wheel.

The Delta 88's all-Morocceen interior was available in black, cranberry red, saddle, and white. Buyers had their choice of sixteen exterior colors.

1973 Pontiac Grand Ville Convertible

Original Price: $4,766
Number Produced: 4,447
Estimated Number Existing in 1979: 3,757
Miles per Gallon: 8–15
Common Trouble Spots: suspension
Availability of Parts: good
Investment Potential: A+

Background: Just five years earlier, Pontiac fans had had their choice of six convertibles. Now there was only one, the luxurious (and big) Grand Ville.

It was powered by a 400 cu. in. V8. Two 455 cu. in. V8s were also available. Turbo Hydra-Matic automatic transmission, power steering, and power disc brakes were standard.

Most full-size 1973 Pontiacs, 94.9%, came with tinted glass, 25% had power windows, 16.3% had power front seat, 28.3% had a tilting steering wheel, and 92.2% were sold with an air conditioner.

Buyers had their choice of sixteen exterior colors.

1973 Pontiac Grand Ville Convertible

PHOTO: PONTIAC MOTOR DIVISION

1973 Oldsmobile Delta 88 Royale Convertible

PHOTO: OLDSMOBILE DIVISION

1974

1974 Buick Le Sabre Luxus Convertible

Original Price: $4,575
Number Produced: 3,627
Estimated Number Existing in 1979: 3,354
Miles per Gallon: 8–15
Common Trouble Spots: none
Availability of Parts: good
Investment Potential: A

Background: The attractive '74 Le Sabre Luxus ragtop was powered by a 455 cu. in. V8 engine. A "Stage 1" version of this engine, featuring electronic high-energy ignition, was optional. Turbo Hydra-Matic 400 automatic transmission, power brakes, and power steering were standard. Many optional accessories were available.

Buyers could choose all-vinyl interiors in three solid colors and three combinations.

1974 Cadillac Fleetwood Eldorado Convertible

Original Price: $9,437
Number Produced: 7,600
Estimated Number Existing in 1979: 6,817
Miles per Gallon: 9–14
Common Trouble Spots: none
Availability of Parts: good
Investment Potential: AA

Background: The new Eldorado was powered by a 500 cu. in. V8 engine. Automatic transmission, power disc brakes, power steering, electric windows, and power seats were standard. Ninety-nine percent of all 1974 Eldorados came with air conditioning, 99.8% had tinted glass, and about 68% had a tilting steering wheel.

1974 Chevrolet Caprice Convertible

Original Price: $4,745
Number Produced: N.A.
Estimated Number Existing in 1979: N.A.
Miles per Gallon: 8–15
Common Trouble Spots: none
Availability of Parts: good
Investment Potential: A+

Background: The new Caprice ragtop was powered by a 400 cu. in. V8. A 454 cu. in. V8 was optional. Automatic transmission, power steering, and power disc brakes were standard.

Over 29% of all full-size '74 Chevys came with power windows, 6.7% had power front seats, 28.3% had a tilting steering wheel, and 92.3% were sold with an air conditioner.

1974 Chevrolet Caprice Convertible

PHOTO: GM PHOTOGRAPHIC

1974 Cadillac Fleetwood Eldorado Convertible

PHOTO: CADILLAC MOTOR CAR DIVISION

1974 Chevrolet Corvette Stingray Convertible

Original Price: $5,864
Number Produced: N.A.
Estimated Number Existing in 1979: N.A.
Miles per Gallon: 8–15
Common Trouble Spots: manual transmission
Availability of Parts: good
Investment Potential: AAA

Background: The new Corvette ragtop was powered by a 350 cu. in. V8. A hotter version of this engine and a 454 cu. in. V8 were available at extra cost. Most 1974 Vettes, 66.3%, were equipped with the optional automatic transmission. The rest had the standard four-speed manual.

Over 95% of new Corvettes had power steering, 88.3% had power brakes, 72.9% had a tilting steering wheel, 63.1% had power windows, and 77.7% were sold with an air conditioner.

1974 Oldsmobile Delta 88 Royale Convertible

Original Price: $4,799
Number Produced: 3,716
Estimated Number Existing in 1979: 3,329
Miles per Gallon: 8–15
Common Trouble Spots: electrical system
Availability of Parts: good
Investment Potential: A+

Background: Sales of the Delta 88 Royale convertible dropped considerably from the previous year. The demise of the Oldsmobile softtop was fast approaching.

The Royale was powered by a 350 cu. in. V8. A hotter version of this engine and a 455 cu. in. V8 were available at extra cost. Automatic transmission, power steering, and power disc brakes were standard.

Most full-size 1974 Oldsmobiles, 61.9%, came with an air conditioner, 51.6% had power windows, 43.5% had power front seats, and 52.5% were sold with a tilting steering wheel.

1974 Oldsmobile Delta 88 Royale Convertible

PHOTO: OLDSMOBILE DIVISION

1974 Pontiac Grand Ville Convertible

Original Price: $5,113
Number Produced: 3,000
Estimated Number Existing in 1979: 2,631
Miles per Gallon: 8–15
Common Trouble Spots: suspension
Availability of Parts: good
Investment Potential: A+

Background: The Grand Ville had a more expensive look this year than last. This was due mainly to its new grille, which resembled the style popular on the high-priced cars of the period.

It came with a 455 cu. in. V8. Two other versions of this engine were available at extra cost. Turbo Hydra-Matic automatic transmission, power steering, and power brakes were standard.

Most full-size 1974 Pontiacs, 93.9%, were equipped with an air conditioner, 34.9% had a tilting steering wheel, 29.6% had power windows, 19.2% had power front seats, and 96.2% had tinted glass.

Some other options included a 60/40 front seat (in saddle, green, burgundy, beige, or white), body side molding, door edge guards, wire wheel covers, striping (in black, red, white, or gold), cruise control, deck-lid release, and remote control outside mirrors.

1974 Pontiac Grand Ville Convertible

PHOTO: PONTIAC MOTOR DIVISION

1975

1975 Buick LeSabre Custom Convertible

Original Price: $5,133
Number Produced: 5,300
Estimated Number Existing in 1979: 4,976
Miles per Gallon: 8–15
Common Trouble Spots: none
Availability of Parts: good
Investment Potential: AA

Background: This was the last Buick convertible. It was powered by a 455 cu. in. V8 engine. Automatic transmission, power steering, and power disc brakes were standard. Buyers had their choice of either standard vinyl notchback or optional vinyl 60/40 notchback seats.

1975 Buick LeSabre Custom Convertible

1975 Cadillac Fleetwood Eldorado Convertible

Original Price: $10,354
Number Produced: 8,950
Estimated Number Existing in 1979: 8,180
Miles per Gallon: 9–14
Common Trouble Spots: none
Availability of Parts: good
Investment Potential: AA

Background: The Eldorado received an attractive face-lift for 1975. It was powered by a 500 cubic inch V8 engine. Automatic transmission, air conditioning, power steering, power brakes, electric windows, and power seats were standard.

1975 Cadillac Fleetwood Eldorado Convertible

PHOTO: CADILLAC MOTOR CAR DIVISION

1975 Chevrolet Caprice Convertible

Original Price: $5,113
Number Produced: N.A.
Estimated Number Existing in 1979: N.A.
Miles per Gallon: 8–15
Common Trouble Spots: none
Availability of Parts: good
Investment Potential: AA

Background: The attractive 1975 Caprice was the last convertible made by Chevrolet. It came with a 350 cu. in. V8. Available at extra cost were a hotter version of this engine and two other V8 engines, a 400 and a 454. Automatic transmission, power steering, and power brakes were standard.

1975 Chevrolet Corvette Stingray Convertible

Original Price: $6,537
Number Produced: N.A.
Estimated Number Existing in 1979: N.A.
Miles per Gallon: 8–15
Common Trouble Spots: none
Availability of Parts: good
Investment Potential: AAA

Background: This was the last year for the Corvette ragtop. It was powered by a 350 cu. in. V8. A hotter version of this engine was optional at extra cost. A four-speed manual transmission was standard. Automatic transmission was optional.

1975 Chevrolet Corvette Convertible

1975 Oldsmobile Delta 88 Royale Convertible

Original Price: $5,200
Number Produced: 7,181
Estimated Number Existing in 1979: 6,649
Miles per Gallon: 8–15
Common Trouble Spots: none
Availability of Parts: good
Investment Potential: AA

Background: This was the last convertible made by Oldsmobile. Ironically, softtop sales were the highest they had ever been for a Delta 88 Royale.

It was powered by a 350 cu. in. V8 with a four-barrel carburetor. A 400 cu. in. V8 with a two-barrel carburetor and a 455 cu. in. V8 with a four-barrel carburetor were available at extra cost. Turbo Hydra-Matic automatic transmission, power steering, and power disc brakes were standard.

Most full-size 1975 Oldsmobiles, 94.6%, came with an air conditioner, 57.7% had power windows, 49.2% had power front seats, 96.5% had tinted glass, and 59% were sold with a tilting steering wheel.

Buyers had their choice of sixteen exterior colors.

1975 Pontiac Grand Ville Convertible

Original Price: $5,858
Number Produced: 4,519
Estimated Number Existing in 1979: 3,994
Miles per Gallon: 8–15
Common Trouble Spots: none
Availability of Parts: good
Investment Potential: AA

Background: Like many other cars for 1975, the new Grand Ville had rectangular headlights. This gave the big car a somewhat sportier appearance.

The Grand Ville came with a 400 cu. in. V8. Another version of this engine and a 455 cu. in. V8 were available. Automatic transmission, power steering, and power disc brakes were standard.

Most full-size Pontiacs, 94.1%, were equipped with an air conditioner, 38.5% had power windows, 26.1% had power front seats, and 44.6% were sold with a tilting steering wheel.

The 1975 Grand Ville was the last convertible made by Pontiac.

1975 Pontiac Grand Ville Convertible

PHOTO: PONTIAC MOTOR DIVISION

1975 Oldsmobile Delta 88 Royale Convertible

PHOTO: OLDSMOBILE DIVISION

1976

1976 Cadillac Fleetwood Eldorado Convertible

Original Price: $11,049
Number Produced: 14,000
Estimated Number Existing in 1979: 13,990
Miles per Gallon: 9–14
Common Trouble Spots: none
Availability of Parts: good
Investment Potential: AA+ (Bicentennial models); AA (the rest)

Background: This was the last year for the Eldorado convertible. It was also considered the last production American convertible made (the four-wheel-drive Jeep softtop is still being produced, and anyone with the money can have a new car made into a convertible by companies that specialize in that sort of conversion). Ironically, because of that fact sales were higher than they had been in years. Even more Eldorados could have been sold if Cadillac hadn't run out of top mechanisms and been unable to obtain more.

Because so many people requested the right to buy (or the more bold, to have) the very last Eldorado softtop, 200 special Bicentennial models were produced. These all were white with white tops and had red-and-blue hood strips. The interiors were white leather with red carpeting and had a unique instrument-panel plaque.

The Eldorado was powered by a 500 cu. in. V8. A hotter version of this engine, with electronic fuel injection, was available at extra cost. An automatic transmission was standard. Most were sold with nearly every available option.

Because of the extensive media coverage, everybody and his grandmother "knew" 1976 Eldorado ragtops were going to be valuable collector's items. It became a self-fulfilling prophecy. For a while, new "used" Eldorados were selling for thousands more than list price. Bicentennial models were going for $30,000 to $40,000. However, by 1977 prices were declining. Regular models were selling for as low as $12,000 and Bicentennial ones for $27,000, and the prices of both types will continue to drop (in 1978, some '76 Eldorado ragtops could be had for under $10,000).

The 1976 Eldorado convertible is a beautiful, luxurious open-air car. That is a good reason for buying one. It also had the distinction of being considered the last American convertible. That adds something to the car's appeal, but not nearly so much as many people believe.

1976 CADILLAC FLEETWOOD ELDORADO CONVERTIBLE

1976 Cadillac Fleetwood Eldorado Convertible

PHOTO: CADILLAC MOTOR CAR DIVISION

3
Should You Invest in an Old Car?

Investing in a convertible or other special-interest car is *not* a sure thing. As with every other type of investment, there are risks involved. To make money on old cars, one must try to minimize these risks as much as possible.

One way to do this is by purchasing the right car. Unrestored cars in good condition are usually the best ones to buy. They cost less to begin with, and so are easier to resell at a profit. A lot of people will admire a perfectly restored 1955 Thunderbird selling for $12,000, but more would be willing to buy a not-quite-so-perfect '55 T-Bird for $4,500 (of course, ten years from now a $12,000 Thunderbird might be a bargain).

This is not to say that you shouldn't purchase a restored car. If it's a car you really love, with good potential for appreciation, and the price is right, get it. But keep in mind that restored cars have the nasty habit of deteriorating into unrestored cars—especially if you drive them much. And they should be driven, because using a special-interest car helps the owner get the most out of his or her investment.

Some people argue that driving a car will devalue it. They are right, up to a point. Any car that is used regularly will gather its share of nicks, little dents, and cracked glass, no matter how careful the driver is. Still, when one weighs the cost of repairing these minor items against the cost of maintaining another, newer model for everyday use, it is minimal.

That is one advantage of buying a very good unrestored car (or an older restoration)—it probably has some nicks already, and a few more won't affect its value. On the other hand, the value of a restored show car, or one with extremely low mileage, is greatly affected by use. Generally, the only time one is likely to see such cars moving under their own power is when they are driven in front of an auction stand. Not only does the owner of such a vehicle cheat himself out of the use value of the car, he also misses out on the fun of driving it.

In northern states, most owners of old cars also keep newer cars which they drive in winter, when the roads are covered with rust-inducing salt. That is a good idea. Otherwise, in most instances, keeping an old car in "protective custody" merely adds to the cost of your investment. A car that is used is at least paying for its keep. A car that is stored and not driven isn't.

If you buy a car, use it for a couple of years, and then sell it for the same amount you paid for it, you will come out ahead on the deal (because of the use value). However, if you sell a car after a couple of years of non-use for what you paid for it, you will have lost money (due to maintenance and storage costs). You will have to sell a car you haven't used for more than one you have used just to break even.

A frequent excuse given for not using a car is the fear that something might go wrong. Well, if you use your car a lot, something *will* go wrong. The transmission might start to leak, the speedometer could stop working, mufflers and tailpipes will certainly wear out. But new cars have their problems too. And if you're going to have to pay money repairing a car, it might as well be spent on a car you can make a profit on than a newer one, which you'll probably end up selling for a loss.

Besides, if you don't make use of your car, there is a very good chance that some of our friends from the "Wild Kingdom" will. There is nothing mice and squirrels love better than an unused car. If you must store a car for any length of time, buy a cat (a good mouser). For problems with squirrels, buy a robust, loud dog (that likes cats). Or a .22 rifle—and develop a taste for squirrel sandwiches.

This doesn't mean you should put 100,000 miles a year on your automobile by cruising around gravel pits with a couple of wild billy goats in the back seat. But making use of your car will, in most instances, help maximize the return on your investment (an added advantage of driving a special-interest car a lot is that doing so will attract potential buyers).

Whether a car is used much or not, it will have to be kept up. Most routine servicing can be done satisfactorily at any garage or gas station. However, it is a good idea to determine first whether the people working there are professional automobile mechanics or grease monkeys (with the emphasis on the monkey).

Some owners of old cars claim to save a lot of money on car repairs by taking their autos to a vocational school. Often, these schools will fix cars in their automobile repair classes. They generally charge only for parts, which is, almost without exception, the cheapest portion of any repair bill. While I know of people who feel this is an excellent way to keep a car in top condition at minimal cost, I would not do it. With my luck, the class clown would be assigned to my car. But it is an idea worth checking out.

Wherever it's done, keep thorough records of all work (including routine oil changes) done on your car. This aids in keeping track of how much your heartthrob is really costing. And when you sell the car, prospective buyers are usually impressed (and rightly so) at seeing evidence of how well the car has been cared for.

One problem with owning a special-interest car is getting adequate insurance. If an old car is stolen or destroyed, the owner may have a difficult time receiving full compensation for the loss. Keeping good records, including the bill of sale, maintenance and repair bills, and some color photos of the car, will help to establish its value.

There are some companies that specialize in insuring special-interest automobiles. Their rates are lower than those of conventional insurance firms. However, they generally place tight restrictions on how a car is used and the number of miles it is driven each year.

Before buying a convertible or other special-interest car, do a lot of research. Know what it should look like, what engine(s) and transmission(s) were available, what options were offered (and which are the rarest), what exterior colors and interior combinations were available, the number of cars produced, and the availability of parts. Much of this basic information is contained in this book. Other places to get detailed data are original sales literature (especially dealer showroom albums), car clubs, present and former owners of that particular year and model of car, and restored and good originals on display at car shows and swap meets. Owners of GM cars can contact the Microfilm Department of GM Photographic (General Motors Corporation, 30001 Van Dyke, Warren, MI 48090). GM sells rolls of microfilm containing all manuals that a given GM division published during a specific year.

Almost without exception, cars that are stock (i.e., have original engine, transmission, interiors, etc.) are worth more than those that have been altered.

Certain postwar special-interest cars are especially susceptible to being faked. Stories of 1960 Ford convertibles being made into "Edsels" are fairly common. The 1954-56 Ford Crown Victorias and Mercury Montereys are easily transformed into the more desirable Skyliners and Sun Valleys by adding Plexiglas roof inserts. The same sort of backyard "reincarnations" are being done on early Mustangs (changing them into Shelby GTs), on 1950-51 Ford two-door sedans (into Crestliners), and 1962-63 Thunderbird ragtops (into Sports Roadsters). So be extra careful when considering purchasing any of these cars.

Another area you should study is the current market value of the car. To find this, read the want-ad sections of *Cars and Parts, Hemmings Motor News,* and *Old Cars* newspaper. Also read what similar examples of the car are bringing at auctions (*Old Cars* regularly runs such information). That way, you will have a good idea of whether the asking price is a bargain or a rip-off.

When inspecting a car, determine its overall quality. Is the body sound and, if possible, rust-free? Are the engine, transmission, and any power equipment in good working order? A weak spot for many cars, especially convertibles, is the interior. If the car has seat covers, look under them to see how good the original upholstery is. Sometimes covers are put on a car to hide damage. Other times they are put on to protect the original upholstery (in fact, during the early 1950s, most new car buyers put seat covers on their cars as soon as they got them).

If you should happen to find such a car, do *not* leave the seat covers off. I made that mistake with an old Ford I bought as a teenager. It had a set of mismatched plaid seat covers that looked as though they had been designed by a color-blind asparagus sorter. When I took them off I was pleased with what I found: the attractive original upholstery looked like new. It had never been soiled. Unfortunately, the fabric was delicate, so it was only a matter of time before the back seat began to look rather ragged. Therefore, always determine whether seat covers have been put on for protection or deception.

Unrestored cars in good to very good condition are generally the best buys. Cars that need a complete restoration are the lowest priced. However, unless you can do most of the work needed to restore the vehicle yourself, you could end up putting more into a car than it is worth. For example, I recently saw a '53 Olds 88 ragtop offered for $8,500. The owner claimed it had received an $8,000 restoration. The car was in beautiful condition, and anyone who wanted a perfect '53 Olds 88 convertible might buy it. However, at the time of the ad, the going rate for '53 88 ragtops in excellent condition was less than $4,000. Those in good original condition could be found for around $1,500 to $2,500.

A person could make more money (per dollar invested) buying a good '53 Olds 88 softtop for $2,500 and selling it later for $3,000. The person with the $8,500 Olds would only make $500 profit (assuming she or he got the car free to begin with). But the lower-priced car would return the same amount of profit, and would be easier to sell, because more people have $3,000 to spend on a ragtop than $8,500.

If you have skills in body work and auto mechanics, you may want to consider getting a car that needs restoration. Restoring postwar automobiles is a very lucrative business. However, it is easy to spend a small fortune fixing up a car—even if you supply the labor.

Should you decide to restore a car, try to get one that still has all the original pieces. Those little items like chrome trim, door handles, grilles, dashes, radios, and speedometer could end up costing a sizable amount of money if you have to buy them one item at a time. And do *not* waste time and money "restoring" things already in good condition.

As a rule, it is *not* a good idea to buy a car for restoration if all or most of the work will have to be farmed out. In most cases, you'll end up sinking a great deal of money into a car and won't really be assured of getting it back (at least in the near future). Even if you have the money to do a complete restoration and aren't particularly concerned with making a profit, you may have a hard time finding competent people to do the work. Those capable of doing a first-class job will probably want (and deserve) a lot of money for it. And a "cheapo" restoration is a lousy investment. By the way, "cheapo" refers not only to price but to the quality of work done. Some high-price shops do low-quality work. So if you are set on restoring a car, do it right, or don't do it at all.

A good place to find one of the cars mentioned in this book is in local newspaper want ads and/or weekly shoppers. Also check papers from communities within easy driving distance.

Used-car lots located in high-income areas are good places to find well-maintained special-interest autos. Most vehicles there were owned by people who didn't put many miles on their cars because they owned several.

Sooner or later, if not now, there will be a special-interest car for sale near where you live. If you don't feel like waiting, or are looking for a specific car, then your best bet is to read the ads in *Cars and Parts, Hemmings Motor News,* and *Old Cars* newspaper. In these publications, literally thousands of desirable (and not so desirable) postwar automobiles are offered regularly—everything from $100 project cars to prize-winning show cars.

In 1975, Bob Latimer, a car collector and free-lance writer, wrote in *Old Cars* newspaper of how he acquires old automobiles simply by asking owners if their cars are for sale. A well-known California collector and dealer leaves his business cards on autos he is interested in buying. Aggressively seeking cars can be successful; a lot of people will decide to sell on the spur of the moment, often because they have lost interest in a particular car, or, more commonly, they just have more cars than they have room for. Most collectors have several cars, so storage is frequently a problem.

Another place to find convertibles and other special-interest autos is at old-car dealers. Many such dealerships are popping up all over the country. Most offer their cars at reasonable prices. Some dealers, and individuals, try to use snob appeal to inflate the value of the autos they sell. Every vehicle they have, from a genuinely nice ragtop to a dead pickup truck abandoned by a migrant worker in 1965, is by their definition a "classic." Such people also tend to overemphasize how rare a car is. Scarcity can and does affect how much a car is worth. However, rarity in and of itself does not necessarily make a car valuable; an automobile could be rare because hardly anyone likes it.

The best way to avoid being ripped off is to do your homework. Know an original example of the car you want when you see one and keep up-to-date with the market.

One of the best places to find a special-interest car at a bargain price is at a swap meet. One reason a person can frequently get a good deal is that sellers are usually in a wheel-and-deal mood. I've seen convertibles and other postwar cars selling for as much as half of what most dealers and individuals were currently asking for cars in similar condition. Of course, there are also people at swap meets asking outrageous prices.

Old-car auctions are becoming a popular source for special-interest automobiles. However, some collectors believe that auctions have brought speculators (and high prices) to the hobby. For this reason, a sizable minority of collectors are anti-auctions.

The best buys at old-car auctions can at times be made at the start and toward the end. Sometimes an auction firm begins with a low-priced car or two to get the bidding warmed up. And toward the end of a long auction people get tired.

Although it is possible to make some very good buys at auctions, there is the danger of catching "auction fever." A buyer may become so wrapped up in the bidding process that he or she ends up paying more than he or she planned. And it is not too uncommon to bid more than a car is currently worth.

Before bidding on any car, check it out. A car that looks nice from a distance may not look so good close up. And just because a car has a high reserve, or the guy in front of you has gone wild over it, doesn't necessarily mean it is a good car. He may want it for sentimental reasons, or he may just be naive.

Talking to gas-station attendants is a good way to find a special-interest car; they usually know of all old cars in their community. College and vocational school bulletin boards can also be an excellent source of old cars, often at bargain prices.

A disadvantage of owning an old car is that when something does go wrong, you may run into a mechanic who will solemnly intone, "They don't make parts for them anymore." Like a doctor informing a patient that the end is near, she or he will tell you that the part your car needs isn't listed in the parts book (perhaps showing you the book to add to the drama). The mechanic usually concludes that the only hope of finding the desired part is to scour some distant junkyard.

The newest car I've owned was eight years old. The oldest (which I am currently driving) is twenty-three. I've never had any problem getting parts without going to a junkyard. The majority of items commonly needed, such as spark plugs, tune-up kits, distributor caps, and the like, can be purchased at most discount stores—especially if the car is less than twenty-five years old. Tailpipes, mufflers, transmissions, rebuilt engines, and other major parts are also readily available for most postwar cars.

Many common parts for old cars can be found at auto-parts stores, which often give discounts of up to 20% to regular customers. There are also a growing number of dealers who specialize in selling parts for old cars. And the parts-for-sale sections of special-interest car publications are filled with ads offering all kinds of parts. Sometimes it pays to go to the new-car dealer of the make of car you own. Occasionally they have some unsold parts around for old cars.

Automobile swap meets are a good place to find parts. Especially things like fenders, grilles, trim, interiors, steering wheels, radios, and the like. It is not unusual to find parts selling there for up to 90% less than what old-car parts dealers are asking.

Whenever you go to a swap meet, come early and stay late. When you first arrive, look around for the best deal on the parts you need most and, assuming the price is right, buy them. Then take your time looking around and visiting with people until it is close to the end of the meet. At that time, go to those dealers that have parts you can use and dicker with them. Often these dealers are willing to take lower offers at the end of a meet than they were earlier. One reason is that whatever they don't sell they have to take back with them (one swap-meet dealer I know is fond of telling prospective customers, "Buy something heavy").

The biggest disadvantage of relying on swap meet for parts is that you never know for sure whether they'll have what you want (it is possible to spend more money looking for a part than what it would cost to buy the item from a parts dealer). Occasionally it helps to ask swap-meet vendors if they know of anyone who has the part(s) you desire. Many have other parts at home or know where to locate what you need.

Most car collectors agree that you should *not* wait until you need a part before buying it. Buy parts (particularly hard-to-find items) whenever you can get a good deal on them; you can usually sell extra parts to other collectors, or trade what you have for those you need. This sort of wheeling and dealing can save an old-car owner hundreds of dollars. It is also a good way to meet and make friends with people interested in the type of car you own. Often these people know where you can find a buyer for your car.

Having lots of extra parts can make it easier to resell a car, especially if it happens to be very rare. So car collectors should become parts collectors. Just as cars appreciate in value, so do parts for them. (For example, in 1972 my brother purchased a set of rust-free fenders for his '55 Chevy for $10. In 1979 those same fenders would probably cost $60 to $100 or more.) Therefore, unless you pay an outrageous price to begin with, it should be easy to recover your investment in parts.

Before buying any special-interest car, make sure that it is original and in good condition, that the price is right (around, or preferably below, current market value) and not overly inflated, that you have room for it (ideally, cars should be stored in a climate-controlled garage—old cars, especially woodies, are affected by the temperature and humidity), that you have realistic expectations as to how much it should appreciate, and that a gut feeling tells you it is the car to buy.

Many decisions based purely on logic turn sour in time. This doesn't mean you should disregard the advice in this chapter or all reason. But it should be remembered that convertibles and other special-interest autos are desirable primarly for emotional reasons, not practical ones. Therefore, when making a buying decision, emotion should not be totally ignored.

4
The Future of Car Collecting

In its twenty-fifth anniversary issue in 1975, *Motor Trend* magazine asked leading authorities on transportation what they thought the future of the automobile would be. Virtually all of them were optimistic. Most believed that the type of fuel might change (although the technology for making gasoline out of coal already exists), but that, even in the year 2000, no one will have to look in a history book to see what a car looks like.

Since most experts agree that personal transportation is here to stay, car collecting should continue to thrive. There are other factors that will contribute to the appeal of special-interest cars.

The percentage of people in the prime auto-collecting age bracket (late 20s to mid-30s) is increasing. More women are working outside the home, so greater numbers of young couples (most collectors are married) will have very substantial joint incomes. Also, greater numbers of married people are choosing not to have children. This too will add to the amount of discretionary income the average family will have.

Nostalgia for the recent past is stronger now than when this trend began in 1969. And cars, primarily because of the annual model changes, have a great deal of nostalgic appeal.

As the population grows and competition for jobs and status increases, more and more people will be concerned with individualism. And one of the best ways to put oneself apart from the crowd is to drive a distinctive automobile. Driving an old car is, and will remain, an overt way of expressing one's individuality.

More and more people are beginning to appreciate quality. Whether it is the quality of the air they breathe, the food they eat, or the way they live, quality is becoming more important. No longer is the newest immediately considered the best.

With the rise in consumerism, people are getting to be smarter shoppers. They are beginning to realize that it is generally cheaper to buy an old car in good condition, and keep it that way, then to waste money on a rapidly depreciating new car.

Perhaps one of the biggest factors assuring the stability of the market for special-interest cars has to do with women. More women are interested in automobiles. This should come as no surprise. According to the Motor Vehicle Manufacturers Association of the United States, Inc., in 1976, 45.6% of all drivers were female. And the percentage of women drivers is going up. So even if the number of men interested in old cars were suddenly to level off, the increasing number of women entering the hobby would ensure its well-being. And, as more and more people seek to own a limited supply of cars, the prices for those autos remaining will naturally go up.

Women had a bigger influence on the postwar automobile than most people realize. As Ford Motor Company's chief stylist George Walker said in a 1957 interview, "Beauty is what sells the

American car. And the person we are designing it for is the American woman. . . . We figure that 80% or better of all car purchases are decided on by women."

As interest in the hobby increases, old cars that have been pretty much ignored in the past will gain in popularity and value. Over the coming years, certain currently hot cars may become too expensive for the average collector. People will begin to discover the merits of other special-interest cars.

All ragtops are desirable, but, as of the late 1970s, the following are some of the best "sleeper" buys (a "sleeper" being defined as a car with more potential than it is currently recognized as having).

Convertibles

Buick: 1949, 1957-60, 1964, 1975 (all series), all Skylarks, all Wildcats, all GS 400s; *Cadillac:* 1954-64, especially 1963-64, (all series), 1969-70 De Ville, 1971-75 Eldorado: *Chevrolet:* 1949-52 Deluxe, 1953 210, 1953-54 Bel Air, 1958-67 Impala, especially Super Sports, 1973-75 Caprice, 1967-69 Camaro, all Novas, all Chevelles, all Corvairs; *Chrysler:* 1956-64, especially 1956, 1960, 1962-64, 1970 (all series); *DeSoto:* 1955-59 (all series); *Dodge:* 1955-59 (all series), 1962-64 Polara 500, 1964 Custom 880, all Dart GTs; *Ford:* 1953, 1957, 1960 Sunliner, 1957-59 retractable, 1962-64 Galaxie 500 XL, 1967 Galaxie 500 and 500 XL, 1972 LTD, all Fairlanes, 1963-65 Falcon; *Lincoln:* 1952-54 Capri; *Mercury:* 1952-56, 1965, 1970 (all series), all Cougars, 1965 Comet; *Oldsmobile:* 1950, 1957, 1960-61 (all series), all Cutlass, all Starfires, all 4-4-2s; *Plymouth:* 1956-59, 1962 (all series), 1963-66 Valiant, all Barracudas, 1965-67 Belvedere, 1967-69 GTX, all Road Runners, all Satellites, all Sport Furys; *Pontiac:* 1955-67 (all series, but especially Bonnevilles and Grand Prix), all GTOs, all Firebirds, all Le Mans, 1975 Grand Ville; *Rambler:* 1964-65 American, 1968 Rebel SST and Rebel 500; *Studebaker:* 1950-51 (all series).

1960 Oldsmobile 98 Sport Sedan

PHOTO: OLDSMOBILE DIVISION

1962 Pontiac Grand Prix Two-Door Hardtop

PHOTO: PONTIAC MOTOR DIVISION

Two-door hardtop body types of the same years and models may also be good "sleeper" buys. So are all muscle cars, all Panteras, 1959-60 GM four-door hardtops, station wagons made in the 1950s and early 1960s that have fake wood trim, Buick and Oldsmobile wagons with "Vista Dome" roofs, four-door hardtop station wagons, 1964-65 Chevelle 300 two-door station wagons, and 1971-73 "boat-tail" Buick Rivieras.

The American convertible may have died in April 1976 when the last Eldorado ragtop rolled off the assembly line. But the desire for open cars lives on. Detroit has tried to satisfy this by introducing sun roofs, moon roofs, and T-roofs. Still, more and more people want the real thing: no roof.

Index